A GENETIC HISTORY OF
BAPTIST THOUGHT

BAPTISTS

History, Literature, Theology, Hymns

General Editor: Walter B. Shurden is the Callaway Professor of Christianity in the Roberts Department of Christianity and Executive Director of the Center for Baptist Studies, Mercer University, Macon, Georgia.

A GENETIC HISTORY OF BAPTIST THOUGHT

With Special Reference to Baptists in

Britain and North America

William H. Brackney

Mercer University Press
Macon, Georgia

ISBN 0-86554-913-3
MUP/

First Edition.

∞The paper used in this publication meets the minimum requirements of American National Standard for Information Sciences — Permanence of Paper for Printed Library Materials, ANSI Z39.48-1992.

Library of Congress Cataloging-in-Publication Data

Brackney, William H.

 A genetic history of Baptist thought : with special reference to Baptists
in Britain and North America / William H. Brackney.— 1st ed.
     p. cm. — (Baptists)
 Includes bibliographical references and index.
 ISBN 0-86554-913-3 (pbk. : alk. paper)
 1. Baptists—United States—History. 2. Baptists—Doctrines—
History. I. Title. II. Series.
 BX6235.B46 2004
 230'.61'09--dc22

                                                2004009008

CONTENTS

Dedicated to

G. Noel Vose, president of the Baptist World Alliance (1985–1990)

Heather M. Vose, historian, colleague, friend (1932–1990)

SERIES FOREWORD

I am delighted for several reasons to have William H. Brackney's pioneering volume on the history of Baptist theology in this series called *Baptists*. First, Professor Brackney is one of the preeminent Baptist historians of our time. His many publications include *The Baptists*, a volume in the distinguished Praeger series of denominational studies, and *A Historical Dictionary of Baptists*, an indispensable tool for those of us who work in Baptist Studies. Historically and theologically, Professor Brackney knows Baptists well because of his painstaking research. Personally, he knows the contemporary profile of Baptists because of his extensive contacts with Baptists throughout the world and especially in North America. He has held administrative positions and taught in influential Baptist institutions among the American Baptist Churches–USA, Canadian Baptists, and Baptists of the South. Few, if any, Baptists with whom I am acquainted know more Baptist names, either in history or in our own time, than does William Brackney. The prestige of this Mercer University Press series is enormously enhanced by its association with his name.

Second, it is a delight to have this volume in the Mercer University Press's series on *Baptists* because it fits the purpose of the series so appropriately. Arguing, and surely to the surprise of some, that Baptists "have an identifiable theological heritage,", Brackney suggests that this theology is derived from "confessions of faith, personal writings of pastors and teachers, and professional theologians." The full title of this particular series by Mercer University Press is *Baptists: History, Literature, Theology, Hymns*. Professor Brackney utilizes all four of the topics in our subtitle to mine the Baptist heritage in order to discover Baptist theology. His volume fits perfectly into the purpose of our series.

Third, I believe this will be a signally important book for Baptists for years to come. To my knowledge, no other book like it exists. We have had books that deal with Baptist theologians, with some specific aspect of Baptist theology, or with the thought of a particular group of Baptists. We have yet to have, however, what Brackney gives us here, a comprehensive historical overview of the development of Baptist thought. By the way, Brackney admits to using the term "theology" in a very broad sense, and so he refers to "Baptist thought" or "the structured study of thinking about God that is expressed in communal and consensual forms."

One of the reasons why this book will last is Brackney's clear understanding and unapologetic affirmation of the diversity in Baptist theology. He never seeks to impose a singular tradition upon the Baptist story. Rather he correctly sees that "assertions of a dominant stream of Baptist theology are inadequate." Brackney contends that the two factors of theological diversity and historical development are essential in adequately assessing Baptist thought across the years. Baptists have had no unchanging "deposit of faith." Regarding the theological diversity, he notes that no single confessional tradition, for example, reflects "anything close to a comprehensive 'Baptist' perspective across time." Compounding the diversity is the fact that Baptists "have had to struggle to secure synthesis—they lack the all-important human administrative authority of an elder, a bishop, or a council.". Regarding historical development, Brackney says that it took "at least two centuries" for the Baptist tradition to solidify around "an adequate literary corpus.." He understands that Baptists have kept historic Christian teachings and vital but constantly changing religious experience in creative tension. These two sources of Baptist thought create problems and possibilities for Baptist life.

A Genetic History of Baptist Thought will be a lasting book because of the methodology Brackney employs. He is not tracing Calvinism or Arminianism or evangelicalism through Baptist life . He takes a "genetic approach" that attempts to connect Baptist ideas historically, while allowing for diversity in evolved thinking. In the face of what appears to be hopeless theological atomization among the Baptists, Brackney has chosen to utilize an approach characterized by interrelationships, dependencies, and cross-fertilization. He believes that a larger tradition of Baptist thought emerges that is biblically oriented, Christologically centered, experientially based, congregationally rooted, all of which celebrate freedom of conscience in a racially and ethnically diverse heritage. The enduring "genes" of Baptist life for Brackney are the authority of Christ as the Living Word, the priority of scripture, Christian experience, a modified Reformed theological tradition, the doctrine of the church, a sense of urgency about the gospel and gospel obligations (evangelical), and freedom or liberty.

All Baptists will learn from this book. All Baptists will have no choice but to interact with this book for the foreseeable future.

Walter B. Shurden
Callaway Professor of Christianity
Executive Director, The Center for Baptist Studies

FOREWORD

John Webster

Good church history has to take seriously both parts of its name. Church history (of which historical theology is a part) is *church* history, because its subject matter is the communion of saints. It is concerned not simply with the history of Christianity outwardly considered, as a form of human culture, a particular concretion of the forces of human action and reaction, but with the history of the church as a 'sanctified' reality. It sees the history of the church and its thinking as the history of the Spirit's sanctifying work—not in the idealist sense that some bit of the church's past can be narrated as a story of achieved perfection, but in the sense that in its secularity and sinfulness the history of the church is a sphere in which the Spirit's converting power is at work. To speak of the history of Christianity and of its theology as *church* history is to try to see that history as caught up in the economy of God's grace. But church history is also church *history*, because the life of the communion of saints and its thinking is not only a spiritual but also a natural reality. The church is human temporal process: people, actions, decisions, ideas, texts, institutions, in all their variety and interconnectedness, inseparably bound up with other human processes and activities in time. The church's sanctification does not mean that its history can be neatly extracted from the wider history of humankind. What marks out church history and historical theology as possessing a certain distinctiveness is not some identifiable point of separation from all other human occurrence, but the fact that in them we study human time, action, and thought standing in a special way under God's determination and promise.

Because of this, church history has to resist the twin temptations of naturalization and mythology. When it falls prey to naturalism, church history refuses to read the church's past under the presupposition that it is the past of the *sanctorum communio*, and instead gives a merely secular rendering of how the church has lived and thought. When this happens, it is no longer a theological enterprise. If it falls into mythology, on the other hand, church history refuses to see that the history of the church and its theology really is an aspect of human time; when that is allowed to happen, then it is no longer an historical enterprise. The dualisms of the natural and the transcendent, built into the fabric of Western culture in the modern period, often encourage church historians (and others) to opt for one or other of these alternatives. But wise historians of the church will refuse to be trapped, and will not allow theological and historical perception to drift apart. If they are to exemplify the coherence of church history as theological and historical enterprise, its practitioners will have to display a range of skills: as historians, a balance of narrative scope and particular incident, a good eye for the telling detail, curiosity, a healthy skepticism about large-scale explanations, and much else; as theologians, that modest and honest faithfulness which sets the history of the church in the sphere of God's providential order without claiming to know how all the bits fit together.

Church history and historical theology are often somewhat marginal in the theological enterprise in the present, in part because they have often taken their self-understanding from secular history, but also because much modern theology sits rather too loosely related to the past traditions of Christian thought and practice. Yet the church's past is an incomparable resource for its present, offering a critical vantage point from which we can become reflectively aware of the limitations and partiality of the way in which we think about ourselves, as well as of the particular opportunities for Christian living and thinking which present themselves to us. The church is now what it has become through time. Not the least of the services of the church historian to the church is to help it see how it has come to be where and what it is, most of all by illuminating the past in all is variety and so inviting us to think differently about ourselves and our present. Though such illumination is sometimes considered iconoclastic, it is in reality a ministry to the church, helping prevent the sclerosis of tradition that often afflicts the life of the people of God.

Professor Brackney's book is best read as this kind of history: as a generous, vivid, and wide-ranging account of the thinking of the Baptist tradition which aims to help its readers think in fresh ways. Its particular concern is with the networks of human relationship—cultural, intellectual, spiritual, ecclesial, institu-tional—which make up the tradition whose story it tells. It is written with erudition, with a certain narrative flair, and with that mixture of love and realistic appraisal that ought to characterize anyone speaking well of the tradition to which they belong. Readers from within that tradition will be invited to reflect on the way in which (particularly in North America) it has sometimes presented its past in over-simplified versions in order to warrant contemporary movements in Baptist life. Readers from outside that tradition will receive much instruction from this portrait of a strand of the life of the church and the ways in which the gospel has been thought about, articulated and lived out.

In his swan song lectures in Basel in 1962, the great Swiss Reformed theologian Karl Barth (himself much drawn to believer's baptism in his later years) reflected *inter alia* on the nature of historical theology. Though sometimes considered to have a hostile attitude to the traditions of the church, Barth was in reality a reverent and deeply knowledgeable student of the theology of the past; and what he has to say may serve as an *envoi* to the study that follows:

[T]heology will...do well to keep in contact with its predecessors. For better or for worse, theology of yesterday is a bubbling source of the community and, above all, of theology itself. We will listen, therefore, with special attention precisely to those fathers of yesterday, interpreting them not only according to the critical rule, *credo ut intelligam*, but also in *optimum partem bona fide*, and making the best of them. By no means will we drop the problems which concerned them; instead we will pursue them further, repeatedly meditating, considering and reconsidering the very problems they posed.[1]

John Webster
Lady Margaret Professor in Divinity
Christ Church
Oxford University

---

[1] Karl Barth, *Evangelical Theology: An Introduction* (London: Weidenfeld and Nicolson, 1963) 47.

ACKNOWLEDGMENTS

In any undertaking of this kind, one that has spanned a decade in the writing, the author is indebted to many people and institutions. I wish to express sincere gratitude to John Irwin and the trustees of McMaster Divinity College, McMaster University, for their support in research leaves and release time around the edges of an active principalship of that great institution. This project was launched while I served at McMaster in the early 1990s under presidents Geraldine Kenney-Wallace and Peter George. Secondly, I am grateful to President Robert Sloan of Baylor University for his support of my research and writing while I was chair of the Department of Religion at Baylor and afterwards as a professor of religion and director of that institution's Program in Baptist Studies.

Several colleagues have read portions of the manuscript. I am grateful for the critiques of John Webster, Walter Shurden, David Bebbington, J. Deotis Roberts, Raymond Bailey, Terry York, J. Daniel Gibson, and Bob Patterson. Across several years other friends and colleagues have offered advice and perspective. They include Robert Torbet, Norman Maring, Gilbert Englerth, Larry Greenfield, Winthrop Hudson, Robert Handy, Clarence Goen, Robert Campbell, Denton Lotz, J. K. Zeman, Millard Cherry, Mark Parent, Theo Gibson, William Wood, Morgan Patterson, Leon McBeth, James Leo Garrett, Glenn Hilburn, John Jonson, Wayne Ward, B. R. White, Keith Clements, Noel and Heather Vose, Stefan Rogazewski, Arlyce Kretschman, and Ronald Vallet.

The library staff at the reference desk in Jones Library, Baylor University, have been most helpful in locating resources and ferreting out details: Phil Jones, Jeff Taylor, and Janet Sheets. Similarly, the staff of the American Baptist Historical Society, Dana Martin, Stuart Campbell, and Karen Sundland in Rochester, New York, and Deborah van Broeckhoven and Betty Layton in Valley Forge, Pennsylvania. In Great Britain, Paul Fiddes, principal of Regent's Park College, and Susan Mills at the Angus Library of the college have over several years been very generous in making available biographical details and space for time to work during off hours. John Nicholson and Roger Hayden have inspired and corrected me regarding British Baptist nuances, as have David Russell, Bernard Green, and John Briggs. Each summer, Patricia Townshend, University Archivist at Acadia University in Wolfville, Nova Scotia, has been supportive and very knowledgeable about Baptists in the Maritimes and beyond. Others who have aided my searches include: Sean Lucas at Southern Baptist Theological Seminary; Margaret Mitchell at John Hay Library of Brown University; Charles Deweese, Baptist History and Heritage Society; Oscar Burdick, formerly at Graduate Theological Union Library; Seventh Day Baptist General Conference; Ken Morgan, Jim and Louise Barber at the Canadian Baptist Archives; Ken Chroniger, pastor at Alfred Station Seventh Day Baptist Church (New York), Jerry Allen, former executive director of the District of Columbia Baptist Convention; and librarians and archivists at the University of Chicago, Yale University, and George Washington University; Andover Newton Theological School and Colgate Rochester Divinity School, Spurgeon's College; Aline Parlier who helped me locate the Primitive Baptist Meetinghouse in Williamston, North Carolina. My nephew, Benjamin Phillips, a doctoral student at Southwestern Baptist Theological Seminary, has assisted me often with difficult to locate sources and theological conversation.

In the final stages of writing, Joyce Chan, my graduate assistant at Baylor, herself a specialist in Baptist thought, has been of inestimable value to me. Erin Brackney kindly assisted in the preparation of the index.

INTRODUCTION

Theology is the articulation of beliefs about or reflection upon God. Christian theology may be derived directly from Scripture, or reflection upon human knowledge, tradition, and experience, or a combination of all of these. It may be expressed in statements like creeds, confessions, or hymns, in formal discourse or conversation, or organized as a "science." As the intellectual life of the Christian Church matured, theology became a formal area of discourse conducted by "theologians," specialists in the categories, substance, and language of the Christian understanding of God. By the thirteenth century, theology had become a highly formalized discipline. Because of its wide field, including matters such as the sovereignty of God, the nature and destiny of humankind, the created order, and the sacraments, theology was the principal science or body of organized knowledge—"queen of the sciences." The Reformations, particularly the Radical movements, opened the way for lay theological discourse by persons not trained in the science of theology, but eager to express their theological views as individuals or congregations.[1] As part of their emphases upon the priesthood of believers and the competency of the individual soul, the Free Churches began to produce a variegated form of theology that reflected a wider variety of sources than the Scholastic or magisterial theologians. At first, academically trained theologians in this tradition were few. Far more numerous were pastors and informed lay students of Scripture. Indeed, even today what stems from the academic community may reflect only a minority understanding within a Free Church denomination, while other sources more popularly reflect theological reflection and understanding. Free Church theology is by its nature more complex, if for no other reason than its many modes of expression, than its counterpart within the magisterial traditions.

Baptists are a major part of the Free Church tradition, along with Congregationalists (Independents), Mennonites, Brethren, Pentecostals, and the Christian Church (Disciples of Christ) to identify the major

---

[1] A helpful introduction to the history and purposes of theology is *Christian Theology: An Introduction to Its Traditions and Tasks*, ed. Peter C. Hodgson and Robert H. King (Philadelphia: Fortress Press, 1982) 1–27.

cousins. Their theological identity is rooted in the Protestant Reformation, yet their relations are multifarious and sometimes conflictual. Baptists and non-Baptists often ridicule Baptist attempts at serious theological discourse. But, the record remains: Baptists do have an identifiable theological heritage. As the eminent W.T. Whitley of the last century put it, "Baptists are recognized by careful enquirers as a body with clear doctrines which are earnestly propagated."[2] This book is first an attempt to describe the complexity of Baptist thought that does justice to a religious movement that is now four centuries old. I will also proceed on the hypothesis that any model of Baptist "theology" worth its salt must begin with a polygenetic base.[3] This is not to diminish any one source, but to recognize the contribution to Baptist theological thought of several sources. Therefore, a second assumption here is: Baptist theology is derived from several sources: confessions of faith, hymns, personal writings of pastors and teachers, and professional theologians. That is the organizing principle of this book. In order to capture the fullness of the Baptist tradition, one must take into account each of these sources. Implicit in this approach is that assertions of a dominant stream of Baptist theology are inadequate. Attempts to mandate a truncated version of Baptist theological identity are harmful to the very freedom Baptists of all kinds have historically affirmed.

Methodology becomes an important issue in theological discourse. One could simply list the theologians in chronological sequence and attempt to make some institutional connections. Many have preferred a biographical approach. Or, one can follow a particular stream, such as Calvinistic Baptists, resulting in an unavoidable neglect or de-emphasis of other categories.[4] An institutional approach may be followed, such as

---

[2] William T. Whitley, *A History of British Baptists* (London: Charles Griffin, 1923), 4.

[3] I have profited in this regard by the evolution of a similar stream of the Free Churches, the Anabaptists. Arnold Snyder's approach in "Beyond Polygenesis: Recovering the Unity and Diversity of Anabaptist Theology," in H. Wayne Pipkin, ed., *Essays in Anabaptist Theology* (Elkhart IN: Institute of Mennonite Studies, 1994) 11–12 is very useful.

[4] This is the great inadequacy of works like *Theologians in the Baptist Tradition*, ed. Timothy George and David S. Dockery (Nashville: Broadman Holman, 2001). The original publication of this volume was highly selective, but its second edition was narrowed even further in its selections. Missing from the second list were John Bunyan, Isaac Backus, Dale Moody, Clark Pinnock, and Eric Rust. More recently, E. Brooks

tracing the "Chicago School." Each of these has its merit, but none alone does justice to the fullness of Baptist thought. I have therefore chosen to try to be inclusive of many Baptist traditions. This suggests a good deal of discontinuity and adversity, given the sharp differences Baptists have had even between each other. This problem is solved in part by a genetic approach that attempts to make a historical connection between the various streams of Baptist thought, while allowing for diversity in evolved thinking. In assessing Baptist life and thought adequately, two factors are absolutely essential: development across time and diversification. In this attempt I have been inspired by three previous resources, Frank Hugh Foster's *A Genetic History of New England Theology* (1907), Claude Welch's *Protestant Thought in the Nineteenth Century* (1972, 2 vols.), and Norman H. Maring's now seminal essays, "Baptists and Changing Views of the Bible, 1865–1918" in *Foundations: A Baptist Journal of History and Theology* (volume 1, numbers 3 and 4, 1958).

Foster's pioneering work traced the development of the New England theology from Puritan thought through Jonathan Edwards to the New Theology of Andover Theological Seminary. In Welch's work, one appreciates the long tradition from the German historians of the intellectual clash and succession of schools of thought named for individuals or institutions, such as the "Ritschelian" or "Hegelian" Schools, Welch used the term, "Protestant thought," to denote relationships of historical dependence, whether in a crystallizing way or for those who are more or less disciples of a prominent figure or institution, or who champion the continuance of a particular religious tradition. While Welch thought his terminology was an indispensable tool of interpretation, he was also careful to warn that this approach can fail to account for a necessary plurality of categories and focus only upon "professional theologians."[5] This would not do for Baptists. I am keenly aware of these pitfalls and consequently will argue from a variety of sources. Building upon Professor Maring's work that demonstrated the interconnectedness of American Baptist theologians and theological

Holifield, *Theology in America: Christian Thought from the Age of the Puritans to the Civil War* (New Haven: Yale University Press, 2003) 11, describes Baptists as part of the spread of Calvinism.

[5] Claude Welch, *Protestant Thought in the Nineteenth Century*, 2 vols. (New Haven: Yale University Press, 1972) 1:18–19.

seminaries around the issue of biblical authority, I can identify clearly "schools of thought" in the Baptist tradition. These are to be understood, of course, as interactive with confessions, pastors, lay expressions, and the general flow of evangelical Protestant thought in context.

In the essay ahead, I use the term "theology" in a particular sense. In this context, theology is the structured study of thinking about God that is expressed in communal and consensual forms. I believe this definition best fits the Baptist circumstance. Baptist theology is referred to in this book by the broader descriptor, "Baptist thought." It often can be understood as a nuance in relation to larger theological trajectories such as "Protestant" or "Reformed." I am not in search of a list of particular ideals that are the sole property of the Baptists. Rather, this is a modest attempt to create a history of Baptist thinking about the major issues of Christian doctrine and experience.

A few words about "genetic" connections and how I treat Baptist thinkers and their literature: In an attempt to establish their antiquity, Baptists have a long history of trying to demonstrate "unbroken lines of succession" in their ideas and origins as a constituted church. While this approach has been shown to be historically false and misleading,[6] many still hold to "successionism"or some version of it, particularly in the American Southern states. My "genetic" approach is altogether distinguishable from any "successionist" theology or "Landmark" theology. I am attempting to show legitimate and demonstrative intellectual/ideological relationships and influences within an expansive religious tradition.[7] I use the term "gene" to mean an entity that is concerned with the transmission or development of hereditary characteristics. I am more concerned with horizontal (among contemporaries) and immediate vertical (from one generation to the next) influences than any notion of any long term/chronological line of connection. The basis of these

---

[6] Compare J. M. Carroll, *The Trail of Blood: Following the Christians Down Through the Centuries, or The History of Baptist Churches from the Time of Christ, Their Founder, to the Present Day* (Lexington, KY: Ashland Avenue Baptist Church, 1931) with W. Morgan Patterson, *Baptist Successionism: A Critical View* (Valley Forge: Judson Press, 1969).

[7] The term "genetic" is not entirely unknown among recent Baptist theologians and historians. See, for instance, Timothy George's characterization: "Historical theology is the genetic study of Christian faith and doctrine," in his article "Dogma Beyond Anathema: Historical Theology in the Service of the Church," *Review and Expositor* 84/4 (Fall 1987): 691.

relationships can be the identification of actual dependency as seen in a person's statements about the derivation of his/her ideas, or a citation of one person's name or work in that of another. In the case of confessional documents, the dependency can be textual; that is, found in the recurrence of phrases from one document to another. Less direct affinities may be suggested by educational context, as in where a person studied, or by his/her working relationships. I have tried wherever possible to avoid speculation. Very few connections are absolutely certain. As I analyze each writer or thinker, I try to assess what the theological contribution of that individual is *in context*. This is not an exhaustive study of each person's theology. I refrain from appealing to preconceived notions or systematic frameworks to draw out artificial categories that a given writer did not mean to stress. This may be disappointing to those who want a neater pattern.

My choices of persons identified as "theologians" are based upon several criteria. First, I selected persons who published theological texts. For pastors this could mean a sermon or a tract. For laypersons it might be a tract or published poem. After the advent of professional theologians in the late-eighteenth and early-nineteenth centuries, I have selected those persons primarily responsible for teaching theology, that is doctrine, systematic theology, or biblical theology. I contend it is most always those who created a theological persona for an institution. I do not disregard others in small faculties who either taught in related fields or influenced the reputation of a school, but I am more concerned with the background and approach of those whose task it was to define and develop doctrine in the Baptist tradition. They were known through their published works and the courses they taught. I know that some critics will be disappointed that there are almost no women included in this approach, but the record among Baptists as a male-dominated tradition, until very recently, stands for itself. It is still the case that there are fewer Baptist women working in theology and ethics than in the historical and biblical fields. Finally, I have chosen to limit my list of theologians from the last two decades to those who had retired from active teaching and writing or who were deceased before 2000. The exceptions are Billy Graham, Harvey Cox, and Jerry Falwell, major influences in the making of contemporary Baptist theological identity.

For many years I have been convinced that there are countless inter-relationships in the Baptist tradition that have been obscured by negative organizational manifestations. Perhaps the following essay will elucidate this "best kept secret" among the Baptists.

CHAPTER 1

FROM THE BEGINNINGS:
THE CONFESSIONS

> We have no itch to clog religion with new words, but to
> readily acquiesce in that form of sound words which hath been,
> in consent with the holy Scriptures, used by others before us.
>
> Second London Confession, 1677

The first category of sources of Baptist theology we shall consider is the confession of faith. Baptists joined other Protestants in issuing personal, congregational, and associational confessions. This tradition of theological expression waned somewhat during the later nineteenth century, but made a comeback among many Baptists in the twentieth century. Thus, confessions of faith are an important place to begin our genetic study.

Among Baptists, confessions may be distinguished from creeds. Creeds (literally from the Latin *credo* = "I believe") evolved from first-century kerygmatic statements to become standards of orthodoxy for the Christian community. Particularly associated with the first five centuries, as Erik Routley has suggested, their purpose was to fulfill a need, namely to objectify the experience of the early church.[1] Examples of historic creeds include the Nicene, Athanasian, and Apostles' Creeds. These statements brought about a collective consciousness of Christian beliefs that had been largely understood in individual terms. Creeds are still used in many contemporary churches as binding acts of allegiance to God. For

---

[1] Erik Routley, *Creeds and Confessions*: *From the Reformation to the Modern Church* (Philadelphia: The Westminster Press, 1962) 1.

many Christians at times the term "creed" has seemed indistinguishable from "confession."[2]

But, as far as many theological specialists are concerned, the difference between a creed and a confession is not to be missed. Strictly speaking, confessions are summations of religious belief in succinct form. They may be contrasted with creeds or doctrinal statements that are used in different ways from confessions.[3] During the Reformation era the term "confession" took on a new substance and purpose, differentiated from the historic creeds. Confessions came to define doctrinal boundaries of the new national and regional churches. While creeds had sought to unify the fractured church, confessions implicitly recognized the divisions among the churches. Exemplary of this meaning of "confession" were the Augsburg Confession, the Helvetic Confessions, the Belgic Confession, and later, the Westminster Confession.[4] Historical theologians believe that confessions were a particular form of theological literature that lasted for a relatively short period of time among mainstream Reformation churches, from about 1530 to 1700.[5]

Out of the tradition of the Reformation, individuals—particularly in the Anabaptist movements characterized by "pure dissent"—took it upon themselves to set out their own statements of belief, calling them

---

[2] See the contemporary Anglican discussion in John Webster, "Confession and Confessions," in *Nicene Christianity: The Future for a New Ecumenism*, ed. Christopher Seitz (Grand Rapids: Brazos Press, 2002) 119–26.

[3] Some Baptists maintain that confessions are a type of creed, along the pattern of the Reformation. While free and democratic, these writers have a higher view of accountability to creeds/confessions than most Baptists would allow. This is particularly true in the American Southern Baptist tradition: See W. J. McGlothlin, *Baptist Confessions of Faith* (Philadelphia: American Baptist Publication Society, 1911) ix–xi. Yet another writer saw creeds as pertaining to the early church, confessions as enforceable by the Catholic Church and the Reformation churches, and a third form, "declarations" as the voluntary statements made by individuals and the New Hampshire Confession. See Ezekiel G. Robinson, *Christian Theology* (Rochester: E. B. Andrews, 1894) 16.

[4] Philip Schaff, *Bibliotheca Symbolica Ecclesiae Universalis, The Creeds of Christendom, with a History and Critical Notes*, vol. 3 (New York: Harper and Brothers, 1877) 11, holds that the differences between the earlier Protestant confessions "pertained to divine decrees, the nature and efficacy of the sacraments, especially the mode of Christ's presence in the Lord's Supper." The later "evangelical" confessions displayed differentiation on matters of anthropology, the Church, and church polity and discipline.

[5] Routley, *Creeds and Confessions*, 1.

"confessions of faith." For many of these Christians, a confession was closely associated with Christian experience. It fit the individualistic nature of Anabaptism perfectly, in that it allowed for one to articulate one's own theological identity. A confession had a devotional dimension to it as well as becoming a voice for a person suffering persecution. The Schleitheim Confession (1527) was an early example. A second noteworthy confession was that of Peter Riedemann (1506–1556), an Anabaptist who became an elder of the Hutterite Brethren. While a prisoner in Hesse in 1540, Riedemann composed his *Rechenschaft unserer Religion, Lehr und Glaubens* ("Account of Our Religion, Doctrine, and Faith"). Analysts are confident that he stood within the tradition of the Schleitheim Confession and that he incorporated a good deal of Hubmaier's thinking.[6] In the foreword to his "confession," Riedemann articulated what a confession meant: "Since it is right, good, agreeable, and well-pleasing to God to confess one's faith," (following St. Paul's advice in Romans 10:10), and "since there is so much blasphemy against the truth..."[7] One may deduce from Riedemann's experience that there have been essentially two important issues in bringing forth a confession in the post-Reformation Free Church tradition: first, the experience of voluntarily affirming one's faith; second, responding to an external stimulus such as "blasphemy" or scandalous and words that misrepresented and defamed an individual. Either circumstance could produce a "confession of faith." Wholly different from devices of doctrinal discipline, confessions in this sense evolved from personal and congregational "testimonies" a kind of "personal apologetic."

The process of producing an historic confession of faith in the later sixteenth century involved four stages. First, there was a stated need for an individual or community to articulate its religious values and propositions. This may have been the process of admission to a congregation or association, or a response to external stimulus. As E. B.

---

[6] Franz Heimann, "The Hutterite Doctrine of the Church and Common Life: A Study of Riedemann's Confession of Faith," *Mennonite Quarterly Review* 26 (January 1962): 142–60; John A. Hostetler, *Hutterite Society* (Baltimore: Johns Hopkins University Press, 1997), 1.

[7] Peter Riedemann, *Account of Our Religion, Doctrine and Faith, Given by Peter Reidemann of the Brothers Whom Men Call Hutterians* (Rifton NY: Plough Publishing House, 1970) 9.

Underhill long ago pointed out, confessions originated in "the false accusations, the calumnies, and misrepresentations of foes."[8]

Next, the confession was composed, that is written out and likely discussed. If by an individual, the person may have sought an existing model to emulate. If by a group, several models may have been employed, and several authors might have had primary and editorial input in a typically voluntary association such as a congregation. The confession was then usually published for the benefit of both the association and any source of external stimulus. Importantly, the original confessions "were not framed to procure unity among the churches that accepted them."[9]

The confession may finally have been employed for purposes beyond its original intention. For instance, some confessions became universally recognized as accepted versions of the beliefs and ethics of a group. This was the case of the early London confessions among Baptists. In some instances, confessional statements took on the facility of providing a standard by which judgements were made to determine doctrinal questions. In this tertiary sense, confessions were no longer confessions of those who produced them nor for the original circumstances for which they were intended, but they came to coerce yet another party or set of circumstances, unrelated to those who first brought the confessions into being. Ironically, such uses have neglected the example of seventeenth-century Baptists "who left the phantom of uniformity to the unavailing search of an establishment."[10]

The development of confessions of faith was a consistent feature of the Anabaptist experience, varied as it was. While they had no generally binding creeds, Anabaptist individuals and congregations issued such statements, some doing so as formulae of union between various branches. Each congregation accepted or rejected what it chose.[11] Balthasar Hubmaier (c.1480–1528), for instance, was among the earliest Anabaptists who created what can be identified as a confession of faith.

---

[8] Edward Bean Underhill, *Confessions of Faith and Other Public Documents Illustrative of the History of the Baptist Churches of England in the 17th Century* (London: Haddon Brothers, 1854) vi.

[9] Ibid.

[10] Ibid.

[11] Williston Walker, *The Creeds and Platforms of Congregationalism* (New York: Charles Scribner's Sons, 1893) 4.

In 1526, while imprisoned in the Watertower of Zurich, he composed "Twelve Articles of Christian Belief" which were formally published the next year in Nikolsburg. Each of the articles was set in the form of a prayer, later causing one writer to speculate that the confession followed a pattern set by Augustine's *Confessions*.[12] Hubmaier's outline, laced with devotional language and personal experiences, [more closely] followed the Apostles' Creed. He affirmed the universal church[13] as well as the importance of water baptism in professing one's faith. The confession ended with a poignant narrative of his persecution.[14]

Similarly, Swiss Brethren leader Michael Sattler (d.1527), met with other Brethren in 1527 at Schleitheim on the Swiss border to address problems associated with unorthodox teachings of South German Anabaptists whom the Swiss thought less biblical and more rationalistic. Sattler was the principal writer of what became known as the "Schleitheim Confession," a document countering the errors of their co-religionists. It became a widely quoted statement of Christian belief. In seven articles dealing with baptism, the ban, the Lord's Supper, separation, the pastorate, the sword, and oaths, the Confession's language was not as devotionally oriented in tone as it was theologically and ethically definitive. Clearly, its signatories wanted to exclude from their fellowship those whose teachings they found erroneous. The Schleitheim Confession became the first of the collective confessional documents issued by a community.[15]

Peter Riedemann, mentioned earlier, provided a lengthy confessional statement. In Book 1 of his confession he commented in over one hundred categories upon classic Apostles' Creed themes, adding Reformed emphases such as the covenants and ethical positions. In Book 2 he covered six areas, including church in the world and the ordinances. Riedemann's work, by many accounts formed a model for early Baptist confessions of faith. Confessions, then, became a more contemporary,

---

[12] Henry C. Vedder, *Balthasar Hubmaier, The Leader of the Anabaptists* (New York: G. P. Putnam's Sons, 1905) 130.

[13] Henry C. Vedder, "What I Teach about the Bible," *The Baptist* (Chicago), 23 October 1920.

[14] "Twelve Articles in Prayer Form," in *Balthasar Hubmaier: Theologian of Anabaptism*, trans. and ed. H. Wayne Pipkin and John H. Yoder (Scottdale PA: Herald Press, 1989) 235–40.

[15] John C. Wenger, "The Schleitheim Confession of Faith," *Mennonite Quarterly Review* 19, 247–53.

less traditionally disciplined means of articulating Christian beliefs. The experience of many Anabaptists was therefore "confessional," meaning that they frequently used the vehicle of a confession of faith to give witness to their views or to correct misrepresentations of their positions.

Whether Anabaptists were direct forbears of Baptists remains a subject of debate. Historical scholarship in the past half century indicates that influences went both ways between Anabaptists and English Puritan/ Separatists, at least geographically. It is likely that Dutch Anabaptists, as part of a Dutch community in exile from the political tyranny of Philip II of the Netherlands, were living and working in England from the 1550s. They immigrated in significant numbers to cities like Norwich, Dover, and Sandwich along the English East coast. It has been estimated that these religious immigrants numbered 30,000.[16] Given the laws under the Tudors for exposing Anabaptist views, they were relatively silent. On the other hand, it is certainly likely that at least the ideas of Anabaptists in England, if not personal connections, were known to Separatists like Robert Browne and Robert Harrison in the 1580s. The extent to which Anabaptist ideas directly influenced English dissenters may never be known with certainty.

Seventeenth-century Baptist thought does bear much resemblance to early English Congregationalism. For example, Robert Browne (c.1550–1633) held to the separation of church and state, the duty of Christians to separate from communion with non-Christians, independence of local congregations, and he rejected the claim of magistrates to coerce consciences. Did Browne receive these ideas from Anabaptists then living in England? If so, it is remarkable that Browne rejected believer's baptism, that he saw nothing amiss in Christians' holding civil office or bearing arms, and that he expressly repudiated alignment with Anabaptists.[17] Rather than insist on a demonstrable connection between baptists and the congregationalist anabaptists, it seems wise to follow the well-worn path of Henry Dexter and Williston Walker. These Congregationalist historians have long believed that the earliest Separatist/Independents "had no consciousness that their views were derived from any other source than the New Testament."[18]

---

[16] Douglas Campbell, *The Puritan in Holland, England, and America*, 2 vols. (New York: 1892) 1:488.

[17] Quoted in Walker, *Creeds of Congregationalism*, 16.

[18] Ibid., 7.

The religious positions articulated by Browne and other Separatists were soon picked up by a London congregation where Francis Johnson was pastor and John Greenwood was teacher. This group issued a confession in 1589 titled "A True Description Out of the Word of God of the Visible Church." This document stressed personal Christian experience, elected church officers, and a body of ruling elders.[19] For their trouble, Greenwood was arrested and executed; Johnson was imprisoned in 1593, along with members of the congregation. Eventually, those who had been imprisoned were released and they imigrated to Amsterdam. They elected Henry Ainsworth (1571–1622) teacher, and following his wise counsel, the congregation prepared a fuller confession of forty-five articles. It was in agreement with continental Reformed thought and the Puritan tradition in the Church of England. Much of "The True Confession" was devoted to defining what a reformed Church of England should look like as "godly congregations." This group of exiled Separates was a part of what William Haller derisively described as Puritanism, as those who were characterized by bibliolatry, an individualistic interpretation of their own authority, a love for civic freedom, and a moral earnestness. Even sharper was Horton Davies' criticism of the "nonconforming Puritans," whom he accused of impatiently wanting reformation according to a misguided grasp of the Word of God and creating illegitimate "gathered churches" to carry forth their ideals. Here was the most likely nesting ground for the earliest Baptists.[20]

Next in theological evolution from Browne, Greenwood, Barrow, Johnson, and Ainsworth was John Smyth of Gainsborough. Trained at Christ College, Cambridge under Francis Johnson, Smyth (fl. 1600–1610) became a pastor in Lincolnshire, his views evolving from those of a displaced Church of England clergyman to Separatist views by 1606, and finally to a "Se-Baptist" stance by 1609 referring either to his self-baptism or his transition from Separatist to Baptist. He expressed his theological views in documents and publications from 1606 to 1612.

From the foregoing discussion, it seems plausible that as a means of articulating theological and ethical affirmations the vehicle of a

---

[19] Dexter referred to the oligarchy of elders in the Congregational tradition as "Barrowism."

[20] Horton Davies, *From Cranmer to Baxter and Fox, 1534–1690*, vol. 1 of *Worship and Theology in England* (Grand Rapids: Eerdmans, 1996) 44.

confession of faith traveled through various forms of radical
Protestantism. These would have included Anabaptists and English
"nonconforming" or congregational Puritans, as well as the earliest
Baptists. Thereafter, Baptists of several types regularly used confessional
statements early in the seventeenth century to define their doctrinal and
ethical views, first for individuals, then for congregations and
associational bodies. McGlothlin observed that Baptists were the last
among mainstream Christians to develop confessions, these coming well
after the great Reformation devices. He rightly pointed out that "they are
not independent productions, but the result of grafting Baptist views of
baptism, church membership, church government, and the relation of
Church and State upon a Calvinistic or Arminian stock."[21]

Baptist confessions of faith exhibit a wide variety of documents,
traditions, purposes, and authors. The major types include: General or
Arminian, Calvinistic, and Mediating. In some instances, confessions
emerged from obvious antagonistic circumstances, while in other
situations individuals placed their ideas on the table for discussion and
negotiation. Some confessions were put forth by groups of churches,
while others were the work of individuals. The documents were
variously published as confessions, private lists of doctrinal formulae,
and tracts or pamphlets exhibiting doctrinal understandings. The period
of confessions of faith stretches from the beginning of the seventeenth
century to the nineteenth century, with an observable resurgence in the
twentieth century as new Baptist groups formed. What is obvious from
the documentary evidence is that there is no one confessional tradition
that reflects anything close to a comprehensive "Baptist" perspective
across time. Rather, Baptist confessional history is rich and varied. To
the various streams, the discussion now turns.

THE GENERAL BAPTIST CONFESSIONAL TRADITION

A succession of General or "Arminian" Baptist confessional statements
emerged across the seventeenth century.[22] These included personal and

---

[21] McGlothlin, *Baptist Confessions of Faith*, xi. This position was an outgrowth of
Philip Schaff's earlier assessment of confessional development among "later evangelical
denominations," that their creeds are "modifications and abridgements rather than
enlargements of the old Protestant symbols." See Schaff, *Creeds of Christendom*, 11.
[22] Underhill included the Confessions of 1611, 1660, and 1678: *Confessions of Faith*,
vi. Here the Orthodox Creed will be treated as a part of a mediating tradition.

collective statements. The earliest legitimately "Baptist-type" confession of faith was written by John Smyth of Gainsborough. There are two important resources on the theology of John Smyth. First was a year of the *Baptist Quarterly* (1984) that contained an exchange of views on the sources of Smyth's thought: Douglas Shantz, "The Place of the Resurrected Christ in the Writings of John Smyth", James R. Coggins, "The Theological Positions of John Smyth"; Stephen Brachlow, "John Smyth and the Ghost of Anabaptism"; B.R. White, "The English Separatists and John Smyth Revisited." The second is a recent thorough study of Smyth, Jason K. Lee, *The Theology of John Smyth: Puritan, Separatist, Baptist, Mennonite* (Macon: Mercer University Press, 2003). With respect to Lee's categorization of Smyth as a "Baptist," I remain unconvinced of the clear identifiability of a mature baptistic position in Smyth, except on the matter of baptism. I agree with Lee that Smyth's arrival at Mennonite views was definitive, and I think it came more closely on the heels of his Separatist identity than his period as a "se-baptist" requires. He and Thomas Helwys, who eventually split from Smyth over doctrinal and ecclesiastical issues in Amsterdam, came to constitute the beginnings of a General Baptist tradition[23]. By the 1620s there were half a dozen congregations of this persuasion in and around London.

John Smyth, a truly transitional thinker, is likely responsible for writing a documented 1609 confession, followed by another in 1610, and a final set of propositions in 1612. A confessional statement of sorts in 1609 was contained in an "Epistle to the Reader," introducing Smyth's *The Character of the Beast*. Smyth demonstrated at least an indirect Mennonite influence in his avowal of the importance of both testaments and the observance of the Sabbath that had drawn criticism over lax observances under the Mennonites. A second issue in Smyth's preface was the authority of magistrates. Here Smyth followed the pattern of many Mennonites in recognizing the magisterial authority in secular matters, while remaining silent about their authority over the populace with respect to religious matters. Smyth responded somewhat vaguely to the accusation that he had adopted the Melchiorite Christology popular

---

[23] Smyth's theology is best understood when contextualized in his Puritan, Separatist, Baptist, and Mennonite phases. In the Mennonite phase his thinking changed under the influence of Hans de Ries. See Jason Lee, *The Theology of John Smyth: Puritan, Separatist, Baptist, Mennonite* (Macon: Mercer University Press, 2003), 35-40, 87-90.

among Mennonites, teaching that Christ's flesh came from heaven and thus Christ was not descended from Mary in the orthodox sense.[24]

In 1610 Smyth and some of his followers issued "Corde Credimus," ("we believe with our hearts") a confessional statement of 20 articles in Latin. At about the same time, a group in Thomas Helwys's church issued a statement known as "Synopsis Fidei." This second statement—whose full English title is "Declaration of Faith of English People Remaining at Amsterdam in Holland"—has been called the first English Baptist confession of Faith.[25] Both confessional statements adopted a Mennonite position on redemption, atonement, and free will. To quote Smyth, who had moved far afield of the Reformed position, "God has created and redeemed the human race to his own image, and has ordained all men (no one being reprobated) to life." Even more strongly, he continued, "That men...are able...to repent, to believe, to turn to God and to attain eternal life; so on the other hand, they are able themselves to resist the Holy Spirit, to depart from God, and to perish forever."[26]

Both documents were presented to the Dutch Mennonites and there was general acceptance of the theological tenets of the English Separatist-Baptist communities.[27] As noted earlier, however, serious difficulties eventually broke out between the expatriated Smyth and Helwys factions with the result that Helwys and his group returned to England and established an ongoing Baptist theological tradition in England. Smyth and his congregation remained in the Netherlands and eventually joined with the Waterlander Mennonites.

Theologically, Helwys's 1610–1611 confession is an admixture of perspectives. For instance, Article 5 declares clearly election and reprobation, while "God is the author of no man's condemnation." The understanding of the atonement is general: "For God would have all men

---

[24] James Coggins, *John Smyth's Congregation* (Scottdale PA: Herald Press, 1991) 74–75; Lee, 209-229.

[25] The fact that it was written originally in Latin is a clue to Helwys's authorship. As a lawyer, his first language was Latin and his correspondence with the Mennonites exhibits this trait.

[26] "Corde Credimus," quoted in William H. Brackney, ed., *Baptist Life and Thought 1600–1980* (Valley Forge: Judson Press, 1983) 26–27; Lee, 87-89.

[27] A useful comparative study of the two documents and Mennonite influences is Goki Saito, "An Investigation into the Relationship Between the Early English General Baptists and the Dutch Anabaptists" (Th.D. diss., Southern Baptist Theological Seminary, 1974).

saved…and would have no man to perish." Likewise, Article 7 is equally clear that "men may fall away from the grace of God." It adds, "Let no man presume to think that because he hath or once had grace, therefore he shall always have grace."[28] The ecclesiological perspective follows Smyth ("the church of Christ is a company of faithful people") and demonstrates Separatist thinking, affirming that "divers particular congregations" are "the body of Christ, and a whole church." Baptism enters into the doctrine of the church as the means to membership upon one's profession of faith. The scriptural reference to baptism is Romans 6, although a proper mode is not suggested. Like the Independents of the Elizabethan era, Helwys urged that ministers are to be chosen by election and approbation of the congregation, with fasting, prayer, and the laying on of hands."[29] Finally, unlike Mennonites, these early "Baptists in exile" believed that it was lawful for church members to serve as magistrates, "and bear the sword of God." Perhaps owing to Helwys' own profession of law, there is a strong statement about the punishment of offenders and the legitimacy of taking up arms in defense of one's country.[30]

Helwys himself made two significant theological contributions to Baptist thought. First was his singular work on religious liberty. In *The Mistery of Iniquity* (1612), he wrote, "Our lord the king cannot as a king have any power over this kingdom, temple, tabernacle, house, and people of God in respect of the religion to God, because our lord the king's kingdom is an earthly kingdom." He continued, "Further, he has no authority as a king but in earthly causes… men's religion to God is between God and themselves. The king shall not answer for it. Neither may the king be judge between God and man. Let them be heretics, Turks, Jews, or whatsoever, it appertains not to the earthly power to punish them in the least measure."[31]

Second, Helwys wrote clearly on the matter of redemption and free will. He reasoned, "[God] by grace in Christ, hath Freed Adam, and in him al man-kind from that sinne off Adam." As for original sin and infants, he responded to the prevailing Calvinism of his time, "al infants are freed by the universall redemption off Christ from that condemnation

---

[28] Underhill, *Confessions of Faith*, 4, 5.

[29] Ibid., 7, 9.

[30] Ibid.,vii., 9–10.

[31] Thomas Helwys, *A Short Declaration of the Mystery of Iniquity*, ed. Richard Groves (Macon GA: Mercer University Press, 1998) 53, 59.

which you (by your opinion off particular redemption) would cast upon most of them."[32]

An interesting theological question that has arisen over the years among Baptist theologians is whether the Smyth/Helwys group or its derivatives were of a genuinely "Arminian" character. The term "Arminian" properly refers to the position of Jacobus Arminius (1560–1609), a Dutch theologian contemporary with the period of Baptist origins. Looking at later General Baptist statements, it became easy to label General Baptists as "Arminian" because of the general atonement and freewill positions held by most General Baptists. James Coggins, however, has again visited the theological indicators in the development of the Smyth/Helwys group and arrived at some useful hypotheses to counter the common supposition.

First, in the context of widespread affirmation of predestination theology as seen in Puritanism, Anglican leadership, and among the Dutch Reformed, John Smyth adopted a free will position by 1610. In effect, he thereby repudiated current Reformed teachings as well as establishing an early contravention to the 1619 Canons of Dort. The Helwys faction that later returned to England clearly favored a general atonement understanding by 1611. The source of their position on the matter, if it can be reduced to any single influence, could have been their own study of the Scriptures or a theological teacher at Cambridge named Peter Baro.[33] The possibility of influence, however, from Dutch Arminians or the Mennonites cannot be ignored.

It seems unlikely that Smyth adopted Peter Baro's position at a later point, when he could have done so in the 1590s as a student at Cambridge. Another possibility was interaction with the Dutch followers of views called "The Remonstrance." while Smyth and Helwys must have been aware of the Remonstrants' position as it raged in Amsterdam, there is no textual dependence upon Remonstrant phraseology. Additionally, Arminius himself at one point rejected the position of the

---

[32] Thomas Helwys, "A Shorte and Plaine Proofe by the Word and Workes of God that God's Decree is not the cause of Anye Mans Sinne or Condemnation; and that All men are Redeemed by Christ; also that no infants are Condemned"quoted in Brackney, *Baptist Life and Thought*, 28–29.

[33] This is the thesis of William T. Whitley, *History of The British Baptists* (London: Carey Kingsgate Press, 1923) xx, and Lonnie D. Kliever, "General Baptist Origins: The Question of Anabaptist Influence," *Mennonite Quarterly Review* 36 (1962): 291–321. More recently, see Lee, *Theology of John Smyth*, 42, 88.

English Separatists. It is more probable was that the Smyth/Helwys group derived its free will and general atonement position and its rejection of predestinarian thought from the Mennonites[34]. The "Short Confession" of Hans de Ries seems much more the likely source of the English group's phrases and doctrine in general. This textual proximity—when coupled with the experiences of Smyth, Helwys, and others who suffered under the arbitrary use of power exercised by a religious authority demanding the embrace of stifling doctrine of determinism—is sufficient grounds to conclude that de Ries may have been a major fountainhead for the theological stance of the early General Baptists. Later, as a generic usage of the term "Arminian" came into vogue,[35] its application to General Baptists seemed appropriate.

William Lumpkin identified a confession issued in 1651 by thirty Midlands congregations as a next stage in the General Baptist confessional tradition. This document he thought to illustrate "soul competency" and theological consensus of an association.[36] He also thought that it demonstrated usage of Thomas Helwys's twenty-seven article confession of 1611. Evidence for a confessional continuity consists of article 17 wherein the authors stated, "that Christ suffered death for all mankind, or every man" and that "he will certainly raise all mankind from that death that fell on them." (Article 18 of the Midlands confession).[37] Articles 31 and 44 reveal a rather sophisticated perception of prevenient grace and human capability, while not using the terms: "That those gifts which God of his free grace gives unto men to the enabling or empowering them to obey or believe in his name, are called the grace of God, as they spring from the spirit of grace"; and, "That God of his free grace or love, called or calleth sinners to repentance and afforded or affordeth them time and opportunity to repent or returne unto

---

[34] Lee, 192-206.

[35] It came to be synonymous with any position advocating some kind of freewill: Underhill, *Confessions of Faith*, v; Coggins, *Smyth's Congregation,* 133. The term was used in the early eighteenth century, if not before, to describe General Baptists pejoratively. For example, in 1740 Thomas Crosby described Benjamin Keach's early associations as "Arminians." Thomas Crosby, *History of the English Baptists* (London, 1740) iv, 272.

[36] William Lumpkin, *Baptist Confessions of Faith*, 173.

[37] *The Faith and Practise of Thirty Congregations, Gathered According to the Primitive Pattern* (London: William Larner, 1651) quoted in ibid., 178.

him."[38] What Lumpkin thought to be evidence of "soul competency" (clearly a late nineteenth-century term coined by E. Y. Mullins), was actually closer to Arminian usage. This confession did move baptismal theology ahead, affirming baptism by immersion in the General Baptist community; this may well have been the document's enduring significance.[39]

Thomas Crosby, E. B. Underhill, and others have identified what may well be the high water mark of the General Baptist confessional tradition, the so-called Standard Confession of 1660. The immediate circumstance that called the confession into being was a series of scurrilous and damaging reports that London Baptists were accumulating weaponry to do harm to persons who opposed Baptist doctrines and, perhaps worse, some secret treasonous plot to overthrow Parliamentary rule. Writers of the confession labeled such rumormongers "lyers and wicked devisers of mischeife, and corrupt designs."[40] Originally forty General Baptist leaders signed it, largely representative of London. Within three years it became broadly acceptable throughout the Connection, as it was referred to in a regional context. Tradition has it that it may have been the work of Thomas Monck of Hertfordshire and Matthew Caffyn of Sussex. Ratified by the General Assembly of General Baptists in 1660, the Confession was presented to Charles II in an attempt to halt the persecution of Baptists. There was little noticeable effect. In 1678 the esteemed Thomas Grantham edited the Confession, adding refinements of explanatory notes and references from the early church literature and the Reformers. Further revisions were made at the request of the General Assembly in 1691 and 1700.

Several parts of the Standard Confession marked its General Baptist character. Article 3 uses the term "freely" twice to indicate the nature of Christ's death for every man, that is, for the sins of the whole world. Human capability is emphasized in Article 6, where "the way set forth for men to be justified...is...by faith in Christ when men shall assent to the truth of the Gospel, believing with all their hearts." In Article 10 the

---

[38] Ibid., 179, 181–82.

[39] It should be noted that the scriptural passages adduced in support of this were the Matthean and Markan gospel narratives of Jesus' baptism, not the more likely passage in Romans 6:1–2 where the symbolism of immersion was clear.

[40] *A Brief Confession or Declaration of Faith* (London: F. Smith, 1660) quoted in Underhill, *Confessions of Faith,* 119.

confessors followed Thomas Helwys in saying that infants were not condemned for original sin. Article 12 affirmed the laying on of hands for the promise of the Holy Spirit. Most significantly, Article 24 clearly embraced liberty of conscience in matters of religion, asserting the inappropriateness of coercion through oppression or persecution.[41]

Within the General Baptist connection there was an identifiable confessional heritage from Smyth and Helwys as individuals to the collective statements of the Midlands churches to the Standard Confession of the General Assembly. The tradition thus identified for the seventeenth century had a modest influence upon General Baptists in the American Colonies and the General Six Principle Baptists in New England. In England the decline of General Baptists at the turn of the eighteenth century was due in part to lesser importance being placed upon doctrine in favor of unitarian and universalist themes. Thus, the oldest confessional tradition among Baptists died quietly.

A MEDIATING CONFESSIONAL TRADITION.

Over the course of the seventeenth century there were several attempts to unite the divergent families of General and Particular Baptists. In some cases this took the form of thinkers who combined other ideas with either General or Particular emphases. While only marginally successful, the mediating confessions illustrate the variety that existed among the types of Baptist confessionalism.

One of the earliest attempts to mediate the differences between the General and Particular Baptists was in 1650 among the churches in Somersetshire. At the root of this attempt was a letter from churches in Ireland to their brethren in London. The letter was apparently circulated broadly among churches in England and this led to discussions in associations of churches. Meetings were held in Wells, Tiverton, and Bridgewater. Underhill believed the resulting statement that came to be known as the Somerset Confession was likely written by Thomas Collier, a General Baptist messenger in Somerset who brought forth the document at Wells in April 1655.[42]

McGlothlin and Lumpkin were both convinced that the Somerset Confession was an attempt at representing both General and Particular

---

[41] Ibid., 109, 113, 124.
[42] Underhill, *Confessions of Faith*, xi.

(Calvinistic) Baptists.[43] Points that support this impression include the moderate Calvinism of the West Country Baptists, the exclusion of certain passages from the well-known London Confession of 1644, and the probable independent thinking of the likely author, Thomas Collier.[44] The Calvinistic quality of the confession is manifest initially in Articles 9, 10, 11, and 15: God chose some to himself (the elect) who "shall never finally fall from him," and that "by his death on the cross, [Christ Jesus] hath obtained eternal redemption and deliverance for his church."[45] The General Baptist tone is seen in phraseology taken directly from Hebrews 6 (though it is not cited): "repented from dead works and have faith towards God, to be baptized," and "the just freedom and liberty in the right worship and order belonging to the church of Jesus Christ" (Articles 24, 30).[46]

In terms of ecclesiology, more of a General Baptist kind is hinted at in the positing of an ordinance "to send forth such brethren as are fully gifted and qualified through the Spirit of Christ to preach the gospel to the world" (Article 34). In response to Quakers and Fifth Monarchists who were complicating theological matters for both General and Particular Baptists, Articles 39–42 detailed a second coming of Christ, the judgment of nations on the earth, the triumph of the righteous, and included a description of heaven and hell as part of an eschatological expectation. Baptism by dipping or "burying under the water" (Article 24) and "several congregations and assemblies, if occasion be, to communicate with each other in things spiritual and things temporal" (Article 28)[47], an associational principle, reflect maturing Baptist emphases common to both traditions by 1650.

The capstone document of the mediating confessions was the Orthodox Creed of 1679. Baptists of the Midlands produced the

---

[43] McGlothlin, *Baptist Confessions of Faith*; Lumpkin, *Baptist Confessions,* 201–202.

[44] Collier was the author of *Several Resolutions and Answers of Queries* (London, 1655). On Collier, See Richard D. Land, "Doctrinal Controversies of the English Particular Baptists 1644–1691, As Illustrated by the Career and Writings of Thomas Collier" (Ph.D. diss., Oxford University, 1979).

[45] Quoted in *A Confession of Faith of Several Churches of Christ In the County of Somerset and of some Churches in the Counties neer adjacent* (London: Henry Hills, 1656).

[46] Ibid..

[47] Ibid., xxviii.

document,[48] perhaps under the direction of Thomas Monck, a messenger of the Buckinghamshire congregation.[49] The use of the terms "orthodox" and "creed" was doubtless to connect with ancient church doctrines, probably in the "orthodox" tradition of the first seven councils of the early church. The stated purpose of the creed was "to unite all true Protestants in the fundamental articles of the Christian religion against the errors and heresies of Rome."[50] In this case, "Rome" was a reference to the established medieval church. Here was an attempt by Baptists to create an English Protestant creedal statement that could be seen as a legitimate successor to the Athanasian, Apostles', and Nicene creeds, each of which was reproduced within the Baptist document.[51] The authors even included a positive assessment of councils or assemblies of bishops, elders, and brethren "of the several churches of Christ" so as to suggest a parity of Baptist organizations with other Protestant bodies.[52]

The contents of the Orthodox Creed reflected both Calvinistic and Arminian statements. For instance, from the Calvinistic perspective, Article 9 gives lengthy exposition to predestination and election, describing "those whom he hath chosen in Christ" as the elect,

---

[48] A comprehensive listing of the signers is found in Arnold H. J. Baines, "Signatories to the Orthodox Confession, 1679," *Baptist Quarterly* 17/1, 2, 3 (January, April, July, 1957): 35–43; 74–87; 122–29.

[49] This is the theory of Lumpkin, who supposed similarities with Monck's work, *A cure for the cankering error of the new Eutychians* (1673). See Lumpkin, *Baptist Confessions*, 295. He was also persuaded that the Orthodox Creed was a step toward Andrew Fuller's evangelical Calvinism, but this is not supported by any evidence in Fuller. Among English Baptist historians, George Gould erroneously ascribed the Creed to Particular Baptists. William Underwood rightly identified it as having likely been composed in response to the Particular Confession of 1688. Underwood also pointed out that no particular Baptist congregations were known to have existed where the signers lived, whereas General Baptists were numerous. Underwood also identified the office of messenger as unknown at the time among Particulars. Most compelling, Adam Taylor, the first General Baptist historian, claimed the Creed as General Baptist in a dispute in 1700 in a church in Wymeswold. See William Underwood, *The General Baptist Denomination, Its Past History, Distinctive Peculiarities, and Present Position* (London: Henry James Tresidder, 1864) 5n.

[50] *An Orthodox Creed, or A Protestant Confession of Faith, Being An Essay To Unite and Confirm All True Protestants in the Fundamental Articles of the Christian Religion, Against the Errors and Heresies of Rome* (London, 1679) reprinted in Underhill, *Confessions of Faith*, 121.

[51] Ibid., 158.

[52] Ibid., 159.

foreordained, and predestinated "to endure forever." But, in the same context, General Baptist terminology derived from Hebrews 6 is evident. For example, "repentance, faith and obedience to God's commandments" was the outworking of Christ's meritorious cause. Original sin was confirmed in Articles 14 and 15. Likewise, Article 26 stated very clearly a doctrine of perseverance of the saints. A softened doctrine of reprobation was included in Article 49, where the writers spoke of hell, torment, and utter darkness with the bodies of unjust persons "being raised to dishonor."[53]

Not surprisingly, other General Baptist qualities were also clearly set forth in the document. As part of a new covenant of grace, freely and fully offered to all men, Christ died for all men, "and there is sufficiency in his death and merits for the sins of the whole world" (Article 18). To carry the General persuasion further, the creed treated the special grace "that frees man from his natural bondage under sin," to will that which is spiritually good. Wrought in humans by the spirit of God, "evangelical repentance" involved a true sorrow of the heart, sincere confession, careful endeavor to leave one's sins, a turning of the whole man to God, to be continued throughout one's life (Article 22). This was, in turn, buttressed by a statement in Article 26 that sanctification involved a continual war in the soul, the believer being enabled by Christ to do good works and exercise piety. Officers in the church of Christ were identical to the General Baptist pattern, including the messenger, and the term "bishop" was used in the sense of "overseer" (Article 31). In view of contemporaneous debates among General Baptists, there was a clear statement (Article 32) that defined prayer with imposition of hands by the bishop as a rite following baptism in order to receive the promised Spirit. Here was a victory for Thomas Grantham's following among the General Baptists. Finally, on the eve of Toleration, the article on "Liberty of Conscience" employed terminology like "God alone is Lord of the conscience" and any thought of requiring an implicit faith was seen to be repugnant to true liberty of conscience and reason.[54]

Mention must also be made of several other elements in this confessional statement that appear to suggest mediation beyond the Calvinistic and General Baptists. For example, the use of the term "one holy catholick church," to be equated with the universal church—as well

[53] Ibid., 128, 133,156, 167.
[54] Ibid., 139, 142, 151–52, 165.

as the visible church on earth being composed of several distinct congregations (Baptist not being particularized)—certainly were openings to other Protestant communions, possibly even the established church. In Article 30 the Reformation rule was quoted: "Where the Word of God is preached and the sacraments truly administered." This certainly would have been attractive to Presbyterians and Lutherans. Hearkening to the decade-old phraseology of the London Calvinistic Confession, the creed acknowledged that errors could exist in a church without its being "unchurched."[55] While believer's baptism was clearly endorsed in Article 31, infant baptism and its connection to original sin was ascribed to Roman Catholicism rather than to Protestant churches that practiced the sacramental liturgy. With respect to the Lord's Supper, the term "sacrament" appeared, but transubstantiation and consubstantiation were associated with the Council of Trent and Lateran theology (Article 33). The Church of England might well have been favorably inclined to Article 42 that affirmed seasons of fasting and "publick humiliation" as an ordinance of God.[56]

One of the often-neglected confessional Baptist groups of the seventeenth century is the Seventh Day tradition. This third major category of early Baptists established a creative theological link with both General and Particular Baptists.[57] Seventh Day preachers often crossed over to fill pulpits of first day congregations such as Mill Yard and Pinner's Hall in London.[58] The Seventh Day position could be summarized as a desire to be faithful to the Ten Commandments as found in Exodus and Deuteronomy. As Thomas Bampfield (1659–1693) put it, "Jesus Christ, the Jehovah of the Old Testament, instituted and sanctified the Sabbath Day in the beginning, before the fall of man; that

---

[55] Ibid., 149.

[56] Ibid., 152–53,162.

[57] A "first day" evaluation is found in Ernest A. Payne, "More About the Sabbatarian Baptists," *Baptist Quarterly* 14/4 (October 1951): 161–66.

[58] Among the "crossover" preachers and writers were Henry Danvers, Vavasour Powell, Peter Chamberlyn and Joseph Stennett. The venerable Calvinistic Baptist, John Gill, preached at Stennett's settlement and recalled him as "an eloquent defender of the doctrines of grace against Socinianism." Another tradition places Stennett with neither the Calvinistic nor General Baptists, but with those "who practice the six principles of the Christian religion," that is Hebrews 6:1–2. See *Seventh Day Baptists in Europe and America,* vol. 1 (Plainfield NJ: American Sabbath Tract Society, 1910) 100; and Joseph Ivimey, *History of the English Baptists*, vol. 3 (London: Holdsworth, 1823) 406.

the Sabbath was not only a seventh day, but the seventh day and was to continue as long as the world lasts;" that the Sabbath was binding upon the Gentiles as well as the Jews, and that it was always to begin at sunset. The Mill Yard (1651) congregation's adopted confession included the Ten Commandments, Matthew 5:19, and Revelation 12:17 and 14:12. At Pinner's Hall where Joseph Stennett was minister, the two great confessional principles from 1676 were, "We own the Lord Jesus Christ to be the one and only LORD and Lawgiver to our souls and consciences, And we own the Holy Scriptures of Truth as ye one and only rule of Faith, Worship, and Life, according to which we are to judge of all our Cases."[59] During the Cromwell Protectorate years, the Fifth Monarchy movement produced a millenarian theology that also brought together General and Particular Baptists with the idea that a "fifth monarchy" would soon be established with King Jesus at its head.[60] The single Baptist church that signed the Fifth Monarchy Manifesto as a unit, according to historian Louise F. Brown, was that of Dr. Peter Chamberlyn, a visionary deeply imbued with Fifth Monarchy views. Chamberlyn was also a leading Seventh Day Baptist.[61]

THE CALVINISTIC BAPTIST CONFESSIONAL TRADITION.

An entirely separate stream of Baptist life and thought from the General Baptists or the Seventh Day Baptists emerged in the greater London region in the 1630s. It had its origins in a congregation that began amidst the Separatists about 1616. Henry Jacob was the movement's first leader, followed by others in course, John Lathrop, Henry Jessey, John Spilsbury, and Samuel Eaton.[62] Once this London congregation declared its baptistic nature (about 1638), other historic personalities were soon associated with the nascent group: William Kiffin, Hanserd Knollys, and Richard Blunt. Daniel Featley, a Presbyterian controversialist of the era,

---

[59] Quoted in *Seventh Day Baptists,* 1:42, 53, 66.

[60] For a connection between Calvinistic Baptists and the Fifth Monarchy movement, consult B. R. White, "John Pendarves, the Calvinistic Baptists, and the Fifth Monarchy," *Baptist Quarterly* 25/6 (April 1974): 251–72.

[61] I am indebted to Dr. Kenneth Chroniger at Alfred Station Baptist Church (New York) for pointing this out. See Louise F. Brown, *The Political Activities of the Baptists and the Fifth Monarchy Men in England During the Interregnum* (Washington DC: American Historical Association, 1912) 59.

[62] Most of what is known about Eaton is in B. R. White, "Samuel Eaton (d. 1639): Particular Baptist Pioneer," *Baptist Quarterly* 24/1 (January 1971): 10–21.

described the congregation as: "tender-hearted Christians who neither teach free-will, nor falling from grace, with the Arminians; nor deny original sin, with the Pelagians; nor disclaim magistracy, with the Jesuits; nor maintain plurality of wives, with the Polygamists; nor community of goods with the Apostolici; nor going naked, with the Adamites; much less over the mortality of the soul, with Epicures and Pschopanychists."[63]

From this one congregation a cluster of churches sprang up to form the London Association of Baptist Churches. It was the forerunner of the dominant group, numerically and theologically, among Baptists in Britain and America. Among the English Calvinistic Baptists, its confessional tradition is represented in the Confessions of 1644, 1656, and 1677. The expansion of this tradition to the United States is a noteworthy feature of later Baptist world-wide expansion.[64]

As congregational life took shape in the 1630s and 1640s, much misunderstanding ensued about Baptists in general, coupled with disinformation provided by other groups with a variety of competing agendas, most notably among the Anglicans and Presbyterians. The misperceptions were at least mischievous, but most often damaging, accusing Baptists of such things as publishing "seditious pamphlets, the tumultuous rising of rude multitudes, the preaching of the cobblers, felt-makers, tailors, grooms, and women; the choosing of any place for God's service but the church; the night-meetings of naked men and women; the licentiousness of spiritual marriages without any legal form..."[65] Among Particular Baptists this prompted the issuance of the first Baptist collective confession of faith by seven London congregations in 1644. It is popularly known as the First London Confession. Editions of the confession, some with changes, were published in 1646, 1651, 1652, and 1653, the last of which was at Leith in Scotland and apparently associated with the New Model Army in that region.

---

[63] Quoted in Thomas Crosby, *The History of the English Baptists from the Reformation to the Beginning of the Reign of King George I*, vol. 1 (London: Crosby, 1738) 171.

[64] For an overall assessment of the Calvinist tradition and its evolution, see F. Townley Lord, "A Moderate Estimate of Calvinism," *Baptist Quarterly* (1928–1929): 82–89; and R. T. Kendall, "The Nature of Saving Faith from William Perkins to the Westminster Assembly" (Ph.D. diss., Oxford University, 1976).

[65] Underhill, *Confessions of Faith*, viii, collected these impressions from authors like Daniel Featley, Edwards, and Robert Baillie.

The First London Confession was a Calvinistic statement of Baptist thought. Historians and theologians have posited the possible influence of several sources upon this key statement. First there was the likelihood of transference of phrases and ideas from earlier personal and collective confessional documents, notably the True Confession of 1596. Among other possibilities was John Spilsbury's published ten-article confession that focussed upon baptism, *A Treatise Concerning the Lawful Subject of Baptism* (1643). Another source that may have contributed to the First London Confession is thought to have been an Aberdeen, Scotland, confession adopted by the Assembly of the Church of Scotland in 1616. Other recently suggested "roots" of the 1644 confession include a synthesis of the Brownist True Confession, some material from William Ames's *The Marrow of Theology* (1629), and perhaps Menno Simons's 1539 *Dat fundament des Christelycken leers (Foundation-Book).* Dependence upon the Mennonite source appears to be in the section devoted to baptism (39), though a recent study concludes that it could have been issued in response to a critique that Praise-God Barebone gave of his former friends in the Separatist congregation.[66] What is conclusive is that seventeen articles of the First London Confession have no identifiable sole source and may be presumed to be original compositions of the London Particular Baptists.[67]

The Calvinistic character of the First London Confession is visible throughout the document. One of the stated purposes of the confession was to address charges whereby Baptists had violated the Reformed tradition. The Preface states, "They finding us out of that common road-way themselves walke, have smote us and taken away our vaile...charging us with holding Free-will, Falling away from grace, denying Originall sinne ..."[68] The Reformed consensus was clear and those outside, including the General Baptists, were pronounced

---

[66] Compare James M. Renihan, "An Examination of the Possible Influence of Menno Simons' Foundation Book upon the Particular Baptist Confession of 1644," *American Baptist Quarterly* 15/3 (September 1996): 190–207 with Glen Harold Stassen, "Opening Menno Simons's *Foundation-Book* and Finding the Father of Baptist Origins Alongside the Mother—Calvinist Congregationalism," *Baptist History and Heritage* (Spring, 1998): 34–38.

[67] Jay Travis Collier, "The Sources Behind the First London Confession," *American Baptist Quarterly* 21/2 (June 2002): 197–214.

[68] "To All That Desire," *London Confession*, 1644 in Lumpkin, *Baptist Confessions*, 154–55.

theologically anathema by the more accepted/established protestant bodies.

Given the social climate of the times, it was appropriate for the London Baptist churches in question to state clearly their collective Calvinistic stance. For instance, in Article 5 of the First London Confession, the writers asserted the importance of "the elect which God hath loved with an everlasting love are redeemed, quickened, and saved, not by themselves, neither by their own workes...but wholly and onely by God of his free grace and mercy through Jesus Christ."[69] Further defining the "particularity" of the atonement, Article 3 added, "God hath in Christ before the foundation of the world, according to the good pleasure of His will, foreordained some men to eternall life through Jesus Christ...leaving the rest in their sinne to their just condemnation to the praise of His justice."[70] In masterful prose, the writers went on to identify the company of visible saints: "that Christ hath here on earth a spirituall Kingdome, which is the Church...called and separated from the world...to the visible profession of the faith."[71] Members of the established church considered many Baptist practices to be "devilish." They took exception to much of what the Baptists affirmed: that church power ought to rest in the hands of the people, that requiring the involuntary payment of tithes to ecclesiastical authority was unlawful, that any gifted member of the church could preach (not necessarily in a steeple house), that it was appropriate to observe the Lord's Supper in common inns, and that preachers should work with their own hands and not go about in black clothes. Clearly, the established church held that the profession of Christian orthodoxy by such people was not to be trusted.[72]

The First London Confession of 1644 and its elaborated derivatives clearly established one branch of Baptists in the mainstream of English Reformed theology. As the Commonwealth dawned, Baptists moved from distant dissenters to leadership in Cromwell's England. This could

---

[69] Ibid., 158.

[70] Lumpkin, *Baptist Confessions*, 157; the theme of foreknowledge is again repeated in article 11, and in article 12 the following is added: "which calling therefore contains in it selfe chusing, foreordaining, sending. Chusing respects the end, foreordaining the means, sending the execution it self, all of mere grace, without any condition fore -seen, either in men, or in Christ, himselfe."

[71] Ibid., 165.

[72] Underhill, *Confessions of Faith*, ix.

not have happened without both accommodations on the part of Baptists to the wider Reformed tradition and some movement toward acceptance by the Puritans on the other side. By using phraseology from Reformed confessions and theological constructs from classic Calvinistic dogma, the first was accomplished. Through public disputations and polemical literature, the Baptist community won a hard-fought battle of acceptance.[73]

Two notable examples of individual confessions of faith belong to the Calvinistic tradition in the period between the First and Second (1677) London Confessions. Vavasour Powell composed what may be the oldest example and John Bunyan wrote the second. Both were widely circulated. Powell (1617–1671), a Welsh evangelist, was a graduate of Oxford University and he was ordained an Anglican priest. He read widely in Puritan literature and became a Baptist. In the 1650s he adopted millenarian views and enjoyed for a time missionary recognition under the Cromwell regime. Later he suffered persecution for his nonconformity. His biography was a spiritual classic among Welsh Baptists for generations, perpetuating his theological views in that region.

Powell's confession of faith consisted of twenty-eight articles elaborated with Scripture texts. The individual articles take up subjects as diverse as the decrees of God, covenants, church life, the Jews, and matters pertaining to the antichrist. The statement, which had a long-lasting currency in Wales, was deeply Christological. It exhibited Powell's preoccupation with Fifth Monarchist ideas, especially issues dealing with the antichrist and the conversion of the Jews. The writer was careful to observe that while many held the Roman Catholic pope to be the antichrist, he thought another might come in the future. With respect to the Jews, he believed they would be restored to Israel "suddenly and strangely." Further, he held they would subsequently

---

[73] There is no available evidence that the First London Confession enjoyed any particular acceptance in the American colonies. This may be attributed to several reasons, including lack of available copies, the overarching importance of the Westminster Confession among American Puritans, and the greater predominance of Baptist emigrants from other than London, such as Somersetshire.

rebuild Jerusalem and there "exercise the first and chiefest power on earth."[74]

Powell's Calvinistic emphases were seen in his discussion of election and reprobation. Of election, he maintained a "prelapsarian" view and attached salvation to "a certain number" who were predestinated and promised eternal life before time began. Consequently, he reasoned, those who were not elected to salvation "were ordained of old to condemnation" (reprobation).[75] Powell's idea of the atonement was consistently "limited" in its application: "The Lord Jesus Christ, by dying and offering up himself as a Sacrifice to God the Father...hath perfectly satisfied for the sins of all that were saved before his coming in the flesh or that shall be saved thereafter." The elect are virtually justified, which is wholly of God's grace.[76] Saints persevere under the New Covenant and good works are considered God's good works to his praise and glory. Powell also included in his ecclesiology a universal church (the elect of all times), a stress upon Christian societies or particular churches, churches being helpful to each other (the principle of association), closed communion, singing of psalms and hymns, and the laying on of hands for both gospel ministers and all believers to signify receiving the Holy Spirit. Powell showed dependence upon the First London Confession in his use of phraseology with respect to the church wherein "particular churches have distinct power, each within itself, of admitting and ejecting members, of choosing their own officers."[77]

The Restoration Period (1660–1688) was for the Calvinistic Baptist community a period of numerical growth, increasing acceptance, and yet renewed persecution under the Clarendon Code. The eminent Bedford pastor, John Bunyan, was moved to write a confession that was published in 1672, at the conclusion of his imprisonment under the Clarendon Code. While it rambled considerably in style and does not demonstrate the theological breadth typically associated with Bunyan (to be discussed below), it does demonstrate his priorities as a Baptist pastor.

The First London Confession had apparently fallen into disuse and few copies were available by the mid-1670s. Prevailing Reformed

---

[74] Vavasour Powell, *A Confession of Faith, drawn Up by Mr. Vavasour Powell, Concerning the Holy Scriptures* (n.p., 1660?) 43, 44–45.
[75] Ibid., 24–25.
[76] Ibid., 27, 29.
[77] Ibid., 36–37, 41.

theology was articulated in the Westminster Confession of Faith (1646), which the Presbyterians accepted and the Congregationalists—with some changes—ratified at their Savoy Conference in 1658. The Baptist community was under no small amount of pressure to demonstrate their proximity to the Westminster Confession. The result was the Second London Confession of Faith (1677), "put forth by the elders and Brethren of many Congregations of Christians…in London and the Country." There were three manifestations of this confession: The first was the original composition, attributed to William Collins, pastor of the Petty France Baptist congregation in London. A body of representatives was called to a general meeting from across England and Wales and approved it. Eleven years later, a second edition was produced and ratified by the Assembly of the Particular Baptists meeting in London. This time 38 pastors from as many congregations, including Collins, signed the confession "in the name of and behalf of the whole Assembly." The third manifestation was produced in 1697 when Benjamin Keach of the Horsleydown, London church, simplified some articles and prepared a catechism to accompany the confession. Among the additional elements of the Keach version were articles on the laying on of hands and singing.

The Second London Confession followed the divisions of the Westminster Confession of Faith and did much to place the Calvinistic Baptist community in line with both Presbyterians and Congrega-tionalists in England.[78] As noted by the preface, "finding no defect in this regard in that fixed on by the Assembly, and after them by those of the Congregational way, we did really conclude it best to retain the same order in our confession…making use of the very same words with them both, in those articles (which were very many) wherein our faith and doctrine is the same as theirs."[79] The essential Calvinism of the Second

---

[78] Howard Osgood, Baptist librarian and historical theologian at Rochester Theological Seminary, identified the exact differences between the Westminster, Second London, and Savoy confessions. Modifications were made to chapter 20; "Of Christian Liberty and Liberty of Conscience"; chapters 21, 23, and 25 were substantially modified by new material, "Of the Church"; chapter 27, "Of the Sacraments," was replaced by "Of Baptism and the Lord's Supper." Finally, the omission of chapters 30, "Of Church Censures," and 31, "Of Synods and Councils," was replaced by material from the Savoy Declaration on the "Gospel and the Extent of Grace Thereof." See Philip Schaff, *Bibliotheca Symbolica Ecclesiae Universalis, The Creeds of Christendom, with a History and Critical Notes*, vol. 3 (New York: Harper and Brothers, 1877) 738–41.

[79] "To the Judicious and Impartial Reader," *Second London Confession*, 245.

Confession was revealed in chapters on "Gods Covenant," the loss of human free will, and especially "effectual calling." They wrote: "This Effectual Call is of God's free and special grace alone not from anything at all foreseen in man, nor from any power, or agency in the creature...the Creature being wholly passive therein, being dead in sins and trespasses." The Baptists' embrace of the doctrine of reprobation was clearly stated: "Others not elected...neither will nor can truly come to Christ; and therefore cannot be saved: much less can men that receive not the Christian Religion be saved." Likewise, "perseverance of the saints" now occupied an entire article. "They can neither totally nor finally fall from the state of grace, but shall certainly persevere therein to the end and be eternally saved." Finally, the nature of the church was understood to be "catholic" or universal, "consisting of the whole number of the Elect, ...saints by calling, visibly manifesting and evidencing ...their obedience unto that call of Christ."[80]

As several modern writers have demonstrated, the theological tradition established by the Second London Confession had a checkered history in England into the early 18th century.[81] The first edition (1677) was signed by participants at a hastily-called meeting and modified slightly eleven years later at the First General Assembly (1688). The second rescension omitted the appendix. Two further printings were made, both of which were overshadowed by the Benjamin Keach version which added articles on the laying on of hands, singing and minor matters of doctrine. Keach's version included a denunciation of infant baptism and an affirmation of closed communion, neither are of which was reproduced by John Rippon or Thomas Crosby. In the eighteenth century, the rise of hyper-Calvinism helped to push the Second London Confession into the background. New editions were published in 1720 and 1791. Curiously, C. H. Spurgeon reproduced the Confession in 1855, referring to it as "an assistance in controversy, a confirmation in faith, and a means of edification in righteousness." Later Baptists in Britain and North America hearkened back to the Confession as a definition of

---

[80] Ibid., 264, 265, 272–73, and 285–86.
[81] Robert W. Oliver, "The Emergence of a Strict and Particular Baptist Community Among the English Calvinistic Baptists, 1770–1850" (Ph.D. thesis, CNAA/London Bible College, 1986) and Lumpkin, *Baptist Confessions of Faith*, 236-240.

moderate Calvinism that satisfied their needs into the twenty-first century.[82]

As a guide to local congregations, the Second London Confession thus had unchallenged reference until the early nineteenth century. When the first attempt at a union of Calvinistic Baptists was made in 1813, however, there was general consensus about a doctrinal basis. Forty-five ministers signed the twelve articles of constitution that included twelve theological points. The "important" doctrines agreed to were: three equal persons in the Godhead, eternal and personal election, original sin, particular redemption, justification through the imputed righteousness of Christ, efficacious grace, final perseverance, resurrection of the dead, eternal happiness of believers and eternal misery of the impenitent, and congregational governance of the churches. In short, every element of the old confession was there, even to the acceptance of reprobation, albeit in a random form and succinctly summarized. No scriptural references were included.[83]

What finally superseded clearly articulated Calvinism, as Ernest Payne and others have argued, was the desire to bring together the Particular and General streams of English Baptists in a common union.[84] In 1832 the Particular Baptist General Union dropped the Confession as a requirement for participating churches, in favor of a statement "who agree in the sentiments usually understood to be evangelical." This effectively ended the confessional era among mainstream British Baptists. A generation later in 1873, Charles Stovel proposed and secured the removal of the phrase "evangelical sentiments" in lieu of a simple Declaration of Principle that "every church has the liberty to interpret and administer the laws of Christ and that the immersion of believers is the only Christian baptism."[85] This effectively set aside doctrinal distinctiveness in lieu of church order.[86] Finally, in 1904, the

---

[82] See for example, Michael A. G. Haykin, *Recovering our English Baptist Heritage*: *Kiffin, Knollys, and Keach* (Leeds: Reformation Today Trust, 1996) 81.

[83] Quoted in Ernest A. Payne, *The Baptist Union*: *A Short History* (London: Carey Kingsgate, 1958) 24. For a theological overview of the Particular Baptists in this period, see O. C. Robinson, "The Particular Baptists in England 1760–1820" (Ph.D. diss., Oxford University, 1963).

[84] Ibid., 61.

[85] Ibid., 109–10.

[86] Payne, *Baptist Union*, 110, concluded that the real issue of strict and open communion congregations was resolved by co-existence, and the matter of Calvinistic

Baptist Union "Statement of Principle" found in Christ the "sole and absolute authority in all matters pertaining to faith and practice as revealed in Holy Scripture."[87] This foundation has held together the British Baptist churches in mission and service ever since.

In its "Keach manifestation," the Second London Confession was transmitted to the American Colonies about the turn of the eighteenth century as the first association was being formed in Philadelphia. There are scattered references to the use of a confession associated with Elias Keach,[88] and later the 1689 edition circulating among the congregations of the Delaware Valley. In 1742 the Philadelphia Baptist Association approved the Confession as its own in the Keach format and ordered Benjamin Franklin of Philadelphia to print sufficient copies for use among the churches. The acceptance of the two additional articles added by Keach is explained by the esteem in which Keach and his father were held, as well as the influence of Welsh Baptists who favored both the articles on laying on of hands and on singing.[89] The Philadelphia Confession of Faith, as it came to be popularly called in the United States, remained the principal Calvinistic statement for most Baptists in all sections until the Second Great Awakenings of the 1820s.[90] A catechism was produced in New England in 1795 to accompany the Philadelphia Confession.[91] It simplified the doctrinal statements and was a popular expression for several generations.

As several historians have pointed out, the Philadelphia Confession of Faith served nobly among various Baptist groups in the eighteenth

---

and Arminian trust deeds was made easier. A third concern, the potential overlordship of a Union, was safeguarded by a statement on the independence of the churches.

[87] Quoted in Roger Hayden, "The Particular Baptist Confession of 1689 and Baptists Today," *Baptist Quarterly* 32/8 (October 1988): 407.

[88] Elias Keach was a son of London Baptist pastor, Benjamin Keach. Elias immigrated to Pennsylvania in the 1680s where he was associated with the Pennypack Baptist Church. Later he returned to England to continue his pastoral career.

[89] See the explanatory note in Lumpkin, *Baptist Confessions*, 349.

[90] McGlothlin states that the Philadelphia Confession was adopted by the Charleston Association in 1767, which commenced its history among the Southern churches. Laying on of hands was omitted but singing was retained. Oliver Hart and Daniel Shepherd issued subsequent editions in the Charleston Association that contained a catechism, summary of church discipline, and Scripture references. McGlothlin, *Baptist Confessions of Faith*, 298.

[91] *The Baptist Catechism, Or a Brief Instruction in the Principles of the Christian Religion, Agreeably to the Confession of Faith* (Boston: Manning and Loring, 1795).

century. It was the basis of each of the new associations formed (Charleston, Warren, and New York) and served the pastor-missionaries effectively as they planted new congregations on the frontier. In 1787 the Philadelphia document was flexible enough to enable the union of the American Regular and Separate Baptists, thus ending the independent heritage of the Separate Baptists. This turn of events was all the more remarkable since the Separates had originally declined to follow any written confession of faith. Finally, to its credit, it is repeatedly referenced in association and congregational records into the nineteenth century as Calvinistic Baptists came to outnumber Arminian congregations.[92]

A unique statement of Calvinistic Baptist belief was issued by the Kehukee Baptist Association, a collection of seven congregations scattered on the Piedmont frontier in Virginia and North Carolina. At its founding in 1765, the Kehukee Association was the fourth oldest in North America. For its theological definition, it followed the original text of the London Confession of 1689 and acknowledged its relationship first to the English General Baptists, and then being firmly established in the doctrine of grace, joined the Particular Baptist stream.[93] The Articles of Faith of the Kehukee Baptist Association, ratified in 1777, thus represent a moderate Calvinistic confession that likely was the first of its kind to be developed on American soil.

The Kehukee confession comprised seventeen articles; the author is not identified.[94] The Calvinistic content of the confession is obvious in

---

[92] See Henry C. Vedder, *A History of Baptists in the Middle States* (Philadelphia: American Baptist Publication Society, 1898) 92–93; McGlothlin, *Baptist Confessions of Faith*, 298; Clifton E. Olmstead, *History of Religion in the United States* (Englewood Cliffs: Prentice Hall, 1960) 109; James E. Carter, "American Baptist Confessions of Faith: A Review of Confessions of Faith Adopted by Major Bodies in the United States," in *The Lord's Free People in a Free Land: Essays in Baptist History in Honor of Robert A. Baker* (Fort Worth: Southwestern Baptist Theological Seminary, 1976) 59.

[93] Sylvester Hassell, *History of the Church of God, from the Creation to A.D. 1885; including Especially The History of the Kehukee Primitive Baptist Association* (Middletown NY: Gilbert Beebe's Sons, 1886) 662. The heritage of the General Baptists was claimed because the earliest Baptists in North Carolina were General Baptists who probably evolved from either the "Regulars" or "Separates" into the "United Baptists" of the late eighteenth century.

[94] Lumpkin, *Baptist Confessions*, 354, argues that the document demonstrates a compromise between Separates who thought the Philadelphia Confession too lax, and the need of some Regulars to declare against Arminianism and lax disciplinary standards.

articles 3, 5, 6, 7, 9, and 10. Election of a particular number is eternal and unconditional; original sin has made men "both filthy and guilty;" and, it is not in the power of men to keep God's law. Further, God's elect are called, justified, pardoned, and sanctified, and it is impossible for them to refuse the call. They will persevere and never fall finally away. There follows an article on everlasting punishment. The only value of good works is a response to the "principle of love."[95] A strong, protectionistic statement of the local congregation is made concerning the ordinances, namely that these belong to the "converted or true believers." Persons who are not baptized after they are savingly converted, by sprinkling or dipping, "continue in unbelief." Significantly, only ministers who are called and ordained (i.e. "come under the imposition of hands by the presbytery") have a right to administer the only two ordinances, baptism and the Lord's Supper.[96] Here were hints of what would blossom later in the South as "Landmarkism."

The historian of the Kehukee tradition was careful to note some nuances of confessions of faith. First was a footnote about what a creed was: "a convenient summary of the religious belief of a particular people at a particular time that may be useful as a bond of union between those who profess to believe it, as an aid to understanding the Scriptures, and as a guard against false doctrine and practice."[97] The Kehukee churches further held that confessions of faith were not absolutely necessary as the Bible was the true confession. "Drawing up a few particulars" has been the prerogative of Baptists in order to make known their faith and practice. "They are not ashamed of their principles," one writer asserted, "neither do they wish to appear under any disguise or false robes."[98] In short, the Kehukee representatives maintained the same understanding of

---

From published associational records, it seems likely that the document was the work of Lemuel Burkitt (clerk) and John Meglamre (moderator). Burkitt (1750–1806) in particular, was the author of the 1782 "Rules of Decorum," he was on the committee in 1789 that created the associational constitution, and finally a popular hymnal. See Lemuel Burkitt and Jesse Read, *A Concise History of the Kehukee Baptist Association, from its Original Rise Down to 1803* (Philadelphia: Lippincott, Grambo, and Co., 1850) 51–54, 66–67, 102–104, 329–30.

[95] The Confession is printed in its entirety in Hassell, *History of the Church of God*, 699.

[96] Ibid., 700.

[97] Ibid., 663n.

[98] Ibid., 702.

a confession of faith as printed on the title page of the First London Confession of 1644.

Two changes in the American Calvinistic community of the early nineteenth century caused movement away from a consistent "Edwardsian" position[99]. First was the influence of New England Theology, as evidenced in Jonathan Edwards, Jr., Samuel Hopkins, Joseph Bellamy, Nathaniel W. Taylor, Lyman Beecher, and Charles G. Finney. These divines softened the old Calvinism to what became an "Arminianized" or evangelical Calvinism that reflected more importance for the part of ministers and evangelists. Second, was the almost complete dismissal of universal or catholic ideas of the Church in favor of "local church protectionism." This influence could be identified in the success enjoyed in the Freewill Baptist Connexion that Benjamin Randal instituted beginning in the 1780s, the rise of Universalism and Universal Restorationism, and the missionary movement spurred on by the theology of Andrew Fuller, Robert Hall, and John Sutcliff in England, and William Staughton, Richard Furman, and Luther Rice in the United States.

These changes in mainstream Baptist thought in the United States elicited a retrenchment confession of Calvinistic Baptist theology, known as the Black Rock Resolutions. A detailed report and six theological and ecclesiastical statements were adopted at a meeting of "Old School" Baptist ministers held at Black Rock, Maryland, on 28 September 1832. By adopting the epithet, "Old School," they wished to distinguish themselves as part of the "school of Christ" in contrast with other modern schools. Reflecting rural and village congregations, there were twenty-two signatories, representing churches from Maryland, Delaware, Pennsylvania, and New York.

Essentially a recasting of eighteenth century English Baptist Calvinism, the Resolutions dictate that the "Baptists require a 'Thus saith the Lord'" as authority in religion.[100] Among those inventions that lacked biblical warrant were tract societies, Sunday schools, the Bible Society,

---

[99] Holifield, *Theology in America*, 282 proposes a four part delineation of Baptist Calvinism in the U.S.: Edwardian, Fullerite, Philadelphia, and "eclectic populist." His types are not clear from the sources, and he misses the overall move away from Calvinism before 1850, particularly among Baptists outside the South.

[100] "Minutes of the Proceedings and Resolutions Drafted by the Particular Baptists Convened at Black Rock, Maryland, September 8, 1832," in *The Feast of Fat Things* (Middletown NY: G. Beebe's Sons, 1832) 6.

colleges and theological schools, and organized missions. With respect to missions, the Old School Baptists propounded a doctrine of the church that was composed of baptized believers only without hierarchies of offices. Church membership and baptism were to be granted only upon evidence of "having been born from above," according to the "ancient principles" of the Baptists.[101] The purpose of associations was entirely non-legislative, rather to "strengthen each other in the good ways of the Lord." Exhibiting an anti-intellectual bias, they held that obedience to Christ and the faithfulness of the Holy Spirit were sufficient for ministry. In response to "four day" or protracted meetings and other New Measures, a clear doctrine of the divinity and sovereignty of the Holy Spirit was evident: "We believe the Holy Ghost to be too sacred a being to be trifled with by trying experiments with him…We believe the Holy Spirit to be God…The purpose of the Father, the redemption of the Son, and the regenerating power of the Holy Ghost, must run in perfect accordance, and commensurate one with the other."[102] The conclusion of the "resolutions" revealed an eschatology that was "realized" in modern terminology: the mass of "human inventions" was connected with the "Man of Sin" that will be "driven away like the chaff of the summer threshing floor."[103]

Four theological emphases were prominent in the Old School Baptist community as evidenced in the Black Rock Resolutions. First, traditional high Calvinist views characteristic of the Second London and Philadelphia Confessions were defended as established "baptistic" doctrines. Second, at least one component of the Baptist community in the United States was unwilling to accept the principles of revivalistic, New School theology, as evidenced in men like Charles G. Finney, Luther Rice, and Jacob Knapp. Third, the inclusion of English Baptist William Gadsby's tract, "An Everlasting Task for Arminians, or A letter to Rev. Edward Smyth, formerly of Trinity College, Dublin," with the publication of the Resolutions, showed crosscurrents of contemporary transatlantic high Calvinism. Gadsby was well known as a Strict Baptist in England. Fourth, the Black Rock Convention sought to create a theological rationale for their ecclesiastical antagonism for the use of any "means" in gospel work. The sovereignty of God stood firmly as a

---

[101] Ibid., 31.
[102] Ibid., 24.
[103] Ibid., 30.

bulwark against any human endeavor. This was to separate out in the North American context a new branch of well-defined Baptist thinking, ultimately to become the Primitive Baptists.[104]

A more reasoned response to the new theological emphases was the New Hampshire Confession of Faith (1833). This statement, produced ostensibly by a select committee of the New Hampshire Baptist State Convention,[105] then later revised by one writer, J. Newton Brown,[106] reflected particularly the ethos of its region. While the precise wording of the original versions do not survive, it may be safely assumed that the objective of a new confession was to bring closer together the main branches of Baptists in northern New England, the Regular or Calvinistic Baptists and the Freewill Baptist Connexion. Particularly in New Hampshire the Freewill group had made great inroads in mountainous rural regions, while elsewhere the two groups ministered in close proximity in small villages. Some leaders doubtless wanted to bring Baptists closer together, luring the Freewillers back from cooperation with, for instance, the Universalists.[107] The New Hampshire Confession was an American version of the mediating type of confessional statement. So moderating was its tone, however, that W. W. Barnes observed the five points that distinguished Calvinism from Arminianism were almost ignored.[108]

---

[104] For a recent excellent study of the formation and doctrinal emphases of Primitive Baptists, see Jeff Taylor, "For Their Rock is not as Our Rock; Primitive Baptist Self-Definition During the Crucial Years of Movement Formation, 1832–1848" (Ph.D. diss., Baylor University, 2000).

[105] The original author, I. M. Person, appears to have been a pastor. The committee was composed of Baron Stow, J. Newton Brown, and Jonathan Going.

[106] Brown was a graduate of the theological program in the second class of Hamilton Literary and Theological Institution. His teachers were Nathaniel Kendrick and Daniel Hascall. On these two, see below, 294–98.

[107] Freewill Baptists, Universalists, and the Christian Church often cooperated at the local level, sharing the use of a meetinghouse.

[108] William Wright Barnes, "The New Hampshire Confession of Faith, Its Origins, and Use," *Review and Expositor* 39/1 (January 1942): 5. The language of this confession was attenuated on several important issues that had been more fully articulated in the Second London (Philadelphia) Confession of Faith. In no way was it in the early-to-middle nineteenth century the *sine qua non* of Baptist "orthodox rationalism," as Grant Wacker has claimed in his *Augustus Hopkins Srtong and the Dilemma of Historical Consciousness* (Macon GA: Mercer University Press, 1985) 17.

The three articles that mark the uniqueness of the New Hampshire Confession are titled "God's Purpose of Grace (ix)," "Sanctification(x)," and "Perseverance of the Saints (xi)" Article 9 dealt primarily with election and demonstrated the admixture of Calvinist and Arminian thinking of the era. On the one hand, the writer asserted that election is the gracious purpose of God, while also recognizing that election is "perfectly consistent with the free agency of man." Further, the legitimate use of "means" is a clear allusion to the New Measures revival techniques employed from the 1820s by Presbyterians Charles Finney and Calvin Colton, and Baptists like Jacob Knapp and Jabez Swan. To counter the tendency among some Freewill Baptists and the Methodists that falling from grace was possible, Article 11 stated unequivocally that real believers may be distinguished from professors and that "a special providence watches over their welfare." A mild statement on "reprobation" (Article 18) asserted "the wicked will be adjudged to endless punishment," a response to the influence of Universalism among Baptists.

In the emerging doctrinal debates of the 1830s, the issue of perfectionism raised by "ultraists" and others was met head on. In the 1853 edition of the confession J. Newton Brown was careful to state that sanctification is a process by which believers are "made partakers of God's holiness." The appointed means of sanctification are application of Scripture, prayer, self-examination, self-denial, watchfulness, and prayer. There was no mention of a "second work of grace," a doctrine embraced by advocates of holiness theology teaching that one could reach a point of "entire sanctification."

Apparently, the "original" final version of the Confession made only a slight impact on the state convention family, in part because confessionalism itself was waning. What gave a new life to the New Hampshire effort was J. Newton Brown's adoption of the document in his manual produced by the American Baptist Publication Society. Given the evangelism and new church development occurring across the constituency between 1840–1880, the printing and distribution of the manual, the confession, and Brown's covenant provided an authoritative ecclesiology and ready reference tool. Produced free of charge with the denomination's imprimatur on the title page, it carried genuine authority. At a time when New Theology and ecumenical expressions were emerging, the New Hampshire Confession became the watermark of the conservative, traditional Baptist community. The fundamentalist faction in the Northern Baptist Convention (known as the Baptist Bible Union) consequently had no reservations in 1922 about proposing that the New Hampshire Confession, with the addition of a premillennial eschatological statement, should become an enforceable standard.[109]

RESURGENT CONFESSIONALISM.

In the twentieth century, serious theological divisions opened up among mainstream Baptists in both Britain and the United States. Some held that Baptists were part of a well-defined confessional tradition that had established theological boundaries across the centuries. Basically, these were Calvinistic Baptists who opposed the "Arminianization" of the mainstream, or those who opposed the ecumenical and cooperative advances of convention and union groups. Once the union between General and Particular Baptists in Britain was finally consummated in 1891, the Strict Baptists redoubled their efforts to articulate an unchanging Calvinistic theology. Likewise, in the United States, as the Northern Baptists coalesced into a national convention, merged with Free Baptists, and joined the ecumenical movement, the ground was laid outside the South for a "regular" Baptist tradition to emerge in favor of an unchanged Calvinistic, local church theology. As an aside, Northern Baptists became convinced officially that the true historic Baptist position was non-confessional and opted to stress the qualities of soul competency and theological toleration.[110] Southern Baptists followed suit, experiencing theological schism externally and internally, revising the New Hampshire Confession of Faith as its standard.

During this period of theological redefinition a scholarly search was made in defense of both positions. Theologians and historians such as E. B. Underhill of Great Britain's Hanserd Knollys Society, American Northern Baptists' Albert H. Newman and Henry C. Vedder, and W. H. Whitsitt and W. J. McGlothlin among the Southern Baptists, published histories and compilations of doctrinal and confessional statements. What emerged from this flurry of "rediscovery" was a sense of the

---

[109] The details of the controversy are excerpted in Brackney, *Baptist Life and Thought*, 356–60.

[110] In the annual meeting of the 1922 Northern Baptist Convention, delegates voted 1264 to 637 "to affirm the New Testament as the all-sufficient ground of faith and practice." Quoted in ibid., 358.

antiquity and variety of Baptist confessional theology. It soon became apparent that no one confession represented even a minority of Baptists across time, and that confessions only ever had a limited usage. As the introduction to the Second London Confession put it, "foreasmuch as our method and manner of expressing our sentiments in this doth vary from the former," and because the earlier confession "was not now commonly to be had," a new statement was in order.

One of the first manifestations of the resurgent confessionalism may be found in the Southern Baptist family. In 1902, with further extension in 1905, a group of churches—reacting against perceived domineering executive leadership in the state conventions of Texas and Arkansas—followed a modified Landmarkist theology and eventually constituted themselves as the American Baptist Association. Ben M. Bogard, one of the leaders, was the principal author of the resultant theological statements. Bogard (1868–1951) was educated at Georgetown College and Bethel College in Kentucky. An active debater on topics of regional interest like Campbellism, evolution, and Christian union, he joined forces with Landmarkism in the Southwest. The Association's "doctrinal statement" commended the New Hampshire Confession of Faith "so long held by our American Baptist people," in addition to twelve additional articles that reflected "attacks" made by "modern science" against the traditional baptistic faith as affirmed by these congregations. The articles affirmed infallible verbal inspiration, the trinity, Creation as Genesis recounted it, the virgin birth and deity of Christ, a vicarious substitutionary atonement, the literal resurrection, ascension, and return of Christ, and reprobation. Landmarkist thinking was illustrated in three articles stressing the local church comprising the Kingdom of God, extra-congregational bodies accountable to congregations, and a succession of missionary Baptist churches from the time of Christ.[111] These articles reflected not only Landmarkist tendencies but also the issues theologically associated with contemporary fundamentalism.

Among Baptists in the Northern Baptist Convention (N.B.C.) family, the resurgence of confessionalism was apparent in the period after 1915.

---

[111] The original statement is found in "Minutes of the Baptist General Association, Texarkana, Texas, November 24–26, 1905, 1–6," and excerpted in Lumpkin, *Baptist Confessions*, 378–79. For a fuller version of these tenets, see *The Baptist Way-Book*, ed. Ben M. Bogard (Texarkana TX: 1946).

Directly attributable to the publication of *The Fundamentals*, efforts were launched to investigate charges of liberalism and unbaptistic teachings in colleges and seminaries. Several Baptists helped to orchestrate the World's Christian Fundamentals Association, formed in 1919. Prominent pastors and leaders corresponded through newspapers in a campaign to organize opinion among Northern Baptists. That came to fruition in 1923 with the establishment of the Baptist Bible Union. It proved to be an event of signal importance in denominational history. The Union was a closely knit fellowship of pastors who wanted to rid the convention of theologically liberal elements, most particularly Cornelius Woelfkin and Harry Emerson Fosdick. They achieved a doctrinal standard in calling for the adoption of the New Hampshire Confession of Faith as the official statement of the N.B.C. This was defeated overwhelmingly in favor of the "New Testament as the sole rule of faith and practice."[112]

The Baptist Bible Union emphasized in eighteen articles the major doctrinal categories they considered orthodox Baptist systematic theology. The phraseology of the New Hampshire Confession is everywhere apparent in the doctrinal declaration, plus the sharpness of fundamentalistic dogma.[113] For example, Scripture was said to be "the supreme standard by which all human conduct, creeds, and opinions should be tried." A subsection on "inspiration" explained that the Scriptures were "supernaturally inspired and free from error, as no other writings have ever been or will be inspired."[114] Of the Holy Spirit, the first line claims "The Holy Spirit is a divine person....who restrains the Evil One until God's purpose is fulfilled." Contemporary thinking about Satan and fallen angels, and an accumulation of the scriptural references to the antichrist, apostasy, and powers of darkness are brought together as one article. In dispensationalist order, the article on Satan precedes the article addressing the doctrine of creation, which is "not a matter of evolution or development through interminable periods of time," but "each after their own kind." On the atonement of Christ, the confession

---

[112] See Brackney, *Baptist Life and Thought,* 356–59. Gilbert R. Englerth, "American Baptists: A Confessional People?" *Foundations* 4/2 (June 1985): 143 argues that the denomination "matured" in its theological understanding to the point of making confessions of faith unnecessary.

[113] Lumpkin thought T. T. Shields of Canada and Des Moines University was the author of the statement; if so, surely he was assisted by William Bell Riley, J. Frank Norris, and other hard-liners.

[114] The best source of the document is Lumpkin, *Baptist Confessions,* 385.

embraces substitutionary theology, coupled with a mediating position between Calvinist and evangelical understandings. "God's grace is made free to all," states Article 10. Justification, repentance, and faith are works of grace rather than human effort. Continuing the essentially Calvinistic tenor, the perseverance of saints and everlasting conscious suffering of the lost is affirmed.[115]

The ecclesiology of the Union statement is probably the clearest example of local church protectionism outside the American South. "The will of the local church is final," the declaration affirms. Without using the language of "autonomy," the statement concludes that the church enjoys the right of absolute self-government. The church of Christ is a congregation whose mission is threefold: to make individual disciples, to build up the church, and to teach and instruct. The order in which the mission of the church is given is purposeful, made all the more emphatic by the included declaration: "We do not believe in the reversal of this order." Appealing to the Pauline text of the Second Letter to the Corinthians, baptism is deemed to be by immersion and a prerequisite to church membership and admission to the Lord's Supper.[116]

The final article of the Baptist Bible Union's confession of faith was a list of the necessary eschatological categories inherent in the return of Christ: bodily resurrection of Christ, second coming, resurrection of the dead, change of the living in Christ, re-establishment of the throne of David, and the millennial kingdom rule on earth.[117] More than any other Baptist confessional statement, that of the Baptist Bible Union is the most clearly premillennial and dispensational. At length, the doctrinal standard of the Baptist Bible Union became that of the newly formed General Association of Regular Baptist Churches in 1933.

A second generation of concern swept through the Northern Baptist Convention family in the early 1940s. The immediate challenge was the lack of doctrinal uniformity in the commissioning of missionaries. A fellowship of Conservative Baptist laymen and pastors pressed for an end to the "inclusive policy." Their statement of faith was prepared by Frank M. Goodchild (1860–1928), pastor at Central Baptist Church, New York City, who was a graduate of Crozer Theological Seminary before its

---

[115] Ibid., 385–87.
[116] Ibid., 388.
[117] Ibid., 389.

reorganization. Goodchild had been instrumental in the establishment of The Eastern Baptist Theological Seminary in 1925.[118]

The preamble to Goodchild's confession revealed a newfound understanding of confessionalism. It cautioned that adopting a creed "would be contrary to our historic Baptist principles and repugnant to our deepest spiritual instincts." On the other hand, adopting a confession of faith "around which our people may rally" was consistent with Baptist practice from the beginning. The immediate need for such a confession (1920s) was a context of "doubt, unbelief and irreligion." Baptists, Goodchild believed, "should reaffirm their faith in the great fundamentals."[119] Consistent with the Philadelphia and New Hampshire Confessions of Faith, Goodchild understood his place in the heritage of Baptist confessionalism.

Goodchild's confessional articles numbered seven and ranged from Scripture to the Trinity, from salvation to the church, and concluded with a voluntarist paragraph on separation of church and state. Using an ancient creedal formulation ("We believe..."), his phraseology was poetic: "God is perfect in holiness, infinite in wisdom, measureless in power" (Article 2). Goodchild's confession exhibited close proximity to the articles of *The Fundamentals*. Of Christ he stated, "miraculous in his birth, sinless in his life, bodily resurrection, ascension, intercession, visible personal return." A general atonement position was clear in Articles 3 and 5, where Christ "died for the sins of the world." Returning to a classic Calvinistic formulation of reprobation, however, Goodchild affirmed eternal separation from God in Article 5.[120] Goodchild softened the local church posture of the New Hampshire Confession, defining the church as "a living spiritual body...of which all regenerated people are members." Moreover, the church is constituted by baptism upon a "credible confession of faith." The final article was obviously composed in light of E. Y. Mullins's work in *Axioms of Religion*: humans have direct relations with God; each church is autonomous; separation of

---

[118] Longtime Eastern Baptist professor of church history, Norman H. Maring, believed that Goodchild was the principal author of Eastern's doctrinal basis. Inspired by the idea in the "Abstract of Principles" of Southern Baptist Theological Seminary, Goodchild stayed close to the New Hampshire Confession.

[119] The Goodchild Confession was originally published in *The Baptist* (Chicago), 2 July 1921. It was quoted in an article "Fundamentals Conference, Des Moines Iowa" *Chronicle*, 1943): 57–58.

[120] Ibid., 57.

church and state. Consequently, churches were to be "free from interference by any ecclesiastical or political control."[121]

Originally written to rally fundamentalists around a standard, Goodchild's Confession became in 1943 the inaugural doctrinal statement of the Conservative Baptist Foreign Mission Society. Within that tradition, the Confession has been used to determine voting privileges and qualifications for office holding or employment of staff or missionaries of the Society. To indicate their acquiescence, adherents have signed the document.[122] With the subsequent breakaway of the Conservative Baptist movement, the confessional tradition largely died among the remaining Northern Baptists.[123]

In its early manifestations, Southern Baptist confessionalism has been largely imitative. Following World War I, Southern Baptist leaders determined to reach out to other Baptists and establish lines of communication. E. Y. Mullins and J. B. Gambrell became traveling statesmen for Baptist ideals. As William Lumpkin has shown, there was a need for a definition of Southern Baptist principles.[124] Coupled with this desire to create a "Baptist Internationale," there were concerns raised over social issues and the threat of the teachings of evolutionary theory. Thus, in 1914 an initial attempt was made to introduce a doctrinal statement, the "Pronouncement on Christian Union and Denominational Efficiency" that was composed within the Convention Efficiency Committee. In 1919 Mullins and Gambrell drew up a summary of Baptist principles to communicate Southern Baptist identity, to which reference was made in the Convention's Fraternal Address that year. The pronouncement was generally well received. In 1922 a group of delegates from both the Northern and Southern Baptist Conventions met

---

[121] Ibid., 58. The phraseology was directly taken from the *Axioms,* the section on "Soul Competency."

[122] This was also the case with the Eastern Seminary doctrinal statement, where new faculty members are required to sign the statement at the beginning of their employment.

[123] It must be noted, however, that institutions officially related to the Northern/American Baptist Convention do have doctrinal statements for faculty assent, for instance, Northern Baptist and Eastern Baptist seminaries. Also, significant numbers of ministry candidates who accept churches related to the Convention come from non-denominational, confessional schools, notably Gordon Conwell, Trinity, and Fuller seminaries. See Donald Tinder, *Fundamentalist Baptists in the Northern and Western United States 1920-1950"* (Ph.D. diss., Yale University, 1969).

[124] Lumpkin, *Baptist Confessions,* 390–91.

at jointly related Stephens College in Missouri to draft a possible common statement on Baptist beliefs. The next year the Southern convention rejected the Stephens commission plan and moved to create a Southern statement. Behind the urging of Oklahoma fundamentalist editor of the *Baptist Messenger*, C. P. Stealey, a committee of the convention was appointed in 1923 to study the work of the Stephens commission, and report to the national convention on a possible *Baptist Faith and Message*. Chosen for the formal task were the most trusted leaders of the era: E. Y. Mullins, S. M. Brown, R. H. Pitt, W. J. McGlothlin, E. C. Dargan, and L. R. Scarborough. In 1925 this distinguished coterie, plus C. P. Stealey, recommended the adoption of the New Hampshire Confession of Faith, with some revisions and additions.[125]

Noteworthy for the purposes of this discussion was the rationale developed during this period around confessions of faith in the Baptist tradition. Most certainly, the rationale was the thinking of W. J. McGlothlin of Southern Baptist Theological Seminary, who less than a decade before had produced a sourcebook of confessional documents that were in widespread use among the Baptist family.[126] The committee argued that confessions "constitute a consensus of opinion of some Baptist body, large or small, for guidance and instruction." Confessions do not add to the "simple conditions of salvation," they reasoned, "nor are they complete statements of faith." Certainly none is infallible or final in authority. Baptists, they believed, are free to revise their confessions as they deem necessary. Further, confessions are drawn from the Scriptures and not to be used to hamper the conscience or freedom of thought in other realms of life. Any group of Baptists has the inherent right to publish to the world a statement of their beliefs whenever they wish to do so. The Baptist churchmen of the era hoped the issuance of a "Statement of the Baptist Faith and Message" would "remove causes of misunderstanding, friction, and apprehension."[127] Significantly, the

---

[125] For a helpful coverage of this development, see Walter B. Shurden, "Southern Baptist Response to Their Confessional Statements," *Review and Expositor* 76/1 (Winter 1979): 71.

[126] See McGlothlin's *Baptist Confessions*, cited above.

[127] "Report of the Committee on Baptist Faith and Message," *Southern Baptist Annual*, 1925, 71. According to Shurden, the addition of the terminology "A Statement on…" was intended to minimize the binding nature of the statement.

committee exhibited its historical consciousness by drawing upon a well-established, generally acceptable confessional statement, adding nuanced articles particular to the Southern Baptist situation.

The revisions to the original New Hampshire document included deleting the articles on harmonizing law and grace and civil government, the last of which was rewritten. Article 7 was revised to delete reference to voluntary obedience and "holy fruit we bring forth," to produce a more Calvinistic statement on regeneration. Similarly, Article 9 was revised to remove florid expressions and repetitious eighteenth century phrases. Still, Southern Baptists were encouraged to the use of means or techniques in the highest degree. Finally, the vague eschatology of the New Hampshire Confession ("Of the World to Come") that swept quickly though Christ's "descension," the resurrection, a "solemn separation," endless punishment or joy, and heaven or hell, was replaced with a more definite exposition on the "Return of the Lord," emphasizing the visible and personal return of Jesus.[128] Here could be seen the pattern of eschatological urgency of the fundamentalists without the specificity of a millennial position.

Additional articles were added in the new statement addressing social issues, including religious liberty, peace and war, education, social service, cooperation, stewardship, the kingdom, science and religion, and creation. Evident in the immediate context was the social gospel which found its way into Southern Baptist usage as "the reign of God in the heart and life of every human relationship and in every form and institution of organized human society."[129] Walter Rauschenbusch's terms were thus drawn upon, but not his strategic initiatives. Instead of public policy change or a socialistic agenda, preaching the gospel and teaching the principles of righteousness and prayer were to bring in the earthly kingdom. In an age of national stewardship drives, Southern Baptists were to contribute "cheerfully, regularly, systematically, proportionately and liberally." With respect to the threat of science upon the miraculous, an article pledged unwavering adherence to supernatural religion including all of the concerns of the fundamentalists: the virgin birth, Jesus' miracles, his resurrection, ascension, and return. The document also contained a disciplinary stream, requiring adherence to

---

[128] Compare the New Hampshire Confession in Lumpkin, *Baptist Confessions,* 363–67 with "Baptist Faith and Message," *Southern Baptist Annual, 1925,* 72–73.

[129] "Report of the Committee on Baptist Faith and Message," 75.

supernaturalism in Baptist schools. A subsequent discussion launched by C.P. Stealey of Oklahoma, attempted an amendment directly rejecting evolution and affirming God's "direct creation," and emphasizing the fall of man, and original sin.[130]

The great contribution of E. Y. Mullins to the *Baptist Faith and Message* was the article on religious liberty. In heroic phraseology, reminiscent of the seventeenth century, the article began, "God alone is Lord of the conscience." It reflected the American doctrine of the separation of church and state and echoed Mullins's *Axioms of Religion* (1908): "A Free church in a free state," and "the right of free and unhindered access to God in a sphere of religion without interference by the civil power."[131]

The first edition of the *Baptist Faith and Message* moved far beyond areas of traditional, orthodox Baptist doctrine to address political and social concerns. Without clear reference to Scripture, the writers assumed a pacifistic position through the "law of love" (Article 19). Unashamedly, the term "enlightenment" was used to describe the Christian religion, although bathed in Southern Baptist terminology of "missions, general benevolence, and the new birth" (Article 20). Their clear response to the social crises that Rauschenbusch and Samuel Zane Batten described, was to urge that "Every Christian is under obligation to seek to make the will of Christ regnant in his own life and human society" and to be "ready to work with all men of good will in any good cause…without compromising their loyalty to Christ and his church." Far from Christian socialism, they asserted that "all means and methods used in social service for the amelioration of society and the establishment of righteousness"[132] must finally depend not upon corporate witness, but upon regenerate individuals. Likewise, while the ecumenical movement was growing in impetus among some kinds of Baptists and many other Christians, Southern Baptists concluded that cooperation meant voluntary engagement in advisory bodies among New Testament churches. Such cooperation, however, should not violate conscience or loyalty to Christ as revealed in the New Testament. Presumably, this was "code language" for Baptist principles.

---

[130] Ibid., 76.

[131] Ibid., 73–74.

[132] Ibid., 74.

The Southern Baptist heart of the 1925 statement was found in Article 23 on "Evangelism and Missions." "It is the duty of every Christian man and woman, and the duty of every church of Christ to seek to extend the gospel to the ends of the earth." Personal evangelism was at the forefront of missionary effort. This was affirmed in Article 25, where the kingdom of God defined as "the reign of God in the heart and life of the individual in every human relationship... and in every institution of human society."[133] The chief means for this attainment are preaching the gospel of Christ and teaching principles of righteousness.

The 1925 *Baptist Faith and Message* produced only marginal results for all of the hopes invested in the process. W. W. Barnes noted that upon its circulation among Southern Baptist congregations, "it met with a tremendous outburst of silence."[134] Barnes' analysis of the process to produce a Southern Baptist doctrinal standard was that it was the product of: a centralization tendency among some Southern Baptist leaders that reflected social and political trends after World War I, the incorporation of the Southern Baptist Convention, the unifying factors in the Seventy-Five Million Campaign, changes in the office of convention president imitating the Interchurch World Movement, and the fundamentalist demands of the 1920s. While Barnes and others lamented the transition from a more voluntary polity of the nineteenth century, the *Baptist Faith and Message* did quietly lay to rest doctrinal disputes during the next three decades of unprecedented growth and missions outreach of Southern Baptists.

Growing patterns of religious conservatism in the United States, a new generation of pastors of large congregations, and a strong voice from the six Southern Baptist seminaries eventually brought forth a desire for revision of the 1925 doctrinal consensus. In the immediate background a controversy over the authorship of Genesis led many conservatives to conclude that the seminaries were slipping into liberal theology.[135] While there were theological tensions, a sense of unity still

---

[133] Ibid., 75.

[134] William Wright Barnes, *The Southern Baptist Convention: A Study in The Development of Ecclesiology* (Fort Worth: Self-published 1934) 8.

[135] In 1961, Ralph H. Elliott, a professor of Old Testament at Midwestern Baptist Theological Seminary, published *The Message of Genesis* in which he wrote of the multiple authorship of the Pentateuch. While this position was hardly new among the seminary faculties, it startled conservative forces who clung to Mosaic authorship. The seminary trustees fired Elliott in 1962 and the event became a rallying point for critical

prevailed. Messengers to the 1962 Southern Baptist Convention meeting in San Francisco voted to reinterpret the 1925 document "in light of the needs of our generation." A committee of twenty-two pastors and laymen chaired by Herschel H. Hobbs of Oklahoma City spent the next year preparing a suitable report. The result was the *Baptist Faith and Message* (1963) adopted that year by the Southern Baptist Convention at Kansas City, Missouri.

The second-generation document made some subtle but significant changes in the articulation of Southern Baptist beliefs. First, on the matter of the Scriptures, the influence of Neo-Orthodoxy was evident: "The criterion by which the Scriptures are to be interpreted is Jesus Christ."[136] In an accompanying guide to the 1963 statement, Herschel Hobbs, in wrestling with terminology such as "inerrancy" and "infallibility," noted: "The Bible then is a book of religion, not of science." To say that the Bible is an authority in every field of human thought is not accurate, Hobbs believed. "It is not an authority in science. It doesn't claim to be." He then went on to use timeworn Baptist phrases about biblical authority, only to conclude, "It is a vital and living authority, and not a mechanical and ecclesiastical one." This new Christological hermeneutic applied to Scripture would bother many conservatives in the convention, but it cheered the scholars in the seminaries, whose training had run along the same tracks.

---

scholarship and fears of increased interference into theological education by conservatives. A second incident occurred with the publication of G. Henton Davies' volume on Genesis in the *Broadman Bible Commentary*. Davies was a tutor at Regent's Park College, Oxford University, well beyond the authority of Southern Baptist conservatives. But, the Sunday School Board in response to pressure from the Convention withdrew the volume and had it rewritten by Prof. Clyde Francisco at Southern Seminary in conformity with historic positions of the SBC. On the Elliott incident, see Ralph H. Elliott, *The Genesis Controversy and Continuity in Southern Baptist Chaos: A Eulogy for a Great Tradition* (Macon GA: Mercer University Press, 1992) esp. 113–26. For both the Elliott and Davies controversies, see Walter Shurden, *Not a Silent People: Controversies that Have Shaped Southern Baptists*, 105–108; 115–17; James Leo Garrett, Jr., E. Glenn Hinson, James E. Tull, *Are Southern Baptists Evangelicals?* (Macon GA: Mercer University Press, 1983) 111–14; 115–17; and Salvador T. Martinez, "Southern Baptist Views of the Scriptures in Light of the Elliott Controversy" (Th.M. thesis, Southern Baptist Theological Seminary, 1966).

[136] Some writers trace this back to E. Y. Mullins, "the forerunner of neo-orthodoxy among Southern Baptists." See W. Wiley Richards, *Winds of Doctrines*, 154.

Articles 3, 4, and 5 reveal much more theological sophistication than any previous Baptist confessional statement. The doctrine of God was expanded to a full-blown Trinitarian treatment. Hobbs's guide spent much of its energy in affirming this article. In the statement on man, the older formulation had focused exclusively upon the fall of man, but the 1963 treatment explained man's creation in the image of God, including his free choice. The currents of New Theology were manifest in phrases like "man's posterity inheriting an environment inclined toward sin," "the sacredness of human personality," and that "every man possesses dignity and is worthy of respect and Christian love." Historical theologians continue to debate whether such interpolations reflect more of E. Y. Mullins, Enlightenment/Personalist thought, Barthian emphases, or all three. In Article 5, the statement on salvation broke out into a specified vocabulary of regeneration, repentance, faith, justification, sanctification, and glorification, reflecting a perception that Southern Baptist appreciation for systematic theology had grown appreciably in the twentieth century. A careful admixture of traditional Calvinistic points (regeneration, justification, sanctification) is made with more "Arminian" nuances: repentance is turning to God, and faith is acceptance of Christ and commitment "of the entire personality" to him as Savior and Lord.

While in the heritage of E. Y. Mullins, terms like "autonomy," "democratic processes," and "equally responsible membership" became canonical, the 1963 *Baptist Faith and Message* moved the doctrine of the church away from the local church-protectionism of the New Hampshire Confession. Significantly, a hint at a doctrine of a universal church concluded the statement on the nature of the church. Readers of this version found affirming the use of the word "ordinance," but it was now styled in light of ecumenical terminology: "an act of obedience, symbolizing..." In trying to respond to long criticisms of Southern Baptists as "closed communionists," Herschel Hobbs moved the question away from the Lord's Supper to the question of what constitutes New Testament baptism. "If Baptists are 'closed anything' at this point," he quipped, "they are closed baptismists." Readers would also note a reversal of "kingdom" emphases from the social gospel influences of the first version in 1925. The kingdom came to be understood as a realm of salvation into which individuals enter "upon childlike commitment to

Jesus Christ," and the full consummation of the kingdom was held to be future, a virtual reversal of Rauschenbusch's thought.[137]

As was the case with the 1925 *Baptist Faith and Message*, the revision of 1963 found new departures and boldness in the articles titled "Education" and "The Social Order." Southern Baptist educators found interesting the discussion of academic freedom in denominationally affiliated schools, a freedom nevertheless cast within the limits of the pre-eminence of Jesus Christ, the Scriptures, and "the distinct purpose for which the school exists." Doubtless this was to assuage fears of faculty in Baptist colleges and universities that the denomination would evaluate them theologically, as had been the situation with Ralph Elliott. The statement, "Denominational cooperation is desirable between various Christian denominations when the end to be attained is itself justified," in some small way reflected a new surge of American ecumenism in the sixties. Importantly, in the midst of the war in Vietnam, the article "Peace and War" remained as it was in 1925; Hobbs added his own pro-national interpretation. The article addressing "Religious Liberty" was moved to the final position, so as to emphasize its critical place in Baptist thinking.

In the 1970s and 1980s, under the influence of a new generation of leaders, the theological tenor of Southern Baptists turned toward biblical conservatism. Those who strongly affirmed the 1963 statement organized themselves in 1973 as the "Baptist Faith and Message Fellowship" and worked to "magnify the Lordship of Christ and reaffirm certain doctrines which Baptists cherish," as articulated in the *Baptist Faith and Message* of 1963.[138] A deep chasm thus opened between "fundamentalists" and "moderates."[139] One by one, beginning with the symbolic presidency of

---

[137] Ibid., 97. The Article on "Return of the Lord" of the 1925 version was greatly truncated to "Last Things," in 1963, doubtless in view of the widespread incursion of dispensational thought entering Southern Baptist life and perceived to be harmful to theological unity. Herschel Hobbs, himself an amillennialist, attempted to posit that one's position on eschatological details "has never been a test of orthodoxy" (105). Here he was either naïve or neglectful of the fundamentalist impact upon Baptists a generation earlier.

[138] Carter, "American Baptist Confessions," 71. Here was the unofficial birth of the "moderate" faction in Southern Baptist life.

[139] A terminology battle raged over the use of the term "conservative" that both sides coveted. For a time the SBC press used the terms "fundamentalist conservatives" and "moderate conservatives."

the convention itself, the institutions and theological seminaries were targeted for unacceptable teaching, the leadership of the national boards and agencies was supplanted, and the theological purge reached even to the state Baptist organizations and foreign missionaries. Theologians and historians of longstanding tenure in Southern Baptist schools responded with warnings about misappropriating Baptist identity and misinterpreting the role of confessional statements in Baptist life.[140] By the late 1990s, however, the administrative reshaping of the Southern Baptist Convention was virtually complete and new expressions of Southern Baptist denominational life were at work.[141] The opportunity was ripe for those who wanted a new confessional statement.

Increased numbers of theological teachers and prominent pastors who were trained in the seventies and eighties in non-Southern Baptist seminaries and graduate schools led in a theological reversal of the trends of the sixties. Their theologies reflected institutions like Dallas Theological Seminary, Trinity Evangelical Divinity School, and Gordon Conwell Theological Seminary in the United States, and from overseas the conservative theologies that had gained prominence at institutions such as Oxford, Basel, and Aberdeen universities, to name a few. Theologians of influence included Carl F. H. Henry, Millard Erickson, Clark Pinnock, and Kenneth Kantzer. On a more popular level, Adrian Rogers, Jerry Falwell, Charles Stanley, Charles Ryrie, and later Ed Young and Max Lucado were popular among pastors and laymen across Southern Baptist life. To no one's surprise, as the new directions of seminaries and program boards were planned, new doctrinal statements were required. The result was the third generation of the *Baptist Faith and Message*, endorsed by the Southern Baptist Convention in 2000.

The authors of the new version were members of a "blue ribbon committee" charged by the 1999 convention meeting in Atlanta, Georgia, "to review the Baptist Faith and Message and report any recommendations to the next meeting." Convention president Paige Patterson appointed a seventeen-member committee of pastors, educators, laymen, and laywomen for the task, including R. Albert

---

[140] See, for instance, W. R. Estep, "Baptists and Authority: The Bible, Confessions, and Conscience in the Development of Baptist Identity," *Review and Expositor* 84/4 (Fall 1987): 500–615.

[141] These include the Alliance of Baptists, the Cooperative Baptist Fellowship, and Mainstream Baptists.

Mohler, Richard Land, T. C. Pinckney, Max Barnett, Heather King, Jerry Vines, with Adrian Rogers as chairman. The final report of the committee to the Orlando, Florida, meeting of the Southern Baptist Convention offered four reasons for revising the statement: Baptists are a confessional people; the church in every age has been called upon to defend its beliefs; each generation of Christians bears the responsibility of guarding the treasury of truth entrusted to it; Southern Baptists must meet the demands and duties of the present hour.[142] Specifically, the report found that: the purpose of the 1925 Statement had been to recover the supernatural nature of the faith; that in 1963, the statement had been revised to address the authority and truthfulness of the Bible much under attack in that era; and, in 1998, an article on the family had been added to the document in light of the prevailing cultural confusion. Boldly, the new committee saw itself in "historic succession" of intent and purpose with the earlier documents, "to set forth certain teachings we believe."[143] For many in the Southern Baptist family, the new revision became the test of "theological integrity." They held that the teachings of the theological schools and the doctrinal basis of the convention agencies should conform to what was endorsed by the convention as the widely held views of the denomination's churches.

An analysis of the content of *Baptist Faith and Message 2000* reveals two trends of a theological character. First, in actual substance, little is changed from the modifications made in the 1963 version. It is, however, increasingly difficult to identify the original wording of the New Hampshire Confession although it is claimed as part of the continuing confessional heritage. Secondly, most of the changes are additional language to underscore or clarify an issue, or to add material of an ethical kind. In Article 1 the words "all Scripture is totally true and trustworthy" are added for extra emphasis of "without error" terminology and to countermand the 1963 perception that Scripture may not be accurate in matters other than religion. There is a marked change from the 1963 guiding Christological hermeneutic to "All Scripture is a testimony to

---

[142] *Report of the Baptist Faith and Message Study Committee to the Southern Baptist Convention*, 1.
[143] Ibid.

Christ."[144] Likewise, the development of the doctrine of God in 1963 is further expanded to three distinct subsections on each member of the Trinity, using much the same language as earlier statement. Doubtless part of the reason for expansion was to elevate Baptist understanding of the Holy Spirit.

Polity and ethical/social issues give the *Baptist Faith and Message 2000* its unique flavor. In Article 6, "The Church," it is asserted: "While both men and women are gifted for service in the church, the office of pastor is limited to men as qualified by Scripture."[145] What is perceived to be a "Zwinglian" understanding of the ordinances is captured in the term "memorialize" concerning the Lord's Supper.[146] The phrase, "all sound learning is, therefore, a part of our Christian heritage" seems reminiscent of the Reformers' principle, "All truth is God's truth"—a dictum quite popular among evangelical educators.[147] In contrast, a Lockean theory of voluntary associations appears in "Cooperation," the revised Article 4: "Christian unity in the New Testament sense is spiritual harmony and voluntary cooperation for common ends by various groups of Christ's people." The phraseology again seems to look toward the so-called parachurch organizations of the evangelical community.[148]

Perhaps the two most telling additions are found in Article 15 ("The Christian and the Social Order") and the final article titled "The Family." Christians should oppose all forms of sexual immorality, "including adultery, homosexuality, and pornography."[149] Significantly, religious liberty is no longer the theme of the statement's final article, but a fully developed position on the family. The family is defined as "persons related to one another by marriage, blood, or adoption." Legitimate marriage is characterized as heterosexual in gender make-up and

---

[144] Ibid., 3 – For a survey of the issues surrounding Scripture, see *Beyond the Impasse? Scripture, Interpretation, and Theology in Baptist Life*, edited by Robinson B. James and David S. Dockery (Nashville: Broadman Press, 1992), 149-169, 278-290.

[145] Ibid., 6.

[146] Many Baptists have mistakenly conceived of Zwingli's view of the Lord's Supper as "mere memorialism," when actually the reformer employed the idea of "anamnesis." See Horton Davies, *Worship and Theology in England: From Andrewes to Baxter and Fox, 1603–1690*, vol. 2 (Grand Rapids: Eerdmans, 1996) 286–87.

[147] Ibid., 8.

[148] Ibid., 9

[149] Ibid.

monogamous in behavioral character. It is "the channel of sexual expression according to biblical standards." The function of sex is reserved primarily for "the procreation of the race." Added to these dicta is a description of the expected nature of the interpersonal relations between husbands and wives, including a controversial and biblically-cast provision, "A wife is to submit herself graciously to the servant leadership of her husband, even as the church willingly submits to the headship of Christ." (Eph. 5:21-24)[150]Further, wives have a God-given responsibility to respect husbands, serving as "helpers in the management of the household and nurturing the next generation." Answering the debate over the moment when life begins, the writers of the 2000 statement unequivocally insist that "children from the moment of conception are a blessing and heritage from the Lord." Moral values are to be passed from one generation to another through the family.[151]

Unlike its predecessors, *Baptist Faith and Message 2000* is being used by the national boards and agencies of the Southern Baptist convention to define acceptable employment as well as "orthodox" teaching in convention-affiliated schools, colleges and seminaries. Whereas the 1963 version spoke of being used as a "guideline for churches," the 2000 Statement speaks of "doctrinal accountability." But, proponents of this terminology speak of maintaining integrity with SBC local Congregations. Its use in this way, and opposition to several of its provisions, has produced widespread fallout from the Southern Baptist family and a renewed interest in non-confessional expressions of Baptist identity. Many are affirming the New Testament alone as the basis of their faith.

Another aspect of Southern Baptist confessionalism is a kind of theologically conservative rationalization that is taking place in the denomination's seminaries and among its loyalist convention groups. One writer has suggested that a literary genre he labels "writings on Baptist distinctives" reveals a confessional identity for Baptists that is both a credible basis for a distinctive Baptist theology and flexible enough to include varying perspectives within the tradition. As a result, "Baptists have a definite, confessional theological tradition," and a

---

[150] Some interpreters take verse 22 as a strict hierarchial relationship, while others place the teaching about wives in the context of vv. 21, 24 which stress mutual subjection to each other.

[151] Ibid., 10–11.

"continuous theological identity" that is "absolute."[152] His organizing principle has two "core" distinctives: biblical authority, from which regenerate church membership and baptism by immersion are derived; and, Christian experience, from which soul competency, religious freedom, believer's baptism, and the lordship of Christ are derived. The nascent movement seems uniformed by the literature of postmodernity.

The last manifestation of resurgent confessionalism to be discussed here has emerged from among more theologically moderate Southern Baptists. It has been labeled the Baptist Manifesto Movement, or colloquially, the "Baptifesto." It appeared in various forms, notably in *Baptists Today*, a moderate [Southern] Baptist newspaper.[153] There are fifty-five signatories listed, fifteen of whom are from a geographical corridor in central Texas, along with a sprinkling of people from across the Southern Baptist family and Canada. Among its principal authors are Michael Broadway, James W. McClendon, Curtis Freeman, Elizabeth Newman, Barry Harvey, and Phillip Thompson. While no one institution is identified as a sponsor of the statement, the influence and prestige of faculty members from Baylor University, Duke University, Houston Baptist University, and Carey Theological College, and other like-minded schools, is noticeable.

Four theological influences played into the Baptist Manifesto. First was a desire to go beyond a "liberal/conservative" paradigm and chart a new course in what has been called "nonfoundationalism." Hans Frei, *Types of Theology* (1992), and Nancey Murphy's work, *Beyond Liberalism and Fundamentalism* (1996), were key resources that influenced the thesis that both fundamentalists and liberals share a commonality in the Enlightenment, one producing an emphasis upon a kind of scientific textualism, the other emphasizing religious experience. Both typify theological "foundationalism," in that each requires adherence to a set of propositions that remain formative or inviolate. By implication, for the Manifesto signatories, both stances are inadequate.

---

[152] R. Stanton Norman, *More Than Just a Name*: *Preserving Our Baptist Identity* (Nashville: Broadman and Holman, 2001) 27–28, 160–63. Norman's list of Baptist distinctives literature is selective by his *a priori* understanding of Baptist distinctives. Excluded are essentially any Baptists outside the acceptable Calvinistic tradition of resurgent Southern Baptist confessionalism or writers with a broad or inclusive view of Baptist tradition.

[153] "Re-Envisoning Baptist Identity: A Manifesto for Baptist Communities in America," *Baptists Today* 26 June 1997, 8–10.

Second was a reaction against modernity and "the Enlightenment Project." The authors are convinced that Baptist identity has reached a crisis stage where "those theologies that depend upon the Enlightenment for their intelligibility cannot successfully negotiate the transition beyond modernity."[154] Third has been an intellectual flow of post-liberal American thinkers. Beginning with the taproot of Karl Barth, and evolving through George Lindbeck, Stanley Hauerwas, George Hunsinger, and William Placher, this school of thinkers has emphasized the role of the church as a faithful witness to Christ in society, rather than making the gospel credible to the world.[155] In one writer's thinking, Barth himself became a free-church [baptistic] advocate as he anticipated the failure of modernity. Devotees of this approach are indebted to Hauerwas in particular and Duke University Divinity School in general.[156]

Fourth, and perhaps most prominently, was a resurrection of an "anabaptist vision" that seemed to some a more generic and counter-cultural approach than a particularly historical approach to Baptist questions. Here the influence of James McClendon was manifest. His pedigree reached back to W. T. Conner of Southwestern Baptist Theological Seminary, and he was a devotee of the Mennonite John Howard Yoder.[157] McClendon had a great appreciation for Yoder's church-against-society model. It emphasized the revelation of God in the person of Jesus Christ who calls the people of God to be Jesus' followers, just as was the primitive church. In the first volume of his *Systematic Theology* (1986), McClendon symbolized his approach in the decapitalization of the proper noun in the term "baptist vision." Theological disciples of McClendon were key to the document, although

---

[154] Curtis W. Freeman, "Can Baptist Theology Be Revisioned?" *Perspectives in Religious Studies* 24/3 (Fall 1997): 293.

[155] Ibid., 299–300.

[156] See the critique of the Manifesto document in Walter B. Shurden, "The Baptist Identity and the Baptist Manifesto," *Perspectives in Religious Studies* 25/4 (Winter 1998): 321–40.

[157] McClendon displays a significant dependence upon the work of his wife, Nancey Murphy.

McClendon himself wanted to be known less as an author and more as a sort of traveling "dispatcher" or promotional agent for the Manifesto.[158]

The Manifesto contained an initial discussion of freedom, followed by a series of five "affirmations." Freedom, declared the document, is a gift of God and "is not to be used for selfish ends."[159] The writers inveighed heavily against narrow biblical interpretation and the application of coercive authority in Baptist life. The five affirmations ranged from Bible study in "reading" communities, to following Jesus in a shared discipleship, to the formation of reforming communities, to preaching, baptism, and the Lord's Supper that seal God's faithfulness, and finally to a renunciation of coercion. Strongly asserted throughout the Manifesto was a rejection of autonomous individualism, soul competency, and faith as a private matter.[160] In many ways, the extreme individualism that characterized Southern Baptist leadership at the turn of the twenty-first century was the catalyst that brought the Manifesto forth from the less conservatively inclined Baptists. In its place, the signers of the Manifesto urged communal discipleship.

The *Baptist Manifesto* received attention among the Southern Baptist-dominated National Association of Baptist Professors of Religion (NABPR) and among the Alliance of Baptists, Cooperative Baptist Fellowship, and readers of *Baptists Today*. It has not yet generated significant response elsewhere in the Baptist family and is thought to be essentially a regionally shaped (Southern), Caucasian statement of theological concern. It is confessional (or as some would characterize it, creedal) in that its authors hold to the value of confessions, they have voluntarily signed the document, and it reflects a variation on theological emphases that have a long currency among Baptists.

SUMMARY

What can be said by way of summary about the confessional development of Baptist thought? First, Baptists followed both

---

[158] James W. McClendon, Jr., "The Voluntary Church in the Twentieth Century," in *The Believer's Church: A Voluntary Church*, ed. William H. Brackney (Waterloo ONT: Pandora Press, 1998) 189.

[159] Freeman, 303.

[160] Freeman, 304–305; 309. Shurden, "Baptist Identity and the Baptist Manifesto" is critical of this direction against what he believes are historic Baptist characteristics. See his *The Baptist Identity:Four Fragile Freedoms* (Macon GA: Smyth and Helwys, 1993) 23–26.

Anabaptists and Puritan/Separatists in writing confessional statements. Importantly, individuals as well as associations or assemblies composed these. This is a point easily missed in modern rationalizations of a unified confessional tradition. Second, the primary purpose of Baptist confessions was to define doctrinal beliefs at a particular time and within a given set of circumstances. None of these confessions was thought to be binding upon any individual until the twentieth century. In the early expressions, those who subscribed to them did so voluntarily and often went on to seek new truth. Third, Baptist confessions of faith reflect a wide variety of theological opinion: general atonement, Calvinistic, and mediating in the early years, and Arminian, Calvinistic, evangelical, landmarkist, hyper-Calvinistic, and post-modern in later development. What Baptists have commonly expressed in confessional documents is an understanding of the sovereignty of God, a high priority on the person and work of Christ, a unique ecclesiology that includes the ordinances, the value of religious experience, and an overall commitment to the authority of the Scriptures in making doctrinal decisions. These constitute the genetic traits revealed in confessions as a source of Baptist thought.

Finally, it was not a particular confession that seemed to prevail among confessional Baptists, but a tradition of confessions. Certain elements in each of the early statements did not hold up under close scrutiny or were inadequate for other groups of Baptists. For example, within three years the First London Confession was found to be lacking in basic Calvinistic substance; a statement on openness to revision was also added to bring along English parliamentary toleration of the young Calvinistic sect. Similarly, there were several attempts to achieve a workable confession among the General Baptists. Each was short-lived. As time went on, attempts to mediate among the Calvinistic and general atonement Baptists achieved little success. The interest in confessionalism waned in the nineteenth century. Revivalism and the "New Theology" resulted in more emphasis among mainstream Baptists upon religious experience than upon theological orthodoxy.

In the twentieth century, a resurgence of confessionalism produced renewed interest in the New Hampshire Confession of Faith, although it was hardly recognizable as such by the end of the century. We have also noted that resurgent confessionalism came to include as much or more emphasis upon social and ethical concerns as upon classical doctrinal formulations.

Over four centuries many Baptists have defined themselves by a confessional statement. Therefore, these statements can be considered more than a source of Baptist thought; indeed theologically they can be a defining element, if understood within their natural limitations.[161] From the record, the confessionally oriented Baptists are significantly of the Reformed or Calvinistic persuasion. Baptist history also reveals that there are numbers of Baptists for whom a confession is too binding and while they recognize the value of doctrinal formulations, they see little disciplinary, liturgical, or educational value in the use of such statements. Instead they prefer a non-creedal, non-confessional orientation that places a high priority upon liberty of conscience.

---

[161] Gilbert Englerth, "Confessions of Faith," 132, wisely pointed out that after over two centuries of evolution, confessions demonstrated the differences of a particular body of Christians from others and that they cannot be separated from the historical context in which they arise.

CHAPTER 2

SINGING THE FAITH

Thank God for hymns! What John Milton says of books is even
more true of hymns: a good hymn is "the precious life-blood of a
master-spirit, embalmed and treasured up, on purpose to a life
beyond life." Who was it that said: "Give me the making of a
people's songs, and I care not who makes their laws." That is
true of the power of the hymn. It comes out of the heart, rather
than out of their head; it abides in the memory when the creed is
forgotten; it subconsciously influences the will, and stimulates
the man to action.[1]

A. H. Strong, 1913.

In addition to confessions of faith that illustrate what Baptist clergy and
interested laypersons want to say theologically, hymns are a second
source of Baptist theology. Perhaps no other source of Baptist thought
better reflects the importance of religious experience than what Baptists
sing. As recent historians have shown, "hymns were probably the most
widely known and memorized of any verbal phenomenon."[2] In the
earliest development of Baptists, singing was a controversial issue. John
Smyth opposed having words in view, even of psalms, when singing.
Eventually, however, Baptists took a lead in advocating congregational
singing and joined other evangelical Christians in composing and using
hymns in worship. What Baptists sing reveals an extension of their
theological identity in a decidedly egalitarian form.[3]

---

[1] Augustus Hopkins Strong, *One Hundred Chapel-Talks to Theological Students
Together with Two Autobiographical Addresses* (Philadelphia: Griffith and Rowland
Press, 1913), 210.

[2] *English Hymns of the Eighteenth Century: An Anthology*, ed. Richard Arnold (New
York: Peter Lang, 1991) xi.

[3] In this regard, Baptists have much in common with the evangelical tradition, so-
defined. Mark A. Noll, *American Evangelical Christianity: An Introduction* (Oxford:

BACKGROUNDS

Music historians argue that the modern singing of hymns[4] probably had its origins in the German Reformation. Wilhelm Staehlin has pointed out that where it was allowed, singing, as opposed to speaking, was the original form of prayer and praise and thus the original theological utterance.[5] Martin Luther compiled the first congregational hymnbook, *Achliederbuch* (1524), and his widespread encouragement to composers and musicians was seen throughout Luther's career.[6] In contrast, however, the Swiss Reformer Huldrych Zwingli eliminated the sensuous elements from worship, including music, and his later co-religionist John Calvin followed in that train.[7] Calvin, who appreciated music in general, was open to choral music and limited hymn singing, as long as it was the words of the psalms.[8] The Geneva community and Calvinists abroad used Theodore Beza's *Psautier Huguenot* (1562) for many generations. But, despite attempts such as those of Miles Coverdale in 1531 to introduce hymns in England, they were left out of Thomas Cranmer's worship agenda. In the reign of Henry VIII the singing of originally composed hymns was frowned upon in the established church and hymn books were banned. Choirs and chants constituted the essence of music among English Christians at worship through the Commonwealth period.[9]

Blackwell Publishers, 2001) 268, asserts "The classic evangelical hymns, contain the clearest, the most memorable, the most cohesive, and the most widely repeated expressions of what it meant to be an evangelical."

[4] I shall use the definition of a hymn offered by the Hymn Society of the United States and Canada: "A Christian hymn is a lyric poem, reverently and devotionally conceived, which is designed to be sung and which expresses the worshipper's attitude toward God, or God's purposes in human life. It should be simple and metrical in form, genuinely emotional, poetic, and literary in style, spiritual in quality, and in its ideas so direct and so immediately apparent as to unify a congregation while singing it." See also, Armin Haeussler, *The Story of Our Hymns* (St. Louis: Eden Publishing Co., 1952) 1.

[5] Wilhelm Staehlin, "The Church Hymn and Theology," *Response* (St. Paul: Lutheran Society for Worship, Music, and the Arts, 1958) 26.

[6] See Paul Nettl, *Luther and Music* (Philadelphia: Fortess Press, 1948).

[7] For Zwingli's perspective, consult Charles Garside, *Zwingli and the Arts* (New Haven: Yale University Press, 1966) 178ff.

[8] A useful essay on Calvin and music is Charles Garside, "The Origins of Calvin's Theology of Music, 1536–43" *Transactions of the American Philosophical Society* 69:4 (1979): 5-33.

[9] Horton Davies, *Worship and Theology in England,* vol. 1 (Princeton: Princeton University Press, 1970) covers this early development admirably.

Some pro-Cromwell "propaganda hymns" appeared during the Interregnum era, but for the most part it was assumed that hymns—presumed of mere human origin—did not enrich worship as did the godly psalms. Hymns were therefore largely absent from both Anglican and Presbyterian public worship. Over time, however, the people tired of the psalter, comparing it to "two hammers on an anvil" or a "cracked bell in a steeple."[10] During the early decades of the seventeenth century, devotional poetry like that of George Herbert filled a spiritual void in private families or gatherings. The established church still banned hymns in public worship. During the Restoration, however, the use of "metrical scriptures" opened the door to the use of hymns. Writers like William Barton argued persuasively that hymn singing was part of the primitive churches (Colossians 3:16), and it appears that hymns gained popularity in private use by the 1690s. Congregational singing nevertheless was frowned upon by Roman Catholics, most Anglicans, Baptists, and Quakers, all of whom considered hymns "promiscuous" and "a form without power."[11] It was left to a minority of Baptists and other nonconformists to start the practice within congregations during the Restoration and to compile a collection of appropriate hymns for Christian worship.

THE BEGINNINGS OF A TRADITION

Benjamin Keach (1640–1704) is usually accorded the place of pioneer among Baptists who favored singing as a legitimate act of worship. As pastor at Horsley-down, Southwark, Keach introduced the practice of singing a hymn at the Lord's Supper.[12] This being well received, he continued the practice on Thanksgiving days and then every Sunday after the sermon. Those who objected left the service early to "go freely forth." Keach himself wrote scores of poems and eventually a collection of hymns in 1691, "Scriptural Melody," that contained three hundred hymns. His justification for hymn singing was published as *The Breach*

---

[10] Quoted in Arnold, *English Hymns in the Eighteenth Century,* 7.

[11] Nicholas Temperley, *The Music of the English Parish Church* (Cambridge: Cambridge University Press, 1971) 89 ff., argues that individual Anglican parishes proceeded to sing within the congregation, in spite of the official decrees.

[12] Thus began a long tradition of hymn composition among Baptists: Michael J. Collis, "The Lord's Supper in British Baptist Hymnody in the Twentieth Century," *Baptist Quarterly* 38/6 (April 2000): 290–305.

repaired in God's Worship, or Singing of Psalms, Hymns, and Spiritual Songs proved to be a holy ordinance of Jesus Christ (1691). His own compositions were of mixed quality and gave pause to those who saw little of doctrine or Scripture therein. The following selection from Keach's compositions demonstrates his penchant for near-doggerel:

> Our wounds do stink and are corrupt,
> Hard swellings do we see;
> We want a little ointment, Lord,
> Let us more humble be.
> Repentance like a bucket is
> To pump the water out;
> For leaky is our ship, alas
> Which makes us look about.[13]

In his better work, Keach's themes followed the psalms, interlaced with Pauline theology, revealing the pastor's understanding of the Christian life as a pilgrimage fraught with dangers:

> The Lord, he is our sun and shield,
> Our buckler and safeguard;
> And hence we stand and will not yield,
> Though enemies press hard.
> Like as a shield the blow keeps off
> The enemy lays on,
> So Thou keeps off all hurt from us
> And Saves us every one.
> Let foes strike at us as they please,
> On the head or the heart;
> This precious shield which we do use
> Secures us every part.
> Our shield and our great reward,
> To Thee all praise be given;
> Who with Thy saving help afford
> Until we come to Heaven.[14]

---

[13] Quoted in Adam A. Reid, "Benjamin Keach, 1640," *Baptist Quarterly* 10/2 (April, 1940): 77.

Keach artfully wove assurance of salvation and eternal security for the believer into the themes of faith's pilgrimage. His "realized eschatology" was obviously a comfort to his fellow nonconformists, who with their pastor faced the continual threat of persecution and imprisonment.

Another well-known early hymnist among the Seventh Day Baptists was Joseph Stennett (1663–1713). Like Keach, Stennett helped to define the role and value of hymns among Baptists. Pastor of a congregation that met at Pinner's Hall in London, Stennett's works were Christological in focus and often emphasized the sacraments. One poem read:

Lord, at thy table I behold
The wonders of thy grace;
But most of all admire that I
Should find a welcome place,
What strange, surprising grace is this,
That such a soul has room!
My savior takes me by the hand,
My Jesus bids me come.
Eat, O my friends the Savior cries,
The feast was made for you;
For you I groaned, and bled, and died,
And rose and triumphed too.[15]

Stennett's poetic theology also helped to define the theology of baptism. One of the earliest Baptist writers, he was likely the first to use the phrase "watery grave" to depict believer's baptism by immersion. In four movements of one poetic enterprise, for example, he developed the metaphor (*divisions mine*):

(*first movement*)
Thus was the great Redeemer plung'd
In Jordan's swelling flood;
To shew he'd one day be baptiz'd

[14] Quoted in Burrage, *Baptist Hymn Writers and Their Hymns* (Portland: Brown, Thurston & Co., 1888) 32.
[15] Quoted in ibid., 35.

In tears, in sweat, and blood.
Thus was his sacred body laid
Beneath the yielding wave:
Thus was his sacred body rais'd
Out of the liquid grave....

(*second movement*)
With thee into thy watery tomb,
Lord 'tis our glory to descend;
'Tis wondrous grace that gives us room
To lie inter'd by such a friend!
But a much more tempestuous flood
O'erwhelm'd thy body and thy soul:
That's plunged in tears, and sweat, and blood,
And over this black terrors roll...

(*third movement*)
The sun of righteousness his beams,
Tho so divinely fair and bright,
Immers'd in Jordan's swelling streams,
Submitting to this holy rite.
O Jordan! Honour'd oft before!
What greater glory would'st thou have,
Than Christ descending from thy shore,
To find in thee a liquid grave?...

(*fourth movement*)
See how the willing converts trace
The path their great Redeemer trod;
And follow thro' his liquid grave,
The meek, the lowly son of God.
Here in the holy laver plung'd,
Their souls are cleans'd from every stain;
They die, descend into the tomb,
By grace they live, and rise again.[16]

---

[16] Joseph Stennett, *Hymns Compos'd for the Celebration of the Holy Ordinance of Baptism*, ed. Don Sandford (Janesville: Seventh Day Baptist Historical Society, 2001) 160, 164, 166.

Stennett was also widely received as a writer of sabbatarian hymns such as, "Another Six Days' Work Is Done." Because the sabbatarian motif was extreme to many mainstream Christians, Stennett's work was rigorously scrutinized for its theology, or often simply ignored.[17] His grandson, Samuel, is still recalled for composing the ever-popular "On Jordan's Stormy Banks I Stand," yet another rendition of pilgrimage themes.

As time went on, Baptists became more refined in their hymnological tastes and recognized the value of hymns from other traditions. A survey of Baptist hymn content suggests that Baptists sought to contemporize and personalize biblical narratives and doctrine.[18] Their poetry reflected their own struggles and their immediate contexts, as John Rippon's own saga related:

Here, Lord, my soul convicted stands
Of breaking all Thy ten commands;
And on me justly might'st Thou pour
Thy wrath in one eternal shower.
But, thanks be to God! Its loud alarms
Have warned me of approaching harms;
And now, O Lord! my wants I see;
Lost and undone, I come to Thee.
I see, my fig-leaf righteousness
Can ne'er Thy broken law redress;
Yet in Thy gospel plan I see
There's hope of pardon e'en for me.

Many churches readily accepted the inspiring lines and theology of the Congregationalist, Isaac Watts (1674–1748). Among his most beloved hymns was the still beloved "Alas! And did my Saviour Bleed?"

Alas! And did my Saviour bleed?
And did my sovereign die?
Would he devote that sacred head
For such a worm as I?

---

[17] Duffield, *English Hymns*, 35.
[18] For a scholarly account, see Robert H. Young, "The History of Baptist Hymnody in England from 1612 to 1800" (D.M.A. diss., University of Southern California, 1959).

Was it for crimes that I have done
He groaned upon the tree?
Amazing pity! Grace unknown!
And love beyond degree!
Well might the sun in darkness hide,
And shut his glories in,
When Christ, the mighty Maker, died
For man, the creature's sin.
But drops of grief can ne'er repay
The debt of love I owe;
Here, Lord, I give myself away—
Tis all that I can do.[19]

As some writers have rightly noted, Baptists have often sung expressions and ideas widely divergent from either Scripture or prevailing confessional theology. For example, early writers liked the idea of a pilgrimage:

Lord, we are pilgrims on the Earth, as all our fathers were,
For this is not our dwelling place, no 'biding for us here.
A Pilgrim loves good company, don't care to go alone;
So do God's saints delight in such who Christ Jesus own;
And walk with them in the same way, if that they be sincere,
They prize their precious company, they helpful to each are.
A Pilgrim, when he's come near home, he greatly doth rejoice;
O let such Saints whose work's near done, lift up with joy their
    voice.[20]

The venerable John Bunyan's hymn (also known as the "Shepherd Boy's Song" from *Pilgrim's Progress*) was written in the same vein:

He who would valiant be
'Gainst all disaster,
Let him in constancy

[19] Isaac Watts, "Alas! And Did My Saviour Bleed?" in *Worship and Service Hymnal*, 64.
[20] Quoted in William T. Whitley, "The First Hymnbook in Use," *Baptist Quarterly* 10/7 (July 1941): 374–75. Benjamin Keach was the author of this poem.

Follow the Master.
There's no discouragement
Shall make him once relent
His first avowed intent
To be a pilgrim.
Since Lord, Thou dost defend
Us with Thy Spirit,
We know we at the end
Shall life inherit,
Then, fancies, flee away!
I'll fear not what men may say,
I'll labor night and day
To be a pilgrim.[21]

THE THEOLOGY OF THE POETIC CANON

In some significant ways, the poetry of the early Baptist and evangelical hymns became for many a kind of theological/experiential canon. It should be remembered that, as poems, hymns were composed before they were necessarily set to music. Common themes began to emerge in Christian history that created a popular theology.[22] S. Paul Schilling has noted seven prominent themes: God, humanity, Jesus Christ, the Holy Spirit, Church and Mission, the Christian Life, and the Consummation.[23] Among Calvinistic Baptists, election, perseverance of the saints, divine sovereignty and watchcare, and the future life were frequently affirmed doctrines. Because Baptists created new understandings of the sacraments as ordinances, these also became a predictable theme of hymnody. Likewise, General Baptists emphasized the fullness of salvation, freedom in Christ, and evangelism. A blending of Old Testament figures of speech with New Testament phraseology constituted many stanzas.

---

[21] John Bunyan, "He Who Would Valiant Be," in *The Hymnal of the Baptist Federation of Canada* (Mississauga: Baptist Federation Press, 1973) 409.

[22] Hugh T. McElrath, "The Hymnbook as a Compendium of Theology," *Review and Expositor* 87 (Winter 1990): 11–31 argues for two streams, Calvinistic and Pietistic. Calvinists, he claimed, stressed objective aspects like the majesty and glory of God and God's mighty acts, while the Pietists emphasized the subjective and human responses.

[23] S. Paul Schilling, *The Faith We Sing* (Philadelphia: Westminster Press, 1983) 13.

The personalization of doctrines and biblical narrative was a prominent feature of eighteenth century Baptist hymnody. The recurring phrases and hymns came to constitute a second canon of acceptable belief and expression in addition to Scripture. Because of the nature of music, it has been speculated that where literacy was low, the phraseology of hymns was more commonly indicative of popular theology than biblical passages or formal confessional theology. To a people who valued religious experience, confessing one's faith through a hymn was an acceptable form of testimony. As Donald Hustad has pointed out, music is a reinforcement of the values of church life involving both revelation and response. God is self-revealed in nature and Scripture and invites a response that can come pleasurably in the form of singing a hymn.[24] Even more to the point is Erik Routley's definition that "a hymn is an opportunity for a congregation to declare its experience and to rejoice in Christian doctrine corporately."[25]

A limited number of Baptist pastors took advantage of the new medium to catechize their congregations in theological precepts. Constant repetition of the hymns led to congregational articulation of great themes of the faith, including sovereign grace, the atonement of Christ, eternal security, the judgement of God through Christ, and the exaltation of Christ. Calvinistic and General Baptists alike developed their poetic gifts and led in the new recognition of the power of singing among their churches. Associational meetings became opportunities for congregations to share their own repertoire and practice what others were doing as well.

Certain theological themes were dominant in early English Baptist hymnody. The eternal security theme for the elect was picked up by early eighteenth-century writers like Benjamin Wallin (1711–1782) at Maze Pond, London:

And when thy victories are complete,
When all the chosen race
Shall round the throne of glory meet
To sing thy conquering grace,
O may my humble soul be found

---

[24] Donald P. Hustad, *Jubilate II: Church Music in the Evangelical Tradition* (Carol Stream IL: Hope Publishing Co., 1981) 27–28.

[25] Erik Routley, *Hymns Today and Tomorrow* (Nashville: Abingdon Press, 1964) 18.

Among the glorious throng;
And I with them thy praise will sound
In Heaven's immortal song.[26]

Among the earliest themes for hymns were the sacraments and
ordinances. In the first Baptist hymn book, Benjamin Keach wrote
several pieces given to the motif. Mingling themes of baptism and the
Lord's Supper, he wrote:

In ev'ry Ordinance also in which we should be found
O Thou art all; for we well know grace in Thee doth abound.
The Sacraments do hold Thee forth and witness bear to Thee;
And we by one to see by faith Thou nail'd wast to the Tree;
Thy body broke, and blood was shed; in Baptism we do espy
Thou in the Grave wast covered, but long Thou didst not lye
But, as the Body raised is that cover'd was all o'er,
So Thou wast raised unto life, and diest now no more.

As Richard Arnold and others have shown, the eighteenth century
witnessed more pastors and laity writing hymns. Eventually, the Wesleys
used singing to maximum advantage to reach thousands.[27] In large part
because Baptists were drawn from the same social classes as those in the
Wesleyan revival, Baptists took note of Methodist singing. In contrast to
the Arminian themes among Methodists, Baptist hymns of this period
were a mixture of orthodox Calvinistic theology and personal narrative.
A dominant theme was the praise of Christ, often interlaced with other
doctrine. Samuel Medley (1738–1799), an eighteenth-century Baptist
pastor at Watford and later Liverpool, wrote,

Dearest of names, our Lord, our King!
Jesus thy praise we humbly sing;
In cheerful songs will spend our breath,
And in Thee triumph over death.

---

[26] Quoted in Burrage, *Baptist Hymn Writers*, 45.

[27] William Vincent, *Considerations on Parochial Music* (London: n.p., 1787) 15,
theorized that tenfold more converts responded to singing than to preaching during the
Evangelical Revival.

In later verses, the Christological theme of the hymn shifted to eschatology:

Death is a sleep; and O how sweet,
To souls prepared its stroke to meet!
Their dying beds, their graves are blessed,
For all to them is peace and rest.
Their bodies sleep, their souls take wing,
Uprise to heaven, and there they sing
With joy, before the Savior's face,
Triumphant in victorious grace.

In the final stanzas of the poetic hymn's lyrics, he drew together the believer's hope and a personal relation with Christ:

Bodies and souls shall then unite,
Arrayed in glory strong and bright;
And all his saints will Jesus bring,
His face to see, his love to sing.
O may I live with Jesus nigh,
And sleep in Jesus when I die!
Then, joyful when from death I wake,
I shall eternal bliss partake.[28]

Benjamin Beddome (1717–1795), another Calvinist Baptist pastor at Bourton-on-Water, wrote with self-assurance in Christ's atonement for himself after recovering from a severe illness:

If I must die, O let me die
Trusting in Jesus' blood!
That blood which hath atonement made,
And reconciles to God.

That perspective inevitably resulted in a form of benign determinism:

If I must die as die I must,

---

[28] Quoted in Burrage, *Baptist Hymn Writers*, 76–79.

Let some kind seraph come,
And bear me on his friendly wing
To my celestial home!
Of Canaan's land from Pisgah's top
May I but have a view!
Though Jordan should o'erflow its banks,
I'll boldly venture through.[29]

Likewise, Edmund Jones (1722–1765), a Welsh Baptist pastor at
Exeter who was educated at Bristol Baptist College, stressed sovereign
grace:

Come, humble sinner, in whose breast
A thousand thoughts resolve,
Come with your guilt and fear opprest,
And make this last resolve.
Prostrate I'll lie before His throne
And there my guilt confess,
I'll tell Him I'm a wretch undone
Without His sovereign grace.
I'll to the gracious King approach,
Whose scepter pardon gives.
Perhaps He may command my touch,
And then the suppliant lives.[30]

The great collector of hymns, John Rippon (1751–1836), also
contributed his own poetry.[31] His presentation of Calvinistic doctrine was
a careful objective in his hymnody:

Here, Lord, my soul convicted stands
Of breaking all Thy ten commands
And on me justly might'st Thou pour
Thy wrath in one eternal shower.

---

[29] Quoted in ibid., 51.
[30] Quoted in ibid., 54.
[31] For a full-scale analysis of Rippon and his contributions to hymnody, see Ken R.
Manley, "John Rippon D. D. (1751–1836) and the Particular Baptists" (Ph.D. diss.,
Oxford University, 1967).

But, thanks to God! Its loud alarms
Have warned me of approaching harms;
And now, O Lord! my wants I see;
Lost and undone, I come to Thee.
I see, my fig-leaf righteousness
Can ne'er Thy broken law redress;
Yet in Thy gospel plan I see
There's hope of pardon e'en for me.
Here I behold Thy wonders Lord!
How Christ hath to Thy law restored
Those honors, on the atoning day,
Which guilty sinners took away.
Amazing wisdom, power and love,
Displayed to rebels from above!
Do thou, O Lord! my faith increase
To love and trust Thy plan of grace.[32]

LAYPERSONS AND VARIETY

In English Baptist life presented frequent instances of laypersons who were inspired to write hymns. John Adams (1751–1835), at one time a member of John Collett Ryland's congregation at Northampton, reflected his beloved pastor's evangelical Calvinistic theological influence. That Calvinism was evident in the themes his hymns addressed: the glory of God, human sinfulness, free election, and the calling and perseverance of the saints. Adams also gave great focus to themes of salvation and redemption through Christ:

Jesus is our great salvation,
Worthy of our best esteem!
He has saved His favorite nation;
Join to sing aloud to Him;
He has saved us,
Christ alone could us redeem.

When involv'd in sin and ruin

---

[32] Quoted in Burrage, *Baptist Hymn Writers*, 100.

And no helper there was found,
Jesus our distress was viewing,
Grace did more than sin abound;
He has called us,
With salvation in the sound.

Save us from mere profession!
Save us from hypocrisy;
Give us, Lord, the sweet possession
Of Thy righteousness and Thee;
Best of favors!
None compared with this can be.

Let us never, Lord, forget Thee;
Make us walk as pilgrims here;
We will give Thee all the glory
Of the love that brought us near;
Bid us praise Thee,
And rejoice with holy fear.

Free election, known by calling,
Is a privilege divine;
Saints are kept from final falling,
All the glory, Lord, be Thine;
All the glory,
All the glory, Lord, be Thine.[33]

Anne Steele (1717–1778) was a prolific Calvinistic Baptist hymn writer of the eighteenth century. She was the daughter of William Steele, a timber merchant and Baptist lay preacher in the congregation at Broughton. She lived as an invalid all of her life in that village. Tragedy struck when just a few hours before her wedding, her fiancé was drowned. She published a book of hymns in 1760 under the pseudonym, "Theodosia." Her personal sufferings are a prominent feature of her poems, many of which were given to devotional topics. Her style moved away from strict biblical language to repetitious, romanticized epithets,

---

[33] Quoted in ibid., 101–102.

though never veering from Puritan thinking.[34] One historian noted that she brought to the genre the quality of introspection, while another non-Baptist found her work "a transcript of a deeply sensitive, humane and pious mind, with little intellectual variety or strength."[35] Her most familiar hymn was "Father, whate'er of earthly bliss," quoted here in part:

> When I survey life's varied scene,
> Amid the darkest hours,
> Sweet rays of comfort shine between,
> And thorns are mixed with flowers.
> When present sufferings pain my heart,
> Or future terrors rise
> And light and hope almost depart
> From these dejected eyes,
> Thy powerful word supports my hope,
> Sweet cordial of the mind,
> And bears my fainting spirit up,
> And bids me wait resigned.
> "Give me a calm, a thankful heart,
> From every murmur free;
> The blessings of Thy grace impart,
> And let me live to Thee.[36]

Steele, like many Baptist hymnists over the years, extolled the person of Christ. Using the language of experience, she wrote with a descriptive and personalized texture reminiscent of Bernard of Clairveaux of the 12th century:

> The Saviour! O What endless charms
> Dwell in the blissful sound!
> Its influence every fear dissolves
> And spreads sweet comfort round

---

[34] Steele was published in the United States in an 1808 edition that included 144 hymns, 34 metrical psalms, and 50 poems on moral subjects.

[35] Ronald W. Thomson, "Anne Steele, 1716–1778," *Baptist Quarterly* 21/8 (October, 1966): 369; Duffield, *English Hymns*, 6.

[36] Burrage, *Baptist Hymn Writers*, 48.

Jesus, the spring of joys divine,
Where all my hopes and comforts flow;
Jesus, no other name but Thine,
Can save me from eternal woe.[37]

There were also examples of General Baptist hymn writers in the eighteenth century whose lyrics articulated their theology. In many ways, General Baptists imitated Wesleyan theological themes of human response and the invitation of the gospel. Samuel Deacon (1746–1816), pastor of the General Baptist congregation at Ratby, openly invited sinners to convert:

Ye heavy-laden souls,
With guilt and fear opprest,
Come! For the Great Redeemer calls,
And calls to give you rest.
Why hesitate and doubt,
Why so unwelcome seem?
When did He shut a sinner out
That ever came to Him?
He stands with open arms
Inviting sinners home;
His voice contains a thousand charms,
And every charm says, "Come!"
Come, then, without delay,
And enter into rest;
With gratitude His voice obey,
And be forever blest![38]

Islington boarding school mistress Alice Flowerdew (1759–1830) was a General Baptist hymn writer who reflected the doctrinal bent of her pastor, London's John Evans, and the literary style of the Age of Romanticism. Her harvest hymn was popular in many collections as it related the passing of seasons to the providence and nurture of God:

Fountain of mercy! God of love!
How rich Thy bounties are!

---

[37] Quoted in Thomson, "Ann Steele," 369.
[38] Quoted in Burrage, *Baptist Hymn Writers*, 94.

The rolling seasons, as they move,
Proclaim Thy constant care.

When in the bosom of the earth
The sower hid the grain,
Thy goodness marked its secret birth
And sent the early rain.

The Spring's sweet influence was Thine,
The plants in beauty grew;
Thou gav'st refulgent suns to shine,
And mild refreshing dew.

These various mercies from above
Mature the swelling grain;
A yellow harvest crowns Thy love,
And plenty fills the plain.

Seed time and harvest, Lord, alone
Thou dost on man bestow;
Let him not then forget to own
From whom his blessings flow!

Fountain of love! Our praise is Thine;
To Thee our songs we'll raise
And all created Nature join
In sweet harmonious praise.[39]

Perhaps the finest hymnic example of nineteenth-century general atonement thinking was found in General Baptist missionary Amos Sutton's (1802–1854) mission hymn:

Men of God, to you we cry,
Rests on you our tearful eye;
Help us Christians, or we die,
Die in dark despair.

---

[39] Quoted in ibid., 109.

Hasten, Christians, haste to save,
O'er the land, and o'er the wave;
Dangers, death, and distance brave.
Hark, for help they call.

Afric bends her suppliant knee,
Asia's woes cry "Pity me"
Hark, they urge the heaven-born plea,
"Jesus died for all."

Haste, then, spread the Savior's name,
Snatch the fire-brands from the flame,
Deck His glorious diadem
With these ransomed souls.

See! the pagan altars fall,
See! the Savior reigns o'er all,
"Crown Him, crown Him Lord of all,"
Echoes round the poles.[40]

EIGHTEENTH AND NINETEENTH CENTURY BRITISH CONTRIBUTIONS

Robert Robinson of Cambridge (1735–1790) brought an unusual expression of Baptist identity to eighteenth-century hymn composition. As a Calvinistic Baptist preacher, he was a pastoral inspiration to the venerable Robert Hall, Jr. Robinson's hymn, "Come Thou Fount of Every Blessing," has been included in virtually every widely accepted English-language Protestant worship hymnal since the eighteenth century. Robinson entered a phase of theological unorthodoxy in the midst of his pastorate in Cambridge. Many thought him to have adopted Unitarian views, especially given his close friendship with Joseph Priestly. His honest poem signaled the possibility of such theological wandering:

[40] Quoted in ibid., 173.

Come, Thou Fount of every blessing,
Tune my heart to sing Thy grace;
Streams of mercy, never ceasing,
Call for songs of loudest praise.

Teach me some melodious sonnet,
Sung by flaming tongues above;
Praise the mount—I'm fixed upon it—
Mount of Thy redeeming love.

Here I raise mine Ebenezer;
Hither by thy help I'm come;
And I hope, by Thy good pleasure,
Safely to arrive at home.

Jesus sought me when a stranger,
Wandering from the fold of God;
He, to rescue me from danger,
Interposed His precious blood.

O to grace how great a debtor
Daily I'm constrained to be!
Let Thy goodness, like a fetter,
Bind my wandering heart to Thee:

Prone to wander, Lord, I feel it,
Prone to leave the God I love;
Here's my heart, O take and seal it;
Seal it for Thy courts above.[41]

Among British Calvinistic Baptists in the nineteenth century, theology flowed in two streams, that of the Strict Baptists and that of the mainstream "union" Baptists. This was reflected in each expression's hymnody. William Gadsby (1773–1844), one of the great Strict Baptist preachers of the North, penned his high Calvinist understanding of the "doctrines of grace" this way:

---

[41] Robert Robinson, "Come, Thou Fount," in *Worship and Service Hymnal*, 104.

Once more, dear God of grace,
Thine earthly courts we tread;
We come to see Thy face,
And banquet with our head.

We long, we faint, we pant for Thee
And hope that with us Thou wilt be.
Though base and vile we are,
No goodness have to bring;

We cannot well despair,
While Jesus is our King.
He welcomes all by sin oppressed,
Upon his grace to come and feast.[42]

But others, such as Solomon S. Alsop (fl.1825), were actively engaged in Sunday School work and encouraged followers to become involved through Sunday School hymns:

Throughout the year we have been blest
With lessons from Thy word,
From teachers, dear, who never tire,
In working for their Lord,
Our minds to train, our souls to win;
O give them their reward.

May we still love the Sunday-school;
Still love Thy word and ways;
And wise unto salvation grow,
In these our youthful days;
Then join the blessed band above,
Who ever sing Thy praise.

Lord, smile upon the friends who come
To aid this work of love;

---

[42] Quoted in Burrage, *Baptist Hymn Writers*, 129.

Their offerings graciously accept;
Thy blessing may they prove
An hundredfold, and may we meet
Teachers and friends above.[43]

As theological emphases became more evangelical, this was reflected in Baptist hymnody.[44] Once the efforts of the Baptist Missionary Society were well established after 1800, Baptist pastors and candidates for overseas service enthusiastically joined the cause of evangelization. John Lawson (1787–1825) was an appointee of the society who served churches in the United States and India. His noted missionary hymn that swept across continents, irrespective of race or culture, was included in John Rippon's "Selection" (see above):

Europe, speak the mighty name
Loud th' eternal Three proclaim;
Let thy deep seraphic lays
Thunder forth the echoing praise.

Asia, bring thy raptured songs;
Let innumerable tongues
Swell the chord from shore to shore,
Where thy thousand billows roar.

Sable Afric, aid the strain,
Triumph o'er the broken chain;
Bid thy wildest music raise
All its fervor in his praise.

Shout, America, thy joys,
While his love thy song employs;
Let thy lovely wilderness
High exalt his righteousness.[45]

---

[43] Quoted in ibid., 191.

[44] For the influence of West Country evangelicalism, see Eric Sharpe, "Bristol Baptist College and the Church's Hymnody," *Baptist Quarterly* 38/1 (January 1979): 7–16.

[45] Quoted in Burrage, *Baptist Hymn Writers*, 145.

AMERICAN NUANCES

As the American Baptist movement matured, so did its interest in congregational worship. Elias Keach may have introduced hymn singing to the Baptist community, following his father's lead in England, but there were likely others in New England and the Middle Colonies that practiced singing outside the church and for individual devotional purposes. A familiar scene among New England Christians was the individual carrying a copy of the Bible and the *Bay Psalm Book* (1640) to meeting, which implied that both were used in the home. Yet, this was not likely the combination that Baptists cherished since the authors/ compilers of the *Bay Psalm Book* had been responsible for ill treatment of Nonconformists.[46] The number of Welsh who settled in the Delaware Valley strongly suggests the presence of singing there in the eighteenth century. Similarly, Baptists commenced singing in the South in the last decades of the 1700s. In any case, the historian Burrage noted sixteen examples of early American Baptist hymn writers (eighteenth century) including, John Leland, Richard Furman, and Andrew Broaddus.

David W. Music at Baylor University has demonstrated the importance of music in the First Baptist Church of Boston and its lead in the American Baptist denomination. Between 1728 and 1771 various books of psaltery served the church adequately until they adopted collections of Isaac Watts and John Rippon. In 1818 pastor James M. Winchell published for the church's use *An Arrangement of the Psalms, Hymns, and Spiritual Songs of Isaac Watts*. Other churches immediately followed suit and this became the standard until two other New Englanders, Baron Stow and Samuel Smith, published the *Psalmist* in 1843. This was arguably the first hymnal produced among American Baptists as a denomination and circulated by the American Baptist Publication Society. The combination of Bostonians William Billings and Oliver Holden in composing music, with Samuel Stillman, the *de facto* Baptist bishop at First Baptist Church, Boston insured the orthodoxy of the theology of the emerging hymnody as well as its acceptance in the larger Baptist community.[47] Hymn singing and a subtle

---

[46] William J. Reynolds, "Baptist Hymnody in America," in *Handbook to the Baptist Hymnal* (Nashville: Convention Press, 1992) 32.

[47] David W. Music, "Music in the First Baptist Church of Boston, Massachusetts, 1665–1820," in Harry Eskew, David W. Music, and Paul A. Richardson, *Singing*

fondness for the expressed theology of hymns, was thus well on its way among nineteenth-century Baptists in the United States.

A flurry of religious poetry was also on display in the nineteenth century. Among the most popular in the Northern Baptist community were Robert Lowry (1826–1899), a professor and organist at Lewisburg (later Bucknell) University, and Joseph Gilmore (1834–1918). Lowry interlaced his understanding of the substitutionary blood-atonement of Christ with his own experience in the hymn titled "Nothing But the Blood":

What can wash away my sin?
Nothing but the blood of Jesus;
What can make me whole again?
Nothing but the blood of Jesus.
For my pardon this I see—
Nothing but the blood of Jesus;
For my cleansing, this my plea—
Nothing but the blood of Jesus.
Nothing can for sin atone—
Naught of good that I have done—
Nothing but the blood of Jesus.
Oh! Precious is the flow
That makes me white as snow;
No other fount I know,
Nothing but the blood of Jesus.[48]

Gilmore likewise used personal narrative to communicate God's sovereign guidance in his pilgrim hymn, "He Leadeth Me, O Blessed Thought":

He leadeth me, O Blessed Thought!
O words with heav'nly comfort fraught!
Whate'er I do, where'er I be,
Still 'tis God's hand that leadeth me.
Sometimes mid scenes of deepest gloom,

Baptists: Studies in Baptist Hymnody in America (Nashville: Church Street Press, 1994) 34–42.

[48] "Nothing But the Blood," in *Worship and Service Hymnal,* 267.

Sometimes where Eden's bowers bloom,
By waters calm, o'er troubled sea,
Still 'tis His hand that leadeth me.
Lord, I would clasp Thy hand in mine,
Nor ever murmur nor repine;
Content, whatever lot I see,
Since 'tis my God that leadeth me.
He leadeth me, He leadeth me;
By His own hand He leadeth me;
His faithful follower I would be,
For by His hand He leadeth me.[49]

Hymn singing became a popular part of Baptist life in the American South. Writers such as Andrew Broaddus wrote of the evangelical purposes of the church:

Restless thy spirit, poor wandering sinner.
Restless and roving—O, come to thy home!
Return to the arms—to the bosom of mercy:
The Saviour of sinners invites thee to come.[50]

Likewise, Basil Manly, Jr., followed his father's lead and in 1850 published a hymnal, *The Baptist Psalmody*, in which he included his own theological poetry addressing doctrines such as grace, holiness, and the person of Christ, and reflecting the evangelical homiletic style of Baptists in his region:

To sin-sick souls He offers grace,
Confined to neither time nor place;
Where'er is offered heartfelt prayer,
The fount of life is open there.
Thou loving, gracious healing Lord,
Speak to my soul the pardoning word;
My sins remove, new strength impart;
O cleanse, and dwell within my heart.[51]

---

[49] "He Leadeth Me, O Blessed Thought," in *Baptist Hymnal*, 469.
[50] "The Wandering Sinner" from Andrew Broaddus, *The Virginia Selection of Psalms, Hymns and Spiritual Songs* (Richmond: n.p., 1835) 708.

Baptists in America followed trends set elsewhere that aided in the "depositing" of theological truths in believers' hearts. One interesting feature that American singers added to emphasize certain themes was the singing of a refrain. This phraseology picked up words from the original poet/theologian's work and added emphasis. Refrains allowed the congregations to participate and underscore their aspirations:

On Jordan's stormy banks I stand
And cast a wishful eye
To Canaan's fair and happy land
Where my possessions lie.
REFRAIN: I am bound for the promised land,
I am bound for the promised land.
O, who will come and go with me?
I am bound for the promised land.[52]

American hymn writers were also well known for writing poetry on occasional topics, such as celebrations of the Bible, anniversaries, patriotic themes, or even in dedication to specific audiences. The venerated Baptist historian David Benedict (1779–1874) wrote in honor of the Scriptures:

Holy Bible! Choicest treasure,
Blest inheritance below,
Purest source of pious pleasure,
Antidote to every woe.
Holy Bible!
Speak to men of every tongue.
Teeming presses all befriend thee,
Countless volumes fly abroad;
Priests and pundits join to aid thee;
Saving, conquering Word of God;
Blessed Bible!

---

[51] Basil Manly, Jr., "Before the Pool A Sufferer Lay," in *The Baptist Psalmist* (Charleston: Southern Baptist Publication Society, 1850) 460.
[52] Quoted in Dickson Bruce, *And They All Sang Hallelujah: Plain-Folk Camp-Meeting Religion, 1800–1845* (Knoxville: University of Tennessee Press, 1974) 90–92.

Send thy saving health abroad.[53]

Samuel Francis Smith (1808–1895), a Harvard College and Andover Seminary graduate who served as a Baptist pastor at Waterville, Maine, and Newton Centre, Massachusetts, was author of one of the best-loved patriotic songs in the United States.[54] His style reflects the romantic or literary type of hymn. Smith's "My Country, 'Tis of Thee" speaks not only of a favored nation, but of the cherished Baptist ideal of freedom, now fused with national identity:

My country, 'tis of thee,
Sweet land of liberty,
Of thee I sing;
Land where my fathers died,
Land of the pilgrims' pride,
From every mountain's side
Let freedom ring!
My native country, thee,
Land of the noble, free,
Thy name I love;
I love thy rocks and rills,
Thy woods and templed hills;
My heart with rapture thrills,
Like that above.
Let music swell the breeze,
And ring from all the trees
Sweet Freedom's song;
Let mortal tongues awake;
Let all that breathe partake;
Let rocks their silence break,
The sound prolong.
Our fathers' God to Thee,
Author of liberty,
To Thee we sing;
Long may our land be bright

---

[53] Quoted in Burrage, *Baptist Hymn Writers*, 256.

[54] For a British assessment, see David Hein, "S. F. Smith and 'America'," *Baptist Quarterly* 32/3 (July 1987): 134–40.

With freedom's holy light;
Protect us by Thy might
Great God, our King![55]

Others like Phineas Stowe (1812–1868), the leader of a well-known Bethel mission to seamen in Boston, wrote the hymn titled "The True Friend" for a collection called "Ocean Melodies:"

There is a Friend, who's always nigh
To those who on His word rely;
When storms arise, and billows roll,
He will protect the humble soul.
When dangers in their pathway lie,
And howling tempests rage and sigh,
He then will keep with watchful care
All those who seek His face by prayer.
Come, then, bold seamen, seek this Friend!
He'll constant prove till time shall end;
And when the voyage of life is o'er.

In the South, scores of graduates of Southern Baptist Theological Seminary sing as their valedictory hymn the words of Basil Manly, Jr. (1825–1892):

Soldiers of Christ, in truth arrayed,
A world in ruins needs your aid,
A world by sin destroyed and dead,
A world for which the savior bled.
We meet to part, but part to meet,
When earthly labors are complete,
To join in yet more blest employ
In an eternal world of joy.

Likewise, a Canadian Baptist institution, McMaster University, adopted as its hymn the lines written autobiographically by its early principal, D. A. McGregor (1847–1890), whose Christology overwhelmed his own

---

[55] "My Country, 'Tis of Thee," in *Worship and Service Hymnal*, 463.

pilgrimage during a terminal illness. McGregor's rich use of metaphors to capture the mysteries of angelic beings, darkness and light, the sea, and music reflect common themes and images in Victorian poetry:

Jesus, wondrous Saviour!
Christ of kings the King!
Angels fall before Thee,
Prostrate, worshipping;
Fairest they confess Thee
In the heaven above.
We would sing Thee fairest
Here in hymns of love.
Sweeter far than music
Quivering from keys
That unbind all feeling
With strange harmonies.
Thou art more and dearer
Than all minstrelsy;
Only in thy presence
Can joy's fullness be.
All earth's flowing pleasures
Were a wintry sea,
Heaven itself without Thee
Dark as night would be,
Lamb of God! Thy glory
Is the light above.
Lamb of God! Thy glory
Is the life of love.
Life is death, if severed
From Thy throbbing heart.
Death with life abundant
At thy touch would start.
Worlds and men and angels
All consist in Thee:
Yet thou camest to us in humility.
Jesus! All perfections
Rise and end in Thee:
Brightness of God's glory

Thou eternally.
Favor'd beyond measure
They Thy face who see:
May we gracious Savior,
Share this ecstasy.[56]

THE INFLUENCE OF REVIVALISM

Revival hymnody has long had as an objective the deepening and renewal of personal Christian experience. Typically, this involves taking the metaphors of Scripture and applying them to one's own personal experience.[57] The Great Revival that began in Kentucky around 1800 was the series of watershed events in the United States that led to widespread use of hymns and gospel songs to indoctrinate hearers with evangelical theology. The revival meetings often began with lively singing. In the Kehukee Baptist Association of North Carolina, singing was described as "a great blessing." Simple verses, refrains, and choruses reduced doctrine to memorized portions. As historians have shown, the officiating minister often would read one line at a time, the congregation would repeat it, after which all would sing a refrain. In pedagogical fashion, preachers would punctuate the verses with exhortative phrases like " Do you know what you just said?" or "How many people really believe what they just sang?"[58] As singing became prevalent and the itinerant revivalists required easily available texts, sales of pocket-sized hymnals increased. These became printed theological texts, with categories like "Awakening," "Providence," "Penitential," and the "Holy Spirit." A variety of composers and lyricists was used, including the Wesleys, Doddridge, and Isaac Watts, as was the proverbial "Author Unknown" that likely referred to the presenting evangelist himself. Given the paucity of lay understanding of musical scores and the scarcity of printed music, emphasis was given to printed poetic texts in the earliest popularly used hymnbooks.

---

[56] "Jesus! Wondrous Savior!" in *Baptist Hymnal*, 4.

[57] Lionel Adey, *Class and Idol in the English Hymn* (Vancouver: University of British Columbia Press, 1988) 22. He also argues that singers in lower socio-economic groups often took the biblical imagery out of its context and created an optimistic world in which to live.

[58] David Singer, "God and Man in Baptist Hymnals," *Midcontinent American Studies Journal* 9 (Fall 1968): 14; John B. Boles, *The Great Revival: 1785–1805: The Origins of the Southern Evangelical Mind* (Lexington: University Press of Kentucky, 1972) 122–24.

By the mid-nineteenth century, as Richard Carwardine and others have shown, revivalism became a transatlantic phenomenon. Not only did evangelists and practices common to British and American evangelicalism appear in Great Britain, but their musicians, music, and the theology they contained did as well. Among the more famous were the team of D. L. Moody and Ira D. Sankey. The latter wrote poetry as well as music for the revival and evangelistic experience. Many Baptist preachers and evangelists were indebted theologically to lines such as:

> I have a Saviour, He's pleading in glory,
> A dear, loving Saviour, though earth friends be few;
> And now He is watching in tenderness o'er me,
> But, oh, that my Saviour were your Saviour too!
> For you I am praying,
> For you I am praying
> For you I am praying,
> I'm praying for you.
> When He has found you, tell others the story,
> That my loving Saviour is your Saviour too;
> Then pray that your Saviour may bring them to glory,
> And prayer will be answered—'twas answered for you![59]

Gradually certain techniques became formulaic in evangelistic proclamation. The "hymn of invitation" was foremost among these. The purpose of invitation hymns was to offer seekers—perhaps moved to conviction during a sermon—the opportunity to declare newfound faith in Christ publicly. The hymns of invitation that grew out of the revivalist tradition in the early twentieth century among North American Baptists became the official way of congregational evangelism. Entire sections of Baptist hymnals were devoted to invitation hymns. Among mainstream Baptists, these hymns began to reflect the human element in salvation and not-so-subtle shifts in theology became commonplace. For example, William Howard Doane (1832–1915), a Baptist lumber magnate from Ohio, intermingled human entreaty with divine sovereignty:

> Pass me not, O gentle Saviour,

---

[59] Words by S. O'Malley Clough and music by Ira Sankey; "I Am Praying for You," in *Worship and Service Hymnal*, 398.

Hear my humble cry
While on others Thou art calling
Do not pass me by.
Let me at the throne of mercy
Find a sweet relief
Kneeling there in deep contrition
Help my unbelief.
Trusting only in Thy merit
Would I seek Thy face;
Heal my wounded, broken spirit,
Save me by Thy grace.
Saviour, Saviour, Hear my humble cry
While on others Thou art calling
Do not pass me by.[60]

Philip P. Bliss (1838–1876) was a Baptist musician, singing-school teacher, and revival performer from Pennsylvania. He had the rare opportunity to distribute his songs throughout a wide region and then publish the selections that were best received. He wrote a famous hymn to express his sense of inner struggle with one's conversion:

Almost persuaded, now to believe
Almost persuaded, Christ to receive;
Seems now some soul to say,
Go, Spirit, go Thy way,
Some more convenient day
On Thee I'll call.

Doubtless the influence of his Methodist upbringing shone through in stanza two where the penitent is anguishing over indecision:

Almost persuaded, come, come today;
Almost persuaded, turn not away;
Jesus invites you here,
Angels are lingering near
Prayers rise from hearts so dear

---

[60] William H. Doane, "Pass Me Not," *Worship and Service Hymnal for Church, School, and Home* (Carol Stream IL: Hope Publishing Co., 1984) 390–91.

O wanderer come.

With the climax of an unsuccessful spiritual conviction, the hymn rendered the expected tragic outcome for the indecisive seeker:

Almost persuaded, harvest is past!
Almost persuaded, doom comes at last!
"Almost" cannot avail;
"Almost" is but to fail!
Sad, sad, that bitter wail,
"Almost"—but lost.[61]

Perhaps no other engine of personal conversion and faith decision among Baptists is as famous as that created by composer William H. Bradbury (1816–1878), "Just As I Am, Without One Plea," the text by Charlotte Elliott (1789–1871). Bradbury took the catchy melodies, simple harmonies, and the refrains of Sunday School songs and presented them to adults as "gospel songs" and invitation hymns.[62] For decades, Billy Graham and thousands of other Baptist evangelists imitating him, could conclude evangelistic sermons with an emphasis upon human response to the theological processes of salvation:

Just as I am without one plea
But that thy blood was shed for me,
And that Thou bidd'st me come to Thee
O Lamb of God, I come, I come.
Just as I am, though tossed about
With many a conflict, many a doubt,
Fightings and fears, within, without,
O Lamb of God, I come, I come.
Just as I am, Thou wilt receive,
Wilt welcome, pardon, cleanse, relieve;
Because Thy promise I believe
O Lamb of God, I come, I come.[63]

---

[61] Ibid., "Almost Persuaded," 208.

[62] Bradbury and other gospel songwriters actually studied in Europe with Robert and Clara Schumann and Franz Liszt. See Hustad, *Jubilate*, 131.

[63] Ibid., " Just As I Am, Without One Plea" 198.

Throughout the twentieth century, Southern Baptists, many Northern Baptists, and large numbers of Independent Baptists[64] in particular adopted the practice of closing each worship service with an invitation to follow Christ or join the congregation's membership. The hymn expresses the invitation on behalf of the congregation. Often, as was the case with Billy Graham,[65] a given invitation hymn was the catalyst to one's own conversion and thus it powerfully recalled Graham's own personal experience. Theologically, hymns of invitation have had a pronounced impact upon the popular theology of many North American Baptists who have adopted an ecclesiology that the church is an evangelizing community and that its primary, if not exclusive, task is offering the gospel and person of Christ to non-believers.

THE AFRICAN AMERICAN CONTRIBUTION

One of the richest treasuries of Baptist thought is found in the surviving African American Baptist spirituals. The spiritual is the root and trunk of American Black music.[66] As Walter Pitts has recently shown, West African poetic features dominated at least three kinds of religious songs: lined hymns learned in the eighteenth century, but modified; camp meeting spirituals that came from the early nineteenth century; and the spirituals that were a product of African heritage and their own experience.[67] Wyatt T. Walker has persuasively argued that the slave songs not only were an emotional release, but a subtle form of

---

[64] I would include here Freewill Baptists, Baptist Bible Fellowship, World Baptist Fellowship, General Association of Regular Baptists, National Baptists, evangelical American Baptists, and Missionary Baptists.

[65] A study of Graham's music displays a conservative style and selection, promoting very little new musical material. Unlike predecessors such as Ira Sankey or Homer Rodehaven in the earlier revival teams, the musician is not a publisher. See George Stansbury, "The Music of the Billy Graham Crusades 1947–1970" (Ph.D. diss., Southern Baptist Theological Seminary, 1969).

[66] Wendel Phillips Whalum, "Black Hymnody," *Review and Expositor* 70/3 (Summer 1973): 353.

[67] Walter F. Pitts, *Old Ship of Zion: The Afro-Baptist Ritual in the African Diaspora* (New York: Oxford University Press, 1993) 63, 82.

communication between slaves.[68] Many of them were shared across the traditional denominational boundaries in the White community. What popularized them was the interaction of Black musicians at the annual meetings of groups like the National Baptist Convention. "In the development of African American congregations, black people can band together to ensure their survival and comfort one another with song and story. Their faith is a matter of survival, a question of life and death," writes Harvey Cox, a Baptist theologian at Harvard.[69]

A popular theme among Black Baptists was the baptism of new believers. Many converts were baptized in cold, wintry weather, often risking their health. Their welfare was in the hands of God, or rather the Black preacher, as the congregation on the banks of the river sang a chorus:

And I'll thank God, almost over,
I thank God, almost over, almost over
My Lord, and I'll thank God almost over.

While the next candidates came forth, they might sing:

Sister if your heart is warm,
Snow and ice will do you no harm
I done been down, and I done been tried,
I been through the water and I been baptized.
O sister, you must mind how you step on the cross,
Your foot might slip, and your soul get lost.[70]

Howard Thurman found a powerful theme of life and death in African American spirituals. For the slave, he wrote, the theme "was extremely compelling because of the cheapness with which his life was regarded." Consequently, slaves sang:
You needn't mind my dying,
You needn't mind my dying,

---

[68] Wyatt T. Walker, *Somebody's Calling My Name: Black Sacred Music and Social Change* (Valley Forge: Judson Press, 1979) 37.

[69] Harvey Cox, *Just As I Am* (Nashville: Abingdon Press, 1983), 56.

[70] Miles Mark Fisher, *Negro Slave Songs In the United States* (New York: Russell and Russell, 1953) 100–101.

You needn't mind my dying,
Jesus goin' to make up my dying bed.

The spiritual seems to suggest that perhaps death was to many slaves a release from their insufferable bondage:

I want to die easy when I die
I want to die easy when I die
Shout salvation as I fly
I want to die easy when I die.

The songs also conveyed a metaphor of the slave's life as pilgrimage:

I've got to walk my lonesome valley,
I've got to walk it for myself.
Nobody else can walk it for me,
I've got to walk it for myself![71]

Eschatological matters were settled in the spirituals. Judgment morning, for example, was an approaching reality:

My Lord what a morning!
My Lord what a morning!
When the stars begin to fall
You will hear the trumpet sound
To wake the nations underground,
Standing at my God's right hand,
When the stars begin to fall.

Heaven was described with the imagery gleaned from the Book of Revelation:

I haven't been to heaven
But I've been told,
The streets are pearl
And the gates are gold;

---

[71] Howard Thurman, "The Negro Spiritual Speaks of Life and Death," in *A Strange Freedom*, ed. Fluker and Tumber (Boston: Beacon Press, 1998) 57, 60, 61.

Not made with hands.

And for the redeemed who had journeyed faithfully through life's trials:

I got a robe,
You got a robe,
All God's children got robes.
When we get to heaven
We're going to put on our robes,
We're going to shout all over God's heaven.[72]

One of the most enduring "Afro-Baptist" gospel songs that is still in vogue is "I Want to Be at the Meeting." This favorite spiritual calls attention to Judgement Day where finally Blacks would not be excluded from those privileges and things reserved for Whites in the Western world. It follows a significantly Christological theme:

After separation of the right from the wrong
I want to be at the meeting when all the saints go marching home.
I'll talk with God the Father.
I'll talk with Christ the Son.
And then we'll have a meeting around God's throne.

The scene is all the more joyous because of the happy reunions:

When I get to Heaven, I'll meet my mother there
She'll say, "God Almighty, here comes my child.
He must have gotten here by prayer."
I'll talk with God the Father.
I'm gonna talk with Christ the Son.
And then we'll have a meeting around God's throne.[73]

As James Weldon Johnson, the great poet of the African-American experience in America, wrote,

---

[72] Ibid., 75–76.
[73] Quoted in Pitts, *Old Ship of Zion*, 88–89.

There is a wide, wide wonder in it all,
That from degraded rest and servile toil
The fiery spirit of the seer should call
Those simple children of the sun and soil
O black slave singers, gone, forgot, unfamed,
You—you alone, of all the long, long line
Of those who've sung untaught, unknown, unnamed,
Have stretched out upward, seeking the divine.[74]

THE CONNECTION OF WORDS AND MUSIC

Singing involves intoning poetry and melody. Early in the development of congregational music, lining out, or forth-singing, proved to be "slow and monotonous." Samuel Pepys recalled that it prolonged the service greatly. To no surprise, familiar tunes were attached to new poetry and musical instruments came into use at the end of the seventeenth century, most notably the organ.[75] Many tunes were not necessarily religious in origin; in fact, in an anthology of English songs produced in 1783, fifty of the best-known tunes came from "drinking songs." These became ingrained in the hearer's mind and identified with particular life experiences. Even today, many religious melodies and songs are learned in childhood, are recounted throughout one's life, and reinforced in daily routine or worship. As is yet the case, for the earlier evangelical Christians of Europe and America, familiar tunes easily became vehicles of personal expression while at work or recreation. They not only called forth emotional responses, but also reinforced impressions. To this was added the value of poetic imagery that deepened spiritual insight and enriched religious understanding.[76] Frederick Swann, a music historian and organist, has observed that a "memory bank" exists in people's consciousness: "A musical performance does not express a present emotion, but rather the recall of a previous emotional experience. In other words, the singer of a happy (or sad) song is not necessarily happy (or sad) at the moment of singing, nor is the listener. Rather, one projects

---

[74] James Weldon Johnson, *The Book of American Negro Spirituals* (Binghampton: Vail-Bollan Press, 1925) 12.

[75] Organ accompaniment, it was observed, muffled the off-key sounds of untrained voices and blended a harmonious result.

[76] Schilling, *The Faith We Sing*, 26–27.

and the other receives a recall of a previous experience of happiness or sadness."[77]

In the later 1600s and early 1700s familiar tunes taken from taverns and workplaces to church meeting houses brought with them the masses of people familiar with the melodies. There also was frequent hymn singing outdoors among English dissenters. Hymns and gospel songs were among the most salient features of the eighteenth-century evangelical revival, according to Arnold and others.[78] Baptists, too, came to believe that everyone should sing simple, spontaneous tunes, as an enhancement of the worship experience. While Baptists certainly pioneered the advance of congregational hymn singing, they were soon overtaken in the experience by Methodists and other dissenters whose tunes were readily passed back and forth between congregations. As one writer has put it of the emerging evangelical communities, "nothing so profoundly defined the *lex credendi* of evangelicalism as the *lex cantandi*; what evangelicals have been is what we have sung." [79]

It is interesting to note that in some cases the original poetic words changed through circumstances or authorial intent, but were nonetheless accepted most readily when accompanied by a familiar tune. For instance, the famous Welsh valley tune, "Cwm Rhondda" was attached among North American Baptists for generations to William Williams' words, "Guide Me O Thou Great Jehovah." In 1931 when Harry Emerson Fosdick penned the words to his poem, "God of Grace and God of Glory" and attached the poem to "Cwm Rhondda," the old tune ratified the new words, and an entirely new generation of Baptists owned the Welsh tune. The theological message of "Guide Me O Thou Great Jehovah" stresses life's pilgrimage and God's nurture, while "God of Grace and God of Glory" emphasizes the social and political agenda of twentieth-century American religious liberalism. Thus, favorite tunes could convey different theological statements and subtly ratify each through the medium of singing.

---

[77] Frederick Swann, as quoted in J. Daniel Gibson, "A Homiletical Hermeneutic for the Re-Writing of Hymn Texts" (M.Th. thesis, Waterloo Lutheran Seminary, 2000) 19.

[78] Arnold, *English Hymns of the Eighteenth Century*, 27.

[79] For an assessment of the importance of hymn singing among evangelicals, see Noll, *American Evangelical Christianity*, 268.

A SOURCE OF ECUMENICITY

Thus far in this discussion we have been considering Baptist hymnody, that is Baptist contributions to theological poetry and expression in music. A much-obscured reality of Baptist use of hymns is the ecumenical character of collections of hymns and this, by implication, introduces the theological ecumenicity that has emerged from this variety. It goes without saying that a strictly Baptist hymnal would be both thin and limited in scope. To add variety and reflect the fullness of artistic expression in the Christian community, compilers of Baptist hymnals have included songs from many Protestant evangelical religious traditions.

Among the ancient selections from the early and medieval Catholic church, one finds "Of the Father's Love Begotten," "All Glory, Laud and Honor," "All Creatures of Our God and King," and St. Bernard's "Jesus, the Very Thought of Thee." The contribution from the Reformation tradition often includes Luther's "A Mighty Fortress Is Our God," the Reformed Church's clarion "All People that on Earth Do Dwell," the Moravian Count Zinzendorf's "Christian Hearts in Love United," Anglican John Newton's "Amazing Grace," and Methodist Charles Wesley's "Joy to the World!" as well as his testimonial, "And Can It Be That I Should Gain."[80]

Viewed from another perspective, Baptist hymns have been included on a limited basis in other traditions. Those poetic songs most widely selected are: "Blest Be the Tie That Binds," "He Leadeth Me, O Blessed Thought," "I Heard an Old, Old Story," "Renew Thy Church," and "God of Grace and God of Glory." A survey found that of the mainstream Christian traditions, the United Church of Christ, Lutherans, and Methodists made the widest use of Baptist hymnody.[81]

SUMMARY

We have briefly surveyed the development of hymnody unique to the Baptist tradition as a source of theological thinking, development, and articulation. Early on in Baptist life, hymn singing became an egalitarian form of theological expression. The selections excerpted above illustrate

---

[80] Milburn Price, "What Every Pastor Should Know About the Hymnal: The Hymnal as a Worship Sourcebook," *Review and Expositor* 87 (Winter 1990): 33–42.

[81] See Paul A. Richardson, "Baptist Contributions to Hymnody and Hymnology," *Review and Expositor* 87 (Winter 1990): 59–74.

how Baptist clergy and laypersons wove doctrine into personal experience to express what they believed and felt about God, Christ, the Spirit, the Church, their own spiritual needs, and the meaning of life. The most often used allusion was that of the Christian life and experience as a "pilgrimage." Repeating these time-worn theological phrases ingrained evangelical thought deeply in the minds and hearts of Baptists. Moreover, the very nature of music as a vehicle of communication ensured that the theological ideas expressed in hymns would endure across generations.

Some writers created hymns as liturgical aids for baptism, the Lord's Supper, or evangelism. In such a context, Baptist theology was expressed collectively through the inspired words of gifted poets. Many of these became standard expressions of a congregation's theology. The process and mode of baptism was expressed in hymnody, as was the fellowship to be experienced in the Lord's Supper. Rich in Scripture-oriented phraseology, Baptist hymns also took one on a personal journey, that of the poet and composer whose experiences came to belong to everyone. For the average Baptist, hymns were a ready source of theology, ranking high on the list of genetic influences.

CHAPTER 3

EARLY BRITISH BAPTIST PASTORS AND WRITERS

> There is nothing more offensive to men, than to dispute their dogmas in religion. Even in the smallest matters connected with this subject, men feel hurt with opposition. To question the truth of their religious opinions, is to insult them; but to suspect that these opinions are dangerous, is to hate them.—
>
> Alexander Carson, 1847[1]

A third source of Baptist theology emanates from the spoken and written words of pastors. Pastors are the primary congregational leaders in the Baptist tradition. Among the major English Baptist groups, beginning in the seventeenth century, the pastoral ministry was defined according to the Puritan tradition as one who had oversight over a congregation, who preached, taught, and acted as a shepherd for a congregation. This had obvious implications for theological articulation and interpretation, and pastors became the primary exponents in oral and written form of Baptist thought. Mention has already been made in connection with the confessions of faith of several Baptist pastors in seventeenth-century England who influenced theological developments. Among these were William Kiffin, Hanserd Knollys, John Spilsbury, and Benjamin Keach. Yet other pastors emerged to debate, write, and reinforce Baptist themes. Some Baptist pastors became catalysts in the development of new theological directions, including John Bunyan, Benjamin Keach, and Thomas Grantham in the 1600s; John Gill, Andrew Fuller, and Dan Taylor were definitive in the eighteenth century. Prominent pastors such

---

[1] Alexander Carson, "The Doctrine of the Atonement, set forth in an Address to the Public, on the Nature and Importance of the Gospel," in *The Works of the Reverend Alexander Carson, LL.D.*, vol. 1 (Dublin: William Carson, 1847) 2.

as C. H. Spurgeon, John Clifford, John Howard Hinton, and J. H. Shakespeare provided leadership from the mid-1800s.

In the discussion of pastoral theological development that follows, several important theological trends are evident. First, early Baptists for the most part accepted a modified Reformed theological system. Within the overall Reformed tradition, there were characteristics that reflected both Calvinism and what would later be called "Arminianism." The General Baptists, for example, reflect congruence in many particulars with their Calvinistic brethren.[2] Where early Baptist pastors spent their greatest theological energy was in matters of church order. To many, this may seem not to be serious theological discussion at all. But to Baptists, whose primary theological distinctiveness was in the area of ecclesiology, church and ministry, discipline, and church order were paramount. Second, Baptist pastors embraced a literal understanding of Scripture that remained the basis for their theological understanding through the seventeenth and most of the eighteenth centuries.

In the last two decades of the eighteenth century, Baptist pastors in England moved to issues of soteriology (matters pertaining to salvation), particularly the idea of the atonement. Andrew Fuller was largely responsible for this shift. In the nineteenth century, the overarching theological issues were authority, religious experience, and the person and work of Jesus Christ. Many Baptist ministers simply chose to retreat to the theological formulae of the previous Calvinistic era and sidestep the contemporary discussions among other Christian theologians. Two groups clearly emerged from among those who did take up the theological discourse, namely the evangelicals and the liberal thinkers. Something of the energy and results of the theological power and prestige of the Baptist pulpit was diminished as academic leaders and alliances assumed the limelight that earlier pastors had shared. By the late twentieth century, the vast majority of theological discussion was absent from the common pulpit and found only in Baptist colleges and seminaries where prominent and theologically trained pastors routinely assumed faculty positions.

---

[2] James Tull makes the point that the prevailing Calvinistic theme was predestination and that a large part of the Baptist family in its early years was "double-predestinarian." See "An Open Question?" in *Are Southern Baptists Evangelicals?*, ed. James Leo Garrett, E. Glenn Hinson, and James Tull (Macon GA: Mercer University Press, 1983) 228.

An assessment of English Baptist pastoral theology has to begin with a collection of first generation of Baptist ministers who defined their doctrine in preaching and infrequently wrote tracts or treatises in defense of theological positions on baptism, the Lord's Supper, salvation, the nature of the church, and related issues of ecclesiology or theology. Among the major pastor-writers of the General Baptists were Thomas Helwys, Henry Denne, and Thomas Lambe. Those to be found among the Particular Baptists included William Kiffin, Hanserd Knollys, and Benjamin Cox.

John Bunyan of Bedford was without doubt the most illustrious pastor of the English Baptist community of the seventeenth century. Controversial in his era, he was the most widely read Baptist of all times but maintained tenuous ties to the denomination in the minds of some of its leaders. Bunyan (1628–1688) emerged from the lowest levels of English working classes as a brazier or "tinker"—in modern terms a handyman— to be heralded as the outstanding Dissenter preacher of the Restoration. Presumably, he had a primary school education after which he served in the army at Newport Pagnall. Sometime between 1644 and 1647 he likely heard the preaching of General Baptist Henry Denne, and some think this was the beginning of his conversion. He married and he wrote of his first wife that she left him two books that were greatly influential in spiritual matters: Arthur Dent's *The Plaine Mans Pathway to Heaven* (1601) and Lewis Bayley's *The Practice of Piety* (1612). Self-taught, his reading list included: Martin Luther, *Commentary on Galatians*; Samuel Clark, *A Mirrour and Looking-glass for both Saints and Sinners*; Richard Bernard, *The Isle of Man*; John Foxe, *The Book of Martyrs*; and, both the Geneva Bible and the Authorized Version. Bunyan himself was to produce about sixty works, beginning with *Some Gospel-truths Opened* (1656) and the posthumous *The Heavenly Foot-man* (1698).[3]

Bunyan was raised a member of the Church of England and converted under the ministry of John Gifford of Elstow to a nonconformist faith, generally referred to as "Separatist." Subsequently, Bunyan referred to the church as related to the "anabaptists." After Bunyan's time, the

---

[3] A very helpful scholarly guide to Bunyan and his works is Lynn Veach Sadler, *John Bunyan* (Boston: Twayne Publishers, 1979) 30–31.

congregation he served in Elstow was identified both with the Congregationalist Union and the Particular Baptist Association.[4]

Bunyan's thought is most evident in five of his principal works. First is *Grace Abounding to the Chief of Sinners* (1666), his reluctant spiritual autobiography. Many scholars are frustrated with Bunyan's imprecise geographic and chronological locators and other lack of details, yet it may be his most revealing work. He records his dependence upon Luther's work, his Puritan leanings, and his obsession with the gospel in Christ. Second and third are Part 1 of *The Pilgrim's Progress* (1678), followed by Part 2 (1684). In this, the legendary English-language allegory, his doctrine of the authority and use of Scripture, his idea of the atonement, and the sovereignty of God are illuminated. Fourth is *The Holy War* (1682), where Bunyan again plumbed his spiritual pilgrimage, demonstrating in another allegory Bunyan's view of history, the establishment of Christ's kingdom, and the final judgment. Last is Bunyan's published *Confession*, commented upon above.

Historian and Bunyan biographer Richard Greaves sketches a theological continuum that provides historical context to Bunyan's doctrinal thinking. In the continuum's bipartite center are the Strict Calvinists and the Moderate Calvinists. On the extreme ends are located the Antinomians and the Arminians. Bunyan seemed mostly a Strict Calvinist, with a few noticeable leanings toward Antinomianism.[5] He was also significantly influenced by Martin Luther's writings and by the consensus reflected in the congregation he joined in Elstow, Bedford. What makes Bunyan's theology difficult to pigeonhole precisely was his own dislike of educated or "syllogistic" theology, preferring to depend upon what he believed to be the direct light of the Word and prompting

---

[4] The issue of Bunyan's denominational identity has long been a subject of debate. For contrasting views, see J. Hobson Thomas, "Bunyan the Baptist," *Baptist Quarterly* 4 (1928): 97–103; A. C. Underwood, *History of the English Baptists* (London: Carey Kingsgate Press, 1947) 98 ff.; Geoffrey Nuttall, *Visible Saints: The Congregational Way, 1640–1660* (Oxford: Basil Blackwell, 1957) 125; J. F. McGregor, "The Baptists: Fount of all Heresy," in *Radical Religion in the English Reformation*, ed. J. F. McGregor and B. Reay (Oxford: Oxford University Press, 1984) 28, 57; N. H. Keeble, *The Literary Culture of Nonconformity in Later Seventeenth-Century England* (Leicester: Leicester University Press, 1987) 9–10; Joseph D. Ban, "Was John Bunyan a Baptist?" *Baptist Quarterly* 30 (1984): 373ff.; Michael Davies, *Graceful Reading: Theology and Narrative in the Works of John Bunyan* (Oxford: Oxford University Press, 2002) 38–42.

[5] Richard Greaves, *John Bunyan* (Abingdon: Sutton Courtenay Press, 1969) 24.

of the Spirit of God, even if it appeared that he was a "dull-sounding Rams-horn." In so positioning himself against "systematic" theology, Bunyan revealed a major trait common to Baptists after him, namely their propensity to believe that correct doctrine emerges directly from Scripture and that all persons can readily and correctly draw from that unchanging well.

Bunyan's theology rested upon a Lutheran foundation. Luther's personal theological narrative was similar to Bunyan's own struggle and Bunyan readily identified with the Reformer. Bunyan adhered to Luther's "wrath and grace" dichotomy with respect to the nature of God, in contrast to Calvin's preoccupation with the divine will. Luther's theology was further manifest in Bunyan's thought in the latter's belief that "for a pilgrim, salvation had to be by Law as well as Grace."[6] Bunyan concurred with Luther that salvation was not a divine transformation, nor the infusion of a divine substance (as in the sacrament), but constituted the forgiveness of God and restoration to Divine favor. The righteousness provided mankind in the person of Christ was all sufficient. Bunyan also held closely to Luther's position on the authority of Scripture and the nature of grace and freedom as characteristic of the Christian life.

As a post-Reformation thinker, Bunyan's theology was eclectic. His most widely-published analyst has observed, "No single theological label without careful qualification will fit Bunyan."[7] His Calvinistic thrusts were evident in his conceptualization of justification, salvation, and the covenants. Bunyan agreed with John Owen, Thomas Goodwin, and others that it was by God's initiative that sinners were pronounced acquitted and justified: "Grace can justify freely, when it will, who it will, and from what it will...grace can comfort, relieve, and help those that have hurt themselves. And grace can bring the Unworthy to Glory."[8]

In *Saved By Grace* (1676), Bunyan defined grace clearly: "It is an act of *God's Will,* which must needs be free, an act of his *own Will,* of the *good pleasure of his Will;* by everyone of these Expressions, is inti-

---

[6] Ibid., 30.

[7] Ibid., 159.

[8] John Bunyan, *The Water of Life: or A Discourse Shewing The Richness and Glory of the Grace and Spirit of the Gospel, as Set Forth in Scripture by this Term, The Water of Life* (London: Nathaniel Ponder, 1688) in *Miscellaneous Works of John Bunyan,* (Oxford: Oxford University Press, 1989) 7:198.

mated, that Grace is a free act of God's goodness towards the Sons of Men."[9] Grace entailed the good will, free mercy, and loving kindness of God. A recent biographer has argued persuasively that grace, spoken of in metaphors of healing, was the permeating factor in all that Bunyan wrote.[10] Sometimes this appreciation of grace was so overwhelming in magnitude as to produce a mild form of antinominanism. Unlike many Calvinists of his era, Bunyan understood human free will as a part of free grace, thus prompting him to invite sinners voluntarily to turn to Christ. His theology did not begin with predestination or election, but with faith in Christ.[11] Very much in keeping with Luther, justification for Bunyan was the work of God. He wrote in *Christ, A Complete Savior* (1692): "He justifies us by bestowing upon us, not expecting from us...He justifies us by his grace, not by our works. In a word then thou must be well grounded in the knowledge of what Christ is, and how we are justified by him, or thou wilt not come unto God by him." His own testimony of free grace in *Paul's Departure and Crown* (1692) illustrated his experience of the teaching: "We are justified in the sight of Divine Majesty, from the whole lump of our sins, both past and present, and to come by free grace...once for all. I bless God, I believe it and that we shall be brought to glory by the same grace."[12] Unlike Luther, however, Bunyan's soteriology was dialectically inclined. Holding to particular atonement, he believed salvation to be a process. It began with predestination on a basis of God's gracious love and was brought to culmination in persons through their ultimate election and salvation in Christ.

Bunyan understood the place of covenants, both of grace and works, and this became a foundational element of his theological treatment. As all Calvinists agreed, the original covenant between God and Adam was broken, thus necessitating a covenant of grace. In his treatise on the subject, *The Doctrine of the Law and Grace Unfolded* (1659), Bunyan took the position that the covenant of grace was between God and the

---

[9] John Bunyan, *Saved by Grace: or A Discourse of the Grace of God* (London: Francis Smith, 1676) in *Works of Bunyan*, 8:183.

[10] Davies, *Graceful Reading*, vii, 21.

[11] Ibid., 48–49. In some places he wrote harshly of predestination, while in others he deplored free will.

[12] John Bunyan, *Paul's Departure and Crown: or An Exposition upon 2 Timothy Chapter 4, Verses 6,7,8.* (London: Charles Doe, 1692) in *Works of Bunyan,* 12:389.

Son, not with a nation or individuals. No conditions were preemptively imposed on humankind. "Now the covenant was not only made on Jesus Christ's side with an oath," he wrote, "but also on God the Father's side, that it might be for the better ground of establishment to all those that are, or are to be, the children of the promise."[13] For Bunyan, the Mosaic Law, that is the Ten Commandments, became a rule of life for the Christian. In this particular perspective, Bunyan was in concert with the strict Calvinism of his era. The role of the law and the covenants was allegorically presented in Bunyan's great work, *Pilgrim's Progress*, illustrating the salvific process by the representation of the various stages of the covenants.[14]

An important nuance of Bunyan's understanding of the covenant of grace was the role of Christ. This covenant, effected through the second person of the Trinity, was made with the elect alone... "else all men would believe." Or to put it succinctly, "The elect, therefore, have the Lord Jesus for their Advocate, then and then only, when they are by calling put among the children; because as Advocate, he is peculiarly the children's."[15] Moreover, like John Owen and Tobias Crisp, Bunyan recognized that the benefits of the covenant of grace came through a promise completely without any merit on the part of the elect.

Ever the eclectic, Bunyan did follow Luther's interest in the relationship of the law and grace for the Christian believer. In his treatise, *Questions About the Seventh Day Sabbath* (1685), he even advanced the terminology "law of grace" which resembled Luther's writings. In one other important respect Bunyan did not follow many of his strict Calvinist contemporaries, that being their understanding that baptism is a seal of the covenant. He applied no particular theological significance to baptism and thus had no difficulty with persons who were baptized as infants but later departed from active Christian lives. The all-

---

[13] John Bunyan, *The Doctrine of the Law and Grace Unfolded; or A Discovery of the Law and Grace; the Nature of the One, and the Nature of the Other, as They are the Two Covenants, etc.* (London: n.p., 1659) in *The Works of John Bunyan*, ed. George Offor (Edinburgh: Banner of Truth Trust, 1991) 1:525, 534.

[14] See John Bunyan, *A Holy Life, The Beauty of Christianity or An Exhortation to Christians to be Holy* (London: Benjamin Alsop, 1684), 36; and Leon J. Trinterud, "The Origins of Puritanism," *Church History* 20 (March 1951): 54.

[15] John Bunyan, *The Work of Jesus Christ as An Advocate, Clearly Explained, and Largely Improved, for the Benefit of All Believers* (London: Dorman Newman, 1683) in *Works of John Bunyan*, 1:170.

important baptism was that of the Holy Spirit. One writer has noted the importance Bunyan placed on covenant theology in the Calvinist tradition, in his very first theological publication.[16]

Another significant source of Bunyan's theology was rooted in his experiences and pastoral ministries among his own congregation. In Bunyan's great allegory, he depicted the church as a palace built for the relief and security of Pilgrims. His doctrine was predicated on the distinction between the church universal, known but to God, and the local congregation. The latter might involve professors not part of the assembly of the elect. Membership in the visible church nevertheless required separation from the world, fellowship with believers, freedom, and a life of holiness. John Gifford had founded the congregation at Elstow as a Separatist body in 1650. Bunyan thereafter became a member, and in 1672 was appointed its pastor. Fellowship, or what Bunyan called the "communion of the saints," was essentially a covenant to be active as a member of the congregation. Love prevailed over all other aspects of outward conformity. Freedom, a third key principle, involved entirely voluntary membership in the church, as well as freedom of polity and doctrine in non-essentials and circumstantial matters. Bunyan was like most Separatists in taking very seriously the strict practice of faith.[17] He underscored the usage of the Pauline term "saints" and called for a life of holiness. "He that keepeth God's commandment," Bunyan wrote, "sheweth his Brother what he must do to honour the Christ that he professeth."[18] For Bunyan the local church was a place of relief for weary pilgrims, a center of genuine camaraderie, a school for students of Scripture, and a believer's armory wherein to be equipped to fight the good fight of faith.[19]

It is theologically surprising to many Baptists that John Bunyan took the position he did with respect to baptism. His disinclination to empowering the ordinance may have come from a combination of his own experience, twice baptized, and the endless argumentation in his day over what he called "shadowish sacraments." Whatever his reasons, he was considered a weak or liberal Baptist among those of the Particular

---

[16] Greaves, *John Bunyan*, 98, 101.

[17] Geoffrey Nuttall, *Visible Saints*, 134.

[18] John Bunyan, *A Holy Life,* x.

[19] Robert Archer, "Like Flowers in the Garden: John Bunyan and His Concept of the Church," *Baptist Quarterly* 36/6 (April 1966): 289.

Baptist persuasion. His own understanding of the sacraments or ordinances as "means to meet with God" was probably a further step beyond the Zwinglian position brought to England by Robert Browne and the Separatists. Bunyan could not bring himself to associate baptism with the covenant, and he insisted that baptism was not required for church membership. Instead, baptism was given to individual pilgrims. After he was strongly admonished in the 1670s by Particular Baptist brethren for not understanding the role of baptism in qualifying for admission to the Lord's Table, he published a response in *Differences in Judgement about water-baptism, No Bar to Communion (1673)*. He wrote, "being assaulted for more than sixteen years; wherein the Brethren of the Baptized way...have fought to break us in pieces, merely because we are not in their way all baptized first...I told you also that Baptism makes thee no Member of the Church, neither doth it make thee a visible saint; it giveth thee, therefore, neither right to, nor being of membership at all."[20]

A significant portion of Bunyan's theological heritage is transmitted through polemical literature. Bunyan was an ardent opponent of Quakerism, as surely as he was of Arminianism. Quakers tended to spiritualize Scripture passages and Bunyan found this hermeneutical practice objectionable. He remonstrated that the Bible is infallible and buttressed his objections with a number of Calvinistic arguments. He openly debated and crusaded against the Quaker doctrine of "Inner Light" and rested his position upon the authority of Scripture.

John Bunyan's place among the shapers of Baptist thought is beyond dispute. Not only did he interact with the major issues of the day that concerned Baptists, he was also the most widely published Baptist during the first century of their history. More subsequent and prominent Baptist thinkers read Bunyan as an exemplar of their faith than they did any other writer. Bunyan posed some challenges, however, that Baptists continued to encounter throughout the course of their theological development. His thought was eclectic, blending the heritages of at least three major Protestant Reformers—Luther, Calvin, and Zwingli—and he held tenaciously to his own selectivity in doctrinal formulation. Additionally, he practiced a highly individualistic form of theological reflection that changed over the course of his ministry, in spite of

[20] John Bunyan, *Differences in Judgement about water-baptism, No Bar to Communion* (London: John Wilkins, 1673) 3–4.

admonitions from other Baptists that he ought to embrace the prevailing confessional tradition. Finally, Bunyan refused to take a firm stance on baptismal theology and church membership, thus presaging the question of closed versus open communion with respect to members of a particular congregation.

Second in prominence in the overall Baptist picture was Thomas Grantham (1634–1692) of Lincolnshire. By all accounts, he was the first organized, comprehensive, published theologian of any of the Baptists. Grantham, a General Baptist, defined the theological position of that part of the tradition. Possibly either a tailor or farmer by trade, he was baptized in 1653 and became a General Baptist pastor within a few years. His leadership was recognized in 1666 when he was elected a messenger and founded several congregations about Lincolnshire. Frequently in prison, he read widely and accumulated material from the Reformers and contemporary writers. Grantham's outstanding contribution was to refocus ministry on the primitive church. Like many writers of his era, he was persuaded of the generally corrupt character of the church's clergy and episcopacy. In response, Grantham sought to lay down strict qualifications for the ministry. His most prominent title was, *Christianismus Primitivus, Or the Ancient Christian Religion in its Nature, Certainty, Excellency, and Beauty (Internal and External) particularly Considered Asserted, and Vindicated from the many abuses which have Invaded that Sacred Profession by Humane Innovation, or pretended Revelation, Comprehending likewise the General Duties of Mankind, in their respective Relations; And Particularly The Obedience of all Christians to Magistrates. And the Necessity of Christian –Moderation about things Dispensible in Matters of Religion. With Divers Cases of Conscience Discussed and Resolved* (1678). The author of twenty-seven individual works, Grantham used the vehicles of debate and polemic to refute equally the Roman Catholic, Presbyterian, and Quaker positions.

Grantham's position on the authority of Bible in *Christianismus Primitivus* was also a denial of Catholic tradition that only the Scriptures in the original are the Word of God. Addressing first part of the essay to the "internal" of religion, he covered Christ, sin, man, and angels. The second part he devoted to the "externals," developing the doctrine of the church, baptism, the laying on of hands, separation, prayer, the Lord's

Supper, singing, the ministry, the office of messenger, and other matters of church discipline.

Grantham strongly affirmed a believer's church position, "no person was admitted to communicate in the ordinances of Christ....but actual believers."[21] The church was congregational and universal: at one point he agreed with the reformers that the true church contained the "whole number of the saved" and was in fact the place where "the Word of God is sincerely taught and the sacraments rightly administered."[22] Even more reflective of the emerging Baptist understanding, he wrote the church was a voluntary assembly "maintained against the force of men, by a free and cheerful obedience to God...nor by any violence or coercive means whatsoever."[23] In addition, Grantham ardently supported the doctrine of general atonement and was often in heated exchanges with Calvinists. "Seeing you think that Christ died but for some only," he wrote to his antagonists, "show me sufficient testimony from Scripture that He died for yourself; and name one (if you can) now living in this great city, for whom Christ died not."[24]

As to the ordinances, after considering pedobaptist arguments, he underscored baptism as submersion or plunging. This was a concession to a practice among the Particular Baptists.[25] More importantly, Grantham became the champion of the practice of laying on of hands as a mark of a true church of Christ, applicable to male and female alike.[26] The laying on of hands made baptism complete in that believers were thereby believed symbolically imbued with the Holy Spirit. Among the General Baptists this was a most controversial issue in the 1650s, while many leading Particular Baptists rejected the rite.[27]

At a time when the foundations of Baptist polity were being shaped, Grantham urged that congregations should respect church councils. His doctrine of the church included congregations, assemblies, and councils.

---

[21] Thomas Grantham, *Christianismus Primitivus*... (1678), Book 2, chapters 1, 7.

[22] Ibid., chapter 1, 2, 3.

[23] Ibid., chapter 1, 58.

[24] Quoted in Underwood, *English Baptists*, 111.

[25] Grantham, *Christianismus Primitivus,* (book 2, chaps. 2, 30.

[26] Ibid., 33.

[27] See the discussion in B. R. White, *The English Baptists of the Seventeenth Century* (Didcot: Baptist Historical Society, 1996) 36–42. Compare William Rider's *Laying on of Hands Asserted* (1656) in favor of the rite, with the position against held by William Kiffin, Edward Harrison, and the Particular Baptists.

In a discussion of the larger church, he defended a "mutual consultation of Churches together, shewing not the superiority of Churches one above the other...but the brotherly Interest which they have in the strength of each other and the duty...to help another in difficulty."[28] A minister, wrote Grantham, should only differ with a council with considerable caution.[29]

Benjamin Keach (1640–1704) was another illustrious early Baptist who served one of the outstanding congregations of the seventeenth century. He suffered much persecution for his religious sentiments. Self-taught, he embarked upon ministry at but sixteen years of age. He was baptized by John Russell and served two General Baptist congregations. Later, he served the London congregation at Horsleydown from 1670 until his death. The author of over forty published works, he was thought of then and later as the most important theologian of the Restoration era among the Calvinistic Baptists.[30]

Initially a General Baptist, Keach was persuaded to join the Calvinistic Baptists, perhaps under the influence of Hanserd Knollys.[31] Keach apparently continued to approve of certain practices drawn from his earlier baptistic affiliation, notably the laying on of hands to signify the coming of the Holy Spirit.[32] He was an avid church planter and preached to hundreds each week at his own church. In the 1680s and 1690s he became embroiled in a defense of traditional Calvinism, specifically the doctrine of salvation. He was a thoroughgoing Calvinist, maintaining a high view of Christ, arguing that human depravity since

---

[28] Thomas Grantham, *Christianismus Primitivus*, chaps. 9, 137.

[29] White, *English Baptists*, 118.

[30] Murdina D. MacDonald, "London Calvinistic Baptists 1689–1727: Tensions Within a Dissenting Community Under Toleration" (Ph.D. thesis, Regent's Park College, Oxford University, 1982) 77, and Michael A. G. Haykin, *Kiffin, Knollys, and Keach: Rediscovering our English Baptist Heritage* (Leeds: Reformation Today Trust, 1996) 83. For an overall assessment of Keach's influence in the Baptist community, see W. E. Spears, "The Baptist Movement in England in the Late Seventeenth Century as Reflected in the Work and Thought of Benjamin Keach, 1640–1704" (Ph.D. diss., University of Edinburgh, 1953).

[31] White, *English Baptists*, 9, points out that while there were several instances of change in this direction, there were few who moved in the reverse direction.

[32] The imposition of hands was more than a matter of polity. It signified the coming of the Holy Spirit into the life of a believer and thus constituted a part of the doctrine of the Spirit and religious experience.

the Fall was total, and championing a doctrine of limited atonement.[33] He relentlessly opposed "Baxterianism," a doctrine suggesting a kind of justification by works that was named for its principal adherent, Richard Baxter. Five of Keach's works were directed against these errors.[34]

In response to the developing moderate tendencies of English Presbyterians who leaned toward Arminian views, Keach articulated a process of regeneration and conversion that affirmed God's sovereignty, yet acknowledged human facility. In a major treatise, *Gospel Mysteries Unveiled* (1701), Keach argued that regeneration was entirely a work of God that preceded conversion. Regeneration was passive, "the act of God's Spirit, by which he infuseth a vital principle." But, conversion is active, "whereby through the power of that grace, the sinner being quickened, is capacitated to believe and return to God."[35] Consequently, he could preach evangelistically: "Our Lord came not to call the Righteous, as such, neither self-righteous ones, nor such who in a Gospel-sense are righteous Persons, but sinners to repentance; to such that were really lost in the first Adam, and under the Bondage of Sin and the law."[36] Whether it was his earlier General Baptist tendencies or his being moderated by changes in prevailing Calvinism itself, Keach thus foreshadowed an evangelical Calvinism later attributed to Andrew Fuller and Robert Hall in the eighteenth-century Baptist community.

John Gill (1697–1771) was the principal Calvinistic Baptist theologian of the eighteenth century on both sides of the Atlantic. Successor to Benjamin Stinton, who followed Benjamin Keach, Gill was pastor of the Horsleydown Church across London Bridge for over fifty years, Gill was an impressive pulpiteer and the leading figure of London Baptist influence. Largely self-taught, he studied for about a year under the Rev. John Davis of Higham-Ferrers. He is said to have read the classics from the age of nine, and later specialized in Greek and Roman

---

[33] J. Barry Vaughn, "Benjamin Keach," in *Theologians in the Baptist Tradition*, ed. Timothy George and David S. Dockery (Nashville: Broadman Holman, 2001) 59–60; Benjamin Keach, *Gospel Mysteries Unveiled* (London: n.p., 1701) 75–76. Keach observed, "the Gospel he doth not give to all, nor his Spirit, Faith, and other gifts that are necessary to Salvation, to many thousands in the world; therefore he did not give his Son to die to save them all."

[34] Vaughn, "Benjamin Keach," 57–59.

[35] Ibid., Book 2, 405–406.

[36] Benjamin Keach, *A Medium Betwixt two Extremes* (London: Andrew Bell, 1698) 31.

historians and seven languages. His dissertation, "Antiquity of the Hebrew Language, Letters, Vowel Points, and Accents" won the attention of scholars throughout England and Scotland. It was the basis for the award of the prestigious degree, doctor of sacred divinity, from Marischal College, the University of Aberdeen, for "distinction in sacred literature, oriental languages, and Jewish Antiquities." His biblical expositions and major theological treatise, *A Body of Divinity* (1769–71), was in circulation well into the nineteenth century. Gill's work was given further impetus in the United States by an abridged edition prepared and endorsed by William Staughton of Philadelphia.[37] His total literary output was in excess of ten thousand folio pages.

To comprehend fully the theological system of John Gill, one must account for its essentially polemical nature.[38] Gill, followed by other Calvinistic pastors—notably John Skepp (1675–1721), John Brine (1703–1765), and John Johnson (1706–1791)—fought a sustained theological battle with the proponents of Arminianism and Pelagianism. Both groups were thought to minimize divine sovereignty and uplift human effort. Gill believed that his exposition of theology was not merely an essay in definition, but "a means of preserving sacred Truths" against those who have "followed their own fancies, and the dictates of their carnal minds", and who have "fallen into labyrinths and cannot find their way." Gill's theological method was to search the Scriptures to see if doctrines advanced were congruous with the Bible.[39] His opponents called him a "botcher in divinity" and his work a "continent of mud." Perhaps unfairly, he earned a reputation in the nineteenth century as the leader of the "hyper-Calvinists."[40]

---

[37] William Staughton, *Gill's Body of Practical and Doctrinal Divinity* (Philadelphia: n.p., 1810).

[38] Olin C. Robinson, "The Legacy of John Gill," *Baptist Quarterly* 24/3 (July 1971): 111–25.

[39] John Gill, *A Complete Body of Doctrinal and Practical Divinity or A System of Evangelical Truths Deduced from the Sacred Scriptures*, introduction (London: John Gill, 1769) lii.

[40] For contrasting assessments of Gill's theology and the question of "hyper" or "high" Calvinism, compare R. E. Seymour, "John Gill-Baptist Theologian" (Ph.D. diss., University of Edinburgh, 1954) with the more recent Curt Daniel, "Hyper-Calvinism and John Gill" (Ph.D. diss., University of Edinburgh, 1983) and George M. Ella, "John Gill and the Charge of Hyper-Calvinism," *Baptist Quarterly* 36/4 (October 1995): 160–77.

Gill's doctrine of the church was definitive. He began with the principle of a divine covenant that affirmed Christ as head of the elect. Distinct from the Old Testament covenants, Christ was the surety of an eternal covenant. The elect make up gospel churches, in contrast to "carnal" churches—meaning the established church and its parochial bodies or presbyteries. A "particular visible church" is, by this contrast, a small congregation of God's elect. The purpose of a church is to glorify God and nurture the saints. "It was not his practice," Gill wrote, "to address unconverted sinners, nor to enforce the invitations of the gospel." What this produced was a quiet, non-assertive form of Christianity that ultimately suffered decline at the end of the eighteenth century.

John Gill enjoyed a wide reception in Great Britain and North America. The influence of his approach was to produce a generation of pastors whose primary task was to maintain the historic faith. As David Benedict, the venerable American Baptist historian put it, "Our old Baptist divines, especially those of British descent, were generally strong Calvinists as to their doctrinal creed...but few of them felt at liberty to call upon sinners in plain terms to repent and believe the gospel. In expatiating on the strong points of their orthodox faith they sometimes ran Calvinism up to seed and were accused of Antinomian tendencies."[41]

In mild contrast to John Gill was Robert Hall, Sr. (1728–1791). The elder Robert Hall was a major catalyst for softening the deterministic outlook of English Baptists in the eighteenth century. Genetically speaking, his work lies between John Gill and Abraham Booth on the one side, and Andrew Fuller and his son, Robert Hall, Jr., on the other. He was raised in a Presbyterian home under the influence of an Arminian minister. His older brother fell in with Baptists and Robert consequently began to study their principles. Robert recalled that Samuel Wilson's *Scripture Manual* was especially helpful in this regard. He was baptized at Juniper-dye-house and received into the church at Hexham in 1752. Again through his brother's connections, he was introduced to a small congregation at Arnsby in Leicestershire that pressed him to consider becoming their pastor because they perceived his gifts. He served that church for almost four decades. His acumen transcended his

---

[41] David Benedict, *Fifty Years Among the Baptists* (Glen Rose: Newman and Collings, 1913) 102.

congregation and he became a preacher of choice in the Midlands as well as a writer for the Leicestershire Association he helped to form.[42]

Theologically, Robert Hall, Sr. was self-taught, to use his son's phrase, "he lacked the benefit of literary culture." He was greatly indebted to the Calvinistic Baptist tradition, but concerned for its lack of burden for the lost. Aware of the theological disputes of his day between Arminians and Calvinists, which many termed sophistry and confused metaphysics, Hall joined others in believing that "the chief praise of metaphysics is the cure of its own life, the repair of the mischief which itself has wrought."[43] Here he exhibited a typical Baptist pastoral attitude among those who lacked a formal education.

In 1776 Hall authored a study of the Trinity and in a second edition included a short treatise on the causes of salvation and damnation. At the 1779 annual meeting of the Northamptonshire Baptist Association, he preached a sermon on Isaiah 52:14, "to take up the stumbling blocks from my people." The famous English Baptist historian Joseph Ivimey considered the sermon "the commencement of a new era in the history of the denomination."[44] In 1781 Hall published a longer version of that sermon as *Help to Zion's Travelers*. The book was his way of responding to objections of Socinians, Sabellians, Arminians, and Antinomians to divine, saving grace. Hall's pastoral perspective led him to believe that the "excreances" of Calvinism had blunted the work of the gospel. He concluded this was due to a lack of appropriate temperate and candid controversy. Calvinism as a system has reduced the Christian religion to one where nothing needs to be explored.[45] On the contrary, an age of religious toleration called for improvements in the knowledge of Christ and the mysteries of the gospel. So he pointed out how questions relating to doctrinal issues could be reduced to the nature of Christ, the love of God, the doctrine of election, and the nature of the atonement. Under the heading of "Experimental Difficulties" he included such seeking out the unconverted, perplexity from misunderstanding, and the often mysterious

---

[42] For a summary of Hall's career and theological emphases, see Gordon W. Hughes, "Robert Hall of Arnesby 1728–1791," *Baptist Quarterly* 10/8 (October 1941): 444–48.

[43] Robert Hall Jr., *Help to Zion's Travelers: Being an Attempt to Remove Various Stumbling-blocks Out of the Way Relating to Doctrinal, Experimental, and Practical Religion* (Boston: Lincoln and Edmands, 1824) xxiii.

[44] Joseph Ivimey, *History of the Baptists* (London: n.p., 1830) 4:41.

[45] Ibid., xv, xxii.

nature of the gospel. Under another topic heading, "Practical Difficulties," he listed evil conduct of professors, errors of false religionists, and the inadmissibility of an apology from moral inability.[46] So cogent was the case Hall made that the book became a formative standard for many important Christian leaders. William Carey recalled that he had read no other book that "caused him such raptures."[47]

Hall's thinking united the doctrinal strength of Calvinism with the urgency of the evangelical appeal. With respect to the atonement, he followed the principle that evolved from the justice of God, that Christ's sacrifice was sufficient and efficacious so as to save all who would turn to the Lord. Closely related was his view of election, whereby he held that God graciously elects persons to salvation, but he rejected the notion that God elects persons to damnation. That occurs, he reasoned by the result of their sinfulness.[48] Implicit in Hall's apologetic is the appointed task of gospel ministers to help the faith and joy of those who believed through grace. Hall lived in a "day of errors," as he observed it, and ministers must remove the stumbling blocks that have done injury to some, confusing and perplexing others. "Hence the servants of the Lord are called upon to cast up and prepare the way, to render it more visible and obvious to every spiritual passenger, to see that it be raised or elevated and thereby be rendered safe…and made as plain as possible."[49] The first step toward softening the rigid determinism characteristic of the period, was to encourage ministers to be assertive and clear in their presentation of the gospel.

Hall felt very strongly that the high Calvinistic approach of exhibiting the mysteries of the gospel without addressing the unconverted unnaturally released ministers from their spiritual duties. He called it a "pernicious tendency." His son, Robert Hall, Jr., noted in the preface to the American edition (1824) that his father was part of a renewal of the practice of piety as the end of theological discussion that was joined by the work of Andrew Fuller. These men wanted to give free scope to the publication of the gospel, and this led to a considerable revolution of doctrinal thought among the Baptists. The result was that "the ministry of

---

[46] Ibid., 269–74.

[47] Quoted in Graham W. Hughes, *Robert Hall* (London: The Carey Press, 1943) 19.

[48] Ibid., 72.

[49] Ibid., 26.

the gospel was rendered more simple, more practical, and more efficacious."[50]

A profound new theological direction began to emerge among English Baptists in the last two decades of the eighteenth century. Brought about in large part by the Great Awakening and the writing of the American Congregationalist Jonathan Edwards, Baptist interpretation of Calvinism was moving toward a gentler Arminian stance. English Baptists began to respond to the criticism of some of their American co-religionists who, while equally Calvinistic, found the former's preaching "selfish, hardening, refrigerant, soporific...Antinomian."[51] Many English Baptists came to believe the atonement applied to all, not merely the elect. Leading Baptist thinkers in Britain adopted a moral governance theory of the atonement in lieu of the formerly widely embraced distributive justice model. The concept of "imputed righteousness" from Christ's sufferings in fulfillment of the law was supplanted by an atonement that substituted his sufferings for the punishments destined to humans for their sins. But most importantly, salvation became effective to those who responded through the grace of God to God's offer. Thereafter, human ability became a factor in evangelical Calvinistic thinking as well as among the largely Arminian evangelicals, such as the Methodists.[52] Several English Baptist pastors played prominent roles in that theological shift.

Among the outstanding English Calvinistic Baptist ministers of the eighteenth century, Andrew Fuller (1754–1815) is typically considered second in prominence only to John Gill. In fact, Fuller was to have the widest transforming influence in the history of the denomination. From a pastoral base, enlarged by voluntary service in the missionary movement, Fuller turned orthodox Baptist thought away from its deterministic obsession to a moderate and engaging evangelicalism. Reared in a high Calvinist Baptist home, Fuller was self-taught. His typically Calvinistic/Puritan conversion experience was informed by reading the works of John Bunyan and Ralph Erskine (*A Gospel Catechism for*

---

[50] Ibid., xxii.

[51] See Cushing Biggs Hassell, *History of the Church of God, from the Creation to A.D. 1885; Including Especially the History of the Kehukee Primitive Baptist Association*, rev. Sylvester Hassell (Middletown NY: Gilbert Beebe's Sons, 1886) 337.

[52] This was a widespread, transdenominational trend as noted in John McLeod Campbell, *The Nature of the Atonement* (London: Macmillan 1869) 76–77.

Young Christians). Turning aside the possibility of a trade, he was encouraged to enter the ministry about 1770. "Being now devoted to the ministry," he wrote in his diary, "I took a view of the doctrine I should preach, and spent pretty much of my time in reading and in making up my mind as to various things relative to the gospel....I earnestly besought the Lord to be my guide."[53] The next five years were spent in occasional preaching and reading authors such as John Gill, John Brine, Jonathan Edwards, and Abraham Taylor. Fuller noted that he could not reconcile the free offer of salvation he found in Bunyan's work with Gill's rigid system that left him without anything to say to the unconverted. He found in Taylor clear evidence of invitations to the ungodly, and Robert Hall, Sr., author of *Help to Zion's Travellers* (1781), further mentored him in this direction.

Fuller's outstanding theological contribution was his understanding of the atonement. His longstanding friend, John Ryland, thought that Fuller was at his best when dealing with the atonement. He stood with one foot in orthodox Calvinism, holding to the particular election of God. Fuller's classic phrase was, "Christ's death was sufficient for all, but effectual only to the elect." His other foot was planted in the presentation of a general offer of salvation. In his classic work, *The Gospel Worthy of All Acceptation*, he asserted no more than he observed in Scripture: people are to proclaim the message of the gospel and many will receive Christ. Additionally, people bear responsibility for their beliefs. To those who reacted in the negative, believing that no one responds to God except those who are chosen of God from eternity, Fuller answered: "No man is an unbeliever but because he will be so, and every man is not an unbeliever because the grace of God conquers some, changeth their hearts, and leads them to Christ." He reminded those who took issue with his biblically derived position, "God's Word, and not his secret purpose, is the rule of our conduct."[54]

Fuller became such an astute student of Calvinism that he was able to distinguish among three types: high, moderate, and strict. The "high" he defined as "more Calvinistic than Calvin himself, bordering on

---

[53] "Memoir," in Joseph Belcher, *The Complete Works of Rev. Andrew Fuller with a Memoir of his Life*, 3 vols. (Philadelphia: American Baptist Publications Society, 1844), 1:12.

[54] Thomas Eakins Fuller, *A Memoir of the Life and Writings of Andrew Fuller* (London: J. Heaton, 1863) 52–53.

Antinomianism"[55] He reckoned moderate Calvinists to be half Arminian, or "Baxterian," a doctrinal position with which he did not wish to be associated. The third category was strict Calvinism, meaning a religious perspective that was true to Calvin's system. As to his own perspective, he offered the following self-assessment: "I do not believe every thing that Calvin taught, nor any thing because he taught it; but I reckon strict Calvinism to be my own system." It may well have been Fuller himself who coined the term "hyper-Calvinist" to denote John Gill, John Brine, and others.[56]

Even during his early pastoral ministry at Soham, Fuller subtly signaled that Baptist theology could change. As he continued to read the high Calvinist classics, he interacted with John Sutcliff and John Ryland, Jr. He came to esteem Robert Hall highly. These men, themselves of the tradition of Bristol Baptist College and the West Country, encouraged Fuller to read the writings of prominent ministers who had moved away from the old order of Calvinism. These included Jonathan Edwards, Joseph Bellamy, and David Brainerd. But, Fuller professed in his memoirs that "I pursued my inquiries by myself and wrote out the substance ...under the title *The Gospel Worthy of All Acceptation*." The ultimate force of this powerful and much-quoted book, that he revised for a second edition in 1801, was to follow Jonathan Edwards's distinction between natural and moral ability. Further, he was also much affected by editorial dialogue with the Arminian Dan Taylor and revised much of what was in the first edition about the limits of the atonement.[57] In the 1790s he read widely among the post-Edwardsean or New Divinity men and came to use more language that indicated a "governmental" understanding of the death of Christ. According to this perspective, God—as a righteous moral governor—had to punish sin. God's mercy,

---

[55] With respect to antinomians, Fuller wrote, "A scheme that sets out with rejecting all obligation to the love of God and man cannot be friendly to either, nor to that gospel whose tendency is to promote them. It must be a mere system of *selfishness*; suited not to the condition, but to the propensities of fallen creatures." Andrew Fuller, *Antinomianism Contrasted with the Religion Taught and Exemplified in the Holy Scriptures* in Belcher, *Works of Fuller*, 2: 751.

[56] Belcher, *Works of Fuller*, 1:77, 16.

[57] Peter Morden, *Offering Christ to the World: Andrew Fuller (1754-1815) and the Revival of Eighteenth Century Particular Baptist Life* (Carlisle, Cumbria: Paternoster Press, 2003), 63-75, 98-99 argues that Fuller moved cautiously toward a general view of the atonement, always keeping Edwards in view.

however, allowed that Christ sacrifice his life on behalf of humankind; an expression of divine love. Sinners were required to read, hear, repent, and pray that their sins be forgiven. As Fuller put it, "If faith in Christ be the duty of the ungodly, it must of course follow that every sinner, whatever be his character, is completely warranted to trust in the Lord Jesus Christ for the salvation of his soul."

Fuller directed a second point at ministers of the gospel: "It is the duty of ministers not only to exhort their carnal auditors to believe in Jesus Christ for the salvation of their souls; but it is at our peril to exhort them to anything short of it, or which does not involve or imply it." In response to John Brine's caution against the general extension of an evangelical exhortation, Fuller retorted, "The truth is, it is never unsafe to introduce this doctrine."[58] Ever true to his eighteenth century heritage, however, he returned to the position that "none ever did or ever will believe in Christ but those who are chosen of God from eternity."[59] Those who adopted this more open style of baptistic faith were "evangelical," he believed, because they approved of addresses to the unconverted. Fuller hoped that no apology was necessary for an attempt to exhibit the Scriptural manner of preaching.[60]

There was a price to be paid for Fuller's theological evolution. His understanding of the imputation of sin to Christ, and consequently the imputation of Christ's righteousness to believers, seemed to some Baptist pastoral colleagues to move away from its obvious and literal biblical meaning. Following conversations with Fuller, Abraham Booth concluded he no longer believed in Christ's death as a full atonement and that he denied imputation. Booth accused Fuller of being an "Arminian" and a follower of Richard Baxter.[61] Fuller denied that Booth's accusations fairly represented him, but the matter was left unresolved from Booth's perspective. At Bourton-on-Water, Benjamin Beddome became critical of Fuller's idea of particular redemption and tried to make the issue a test of orthodoxy. Similarly, other strict Calvinists like

[58] "Gospel Worth of All Acceptation," in *Works of Fuller,* 2:383, 387, 391.
[59] Ibid., 330.
[60] "Concluding Reflections," in ibid., 387.
[61] On Baxterianism, Fuller wrote, "Mr. Baxter pleads for universal redemption; I only contend for the *sufficiency* of the atonement...for the redemption and salvation of the whole world; and this affords a ground for a universal invitation to sinners to believe; which was maintained by Calvin and all the old Calvinists." See "Letter VI-Baxterianism," in *Works of Fuller,*714.

William Gadsby and J. C. Philpot stepped up criticism of Fuller and labeled him the "greatest enemy the church of God has ever had."[62] His response in large part came in the form of *Six Letters to Dr. Ryland Respecting the Controversy with the Rev. A. Booth* (1803) and *Three Conversations: Imputation, Substitution, and Particular Redemption* (1806). Fuller concluded that Booth in particular was too close to the atonement theory of Tobias Crisp (1600–1643), a seventeenth century Puritan who thought that Christ actually became a sinner. He countered his critics by following John Calvin's lead that imputation was to be understood subjunctively or figuratively: "To say that Christ was reckoned or counted in the Divine administration *as if he were the sinner,*" he reasoned, "and came under an *obligation* to endure the curse for us is one thing; but to say that he deserved the curse is another. To speak of his being guilty by imputation is the same thing, in my ear, is to say he was reckoned, *as if he were so,* is just; but if properly for his being so, is inadmissible."[63] The matter did not end with Fuller's death. Modern Calvinistic Baptist theologians continue to debate Fuller's shifts in orthodoxy as a sign of the eighteenth-century revival or the declension of Calvinist Baptist thought.[64]

What is missed in the often-turgid theological discussions focused on Andrew Fuller is that he signaled a number of macrocosmic changes in the course of Baptist thought. For instance, Fuller discovered in his theological pilgrimage that there was often a difference between one's practices and one's principles; and he dared to say so. He observed, "I perceived that men's characters were not always formed by their avowed principles...we may profess an erroneous creed, and yet our spirit and conduct may be formed irrespective of it." Fuller concluded somewhat "tongue-in-cheek" that opinions are the actual moving causes for one's

---

[62] On the fairness of Fuller's critics and their comprehension of his work, see Morden, *Offering Christ*, 100-101.

[63] "Letter 2-Imputation," in *Works of Fuller*, II:705.

[64] A recent essay summarizes this controversy: Michael A. G. Haykin, "Particular Redemption in the Writings of Andrew Fuller (1754–1815)," in *The Gospel in the World*: *International Baptist Studies*, ed. David Bebbington (Carlisle, UK: Paternoster Press, 2002) 107–129. More extensive examinations are found in Robert W. Oliver, "The Emergence of a Strict and Particular Baptist Community among the English Calvinistic Baptists 1770–1850" (Ph.D. diss., CNA, 1986), and R. Philip Roberts, *Continuity and Change*: *London Particular Baptists and the Evangelical Revival 1760–1820* (Wheaton IL: Richard Owen Roberts, 1989).

actions, while theological principles often float in the mind, without being reduced to practice.[65] He could readily see that religious culture was moving in new directions and new challenges were soon to confront the principles of orthodoxy, thus change was likely. He pursued new ideas in practice (e.g. evangelism) and later worked out the theological foundations. What saved Fuller from charges of extreme heterodoxy, or even heresy, was his continual retreat to a strong affirmation of the doctrine of salvation by grace.[66]

Fuller's theological perspective was an important element in giving sharp definition to Baptist theological identity at the turn of a new century. Often called the "Benjamin Franklin of theology" because of his clear, plain, practical, and judicious theological observations, he was a mighty apologist, publishing a number of rejoinders countering his critics and others who challenged what he considered the boundaries of a biblical understanding of Christianity. His most direct and vitiating attacks were upon Joseph Priestly, Robert Robinson,[67] Archibald McLean, and William Vidler. He thought Priestly's Unitarianism was "another gospel" and a "bye-path of error," that Robinson at Cambridge had turned to infidelism, and that Vidler engaged in "animadversions" of Scripture.[68] In response to Archibald McLean's idea that faith belonged merely to the intellectual capacity, a matter of examining the evidence, Fuller argued that faith in Christ is a persuasion influenced by the moral state of the heart. He was repulsed by Robert Sandeman's notion that gospel invitations exhibited "priestly pride, and strutting self-importance." While he had great respect for Baptist colleagues like McLean and Abraham Booth, he stood firm: "Truth ought to be dearer to us than the greatest or best of men."[69]

---

[65] Belcher, *Works of Fuller,* 1:16.

[66] Morden, *Offering Christ to the World*, 96-97 follows David Bebbington and others in asserting Fuller's "vibrant Evangelical Theology."

[67] Belcher's account of Robinson's theological lapse into Sabellianism is the best account of the prominent pastor's pilgrimage. See "Tendency Toward Infidelity," in *Works of Fuller*, 2:223–24.

[68] Ibid., 233. See also Fuller's *Calvinistic and Socinian Systems Examined and Compared, as to their Moral Tendency, in a series of Letters* (1793); *Strictures on Sandemanianism, in Twelve Letters to a Friend* (1810); and, *Letters to Mr. Vidler on Universal Salvation* (1803).

[69] Ibid., 336–37.

Later in his career, Fuller attempted a systematic theology that he called "a connected view of the gospel." It was actually a series of letters requested by John Ryland. Fuller's failing health and lack of leisure prevented their completion.[70] He chose to begin with the doctrine of the cross as the heart of Christianity, through which "all the veins and relations trace." He planned to use the familiar territory of the General Six Principle Baptists, drawn from Hebrews 6:1–2, as his foundational set of principles.[71] In the extant portions, Fuller spoke of his understanding of the authority of Scripture: "The Old and New Testaments are dictated by one and the same Spirit...If the Bible be of God, perfection must be one of its properties."[72] He proposed to build on the being of God, and then move to God's creative acts. "The person of Christ," he believed, "was the principle upon which Christianity rests." Beyond that point, Fuller explicitly affirmed the Trinity, saying, "It is a subject of pure revelation. If the doctrine be not taught in the oracles of God, we have nothing to do with it; but if it be whether we can comprehend it or not, we are required humbly to believe it...We are not required to understand how three are one; for this is not revealed."[73]

From John Ryland's comments and Fuller's sketched plan, it can be concluded he likely would have developed a major section on the atonement. Looking ahead, Fuller observed, "If the doctrine of the atonement be viewed in the connections in which it stands, in the sacred Scriptures, it is the life-blood of the gospel system. Consider it as a method devised by the infinite wisdom of God by which he might honour his own name by dispensing mercy to the unworthy in a way consistent with righteousness."[74] His thinking was much influenced by Jonathan Edwards and the New Divinity writers, but he did not accept American theologians uncritically. Had Fuller been able to complete the work, it would have been the first evangelical full systematic theology among the Baptists.[75]

---

[70] At the time of his death, only nine installments had been completed. See Belcher, 684 ff.

[71] "The Nature and Importance of an Intimate Knowledge of Divine Truth," in *Works of Fuller,* 161–62.

[72] Letter 6 in "Letters on Systematic Divinity," in *Works of Fuller,* 700.

[73] Letter 9 in ibid., 708.

[74] Letter 2 in ibid., 687.

[75] For evolving assessments of Fuller, Fullerism, and "evangelical Calvinism," see Gilbert Laws, "Andrew Fuller 1754–1815," *Baptist Quarterly* (1924–1925): 76–84;

Andrew Fuller's impact on Baptists in the United States has been profound. An edition of his complete works was edited by an immigrant Baptist, Joseph Belcher, and published by the American Baptist Publication Society in 1844. Francis Wayland, in the Northern states, and James P. Boyce among Southern Baptists understood Fuller as a watershed of theological thought in Baptist life.[76] The American "Old School Baptists" who quarreled with many of his conclusions, recognized him as "the sledge-hammer who beat Methodist fervor into the cold Baptists."[77] Among those who recognized the reputation of Andrew Fuller were the College of New Jersey that in 1800 offered him an honorary degree, and Yale College that did likewise in 1805 over the signature of Timothy Dwight.[78] Even in the late twentieth century, some Southern Baptists in the United States insist Fuller be included in the orbit of acceptable Calvinism.[79]

Standing in stark contrast to the general trend of the later eighteenth century toward evangelical witness was Fuller's contemporary, William Vidler. Vidler (1758–1816) demonstrated the diversity that existed within Baptist ranks and was even more of a radical departure from older orthodoxy than Elhanan Winchester would become in the American Baptist context. Apprenticed as a bricklayer, Vidler was self-taught. He became a Baptist under the influence of Thomas Purdy in 1780; he was baptized and ordained to the ministry the same year. Called to a small English congregation at Battle, Vidler traveled in the region to raise funds for a new church building. During his travels he met General Baptists and some restorationists. In 1792 he professed universalism, but continued to serve his Baptist congregation. He met Winchester and became the latter's assistant at Parliament Court Church in London.

Arthur H. Kirkby, "Andrew Fuller-Evangelical Calvinist," *Baptist Quarterly* 15/5 (January 1954): 195–202); and E. F. Clipsham, "Andrew Fuller and Fullerism: A Study in Evangelical Calvinism," *Baptist Quarterly* 20 (1963–1964): 99–114; 146–54; 268–76. Clipsham includes a good analysis of Fuller's use of Calvinism and his ability to deal with paradox.

[76] Noted in Haykin, "Particular Redemption," 109.

[77] Hassell, *History*, 337.

[78] See the letter from Fuller to Dwight declining the honor, and extolling Dwight's predecessors, Jonathan Edwards, Sr., and the younger Edwards, in ibid., 85.

[79] See Tom Nettles, *By His Grace and for His Glory: A Historical, Theological, and Practical Study of the Doctrines of Grace in Baptist Life* (Grand Rapids: Baker Books, 1986) and Phil Roberts, "Andrew Fuller," in *Theologians of the Baptist Tradition*, 34–47.

Upon Winchester's return to the United States, Vidler became his successor in the London congregation. Vidler also launched a journal, *The Universalist's Miscellany*. His role as editor gave his views wide exposure in Britain until 1806 when he sold the journal to John Asplund.[80]

As Andrew Fuller saw it, Vidler's theology was a serious threat. First, Fuller held that there was no passage in Scripture that supported Vidler's interpretation of universal restoration allowing men to continue in their sins. Everywhere people are admonished to repent and turn from their evil ways. Thus, he declared Vidler's system to be "antiscriptural." Second, Fuller feared for the minister who declared false doctrine and who would some day face both the lost person and God over the matter. He called upon Vidler to jettison his system. Finally, he thought Vidler propounded many perversions of the plain meaning of Scripture. For instance, Fuller questioned the interpretation Vidler gave to translated terms such as "eternal" and "everlasting," rendering meanings such as not "unending" or "forever." In the end, he thought Vidler's real difficulty was that he had been sucked into the whirlpool of Socinianism. To Vidler's comment that "truth courts the public observation of men," Fuller replied, "folly is loud and stubborn."[81]

Unlike Andrew Fuller, Archibald McLean (1733–1812) is often overlooked as a key figure in the genetic development of Baptists in Britain. He is linked to mainstream English Calvinistic Baptists and is the parent of one type of Baptist in Scotland. He was reared in a Scottish Calvinistic home according to the accepted catechism, and received a commendable primary school education. He heard George Whitefield preach and was much impressed with Whitefield's style and message. He was apprenticed to a Glasgow printer and this became his trade. He read theology as a past-time and became active in a Church of Scotland parish church in Glasgow. He was well-read in William Paley's *Moral Philosophy*, George Campbell's *Lectures on Ecclesiastical History*, and John Gill's *Body of Divinity*.

McLean's religious pilgrimage took a dramatic turn in 1762 when he read the work of an Independent thinker, John Glas, of Edinburgh. The latter was a Calvinist who held that faith is a belief in the facts of the

---

[80] Little has been done on Vidler. See F. W. Butt-Thompson, "William Vidler," *Baptist Quarterly* 17/1 (January 1957): 3–10.

[81] "Letters to Mr. Vidler," in *Works of Fuller*, 2:295–327, esp. 302.

gospel. Glas had published a book, *The Testimony of the King of Martyrs,* which won acclaim as a statement of Independent principles. He derived his ecclesiology and church polity from a literal reading of the New Testament Book of Acts.[82] McLean followed Glas for about a year, but broke with the latter over a matter of church polity. McLean was soon joined by Robert Carmichael, the minister at Cupar-in-Angus. Carmichael had joined the 1747 secession Church in Scotland (the Antiburghers) over opposition to taking oaths. The two dissenters examined the issue of baptism. Claiming that he was not influenced on the subject by any Baptist writer, McLean achieved a theological position in support of believer's baptism from reading his New Testament. McLean and Carmichael contacted the venerable John Gill in London to request that he come to Edinburgh and baptize the congregation that Carmichael had gathered. Gill declined and Carmichael went to London, conferred with Gill, and was baptized at the Barbican.[83] Upon his return to Scotland, he in turn baptized McLean. In 1768 the two became co-pastors of the Edinburgh congregation and leaders of a new "Baptist" movement in Scotland.

Once constituted, the Scotch Baptists attempted to connect with the Particular Baptists of England in every important way.[84] McLean devised a set of beliefs that espoused sovereign free grace, the full deity of Christ, justification by faith alone, particular election, the perseverance of the saints, strict communion, and the need to be faithful witnesses of the gospel to the heathen. In fact, one of McLean's leading passions in ministry was his support for the Missionary Society of the English

---

[82] Among Glas's traits were particular redemption and congregationally appointed elders who were gifted but not necessarily trained. The best account of the interplay between Glas and McLean is Derek Murray, "The Scotch Baptist Tradition in Great Britain," *Baptist Quarterly* 33/4 (December 1987): 186–98.

[83] This circumstance involved Gill in an extensive editorial and pamphlet war with other dissenters in London over the issue of believer's baptism. See *History of the Baptists in Scotland,* ed. George Yuille (Glasgow: Baptist Union Publication Committee, 1926) 45–46.

[84] Throughout his career, McLean tried to accommodate himself theologically to the English Particular Baptists. Concerning novel views on baptism, Carmichael wrote to McLean in a letter dated 12 June 1766, "I am not willing to have any controversy with the brethren who are agreed with us in the same cause against Infant Baptism." See *The Works of Mr. Archibald M'Lean, Late Pastor of the Baptist Church, Edinburgh, with a Memoir of His Life, Ministry, and Writings in Six Volumes,* William Jones, comp. (London: William Jones, 1823) Vol 6, cxi-cxii.

Baptists.[85] Despite his hopes for inclusion among the English Baptists, McLean nevertheless spent a good deal of his effort defending his views and practices against critics from within that tradition. It was especially in the area of church order that he followed divergent paths. The McLeanites, or Sandemanian Baptists as some called them, celebrated the Lord's Supper weekly, they fiercely defended the independence of each local congregation as complete in itself, they observed strict dietary rules and dress codes, and eschewed popular forms of amusements. McLean himself developed a literalistic understanding of Scripture and also a view of Christ that maintained that Jesus was not the Son of God before the Incarnation. Many of the theological deviations from more commonly accepted doctrine in the movement were attributable to overreactions of McLean and Carmichael against the Glasites, as well as the result of McLean's self-taught theological breadth and somewhat naive perspective.[86]

Andrew Fuller, who connected positively with Archibald McLean for many years because of McLean's ardent support for the missionary cause, finally broke ranks with his Scottish colleague. Issuing a stinging denunciation of McLean's positions in a tract titled *Strictures on Sandemanianism* (1810),[87] Fuller attacked the Scotch Baptists as "Sandemanians plus believer's baptism." McLean's biographer reckoned Fuller's attacks "extremely unfair and disingenuous" and ultimately harmful in building a relationship with the English Baptists. Fuller and other critics of McLean freely fused their impressions of the Glasites with McLean's thinking, particularly in the matter of the meaning of personal faith. Fuller maintained that McLean held that faith was essentially an intellectual act, nothing more. McLean supposedly robbed the gospel of its moral content and imperatives. To this McLean constantly responded that he believed there were three components to "simple faith," namely faith, hope, and charity, and that Fuller did not understand the fine distinction. McLean thus went to great efforts to

---

[85] *Works of Mr. Archibald M'Lean,* 6:74, 76–78.

[86] For a fuller treatment of McLean's beliefs and variations, see Percival Waugh, "The New Dawn and the Rise of the Scotch Baptists," in Yuille, *Baptists in Scotland,* 44–50, and *The Baptists in Scotland: A History,* ed. D. W. Bebbington (Glasgow: Baptist Union of Scotland, 1988) 21–23.

[87] John Glas's son-in-law, Robert Sandeman, took Glas's religious views to England where a small following responded. Thus, on the English side "Sandemanians" were considered dangerous, unorthodox sectarians.

distance himself from the Phariseeism and censoriousness of the Glasites, later known as Sandemanians. Fuller remained critical of the demanding lifestyle expectations and of the exclusivity of the Scotch Baptist ecclesiology, as well as his sense that they lacked proper assurance of their salvation.[88]

McLean was also involved with others in doctrinal controversy, much of which stems from his literalistic hermeneutical method. Against Ralph Wardlaw's treatise connecting the Abrahamic covenant with infant baptism, McLean followed John Gill in asserting that there was no connection with the covenant nor between circumcision and baptism. Rather, he taught, baptism was properly the privilege of the New Testament church. To James Watt's tract defending the pastoral office as the only legitimate persons to administer the Lord's Supper, McLean countered that there was no work or function peculiar to the pastoral office. He argued that where there are two or three believers constituting a church, they can do every thing without pastors that they can do with them.[89]

McLean made some important contributions to the transitions in Baptist theology from the old Calvinist system to the evangelical stage. In his first theological treatise (1766), he responded to John Glas's *Dissertation on Infant Baptism.* The standard Baptist position was to deny that baptism became the initiatory rite for the church, in place of circumcision for Israel. Gill and others argued that infant baptism was nowhere taught in Scripture as an initiatory rite for anything. McLean, following a suggestion from Robert Carmichael, partially conceded the pedobaptist argument connecting circumcision and baptism, while also positing that baptism was for believers only who clearly possessed their faith, and for no one else. Theologically cogent and biblically informed, McLean's published letters on baptism were an instant novelty in Scotland as the first direct attack on infant baptism made in the country.

Following the lead of Fuller and others, in 1786 McLean published a tract entitled *The Commission Given by Jesus Christ to His Apostles, Illustrated.* Therein he asserted that the Apostles were commanded to state and explain the doctrines of the Gospel, the proper mode of baptism with its appropriate subjects and doctrinal import, and the nature of the

---

[88] Underwood, *English Baptists*, 190, contains an account very much prejudicial to Andrew Fuller.

[89] Ibid., 63.

Kingdom of Christ with its peculiar laws and institutions. These he included under Jesus' terminology "all things" (Matthew 28:19). Critics hailed this work with unqualified commendation as doing more to recall original Christianity than any "human production" then extant.[90] In 1797 he wrote *An Essay on the Calls and Invitations of the Gospel* in which he pointed out that the Gospel contains not only a declaration of facts about the person and work of Christ, but also kind and gracious invitations, calls, and exhortations to unbelievers to be saved. McLean thought the lack of this evangelizing emphasis a major shortcoming of John Gill and John Brine in the former generation, as well as with his contemporary Abraham Booth (*Reign of Grace*).

While somewhat isolated in Scotland from the epicenters of Baptist life and thought, unaware of earlier and contemporary Baptist developments in Scotland, and self- taught, Archibald McLean nevertheless made important, lasting contributions to the evolving Baptist identity. He followed a typical pattern of searching the Scriptures for doctrinal teachings and practices. This led him to a more or less literal interpretation that attracted many hearers. His doctrine of the church centered on believer's baptism and this he would not compromise. His evangelical commitments led him to leadership in the advancement of Baptist missionary activity and church planting. Finally, the publication of six volumes of sermons, treatises, and a full memoir guaranteed his connections with the Baptist movement.[91] In the strictest sense, his Scottish Baptist legacy was short-lived as such (evolving into the Churches of Christ), while in other manifestations it was carried South to England in Liverpool, Manchester, and Newcastle, to Wales among the Particular Baptists and Churches of Christ, and in Canada and the United States via the influence of Alexander Campbell and the Disciples of Christ.[92]

A second important stream of Baptist thought that originated in Scotland and had a wide influence was that of Robert and James Haldane. Robert (1764–1842) originally wanted to prepare for ministry in the Church of Scotland and attended the University of Edinburgh.

---

[90] Ibid., 54–55.

[91] In recognition of his literary achievements and their desire to raise funds in Scotland, the College of Rhode Island conferred an honorary degree upon McLean, which he promptly refused and ridiculed.

[92] Underwood, *English Baptists*, 192.

Owing to his upper class prerogatives and a desire to travel, however, he entered the Royal Navy in 1785. He settled near Stirling, managing his estate and from time to time attending theological lectures. James (1768–1851) followed a similar path, also serving in the Royal Navy, with duty in the Far East and Africa. He later returned to Edinburgh. Both Robert and James became interested in Christian missions as laymen and embraced the vision of overseas work. They were among the earliest supporters of the London Missionary Society (Congregationalist), and they both became involved in a variety of benevolent projects in Scotland, notably the Sunday School movement of John Campbell. In the late 1790s James Haldane left his life as a quiet country gentleman to conduct lay preaching tours that won him much acclaim among evangelicals.[93]

In 1797 the brothers Haldane established a domestic missionary society, the Society for Propagating the Gospel at Home, and continued evangelistic efforts in Scotland and England. Their plan followed that of George Whitefield in establishing preaching chapels throughout the countryside. A shortage of evangelists led in 1798 to the establishment of regional theological schools. In 1799, with the assistance of brother Robert, James Haldane established the Tabernacle or Circus Church at Edinburgh. Having previously withdrawn from the Church of Scotland, James was ordained at the Tabernacle as the first minister of the first church of a new movement, the Congregational Churches of Scotland. Under the supervision of the Haldane brothers, sister tabernacles sprang up across Scotland's urban centers. Over a ten-year period, the brothers contributed upwards of seventy-thousand pounds to Christian missions in Scotland.[94]

The pattern of theological education initiated by the Haldanes brought significant transformation to Baptist and evangelical life in Scotland and beyond. By design, it was church-based and practical. Much influenced by David Bogue, a learned Presbyterian and later Independent pastor at

---

[93] A good, brief survey is found in William W. Lawson, "Robert and James Haldane," *Baptist Quarterly* 8 (1934–1935): 276–86.

[94] Alexander Haldane, *The Lives of Robert Haldane of Airthrey and His Brother James Alexander Haldane* (London: Hamilton and Adams, 1853) 367. For a more recent assessment that stresses the theological and organizational difficulties of the Haldanes, see Bebbington, *Baptists in Scotland*, 30–32.

Gosport,[95] the brothers utilized a collection of capable pastors including Greville Ewing[96], John Aikman, William Walker, G. Cowie, and William Innes as instructors. In Ireland, Alexander Carson also served as a pastor-instructor. The course of study lasted for two years, embracing English grammar, Greek and Hebrew, preaching and systematic theology. Over three hundred students attended the seminaries, which ultimately closed in 1808.[97]

About 1808 James Haldane began to explore matters of church polity and discipline with several of his Congregationalist colleagues. These explorations included the terms of communion, infant baptism, plurality of leadership, and support for the ministry. From the establishment of the Congregation Union, it was agreed that none should be admitted to the Lord's Supper but those who gave evidence of vital Christianity. Here was evidence of New School theology. Based on the apostolic model, the practice of celebrating the Lord's Supper every Lord's Day was soon instituted. Thereafter, the use of lay exhorters was allowed for purposes of mutual edification and this led to a debate over plurality of elders. In that same year, after protacted personal study on the subject, James Haldane accepted believer's baptism as the teaching of Scripture and for all purposes became a Baptist. Robert was immersed before the year was out. Apparently both had been influenced by John Young, author of *Thoughts on Baptism* (1801).[98] As James moved in the direction of becoming Baptist, he and Robert were embroiled in a controversy among their connection over local church government, both baptism and polity relating to their evolving doctrine of the church. Atypical of other Baptists of the era, Haldane refused to dwell on what he considered "the barren controversy about the meaning of "bapto" and "baptidzo," or even the proper objects of baptism. Ever the evangelist, he preferred to

---

[95] Bogue's domestic missionary effort, the Hampshire Association for Itinerant Evangelism, had been a model for the SPGH.

[96] Ewing was formerly the minister of Lady Glenorchy's Chapel in Edinburgh.

[97] Haldane, *Lives*, 330–31. See also R. F. Calder, "Robert Haldane's Theological Seminary," *Transactions of the Congregational Historical Society* 13 (1937).

[98] Young was a graduate of the first class in the Haldane Seminary. He became pastor of the Congregational/Haldanite church at Paisley. About 1801 he adopted Baptist views and composed his treatise. Young likely baptized both James and Robert Haldane. See Yuille, *Baptists in Scotland*, 58n.

emphasize the thing signified, namely the eternal welfare of souls.[99] Haldane was also weary of the problem of the Scotch Baptists (whom he called Glasites or Sandemanians), who in his mind exhibited a bitter and intolerant spirit, and whose "expansive powers were contracted and dwarfed."[100]

In his later years, Robert Haldane engaged in strenuous efforts on behalf of the emerging evangelical community in Europe. Though a Baptist in his personal views, "one of the most remarkable features of Mr. Haldane's teaching," wrote a European friend, "was that not a shadow of sectarianism was mixed up with it."[101] He channeled much of his philanthropy through the Continental Society, his personal interests being France and Switzerland. He published a widely circulated commentary on the Letter to the Romans and a monograph entitled *Evidences of Divine Revelation* (1816). He lectured at universities across Europe and drew to his circle a collection of outstanding scholars, including Louis Gaussen at Geneva, Henri Pyt in Paris, and Merle D'Aubigne of Geneva. His passions included able defenses of the doctrine of verbal plenary inspiration of Scripture and the canon of Scripture against "the intermixture of Apocryphal fables or the writings of lying prophets."[102] In his lectures he inveighed against "neologians," who diminished the majesty of the Word of God. In a revised edition of his Romans commentary, he attacked what he considered the grievous errors of Moses Stuart (who trained American Baptists at Andover) and Professor Tholuck at Halle (a German Lutheran much esteemed by contemporary American and British Baptists), whom Haldane considered "lamentably deficient, and full of false doctrine and startling neology."[103] Not only did Robert publish a spate of his own rejoinders to liberal scholarship, he also underwrote the work of the evangelical community in publications such as Louis Gaussen's *Theopneustia* and eight of Alexander Carson's pamphlets.[104]

---

[99] Haldane, *Lives*, 375 gives the account of the sermon he delivered to his 4000 member congregation.

[100] Ibid., 381.

[101] Ibid., 454.

[102] Ibid., 514.

[103] Ibid., 606–607.

[104] On this aspect of his work, see ibid., 546–56.

The theological impact of the Haldanes upon mainstream Baptist thought was significant. The attachment of Baptist principles to an aggressive revivalist tradition in Scotland affected many immigrants to the United States, British North America, India, Australia, and Africa. In the later career of Robert Haldane the diminution of sectarian Baptist views in favor of Evangelical emphases caused many Baptists in Britain and the United States to gravitate theologically to the Evangelical Alliance and away from the New Theology fostered in Germany. Robert Haldane's commitment to the verbal plenary inspiration of Scripture carried many Baptists with him and laid the foundation for later fundamentalist positions in the United States and Canada. As for James Haldane, his role in creating a viable Baptist community is part of the theological heritage of modern Baptists in Scotland. Moreover, his idea of church-based theological education taught by pastors offset the emphases of college and university-based theological education elsewhere in Britain. Finally the literary output of the brothers was phenomenal. Robert published fifteen titles, the most influential of which were *Evidences and Authority of Divine Revelation,* 2 volumes (1816, three editions), *On the Inspiration of Scripture* (1828, seven editions), and *Exposition of the Epistle to the Romans,* 3 volumes. (1835–1852, seven editions). Likewise, James wrote twenty-seven titles, the most prominent of which were *Views of Social Worship* (1805, two editions), *Reasons for a Change of Sentiments on the Subject of Baptism* (1808, two editions), *On the Dignity and Person of Christ* (1813), and *Doctrine of the Atonement* (1845–47, two editions). Robert's *Commentary on Romans* continues to be in print in the late twentieth century.

An interesting outgrowth of the Haldanite theological tradition was the work of Alexander Carson. Carson (1776–1846) was Scotch-Irish and educated at Glasgow University. Initially he entered the Presbyterian ministry, but left on principle of evangelical church discipline. He was ousted from his church at Tubbermore, and met in the open air for some years. He became a well-known controversialist through his pastoral work, his engagement of university scholars, and his friendship with the Haldane brothers. In his lifetime he was dubbed the "Jonathan Edwards of the nineteenth century." Carson's arguments against what he termed the "absurdities" of transubstantiation and his "demolition" of Unitarian premises earned him a transatlantic reputation as a first rank biblical scholar and philosopher.[105]

Carson's outstanding work was *Baptism: Its Mode and Subjects* (1831).[106] He also wrote extensively on the Trinity and the doctrine of the atonement. His classic style of argument was most evident as he delved into the subject of baptism. In response to the Archbishop of Dublin, who argued that the burden of proof on matters baptismal lies with those who oppose a long church tradition, Carson retorted: "The side that affirms needs the proof; and the side that needs the proof must produce it. Infant baptism and episcopacy, and all religious rites must show their authority in Scripture, or perish with the other human inventions discontinued at the Reformation."[107] Like other writers before him, he clearly laid out the scriptural and linguistic evidence for the proper mode of baptism, taking into account prominent pedobaptist authors. Next, he denied the purported Old Testament connection of baptism with circumcision, or more generally the Abrahamic covenant. Finally, he also set aside traditional pedobaptist arguments evoking New Testament passages concerning the baptism of families and children. To the assertion by Independents that they were guided solely by the Bible in the practice of infant baptism, Carson admonished, "Let our ancestors have all the esteem and gratitude to which they are entitled... It is disgraceful to Christians, that they continue to hold the errors of their unworthy ancestors and to feel a reverence for the unscriptural phraseology of ancient divines."[108]

Of Christ's atonement, Carson espoused a substitutionary understanding based primarily upon Hebrews 9:11–15: "If there be any meaning in language, Jesus Christ is represented in this passage as a true and proper sacrifice, and that through this, the conscience of the believer is purged from all the sins of which he is guilty... Christ's work is

---

[105] See the various reviews of his work cited in "Opinions of the Press on Dr. Carson's Merits as an Author," in *Works of the Rev. Alexander Carson (Dublin: William Carson, 1847-63)*, 2:457.

[106] The book is still held in high regard by Reformed Baptists who produced a reprint edition in 1983 in their "Sovereign Grace Series," as well as a Kregel Publisher's edition in 1981.

[107] Alexander Carson, *Baptism: Its Mode and Subjects Considered and a reply to the Arguments of Mr. Ewing and Dr. Wardlaw Refuted* (Edinburgh: Waugh and Innes, 1831) 17.

[108] Ibid., 235.

imputed to us (not as a matter of course), in God's sovereignty."
Unquestionably of the "sacrifical" school, Carson promulgated his view
as "saving faith."[109]

Carson was a tough-speaking apologist for his tradition. There was
little that was ground-breaking in his work, but what was relevant to the
Haldanite tradition was his combative stance, particularly against
university-trained, "enlightened" theologians. In a mid-century rebuttal
to growing unitarianism[110] and particularly the influence of Joseph
Priestly, Carson was direct: "I cannot conscientiously call a man a
Christian, who does not believe Jesus Christ to be what the Scriptures
represent him to be; and as I believe the Scriptures represent him to be
God, I cannot believe him a Christian who denies this."[111] His apologetic
was starkly biblicist, like that of the Haldanes: "If the Scriptures are not
true, then the institution of religious teachers of every kind is a forgery of
priestcraft. What higher credentials can religious teachers plead than the
Word of God?"[112] In like manner, with respect to the sovereignty of God,
Carson answered an important question: "Why did God save sinners of
Adam's race, and leave all the sinning angels to perish? Because it was
his sovereign pleasure. It is not my business to justify God, for he scorns
to give any account of his matters. If there is anything plainly taught in
Scripture, it is that the sacrifice of Christ was made for those only who
shall eventually be saved by it."[113] To those who scorned traditional
Calvinist thought, he wrote, "Why then, that sarcastic leer? Why those
derisive appellations for Christians? No more of your petulance; the
knowledge of Jesus is the noblest of the sciences." To those of high
social status, Carson warned, "And ye infidel Christians, ye men of

---

[109] Alexander Carson, "The Doctrine of the Atonement, Set Forth in An Address to
the Public on the Nature and Importance of the Gospel," in *The Works of the Reverend
Alexander Carson, LL.D.* (Dublin: William Carson, 1852) 1:51, 103, 124. To underscore
his position, "in the atonement of Jesus, mercy and truth meet together, righteousness and
peace kiss each other...justice and the law have received full and perfect satisfaction..."
(126).
[110] Carson distinguished between "Unitarians," Arians, and Socinians. He preferred
to use the older terminology because for him it rooted modern distortions in earlier
heretical thought. See "Doctrine of the Trinity," *Works of Carson* 2: 203–205.
[111] "A Reply to Doctor Drummond's Essay on the Doctrine of the Trinity in a Letter
to the Author," in ibid., 2:204.
[112] Carson, "Doctrine of the Atonement," 103.
[113] Ibid., 125.

merit, who intend to storm heaven by your arrogant virtue, what is your paradise compared to that of the ransomed of the Lord?"[114] He was a master at delivering biblical ideas in Elizabethan-style biblical polemic.

Like the Haldanes, Carson was often accused of being a theological bigot, an intolerant evangelical, and a Baptist. He said in response, "So far from fostering a sectarian spirit, no one can more thoroughly abhor it than I do.... While I defend what I consider truth with respect [to baptism], I cordially embrace every lover of the Lord Jesus."[115]

Robert Hall, Jr., was also in the transforming tradition of Fuller. One of the most unsung Baptist thinkers of the early nineteenth century, Hall (1764–1831) was a member of the second generation of transitional theologians. The son of Robert Hall, Sr., he was reputed to have read the works of Joseph Butler and Jonathan Edwards by the age of nine. He received one of the best educations of any Baptist of his era: a year at John Ryland's academy at Northampton, the course at Bristol Baptist College, and subsequently an M.A. in classics at the University of Aberdeen (he was awarded a John Ward Scholarship to study at Aberdeen). At Bristol he was much enamored of Caleb Evans and liked theology. At Aberdeen his interests were science, mathematics, and the Greek classics. He was one of the most distinguished students in his Aberdeen class. Hall served as pastor at Broadmead Church, Bristol, at Cambridge, and at Harvey Lane, Leicester. While serving as assistant pastor at Broadmead, he became tutor in classics at Bristol College.

Hall's theology was much influenced by his father. The elder Hall had discarded some opinions formerly embraced, and his son esteemed his father to the point of having an ambition to imitate him theologically.[116] Specifically, this meant addressing the issue of the unconverted and infidelity. Hall's much-renowned sermon, "Modern Infidelity," was a second volume to his father's *Help to Zion's Travelers*. In the sermon, the younger Hall identified various sources and forms of rationalism, irreligiosity, and impiety. He spoke out emphatically in support of a faith wherein millions had found inspiration for life, consolation in death, excellence of character, and that had claimed the allegiance of the greatest names in history. He was especially persuasive on the point that Christianity had vindicated itself in the moral and

---

[114] Ibid., 186–87.

[115] Ibid., xv.

[116] Hall, "Preface," in *Help to Zion's Travelers*, xvii, xxiv.

ethical sphere.[117] Unlike his father, he had the clear example of the effects of the French Revolution and the social unrest of the Napoleonic Wars upon which to draw. Stretching beyond his father's Calvinistic boundaries, Hall did not hesitate to offer clear evangelistic invitations: "The kingdom of God is indeed come nigh unto you: it is nigh you in the gospel, it is nigh you in the efforts of the present time, it is nigh you in the endeavours of your ministers, it is nigh you in every sermon you hear and in every ordinance you attend."[118] Contemporary observers recognized it was not only the substance of his message, but his incarnation of gospel urgency and unsurpassed oratory that brought life to his theological interpretations. "Surely like no other dissenting bishop in England, his diocese is limited only by Christendom."[119]

In light of eighteenth-century Particular Baptist thought, the younger Hall was a "new" type of Calvinistic thinker. He read the works of John Gill, and like Andrew Fuller, he found little useful in the many pages. In a much-quoted interchange between Hall and the celebrated evangelist, Christmas Evans, who wished that John Gill's work had been published in Welsh, Hall retorted, "I wish they had sir. I wish they had with all my heart, sir, for then I should never have read them. They are a continent of mud, sir!"[120]

Perhaps Hall's most memorable theological contribution was in developing a new Baptist position on the sacraments/ordinances. It followed predictably upon his "opening up" of the gospel message. From a pastoral point of view, he found it difficult-to-unacceptable to exclude persons from the Lord's Table who were non-Baptist, professing Christians. He reasoned, "the rite which of all others is most adapted to cement mutual attachment should not become a line of demarcation or an impassible barrier to separate and disjoin the followers of Christ."[121] Here he was a true son of John Bunyan.

In response to Hall's position on "open communion," Joseph Kinghorn (1766–1832), pastor at the Particular Baptist Church at

---

[117] Robert Hall, Jr., *Modern Infidelity, Considered with Respect to Its Influence on Society in a sermon preached at the Baptist Meeting in Cambridge* (Cambridge: n.p., 1799).

[118] Quoted in Hughes, *Robert Hall,* 97.

[119] *New York Observer* quoted in Hughes, *Robert Hall,* 99.

[120] Quoted in Underwood, *English Baptists,* 170.

[121] Quoted in Hughes, *Robert Hall,* 64.

Norwich, responded with an important rejoinder, *Baptism a Term of Communion at the Lord's Table* (1816). The Norwich pastor sided with Abraham Booth and others in the classic argument that the law of Christ demanded that only baptized persons come to the Lord's Table and that persons baptized in infancy were not baptized. Hall's response was to point out that no group or society of men had the authority to determine who was welcome at the Lord's Table. Here was an outrage not unlike transubstantiation, that "every little Baptist teacher" should have the right of repelling people from communion.[122] Hall's thinking called for a new view of the church and society: more open, accepting, and inclusive. For him, the church was redefined as an association of people with a common intention to pursue a particular work. Being "Baptist," Hall's ecclesiastic perspective favored individuals rather than churches.[123] He was simply unwilling to exclude from fellowship Anglicans, Methodists, or other nonconformists. His more liberal thought applied to other contemporary causes as well, from voluntary religion to the rights of framework knitters to bargain collectively, to advocacy of a free press. His social conscience and political savvy was to presage later advocates of a social gospel.

In contrast to Robert Hall and his son Robert Hall Jr., Abraham Booth of Kirkbywood House, and later of Sutton Ashfield, was one of the key determinants of a stricter eighteenth-century Calvinistic Baptist identity. Booth (1734–1806) was a farmer who learned the trade of weaving stockings. He was converted during the Evangelical Revival in the Midlands, a movement sparked in large part by the Wesleys who stressed Arminian themes[124] and began to preach among New Connexion of General Baptist gatherings. Self-taught by reading the works of European theologians and historians, and from the Jewish antiquities, he became a General Baptist pastor for about six years at Kirkbywood House. He recognized the inadequacy of his education and sought tutelage under a Roman Catholic priest. Booth soon became proficient in classical authors in theology and church history. His studies caused him to modify his thinking about the nature of God's sovereignty and salvation. He soon

---

[122] Ibid., 172.

[123] Hall, *Works*, 3:97.

[124] On the evangelical revival, the Wesleys and the impact from other groups, see Gordon Rupp, *Religion in England 1688-1791* (Oxford: Clarendon Press, 1986), 399-400.

dissociated himself from the General Baptists and worked on a major writing project to define his new views.[125]

In 1768 Booth became pastor at Prescot Street, Goodman's Fields in London and over the next three decades became the preeminent Baptist in London after John Rippon.[126] What made Booth important to the development of Baptist thought was his shift from Arminian theology as a General Baptist to a moderating Calvinist position among the Particular Baptists. His first publication was a poem critical of Calvinism, entitled "Absolute Predestination." After his theological change of heart, he wrote the much-quoted *Reign of Grace* (1768). He described his earlier poetic criticism of the Calvinistic stance as "an impotent attack on the honour of divine grace...and a bold opposition to the sovereignty of God, and as such I renounce it." Booth became a major apologist for Particular Baptist beliefs. "Many reflections are cast on the Baptists," he wrote, "and various charges are laid against them; reflections and charges of such a kind, as greatly impeach the truth of their doctrinal principles, and the candor of their Christian temper. They are frequently represented by their Paedobaptist brethren, as uncharitably rigid, as incorrigible bigots to a favourite opinion, and putting baptism in the place of our Lord's atoning blood and the sanctifying agency of the divine Spirit."[127] He thus took up the cudgel of the apologist and managed not only to provide an adequate defense of the Particular Baptist tradition, but to create a self-consciousness that resulted in a highly-defined subcategory known as "Strict Baptists."

Like Andrew Fuller, Booth was a proponent of "close communion." Booth was among those who would define a "strict" communion position, namely that baptized believers only should be admitted to the Lord's Supper. Consistent with contemporary Baptist doctrine and practice of the period, only baptism by immersion was considered legitimate. Booth reasoned those who had not been baptized in the proper way were not admissible to the Lord's Supper in any church that sought

---

[125] A new look at Booth is found in Ernest A. Payne, "Abraham Booth 1734–1806," *Baptist Quarterly* 26/1 (January 1975): 28–42. Payne argued that Booth steered a middle course between Gill and Fuller.

[126] One of Booth's prominent deacons was William Fox (1736–1826), who advanced the cause of Sunday Schools. The congregation was renowned for its support of voluntary societies, education, and benevolent enterprises.

[127] Abraham Booth, *An Apology for the Baptists* (London: E. and C. Dilly, 1778) 1.

to be consistent in its witness to the Scriptures. He further argued that the Lord's Supper was not intended to be any sort of test among Christians, but a continual memorial of a stupendous act of God in Christ.[128] Booth, like others of his Particular Baptist persuasion, contended that New Testament order placed baptism before fellowship, which included the Lord's Supper. By linking the Great Commission (Mathew 28: 19, 20) with passages in the Acts (16:31-34; 18: 8-11; 19: 4-7) this seemed obvious to his position. He referred to baptism as the sacrament of regeneration or initiation, whereas the Lord's Supper was the "sacrament of nutrition."[129] Against even the venerable John Bunyan, who railed against "obedience to water,"[130] Booth argued that those not baptized were guilty of sinning against a clear injunction of the Lord. Further, those who admitted such persons to the Table were sinning as well in giving solace to the unbaptized. Booth argued that if Scripture's instructions were not taken as the rule for admission to the Table, then a candidate's testimony had more authority than the Bible.[131] His sacramental theology was actually a disguised argument for the authority of Scripture. In the end, Booth contended, "Either Jesus Christ has informed us in the New Testament what baptism is, and what is requisite to communion at his table, or he has not." [132] The consistency of his Bible literalism could not be assailed, even though critics reviled Booth and others of his doctrinal ilk as "watery bigots." To those critics who referred to him pejoratively as a "Strict" Baptist, Booth replied, "We are not ashamed to be called Strict Baptists: we cheerfully adopt the character."[133]

Also like Fuller and Hall, Booth came to appreciate the urgency of evangelical preaching. Regarding the doctrine of "reigning grace" he wrote: "It is the grand instrument ordained by a holy God, for informing the ignorant, comforting the disconsolate, and rescuing the profligate from that worst of vassalage, the servitude of sin and subjection to Satan." Of the effects of a freely given evangelistic offering of Christ to non-believers, he wrote, "Now, it is evident, he invites us by the name of

---

[128] Ibid., 16.
[129] Ibid., 37.
[130] Ibid., 132.
[131] Ibid., 47, 57.
[132] Ibid., 70.
[133] Ibid., 101, 138.

sinners. As sinners, therefore, miserable, ruined sinners, we must come to him for life and salvation. The gospel of peace is preached to such, and them the gospel calls; even those who are not conscious that they are the objects of any good disposition."[134] He retained his belief theologically in election as his literary mentor John Owen would have had it, but this in no way hampered his ability to "commend himself to every man's conscience, by manifestation of the truth." If ministers had any reason to expect success, it must be by a faithful and simple promulgation of revealed truths.[135]

One of the unique contributions that Abraham Booth made to Baptist thought pertained to his theology of the kingdom. Rather than radically separating the economies of the Old and New Testaments, he saw in the kingdom of Christ a unifying principle of the entirety of Scripture and human history. In contrast to the earthly kingdom of Israel, the Kingdom of Christ is spiritual and coequal with the true church. It is always separate from worldly kingdoms or churches that are governed by worldly standards. Those who are part of the Kingdom of Christ are in a state of preparation for heaven, and none but believers comprise the Kingdom of Christ. Their worship and service must be pure and as given to the Messiah who reigns over the kingdom that is presently in place and the kingdom yet to be established. Here was a theme that not only reinforced the purity of the nonconforming churches, but also a strong Christological statement about the Lordship of Christ in his church and the life of believers.

Booth is genetically important to Baptist thought for three reasons. First, he represents a crossover from the Arminian category to evangelical Calvinism. Second, he was one of the most respected pastor-theologians of his era and promoted the missionary and itinerant causes from his base in London. Third, he was a theological fountainhead for the emerging Strict Baptist movement of the nineteenth century. His works were well referenced in their literature. William Gadsby, for

---

[134] Abraham Booth, *The Reign of Grace, from Its Rise to Its Consummation* (Grand Rapids: Eerdmans, 1949) 44, 107, 185.

[135] Booth's book published in 1796, *Glad Tidings to Perishing Sinners; or The Genuine Gospel, a complete Warrant for the Ungodly to believe in Jesus Christ,* made his position abundantly clear.

instance, took similar positions to Booth, though far less charitably.[136] Finally, Booth's writings have endured to the twentieth century as an able apologist of Calvinistic or Strict Baptist thought. An American publisher of Primitive Baptist classics issued a new edition of Booth's work in 1985.[137]

General Baptist Dan Taylor was another key figure among English Baptists of the eighteenth century. A coal miner's son, Taylor (1738–1816) was a native of Northowram. He learned to read by age five, but was denied any consistent education until he managed to learn Latin, Greek, and Hebrew from Titus Knight, a Methodist tutor in Halifax. He joined the Methodists and prepared himself to be a local preacher. Familiarity with the Methodists, however, bred disinclination for young Taylor. He could not accept Mr. Wesley's rigid conference system, nor the superintendency of the Connection. He broke off his association with the Methodists and, reading Dr. William Wall's *History of Infant Baptism* (1705), sought a relationship among the Baptists. Rejecting the Calvinist doctrine of election, he was introduced to the General Baptists, baptized among them, and called to be a pastor at Wadsworth in Yorkshire in 1763. His popularity increased and in 1770 he organized the New Connexion of General Baptists, destined to become a revival of Arminian Baptist thought in Britain.[138]

Taylor was a self-taught theologian, typical of many Baptists of his era. A school teacher, he read classical literature and was acquainted with Virgil and Xenophon. His theological reading was in part devotional, in part given to the more studious contemporary dialogues. Across the years of his pastoral ministry he read Philip Doddridge's *Growth in Grace*, Walter Marshall on sanctification, John Owen, Henry

---

[136] Gadsby was said to be unlettered to the point of being uncouth in oral expression. According to Robert Halley, a ministerial colleague in Manchester, he was well-versed in John Bunyan. See Halley's characterization in A.C. Underwood, *A History of the English Baptists* (London: Kingsgate Press, 1947), 185-86.

[137] Abraham Booth, *A Defense for the Baptists, Being A Declaration and a Vindication of Three Historically Distinctive Baptist Principles, Compiled and Set Forth in the Republishing of Three Books* (Paris AR: The Baptist Standard Bearer, 1985). The three works republished were: *An Apology for the Baptists* (1778), *An Essay on the Kingdom of Christ* (1788), and *Pastoral Cautions* (1805).

[138] On Taylor and the New Connexion, see F. W. Rinaldi, "The Tribe of Dan: The New Connexion of General Baptists 1770–1891: A Study in the Transition from Revival Movement to Established Denomination" (Ph.D. diss., University of Glasgow, 1996).

Venn, John Cotton, and Isaac Watts. In preparation for teaching, he immersed himself in Bible history and geography. "Mr. Taylor's knowledge of the doctrines of the Bible was remarkable," exclaimed one observer, "his general, extensive and critical knowledge of the Scriptures, rendered him truly eminent."[139] Like many Baptists before and since, eminence rested upon one's knowledge of the content of Scripture.

Taylor's own theological works were of a practical bent: *Scriptural Account of the Way of Salvation* (1772); *Fundamentals of Religion in Faith and Practice* (1775); *A Catechism or Instructions for Youth* (1780); *Dissertation on Singing in Public Worship* (1786; 1789); *Essay on the Truth and Inspiration of the Scriptures* (1790); and *Principal Parts of the Christian Religion* (1802). He also edited the *General Baptist Magazine* 1798–1800. In his first book he detailed his evangelical views, demonstrating an advanced understanding of the *ordo salutis* or process of conversion, the atonement, and his acceptance of classic positions on eschatological subjects and holiness.

Taylor was a controversialist and interacted with a number of significant eighteenth-century writers. For instance, he arrived at an agreeable counterpoint with Particular Baptist Robert Hall, Sr., author of *Help to Zion's Travelers* (1781). While he liked Hall's evangelical side, he strongly opposed him on election and reprobation. He exchanged letters with Andrew Fuller on the universality of the atonement, free moral agency, and human inability where he opposed Fuller's modified Calvinism and reliance upon the moral argument that all men had an obligation to believe and accept salvation.[140] Rather, Taylor argued for the universality of Christ's atonement based on universal calls and invitations of the gospel.[141] This work proved to be defining theologically, not only for Taylor, but for the New Connexion Baptists as

---

[139] Adam Taylor, *Memoirs of the Reverend Dan Taylor, with Extracts from His Diary, Correspondence, and Unpublished Manuscripts* (London: Adam Taylor, 1820) 295.

[140] "The Reality and Efficacy of Divine Grace, with certain success of Christ's Kingdom, Considered in A Series of Letters Containing Remarks upon the Observations of the Rev. Dan Taylor on Mr. Fuller's Reply to Philanthropes, by Agnostos" in *Works of Fuller*, II: 512-560.

[141] Compare for instance Taylor's *Universality of the Savior's Death* (London: 1796) with Fuller's *A Defense of a Treatise Entitled The Gospel Worthy of All Acception* (London: T. Dicey, 1787).

well. In 1789 he published a treatise on the inspiration of the Scriptures, which reviewers hailed as perspicuous, concise, and well-versed. When the American Baptist Elhanan Winchester arrived in England about 1790, teaching universal restoration, several prominent friends of Taylor urged him to address the topic. After much study, he concluded that Winchester's position required too much theological labor and "shuffling," and "had lost all sense of evangelical religion and acceptance with God." Except for two published tracts on future punishment, Taylor graciously and tactfully declined to do battle with Winchester, "so as not to expose him."[142]

As a role model for the New Connexion, Taylor was an obvious choice to be tutor of the General Baptist Academy at Church Lane, London. He developed a theological curriculum suited for General Baptist candidates for ministry. His lectures covered topics that included Christian Evidences (apologetics), Study of the Scriptures, Preaching (method and practice), Bible geography and chronology, Jewish antiquities, prophecy, logic, and rhetoric. Taylor assumed that few of his students had any previous education and that their chief needs were preaching, evangelism, and Bible exposition.[143]

It was a collection of pastors across the greater part of the eighteenth century that brought about the transformation of the church, as W.R. Ward has characterized their influence.[144] Fuller, McLean, the Halls, Booth, Kinghorn, and others nudged along subtle modifications in the basic doctrinal foundations of the Particular Baptists, while William Carey, Joseph Ivimey, and Joseph Hughes afterwards created a new institutional network to carry forth the new theological emphases. The transformation would be complete as the old guard, particularly John Gill, slipped into the twilight (remembered for the most part only by the "hypers") and as Baptist development and proliferation on the other side of the Atlantic made headway in helping to define the future of Baptist theological identity.

As the nineteenth century dawned in Britain, another era in the evolution of Baptist thought was begun. The over-arching issue driving the new impetus of theological discussion was to be the matter of the

---

[142] Ibid., 188–91.

[143] The curriculum is detailed in Taylor, *Memoirs*, 315.

[144] W. R. Ward, "The Baptists and the Transformation of the Church, 1780–1830," *Baptist Quarterly* 25/4 (October 1973): 167–84.

Bible's authority, and the reaction of British Baptists was largely negative.[145] Two towering pastoral figures emerged within the English Baptist community to represent the polarities created by the dispute: C. H. Spurgeon and John Clifford. Charles Haddon Spurgeon (1834–1892) was acclaimed as the outstanding Baptist pulpit master of the period and included among the most illustrious Christians of the modern era. In his case, personal narrative played a much more significant role in shaping his thought than educational preparation or mentoring by another. Such personalized experience and its consequent expression was and would continue to be genetically important to Baptist theology.

Spurgeon was initially reared by godly grandparents in the context of an Independent setting near Colchester. This was due to "unfavorable circumstances" in Colchester—probably inadequate housing. Upon his return home, his deeply religious parents continued his care and nurture. In this atmosphere he was introduced to reading the Puritan classics: first John Bunyan's *Pilgrim's Progress*, later the works of Richard Alleine and Richard Baxter. His conversion was according to a classic Puritan "morphology" or pattern of conversion[146]:

> When but young in years I felt much sorrow for sin. Day and night God's hand was heavy on me. If I slept at night I dreamed of the bottomless pit, and when I awoke I seemed to feel the misery I had dreamed.... I used to say "If God does not send me to hell, he ought to do it"...When I was in the hands of the Holy Spirit under conviction of sin, I had a clear and sharp sense of the justice of God... Though I dearly venerate the men that occupy those pulpits now, I am bound to say that I never once heard them preach the gospel. I mean by that they preached truths, great truths that were fitting to many of their congregations, spiritually minded people; but what I wanted to know was—How can I get my sins forgiven? And they never once told me that.

---

[145] See the discussion in Ernest A. Payne, *The Baptist Union: A Short History* (London: Carey Kingsgate, 1958), 121 ff. for a fuller treatment.

[146] The term "morphology" has been useful among scholars of Puritanism where clinical analyses of conversion experiences were common among Puritans. See Jonathan Edwards, *The Great Awakening*, edited by C.C. Goen (New Haven: Yale University Press, 1972) 25-32.

Blessed be God for that poor local preacher. He read his text. It was as much as he could do. The text was: "Look unto me and be ye saved, all the ends of the earth." He was an ignorant man, he could not say much, he was obliged to keep to his text…Now that simple way of putting the Gospel had enlisted my attention, and a ray of light poured into my heart. Stooping down, he looked under the gallery and said, "Young man, you are very miserable…" And he called out with all his might, "Young man, look! In God's name look, and look now. Look! Look! Look! You have nothing to do but look and live…" I thought I could dance all the way home. I could understand what John Bunyan meant when he declared he wanted to tell all the crows on the ploughed land about his conversion… Between half past ten, when I entered that chapel and half past twelve, when I returned home, what a change had taken place in me.[147]

All of the emphatic elements in Spurgeon's unique ministry could thus be found reflected in his own conversion. He was guilt-ridden, faced with the justice of God, and confronted with an ultimatum. He searched the existing mainstream churches and found them wanting. He became critical of "non-evangelical" pastors. And, finally, he had a demonstrative conversion experience that transformed his outlook and behavior.

Spurgeon's schooling included primary school and another school at Newmarket in Cambridgeshire. He yearned to take up studies in a theological college, especially impressed with the Puritan heritage of several of the Cambridge University colleges, notably Emmanuel and Sidney Sussex. His closest but failed possibility came in an aborted interview with Joseph Angus of the Baptist College at Stepney. Spurgeon took the event as a sign that he should not tarry in college, but go directly into ministry. He began to preach through a ministry of outreach sponsored by St. Andrews Baptist Church in Cambridge and soon moved to London. Beginning in 1854, he served the New Park Street Congregation for thirty-eight years, thirty of which were in the Metropolitan Tabernacle, that Spurgeon built for the church, one of the most unusual worship structures in the Baptist world.

---

[147]Excerpts quoted in Ernest W. Bacon, *Spurgeon: Heir of the Puritans* (London: George Allen and Unwin, 1967) 20–24.

152 Genetic History of Baptist Thought

Shaped largely by Calvinist theology and the Puritan tradition in particular, nine recurring themes emerge in Spurgeon's thought.[148] These are the divinely inspired, fully authoritative Scriptures; the sovereignty of God; predestination and election; the deity of Christ; substitutionary atonement; justification by faith; practical holiness; perseverance of the saints; and the return of Christ. He was especially drawn to the Puritan Richard Sibbes, who declared that "the special work of the preacher is to lay open Christ, to hold up the tapestry and unfold the mysteries of Christ himself."[149] His appreciation of Calvinism was deep: "We believe that Calvinism has in it a conservative force which helps to hold men to the vital truth, and therefore we are sorry to see any quitting it who have once accepted it."[150] As Willis Glover and others have pointed out, Spurgeon's Calvinism was nonetheless decidedly tainted by evangelistic preaching. The oft-quoted line from Spurgeon illustrates the point: "Lord, hasten to bring in all Thine elect, and then elect some more."[151] All commentators on Spurgeon agree that love for Christ was his greatest passion: "In his first sermon in the Metropolitan Tabernacle he had said: 'I would propose that the subject of the ministry of this house should be the Person of Jesus Christ, the only mediator between God and man.... in the solitariness of His redemptive work, and as the sole King of His church.'"[152] The person and work of Christ was also the topic of his last public sermon.

Not only did Spurgeon preach on these great themes, he built a library of Puritan works that rivaled any collection in Britain.[153] This library became a reference point for students who came to study with Spurgeon

---

[148] Ibid., 110–19. This is an abridgement of Bacon's helpful categories. For a study of Calvinism in Spurgeon, see Kent E. Sweatman, "The Doctrines of Calvinism in the Preaching of Charles Haddon Spurgeon" (Ph.D. diss., Southwestern Baptist Theological Seminary, 1998).

[149] Cited in Lewis Drummond, "Charles Haddon Spurgeon," in *Theologians of the Baptist Tradition*, 132.

[150] *The Downgrade Controversy: Collected Materials Which Reveal the Viewpoint of the Late Charles Haddon Spurgeon* (Pasadena TX: Pilgrim Publications, n.d.) 15.

[151] Quoted in Willis B. Glover, *Evangelical Nonconformists and Higher Criticism in the Nineteenth Century* (London: Independent Press, 1954), 92.

[152] Ibid., 119.

[153] Ibid., 133. Lewis Drummond demonstrates how broad Spurgeon's reading list of Christian classics was: Tertullian, Origen, Gregory of Nazianus, George Fox, the Quakers, John Howe, and John Owen. Among the Baptists found in his sermons were John Gill and Andrew Fuller.

at the Pastor's College. Here was an educational program that directed theological discourse to the practical needs of church and ministry.[154] During his lifetime, Spurgeon himself lectured on preaching, witnessing techniques, pulpit gestures, and the life of prayer, as well as Christian classics from Augustine to Thomas a' Kempis, poetry from Milton to Coleridge, and books of the Bible. Though criticized by no less than T. R. Glover, Public Orator of Cambridge University and president of the Baptist Union, as "theologically amateurish," over nine hundred students passed through the College in Spurgeon's ministry and he continued to enjoy an ever-widening influence through editions of his *Lectures to My Students* (1890) and *The Sword and Trowel* (1865-1892).

C. H. Spurgeon also left behind a theological legacy that was not as readily evident as his other contributions to the religious dialogue of the era. He was not timid about theological controversy and confrontation. In 1864 Spurgeon preached a memorable sermon on the gospel-order of faith's profession followed by baptism. He strongly attacked the liturgical churches that practiced infant baptism, openly criticizing the Book of Common Prayer wherein it stated that through baptism a child is made a member of Christ, a child of God, and an inheritor of the kingdom of heaven. Spurgeon pointed out the fallacy of the prayer book's assertion that the act of baptism regenerates and grafts candidates into the church. At one juncture he exclaimed, "That baptism saved the soul was the most atrocious lie that had dragged millions down to hell!"[155] Not only did he antagonize clergy in the liturgical churches with his public rejection of the traditional sacramental theology, Spurgeon also alienated ecumenically-inclined friends among Baptists and his own theological coreligionists in the Evangelical Alliance who thought themselves "evangelical" but not Baptist.

In the 1880s he became embroiled in a another public theological dispute. This was an editorial war over what he called liberal, destructive theological positions in the leadership and colleges of the Baptist Union. Dubbed the Downgrade Controversy (taken from an 1887 comment in

---

[154] For a full discussion of Spurgeon's unique ideas on theological education see Nina Reid Maroney, "Spurgeon and British Evangelical Theological Education," in *Theological Education in the Evangelical Tradition* (Grand Rapids: Baker Book House, 1996); and, Michael J. Quicke and Ian M. Randall, "Spurgeon's College," *American Baptist Quarterly* 18: 2 (June 1999): 118–31.

[155] Quoted in ibid., 125.

his periodical *The Sword and Trowel*), Spurgeon virtually declared war
on the Union.[156] He declared that, theologically, the Union was "going
downhill at breakneck speed."[157] He noticed less veneration for the
Scriptures, a lessening of the importance of Christ in Arian and Socinian
tendencies, an emphasis upon the theory of evolution, the introduction of
the New Theology in Baptist colleges, and a general belief in the
evolution of the spiritual life from human nature.[158] Additionally, he
accused the Union of widespread ethical and moral lapses among its
membership, such as increased theatre attendance, card playing, and
dancing.

Spurgeon characterized what he asserted was the liberal direction of
the Union as follows: "A new religion has been initiated, which is no
more Christianity than chalk is cheese."[159] He blamed in particular the
insidious influence of German higher criticism of the Bible, referring to
it as "the German poison," or the cutting up the Bible with "German
scissors."[160] As Willis Glover has shown, Spurgeon charged that specific
doctrinal substitutions were taking place: the atonement was less
emphasized than the incarnation, eternal punishment or the annihilation
of the wicked was being replaced by universal salvation, and most
troubling, the inerrant Scriptures were being interpreted in an
evolutionary, historical sense.[161] Throughout this and other debates,
Spurgeon gradually began to define his version of an "evangelical
theology"[162] as he defended what he thought to be the essentials of
orthodox Calvinism.

---

[156] The first two articles that appeared unsigned, but under the title "Downgrade,"
have been attributed to Robert Shindler, the Baptist pastor at Addlestone. Spurgeon
followed with additional articles on the topic. See Payne, *Baptist Union*, 131 ff.

[157] See Mark T. E. Hopkins, "Spurgeon's Opponents in the Downgrade Controversy,"
Baptist Quarterly 32 (1988): 274–94; and his sequel, "The Downgrade Controversy: New
Evidence (S. H. Booth Correspondence)," *Baptist Quarterly* 35 (1994): 262–78.

[158]"Our Reply to Sundry Critics and Enquirers," in *Downgrade Controversy:
Documents*, 25.

[159] "Another Word Concerning the Down-Grade," in ibid., 17.

[160] Glover, *Evangelical Nonconformists*, 40.

[161] Ibid., 163.

[162] For a unique view from the standpoint of William Landels, see Michael Nichols,
"The Downgrade Controversy: A Neglected Protagonist," *Baptist Quarterly* 32/6 (April
1988): 260–73.

Ultimately unsatisfied with the Union's inability to achieve an acceptable doctrinal consensus, Spurgeon pulled the Metropolitan Tabernacle out of fellowship with the association and Union. "To pursue union at the expense of truth is treason to the Lord Jesus," he claimed.[163] What this produced was a legitimization of schism for the sake of theological beliefs. There was no use in further contending for the Union after 1890, because Spurgeon thought it "without form and void, and so it must remain." Spurgeon consequently told his readers in December 1888: "Cost what it may, to separate ourselves from those who separate themselves from the truth of God is not alone our liberty, but our duty."[164]

It has been noted from Spurgeon's position in and prior to the Downgrade Controversy, that he was confessional, that is, he believed a confession of faith would guarantee doctrinal purity and solidarity. He used the Second London Confession of Faith and agreed with much of the scope of the theological position taken by the Evangelical Alliance. In 1891, he and 29 others signed a three-paragraph statement that has come to be called "Mr. Spurgeon's Confession of Faith." The first paragraph was devoted entirely to Scripture, declaring: "the Bible does not merely *contain* the word of God, but *is* the Word of God." They further affirmed: "We accept Christ's own verdict over against the supposed discoveries of so-called higher criticism." Second, the confession dealt with "doctrines of grace." Listed categorically were the electing love of God, the propitiatory and substitutionary sacrifice of Christ, regeneration by the Holy Spirit, imputation of Christ's righteousness, justification, indwelling of the Holy Spirit, the hopeless perdition of all who reject Christ, and the personal pre-millennial return of Christ.[165] The confession was actually the work of an interdenominational "fraternal" or committee composed of Archibald Brown, G. D. Hooper, and H. Sinclair Patterson. Spurgeon did sign it, it was published widely, but Spurgeon's closest associates denied that it was his own particular confession of faith. The document was roundly

---

[163] "A Fragment Upon the Downgrade Controversy," in *Downgrade Controversy, Documents,* 34.

[164] "Attempts at the Impossible," in ibid., 36, 72.

[165] "Mr. Spurgeon's Confession of Faith," in *Downgrade Controversy: Documents,* 85–87.

denounced by Baptist editors as "Shibboleth," a step backwards toward the Dark Ages, and notable for who was not among the subscribers.[166]

Spurgeon's theological genes were clearly seen in several enduring patterns. First, he linked Baptists with the Puritan tradition and caused a revival of interest among Baptists in that literature. Second, he gave renewed impetus to conservative thinking about the Scriptures and modern theology. He boldly opposed higher criticism and what he broadly termed the destructive influences of theological education. Not only did the Strict Baptists take heart from Spurgeon, the seeds were laid for the next generation to be labeled as "fundamentalists." Third, he emphasized a simplistic evangelical theology devoid of the thorny issues raised in the New Theology. Finally, he gave license and example to those who found the newer alternative theological perspectives intolerable and sought to separate themselves from the more liberal Christians who embraced the trends. Lastly, Spurgeon continued to demonstrate the remarkable theological influence of an eminent pastor and vibrant congregation upon published theology and theological education.

John Clifford (1836–1923) was the second major figure among nineteenth-century British Baptist pastor-theologians. Of Methodist upbringing, Clifford was joined to the General Baptist congregation at Sawley while attending a Wesleyan school. Under the personal influence of his pastor, Richard J. Pike (also the first secretary of the General Baptist Missionary Society), he sensed a call to ministry and studied at the Midlands Baptist College at Leicester. During his three-year course of study, he was most influenced among the faculty by William Underwood, the principal, and Thomas Stevenson, a tutor. Though Clifford won prizes in Greek, history, and Latin, he complained there were no textbooks and that examinations terrified the students. He read heavily in John Bunyan and John Wesley, a preference he maintained throughout his life. He was much impressed with visiting clergy-instructors, including John Angell James, James Parsons, and J. P. Mursell. Clifford served Praed Street Baptist Church in one of London's working class districts, and later Westbourne Park, a well-to-do congregation that he served until retirement. While at Praed Street, Clifford earned the B.A., B.Sc., and M.A. degrees, as well as a degree in

---

[166] Ibid., 86.

law from the University of London. One of the cleverest clergy of his era, a fellow member of a ministerial club characterized him as having an "adventurous intellect, bringing a touch of incandescence to everything he wrote and said."[167]

Doctrinally, Clifford was in tune with the times. His interest in education kept him abreast of biblical scholarship and theological trends. His proximity to Parliament gave him an exposure to world order and social needs. Much influenced by German scholarship, he moved from a progressive to a liberal stance over the course of half a century of ministry, and in so doing became the particular nemesis of evangelicals like Charles H. Spurgeon. He entered the controversy over the critical investigation of the Bible in support of scholarship: "We must study the contents of the Bible in the same way as we do those of any book...with the same detachment of mind; the same readiness to defer to rightful authority; and the same use of the best tools which can be had." He declared openly the intermingling of the historical disciplines and biblical scholarship.[168] His view of inspiration affirmed the "earthen vessel" nature of the Bible and he rejected many of the prevailing evangelical theories about the composition and inspiration of Scripture. Somewhat disingenuously, Clifford advised young ministerial students to avoid discussion of apparent discrepancies in the Bible with potential converts to the faith because he thought the difficulties to be of a "surface nature."[169] Following many continental and British liberals, Clifford saw the greatest value to be drawn from the Scripture was "to see God in Christ reconciling the world to himself."[170]

Clifford's doctrine of the church proceeded from his General Baptist perspective. He rejected Calvinist teachings for a thoroughgoing Arminian principle that Christ made atonement for all men. Concomitant was his view that the gift of the Holy Spirit could be lost if not rightly reverenced and humbly obeyed. He embraced three principles regarding the church. First, the church was an independent and its membership open to all who confess faith in Christ. Second, baptism is the privilege of every believer but subject to every man's conscience. Third, the nature

---

[167] Ibid., 243.

[168] John Clifford, *The Inspiration and Authority of the Bible* (London: 1895) 34.

[169] Glover, *Evangelical Nonconformists*, 82.

[170] Quoted from Clifford's *Inspiration and Authority* (1892) in G. W. Byrt, *John Clifford: A Fighting Free Churchman* (London: The Kingsgate Press, 1947) 96–97.

of membership implies a brotherhood of workers, each of whom has individual gifts.[171] The openness of his polity and doctrine illustrated his own General Baptist background, but flew in the face of both Strict Baptists and Spurgeon's following of Puritan/Calvinistic teachings.

Clifford's theological influence reached far beyond his own pulpit. In 1870 he was appointed editor of the *General Baptist Magazine* and thereby given the opportunity to express his theological views and influence the merger of General and Particular Baptists in the Baptist Union during the subsequent fourteen years. As an outgrowth of his editorship and pastorates he published several titles of a popular theological kind, again building a following for a progressive Baptist theology.[172] As president of the General Baptist Union, the London Baptist Association, and the Baptist Union of Great Britain, Clifford brought a sense of statesmanship to the organizations' responses against the sharp rebukes and grave charges of heresy emanating from C. H. Spurgeon. When Spurgeon resigned from the Baptist Union in 1888, it was Clifford and two other leaders who met with Spurgeon to dissuade him.[173]

Clifford reduced Spurgeon's theological concerns to four: the atonement, Holy Scripture, referring to the fall of humankind as a fable, and denying the personality of the Holy Ghost. Clifford held that the general state of the Baptist ministry in Britain was much more theologically sound than Spurgeon thought, and "that nothing had been shed except the metaphysical conceptions of medieval philosophy"[174] as the basis of the Union. At the 1888 meeting of the Assembly, Clifford presided over the proceedings and was the principal author of the propounded theological declarations.[175] In his speech, he inveighed

---

[171] Ibid., 61–62.

[172] These titles include *Starting in Life, The Inspiration and Authority of the Bible, Is Life Worth Living,* and *The Gospel of World Brotherhood, According to Jesus.*

[173] Clifford recalled that Spurgeon appeared to hold little personal animosity, believing that he and Clifford held "vital evangelical truth" in common. Spurgeon did point out that he disliked a recent book of Clifford, doubtless *Battle of the Sacred Books* (London: E. Marlborough, 1888). Remarks recorded in Payne, *Baptist Union,* 129.

[174] James Marchant, *Dr. John Clifford, c.h.: Life, Letters, and Reminiscences* (London: Cassell and Co., 1924) 159.

[175] There is an interesting pro-Clifford account of the Baptist Union proceedings in Glover, *Evangelical Nonconformists,* 173–76, in which he points out that Spurgeon's opponents in the Baptist Union Council included Alexander Maclaren and James Culross

against creeds, clerical absolutism, theological tyranny, and "padlocks on the Bible." Instead, Clifford called upon his fellow ministers to "stand for Christ and Christ crucified...united by experience...opinions may divide, but life in Christ by the cross makes us one." When the vote came on a creedal statement styled after the likes of Spurgeon's confession, it was defeated almost unanimously.[176]

Freed from creedalism in his own denomination, Clifford moved ahead officially to affirm open communion among the churches. He saw in this a potential bond with the Congregationalists. Further, as he had become a leading nonconformist in the Protestant Christian community, he contended fervently for a united Free Church movement against Anglican Romanism. In the waning years of the Victorian era, his Baptist voice was heard advocating an egalitarian school system, temperance, passive resistance against the Great War (World War I), and religious liberty and humanitarianism following the cessation of the war.[177] As the first president of the Baptist World Alliance, John Clifford established an indelibly progressive-to-liberal quality to the emerging international identity of Baptists. His publications, numbering over one-hundred, spanned the years from 1872 to 1920 and touched upon every conceivable theological topic.[178] As his long career drew to a close, he summarized in six urgent principles a Baptist interpretation of Christianity much needed to address a new world order: the absolute authority of Jesus Christ; complete liberty of conscience; insistence upon personal faith as the basis of the Christian church; the autonomous character of religious societies; thoroughgoing repudiation of sacerdotal ministry as a means of grace; the love of God for all humankind, coupled with the sacrifice of Christ, and the gift of the Spirit to convince the world of sin.[179]

Throughout his ministry, John Clifford developed an antagonism to systematic theology that was to become increasingly influential in British Baptist life. "Systems of doctrine," he wrote, "are trifles light as air to

---

(neither of whom accepted scriptural inerrancy), as well as Samuel Cox, a well-known exponent of universal restoration.

[176] Marchant, *Dr. John Clifford,* 109, 111.

[177] See David Thompson, "John Clifford's Social Gospel," *Baptist Quarterly* 31/5 (January 1986): 199–218.

[178] There is a complete list in Marchant, *Dr. John Clifford,* 291–93.

[179] Clifford's speech to the Baptist World Alliance, 1923, quoted in ibid., 158.

souls that see God face to face in immediate fellowship with the Eternal Spirit."[180] He valued religious experience more highly than confessionalism. His open heritage as a General Baptist, what he perceived to be the burden of a confining theology in Spurgeon, and his own pastoral proclivity for the practical, pushed him away from traditional doctrinal formulations. His position and resulting influence among many Baptists in Great Britain caused him to become one of the most important theological influences of the era.[181]

There were other Baptist pastors in the late nineteenth century who engaged in theological reflection or work, but who were not necessarily pioneering in their approaches nor paradigmatic. Among these mentioned by historian John Briggs were James Martin (1821–1877) and Samuel Cox (1826–1893). A Stepney graduate under Gotch and Davies, Martin was a Ward Scholar at the University of Bonn who later translated substantial German theological scholarship for the English publisher, T. and T. Clark. A leading conservative evangelical thinker, Martin was devoted to biblical works and was avowedly anti-creedal. He was pastor at Derby Road, Nottingham, and later in Australia. Cox, also a Stepney graduate, served Mansfield Road, Nottingham, for a quarter of a century. As pastor, he founded and edited *The Expositor,* whose pages introduced many English pastors to German scholarship. Cox ventured into difficult theological questions such as the finality of Christ, new concepts of the atonement, the nature of eternal life, and the teaching of hell, the last of which he found unbiblical. The author of twelve volumes of Bible exposition, Cox was dismissed as editor of the paper he founded for heterodox views on the inspiration of Scripture and eschatology.[182]

Other pastor/theologians worthy of note were J. G. Greenhough (1843–1933) and John Howard Hinton (1791–1873). Greenhough was born in Germany, educated at Rawdon College, and took two degrees at London University. In 1879 he became F. B. Meyer's successor at Victoria Road, Leicester, and won acclaim for his preaching capacities.

---

[180] John Clifford, "Baptist Theology," *Contemporary Review,* 53 (1888): 505–506 quoted in Glover, *Evangelical Nonconformist,* 94.

[181] On Clifford, see W. S. Stroud, "John Clifford," *Baptist Quarterly* 6 (1932–1933): 304–311); and J. H. Rushbrooke, "John Clifford: Pastor, Social Reformer, National Leader, First President, the Baptist World Alliance," *Baptist Quarterly* 11/11 (October 1944): 288–94.

[182] Briggs, *English Baptists in the Nineteenth Century,* 167–71, 194–95, has a useful assessment of Cox's work.

He inclined toward the new theology and drew the ire of none other than C. H. Spurgeon. While many characterized Greenhough as "intensely evangelical," Spurgeon disliked his Arminian tilt and his tendency toward euphemistic language. For example, when speaking of the socially upscale setting in which he led worship, Greenhough said, "We should never forget that the gospel we preach is a gospel of radiant gladness and confirmed optimism, and he who makes a doleful song of it, has never read its deeper meaning."[183] He obviously was not enamored with the Puritans or with their most devoted contemporary protégé. Regarding those who turned on Spurgeon's every word, he mused, "We need as far as possible to drink our inspiration, not through human channels however amazingly made or bravely carved by doctors and reformers and sympathizers, but at the fountainhead."[184] Spurgeon's response was to call for the expulsion of Greenhough from the Union.[185]

John Howard Hinton was pastor of congregations at Reading and Devonshire Square in London, also serving as secretary of both the Baptist Union and the Baptist Missionary Society. Hinton claimed his theology was entirely his own creation, having trained in medicine at Oxford, with two years at Bristol Baptist College and later at the University of Edinburgh. He produced a voluminous amount of published writing on a wide variety of topics, including voluntarism, morals, and religious experience. Claiming to be a moderate Calvinist in the tradition of Jonathan Edwards and Andrew Fuller, Hinton veered between Calvinism and Arminian tendencies, hoping to receive the mantle left by Fuller.[186] He publicly announced, "the creedal inheritance of the past...is no longer authoritative," demonstrating theologically iconoclastic tendencies. He wrote that original sin was not a valid

---

[183] J. G. Greenhough, *The Conduct of Public Worship* (London: Baptist Union, n.d.) 57.

[184] *Inaugural Address of Reverend J. G. Greenhough* (Darby: Williams Printing, 1893) 17.

[185] Payne, *Baptist Union*, 133.

[186] Hinton offered a cogent analysis of the theological differentiation among Baptists in England about 1860: General Baptists who preached general redemption; Particular Baptists who preached particular redemption, but who were first subdivided among high and moderate Calvinists, and secondly among those who practiced open communion and others who were strict communionists; six types in all. See his remarks in ibid., 85–86.

teaching, rather that "man is in a state of benignant probation."[187] Here
he reflected the theology of the New Measures from Charles Finney and
Calvin Colton in the United States, two for whom he held much
esteem.[188] In his *Essay on Man's Moral Responsibility*, Hinton concluded
that man is morally free, can act independently, possesses a competency
to perform the conduct required of him, and has a capacity to act on the
motives that inspire him. Further, Hinton believed man has an adequate
impulse that he called "conscience," reflecting some of the style of the
American educator-theologian, Francis Wayland.[189] This theological re-
positioning even from Fullerism, would provide Hinton with a
theological foundation for promoting the union of General and Particular
Baptists in the organization he served, but it would also draw ridicule
and criticism from both stalwart Particular Baptists and General Baptists
who could not accept his idea of redemption. Hinton persevered,
however, in his mediating theological stance, as Ian Sellers has argued,
because he recognized the tide of his era was against authoritative
religion. He also disliked the resurgent orthodox Calvinist position of
theologians in his own denomination such as the Haldanes and
Alexander Carson, theologians he considered "wooden and
impossible."[190]

In the end, Hinton was "rebuked by his elder brethren for innovations
in doctrine," only later again to be chastized for his vindication of
orthodoxy.[191] As he watched the effects of German scholarship and
British academic theologians, particularly A. B. Davidson at New
College, Edinburgh, he saw a sort of theological downgrading that
ultimately caused him to retreat from his earlier openness. By the 1870s
he was advocating more traditionally conservative dogma with respect to
topics such as sin, atonement, saving faith, and evangelism. Against a
tide of denominational ecumenism, particularly involving the
Congregationalists, Hinton held on to a belief in the primacy of gathered

[187] Quoted in Ian Sellers, "John Howard Hinton: Theologian," *Baptist Quarterly* 33/3
(July, 1989): 123.
[188] See his work, *The Test of Experience or The Voluntary Principle in the United
States* (1851).
[189] Sellers, "John Howard Hinton," 123–24. David Bebbington at the University of
Stirling believes that Hinton displayed influence from Dugald Stewart, the Scottish
rationalist at the University of Edinburgh, whose lectures Hinton knew as a student.
[190] Ibid, 121.
[191] Payne, *Baptist Union*, 85.

churches, built as they were on similar principles and character of those who belong to them.[192] He was combative, individualistic, evangelistic, and rationalistic—adjectives that his friend, C. M. Birrell, thought precursors of the "Age of Spurgeon." Later observers saw in Hinton the future of twentieth-century British Baptist life.[193]

Pastors were crucial in the making of the first three centuries of British Baptist thought. Their contributions included a fully orbed doctrine of the church, an evolved understanding of the atonement of Christ, and a changing doctrine of Scripture that either embraced or challenged higher critical methodologies. Some pastors remained committed to the older formulations, sustaining a Calvinism that seemed virtually unchanged from its seventeenth-century moorings. As servants of various organizations in Baptist life, pastors gave a defined shape to Baptist mission and ministry, and they created an identifiable corpus of significant theological literature. Most of all, pastors were spokesmen for their local congregations, the fundamental units of Baptist polity.

SUMMARY

Across three centuries, the English Baptist pastoral ministry was a definable source of Baptist theology. Baptist ministers were "carriers" of genetic traits. Some they transmitted, as it were, *in toto*. Others they modified within the context of their pastoral ministries. Pastors even created new genetic characteristics that subsequent Baptists would receive as a legacy. Theology for the typical pastor was applied in context. Thus, questions of order and organization more often dominated their thinking and writing than did speculative or doctrinal issues. As we have seen, those questions most often included sacramental concerns such as the meaning of baptism, who should be admitted to the Lord's Supper, and whether to employ the imposition of hands. Other polity questions included church discipline, authority, and congregational life. First day worship versus sabbatarian practice was a viable issue in the first century of Baptist life. Later, Baptist pastors debated the atonement of Christ, itself in reality a disguised question of evangelism versus Christian nurture in the mission of the church. And still later, English Baptist ministers spoke out on the person and work of Christ, in response

---

[192] Here he reflected an uncanny sociological understanding of church and society that was advanced well beyond any of his Baptist contemporaries.

[193] Noted in Sellers, "John Howard Hinton," 129.

to leading Christian thinkers in other traditions in Europe and North America.

It would be both unfair and inaccurate to argue that Baptists were not concerned with serious theology but merely with matters of church order. To underscore the assertion of William T. Whitley, their distinctive theological feature is the doctrine of the Church.[194] To them, the visible church was the kingdom of God, the very center of God's redemptive purposes. The Bible was the sole source of Christian doctrine and their approach to understanding the faith was "biblical" theology, that is, theological reflection upon the text of Scripture. The essential purpose of theology for these ministers was typically a search for a theological basis in Scripture regarding the life of the church, ministry, and mission. For example, to these Christian leaders the imposition of hands was not merely a liturgical act as it was practiced in the Establishment church. For Baptists it signified the presence and empowerment of the Holy Spirit, upon which they built their doctrine of the Spirit. If God speaks through his Word to his people the church, then, the task of theology, especially for a Baptist minister, was to derive the message and purposes of God from Holy Scripture for the enlightenment of the saints. "Jesus as Lord of the church" became for such Baptists the all-empowering source of authority in Scripture.

As a source of Baptist thought, British Baptist ministers represented a variety of theological orientations. From the outset there was friction between advocates of limited and general atonement, leading to fracture and pejorative labeling between the Arminian and Calvinistic factions. There were also represented among Baptists sabbatarian thinkers, universalists, unitarians, hyper-Calvinists, and evangelical Calvinists. The spectrum of Baptist thought exhibited in British pastoral ministries during the eighteenth and nineteenth centuries was indeed broad.

---

[194] Whitley, *History of British Baptists*, 4.

CHAPTER 4

BRITISH BAPTIST ACADEMIC
THEOLOGIANS

> The universities are not quite designed and furnished as
> schools of the prophets. I do not think they are best calculated to
> supply that peculiar kind of inspiration which the Nonconformist
> ministry needs. They are well fitted for the making of gentlemen
> and scholars; but pastoral experience and preaching fervour are
> better found elsewhere...If we could combine the advantage of
> Oxford with the training and experience furnished in one of our
> theological halls...that would be the best thing possible.[1]
>
> J. G. Greenhough, 1893

Increasingly, serious theological reflection took place within small
college faculties closely related to both the churches and Baptist
organizational life. Here was to be found a fourth major component of
the genetic history of Baptist thought. Those who taught in the academies
and colleges sought training in the universities and colleges of the day,
where theological questions drove the discussions to broader areas of
interest than those having a perceived immediate impact upon the local
congregation. One contemporary historian has listed at least two salient
reasons for the founding of nonconformist colleges by the eighteenth-
century Baptists: first, to provide a committed ministry that would
advance evangelical religion; second, to improve the capacities of those
who entered the ministry.[2] Issues raised by the Reformers and the early
church came to be of interest to Baptist academic theologians.
Importantly, they came to employ the most advanced methods of biblical

---

[1] J. G. Greenhough, *Inaugural Address of Reverend J. G. Greenhough as Warden of
Midland Baptist College, 1892–93* (Derby: Williams Printing, 1893) 10.

[2] Dale A. Johnson, *The Changing Shape of English Nonconformity, 1825–1925* (New
York: Oxford University Press, 1999) 20.

criticism to ascertain the meaning of the Scripture, always a hallmark of
Baptist interest. In some key areas scholarly theologians led their
constituencies into new doctrinal understandings and theological
emphases. Among the salient topics that these educated Baptist
theologians addressed were matters of epistemology, as well as an
exploration of whether Baptists could build and maintain a theological
system.

Among Baptists, Christian "higher education" generally meant some
manner of training for ministry.[3] This came first in the form of
mentoring, whereby candidates for pastoral ministry served under a
senior pastor. Prominent examples of this were found in the ministries of
John Gill in London, and William Steadman in the North. As more
candidates came forth and the limited number of qualified mentors
available to protégés became more evident, the need for institutions
devoted to education was increasingly recognized. The first such
institution was Bristol Baptist College, evolved from the Broadmead
Church and given lasting financial support through a trust bequeathed by
layman Edward Terrill. In London both the General Baptists and the
Calvinistic Baptists started academies.[4] The first faculties were pastors
who took on the teaching load in addition to serving their congregations.
As permanent facilities were provided and the curricula grew from year
to year, the academies evolved into colleges specializing in their
particular courses of training. In some instances, arts courses
supplemented theological courses. After the mid-nineteenth century,
following the lead of Congregationalists, Baptist theological educators
looked for ways and means to upgrade their schools to provide the
churches with a more academically trained and learned ministry. Some
thought the answer was H. R. Reynolds's 1865 proposal to set up an
independent *Senatus Academicus* that would administer examinations

---

[3] Several of the schools in the twentieth century experimented with general education
and housed students from other curricula in nearby universities, essentially providing a
Christian setting for university studies. Spurgeon's College offered courses for various
Christian workers other than pastors, and in the late 1980s Regent's Park, Oxford, offered
integrated programs of theology, literature, and culture.

[4] The first school of its kind to receive the official blessing of the denomination was
Trosnant Academy in Wales. It was founded and opened in 1732. See Selwyn Gummer,
"Trosnant Academy," *Baptist Quarterly* 19 (1938–1939): 417–23.

and issue diplomas.[5] Others, such as Andrew Fairbairn, suggested the integration of theological training for pastors more fully into the standing curricula of the universities. Still others wanted the churches and/or the Baptist Union to take greater responsibility for the funding of colleges. As we shall see, Baptists went in all three directions.

Moving with the times, the stronger Baptist colleges sought affiliation with existing universities, particularly the "red-brick" institutions like Bristol, Leeds, Nottingham, and Manchester. Baptists enjoyed demonstrable success with this transition in Manchester and Bristol. With much hope, Baptists were proactive in founding London University, although their real influence was limited. The plan to institute a Nonconformist theological faculty at London did not materialize. Eventually, Regent's Park College in London moved to Oxford as a permanent private hall, and a connection for Baptists within the ancient university framework was solidified.[6]

The transition from pastor-theologians to academic theologians took place over several generations, from about 1780 to 1850. In many instances, pastors led in the development of the academies and colleges, while encouraging biblical scholars, theologians, and historians to seek higher education and fill the ranks of the faculties. Historian Deryck Lovegrove attaches the emergence of new academies to evangelical Calvinism that brought with it emphases of preaching and personal devotion. An important model behind the Baptist schools was the Countess of Huntingdon's institution at Trevecca, inspired by George Whitefield. The first professional theologians among Baptists began to appear in the British tradition associated with Bristol and Stepney Colleges.[7]

---

[5] In 1879, eight congregational colleges agreed to constitute the *Senatus Academicus* and eventually seven Baptist colleges joined the scheme that survived till just after 1900. For a discussion of the *Senatus* proposal, compare H. R. Reynolds, ed., *Ecclesia: A Second Series of Essays on Theological and Ecclesiastical Questions* (London: Hodder and Stoughton, 1871) with Johnson, *English Nonconformity*, 39–47.

[6] On the Baptist contribution in ministerial education, see J.H.Y. Briggs, *The English Baptists of the 19th Century* (Didcot: The Baptist Historical Society, 1994), 70-95.

[7] An important debate among historians prevails over whether an older form of academies faded as the newer evangelical types emerged. Deryck Lovegrove, *Established Church, Sectarian People: Itinerancy and the Transformation of English Dissent 1780–1830* (Cambridge: Cambridge University Press, 1988) 67–68 follows the earlier thesis of Elie Halevy, *England in 1815*, trans. E. I. Watkins and D. A. Barker (New York:

BRISTOL BAPTIST COLLEGE

In many ways, the college at Bristol was an outgrowth of an extended pastoral ministry. Located in the commercial section of Bristol, Broadmead Church evolved as a congregation of well-to-do, socially informed persons who were leaders in the religious community. Among the church's first pastors was a courageous woman, Dorothy Hazzard. Other pastors included Thomas Hardcastle, Andrew Gifford, Bernard Foskett, and Hugh Evans. A prominent layman, Edward Terrill, recognized the particular mission of the Broadmead church within its region of influence. He made it possible through a bequest in his estate for the pastors of the church to train younger men in the ministry. A permanent program of mentorship thus began. Terrill especially favored instruction in the biblical languages and an outreach among the smaller churches.

Under the presidency of Caleb Evans, the Bristol Academy evolved into a College, supported by the Bristol Baptist Education Society. Evans required fifteen to twenty students at a time to read the elementary Latin classics, while he lectured on theological topics. As part of their curriculum, each preached at the Broadmead Church, to be critiqued by Evans. The course of study at this time was hampered by the predominance of Welsh students who spoke English poorly. Evans' pedagogical method was recitation, which inhibited progress among the keener students. Few went on to advanced studies in Greek and Hebrew.[8] Some felt the literary work burdensome and formed associations for experiential conversation.

Recent historians have pointed out that a peculiar kind of theology developed at Bristol that transformed the West Country and beyond.[9] Against a backdrop in the mid-eighteenth century of lifeless, doctrinaire Calvinism, Unitarianism, Arianism, and anti-trinitarian thought, coupled

---

Peter Smith, 1949) 418–19. Bristol historians like Norman Moon and Roger Hayden argue persuasively that the evangelical ethos had long resided in Bristol Academy, founded in 1679, and its antecedents. The issues are well summarized in Briggs, *English Baptists*, 74–75.

[8] Thomas Steadman, *Memoir of the Reverend William Steadman, D.D.* (London: Thomas Ward and Co., 1838) 37.

[9] Roger Hayden, "Evangelical Calvinism among Eighteenth Century Baptists, with Particular Reference to Bernard Foskett, Hugh and Caleb Evans, and the Bristol Baptist Academy" (Ph.D. diss., Keele University, 1991).

with dry intellectual communication, the leaders at Bristol stressed an evangelical form of Calvinism. Their objective was to train "able and evangelical men." Closely akin to John Wesley's thought, that had roots just around the corner from Broadmead in Wesley's New Room, plus Andrew Fuller's works, the Broadmead pastors stressed mission and conviction. One writer pointed out that as early as the mid-seventeenth century, the writers of article 34 of the Somerset Confession in the West Country thought it was the duty of churches to "send forth such men as are fitly gifted and qualified through the Spirit of Christ to preach the Gospel to the world."[10] Caleb Evans, the leading faculty member of the eighteenth century, openly acknowledged the "heart-cheering doctrine as worthy of all acceptation."[11] Little wonder that Bristol graduates emerged imbued with a church-planting conviction, a zeal for missions, and a characteristically deep sense of piety. These included Benjamin Francis, John Ash, Samuel Pearce, John Fawcett, and John Sutcliff. Perhaps the most influential of all the early graduates were Morgan Edwards and William Steadman. Edwards would leave a deep impression upon the American Baptist scene and Steadman would pioneer his own theological school in the north of England.

Caleb Evans's successor was John Ryland who cast a long shadow as pastor of Broadmead Baptist Church and principal of the College for over twenty-five years. Ryland (1753–1825) was the son of John Collett Ryland, a high Calvinist in the tradition of John Brine and John Gill. The father served Carter Lane Church in Northampton and taught school. In addition to his father's tutelage, young John Ryland read with appreciation Robert Hall, Sr.'s *Help to Zion's Travellers* and the works of American Jonathan Edwards, particularly his *Treatise on Religious Affections*. He corresponded widely with religious luminaries such as the Anglican evangelical John Newton, Andrew Fuller, John Sutcliff, and William Carey. A person of national and ecumenical importance, Ryland was one of the leading evangelicals of his era.[12]

---

[10] Somerset Confession, XXXIV.

[11] Norman S. Moon, *Education for Ministry: Bristol Baptist College 1679–1979* (Bristol: Bristol Baptist College, 1979) 18–21.

[12] Leonard G. Champion, "The Theology of John Ryland: Its Sources and Influences," *Baptist Quarterly* 38/1 (January 1979): 17–29, develops the major themes and relations in his life.

Ryland was an effective apologist for the Baptists at a crucial point in their development. He stood clearly against Arminianism, holding fast to the sovereignty of God and efficacious grace. Against the Socinians and Unitarians, he maintained the full deity of Christ. Like Robert Hall, Sr., he held that ministers had an obligation to preach the gospel to all mankind and that hearers had an obligation to respond to the gospel or receive the condemnation that fell consequently upon them. To the antinominan charge, he preached of moral obligations in the life of faith. In general, for Ryland, the overwhelming sovereignty of God was the most powerful incentive one needed in evangelism. He was paradigmatic of the eighteenth-century Particular Baptist tradition, evincing clear genetic traits from prominent predecessors in the faith.

Ryland's influence in Britain and elsewhere was profound. It was likely Ryland who introduced Andrew Fuller to the writings of Jonathan Edwards. Following a lifelong friendship, he preached Fuller's funeral in 1815. Ryland was also a primary influence upon William Carey, having baptized him. Carey was much taken with his interpretation of Calvinism and its effects upon missions. Their correspondence, that spanned the seas between Britain and India, lasted until Ryland's death. As principal of Bristol Baptist College for over three decades, Ryland continued the academic regimen of Evans but introduced a new missionary zeal in the context of the Baptist Missionary Society. His grand design for theological education was "to make young ministers better scholars." His students included eight graduates who went on to advanced studies and/or leadership in the Baptist Union, including Francis A. Cox, John Howard Hinton, James Acworth, and Edward Steane. As Bristol's principal, he led the college beyond its character as a mentoring program and oversaw the building of the first collegiate building dedicated to academic use among British Baptists. When the foundation for the Stepney institution was laid in 1810–1812, it was the eminent John Ryland of Bristol who told subscribers, "the minister must be influenced by an ardent desire to know, enjoy, resemble, serve and glorify God himself."[13]

The next principal of Bristol College led it into a "quiet period." Thomas S. Crisp (1788–1868) was diligent, but unremarkable in his leadership. He had worked with John Ryland and was expected to carry

---

[13] Quoted in Champion, "Theology of Ryland," 24.

on his direction. Crisp had a Congregational background and spent two years at Glasgow University. He was well connected with Anglicans and Congregationalists and steered the college on a conservative course for over four decades. Often in poor health, he managed the few students who enrolled at Bristol in biblical languages but left the theological subjects to his tutors, Edgar Huxtable and F. W. Gotch. It is easy to conclude that it was during this period that Bristol's historic leadership among the Baptist theological colleges slipped behind the more recently established institution at Stepney.[14]

Bristol's congruency with the new theological trends began with Frederick William Gotch (1808–1890). Gotch was descended from a Kettering family that was integrally involved in the mission of William Carey. He was educated at Bristol College (2 years), then at Trinity College, Dublin, where he received two degrees. He taught philosophy and science for two years at Stepney, afterwards returning to Bristol to lecture in the classics, logic, and rhetoric. Through Gotch's relationships while in London, Bristol achieved the right to present students for University of London degrees. This enhanced its academic standing. After several years as tutor, Gotch became principal of the college in 1868, concurrent with his presidency of the Baptist Union.

A scientifically oriented thinker, Gotch was most interested in biblical studies. He set the stage for the debate of several important theological issues of the day. First, bowing to the higher critics, Gotch saw no future in any theory of verbal inspiration of Scripture. He wrote of Louis Gaussen's position on verbal plenary inspiration, "It is a useless and illusory statement." Instead, Gotch stressed the inspiration of those who wrote the words of the Scripture. "Inspiration pertains to the teachers of the truth, and in a secondary and derived sense, the truths they taught."[15] He openly recognized multiple authors for Old Testament books and declared that the Christian faith stood on a foundation of Christocentric reconciliation rather than upon a series of ancient presuppositions. "Christ is the centre of the revelation God has given to us... the Bible

---

[14] Moon, *Education for Ministry*, 42–47.

[15] F. W. Gotch, "The Inspiration of the Holy Scriptures," *A Discourse Delivered before the Bristol Association of Baptist Churches June 12, 1851* (London: Hamilton, Adams, 1851) 7, 23, 25. Gotch preferred to speak of inspiration only with respect to the New Testament.

speaks to man in popular, not in scientific language."[16] This second contribution, a response to biblical criticism through a new doctrine of Christ, much resembled that of the American Baptist William Newton Clarke, who arrived at much the same theological place at about the same time. Third, Gotch embraced evolutionary theory because of his fondness for free scientific enquiry. His influence in this regard on behalf of Baptists was broad, serving as one of the most respected members of the ecumenical Old Testament Revision Committee charged with preparing an up-to-date translation of the Bible in the 1870s. This proved, however, to be a bit of theological embarrassment because of the identification of the Unitarian Vance Smith with the translation and its relative unpopularity in Baptist church life.[17]

In a very real sense, Gotch was among a handful of English Baptist leaders who signaled an end to the era of theological confessions. He stressed the principle of individuality that he held distinguished Baptists from other denominations: "A Christian nation as distinct from individual Christians that compose the nation is, from my point of view, an impossibility. A Christian family, as distinct from the individual Christians that compose the family, is equally impossible." Here was an important indicator of the individualistic, voluntaristic ecclesiology and soteriology that would characterize many non-creedal Baptists in Britain and North America in the early twentieth century. The very essence of their creed was that Christianity is simply and solely personal, to use Gotch's words.[18]

James Culross (1824–1899) followed Gotch as principal of the College in 1883. A Scot, he had a master's degree from St. Andrews University, which also awarded him the Doctor of Divinity degree. He came directly from distinguished pastorates at Stirling and London and encouraged a number of Bristol men to serve in the Baptist Missionary Society He taught a wide range of courses, including New Testament, biblical languages, church history, theology, Christian apologetics and world religions. During Culross's principalship the Downgrade Controversy dominated the Baptist Union, over which Culross presided

---

[16] Quoted in Moon, *Education for Ministry*, 54.

[17] Ernest A. Payne, *The Baptist Union: A Short History* (London: Carey Kingsgate, 1958), 121–22.

[18] F. W. Gotch, *On the Mid-Century Disestablishment Question* (London: n.p., n.d.) 11–12.

for part of the time. When Spurgeon attacked the Union for preaching liberal doctrines, Culross responded with a set of affirmations characteristic of Bristol's historic evangelicalism: personal faith in Christ, believer's baptism, the Trinity, forgiveness through Christ—but he stopped short of allowing the statement to become creedal. He believed Spurgeon and himself to be essentially agreed as "evangelicals," but would not favor any such resolution to be doctrinally binding.

Within the Bristol community itself, Culross and his successor, W. J. Henderson (1843–1929), presided over significant changes in the College curriculum. First was the establishment of University College, Bristol, that took responsibility so far as ministerial students were concerned for instruction in general arts subjects. That allowed an already stretched staff to reduce its teaching and the College moved ahead for the next several generations with only two tutors. Generally, the principal taught the theological disciplines and the second tutor taught the biblical languages. The second important change was the cooperative agreement with Western Congregational College that relocated to Bristol in 1901. Under the arrangement, the Baptist College provided lectures in biblical subjects and languages while the Congregationalists provided theology, apologetics, philosophy, and comparative religions. This agreement lasted until 1966 when an amalgamation of declining Congregational colleges at Manchester occurred. Bristol Baptist College continued its specialization and became enamored of its reputation as part of the Faculty of Theology of Bristol University, with its faculty recognized in the broader sphere. On balance, however, the net result was that the historic evangelical fervor and reputation of the College seems to have been lost in the academic mix. A good deal of effort was placed upon qualifying students for Bristol University degrees in theology.[19]

In the twentieth century, five principals brought their own scholarly and professional emphases to the oldest Baptist college. C. D. Whittaker, a secondary school administrator with degrees from Cambridge and London, served for only two years 1922–1924. Next was the long tenure of Arthur Dakin from 1924–1953. Dakin (1884–1969), a Rawdon graduate who studied at Halle, was a specialist in New Testament and church history whose 1911 thesis at the University of Heidelberg was

---

[19] See Moon, *Education for Ministry*, 68.

"Die Beziehungen John Wiclife und der Lollarden zu den Bettelmochen" ("The Relation of John Wiclife and the Lollards to the Friars"). He produced a useful study on Calvinism (1940) and essays on Baptist views of church and ministry (1944). During Dakin's term the college entered an agreement with Regent's Park, Oxford, whereby Bristol would qualify students for Oxford and Bristol graduates could go on to Oxford degrees.[20]

Leonard G. Champion (1907–1997) succeeded Dakin, and brought outstanding credentials to the College.His tenure covered the years 1953-1972. He earned a Bristol Bachelor of Arts, a London University Bachelor of Divinity, and then received a Baptist Union scholarship for post-graduate work at Marburg and Heidelberg. At the latter institution, under the mentorship of Martin Dibelius, he was awarded the Doctor of Theology for a dissertation entitled, "Doxologies in the New Testament." Champion was an eighteenth-century specialist who continued to challenge younger scholars to consider the unique role that evangelical Calvinists of the West Country played in making British Baptist identity.[21] Later in his career, he represented British Baptists in ecumenical discussions and pointed out the inadequacy of Baptist doctrines of the church, ministry and the Spirit. In so doing, he reflected a larger British interest in liturgy, the universal church, and the diversity of Christian traditions.[22]

The most impressive expansion of the College took place under Champion's successor, Morris West, principal from 1972 until 1987. West was a graduate of Bristol and Oxford and completed a Doctor of Theology at the University of Zurich. His doctoral dissertation was titled "John Hooper and the Origins of Puritanism". An understudy of Ernest Payne,[23] and a longtime personal friend of Robert Runcie, Archbishop of Canterbury, he was active in ecumenical discussions, particularly the

---

[20] See the brief obituary by Ernest A. Payne, "Dr. Dakin," *Baptist Quarterly* 23:1 (January 1970): 193–94.

[21] There is a brief obituary by Roger Hayden, "Leonard George Champion," *Baptist Quarterly* 37/1 (January 1998): 211–12; and a festschrift, *Bible, History, and Ministry*, ed. Brian Haymes and Roger Hayden (Bristol: Bristol Baptist College, 1997).

[22] See his article, "The Baptist Doctrine of the Church," in the inaugural issue of *Foundations*, 1/1 (January 1958): 27–39.

[23] See the biography by Morris West, *To Be a Pilgrim: A Memoir of Ernest A Payne* (Guildford: Lutterworth, 1983).

Faith and Order Commission of the World Council of Churches.[24] The staff at Bristol increased with tutors in practical and speculative theology, though student enrollment did not materially increase. Serious decline in the student population ensued under West's successor John Morgan-Wynne (New Testament), and through the principalship of Brian Haymes (philosophy of religion), who arranged to relocate the campus to be in proximity with Trinity College, Bristol, an evangelical Anglican institution.

Bristol Baptist College followed a predictable course in its development. From an emphasis upon a learned ministry, it forged an unmistakable reputation for an evangelical Calvinism that reached virtually around the world. As the demands of university scholarship pressed upon the college, its tutors increasingly stressed academic rigor and university degrees. Its agreement with other schools to share its curricular teaching assignments, particularly in the area of theology, led to a diminution of its particular theological ethos, in favor of a theological tradition informed by general English and European Protestant developments. By the 1960s Bristol was not theologically distinct from Regent's Park, Northern, or Cardiff. Admittedly, Bristol University was neither Oxford nor Cambridge, nor Manchester or London. Enduring declining ministerial demand within its Baptist Union constituency, Bristol also felt the strong impact of Spurgeon's College and London Bible College which enjoyed greater success drawing candidates of evangelical conviction.

MIDLAND BAPTIST COLLEGE

An often-overlooked educational tradition early in the development of Baptists in England was the General Baptist school that Dan Taylor founded in 1797 in London. It was located successively in London (1797–1813), Wisbech (1813–1837), Loughborough and London (1838–1843), Leicester (1843–1857), Nottingham (1857–1862), Chilwell (1862–1883), and again in Nottingham (1883–1920). In 1920 the school merged with the Baptist College at Manchester.

As noted above, Taylor's theological emphases were of the Arminian type and more pastoral than speculative. His self-ascribed vision was to train preachers for the New Connection, much as John Wesley had done

---

[24] West played a major role in the writing of the World Council of Churches 1972 *Baptism, Eucharist, and Ministry* statement.

for the Methodists. In fact, Taylor's idea of theological education was likely much influenced by Mr. Wesley. He lectured on the content of the English Bible and drew application to personal spirituality and pastoral needs.

After Taylor, the school's tutors tended to be General Baptist ministers and laymen trained in the classics or natural philosophy.[25] Joseph Wallis (1796–1857) was tutor from 1843 to 1857, while also serving as the editor of the *General Baptist Repository* for five years. A graduate of Glasgow University, Wallis was critical of continental rationalism and he greatly strengthened the curriculum around Latin and Greek authors and biblical books in the original languages. The course also included lectures in ethics, rhetoric, logic, church history, and theology. One of Wallis' outstanding students was John Clifford. William Underwood (1812–1898) followed Wallis. Though having attended Midland College, he was largely self-taught and stressed Butler's *Analogy*, Seneca's *Works*, and the writings of Robert Hall. He later set up an important trust, the Robert Pegg Scholarship.[26]

Uncertainty about the best geographical location for the school was the prominent issue characterizing the institution's story at mid-century under Thomas Goadby's leadership. Goadby (1829–1889) studied under Wallis, then pursued an undergraduate degree at Glasgow University, earning distinction in several disciplines and honors in logic and philosophy. Characterized as a Platonic thinker, Goadby defended the evangelical cause against philosophical skepticism and made several attempts to bridge theology and the "modern spirit." He taught languages, theology, philosophy of religion, pastoral theology, biblical theology, and homiletics. During the 1860s, Midland College cooperated with Paton Theological College in Nottingham, a Congregationalist school, again demonstrating the crosscurrents of Nonconformity.

Other outstanding theologians associated with Midland were Thomas Witton Davies and Arthur C. Underwood. Davies (1851–1923), a graduate of Pontypool College and Regent's Park, went to the college as principal from Haverfordwest College. While in Nottingham Davies lectured in oriental languages at the University of Nottingham. Among

---

[25] A helpful introduction to the Midlands story is A. C. Carter, *A Popular Sketch Historical and Biographical of the Midland Baptist College* (London: Kingsgate Press, 1925).

[26] *Handbook of the Baptist Union* (London, 1899).

his notable students was J. H. Rushbrooke. After seven years of service, Davies left the General Baptist College in 1899 to teach Old Testament at North Wales Baptist College and Bangor University. He was widely recognized for his work in Arabic and Syriac, receiving honorary degrees from Leipzig, Durham, and Geneva universities. In an attempt to upgrade the scholarly reputation of the Midland school, a string of short-term scholar-principals followed Davies and this proved less than successful. Cooperation with Rawdon College ensued and the two institutions merged in 1920 to form the Manchester Baptist College. Among the last of the distinguished Midland men was A. C. Underwood, who upon moving to Rawdon took up the John Clifford Chair in Theology, carrying forth the General Baptist educational tradition.

While never having the scope of the Particular Baptist institutions at Stepney or Bristol, the General Baptist theological tradition must not be neglected in the genetic history of British Baptists. It nourished Arminian Baptist scholarship and gave it educational credibility, its graduates having an important theological impact upon British Baptist life and thought.

THE BAPTIST ACADEMICAL INSTITUTION AT STEPNEY

As early as the first decades of the eighteenth century, Particular Baptists in London, debated about the need for a school to train ministers. In 1810 a school in Stepney, a London suburb, known as The Baptist Academical Institution, was created for "the education of pious young men for the ministry." In support of the venture, the eminent pastor at Leicester, Robert Hall, Jr., made a convincing case for a theologically learned ministry, "challenged in various departments of science." The Stepney tradition in theology was not necessarily set and nurtured by theologians *per se*; rather it represents in the British context an academic theology that soon evolved from a small college of pastoral faculty into a university-affiliated context. Those behind the Stepney venture had a sophisticated idea of the future of the Baptist denomination, hoping through an educated ministry "to reach the higher classes, whose salvation was no less important than that of the lower orders."[27] Hall thought the proximity to London was important for the growing

---

[27] Briggs, *English Baptists*, 78, quoting Robert Hall of Leicester.

denomination, and he thought the curriculum should be informed by the sciences, a unique approach to dissenter theological schools of the era.

The first principal of Stepney, William Newman (1773–1835), was lacking in academic qualifications, but stressed the piety needed to be a minister.[28] He was joined by Solomon Young (1783–1827) in Greek and Latin, and Francis A. Cox (1783–1853) in "mathematics." Young and Cox had completed the course at Bristol Baptist College. Young died prematurely, but Cox went on to be a leader in promoting the Nonconformist interests, ultimately leading to the beginnings of what became London University. The first faculty, much akin to the Rhode Island College, operated on the premise that theological subjects should be cradled in a general arts course. The Bible was the chief textbook under Newman, with students expected to think for themselves. In the original four-year course, students took theology and biblical exegesis, classics, philosophy, and mathematics. Among the students of the college during its early years were Charles Stovel, John Mockett Cramp, and Joseph Hughes.[29]

In later generations, W. Harris Murch (1784–1859) was joined by Samuel Tompkins in delivering the four-year program. In the first year Greek and Latin classics were read; Hebrew, philosophy, and lectures on divine revelation that one supposes was theology, were pursued in the second year. Along with more language study, the third year featured history and doctrines of Christianity. In the final year, ecclesiastical history and "doctrines and duties of Christianity" were again coupled with Hebrew, Latin, Greek, and after 1829, Syriac. During Murch's years, students were exposed to modern thought, as seen in their use of Richard Whately's work on rhetoric, James Mill's psychology, and Herbert Marsh's biblical criticism. As John Briggs has shown, Whately was one of the "Noetics"—a cluster of liberal thinkers at Oxford's Oriel College—Mill was a utilitarian, and Marsh was a "sworn enemy of evangelicals." Other non-Baptist texts used included Samuel Davidson,

---

[28] Newman was offered an honorary degree by the College of Rhode Island in recognition for his work in beginning the Stepney Institution.

[29] Ernest A. Payne, ed., "The Development of Nonconformist Theological Education in the Nineteenth Century, with Special Reference to Regent's Park College," in *Studies in History and Religion, Presented to Dr. H. Wheeler Robinson, M.A. on His Seventieth Birthday* (London: Lutterworth, 1942) 229, 232; Briggs, *English Baptists*, 189.

J. B. Lightfoot, Henry Sidgwick, and R. W. Dale.[30] During this period, outstanding Stepney graduates included C. M. Birrell, Thomas Thomas, and Joseph Angus. In 1836 the annual academic visitors included F. A. Dorner of the University of Tuebingen.[31]

Ernest Payne has suggested that a new era of theological education at Stepney commenced in 1841 with the establishment of an affiliation to London University. Written examinations were held, the curriculum was broadened to include natural science, chemistry, physics, and the German language. Baptists joined other dissenters in supporting the charter of the University of London, in which the former "London University" evolved as University College. A number of Baptist ministerial students qualified for degrees and a few found their way to German universities. Although the beginnings of suspicion against German theology were noticeable by the 1850s, Stepney stayed its course of emphasizing scholarship and ministry.[32] Typical of the affiliated college affiliation was Benjamin Davies (1814–1875), who was recalled from Canada to be principal at Stepney. He was educated at Bristol, then at Dublin, Glasgow, and Leipzig, where he earned the first Ph.D. in the Baptist theological enterprise. George Small, tutor in Sanskrit and Indian languages whose pupils intended service in India as missionaries or civil servants, was another example of Stepney's contribution to the religious arena through advancing education.

Under the leadership of Joseph Angus (1816–1902) that lasted forty-four years, theology at Stepney became increasingly academic and scientific. In many ways, Angus was to Regent's Park what Gotch was to Bristol. Angus was educated at Stepney, after which he enjoyed a Ward Scholarship at the University of Edinburgh, where he took a degree in moral philosophy. Following the textual interests of Angus and Davies, specialization in biblical studies took place at the college, admission came via classical studies, lay students in various fields mingled freely with ministerial students, and the emphasis was upon qualifying for the university degrees. Even more significantly, after the institution moved to Regent's Park's Holford House in 1856, cooperation ensued with the Congregational New College that created an ecumenical community within the dissenting traditions. Angus himself was interested in biblical

---

[30] Briggs, *English Baptists,* 189.
[31] Payne, *Studies in History and Religion*, 234.
[32] Ibid., 237–39.

scholarship and produced the *Bible Handbook* (1853), a summary of
material for theological studies at Regent's Park College. He had
personally signaled his evolving view of the Bible when he offered
criticisms of the Authorized Version and agreed to serve on the
Committee for a Revised Version. With a nationally reputable faculty,
Regent's Park thus became the institution of choice for many leaders of
the Baptist Union, such as S. G. Green, Alexander MacLaren, W. E.
Blomfield, James Sully, and T. Harwood Patterson. Patterson taught at
Rochester Seminary in the United States. Sully distinguished himself at
the University of Goettingen and later taught within the academic
curriculum of "Mind and Logic" at University College, London.

In the 1880s, Principal Angus led the college to join efforts with
Congregational and other Baptist colleges in launching the *Senatus
Academicus*. Regent's men could prepare for the A.T.S (Associate of the
Theological Senate) and F. T. S. (Fellow of the Theological Senate)
diplomas by taking examinations in the classical fields of theological
studies. The examiners included prominent Free Church and Anglican
scholars, and this upgraded perceptions of Nonconformist preparation for
ministry. Professors Gould (see below) and Green were especially active
in *Senatus* work and were responsible for several prizes being awarded to
Regent's students.[33]

At the turn of the twentieth century, George P. Gould (1848–1921)
became principal and continued the college's relationship with the
Congregationalists. Gould was a graduate of Glasgow University, later
winning a Hibbert Traveling Fellowship to study theology at Berlin,
Goettingen, and Leipzig. He "gloried," it is said, in the non-creedalism of
Baptists of the nineteenth century. Gould went to the college from the
pastorate to be tutor in Hebrew and Old Testament. His biblical
scholarship ran apace with the New Theology, as evidenced in a revision
of Angus's Bible handbook that included the Graf-Wellhausen theory of
Pentateuchal origins.[34] Gould also pressed for a distinct Baptist sense of
identity, calling upon his Union friends to recognize four basic Baptist
tenets: religious liberty, the church as a faithful company of believers,

---

[33] Ibid., 244–45.
[34] Briggs, *English Baptists*, 190. The revisions were made after Angus died and under
the supervision of one of his top students, Samuel Gosnell Green.

baptism only upon profession of faith, and the autonomy of each congregation under the headship of Christ.[35]

Along with S. W. Green, Gould was one of the representatives of the affiliated colleges that helped shape the Faculty of Theology of London University under the Parliamentary Act of 1898. This led to the offering of Bachelor of Divinity and Doctor of Divinity degrees, with Regent's Park College faculty formally included among seven recognized divinity faculties.[36] However, during the First World War, Regent's Park College languished practically to the point of closure. Gould resigned the school's presidency in 1919.[37] The curricular pattern that Regent's Park achieved in this period—emphasizing biblical studies with supplemental lectures in theology, church history, and pastoral subjects in relationship to a general university program—would have profound meaning for both the course of academic theology and its institutional aspects in Britain and Canada.

A new era for Regent's Park College dawned in the person of H. Wheeler Robinson (1872–1945).[38] Robinson occupies a unique place in British Baptist life and thought. Trained briefly at Regent's Park College in London and graduated from the University of Edinburgh with a Master of Arts in classics and philosophy, he later studied theology under Andrew Fairbairn at Mansfield College, Oxford University. Among his faculty at Edinburgh was Marcus Dods, and at Oxford, S. R. Driver, Francis Brown, and C. A. Briggs. The work at Mansfield College opened up further studies at Strassbourg and Marburg in Europe. His first teaching position was at Rawdon College, where he lectured for fourteen years in various subjects including church history, theology, and New Testament. In 1920 he began a three-decade stint in London, ultimately becoming principal at Regent's Park College in Oxford.

Robinson's tenure was in some key aspects a break with norms of Baptist tradition. Having studied in Europe, he unashamedly introduced

---

[35] George Gould, "The Origins of the Modern Baptist Denomination," *Transactions of the Baptist Historical Society* 2 (1911): 193–212; Johnson, *Nonconformist Colleges*, 172.

[36] Ibid., 244–45.; Briggs, *English Baptists of the 19th Century*, 83.

[37] A positive assessment of Gould is found in Theodore H. Robinson, "Reminiscences of George Pearce Gould," *Baptist Quarterly* 9 (1938–1939): 311–13.

[38] This period of the College's history has been covered in Ernest A. Payne, "Regent's Park College, Oxford: The First Half-Century," *Baptist Quarterly* 27/5 (January 1978): 225–33.

positive aspects of the "New Theology" and higher critical views of Scripture studies. A. M. Fairbairn, whom Robinson much esteemed, played a primary role in introducing German New Testament criticism to British scholarship and this was to be transforming in Robinson.[39] Fairbairn was particularly enamored of the Fatherhood of God and the eternal sonship of Christ as a basis for Christian theology, rather than the more traditional theological pillars of the atonement and incarnation.[40] Fairbairn had masterminded the establishment at Oxford of Mansfield College that clearly pioneered a new role for Nonconformist theological education. Like his mentor, Robinson firmly believed in a learned ministry and nurtured a plan to move Regent's Park College to the campus of Oxford University. In so doing, he built on the foundation laid in 1841 with the university affiliation in London. This single project did more to raise standards for the Baptist ministry and public perceptions of Baptists than perhaps any single circumstance. Among Baptists, Robinson was this movement's chief advocate.[41] Robinson also contributed directly to the articulation of Baptist principles. He maintained an active dialogue with American Baptist thinkers, notably E. Y. Mullins. Finally, Robinson offered a new approach to the doctrine of the Holy Spirit that demonstrated his conversancy with modern trends.

The question of Baptist origins was dominant at the height of Robinson's career. Some writers stressed the continental Anabaptist origins of Baptists. Others posited that Baptists were heirs of a Puritan ancestry, concluding the former were "Protestants of Protestants." Robinson followed J. H. Shakespeare, James Rushbrooke, William T. Whitley, and Champlin Burrage in finding evidence of Congregationalist

---

[39] According to one observer, Fairbairn's own scholarship was overrated and he remained pre-Wellhausen in his thinking. Pompous and verbose, his great contribution was to expose Free Church students to the new methods. See Willis B. Glover, *Evangelical Nonconformists and Higher Criticism in the Nineteenth Century* (London: Independent Press, 1954), 111, 140.

[40] See the discussion of Fairbairn's thought in Johnson, *Nonconformist Colleges*, 149 ff.

[41] Thereafter the other Baptist colleges moved to affiliate with universities: Bristol with the University of Bristol, Rawdon with Manchester University, and eventually Spurgeon's College with the University of Wales. The Baptist affiliation with Oxford became a symbol of denominational maturation. On the role of Fairbairn and Mansfield College see Johnson, *English Nonconformity*, 43.

influences at work in the life and ministry of John Smyth.[42] Robinson found characteristics paradigmatic of Baptist thought in Smyth and other historic Baptist forebears: the authority of the Bible, the priesthood of all believers, the moral holiness required of believers, and a regenerate church membership. In the midst of the outbreak of fundamentalism in the United States, Robinson declared that rather than a "textbook," the Bible is a "sourcebook of Christian experience." Here he acknowledged the foundations of the New Theology that stressed experience over doctrinal authority. Robinson bridged the obvious gap between new and older conceptions of biblical authority by adding that the Bible requires that the testimony of the Holy Spirit in concert with the believer's spirit be rightly understood. Further, he attached the practice of believer's baptism to the interpretation of Scripture as the element that constantly called believers back to the death and resurrection of Jesus. He held tenaciously to the position that believers in every generation must be free afresh to interpret the meaning of Christ's redemption.[43] From his critical/historical Old Testament studies,[44] he prioritized the office of prophet over priest, and built a case for the priesthood of Jesus and all believers in the line of the prophets who spoke freely to and for God.[45]

Robinson's doctrine of the church commenced with a view of believers as consecrated persons. Whether Israel or England "what whole nation has ever been a true church?," he wrote. The nature and ideals of the true church are derived from critical study of the Bible by the "community of the regenerate."[46] He openly accepted his Congregationalist teacher's definition of a true church: "a society of the godly who truly believe and piously live...autonomous and authoritative...possessed of the freedom necessary to the fulfilment of its mission."[47] But, he went further to a more baptistic perspective in deserving that the Free Church stands or falls by the doctrine of the Holy

---

[42] H. Wheeler Robinson, *The Life and Faith of the Baptists* (London: Methuen, 1927) 2–5.

[43] Ibid., 8.

[44] His role in the academy of Old Testament scholars was large according to Rex Mason, "H. Wheeler Robinson Revisited," *Baptist Quarterly* 37/5 (January 1998): 213–26.

[45] On Robinson's view of revelation, see W. T. Early, "The Doctrine of Revelation in the Theology of H. Wheeler Robinson" (Th.D. diss., Union Theological Seminary, 1963).

[46] Robinson, *Life and Faith of the Baptists*, 20.

[47] A. M. Fairbairn, quoted in ibid., 17.

Spirit. Here was the germ of a doctrine of the Spirit for a new age.[48]
Some see in Robinson an affinity for the Oxford Movement, as he
observed the clarity of a doctrine of the Church among Catholics and
Anglicans and yearned for an appreciation of Nonconformity's rise in the
seventeenth century, a more universal idea of the Church, and some
understanding of liturgy.[49]

The success of the Baptist World Alliance (BWA) provided Baptists
with an opportunity to exchange theological ideas on a regular basis. A
prime example of the British-American exchange through the auspices of
the Alliance was that between Robinson and E. Y. Mullins at Southern
Baptist Theological Seminary in Louisville, Kentucky. In his much-
quoted book, *The Life and Faith of the Baptists* (1927), Robinson
displayed direct dependence upon Mullins's book, *The Axioms of
Religion,* published nineteen years earlier. With Mullins, he afffirmed
that the distinguishing significance of the Baptists was the doctrine of the
soul's competency. In describing Baptist polity, he followed Mullins's
profile of non-legislative and non-judicial administrative denominational
structures. To understand individual Christian experience, Robinson
agreed with Mullins that "fatherhood and sonship" were expressive of
individual rather than corporate relations. And finally, he commended
Mullins's book to his British audience as "indicative of a useful
American viewpoint."[50]

Like Mullins and other prominent Baptists in the United States,
Robinson was greatly persuaded of the importance of religious
experience. One writer has observed that as a Baptist, Robinson "was
very much a theologian of experience and the heart."[51] Rather than
relying upon the authority of the church or older concepts of the Bible,
Robinson sought to build upon the authority of the "Christ of
experience" that is made real to humans through the activity of the Holy
Spirit.[52] Religious experience was the emerging factor of validation:

---

[48] H. Wheeler Robinson, *The Christian Experience of the Holy Spirit* (London: Nisbet, 1928) 154-55.

[49] Johnson, *Nonconformist Colleges,* 174–75.

[50] Robinson, *Life and Faith,* 18, 110, 173, 184.

[51] Duane A. Garrett, "H. Wheeler Robinson," in *Theologians in the Baptist Tradition,* ed. Timothy George and David S. Dockery (Nashville: Broadman Holman, 2001) 410.

[52] Carl F. H. Henry, *Fifty Years of Protestant Theology* (Boston: W. A. Wilde, 1950) 53, argued that Robinson, equally opposed to pantheistic immanence and Barthianism,

> The religious experience of others can similarly be studied as so many objective data...this applies underlying the revelation of God found in the Bible, the experience of those who had earthly fellowship with Him in the days of His flesh, the experience of the whole Church in the widest sense, and our own personal fragment of such experience, always needing to be revised and enlarged through the experience of others.[53]

In all of his discussion of the relevance of religious experience, Robinson was careful to underscore the active partnership of the Holy Spirit. For him, the Holy Spirit revealed God in nature, history, and personality. He developed a *"kenosis* theory" in his 1928 work, *The Christian Experience of the Holy Spirit*, that followed a sacramental principle of "the mediation of the higher through the lower" and the "transformation of the lower by the higher." Robinson believed the theory was an intellectual and spiritual landmark. Ernest Payne, a student of Robinson at Oxford, thought the work Robinson did on the Spirit and experience established his reputation as a recognized constructive theologian.[54]

H. Wheeler Robinson truly cast a long shadow over Baptist thought. He was at one time a member of the prestigious London Society for the Study of Religion, sharing prominence with R. N. Flew, C. H. Dodd, and Claude Montefiore. An Old Testament theologian at Oxford in 1938, he was asked to edit a volume titled *Record and Revelation*, which included contributions by prestigious critical scholars such as Otto Eissfeldt, Johannes Hempel, and J. A. Montgomery. In time, generations of American Baptists and others from around the globe would travel to Regent's Park College to study under British teachers at Oxford. That pilgrimage began under Robinson's influence. The tall portrait of H. Wheeler Robinson in the refectory of Regent's Park College that students pondered at mealtimes has come to symbolize the academic Baptist

---

was no supporter of evangelical views of Scripture. He rejected external biblical authority and propositional divine revelation in favor of human response and interpretation.

[53] H. Wheeler Robinson, "The Principle of Authority in the Christian Religion" (paper read at Regent's Park College, 13 April 1942), in Ernest A. Payne, *Henry Wheeler Robinson: Scholar, Teacher, Principal* (London: Nisbet, 1946) 176–77.

[54] Payne, *Henry Wheeler Robinson*, 81–82.

theologian: university trained, erudite, conservative, and robed in authority.

While not possessing advanced academic degrees, Ernest A Payne (1902–1980) was nevertheless an erudite scholar and a defining theological personality of his generation among British Baptists. His career involved teaching at Regent's Park College and service as general secretary of the Baptist Union of Great Britain. Payne was educated at King's College, London University and Regent's Park College, and Mansfield College, Oxford University. At King's he was influenced by Wilden Carr and W. R. Mathews-especially in the field of philosophy-who exposed Payne's Baptist faith to broader ideas. Descended from ministerial forbears of the Baptist Union tradition, he opted in 1922 for ministerial studies and entered Regent's Park at the peak of H. Wheeler Robinson's influence as principal. Robinson was for Payne a role model as a scholar-churchman who stressed Trinitarian theology and Free Church ideals. Later at Mansfield College, Payne enjoyed an advanced ecumenical experience that laid a foundation for his Free Church identity as well as overseas study. He was introduced to Karl Barth and Rudolf Bultmann in Marburg, as well as professors Friedrich Heiler and Heinrich Hermelink who had involvement in the 1927 Lausanne Conference on Faith and Order. He confessed later to having more appreciation for Barth than Bultmann, the latter whose work he little understood.[55]

Payne joined the staff at Regent's Park in 1940 following service in the Baptist Missionary Society and the Baptist World Alliance. He was not chosen principal upon Robinson's retirement—that honor went to his classmate, Robert Child. Instead, Payne lectured in historical theology, Baptist thought, and missions. His scholarly publications poured forth, including *The Church Awakes* (1942), *The Free Church Tradition in the Life of England* (1943), and *The Fellowship of Believers: Baptist Thought and Practice Yesterday and Today* (1944). The last was a response to a work in process by Arthur Dakin on church and ministry that advocated an extreme local congregational view of the Baptist church. Payne espoused a much wider view of churchmanship, fully supporting ecumenical relations. With a keen interest in missions, Payne was a significant influence upon students from across the globe and was

---

[55] W. M. S. West, *To Be a Pilgrim: A Memoir of Ernest A. Payne* (Surrey: Lutterworth Press, 1983) 33–34.

himself involved in the Baptist Missionary Society, World Council of Churches, and Student Christian Movement organizational affairs. He departed Oxford in 1951 to begin fifteen years as general secretary of the Baptist Union, at a time of denominational statistical decline but increased involvement in world ecclesial affairs.

Payne made several important contributions to Baptist thought. Importantly, he broke with his teacher, H. Wheeler Robinson, in one respect and carried forth a lifelong project to connect Baptists with Anabaptist writers and thought. In an essay on contacts between Baptists and Mennonites, Payne unabashedly argued, "Both Christian groups owe their origin to the Reformation and to its left wing...there have been far closer contacts than is generally realized." Here was a clear affirmation of the "Anabaptist kinship" theory of Baptist origins. Payne believed the points of doctrinal dependence or convergence included baptismal theology, the church, religious freedom, and issues of Christology.[56]

Contravening the work of Congregationalist historian Douglas Horton and American historians whom he characterized as "misguided and erroneous," Payne asserted that Baptists and Congregationalists shared common roots in Separatism. Perhaps owing to his hope that Congregationalists and Baptists would draw together in the English Free Church tradition, Payne went to great historical and theological efforts to demonstrate their commonality.[57] In 1954 he defended the Baptist practice of "laying on of hands" as an important gesture emphasizing the gift of the Holy Spirit. Here again, he was not only concerned for the dearth of emphasis upon the doctrine of the Spirit, but recognized the possibility of another entry point for Baptists in the ecumenical discussions regarding Christian initiation.[58]

As an ecclesiocrat, Payne also influenced Baptist life theologically as did few other leaders of his generation. In numerous essays, he reminded readers of the dependence of Baptists in worship upon Protestants and particularly other Free Churches.[59] Payne was convinced that a doctrine

---

[56] Ernest A. Payne, "Contacts Between Mennonites and Baptists," in *Free Churchmen, Unrepentant and Repentant, and Other Papers* (London: Carey Kingsgate Press, 1965) 75, 83–85.

[57] "Baptist–Congregational Relationships," in ibid., 94–96.

[58] "Baptists and the Laying on of Hands," in ibid., 105–119.

[59] See, for instance, "The Free Church Tradition and Worship" and "The First Free Church Hymnal," in ibid., 15–45.

of the church that rests solely on the autonomy of a local congregation was inadequate.[60]From his larger ecclesiology he led the Baptist Union in engaging the Faith and Order Movement and the formation of the World Council of Churches. In Britain he continued the early leadership toward the ecumenism of J. H. Rushbrooke through the National Free Church Council. He encouraged contacts between Baptists and Mennonites and closer cooperation with the Congregational Union. While he understood Baptist reluctance on the grounds of evangelical witness toward organic union, he urged constant dialogue and appropriate cooperation. One of Payne's enduring legacies was the mentoring he provided the next generation of Baptist leaders. Educators like W. M. S. West and Barrington R. White would carry forth as Baptist college principals at Bristol and Regent's Park, respectively. D. S. Russell, John Nicholson, and Bernard Green owed Payne a great professional debt, particularly in the ecumenical arena. British-Canadian Baptist theologian Russell Aldwinckle credited Payne as a foundational figure in the formation of his theological identity.

Following the era of Ernest Payne, Regent's Park competed favorably as a college with its sister schools, Bristol and Spurgeon's. The attraction for study at Oxford was heady for British students and those from overseas. Less a matter of theological tradition than the vast resources of an ancient university, the strength of Regent's was found not in theology during the principalships of G. Henton Davies and B. R. White, but in biblical studies and church history. Davies was to earn a reputation as a critical Old Testament scholar, whose ideas on Pentateuchal origins repulsed some Baptists in North America.[61] Later his colleague, Rex Mason, formerly at Spurgeon's College, supervised several doctoral students in the same field. Ties were forged with Southern Baptist institutions in the United States, and a string of graduate students from America traveled to Oxford to study with White in particular. Those who exercised some influence in the shadow of their "simple Bible-believing" seventeenth-century specialist mentor included Horace Russell, Stephen Brachlow, Morgan Patterson, John Gladstone, Richard Land, and Karen

---

[60] "Baptists and the Ecumenical Movement," in ibid., 129.

[61] Davies's commentary on Genesis in the *Broadman Bible Commentary* was withdrawn after its initial printing and reassigned to Professor Clyde Francisco at Southern Baptist Theological Seminary.

Smith.[62] White's successor, Paul Fiddes, a contemporary theologian, much influenced by White's historical perspectives, has attempted to create a Christian studies idea for the college as well as recovering its prestigious position as a premier theological training ground for graduate students.

BRADFORD ACADEMY / NORTHERN EDUCATION SOCIETY

An important theological school tradition emerged among the northern churches of England, spearheaded by William Steadman (1764–1837)of Bradford, Yorkshire. Steadman taught school for a time and read theological works by John Bunyan, John Gill, and John Newton under the direction of the celebrated Joshua Thomas of Leominster (1719–1797). Having prepared himself for formal study, he entered Bristol Baptist College in 1788 under Caleb Evans. He found Evans a man of high literary attainments, a popular preacher, pious, and amiable.[63] The other tutors were Robert Hall and James Newton, neither one of whom at first made deep impressions upon Steadman. He recalled that most students were Welsh, his close friends being Benjamin Evans and Samuel Pearce.

The young preacher entered pastoral ministry, but enjoyed only modest results at several churches. Steadman continued to read widely, especially among American and English Puritan divines, notably Jonathan Edwards, David Brainerd, and John Owen. For several years he itinerated widely in a kind of evangelistic ministry, a pattern he would co-mingle with his idea of theological education. Among his close friends were Samuel Pearce and Andrew Fuller. His son categorized him as a moderate Calvinist, one of the early disciples of Fuller.[64]Upon settling at Bradford in 1805, Steadman opened an academy for "the preparation of pious young men for ministry" at Little Horton. A new and arguably unique theological tradition was born under his tutelage.

---

[62] Not all those who benefited from White's tutelage were degree candidates. Some came to spend sabbatical terms and did guided readings courses in Baptist, Puritan/Separatist thought.

[63] Steadman, *Memoir,* 36.

[64] Ibid., 459. See the contemporary assessment in Sharon James, "Revival and Renewal in Baptist Life: The Contribution of William Steadman 1764–1837," *Baptist Quarterly* 37/6 (April 1998): 263–82.

From his experience as a theological student, Steadman built his curriculum upon a strong practical base, requiring preaching in local churches and time for student interaction. Although formally trained at Bristol, much of Steadman's previous learning was self-taught. His memoir indicates that his Greek skills were stronger than his facility with Hebrew. His historical repertoire included Justin Martyr in Latin, Johann L. Mosheim's history, Rene Rapin's comparison of Greek philosophers with the church fathers (he considered this work difficult), fellow Baptist Robert Robinson's *Ecclesiastical Researches*, and Foxe's martyrology. He relied heavily upon John Gill, Matthew Poole, Philip Doddridge, and John Newton, the last of whom he greatly esteemed. More "evangelical and experimental" than philosophical in his classes, Steadman made continual reference to John Bunyan and to both the biographical and theological works of Jonathan Edwards. Of Edwards he wrote, " …even where he is abstruse and metaphysical, he excites spiritual affections in my soul."[65]

The curriculum at Little Horton called for one year of Latin, one year of Greek, and one year of Hebrew. Lectures were also given in geography, natural philosophy, and chemistry. Jonathan Edwards Ryland of Bristol, and later B. Godwin of Great Missenden, assisted the principal in teaching. Beginning in 1807, Steadman embarked upon a course of lectures in theology, ecclesiastical history, and the practice of ministry for which he alone was responsible. In theology, he developed a system that covered all the major doctrines and practical questions, plus an exposition of the Bible. He covered Christian evidences, God, the Trinity, Scripture, man, redemption, the major Reformed categories, and eschatology.[66] In discussing the church and ministry, he was a Christian of a catholic perspective, maintaining good relations with local Anglican and nonconformist pastors. He nevertheless held tenaciously to strict communionism as a doctrine of church discipline.[67] With a style of extemporaneous commentary under topical headings, Steadman exhibited his current reading as well as from the classics in copious lists of references. The real "test" of student comprehension was in an assigned sermon, in which the student was expected to give evidence of readings and integration. Steadman was a gracious but demanding

---

[65] Ibid., 140.
[66] Ibid., 320.
[67] Ibid., 473–74.

taskmaster. His influence was certainly widely felt. He preached about 11,000 times, baptized over 600 declared candidates, supervised 160 graduates of his academy, and spoke at more than 100 ordinations.[68]

Upon Steadman's retirement, James Acworth (1798–1883) became principal at the academy. He graduated from Bristol College and was a Ward Scholar at Glasgow University. Under his guidance the Horton school moved to Rawdon and grew in academic prestige. His principal theological work was *Internal Witness to Christianity; A Discourse before the Ministers & Delegates of the Yorkshire Associated Baptist Churches* (1856). Tackling one of the larger theological issues of his day, he wrote of the Trinity, "It is thus, in connexion with the scheme of human recovery, and as necessity involved in its execution, the fact of a plurality of subsistences, or of persons in the Godhead becomes known to us...the doctrine is far from being a theoretic one."[69]

Following Acworth, came in turn, Samuel G. Green (1822–1905), Thomas G. Rooke (1837–1890), and T. Vincent Tymms (1842–1921), each of whom contributed to the modernization of the Rawdon College and English Baptist thought. Green, a biblical scholar, was well-known for his handbooks on the grammar of biblical Greek and Hebrew. In his inaugural address he called attention to Rawdon's lack of a creedal foundation, and he took the Christological route for himself.[70] He was indebted to John Calvin ("the man from whom the whole of our modern theology, worthy of the name, has taken its shape and tone")[71] and he was thoroughly individualistic. Testifying against sacramental efficacy or hereditary claims to religious authority, he was prepared to take his stand as an ardent Congregationalist and Baptist, marks of his growing ecumenicity within the Free Church tradition. Green's real modernity

---

[68] James Acworth, *A Discourse Occasioned by the Decease of the Reverend William Steadman, D.D.* (London: Simpkin, Marshall & Co., 1837) 21.

[69] James Acworth, *The Scripture Doctrine of the Trinity, in A Circular Letter of the East and West Ridings of the Yorkshire Baptist Associations of Baptist Churches* (Bradford: Scarlett and Northgate, 1857) 4.

[70] *Inaugural Address of the President, the Reverend Samuel Green, B.A., September 1863* (London: J. Heaton & Son., 1863) 4.

[71] Ibid., 6–7. Green envisioned a three-year course for theological studies following a literary course in a university, a plan remarkably similar to the emerging pattern in the United States. See his *Education for the Ministry, Being One of the Papers Read to the Baptist Union of England and Wales, At Its Annual Session in Northampton, September 1871* (London: Yates and Alexander, 1871) 11–12.

showed in his design of the Rawdon curriculum, listing courses in biblical criticism, systematic theology, ecclesiastical history, Greek, and Hebrew. Of them all, he placed the highest emphasis upon biblical criticism.[72] Rooke authored works on baptism, inspiration, and supernaturalism.

T. Vincent Tymms, pastor for a quarter-century at Victoria Road, Leicester, was known for his works titled *The Mystery of God: A Consideration of Some Intellectual Hindrances to Faith* (1885) and *The Christian Idea of Atonement* (1904), the latter a published version of the 1903 Angus Lectures delivered at Regent's Park College. His view of scriptural authority claimed the general reliability of the Bible, while acknowledging among his "hindrances to faith" discrepancies in detail, and importantly, the absence of original autographs.[73] He opened up the question of the interpretation of the atonement among Baptists, first rejecting the Anselmian view because it dwelt too much on punishment, and the governmental hypothesis because it was too calloused and irreverent. Instead, he argued for a view of the atonement based in the love of God that also recognized God's sovereignty.[74] With respect to infant baptism, he used critical historical skills to demonstrate that it was not a part of the original Christian tradition, but was adopted in the fifth century. He used baptism to illustrate what he called an "evolutionary process" distinct in early Christian literature.[75] Like Green, Tymms was ecumenically inclined. In a published sermon, he exclaimed, "Let me recognize as brethren all who hold Christ as the Head over all things to His church, although they call us not brother." He declared further, "Let us open our hearts and minds to learn truth through any channel and to serve Christ in union with all disciples."[76]

Rawdon College enjoyed even more prestige as a theological institution under the eighteen-year principalship of H. Wheeler Robinson (1906–1920). Robinson began his educational career in Hebrew lectures,

---

[72] Ibid., 7, 16.

[73] T. Vincent Tymms, *The Mystery of God: A Consideration of Some Intellectual Hindrances to Faith* (London: Elliot Stock, 1885) 201.

[74] T. Vincent Tymms, *The Christian Idea of Atonement* (London: Macmillan, 1904) 437. (There is a useful discussion of Tymms's view in Johnson, *Nonconformist Colleges*, 156.)

[75] Ibid., 445. He showed a marked dependency on Wall's study of baptism.

[76] T. Vincent Tymms, *First Principles of a Christian: A Sermon Preached at the Downs Chapel, Clapton October 17, 1875* (London: Yates and Alexander) 9.

but branched out into theology as well. He was particularly interested in the interplay of psychology and Pauline theology. He produced a widely acclaimed work, *The Christian Doctrine of Man*, in 1911. Later, while at Rawdon, he finished *The Religious Ideas of the Old Testament* (1913) dealing with some of the same themes being explored by the Chicago School in the United States, namely the moral emphasis of Israelite religion and the evolutionary nature of Israel's history and theology. Robinson's critics would have enjoyed greater response to their concern for his "modern handling of the Bible" had it not been for his pastoral and devotional character. While he did not embrace sentimentalism in religion, he relentlessly called for a renewed attention to the doctrine of the Holy Spirit. He won great respect for the little school at Rawdon, earning recognition at the University of Leeds for a four-year cycle of lectures on the Bible. At the conclusion of the first World War, however, his academic career was diverted to London and Regent's Park College. His students, A. C. Dakin, and L. H. Marshall, would carry on his scholarly emphases in the continuing saga of Rawdon/Manchester as a ministerial training school of the North.[77]

In 1866 another attempt at theological education began at Bury with the Baptist Theological Institution at Chamber Hall. Its uniqueness included a non-residential program and stress upon practice of ministry. A theological imitation of Spurgeon's Pastor's College in London, its *raison d'etre* was to propagate a strict form of Calvinism. The school prospered under the tutorship of Henry Dowson and relocated to Brighton Grove, Manchester, where it became popularly known as "Manchester Baptist College." This program evolved as part of Victoria University of Manchester that called for an integration of denominational theological colleges to comprise a Faculty of Theology. The historian of the college notes that the Manchester school created an alliance between liberal politics and conservative religion."[78] Consistently Calvinistic in outlook, it enjoyed a limited but identifiable following. C. H. Spurgeon

---

[77] On Marshall, who had a stormy interlude at McMaster University in Canada, see his relatively conservative essay in his mentor's festschrift, "Formgeschichte and its Limitations," *Studies in History and Religion, Presented to Dr. H. Wheeler Robinson M.A. on his Seventieth Birthday*, ed. Ernest A. Payne (London: Lutterworth Press, 1942) 69–86 and Gerald T. Rimmington, "L. H. Marshall's Ministry in Leicester 1930–1936," *Baptist Quarterly* 36/8 (October 1996): 404–412.

[78] Richard Kidd, "Northern Baptist College," *American Baptist Quarterly* 18/2 (June 1999): 98.

himself gave an address at the cornerstone laying of the college building in Manchester in 1872.

In 1920 the Midland Baptist College in Nottingham merged its assets with Rawdon College, and thus a General Baptist theological tradition was blended with the Particular Baptists, reflecting the practical realities of the Baptist Union. One of the ongoing evidences of the General Baptist legacy in Rawdon was the establishment of a John Clifford Chair. As it thus moved into a new century, the Rawdon college represented two theological traditions among Baptists.

The final amalgamation of institutions in the North of England ensued in 1964 when Manchester Baptist College (formed in 1866 on closed or strict communionist priciples)[79] merged with Rawdon College to form Northern Baptist College on the Brighton Grove site. This occurred under the leadership of David S. Russell (1953-1957), an internationally known Bible scholar and expert in the area of apocalyptic literature who followed L. H. Marshall as principal at Rawdon. Russell, a Glasgow University and Rawdon graduate, went on to give stellar service as general secretary of the Baptist Union and was succeeded by Michael Taylor (1969-1985). Taylor, a graduate of Manchester University (B.D.) and Union Theological Seminary in New York (S.T.M.), had many contemporary ideas and a theological perspective that often exceeded typical Baptist outlooks. At the annual assembly of the Baptist Union in 1971, President G. Henton Davies from Regent's Park College, asked Taylor to give an address on Christology. Taylor titled the address, "How Much of a Man Was Jesus Christ?" His remarks seemed to many evangelicals a renewed form of Docetism and created great controversy in the Union. As a result of the polemics, chances for growth at Northern Baptist College appear to have been doused. Although Taylor continued as principal until 1985 and initiated new models for training candidates for ministry, the school's enrollment continued to plummet. It was evident that the school could not overcome its principal's damaged reputation among traditional Baptists and other evangelicals. Succeeding Taylor were Brian Haymes, a tutor in philosophy of religion, and Richard Kidd, a theologian trained at Oxford. They redirected the program at Northern toward a non-residential curriculum with an

---

[79] Briggs, *English Baptists of the Nineteenth Century*, 80-81.

ecumenical character. Taylor went on to lead Christian Aid, an ecumenical world relief agency.

SPURGEON'S COLLEGE

The last of the scholarly traditions in the English Baptist family that had a unique impact upon Baptist theological development was that emanating from Spurgeon's College. Keeping well within the traditions Spurgeon himself articulated, the college came to be the center of evangelical thought in the Baptist family.[80] Not only has Spurgeon's College come to reflect this posture in Britain and Europe where many Spurgeon's graduates have served, but its impact also has been felt among Baptists and evangelicals in the Americas, South Africa, and Australia.

Spurgeon was not satisfied with the existing theological colleges and faculties of his day. In fact, he was openly critical of the majority of those institutions. To no one's surprise, he started a school in 1856 to train preachers and pastors for congregations of the Union. While he declined personal initiative in starting the school, Spurgeon was intimately involved in the design of the curriculum, its theological outlook in the Reformed tradition, and the guaranteed piety of the students. For over a decade, the name of the institution was "Pastor's College," denoting his proprietorship of the school.[81] The students were clearly expected to be representative of the views and practices of the Metropolitan Tabernacle.

Spurgeon taught many of the courses in the school's early years. His first choice to provide administrative leadership as the college's principal was Congregationalist George Rogers (1799–1892) of Albany Chapel, Camberwell. Rogers, whose long pastorate brought him regional distinction, shared Spurgeon's enthusiasm for Calvinistic doctrine. Spurgeon knew him as "a man of Puritan stamp, deeply learned, orthodox in doctrine, devout, earnest, liberal in spirit, and withal juvenile in heart." In its first decade, Rogers ensured that "Calvinistic theology was dogmatically taught" by the school. Courses were diverse but not

---

[80] A useful analysis of Spurgeon's in its early years is David Bebbington, "Spurgeon and British Evangelical Theological Education," in *Theological Education in the Evangelical Tradition*, ed. D. G. Hart and R. Albert Mohler, Jr. (Grand Rapids: Baker Books, 1996) 217–34.

[81] Ibid., 220.

advanced in any given area. Mathematics, geography, history, English composition, and ancient languages—particularly Latin—were offered. Spurgeon thought science should be included for the purpose of enriching sermon illustrations. The founder took pleasure in advertising that "free inquiry" was encouraged and he often engaged the students in discussion of contemporary moral and political concerns at weekly meetings.[82] In its early years, the college appeared to some to be a center of anti-intellectualism, but its leaders countered that they were training preachers, not scholars. Theirs was, they asserted, a middle way between classical instruction and practical application. Each student was heavily involved in ministry, and the graduates went in large numbers directly to churches. Spurgeon's sons served as "ministry directors" and Spurgeon made an attempt to organize an ongoing association of college alumni to carry forth the school's ideals. The college's impact on the Baptist Union was pronounced, causing other schools to complain about "overstocking the market."[83]

David Gracey (1841–1893) followed Rogers and brought renewed theological energy to the school. He had been converted during a revival in the north of Ireland and met Spurgeon when he was in Glasgow. Gracey's theological lectures survive in published form and reveal his characteristic biblicism: "The Word of God is the primary and the only foundation from which we would draw...if we admit development, it is the development of truth within the bounds of revelation."[84] He exhibited dependency upon Calvin, Turretin, Charles Hodge at Princeton, and Pye Smith, an English Congregationalist. Gracey believed his theology was consistent in character with the theological perspectives of Jonathan Edwards, Timothy Dwight, and especially that of Andrew Fuller.

Among mainstream Calvinistic Baptists in Britain at mid-nineteenth century, Andrew Fuller's evangelical divinity system was widely regarded. Since Fuller had not completed his system, it remained for others to extend his foundation. Building upon Fuller, Gracey sketched a soteriological flow of sin, salvation, the Savior, Redeemer, and

---

[82] The "Outline" of the College is treated in ibid., 221.

[83] Ibid., 231. The organization was called the Pastor's College Evangelical Association.

[84] David Gracey, *Sin and the Unfolding of Salvation, Being the Three Years' Course of Theological Lectures Delivered at the Pastor's College, London* (London: Passmore and Alabaster, 1894) 14.

atonement.[85] He accepted Fuller's dictum that the mercy of God is turned towards the world, the human race, and the church. "Inviting the sinner," he wrote, "is the great aim of preaching the gospel."[86] The curriculum he developed reveals his dependence on Elisha Coles's *Treatise Upon Divine Sovereignty*, Thomas Watson's *Body of Divinity*, and A. A. Hodge's *Outline of Theology*. Much attention was given also to the writings of Jonathan Edwards. In ethics and moral theology, Gracey exhibited an affinity toward Sir William Hamilton and the Scottish Common Sense School, as well as Francis Wayland's *Elements of Moral Science*. Among Gracey's concerns for the program of the college were the need to raise its academic standards and to communicate that the school's standards were commensurate with other church colleges. When the idea of "Senatus Academicus" was proffered among Nonconformists, Spurgeon's leadership—not unexpectedly—dismissed the idea.[87]

Two significant changes occurred following the days of the first generation of students and the death of Mr. Spurgeon. First, in 1923 the college moved to South Norwood and severed its ties with the Metropolitan Tabernacle. Second, in 1939 it re-affiliated with the Baptist Union of Great Britain and Ireland. A succession of principals gradually eased the program into the conservative mainstream. Two of these served for lengthy periods: Archibald McCaig (1852–1936) was principal from 1898 to 1925 and P. W. Evans (1882–1951) served in the senior capacity from 1925 to1950. McCaig had been a colporteur pastor in Scotland who attended Spurgeon's and then completed the B.A., LL.B., and LL.D. degrees at Queens University, Belfast. A significant portion of his academic work was in response to German criticism and in defense of biblical inspiration.[88] He had a special interest in Russian Baptist life. Similarly, Evans, who was educated at Birkbeck College, London, Spurgeon's College, and the University of London (B.A., B.D.), was at home in Hellenistic Greek and wrote on the subject of infant baptism as he engaged in ecumenical discussions.[89] He was much involved in work

---

[85] For a summary of the rest of his system, see David Gracey, *Precision in Doctrine: A Paper Read at the Baptist Union 1869* (London: n.p., 1869).

[86] Ibid., 289–90.

[87] Bebbington, "Spurgeon," 222, 228.

[88] Archibald McCaig, *The Grand Old Book, Being Lectures on Inspiration and the Higher Criticism* (London: n.p., 1923).

[89] Percy Evans, *Infant Baptism Today* (London: Carey Kingsgate Press, 1948).

beyond the confines of Spurgeon's College, including responsibilities with the Senate of London University, serving as moderator of the Free Church Federal Council, and acting as a Baptist representative to the World Council of Churches General Assembly in 1948. An outwardly focused evangelical, he was the driving force behind the revised understanding of the ministry in the Baptist Union. During this time, Spurgeon's College developed an identity in evangelical biblical studies and missions much along the pattern of several like-minded Bible colleges in the United States.

From 1950 through the 1980s the college developed a more classically educated faculty under the principalships of Frederick Cawley (1950–55), Eric W. Worsted (1955–57), and George R. Beasley-Murray (1958–1973). Each of these men earned multiple academic degrees, culminating in research doctorates. Cawley was initially a librarian and after graduating from Spurgeon's he became a missionary to India. His Ph.D. dissertation at the University of Edinburgh under H.R. Macintosh was "The Transcendence of Jesus Christ." Worsted's tenure was short due to his involvement in a group called "Moral Re-Armament" that galvanized evangelicals against the college and eventually led to his resignation.

Beasley-Murray (1916–2000) was the most scholarly of the three. He had a diploma from Spurgeon's, held the B.D., Th.M., and Ph.D. from London University, and an M.A. (first degree) from Cambridge University. At London, his dissertation under R. V. G. Tasker of Kings College was entitled "The Eschatological Discourse of Mark 13: Its Origin and Significance." He acknowledged being much influenced by C. H. Dodd and R. Newton Flew at Cambridge, both critical scholars.[90] His teaching career included serving as tutor at Spurgeon's, then New Testament professor at Rüschlikon,[91] Switzerland, and again a period at Spurgeon's as principal. The thesis of his dissertation—that from a human standpoint Jesus did not exhibit chronologically accurate information about the end times consistent with other apocalyptic passages—had profound Christological and eschatological implications

---

[90] The Beasley-Murray era moved beyond the image of "a fundamentalist institution that had no time for biblical criticism," as one writer characterized it in the 1920s: Bebbington, "Spurgeon," 234.

[91] At Rüschlikon, Beasley-Murray developed a life-long friendship with the University of Zurich New Testament scholar, Eduard Schweizer.

and greatly exercised many evangelicals.[92] Through his teaching and writing, Beasley-Murray's work on baptism reached many parts of the Baptist family. He developed an ecumenical position, "evangelical sacramentalism," that found infant baptism acceptable. He moved in the direction of understanding baptism as a sacrament, something he recovered from the earliest Baptists and, more recently, from H. Wheeler Robinson and H. H. Rowley.[93] His tireless efforts as a popular preacher and evangelist, with friends like F. F. Bruce at Manchester, made his theology more acceptable than earlier generations of Spurgeon's theologians might have found him. During Beasley-Murray's tenure, Spurgeon's College clearly became the leading Baptist theological college in Britain, assisting students to prepare for degrees at the University of London and later the CNAA (Council for National Academic Awards) and the University of Wales. In 1973 Beasley-Murray accepted the James Buchanan Harrison Professorship in New Testament at Southern Baptist Theological Seminary in Louisville, Kentucky. This greatly expanded his intellectual influence in the United States, mostly in the area of biblical studies.[94] His legacy at Spurgeon's was one of rigorous scholarship, European influences, American connections, acceptance of higher criticism of the Bible, and ecumenical interests.[95]

With Beasley-Murray's principalship, Spurgeon's College could rightly be said to have joined the theological stream of the other Baptist colleges, with a strongly evangelical ethos. The evolving curriculum at Spurgeon's reflected the maturing nature of British evangelicalism. Guided by the standards of the University of London, lectures in Old Testament, New Testament, biblical languages, historical theology, and

---

[92] Paul Beasley-Murray, *Fearless for Truth: A Personal Portrait of the Life of George Beasley-Murray* (Carlisle: Paternoster Press, 2002) 71–75. One New Testament scholar and recent biographer of Beasley-Murray claims that he modified his controversial position by adopting J. A. Bengel's metaphor about distant perspectives. See R. Alan Culpeper, "George R. Beasley-Murray," in *Baptist Theologians*, 573.

[93] For his work on baptism, London University awarded him an honorary doctorate in 1963, clearly marking him as the premier theological teacher of his day in the British Baptist family. Later, Cambridge University similarly awarded him the D.D.

[94] He continued to visit Southern Seminary as an Elrod Senior Professor after 1980.

[95] Primarily a New Testament scholar rather than methodologically a theologian, he was celebrated in an American festschrift: Hulitt Gloer, ed., *Eschatology and the New Testament: Essays in Honor of George Beasley-Murray* (Peabody: Hendrikson, 1988).

systematic theology became the foundation of the course of study. Particular attention also was given to the doctrines of church and ministry, Baptist history, ethics, and ministerial arts such as counseling, youth work, and elocution.[96] Gradually, faculty with appropriate degrees would be recruited to teach at the College, and it came to reflect the overall evolution experienced by other similarly evangelical schools in Great Britain.[97]

SUMMARY

The evolution of a scholarly tradition in British Baptist life was important for several reasons. First, the academic institutions translated the compelling theological questions of the day to the local Baptist congregation. These included:

—Is the sole source of theological truth the revealed Scripture?
—Had God predetermined some souls to damnation or provided salvation for all?
—How does one understand God's requirement in the sacrifice of Christ?
—What constitutes a true gospel church?
—To what extent has history shaped the doctrines of the church?
—What is the obligation of the Christian community to the world's heathen peoples?

The resulting circumstances were not always happy, producing conflict between the educated and the self-taught pastors or between the ecumenically inclined and the stricter forms of Baptist life.

Second, the standards and expectations for ministry itself were substantially raised as colleges opened. By the nineteenth century, British Baptists could rightly point to the beginnings of a learned ministry in a Nonconformist context. Those teaching in the colleges and

---

[96] A. E. Wilmott, *Greater Things: A Popular History of Spurgeon's College* (London: The College, n.d.).

[97] A genuine spirit of cooperation among the colleges emerged in the 1990s as witnessed in *Something to Declare: A Study of the Declaration of Principle jointly written by the Principals of the four English Colleges in membership with the Baptist Union of Great Britain*, ed. Richard Kidd (Oxford: Whitley Publications, 1996) that stressed the similarities rather than theological differences among Baptist schools.

their students were exposed to European scholarship. Biblical studies and theology were most profoundly affected. This inevitably led to the modernization of Baptist thought according to lines drawn in other denominations and trends. Third, the development of these schools influenced the creation of institutions elsewhere in the Baptist family. These included colleges and seminaries in the United States, British North America (Canada), the Caribbean, Australia, India, Africa, and China.

What was the overall impact of the scholarly tradition among British Baptists? Certainly, Baptists developed a much keener appreciation for the Bible and for the study of the ancient biblical languages. Baptist luminaries such as Joseph Angus, Frederick Gotch, and H. Wheeler Robinson made significant contributions to that scholarship. Baptists also joined the currents of Protestant thinking in ways previously unknown among local congregations. C. H. Spurgeon and John Clifford are representative of Baptist leadership that brought congregational attitudes closer to that of other Protestant groups. Finally, Baptists could with pride increasingly claim a coterie of respected, professional theologians who addressed contemporary matters and represented the tradition in the larger, ecumenical councils of Christian leaders. Contributions to social concerns, the Evangelical Alliance, political questions, and missions are important examples of this participation. Here, Baptists Ernest Payne, Morris West and David S. Russell were without peers.

CHAPTER 5

AMERICAN BAPTIST PASTORS
AND EDITORS

> When preachers are willing to leave unscriptural words, and
> unscriptural doctrines, for the words of Christ, and the plain
> express doctrines of Christ and the apostles, jars and contentions
> will cease, and all will consent to wholesome words, and the
> doctrine which is according to godliness.[1]
>
> Elias Smith, 1816

The discussion of Baptist theologians is now extended to the community
in the United States. As with the British Baptists, the pastor-theologians
are considered first and then the emergence of academic theologians.
There is a demonstrable dependence of American Baptist thinkers on
their British forbears and a rich transatlantic interaction among
contemporaries. The development of Baptist thought in North America
follows typically the same patterns and reflects similar genetic influences
as that in the British experience. Not to be overlooked was the example
and influence of New England Congregationalist ministers upon Baptist
thought; indeed, it is not overstating the case to say that the evolution of
New England theology provided as well the cradle for Baptist
development. Pastors played a crucial role in that development through
preaching and writing, by their personal efforts in mentoring young men
for the ministry, and with their efforts to establish schools of higher
education. More than in Great Britain, scholarly Baptist theology in
America flourished with unusual vigor. Confessions of faith must not be
neglected as transatlantic bridges of Baptist thought. American pastors

---

[1] Elias Smith, *The Life, Conversion, Preaching, Travels and Sufferings of Elias Smith*
(Portsmouth: Beck and Foster, 1816; repr. New York: Arno Press, 1980) 141.

lived within these confessional boundaries and later modified them to suit congregational, associational, and mission circumstances.[2]

The earliest influence upon American Baptist thought was from pastors who led strategic congregations or who became involved in important debates or issues, or who wrote about themes important to the Baptist community. They were carriers of theological genes that influenced a wide circle of churches and other pastors. John Clarke, John Myles, and Thomas Goold define the seventeenth-century New England Baptist tradition. In the next century, Isaac Backus, Samuel Jones, Morgan Edwards, Benjamin Randal, Elhanan Winchester, Richard Furman, David Jones, and Oliver Hart helped set the Baptist theological identity in all three sections of colonial America. Pastors and editors like Samuel Stillman, Thomas Baldwin, Elias Smith, and Baron Stowe continued to shape Baptist thought into the first decades of the nineteenth century. Gradually, the academician-theologians of the nineteenth and twentieth centuries took the lead in giving form to the evolving American Baptist theological identity.

John Clarke (1609–1676) was the pre-eminent pastor-theologian in early American Baptist life. Born in England, some think he was educated at Oxford or Cambridge. A plausible theory is that his medical education was taken at the University of Leyden where he received the Master of Arts degree. There is no record of his being baptized as an adult or of his ordination to the ministry. His Baptist identity and influence stem from the role he played in the congregation he founded at Newport, Rhode Island. He was truly a "work in progress."

Clarke arrived in Boston (Massachusetts Bay Colony) in 1637 at the height of the Antinomian Controversy. This challenge to the "Bible Commonwealth" produced two theological parties, one affirming the covenant of grace, the other the covenant of works. The intensity of adversity over theological matters troubled Clarke. He wrote of his consternation in *Ill Newes from New England* (1652): "They were not able so to bear with others in their different understandings and consciences, as in these uttermost parts of the world to live peaceably together." Clarke's desire to live under a government that allowed differences of opinion led him to Newport on Aquidneck in Rhode Island. The eminent Roger Williams advised him in this matter. By 1663

---

[2] See the Philadelphia Confession of Faith, the Kehukee Statement, the Black Rock Resolutions, and the New Hampshire Confession of Faith, all discussed above.

Clarke became the "trusty and well-beloved subject" of King Charles II, who granted through him a charter for the founding of the Colony of Rhode Island.

Clarke's theological disposition is ascertained from his historical context as much as from his scant writings. For instance, in contrast to Quakers who gave priority to the Spirit and Antinomians who rejected the law of God, Clarke upheld the sufficiency of the Scriptures. Against those who required the baptism of infants, Clarke took an anti-pedobaptist position. Clarke is difficult to categorize theologically with respect to the formative period of Baptist identity. At the same time that he was establishing the congregation at Newport, English Calvinistic Baptists were in the nascent stages of their development (1638–39). He did not have any known interaction with the General Baptists. His congregation lacked a sharp creedal statement as it took shape. Further, there was no church covenant nor any record of ordination of its multiple pastors. Clarke came to be classed with the Calvinistic or Particular Baptists because upon his return to England in the 1650s he developed friendships with their leaders, including Hanserd Knollys.[3] Many of his theological stances were replicated in other emerging New England "baptists," Henry Dunster being one example.

Clarke's theological tendencies may be determined by a careful reading of what he did not mention in *Ill Newes from New England*.[4] For example, he seemed not to have pursued re-baptism vigorously and it appears he practiced closed communion. The latter position was based upon the Puritan concept of the covenant and assurance of grace. The Holy Spirit was the guide in confessional matters, not a creed. A biblicist at heart, he encouraged lay exhortation on an egalitarian basis. With Roger Williams, Clarke distrusted a "hireling ministry" and felt "every believer ought to improve the talent the Lord hath given him, and may

---

[3] It is interesting to speculate that Clarke may have been influenced by Knollys and Mark Lucar during the three years they spent in New Hampshire and Massachusetts 1638–1641. He turned to Knollys later in England, the latter having become a leader in the Particular or Calvinistic Baptist movement there in the 1640s. See William G. McLoughlin, *New England Dissent, I: 5-6. 2:834* and Henry S. Burrage, *A History of the Baptists in New England (Philadelphia: American Baptist Publication Society, 1894)*, 25-26.

[4] Sydney V. James, *John Clarke and His Legacies: Religion and Law in Colonial Rhode Island 1638–1750* (University Park: Pennsylvania State University Press, 1998) 26.

speak by way of prophecy...for the comfort of the whole."[5] Here he clearly exhibited an advanced understanding of the Holy Spirit derived from 1 Corinthians 14. With the arrival of Mark Lucar[6] in the 1640s Clarke moved toward baptism by immersion as a form of witness. It may be an overstatement to say that the characteristic divisions over general and particular understandings of the atonement were unimportant to Clarke, but there were both kinds of thinkers in his congregation.[7] His kind of Baptist experience opposed doctrinal rigidity, and rightly so in the confused web of theological opinions that marked the Bay Colony at mid-century.

Another telling characteristic of John Clarke's theology was his understanding of the Christian witness. In 1651 he learned of a group of dissidents in nearby Seekonk, Massachusettts. Clarke and Mark Lucar visited them to welcome them into the new Baptist fold and introduce them to baptism by immersion. There he met the redoubtable Obadiah Holmes. On a second excursion in 1651, Clarke, Holmes, and John Crandall paid a visit to William Witter of Lynn, Massachusetts, for what became a celebrated case of pastoral care and public witness. When the constables arrived to arrest the Baptists, Clarke behaved with acumen and poise. The accused were taken to a local Standing Order meeting house for a service, where Clarke refused to take off his hat during the service and defiantly read a book, probably the Bible! A trial ensued in which the three "evangelists" were fined. Clarke's fine was paid and he returned to Newport to include the incident in his forthcoming *Ill Newes From New England* (1652). He protested (but did not refuse!) the payment of the fine because he wanted a public debate about his theological positions. Obadiah Holmes refused payment of his fine, was whipped, and became a hero in Clarke's narrative.[8]

---

[5] John Clarke, *Ill Newes from New England*, 10, 62.

[6] Lucar was among the original Particular Baptists of England. He may be credited with introducing believer's baptism by immersion among them. See Champlin Burrage, *The Early English Dissenters in the Light of Recent Research (1550-1641) 2 vols.* (Cambridge: Cambridge University Press, 1912), II: 296, 299, 302.

[7] Ibid., 40. I think James may misunderstand and thus devalue to a large extent important theological distinctions already emerging among various sorts of Baptists.

[8] For a full contemporary account of the incident, see Edwin S. Gaustad, *The Last Will and Testimony of Obadiah Holmes* (New York: Arno Press, 1980) that brings together all of the relevant original sources.

Of course the question arises about the theological bases of Clarke's religious toleration. Here he shared with Roger Williams the lead among New England and American Baptist thinkers. Part of Clarke's mindset may be determined from his understanding of the Church. Unlike Puritans who allowed that the visible church might include "wolves," or the Separatists who thought they could determine precisely who were children of the covenant, Baptists like Clarke based their view of church membership on profession of faith. Eschewing probationary periods of membership, they merely trusted the sincerity of profession. Baptists interpreted the Wheat and Tares parable of Matthew 13: 24–30 differently from Puritans. Puritans thought Jesus meant that any attempt to keep hypocrites and others out of the church were futile, while Baptists argued in favor of toleration because the parable pertained to the world and that only the angels could separate the saints from the heretics at judgment day.[9] Clarke further realized that the Puritan oligarchy in New England was prepared to wink at "non-fundamental" differences of opinion. Thus, he and others "connived at toleration" by pushing the boundaries. His *Ill Newes from New England* was an attempt to soften the relative intolerance of Massachusetts Bay in order that they become "nursing fathers to the children of God" that propagated the gospel of Jesus Christ and suffered the tares of heresy with the wheat of truth as Scripture provided.[10] As was the case with Thomas Helwys and others in the English General Baptist tradition, Clarke's theology of religious toleration grew out of experience rather than theological speculation.

The contributions of John Clarke to Baptist identity must be seen in the context of an evolving theology. He was shaped by his context and he listened to those who crossed his path. Rather than defining a sharp doctrinal stance, he exhibited openness to dialogue and consequent theological growth. Moreover, his penchant for religious liberty became the basis of public policy in a colonial outpost. These characteristics certainly earned him a place in the genetic traces of early American Baptist life and thought. More than Roger Williams, John Clarke is the true democrat and religious libertarian among early Rhode Island

---

[9] McLoughlin, 1:44n.

[10] Clarke was apparently limiting his case for toleration to Christians and probably Protestant groups, as he made no claim for toleration of Jews, Turks, or papists as Thomas Helwys had. See ibid., 1:97, and *Ill Newes from New England*, 39–76.

Baptists.[11] The spirit he brought to religious and public discourse has long characterized the American Baptist theological disposition.

John Myles (c.1621–1682) was the second of the determinative pastoral and theological influences of the seventeenth-century American Baptist experience. The early years of John Myles are obscure. Likely he was an Oxford graduate who joined the Baptist movement while he was at Brasenose College. He may have been baptized in the London Particular Baptist Church led by William Consett and Edward Draper. While English by birth, he was an adopted Welshman, probably volunteering for missionary service on behalf of the London Baptists. By 1651 he was the leading Baptist minister in Wales and the original force behind the establishment of numerous congregations, notably at Ilston, Caermarthen, and Abergavenny. He apparently was of the Calvinistic Baptist tradition, taking a closed communion position. During the Cromwell Era, he was paid to evaluate clergy as a government "tryer," thus revealing a more cooperative than separationist stance with the state. In 1662, however, the St. Bartholomew Day (or Conventicle) Act deprived Myles of his government support and he determined to emigrate to the American colonies. Landing at Plymouth, Massachusetts, he founded a congregation at Rehoboth. Following some intense persecution, the congregation re-settled at Swansea, near the Rhode Island boundary. There he ministered according to open communion practices until his death in 1683.[12] In 1676–1678, following the burning of his church during King Philip's War, Myles served the congregation at Boston. He influenced them on the open communion question, and baptized among others, William Screven, pioneer of Baptist life in the South.

The covenant that the Myles church drew up reveals its formation and character. They "protested against all rending or dividing principles or practices from any of the people of God." These Myles believed were

---

[11] One is tempted to include here Obadiah Holmes (c.1607–1682), who in the theological tradition of John Clarke, made a lasting contribution to the religious liberty motif in American Baptist experience. Holmes's 1651 episode at Lynn, Massachusetts, was well-heralded in accounts and later picked up by Isaac Backus and still later by Edwin S. Gaustad, *Baptist Piety: The Last Will and Testimony of Obadiah Holmes* (Grand Rapids: Eerdmans, 1978). There is, however, too little documentation of Holmes's developed theology and virtually no trace of his theological impact upon anyone else.

[12] William Henry Brackney, "John Myles," in *The Baptists* (New York: Greenwood Press, 1988) 235–36.

utterly inconsistent with that Christian charity which declares men to be Christ's disciples. Thus they practiced communion with "all such fellow-members in Christ, with liberty in controversial points not essential to salvation."[13] In the organizing principles of New Swansea, Myles defined orthodox doctrine as Trinitarian and Chalcedonian on the doctrine of Christ; affirming the priestly work of Christ, his personal return, and the resurrection of the dead; upholding the celebration of the Lord's Day. The congregation rejected meritorious works as a means of salvation and disavowed the doctrine of transubstantiation. Positions such as pedobaptism and matters of church discipline were left to the discretion of the consciences of the town inhabitants.[14] Myles was close enough to the prevailing Calvinism of the Puritan Commonwealth to be acceptable as a recognized pastor. He was hostile to the same groups of religious heretics as the Congregationalists: Papists, Jews, Arminians, Lutherans, Quakers, sabbatarians, Anglicans, and radical separationists such as John Clarke.[15] It is to be noted that Myles's open communion stance was directed toward communion with Congregationalists.

Myles's theological legacy lay in its connection with the Reformed tradition. He was theologically astute about matters of the covenants, tenets of prevailing Calvinism, and the biblical emphases of the Puritans. His experience in England and Wales point to his complicity with Cromwellian Calvinism, as defined in the Westminster Confession of Faith and the London Baptists's 1644 Confession. His long-lasting influence in American Baptist thought lay in his proximity to prevailing Calvinism and his irenic spirit. That proximity also helps to explain why Myles fared better in the hands of the Standing Order than his Baptist cohorts at Boston and Newport during the era of the earliest American Baptist witness.

The first pastor of the first Baptist church in Boston was Thomas Gould (c. 1615–1675), third in preeminence among American Baptist pastor-theologians. The congregation in Boston was as strategically placed with respect to theology as was the city in terms of geography. Founded through adverse circumstances, the church had close ties to English Baptist precedents. Boston was the parent church to most Baptist

---

[13] Quoted in Thomas W. Bicknell, *John Myles and Religious Toleration in Massachusetts* (Boston: n.p., 1892) 13–14.

[14] Ibid., 19–20.

[15] McLoughlin, *New England Dissent*, 1: 133–34.

churches of eastern Massachusetts and beyond in Maine and New
Hampshire. The congregation was also connected with early churches in
Rhode Island.

Thomas Goold remains somewhat of an enigma, in part because he
was a lay preacher who was on occasion overshadowed by others. What
he studied in preparation for ministry is not known, nor is it clear who
most directly influenced him.[16] Goold's theological contribution was
mediated through his experience, as a fairly well-to-do farmer and wagon
maker who reflected theologically upon his immediate circumstances. In
this regard, he represents the rank and file of early New England
Baptists, characterized as "honest, hard-working plowmen, artisans,
mechanics and day-laborers."[17] From the Congregationalist records, we
learn that Goold absented himself from Sabbath meetings in his church at
Charlestown and was admonished for such breaches. With respect to
infant baptism, Goold himself recalled that on the birth of his child in
1655, "God was pleased at last to make it clear to me by the rule of the
gospel that children are not capable nor fit subjects for such an
ordinance."[18] Goold was brought before church leaders and a debate
about baptism ensued. The Scripture passage referred to for over five
hours was Acts 2:39–40. Goold maintained the Congregationalists had
misquoted and misappropriated the passage in favor of infant baptism.
After a second altercation in the Cambridge Church, several Baptists
began meetings in Goold's home. "We consulting together what to do,
sought the Lord to direct us…they gave us counsel to congregate
ourselves together; and so we did, being nine of us to walk in the order of
the gospel according to the rule of Christ, yet knowing that it is a breach
of the law of this country."[19] The nine have been identified as emigrants

---

[16] The story of Goold is derived from original manuscripts he created plus official
records of proceedings against him and local church records. Isaac Backus used
manuscripts in *A History of New England with Particular Reference to the Denomination
of Christians Called Baptists*, ed. David Weston (Newton: The Backus Historical Society,
1871) 1:288–327. An interpretive version, plus a photostatic reproduction of Goold's
covenant/confession, are found in Nathan E. Wood, *The History of the First Baptist
Church of Boston, 1665–1899* (Philadelphia: American Baptist Publication Society,
1899) 31–96. McLoughlin accumulates much of the detail on Goold and makes sense of a
shadowy career. See McLoughlin, *New England Dissent*, 1:49–78.

[17] McLoughlin, *New England Dissent*, 1:77.

[18] Backus, *History*, 290.

[19] Ibid., 296.

of various Baptist backgrounds in England from London and Dartmouth, most of whom fled the Clarendon Code.[20] Goold and others were eventually imprisoned. To deal with their obstinacy, Massachusetts Bay authorities staged a debate with prominent Puritan ministers. At length, Goold was released and fled to Noddles Island in Boston Harbor where he held religious services until the authorities ceased pursuit 1670–71. The last four years of Goold's ministry to his death in 1675 were spent 'peaceably enjoying liberty" in rented quarters back in Boston.[21]

Goold's theological contribution to Baptist identity can be seen through three products of his work and ministry. First was the covenant or statement of faith that he wrote at the founding of the congregation in 1665. Composed of twenty-five articles, it takes a Christological and evangelical perspective, holding that "Christ's commission to his disciples is to teach and to baptize." The use of terminology such as "saints by calling" and his description of fellow believers as "joined together in covenant and fellowship are a gospel Church of Christ"[22] is reminiscent of earlier confessional language, notably the first London Confession. The document is replete with matters of church order, such as the process to select officers, discipline of membership, the first day meeting, and a clear statement on recognition of the "things of ceasere," by which they meant the magistracy and the laws of the Colony. There is a hint of Calvinistic dogma in the affirmation of "the resurrection of the just unto life and the unjust unto condemnation everlasting."[23]

The second product of Goold's work helping to shape the American tradition of being Baptist came in the form of testimony at the trials and debates held between 1665–67. While not practiced theologians, Goold and his colleagues argued for an individualistic form of Christianity, relying upon what they held was the direct empowerment of the Holy Spirit. Spiritual community was to be had within churches and between churches, rather than as a Bible Commonwealth. Small, voluntary gathered churches of professed believers, symbolized in believer's baptism, constituted a gospel ecclesiology. As William G. McLoughlin so aptly put it, "The covenant of God with a chosen people could better

---

[20] See McLoughlin, *New England Dissent*, 1:55.
[21] Nathan E. Wood, *The History of the First Baptist Church of Boston* (1665-1899) (Philadelphia: American Baptist Publication Society, 1899), 121.
[22] Wood, *History*, 65–67.
[23] Ibid., 66.

be sustained by numerous spirit-filled raisins giving savor to the national cake than by trying to leaven the whole fruit cake."[24] Finally, the theological makeup of the Bostonians was directly linked to the English Baptist confessional tradition. The congregation first used the 1644 London Confession and later the 1677 London Confession of Faith to ratify theological positions.[25] If recent historians are correct, there was also evidence of the Somerset Confession signers and their relatives in the Boston congregation.[26]

As others have pointed out, Thomas Goold was not a religious libertarian like Roger Williams. He was not a radical civil remonstrator, as was Henry Dunster. Goold represented the self-taught lay tradition in theology. It is obvious that he was clever enough to draw upon other resources to create his confession. His emphases clearly mark his tradition within the Puritan/Separatist tradition of Massachusetts Bay and English Particular Baptists. The influence of the Boston congregation, even within its first generation, is a matter of historical record. The congregation, it may be noted, continues to use Goold's confession at the present.

Collectively, then, the theological legacy of New England Baptist pastors in the first century was seen in Thomas Goold, John Clarke, and John Myles. Goold represented an anti-pedobaptist form of dissent of individual, voluntary congregations. In establishing the first Baptist Church in Boston, he laid the groundwork for a theological heritage that spawned numerous congregations across New England and beyond. Similarly, John Clarke represented the foundation of religious toleration in the colonies, as it eventually would be applied to congregational and

---

[24] McLoughlin, *New England Dissent*, 1:69.

[25] The application of William Screven's congregation in Kittery, Maine, for recognition of officers, baptism, and validity of covenant to the Boston church indicated conformity with this recent confession of faith. See "Selection of the Minutes of First Baptist Church," quoted in Wood, *History*, 180.

[26] A. H. Newman, Henry S. Burrage, Richard D. Land, and Robert Baker all hold that William Screven and/or his son who immigrated to New England about 1668, were from the Somerton Church, Somersetshire. See Albert H. Newman, *History of the Baptist Churches in the United States* (Philadelphia: American Baptist Publication Society, 1898) 218; Henry S. Burrage, *History of the Baptists in Maine* (Portland: Marks Printing House, 1904) 24–25; Robert Baker, *Adventure in Faith: The First Three Hundred Years of First Baptist Church, Charleston, South Carolina* (Nashville: Broadman Press, 1982) 33–40. The Land evidence is discussed on page 34 of Baker's work.

political life. Finally, John Myles built an early case for open communion in an enlarged Reformed Tradition that appreciated liberty in non-fundamental doctrines. Each would be "rediscovered" in Isaac Backus's history during the next century. An often-overlooked genetic connection with the New England Baptist tradition was that of William Screven, pioneer Baptist of the American South. Screven visited the Baptist Church in Boston on numerous occasions in the 1670s when Thomas Goold and for a short time, John Myles, were pastors. As Robert Baker has adeptly shown, Screven was baptized in 1681, likely by John Myles.

As the eighteenth century dawned, the Baptist movement in America was made up of scattered congregations in New England, the Middle Colonies, and very sparse pockets in the South. Strong pastoral leadership and missionary endeavors of pastors would greatly extend the Baptist witness. Great theological diversity would manifest itself as the new century grew to maturity.

Isaac Backus (1724–1806) was the outstanding American Baptist pastor of the eighteenth century colonial period. Backus rose from a modest upbringing and a self-instructed education to theological leadership in his community, had a profound effect upon public affairs, and made significant contributions to the creation of an identity for the emerging American Baptist denomination. He was a self-educated farmer who in 1741 was caught up in the Great Awakening and experienced a religious conversion. He was much influenced by his pastor, Benjamin Lord, who followed the path of the Separates to form a new congregation in Norwich, Massachusetts. Apparently Backus's mother, Elizabeth, was also an important source of his spirituality. In the mid-1740s Backus began preaching to various Separate congregations in the area, finally settling in Titicut in 1747, where he was called to organize a New Light congregation and become its pastor. He became a leader of the Separates in the colony, appealing to the General Court for exemption rights. At length, in 1751, he led the Titicut congregation to adopt Baptist principles and thereafter became a leading spokesman for the Separatist Baptist movement. In 1756 he again reorganized the principles of his congregation to adopt a closed communion stance, typical of older Calvinistic Baptist congregations in Massachusetts.

Backus's own ecclesiological pilgrimage was a paradigm of the larger movement taking shape across New England.[27]

Over the next five decades, Isaac Backus became one of the leading theologian-apologists for Baptists in America. He built a strong ministry base in his own congregation, assisted in the development of the Warren Baptist Association—first of its kind in New England—and lent his ardent support to education in the founding of the College of Rhode Island. When the issue of taxation to support religious institutions came up, Backus emerged as an articulate defender of the separation of church and state.[28] His writings placed him at the forefront of Nonconformist theology in New England. His history of New England Baptists did much to define the theological identity of the Baptist movement in his region. Backus's understanding of the "doctrine of the church" often involved issues of polity, governance, and practical experience.[29]

Isaac Backus's theology was often revealed in response to a tract or statement from the Standing Order ministry. What emerges from a reading of his works is a Calvinist in transition, much affected by Jonathan Edwards on the one hand and the Enlightenment on the other hand.[30] For instance, on the contemporary thorny issue of free will, Backus opined, "We know and as firmly hold as any free-willer on earth that all men are under moral government where precepts and promises,

---

[27] For a sense of the lineage and spread of the Separatist movement to the Baptist persuasion, see C. C. Goen, *Revivalism and Separatism in New England 1740–1800* (New Haven: Yale University Press, 1962).

[28] The place of Backus in the debate of separation of church and state continues to spark debate. Edwin S. Gaustad in a seminal article, "The Backus-Leland Tradition," *Foundations* 2/2 (April 1959): 147–50 saw Backus and Leland constituting a kind of unified vision of church/state relations. Lately, John Witte, Jr. in "The Theology and Politics of The First Amendment Religion Clauses: A Bicentennial Essay," *Emory Law Journal* (1991): 490–507 has lumped Backus and Leland together as "accomodationists," while Joe L. Coker, "Sweet Harmony vs. Strict Separation: Recognizing the Distinctions Between Isaac Backus and John Leland," *American Baptist Quarterly* 16/3 (September 1997): 241–49, argued for Backus as an accomodationist and Leland as a strict Enlightenment separationist.

[29] Robert G. Torbet, "Baptist Thought About the Church," *Foundations* 1/2 (April, 1958): 24–25.

[30] Backus frequently directly quoted Jonathan Edwards. See various Backus titles excerpted in McLoughlin, *Pamphlets*, 210, 221, 404, 413. Backus likewise quoted John Locke: see *Pamphlets*, 357, 376; in the latter he quotes Locke's famous definition of churches as voluntary societies.

exhortations, warnings, etc., have their proper place and ought to influence us in all our conduct. And I believe from the bottom of my heart that God never did nor ever will punish any but the guilty." He held those Calvinists who insisted upon double-predestination blessing of the righteous and condemnation of the non-elect to be "blasphemers of God's sovereignty."[31] Yet, his view of the atonement was decidedly beyond orthodox. "God was so far from ever proclaiming atonement for all men, without any exception," he deduced from Scripture. He reasoned that not all were saved and that several classes of ungodly men, heretics, and the fallen angels are reserved for eternal torment.[32] In this context, Backus greatly modified the prevailing covenant theology of the Standing Order. Puritan Congregationalists held that there was one covenant between God and humans, seen in the Old Testament and continued in the New. But, Backus maintained there were two covenants, one of works, made with the Jews, and a second the covenant of grace, made with those who believe in Christ. The discontinuity was important because it meant that the church and baptism were parts of an entirely new economy, and the new covenant looked entirely to the future. It has been rightly argued that this may well have been a theological reason for American acceptance of the Baptist persuasion, namely that it symbolized a break with Old World, medieval, and Puritan thinking, in favor of a new vision in a new land.[33]

In *The Bondwoman and the Free* (1756), Backus gave his understanding of the nature of the church and its relation to believer's baptism: "It is evident that as the branch must have a living union to the tree or vine in order to receive nourishment therefrom, so every person, both great and small, must by faith be united to Christ, in order to partake of them favors; which shows that no arguments can be drawn from hence to prove that any others are subjects of baptism but real saints."[34] His

---

[31] Isaac Backus, *The Sovereign Decrees of God* in *Isaac Backus on Church, State, and Calvinism: Pamphlets* , ed. William G. McLoughlin (Cambridge: The Belknap Press, 1968) 296.

[32] Isaac Backus, *The Doctrine of Election and Final Perseverance* (1789) in ibid., 454.

[33] William G. McLoughlin, *Isaac Backus and the American Pietistic Tradition* (Boston: Little, Brown, 1967) 74.

[34] Isaac Backus, *A Short Description of the difference between the Bond-woman and the Free*; *As they are the two Covenants, with the Characters and Conditions of each of*

1783 tract, *A Door Opened for Equal Christian Liberty,* was his theological underpinning of religious liberty, buttressed by New Testament passages such as Luke 9:49, Galatians 5:1, 13, and 1 Peter 4:10–11: "Since religion is ever a matter between God and individuals, how can any man become a member of a religious society without his own consent? And how can a man who believes it to be impossible practically say that it is possible without contracting guilt to his conscience?"[35]

At the root of Isaac Backus's theology was a radical pietism. His major contemporary interpreter, William G. McLoughlin, argued that from this taproot sprang his ideas of the separation of church and state, the priesthood of all believers, a gathered voluntary church, and a confidence in the trustworthiness of the conscience of the common man.[36] Further, Backus saw in the not too distant future a realization of millennial hopes that gave the United States a role as a truly Christian society. In America, there would be no hierarchical, establishment church, no elite learned ministry, and no overarching public policy respecting religion. In Backus was an evolved wedding of John Locke's theory of religious societies and the experiences of New Birth revivalism. As McLoughlin has shown, behind Backus's leadership the revival was not a backward-looking reaction against enlightened religion, but a form of experimental religion every bit as scientific and defensible as the discoveries of Newton or Boyle. Backus even went so far as to write about "scientific doctrines of grace."[37]

There are other clues to the theology of Isaac Backus in his interaction, sometimes heated, with other Christians in New England. For example, by the 1770s there was an increasing interest among intellectuals in deism as a convenient successor to Calvinism. Men like Thomas Jefferson and Thomas Paine reflected discontent with the old theological systems. Not a few persons in New England shifted from Congregationalism to Unitarianism. More than once, Backus showed his scorn for deistic and Unitarian forms that he thought the essence of

---

their children; *Considered in a Sermon, delivered at Middleborough,* in McLoughlin, *Pamphlets,* 151.

[35] Isaac Backus, *A Door Opened for Equal Christian Liberty, and No Man Can Shut It. This Proved by Plain Facts,* in McLoughlin, *Pamphlets,* 432–33.

[36] McLoughlin, *Isaac Backus,* 232–33.

[37] Ibid., 232.

infidelity. But he was equally critical of hyper-Calvinism, especially as the Sandemanians and Glasites had articulated it. His tract, *True Faith Will Produce Good Works* (1767) was to be an antidote. The tract also had in its purview the groups like the General Six Principle Baptists and the Methodists that stressed general atonement and/or freewill. Backus referred the latter groups to Jonathan Edwards's discourse, *The Freedom of the Will,* and warned against confounding works and grace. He stoutly condemned the universalist thought of John Murray and James Relly, as well as that of fellow-Baptist Elhanan Winchester. He thought Relly was wrong in holding to an imaginary union with Christ, and that Winchester overemphasized God's benevolence. Backus embellished Locke in holding that God was the owner of the property of the universe and all its inhabitants and could show mercy to whom he wanted. Backus's most vitriolic attacks were reserved for the Shakers who, according to his perspective, totally perverted the Christian faith. He even called upon the town council of Pittsfield, Massachusetts, to outlaw them. He referred to Mother Ann Lee as "nothing but a common prostitute."[38] Finally, Backus had no affinity with the following of Samuel Hopkins and the "New Divinity" theology because they misunderstood the venerable Jonathan Edwards in setting up a deterministic theology in some sort of "consistent Calvinism." In his senior years, he seems not to have understood the powerful reshaping of the New England theology at work among Congregationalists Joseph Bellamy, Samuel Hopkins, and Jonathan Edwards, Jr., giving new interpretation to the doctrines of efficient causation, atonement, sin, conversion and holiness.[39]

Mention must also be made of Backus's contributions to creating ideological and theological heroes of Baptist thought. The premier of these was the venerable Roger Williams (1603–1684). Williams had lived well into old age and was uninvolved in Baptist life and thought after 1650. He was not a pastor nor did he contribute to the theological development of the Baptist community. In his *History of the Baptists in New England* (1777), Backus recovered the life of Roger Williams and extolled his virtues as a Baptist statesman in the religious libertarian tradition. Agreeing with John Callender, Backus wrote of Williams: "Thus lived and thus died the first Baptist minister in New England and

---

[38] Quoted in ibid., 182.

[39] Frank Hugh Foster, *A Genetic History of the New England Theology* (Chicago: University of Chicago Press, 1907) 116–17, 180–86, 240.

the first founder and supporter of any truly free civil government upon earth, since the rise of antichrist; and he was buried with all the solemnity the colony was able to show."[40] A second heroic figure for Baptists that Backus recovered was Obadiah Holmes (1607–1682). Holmes became involved with John Clarke and moved along the continuum of Puritan/Congregationalist to Baptist. In 1651 he, Clarke, and John Crandal were apprehended for evangelical purposes (see earlier, p. 205). These incidents spread through both Massachusetts and English Puritan society. Backus wove the fabric of the historical narrative artfully: "As the sentiments of the ancient Baptists in this country have been grossly misrepresented, and as Mr. Holmes was no small sufferer in that cause, I thought it expedient to let the reader thus far hear him speak for himself, and tell his ideas about the nature of true religion."[41] With the passing of time into the eighteenth century, Holmes's story might well have been forgotten had Backus's history not brought it to life again.[42]

A true child of the Awakening and the Enlightenment, Backus emphasized an evangelical Calvinism that was bathed in piety: the experience of the New Birth symbolized in believer's baptism, family devotions, a pure and voluntary church of gathered saints, and a lively preaching of the gospel as a "means of grace." The triumphs of the American Revolution, the separation of church and state, yet the continuation of a godly commonwealth, all signaled to Backus a validity to his post-millennialism. America was the hope of the world, and soon the kingdom of Christ was to be made manifest. "Since a door is now opened for a clear deliverance from these evils," he wrote, "...we shall be the happiest people upon earth."[43]

Samuel Jones (1735–1814) was one of the most influential ministers of the Philadelphia Baptist tradition in the eighteenth century. Born in Wales of Baptist parentage, he immigrated to Pennsylvania at an early age. He was educated at Isaac Eaton's Hopewell Academy in the

---

[40] Backus, *History*, 1:413.

[41] Ibid., 1:176.

[42] A second generation of appreciation for Holmes began with the retelling of the stories in Edwin S. Gaustad, *Baptist Piety: The Last Will and Testament of Obadiah Holmes* (New York: Arno Press, 1980).

[43] Isaac Backus, *Church History of New England* (Philadelphia: Baptist Tract Repository, 1839) 239–46.

company of James Manning, Isaac Skillman, David Jones, and David
Howell—all themselves destined to become leaders in the Baptist
movement. He graduated from the College of Philadelphia, was ordained
in the Philadelphia Association, served the Southampton Baptist Church,
and later Pennepack or Lower Dublin. Jones's leadership in the
developing Philadelphia Association became evident after he wrote a
definitive annual letter on the nature of Baptist associations.

The influences upon Jones were an intricate interplay of elements
from eighteenth-century Baptist life. He was descended from a long line
of Welsh Baptists, sturdy in their Calvinistic theology. At the College of
Philadelphia he was deeply influenced in Enlightenment philosophy by
Glasgow University alumnus, Francis Alison. His community of support
in Philadelphia included Bristol graduate Morgan Edwards, Isaac Eaton,
Ebenezer Kinnersley, and Samuel Stillman, all adherents of the
Philadelphia (Second London) Confession of Faith. Jones himself
recognized the importance of the confession, but refused to treat it as any
form of "human establishment."[44] Clearly as Hywel Davies believes,
Morgan Edwards was the leading influence upon Jones, certifying his
ordination, preaching at the service and reminding him of their common
Welsh heritage. Jones enjoyed a lifelong friendship with Edwards, even
during the dark period of Edwards's life when he was banished from
Philadelphia.[45] The two men were to become synonymous with an
educated Baptist ministry in the United States, much of which was
associated with the Rhode Island College.[46]

Jones's ministry in Southampton was played out against a background
of the Great Awakening. While he later reminisced about the effects of
that revival, of George Whitefield and Gilbert Tennent, he was not an
enthusiastic evangelical. Like Morgan Edwards, he used a sermonic
manuscript and was steeped in the Calvinist tradition of John Gill, whom

---

[44] Hywel Davies, *Transatlantic Brethren*: *Reverend Samuel Jones and His Friends*;
Baptists in Wales, Pennsylvania, and Beyond (Bethlehem: Lehigh University Press,
1995) 93.

[45] Ibid., 94–95.

[46] It will be noted that the Philadelphia Baptist Association founded the Rhode Island
College because Rhode Island alone of the colonies in 1764 lacked an institution of
higher education. Morgan Edwards was the prime mover of the project.

he considered a "great luminary."[47] When Jones heard of the effects of "Fullerism" among the English churches, he was dismayed and defended traditional Calvinism against the so-called "New Divinity" that he thought was "freewillism" in disguise and symptomatic of the decline of the power of true religion. He differed with men like Isaac Backus, whom he thought too close to Andrew Fuller theologically, and against whose more open positions he articulated a continuing high Calvinism.[48] His favorite theme was sovereign grace, and he was more remembered for what he wrote than for his preaching.

Perhaps the most important theological contribution to Baptist life made by Samuel Jones was his own transformation in the sacramental matter of the "laying on of hands." This teaching was of primary importance to the Welsh Tract congregation; there it was a symbol for the reception of the Holy Spirit and "foundational" to the Baptist principles. Seemingly based on apostolic practices hinted in Acts 8:12 and 19:6–7 as well as in Hebrews 6:1–2, the Welsh churches from the mid-seventeenth century practiced it. It was primary to their doctrine of the Holy Spirit. Yet, in the colonies there was disagreement about its purposes and by the mid-eighteenth century many congregations discontinued its practice. From the illustrious Welsh Baptist theologian and historian, Joshua Thomas, Jones became convinced that the laying on of hands was more of a Welsh custom than a scriptural ordinance. Following Joshua Thomas's tract, *Historical Sketch of the Debate upon the Laying on of Hands*, more particularly among the Baptists in Wales through the seventeenth and eighteenth centuries (1782), Jones made his case to the Philadelphia Association to cease the practice. He wrote his own tract, *Brief History of the Imposition of Hands on Baptized Persons* (c. 1787), in which he investigated the scriptural bases for the rite and concluded it was an ethnically motivated practice from a time when Welsh pastors dominated the Association.

Jones spearheaded a change in the Association's confession of faith, deleting from it the article referring to the imposition of hands. His former classmate, David Jones, the pastor at the Church in the Great

---

[47] When Gill died, Jones thought the future of Baptist theology was static, and he unsuccessfully attempted an American edition of Gill's *Exposition of the Bible* to continue the high Calvinist tradition.

[48] See Samuel Jones, *The Doctrine of the Covenants. A Sermon Preached at Pennepack in Pennsylvania, September 14, 1781.* (Philadelphia: F. Bailey, 1782).

Valley, immediately opposed the deletion. David Jones argued that this was a dangerous theological precedent, which could lead to other fundamental changes in the doctrinal understanding of the Association. He even attacked the venerable John Gill, who had also disputed the relevance of the practice. David attacked Samuel for "impudent conduct" and the ensuing relationship between the two reflected a serious schism that existed for over a decade in the strongest Baptist community in the United States.[49]

Samuel Jones also became embroiled in the theological controversy surrounding Elhanan Winchester. When Winchester's proclivity toward universal restoration became evident at First Baptist, Philadelphia, his congregation split and the Association was asked to intervene. A Committee consisting of Abel Morgan, James Manning, Oliver Hart, and chaired by Samuel Jones was deputed to investigate the controversy. Under Jones's astute leadership, the Committee adjudicated on the basis of the Philadelphia Confession of Faith. In the Association's Circular Letter of 1781, Jones responded to Winchester's positions by clear statements on the atonement using the very biblical passages Winchester had appealed to in support of universal restoration. Jones denied there was any covenant between God and man with respect to salvation, thus vitiating Winchester's theological case. Later in the decade, Jones went on to define theological positions related to freedom of the will and the nature of the church.[50]

Jones's influence on other Baptist ministers, North and South, could hardly have been greater. He corresponded with Isaac Backus, Hezekiah Smith, and James Manning in New England, with pastors throughout his own association in Pennsylvania, and with ministry leaders in New York and New Jersey. In the South, he had a lively interchange of correspondence with pastors such as Oliver Hart and Richard Furman. Further, through the publication of *A Treatise of Church Discipline, and a Directory* (1798), he became a recognized authority on doctrine and polity for those of the Philadelphia persuasion well into the nineteenth century.

Morgan Edwards (1722–1795) was a prime example of the trans-atlantic connection of Baptists in the eighteenth century. He was born in

---

[49] The controversy is covered adequately in Davies, *Transatlantic Brethren,* 150–60.
[50] Refer to the *Minutes of the Philadelphia Baptist Association1707–1807*, ed. Abram D. Gillette (1781–1787).

Wales, educated at Trosnant Academy under John Mathews, and at Bristol Baptist College under Bernard Foskett. At Bristol he became one of the proponents of the new evangelical Calvinism that opened new opportunities for Baptist witness. At a strategic point in his development he took the advice of Dr. John Gill in London and immigrated to the colony of Pennsylvania. Edwards served only one congregation, First Baptist Church in Philadelphia, and that was an uneven experience. His influence was largely channeled through published historical essays, his itinerancy as an evangelist, and his advocacy of a style of ministry that self-conscientiously reflected upon the implications of serious theological dialogue.

Edwards greatly strengthened the theological constitution and reputation of ministers in the Philadelphia Baptist Association. He advocated an educated clergy and particularly championed knowledge of the biblical languages. A survey of his beliefs by his most recent biographers reveals that on major doctrines dealing with God, Scripture, Christ, and salvation, Edwards was consistent with the theological tradition of the Second London Confession of Faith. His influence may have helped its adoption by the Philadelphia Baptist Association.[51] Two defining doctrinal concerns were given specific emphasis in Edwards's thought: eschatology and ecclesiology. He held to a kind of chiliastic scheme for interpreting the Book of Revelation, in which there are to be two returns of Christ, a literal millennial kingdom, and the appearance of a literal antichrist. He calculated that the beginning of the Kingdom would come in 1996 and that the Lake of Fire was located on the moon.[52] What his work indicates as much as anything else is the Baptist preoccupation with the details of Scripture. In this regard his musing led a host of similar Baptist prophetic speculations in the next century.[53]

Edwards's doctrine of the church was influential in building a broader idea of the church and in strengthening local congregations. First, he

---

[51] Thomas R. McKibbens and Kenneth L. Smith, *The Life and Works of Morgan Edwards* (New York: Arno Press, 1980) 113–23.

[52] Morgan Edwards, *Two Academical Exercises on Subjects Bearing the Following Titles: Prescience, God's Purpose. Predestination, Election, Reprobation, Regeneration, Conversion, Holy Lump, Delivered in 1742 and 1743* (Philadelphia: Dobson & Lang, 1788?) 33–34, 48.

[53] One unique area in Edwards' theology was his conclusion that to be created in Christ before the foundation of the world, must imply the pre-existence of human beings before creation. See *Academical Exercises*, 37.

understood the church to be composed of only those persons who repent and are forgiven; "such as are regenerate or have the law in their minds; such as believe, and, in a word, such as savingly know the Lord."[54] He understood the church to be local and universal. He was among the first to apply "denominational" terminology among Baptists. This use led to his ecclesiology, connecting churches with associations that in turn might comprise a general union. His sacramental theology expanded well beyond traditional Baptist perspectives. Edwards identified nine "rites" he thought scriptural: baptism, Lord's Supper, love feast, laying on of hands, foot-washing, anointing the sick, right hand of fellowship, kiss of charity, and dedication of children.[55] In fact, he developed a clever typology for local churches by their observance or practice of the rites. Lastly, Edwards believed that every congregation should write a covenant as a theological statement of its beliefs and practices.

Edwards's work in compiling a series of treatises on Baptist development throughout the colonies did much to illustrate the diversity of the group by the 1770s. In the Carolinas, he noted the presence of Calvinistic, New Light revivalist, and older General Baptists. In Pennsylvania, he made account of the German Baptists or Tunkers. His staunch Calvinistic bias was revealed in his disdain for those holding the general atonement view. He also held little affection for the Separate Baptists in the South, thinking they should put aside their differences and unite with the Regular Baptists. He frequently had harsh words for Presbyterians, Congregationalists, and Quakers, all of whom were involved in debates with the Baptists.

Morgan Edwards's great genetic value to the Baptists was his bridging connection between the Bristol/West Country English Baptist tradition and the colonial Middle States. His work to establish the College of Rhode Island and his penchant for an educated ministry are tributes to the American Baptist tradition that was to a notable degree rooted in his sometimes-controversial career.

Benjamin Randal (1749–1808) was a short-lived but extremely influential leader in the differentiation of Baptist thought in the United States and Canada. His theological genes reached well beyond his region

---

[54] Morgan Edwards, *The Customs of the Primitive Churches, or a Set of Propositions Relative to the Name, Materials, Constitution of a Church* (Philadelphia: Andrew Stuart, 1768) 5–6.

[55] Cited in McKibbens and Smith, *Morgan Edwards*, 129–30.

and lifespan. Working with a rudimentary primary school education, he became a sailmaker and tailor by trade in his native New Hampshire. He attended a meeting in Portsmouth about 1770 where George Whitefield preached and Randal was converted, making him a direct product of the Great Awakening. He first joined the Congregationalist movement, but was rebuffed by the elitism that characterized the churches he attended. He found others in upstate New Hampshire who struggled both with the baptism issue and with Standing Order Calvinist theology. Baptized by immersion in 1777, he began to preach in various places, sometimes in the open air without benefit of a church building or pulpit. He was called to New Durham where he joined a Separate congregation. Within two years he re-gathered the congregation in covenant on the basis of "free grace, free will, and free communion." Randal arrived at these understandings largely through his own experience and study of Scripture.

Randal's theology was apparently self-defined. When interviewed in 1779 by Calvinistic Baptist ministers in New Hampshire about his understanding of Calvinistic orthodoxy, he replied that he did not believe it and furthermore that "the Lord had shewed me an universal atonement and fullness enough in Christ for all men—the appearance of grace to all men—that the call of God was to all."[56] What he actually objected to was "eternal, particular, personal unconditional election and reprobation."[57] Randal also revealed that God had called him to go out and call all men to be saved. As others have shown, it would be a misstatement to call Randal an Arminian, for he did not use the term and little understood what it meant. Instead, he preferred the term, "universal":

> I saw the Scriptures in perfect harmony; and those texts, about which my opposers were contending, were all opened to my mind; and I saw that they ran in perfect connection with the universal love of God to men—the universal atonement in the work of redemption by Jesus Christ—who tasted death for every man—the universal appearance of grace to all men and with the universal call of the gospel.[58]

---

[56] Buzzell, *Freewill Baptists,* 75.
[57] *Religious Magazine,* no. 1 (1811): 2.
[58] Buzzell, *Freewill Baptists,* 89.

Randal recreated Baptist ecclesiology by syncretizing Methodist, Quaker, Calvinistic, and General Baptist polities. Rather than stressing the independence of each local congregation or the associational principle *per se*, he moved in a connectional direction. Because his preaching purposely extended beyond the New Durham congregation, he made regular itinerant tours to an ever-widening circle of congregations. Here was the beginning of a ruling eldership not unlike the Methodist superintendents or the messengers of the English General Baptists. As this individual met with each congregation on a regular basis, perhaps to celebrate the Lord's Supper, it became a "monthly meeting." Every three months Randal or his successors met with several congregations in an area, usually for the purposes of holding a revival; these became "quarterly meetings." When he met with representatives of the quarterly meetings in a state, that session became a "yearly meeting." Eventually in 1827, all the Freewill congregations met through representatives in a "general conference". This general conference developed legislative capabilities, authorized an integrated denominational series of societies and achieved far-reaching stances addressing social reform. Here was an ecclesiology that carried genuine accountability amidst and beyond the local church, similar to the General Baptists in England.

Of course, the most outstanding contribution that the Freewill Baptists made was in the promulgation of the doctrine of the authentic freedom of the human will. Randal refused the notion that because Adam sinned, so the entire posterity is condemned. Instead, he taught, persons are condemned for their own unbelief and he urged his hearers to believe the gospel in order to be saved. Three propositions were implicit in Randal's beliefs. First, salvation is offered freely to all persons. Second, each person has the choice of accepting or rejecting salvation. Third, once converted, the sinner nevertheless might backslide and fall from grace. The lack of documents and records from Randal's writings suggest he had little opportunity during his lifetime to articulate more fully Freewill doctrines.

Randal and his followers seemed to lay greater stress upon ethics than doctrine. This may have been due to their lack of theological sophistication, or it was a reaction to a perception that Calvinistic Christians were obsessed with continual theological debate. Whatever the reason, Freewill Baptist periodicals, sermons, and statements abound with commentary on lifestyle issues, discipleship, and reformation. Little wonder that the Connection produced early opposition to slavery, recognition of women in ministry, and temperance.[59]

What Benjamin Randal did was to call into question the prevailing theological traditions of his time and announce the inauguration of a new, egalitarian theology that matched Methodism and Universalism in its popular effects. Later, as the sect matured, it achieved a more sophisticated theological understanding and established connections with other "Arminian" Baptist bodies in England, Canada, and the United States.[60]

Boston became for the Baptists a center of Calvinism. By mid-century Samuel Stillman (1737–1807), a protégé of Oliver Hart, was the outstanding Baptist spokesman, moving about the Baptist constituency with nearly an episcopal standing.[61] Stillman was known for his theological congruency with the New England Standing Order, but he was essentially unlettered.[62] It was his colleague at Second Baptist, Boston, Thomas Baldwin (1753–1826), who displayed a well-articulated theological system in several publications. Baldwin was a self-educated minister, originally trained for the law. He served the Baptist church in Canaan, Connecticut, and from 1790 to 1826, Second Baptist Church in Boston. Baldwin was one of the most influential Baptist ministers in New England during that time, the leader of a large congregation. He actively promoted the Massachusetts Baptist Missionary Society, the *American Baptist Magazine*, the General Baptist Missionary Convention,

---

[59] A list of Conference statements on reform issues is found in William H. Brackney, ed., *Baptist Life and Thought 1600–1980* (Valley Forge: Judson Press, 1983) 203–206.

[60] These include the English General Baptists, the New Connexion of General Baptists, General Six Principle Baptists, the General Association of General Baptists, the National Association of Freewill Baptists, and smaller bodies.

[61] According to Elias Smith, "He was a small man, but he looked very large to me. He was dressed in black, wore a large white wig, and three cornered hat." Elias Smith, *The Life, Conversion, Preaching, Travels, and Sufferings of Elias Smith* (Portsmouth: Beck and Foster, 1816) 224.

[62] One of Stillman's later detractors noted in 1804, "Next he undertook to extol Calvinism. He told the people the land on which the meetinghouse stood, was to remain theirs, so long as there were three Calvinists; though there was no such thing mentioned in the deed, which was afterwards proved to his face. He harangued upon sovereign grace; and talked loudly of Arminian doctrine; and with a loud voice, said it was free-will doctrine!" See Smith, 335.

and the Newton Theological Institution.[63] Although ridiculed by
Congregationalists as "illiterate and a blacksmith by trade," Baldwin was
given an honorary M.A. by Rhode Island College and a D.D. by Union
College.[64] He was chaplain to the Massachusetts Legislature and the U.S.
House of Representatives, and served as a delegate to the state
Constitutional Convention of 1820.

Like many converts from Congregationalism, Baldwin was deeply
committed to Baptist principles. His combined essays on baptism, his
only major published work among about three dozen less developed
tracts, were the most widely published polemic on baptism and
communion until the release of Anders Wiberg's work and the manual of
J. Newton Brown in the 1840s. The first part, *The Baptism of Believers
Only and the Particular Communion of the Baptist Churches, Explained
and Vindicated* (1789), was written at the request of the Woodstock,
New Hampshire Baptist Association as a defense of closed communion.
In 1791, a trinitarian Congregationalist pastor at Thornton, Noah
Worcester, published a response to Baldwin's work, *A Friendly Letter*,
that Baldwin felt misrepresented certain facts. Consequently, in 1794,
Baldwin responded with Part Two, published as *A Reply*. In the next
decade, the dialogue continued, spurred on by the publication of Peter
Edwards's tract, *Candid Reasons*, to which Baldwin again felt obligated
to respond. The result was Baldwin's *Appendix,* issued with parts one
and two in 1806. Together. Baldwin's work on baptism and communion
became texts for Baptists and non-Baptists on the topic.

Baldwin's theological case for baptism began with a high
confessional affirmation of Scripture: "We profess to take the word of
God for a perfect rule of faith and practice," he wrote. "If so, we are not
to follow the opinions of the best of men, though ever so learned and
great."[65] Next Baldwin reasoned, baptism is a positive institution of
Christ, revealed in Scripture. He thus rejected sincerity as a substitute for

[63] The others included Lucius Bolles of Salem, Caleb Blood and Joseph Grafton of
Newton, Daniel Sharp and James D. Knowles of Boston. Of these, one historian has
commented, "despite their unquestioned devotion to their cause, none of them left any
distinctive or lasting mark behind them." See McLoughlin, *New England Dissent*,
2:1114.

[64] Ibid., 1069.

[65] Thomas Baldwin, *The Baptism of Believers Only, and The Particular Communion
of the Baptist Churches Explained and Vindicated in Three Parts* (Boston: Manning and
Loring, 1791) 35.

Scripture, as well as superstition, or consistency, or parallels with heavenly fellowship, or charity out of ambiguity in the interpretation of Scripture. In the conclusion to his first treatise, he summarized on the basis of 2 Thessalonians 3:6, that it is the duty of servant/disciples to withdraw from those considered not conforming to the tradition of the apostles, and not to partake together at the Lord's table.[66]

In his 1794 installment, Baldwin investigated the biblical and historical nature of baptism. Following the lead of Robert Robinson in *History of Baptism*, and William Wall's book, *History of Infant Baptism* (1705), with some Hebrew linguistic assistance from John Gill's publications, he expanded on his earlier expositions. Two additional arguments were advanced, one having to do with Baptist identity, the other with "child damnation." Baldwin noted that one attack of pedobaptists had been to suggest that too many Baptists had slipped into the errors of Shakers, Universalists, and Deists. To this charge Baldwin responded that "The churches of our denomination in America, contain upwards of sixty thousand members, which hold visible communion together; nor did I ever know, that any attempt had been made on our part, to destroy the visible communion of Christians in general.[67] Further, Baldwin added "we have an annual correspondence with brethren from the district of Maine to the state of Georgia; and also with our brethren on the other side of the Atlantic."[68] Numbers of dissenters from the Baptists would be very small, he surmised. To the concern over the damnation of infants who are not baptized, Baldwin retorted that this was an "audacious cruelty," especially in light of Episcopalian and Presbyterian statements about the efficacy of baptism, it would be unfair to argue that Baptists laid undue stress upon baptism and thus undue condemnation upon the unbaptized (or the improperly baptized, as Baptists held infant baptism).[69] Baptists like other Christians could hardly make any guarantees about persons outside the household of faith.

The final part of Baldwin's treatise focused on matters raised in the intervening years since the 1790s. First, James Pierce of Exon, New Hampshire, held that on the basis of Christ's invitation to little children, infants should be admitted to communion as well as baptism. Baldwin's

---

[66] Ibid., 51.
[67] Ibid., 1794, 152.
[68] Ibid., 158.
[69] Ibid., 156–58.

response was that to admit either infant baptism or infant communion was a subversion of the great design of the gospel, which was to form a church distinct from the world.[70] Against Noah Worcester's reasonings that Baptists in being baptismally exclusive, deny God's "superabounding covenant of grace" designed to be a blessing to all the earth's peoples, Baldwin argued that Baptists denied no covenant from the Bible. Worcester erroneously charged Baptists with making baptism the distinguishing mark of the Christian faith. Baldwin's response was that the suggestion was a slander and that Baptists emphasized believer's baptism no more than others preached and wrote on infant baptism.[71] Moreover, Baptists preferred to lay the order of stressing a profession of faith before baptism. Finally to Worcester's defamatory accusation that Baptists were intimately connected with earlier Anabaptist doctrinal error, Baldwin quipped, "Hard names and hard arguments were very different things!"[72]

Thomas Baldwin's contributions to Baptist thought had continuing impact into the first two decades of the nineteenth century. While he grew in his reading of extant scholarship, his own educational capacity was limited. During his lifetime, theological institutions like Newton took Baptist thought well beyond the traditional self-taught pastor. Even so, Baldwin was one of the last mainstream American Baptist pastors to engage in polemical theology. His role, like many before him back to the seventeenth century, was to respond to critics of the Baptist position. As his major works well illustrate, organization, quotation, repetition, and strongly-toned rhetoric predominated over creativity and experimentation. As scholarship advanced and new questions were set, Baldwin's genetic influence had lessening influence.

Elias Smith (1769–1846) must be included in any list of influential later-eighteenth century American Baptist thinkers. He is representative of the self-taught dissenter who could not compromise with the doctrinal majority in the mainstream. Smith was converted in a New Light family and early experienced a call to ministry. He read what was available in local farm communities, including Jonathan Edwards's *History of the Work of Redemption* (1774); John Norton's *A Discussion of that Great*

---

[70] Ibid., 1806, 187.

[71] Ibid., 299.

[72] Ibid., 298. Worcester reclaimed the title "Baptist" for all Christians who baptized. He referred to Baptists as "Dipping" or "Duck-dipping" Baptists.

Point in Divinity, The Sufferings of Christ; and the Question about his Righteousness and the Imputation thereof (1653); Jean F. Osterwald's *A Compendium of Christian Theology* (1785); and John Flavel's *The Fountain of Life Opened; or a Display of Christ in His Essential and Mediatorial Glory; Containing Forty Two Sermons* (1671).[73] He followed the advice of mentors Thomas Baldwin, Samuel Stillman in Boston, and Samuel Shepard of New Hampshire. Originally a theological hybrid to be located somewhere between the Freewill Baptists and the regular Baptists, he rejected the harsh predestinarianism of Calvinists. At one point early in his ministry, Smith declared "Though God has determined that a certain part shall be saved; yet he has determined they shall be saved through faith in Christ; and though God has determined that some shall be damned, yet he determined they shall be damned for unbelief."

The Calvinistic system was so fixed in Smith's mind that he kept it for "ballast" and was able to relate to varying theological situations in Massachusetts and New Hampshire: "By keeping my fatalism so, I ever preached a free gospel to all...while my Calvinism for ballast preserved my reputation among the Calvinists who considered me sound in the faith."[74] Eventually he jettisoned the doctrines of original sin, the Fall, the covenant of grace, the Trinity, reprobation, eternal torment, foreordination, and election in favor of being free from the commandments and doctrines of men. He eventually became an itinerant and joined a voluntary association he called "Christians."[75] Like so many of the self-taught Baptist ministers of the era, Smith wanted to be free of the categories and the trappings of established ministry, "reverend, parsons, chaplains, doctors of divinity, clergy, bands, surplices, notes, creeds, covenants, platforms, and the spirit of slander." Most of all, however, it

---

[73] These were all classics in the Reformed tradition: Edwards, the Congregationalist pastor at Northampton; Norton, *Puritan Minister at Dartmouth*, Englands seventeenth-century Congregationalist teacher at Ipswich; Ostervald, a Swiss pastor at Neuchatel; and John Flavel, a Puritan minister at Dartmouth, England.

[74] Smith, *Elias Smith*, 242, 322–23.

[75] Ibid., 298, 339. Smith's reasons for withdrawal had much to do with the ill personal treatment he suffered, particularly over financial obligations he was unable to honor. In 1804, when the first meeting was held of the new movement in Boston, Smith declared it was "a little like the declaration of independence once made by the Americans."

was the "Calvinism of Boston" that he held to be "an abomination in the sight of God."[76]

Elhanan Winchester (1751–1797) is an example of both an influential pastor and one whose theological self-understanding evolved into heterodoxy, if not Baptist heresy. A bright and voracious reader as a child, he had only a primary school education. He was reared in a typical eighteenth-century Calvinistic religious environment in Brookline, Massachusetts, with paternal encouragement to seek a vivid spiritual conversion. This finally occurred in 1769 when he was nineteen, after which he joined a Separate Church in Brookline, where Jonathan Hyde was minister. He later acknowledged his debt to consistent Calvinism, understanding his own election and the complete sovereignty of God in salvation.

Winchester became a Baptist about the time of his first marriage. He was baptized by an open-communionist Baptist, Ebenezer Lyon of Canterbury, Connecticut. By 1771 young Winchester had moved to Rehoboth, Massachusetts, where he began preaching. His eloquence attracted a significant following. He formed an open communion congregation and was ordained a Baptist. At length the communion issue was agitated in the new congregation, with the result that Winchester moved to a closed communion position, for which he was eventually excluded by the congregation. His theological struggle did not end with this episode. A brief interlude in Bellingham, Massachusetts, found him renouncing Arminian tendencies for an avowal of John Gill's system. He moved to South Carolina in 1775 and was called to be pastor in 1776 at Welch Neck. In the five years he was attached to that church, he earned a reputation as a revivalist and church-growth pastor. He was also open to the plight of the slave population. In 1780 he accepted a call to be minister at First Baptist Church in Philadelphia, one of the oldest and most prestigious congregations in the Middle States. In Philadelphia Winchester was to experience major changes in his theological outlook.

Winchester's engagement of the revivalist tradition was the starting point for his transformation. "Before he was aware," his biographer noted, " he was preaching a general provision and a universal call...he actually made such progress in the doctrine of salvation as to be fully persuaded that the number of the saved would fully equal if not exceed

---

[76] Ibid., 342.

that of the lost."[77] Two years into his pastorate in Philadelphia, and under the influence of colleagues like Benjamin Rush and John Redman at the University of Pennsylvania, he moved toward the doctrine of "restorationism." Winchester thought it began with his reading of Paul Siegvolk's *The Everlasting Gospel* (1753) while he was in South Carolina, a work which argued that all fallen creatures would be restored by Jesus Christ to a state of holiness and happiness. Secondly, in the 1770s Winchester came under the influence of an Episcopalian minister in Virginia who preached universal restoration. The third influence on his thinking was George Stonehouse's *The Restitution of All Things* (1761). Stonehouse was an original participant in John Wesley's Holy Club at Oxford University, yet he held to the doctrine of universal "restitution" and wrote widely on the scriptural bases of the principle. A fourth factor, also of a literary nature, was Andrew M. Ramsay's *Philosophical Principles of Natural and Revealed Religion* (1748–49). Winchester considered it "one of the best books in the English language." By 1781, Winchester's growing universalism led to a deep disagreement within the First Baptist congregation. His supporters turned out on Sunday evenings for "lectures" in which he discussed his evolving theological perspectives. His opponents generally supported the orthodoxy of the Philadelphia Baptist Confession of Faith. These included stalwarts of the Philadelphia tradition, such as Samuel Jones, Oliver Hart, William Van Horn, and John Boggs. When the controversy peaked in 1782, Winchester and his friends were denied use of the meeting house and he was terminated as pastor of the church. The remainder of his career was spent as a traveling lecturer and sometime preacher.

The essence of Winchester's case for universal restoration was straightforward, both theologically and empirically. First, he held that the essence of God is love and that God seeks to do his creatures good. Second, God created intelligent beings and he desires them to be happy in knowledge and "perfections." Third, hearkening back to John Gill, God's eternal designs cannot be frustrated. Fourth, Christ died for all, and did not do so in vain. Finally, Christ destroyed the evil principle in the universe, and the misery of the fallen will be no more. He concluded

---

[77] Edwin Martin Stone, *Biography of Reverend Elhanan Winchester* (Boston: H. B. Brewster, 1836) 27.

his case by rejoicing in the goodness of the Lord.[78] Ever a careful student of the Scriptures, Winchester added his own theological contribution to Restorationism. He asserted that by the "law of correspondence," God—who had confounded human speech at Babel—would restore not only one language, but also universal salvation through a gift of tongues. He understood Pentecost to be a "specimen" of what was to take place in the last days, or at the dawning of the millennial kingdom: "Christ's ministers shall see eye to eye, and those that believe shall be one as the Father and Son are one...then the knowledge of God becomes general and all nations shall join together to serve the Lord...and doubtless be restored."[79] Winchester also reached into practical experience to make his case. In the benevolent institutions of the day, among which he considered houses of reformation, associations for relief of penury and disease, as well as missionary efforts, he found the seeds of the conversion of the world. Observing specifically in Central Pennsylvania the German Baptists or Tunkers, he was advised by his predecessor at First Baptist Church, Morgan Edwards, that these folk were a "harmless" group of meek and pious Christians who held to general redemption and general salvation.[80] Winchester thus oddly reflected a case supposedly dedicated to a form of Restorationist theology in the midst of a changing theological order. Because the case that he made was so comprehensive, Winchester's theological adversaries claimed he supported the restoration of "bad men and angels," and they declared his position a "most dangerous heresy."[81]

Although his life was short, Elhanan Winchester enjoyed wide noteriety in the international Christian community. He was the author of over thirty published writings, a considerable achievement among Baptists in the late eighteenth century.[82] In the United States, he claimed James Manning, president of Rhode Island College, a "dear friend" (though Manning's arguments for "endless misery" did not convince him). In Philadelphia, and later London, he interacted closely with

---

[78] His case thus made was the essence of a famous sermon he delivered in 1781: "The Seed of the Woman Bruising the Serpent's Head." It was locally published in Philadelphia and is quoted here from Ibid., 51.

[79] Ibid., 171.

[80] Ibid., 74–75. Edwards was the first Baptist writer to take note of this group, identifying its theological peculiarities, some of which he objected to.

[81] Ibid., 54.

[82] These are listed in ibid., 250–51 and partially excerpted therein.

Joseph Priestly, a well-known religious dissenter. Likewise, he had a long friendship with John Wesley and affirmed Wesley's opposition to Calvinistic doctrines. John Murray, the leading Universalist of the era, considered him "one of the best hearts he had ever known" and carried on extensive correspondence with Winchester. During the six years Winchester spent in England he preached in numerous General Baptist churches and was cordially welcomed. But, Baptist leaders gave Winchester mixed reviews: Dan Taylor, the General Baptist, whose sermon on endless misery called forth five letters from Winchester, opposed the latter's universalism. Robert Robinson, a Particular Baptist in Cambridge—also on a theological pilgrimage toward heterodoxy—defended Winchester against "phonies" and theological arrogance.[83] Likewise, British-American pastor Morgan Edwards was charitable towards Winchester. A modern study argues that "in other particulars," Winchester remained as orthodox as his former Baptist friends."[84]

Genetically speaking, Elhanan Winchester was connected to an American revivalistic tradition of a Calvinistic bent. His lack of formal education, coupled with considerable gifts of oratory and persuasion, posed a serious problem for local congregations. Leadership was needed for an emerging movement, yet unsophisticated theological understanding could lead far from the Christian mainstream. The self-taught preacher seemed to some obscurantist, to others heretical. In this regard, Winchester was a harbinger of a coming increase in challenges to traditional orthodoxy.

Richard Furman (1755–1825) was a significant bridge in moving the Baptist heritage from the eighteenth to the nineteenth century. He was also a trans-regional figure, having contributed to Baptist ministry in South Carolina, Virginia, and nationally in the development of the Triennial Convention. Furman was taught largely under his schoolteacher-father's auspices. It is likely that he originally planned to pursue a career in law. He experienced a religious conversion in 1770 under the revival preaching of Joseph Reese of Congaree Church.

---

[83] Ibid., 180.

[84] Joseph R. Sweeny, "Elhanan Winchester and the Universal Baptists" (Ph.D. diss., University of Pennsylvania, 1969) 64, is a reminder that Winchester continued to preach the doctrines of revelation, the trinity, the divinity of Christ, substitutionary atonement, the resurrection, and the second coming of Christ.

Furman thus moved from an Anglican upbringing into the ranks of the Separate Baptists. His biographer notes that while Furman's conversion experience was genuine and baptistic in nature, he was also inclined toward a deeply reflective approach—in contrast to the more experiential—to doctrinal issues, including the justice of God, the universality of grace, justification by faith, and human choice.[85]

Furman came early under the influence of the Regular Baptist tradition. In 1773 he met Oliver Hart, pastor of the First Baptist Church of Charleston, and the two began a lifelong friendship. At the outbreak of the Revolution, Furman became devoted to the Patriot cause and his travels brought him into a circle of important Regular Baptist ministers, including John Gano, whose church in New York allowed him to take evangelistic trips South, Edmund Botsford of Welsh Neck and later Georgetown, South Carolina, Elhanan Winchester of Philadelphia, and the celebrated Daniel Marshall. Also among these was Joseph Cook, a convert under George Whitefield who left Anglicanism for the Baptist faith and was an ardent advocate of religious liberty. In 1787, following the war for American independence, Furman was called as pastor to First Baptist Church, Charleston, South Carolina, where he remained the rest of his life.

During the first years in Charleston, Furman began corresponding with Particular Baptists in England such as John Rippon, John Ryland, and Samuel Pearce. He also established the same with many in the Northern states, including William Rogers, James Manning, and Samuel Stillman. One may assume from the content of his letters that while he was self-taught theologically, Furman adopted and propagated main-stream Particular/Regular Baptist views. For example, he took special interest in the Bristol Academy and was solicitous of William Staughton's immigration to America. Furman became a devoted supporter of Rhode Island College through his acquaintance with James Manning and the Philadelphia Baptists. He sent two students to Providence, and the institution conferred upon him an honorary master's degree in 1792 and the Doctor of Divinity degree in 1800. Later he recommended Jonathan Maxcy, former president of the College, as president of South Carolina College.

---

[85] James A Rogers, *Richard Furman: Life and Legacy* (Macon GA: Mercer University Press, 1985) 18.

Furman's theological identity matured as the new century dawned. When the Great Revival broke out in 1800 that swept across the South, he cautioned against potential excess in revivalism: "I hope the direct good obtained from these meetings will much more than counterbalance the incidental evil."[86] As a biographer observed, "He was enough Separate Baptist not to condemn, and enough Regular Baptist to be concerned."[87] Furman's own theological emphases turned to missions and education. He supported the English Baptist Missionary Society and was friendly toward William Carey's Bible translation projects. Like Jonathan Edwards of old and the British Baptists, he instituted "concerts" of prayer for foreign missions. In the context of the United States, he welcomed the Massachusetts Baptist Missionary Society, the Catawba Indian mission, preaching to Negroes, and the General Convention over which he presided in its formative years. Luther Rice and Adoniram Judson also had regular correspondence Furman.

Like other Baptist ministers who had participated in the great events of the Revolutionary War, Furman exhibited a theological trait best described as "patriotic millennialism." Contemporaries like Henry Holcombe of Savannah and later Philadelphia, wrote of the end times for a remnant people that envisioned a pessimistic outcome. But others like Isaac Backus and Furman saw a golden age with its foundations in the future of the United States. For Furman, that perspective may have been a by-product of his revival experiences where the increase of conversions and the spread of the revival seemed to suggest the wholesale Christianization of America. It also appeared to signal America's leadership among the nations, as usher to a new era. In a sermon preached on 4 July 1802, Furman spoke of a day "when America will be the praise of the whole earth, and shall participate largely in the fulfillment of those sacred prophecies which have foretold the glory of Messiah's kingdom."[88] Furman's optimistic and nationalistically inclined millennial outlook explains why he strongly urged the expansion of the Baptist missionary enterprise and the strengthening of pastoral leaership.

---

[86] Richard Furman to John Rippon, 11 August 1802, quoted in Rogers, *Richard Furman*, 109.

[87] Ibid., 113.

[88] Richard Furman, *America's Deliverance and Duty: A Sermon Preached at the First Baptist Church of Charleston, on the Fourth Day of July, 1802* (Charleston: n.p., 1802).

Furman's investment in literary and theological education revealed much about his theological orientation. In his region of the country, Baptists lacked direct formal opportunities for education, and this caused Furman to become a devotee of denominational education. He fought to have an institution included in the plan of the General Missionary Convention and rejoiced at the establishment of Columbian College in Washington, D.C. His old friend William Staughton had fused his theological school from Philadelphia with a classic undergraduate department in the Nation's Capital and this pleased Furman greatly. In fact, Furman seemed to adopt Staughton's idea of theological preparation without revision: learned, pious professors were to direct studies such as "theology in its various branches, church history, the Hebrew language, and other Oriental languages, the knowledge of which is favorable to a right understanding of the sacred Scriptures... together with biblical criticism and pulpit eloquence."[89] Later, he desired the same plan for South Carolina.[90]

Furman foresaw the evolution of a refined ministry, "gentlemen-theologians" to use Brooks Holifield's term, that recognized the progress of the arts and sciences, the subtleties of reasoning, and logical deduction. Against the "powers of darkness," Furman beseeched his South Carolina brethren to educate by the aids of grace and learning, "to put silence to the proud philosopher, the artful sophist, who would oppose Christ's divine character, and many of the essential doctrines of Christianity."[91] Richard Furman's interest in advanced theological education would insure that the Baptist community in the South would enjoy the benefits of scholarly theology. It would also highlight the limitations of pastoral theologians.

At the turn of the eighteenth century, Daniel Parker (1781–1844) was as far to the right on the theological spectrum as Elhanan Winchester was to the left. He was self-educated on the Georgia and Tennessee frontiers

---

[89] "Proposed Resolutions, including a scheme of Education, having for its subject the assistance of pious young men designed for the gospel ministry, which were laid before the Baptist Convention at Philadelphia, in May, 1817," quoted in Rogers, *Richard Furman*, 295. The connection of Furman with Staughton at this point stems from Furman's rooming with the Staughtons while in Philadelphia at this time, and Furman's lack of any formal theological education himself.

[90] Ibid., 193.

[91] "Address to the Churches," 4 December 1824, attributed to Richard Furman and quoted in ibid., 307–310.

and gravitated toward a ministry in the Baptist movement. Ordained at Turnbull's Creek Church in Dickson County, Tennessee, he served several small, isolated churches and frequently debated Methodists about theological issues. He moved about frequently in Indiana and Illinois, eventually reaching Texas. He was an antislavery reformer, elected to the Illinois legislature, and a popular writer on dissenting topics.

At the heart of Parker's theology was a creative apologetic for hyper-Calvinism. He was particularly concerned about the growth of universalism, Arminianism, and antinomianism. Using Genesis 3:15, he deduced that there are two seeds that come to moral fruition in God's purposes. The first germinates through Adam, Christ's body, the true church, and the elect. The second is the seed of the serpent, the non-elect that came through woman. As the sons of God married the daughters of men, the two were mixed together. The Serpent's seed was especially evident in the offspring of Ham, and later of Ishmael. Parker believed that God would display his justice in the redemption of the elect, while the seed of Satan would be defeated and overthrown.[92] The Baptists, he held, were the only true church, uncorrupted by "old mother Rome" or other antichristian churches. Inveighing heavily against the "invisible Church," he said: "There is no such thing…Thus the members of Christ's church are visible…all who fail to produce the evidences of grace…we have no scriptural knowledge of them as Christ's church; and it becomes our duty to let them know they are not part of us."[93] In the end, his eschatology involved the elect being brought home, while "Satan and his seed will be banished from God and his people forever, to bear the wrath of God."[94]

While in most instances, Parker seemed to adhere to the eighteenth century Philadelphia confessional tradition; there was one interesting exception. Understanding that Baptists held God could not be the author of sin, he thought it inconsistent to hold that the existence of the devil—a creature of God—did not, by logical deduction, make God indirectly the

---

[92] Daniel Parker, *Views on the Two Seeds, Taken from Genesis 3d chapter, and Part of the 15th Verse* (Vandalia: Robert Blackwell, 1826) 8–10. Parker built his scheme to be followed throughout Scripture, a popular study strategy for Baptist interpreters.

[93] Ibid., 20.

[94] His position on reprobation was in keeping with chapter 32 of the Second London (later Philadelphia) Confession of Faith.

author of sin.[95] He believed that sooner or later other Baptists would understand this important point, validated by his understanding of the doctrine of the "two seeds."

Parker took it upon himself to advocate a practical response to theological heterodoxy. Beginning in 1820, and largely in response to visits of Luther Rice, he became a staunch opponent of the Baptist Board of Missions. In support of God's sovereignty, Parker held that education had produced more bad men than good and "we had better leave it to God's work to call men of education than to undertake to make preachers by giving them education."[96] He firmly believed there was no scriptural basis for the mission system in the Bible and that it was an act of rebellion against the King of Zion, "inasmuch as they have assumed an authority that Christ has reserved alone to himself."[97] Here he adeptly co-mingled his doctrines of divine sovereignty with his Christology.

Daniel Parker demonstrated the capability of "farmer-preachers" to derive, simplify, and propagate theological premises from literalistic readings of the Bible. It was estimated that by 1830 a majority of the Baptist associations in Illinois were hyper-Calvinistic in theology due to "Parkerism." Somewhat unexpectedly, Parker's Pilgrim Church reached into the territory of Texas, thus claiming its place as the first Baptist presence in that important frontier region.

Another Baptist pastor of the hyper-Calvinistic persuasion in the early nineteenth century, whose ministry and tenure as a religious editor had an impact exceeding Parker's, was Gilbert Beebe (1800–1881). Beebe was baptized in Norwich, Connecticut, in 1811. By 1816 he moved to New York City where he united with Ebenezer Baptist Church and was licensed to preach in 1818. Though lacking formal education, Beebe became a popular preacher. He traveled in the Middle Atlantic States, serving Third Baptist, Baltimore, Maryland, as a supply preacher, as well as several other preaching points in the region. In 1823 Beebe was ordained to serve the Baptist Church of Ramapo in Rockland County, New York, where he remained through 1826. He was next called to the Baptist Church at Mt. Vernon, New York, where he served with only

---

[95] Ibid., 11.

[96] Daniel Parker, *A Public Address to the Baptist Society and Friends of Religion in General, on the Principles and Practices of the Baptist Board of Foreign Missions* (Vincennes IN: Stout and Osborn, 1820) 46.

[97] Ibid., 39.

brief interruptions for fifty years. His pastoral career touched churches in Virginia, Washington D.C., and New York. It was from Middletown, New York, due to the proximity of the railroad, that he managed and edited the *Signs of the Times*, the official paper of the Old School or Primitive Baptist cause.

Early in his ministry among small congregations, Beebe became convinced that there were serious departures among his fellow Baptists from the order of the church of God as organized on the Day of Pentecost. The Apostles' doctrine and fellowship, he maintained, did not give place to mission boards, Sunday schools, theological schools, or the religious rites and formalities of denominationalism. "I have never been identified with, nor have I had any fellowship for, any religious titles, forms, fashions, or customs which cannot be found in the laws of Christ, and practice of the Apostles and primitive saints," he wrote.[98] His own ministry became that of "protesting solemnly and soberly...against spiritual wickedness in high places."

Beebe was a thoroughgoing predestinarian. In accord with the Philadelphia and London Confessions of faith, he held that "every Bible Baptist believes that God is the All-mighty, All-Wise, and All-Holy Sovereign of the Universe...who foreknew the fall and the wickedness of men; that he had a purpose worthy of himself." [99] In a piece written at an advanced age, Beebe was even more deeply convinced that "to admit the universal government of God, is to admit the predestination of all things, from the falling of a sparrow to the dissolution of a world." [100] Doctrinally, it seemed perfectly clear that nothing could be foreknown that was undetermined and that foreknowledge and the determinate counsel of God were inseparable. The doctrine of predestination was for Beebe so characteristic of the Old School Baptists, that he preferred the name "Predestinarian" Baptists to other designations.[101] He and his

---

[98] "Autobiography of Elder Gilbert Beebe," in Sylvester Hassell, *History of the Church of God, from the Creation to A.D. 1885; including Especially The History of the Kehukee Primitive Baptist Association* (Middletown NY: Gilbert Beebe's Sons, 1886) 935.

[99] "Predestination," editorial in ibid., 942.

[100] Ibid., 946.

[101] Ibid., 943. The name is understood in the context of "New School" or "Missionary Baptists" who claimed to have an unbroken succession from the Primitive Baptists of the Apostolic Age. At the time of the Black Rock Resolutions in 1832, many churches consented to be known as "Old School," and later the "true" Primitive Baptists. Once

adherents wrote "they never did consent to any of the antichristian doctrines of the new order, even when mixed up with them in denominational connection."[102] Beebe is said to have had few equals among the Old School Baptists, having preached about 10,000 sermons and having traveled over 200,000 miles, sustained not by "missionary funds, but by the God of Providence."[103] Beebe's publications included two volumes of his editorials and a hymnbook. His sons, William and Benton, carried on his publishing work in the nationally distributed *Signs of the Times*. Beebe's counterpart in the South was Elder Cushing Biggs Hassell (1809–1880) of Williamston, North Carolina, the leading Primitive Baptist of Kehukee and surrounding regions. Hassell's mantle was assumed by his son, Sylvester Hassell, who completed his father's history and brought together the various strands of Old Schoolism into a relatively united theological tradition.

At the same time Gilbert Beebe and others were defining a hyper-Calvinist position, John Newton Brown (1803–1868) was moving mainstream Baptists in a more moderate direction. He was educated at Hamilton Literary and Theological Institution, graduating in the second class. He served congregations in New York, Rhode Island, and Massachusetts. In 1829, he went in failing health to Exeter, New Hampshire, to serve a small church and work on compiling the *Encyclopedia of Religious Knowledge*. From 1838 to 1844 he was professor of theology at New Hampton Institution. As it turned out, he was the principal author of the New Hampshire Confession of Faith, generally accepted among churches of his state. He went South for health reasons in 1845 and was pastor for a time at Lexington, Virginia. From 1849 to 1859 he served as editorial secretary of the American Baptist Publication Society, earning a wide reputation for personal piety and his knowledge of Baptist principles. Brown was one of the most devoted alumni of Hamilton who studied with Kendrick, Hascall, and others of the school's original faculty.[104]

---

defined, they even claimed such libertarian luminaries as John Leland of Connecticut and Virginia. See Ibid., 622–23.

[102] Ibid., 356.

[103] Beebe's influence may be considered international, as copies of his paper, *Signs of the Times,* reached Upper Canada in the 1850s, where several congregations identified with the Old School cause and in 1857 produced a Confession of Faith. See Ibid., 881–85.

[104] Hezekiah Harvey, "Historical Discourse," 103–104.

Until the mid-nineteenth century most Baptist ministers in the South were self-educated and served smaller rural congregations. Some read classic Baptist, Presbyterian, and Episcopalian authors, while most learned their theology from what they heard other ministers preach. Andrew Broaddus was an exceptional Baptist minister of the era, widely read and published throughout the Baptist family in the United States. Broaddus (1770–1848) was self-taught and served small congregations in the Tidewater region of Virginia: Upper King and Queen, Bethel, and Fredericksburg. He was widely sought as an evangelist and declined some of the most prestigious churches in Baptist America. Among his published works were *Age of Reason and Revelation* (1795),[105] *Bible History, with Occasional Notes to Explain and Illustrate Difficult Passages* (1816), *Catechism for Children*, and a manual of church polity and discipline. His *Reply to Mr. Campbell's Millennial Harbinger* (1831) was one of the first Baptist responses to Alexander Campbell's writings on redemption.

Another influential nineteenth-century American Baptist pastor was James R. Graves (1820–1893). Born into a poor family in Vermont, Graves moved early in life to Ohio. He educated himself, taught school, and continued to read widely on biblical topics and others related to the humanities. In 1845 Graves moved to Nashville, Tennessee, where he eventually became a Baptist minister and assistant editor for the Baptist newspaper. Graves soon became the sole editor of *The Tennessee Baptist* and used its pages for decades to launch editorials.[106]

Graves is the father of the "Landmarkist" movement among Southern Baptists. Inspired by the Old Testament passage, "Remove not the ancient landmark, which thy fathers have set" (Prov 22:28), Graves pursued a doctrine of the church that was exclusive and Baptist. Appropriately labeled "local church protectionism", Graves joined others in the first decades of the nineteenth century in reducing the Baptist understanding of the true church from a universal dimension to the local

---

[105] In this first title, he rebuffed the work of Thomas Paine.

[106] Unfortunately Graves is not well known outside Southern Baptist life. Two useful, somewhat dated studies of his theology are T. A. Patterson, "The Theology of J. R. Graves and Its Influence on Southern Baptist Life" (Th.D. dissertation, Southwestern Baptist Theological Seminary, 1944) and Harold S. Smith, "A Critical Analysis of the Theology of J. R. Graves" (Ph.D. dissertation, Southern Baptist Theological Seminary, 1966).

congregation.[107] Using a series of "axioms"[108] and "marks," he questioned the validity of other churches—which he scornfully called "societies"—discouraged Baptists from fellowship with non-Baptists or from allowing non-Baptists into their pulpits. As time went on, Graves added to his theology a successionist idea of Baptist history that constituted "a visible kingdom on earth, and that this kingdom has never yet been 'broken in pieces' or given to another class of subjects—and had never for a day 'been moved,' or ceased from the earth and never will until Christ returns."[109] To this were also added denying "alien immersion," close communion, and local church control over the ordinances and the preaching of the gospel. James Tull, the principal contemporary interpreter of Landmarkism, characterizes it as "a denial of the New Testament principle of the Universal Church."[110]

Graves's principles could be easily construed as issues of polity and practice were it not for the importance of the doctrine of the church to Baptists. His ecclesiology was a further "refinement" of Baptist doctrine and is worthy of discussion. Like John Smyth and the writers of the First London Confession, Graves believed the church is composed of regenerate persons. Such persons comprise local congregations that in turn amount to the visible Body of Christ. Graves equated the sum total of true churches with the Kingdom of God that has existed continuously since its founding in the New Testament.[111] Tull characterizes Graves's thought as Baptist "high churchism" or "a compact, hard-hitting ecclesiology."[112] What Graves attempted to arrive at was a doctrine of the church that only could be realized by the contemporary Baptist community. The ultimate test of theological acceptability for Graves was "blood before water," by which Graves asserted that counterfeit churches placed water baptism before the person's acceptance of the blood

---

[107] Others rightly placed in this tradition were J. Newton Brown, John L. Waller, Francis Wayland, George H. Orchard, and John T. Christian (1854–1925).

[108] He obviously borrowed the terms "axiom" and "corollary" from the vocabulary of Euclidian geometry, doubtless a part of his self-taught education.

[109] James R. Graves, *Old Landmarkism: What Is It?* (Memphis: Baptist Book House, 1880) 122–23.

[110] James Tull, *High Church Baptists in the South: The Origin, Nature and Influence of Landmarkism* (Macon GA: Mercer University Press, 2000) 173.

[111] Ibid., 121–23.

[112] Tull, *High Church Baptists*, 1.

atonement of Christ, whereas churches of Christ placed "Christ before the church and blood before water."[113]

An important theological distinction missed by modern commentators on Landmarkism and Graves was his employment of the term "evangelical." It was becoming common in the 1840s to distinguish between evangelical and non-evangelical churches. Typically that distinction meant differentiating between the voluntary, revivalistic, Free Church groups (the evangelicals) and defining non-evangelicals as a wholesale grouping of the established reformed mainstream and the sacrament-observing churches in the Protestant tradition.[114] Graves used the term "evangelical" as a kind of synonym for his interpretation of New Testament faith and practice. In *Old Landmarkism* he put it clearly: "Those religious organizations that...do admit infants and the confessedly unregenerate to baptism and church membership, are not and should not be considered, called, or by any act recognized as churches of Christ or evangelical bodies." He especially distinguished between Pedobaptists and Campbellites on the one hand, and Baptists on the other: "If Baptist churches are evangelical, as all Baptists believe, then all Pedobaptist and Campellite societies are not evangelical, and vice versa."[115] In using the term in this way, Graves and other Baptist Landmarkists began to separate themselves from other experiential, biblically-defined groups over the issue of believer's baptism.[116]

Graves was joined in the Landmarkist movement by Amos Cooper Dayton (1813–1865) and James Madison Pendleton (1811–1891). Dayton, the author of *Theodosia Earnest* (1856–57) was milder than Graves in his Landmarkist stance. For example, he refused to equate fully the local church and the Kingdom of God. He preferred instead to stress the voluntary nature of faith and that a true church of Christ never persecutes other professing Christians for conscience's sake. Pendleton, who had a widely-circulated tract, *An Old Landmark Re-Set* (1854),

---

[113] Ibid., 79.

[114] See the breakdown in Robert Baird, *Religion in America, or An Account of the Origin, Relation to the State, and Present Condition of the Evangelical Churches in the United States* (New York: Harper and Brothers, 1856) xvi-xvii.

[115] Graves, *Old Landmarkism*, 22–23, 63.

[116] This would not long stand, however, because other non-Baptist evangelicals were already coalescing around doctrines like the authority of Scripture, the deity of Christ, and the necessity of regeneration in organized forms like the Evangelical Alliance, formed in 1846.

influenced many in the Southern Baptist family and ended his career as pastor in Upland, Pennsylvania, and an adjunct professor at Crozer Theological Seminary. Among other matters of doctrine Graves held in contrast to Graves and Dayton were his continuing understanding of the universal church, his rejection of church successionism, and his refusal to localize the Kingdom of God.[117]

One last figure requires mention to round out the Baptist pastoral theological contribution of the nineteenth century. Adoniram Judson Gordon (1836–1895) was a premier example of the New England pastoral tradition. Educated first at Brown University, where he excelled in classical languages, he made friends with future influential denominational leaders such as Henry S. Burrage. His education continued at Newton Theological Institution where he was greatly drawn to Horatio B. Hackett in biblical languages and Alvah Hovey in theology. He was especially indebted to Hackett for conveying to him a deep reverence for divine revelation, as well as his baptistic orientation.[118] Gordon's first pastorate was at Jamaica Plain, Massachusetts, outside of Boston, and in 1869 he moved to the inner city's Clarendon Street Baptist Church. There he built a large congregation and an international reputation.

Gordon's theology in large part was indebted to traditional Calvinism, but it was also modified by nineteenth-century revivalism. Three theological emphases characterized his thinking: premillennial eschatology, the Holy Spirit, and missions. In each case, Gordon responded to environmental factors in creating his theological statements. As early as his Newton years, Gordon began to question the prevailing postmillennial eschatology of most American Baptists and, in particular, of his professors at Newton. He found the position unattractive for preaching and began to study the premillennialist scheme. He was definitely influenced by Plymouth Brethren and through study arrived at an "historicist" premillennial position by the early 1860s. He told the first meeting of the Baptist Congress in 1882, "The Plymouth Brethren have given us a great number of Biblical works. Nowhere have I seen the gospel so luminously presented."[119] Gordon's approach was

---

[117] See the discussion in Tull, *High Church Baptists*, 44 ff.

[118] Ernest B. Gordon, *Adoniram Judson Gordon: A Biography* (New York: Fleming H. Revell Co., 1896) 37, 49–51.

[119] A. J. Gordon, "Modern Evangelism," in "Minutes and Proceedings of the First Annual Autumnal Conference Held at Brooklyn, New York, 1882" (Typescript,

distinguished from dispensational premillennialism by his belief that certain prophecies had been fulfilled in history, notably the antichrist's appearing in the shape of the Roman Catholic papal system.[120] This nativistic, anti-Catholic interpretation had been popular among Baptists like William Cathcart in Philadelphia and John Mockett Cramp in England and Nova Scotia in the earlier 1800s.[121] In due course, Gordon's stance became virtually synonymous with premillennial thinking among Baptists, and his book, *Ecce Venit* (1889), won national attention. A biographer asserted, "The Second Coming was Gordon's passion—it consumed his thinking, his theology."[122]

Revival in Boston in 1877 had a good deal to do with Gordon's ideas of spiritual renewal. Dwight Moody and Ira Sankey held a three-month campaign that year that extended into churchly meetings. Clarendon Street Church was greatly affected. Gordon wrote of his own transformation: "The church of Jesus Christ is builded together for an inhabitation of God for the Spirit....when I awoke to this fact, and began to preach it...then began the real progress in this church." The filling and indwelling of the Spirit led inevitably to what Gordon referred to as "consecration" or in the parlance of the Phoebe Palmer and Wesleyans, "entire sanctification." He also concluded there was a second step after conversion, a "higher life" could be attained by the Holy Spirit falling upon believers and filling them with divine power.[123] Gordon wrote hymns to express and induce this revivalistic experience that was not "gradual," as most Baptists understood it, but instantaneous. In his book, *The Ministry of the Spirit* (1894), he spoke of the baptism of the Spirit at salvation (where one is sealed with the Spirit), followed by consecration (where one is filled with the Spirit), and finally of growth (where one is anointed with the Spirit to live the Christian life).[124] The entire process

---

American Baptist Historical Society) 19. He also hastened to note that "The sect has done its work and is fast falling to pieces, as it ought."

[120] On the particulars of his interpretation of Revelation, see Gordon, *Adoniram Judson Gordon,* 310–329.

[121] See for instance, William Cathcart, *The Papal System* (Philadelphia: Griffith and Rowland Press, 1872).

[122] Scott M. Gibson, *A. J. Gordon: American Premillennialist* (Lanham: University Press of America. 2001) 35.

[123] A. J. Gordon, *The Twofold Life* (Boston: Howard Gannett, 1882) 15.

[124] A. J. Gordon, *The Ministry of the Spirit* (Philadelphia: American Baptist Publication Society, 1894) 67 ff.

Gordon referred to as "enduement." As a recent biographer puts it, "By the 1880s Gordon was one of the authorities on the ministry of the Spirit," speaking nationally on the theme and writing scores of articles on the topic.[125]

Gordon's premillennial views gave him a sense of urgency about the missionary task of the church. The time was short, he believed and the church's responsibility was to take Christ to the world. According to Acts 24:14, missionary activity was a sign of the imminent end and Gordon pushed hard at a "hermeneutic of haste." He dismissed educational ventures in mission for pure evangelism. Speaking to a group of seminarians in 1892, he declared: "the Holy Spirit is the 'president' of this age who dictated and revealed this programme of missions, whose office it was henceforth to carry out its specifications to the end of the age."[126]

Gordon carried that strong message to mission conferences, student-worker rallies, and in his widely circulated book, *The Holy Spirit in Missions* (1893). He drew frequent opposition to his premillennial approach, including from George W. Northrup of the University of Chicago and John W. Nevius, the famous Presbyterian missionary to China. His great contribution to the cause of Baptist missions was his leadership in resurrecting the American Baptist Missionary Union program from its doldrums by assuming control of the Livingstone Inland Mission in Africa and drawing national American Baptist attention to new possibilities in overseas work.[127]

Like his contemporary, C. H. Spurgeon, Gordon came to the conclusion through his premillennial perspective that a large part of the problem for the church, and Baptists in particular, was a diminishing of the authority of Scripture. He was concerned about the situation in his

---

[125] Ibid., 70.

[126] A. J. Gordon, *The Holy Spirit in Missions* (New York: Fleming H. Revell, 1893) 8, and quoted in Gibson, *A. J. Gordon*, 82.

[127] On Gordon's contribution to missions, see Dana L. Robert, "The Crisis of Missions: Premillennial Missions Theory and the Origins of Independent Evangelical Missions," *Earthen Vessels: American Evangelicals and Foreign Missions 1880–1980*, ed. Joel A Carpenter and Wilbert R. Shenk (Grand Rapids: Eerdmans, 1990) 29–46; and Robert G. Torbet, *Venture of Faith: The Story of the American Baptist Foreign Mission Society and the Women's American Baptist Foreign Mission Society 1814–1950* (Philadelphia: Judson Press, 1955) 198, 323. For coverage of his investment in the Congo, see Gordon, *Adoniram J. Gordon,* 158–72.

own theological seminary. As a student, he had imbibed a love for Scripture from his New Testament professor, Horatio Hackett.[128] Although President Hovey at Newton seemed to shepherd the school in an essentially conservative path, Professor Ezra P. Gould had made headway in introducing higher critical methods. As president of the Newton Alumni Association in 1894, Gordon likened the situation to "Christians riding in the parlor car while the higher critics sounded the wheels and oiled the tracks." Convinced that these methodologies were "liberal" or associated with "new theology," Gordon associated them with mere elitist diversions for learned and advanced theologians affording little to devout and serious students of Scripture and ministry. Also of concern was the advance of social Darwinism that Gordon thought altogether without foundation. He preferred to opine somewhat piously that Scripture was inspired, and is inspired, "because the Spirit of God lives and breathes in its letters and sentences."[129] Here the pastor was not to be confused with being a biblical scholar or a theologian.

Gordon's influence extended in several important directions across the religious landscape in America and beyond. First, as a close confidante of D. L. Moody, he was a supporter and leading teacher at Moody's Northfield Bible Conferences in Massachusetts.[130] These became national training and spiritual-life events similar to the Keswick movement in England. He was also active in the Niagara Bible Conferences that introduced him to the Canadian community of evangelical premillennialsts. During a trip to Britain in 1888 he was introduced to the evangelical and holiness circles there. Second, he was known widely in his denomination for improving the prospects of overseas missionary work by fundraising and holding offices in the American Baptist Missionary Union. It is noteworthy that few people of Gordon's era among Northern Baptists enjoyed his prestige, as witnessed in the number of books he published in the denominational press. Third, much of his legacy was ensured with the establishment of the Boston Missionary Training School that became Gordon College and Gordon Divinity School. While baptistic in outlook, the schools became the

---

[128] Gordon, *Adoniram J. Gordon*, 37.
[129] Quoted in Gibson, *A. J. Gordon*, 192, 195; 317.
[130] Compare Gordon, *Adoniram J. Gordon*, 173–79.

epicenters of a more independent stream of evangelical thought and training in the New England area.[131]

An important theological transition occurred among Baptist pastors in the United States between 1800 and 1850. As David Benedict noted, "Our old Baptist divines, especially those of British descent, were generally strong Calvinists as to their doctrinal creed."[132] In application this meant that while they might preach the gospel to the unconverted, they did not invite them to Christ. The strongest stream of confessionalism was to be found in the Middle Atlantic States and the South, while New England pastors were less emphatic about such matters. Preachers dwelt much on themes of the decrees and purposes of God, "the hidden treasures of the gospel." Freewill and Seventh Day Baptists, however, were noted as opposed to some of the distinguishing doctrines of the Calvinistic creed. Likewise on the frontier, circuit riders and other itinerants often openly vacillated between Arminianism and hyper-Calvinism. As a result of the wide distribution of his books, the impact of Andrew Fuller's theological turns was broad. It was especially so in preaching, where a general understanding of the work of Christ gradually led to an open invitation to all sinners. More and more "heralds of the gospel" felt the obligation to call upon men everywhere to repent. Some even resorted to using the "New Measures." The debates in the first three decades of the century between Gillites and Fullerites were fierce, with the result being in favor of the Fuller position, and to some observers, a lowering of the standard of orthodoxy. Preaching on doctrinal subjects thus became less common, with a general Calvinism implicit in the background. As the Calvinist John Leland put it, "Two grains of Arminianism, with three of Calvinism, would make a tolerable good compound."[133]

---

[131] One of Gordon's purposes in starting the Institute was to train lay workers for the Congo mission. Because of its avowedly premillennial basis, it drew the criticism of numerous Baptist educators, notably E. H. Johnson and Henry Vedder at Crozer Seminary. The Institute became an epicenter of premillenial Baptist life supported by pastors like Clarence Larkin of Pennsylvania and Henry C. Mabie in Minnesota. Beginning in the 1960s, Gordon Divinity School began to outdistance Andover Newton as the seminary of choice among New England Baptists. It had a similar attraction among Maritime Baptists in Canada. See Gibson, *Gordon*, 132–40.

[132] David Benedict, *Fifty Years Among the Baptists* (Glen Rose: Newman and Collings, 1913) 102.

[133] Ibid., 108.

SUMMARY

The pastoral ministers of the Baptist community in the United States constituted an important resource for defining Baptist theology. Their sermons, opinions expressed in debates, and fidelity to confessional traditions formed a resource for congregational theology. Pastoral mentors, regional role models, and widely published writers demonstrated genetic theological connections. The readiness of pastors to be sharply critical of each other reveals much about the day-to-day theological mindset of the churches. Across a vast geography and a dispersed population, Baptist pastors became agents of genetic transmission of theological genes. Significantly, they both carried and transformed these genetic Baptist traits.

Most Baptist ministers were not formally educated. The result was a developing popular theology that was often piecemeal and imitative. A pastor's theology might be derived from a perceived literal understanding of Scripture and further informed only by what paucity of reading material was at hand. Most firmly embraced a confessional tradition, like the London (later Philadelphia), and the New Hampshire Confession. When confronted with new ideas the real possibility for theological heterodoxy arose, as in the exposure of some pastors to universal restorationism, apocalypticism, or radical biblical criticism that produced anti-trinitarian thinking. A favored few were educated in the New England tradition of a classical four-year baccalaureate degree and the addition of two-to-three more years in a theological school. Ironically, even some of these well-educated pastors adopted theological positions untenable among the Baptist churches in which they had their roots. Very few ministers, however, had the time, money, education, or social standing required to gain entrance to the loftiest levels of ministerial training. By the nineteenth century an increasing number of Baptists nevertheless received some level of formal theological education from one of the literary and theological institutions that combined arts courses with theological subjects, Bible, theology, languages, history, and the pastoral arts. In this regard, Baptists in the New England and Middle Atlantic states fared better than those in the South and West where the farmer-preacher was a dominant presence among the churches.

Generally speaking, it was the pastors of congregations in urban centers whose theology was committed to literature. Printed sermons, tracts, and a few serious books took up the Baptist understanding of the church, biblical questions, and sometimes relations with other Christian groups and their tenets. Pastors like Thomas Baldwin and Samuel Stillman, Morgan Edwards and Isaac Backus, Andrew Broaddus and William Bullein Johnson, came to theological leadership because their pastoral voices were influential and consistent with what appeared to be both Baptist orthodoxy and evangelical truth. In the establishment of the first theological courses and schools, these men were selected to lead the curricula because of their proven experience in the pastorate. Others promoted their views through editorial writing and debates, as readily seen in the case of Landmarkism's important place in the history of Baptist thought.

Finally, it is accurate to note that Baptist thought in the United States, as articulated by pastors before 1900, was largely in the Reformed or Calvinistic tradition. Some exhibited extreme Calvinistic tendencies, others reacted against harsh determinism but accepted other tenets, while most operated within a moderate or evangelical Calvinist viewpoint. Because this was the basis of acceptability in the ordination process and the call of a new pastor among "Regular Baptists," it constituted "Baptist orthodoxy." It was in the definition of a doctrine of the church, including the sacraments/ordinances and membership, that Baptist ministers most clearly delineated themselves from other denominational traditions. In most ways, Baptist pastors in mainstream congregations followed the trends of evangelical Protestantism, softening their determinism, using revivalistic measures, and from time to time exhibiting flourishes of millennialism and perfectionism.

CHAPTER 6

AMERICAN BAPTIST SCHOOLMEN

> The theology of any age is largely an expression of the Christian experience of that age. The general experience of any given time, with its characteristic peculiarities, grows up into a style of thinking, a moral and spiritual consciousness, from which there is no escaping.[1]
>
> William Newton Clarke, 1899

As was the case during approximately the same era with their British colleagues, the primary theological influence of American Baptist pastors over the denomination gradually gave way to teaching theologians in Baptist colleges and theological schools. In 1800 there were slightly more than thirty pastors in all the United States who had a collegiate education, and only eight upon whom a doctor of divinity degree was conferred. Within a half century, however, it became common to have churches express their interest in education for pastoral candidates.[2] The impact of this change was felt not only among pastors who upgraded their educational attainments, but also in the transformation of certain theological ideas and development of entirely new genetic traits in Baptist theological life. Overall, the contribution of Baptist schools to the making of a Baptist theological identity mirrored trends in American Protestantism, particularly among the Congregationalist and Presbyterian communities.[3]

---

[1] William Newton Clarke, *An Outline of Christian Theology* (New York: Charles Scribner's Sons, 1899) 19.

[2] David Benedict, *Fifty Years Among the Baptists* (Glen Rose: Newman and Collings, 1913) 50, 218.

[3] See Holifield, *Theology in America*, 15 on this point. Baptists were slower to evolve, more institutionally diverse, and continued to value pastor – theologians well into the nineteenth century.

">252   A Genetic History of Baptist Thought

Early in the nineteenth century the task was to define theology. Christology and soteriology were the dominant questions. Later, under the influence of German and British thinkers, Baptists in North America took up the challenge of Christianity and culture. This meant scrutinizing history and applying new techniques to understanding contemporary society. More often than not, scholarly Baptist theologians looked for direction to the most progressive and liberal Protestants of Europe. American Baptist theologians were exposed to German theologians through journals such as *Christian Review* and *The Baptist Quarterly*, as well as travel and study leaves spent mostly with moderate and conservative representatives of German thought.[4]

The roots of the scholarly Baptist tradition lay in the late eighteenth century with the Rhode Island College. As the growth of the denomination took place on the Great Lakes and Southern frontiers, schools and colleges were founded in greater numbers, increasing employment opportunities for theological teachers. A second "type" of church-affiliated school emerged with a blended curriculum to train ministers and other students in the arts and applied sciences. The first of these was Maine Literary and Theological Institution (later Colby College), founded in 1817. The faculties of these "L&T" schools always included a theological teacher. Based upon the Andover model of a post-undergraduate theological seminary, a third kind of institution developed among Baptists, beginning with Newton Theological Institution in 1825. A cluster of theological teachers gathered in these "seminaries," including classic theologians, biblical specialists, and applied "theologians," the last who sometimes taught church history as well.

The developing tradition of an academically informed theology was at first centered within institutions largely devoted to the training of pastors, as well as in a select few colleges and universities. Among those schools were Hamilton (later Madison, Colgate), Columbian, Franklin, Kalamazoo, Shurtleff, Richmond, Wake Forest, Furman, Mercer, and Baylor. In several cases the theological studies programs were discontinued or rechartered to become separate theological schools. Colgate best exemplified this evolution. In Newton's wake came Western Baptist Theological Institute (1845), Rochester Theological Seminary (1850), Southern Baptist Theological Seminary (1859), Crozer

---

[4] Norman H. Maring, "Baptists and Changing Views of the Bible, 1865–1918" (Part 1), *Foundations* 1/3 (July 1958): 53.

Theological Seminary (1867), and Baptist Union (later Morgan Park) Theological Seminary (1867). Trained theologians gravitated to these schools to teach aspiring pastors and the few who would follow them into a teaching ministry. Definite traditions or "schools of thought" came to characterize the institutions. The high water mark of scholarly American Baptist theologians occurred in association with these schools between 1850 and 1940.

As time went on, the evangelical community among American Baptists established additional schools and developed new theological traditions. The most prominent of these were Central Baptist Theological Seminary (1901), Northern Baptist Theological Seminary (1913), Eastern Baptist Theological Seminary (1925), and California Baptist Seminary (1944), later called American Baptist Seminary of the West (when formally merged with Berkeley Baptist Divinity School in 1968). Related to the denominational schools in the evangelical tradition were other institutions of a baptistic flavor, where evangelical Baptists taught: Gordon Divinity School in New England and Fuller Theological Seminary in California. Baptists also were found in smaller but academically prominent schools such as North American Baptist Seminary and Bethel Theological Seminary.

Recruitment of faculty personnel became a major issue for Baptist schools concerned with upgrading their theological disciplines. With the advent of the post-undergraduate theological seminary as a training school for ministers, Baptists followed other Protestant denominations in expecting their leading pastors and teachers to gain a seminary diploma. Newton, Colgate, Rochester, and Southern pioneered this direction. A first step toward more advanced specialized theological work was taken in faculty travel for overseas study. This amounted to a semester or a summer of visiting British or more likely German universities where American faculty sat in on lectures. The value of this exposure was directly related to the comprehension of German. Barnas Sears stands out as one who had the capacity to do first-rate study overseas. Next were those seminary graduates who had the resources to take advanced degrees in Europe before beginning their teaching careers in earnest. By the 1890s with the rise of doctoral programs in select American universities, Baptists went off to Yale and the University of Chicago. In the South, Southern Baptist Seminary and Southwestern Baptist Seminary began graduate schools to provide theological doctorates for their constituency. By the mid-twentieth century a great variety of graduate schools could be noticed among the rosters of Baptist colleges and theological schools, including Boston University, Vanderbilt, Duke, Harvard, the University of Pennsylvania and Temple University. Beginning in the 1960s a few American students determined to study overseas and settled into graduate programs at Glasgow, Edinburgh, St. Andrews, Aberdeen, London, Oxford, and Cambridge. Karl Barth and Emil Brunner attracted a few to Basel and Zurich, respectively. The graduate theses and dissertations completed by Baptist theologians represent a major body of theological research done from a Baptist perspective.

BROWN UNIVERSITY

The rich theological heritage of Brown University emanates mainly, though not exclusively, from its presidents. In its first charter, Rhode Island College had as its purpose "education in the vernacular and learned languages, and in the liberal arts and sciences...to provide a succession of men duly qualified for discharging the offices of life with usefulness and reputation."[5] At the heart of this egalitarian mission, Baptists had as their "main design" a Baptist college, especially for the education of their ministry.[6] As a consequence, the appointment of theologically orthodox leadership was of the essence to those who first labored to establish the school. The college invited as its first teacher and president, James Manning, a top student at Princeton College.[7]

James Manning (1738–1791) was the fountainhead of Baptist education in the United States. Although Rhode Island College was a

---

[5] Reuben Aldridge Guild, *Early History of Brown University, Including the Life, Times, and Correspondence of President Manning 1756–1791* (Providence: Snow and Farnham, 1896) 534.

[6] So observes the college historian, Guild. Ibid., 515.

[7] Contrary to this long held historical opinion, Glenn T. Miller wrote in his *Piety And Intellect: The Aims and Purposes of Ante-Bellum Theological Education* (Atlanta: Scholars Press, 1990) 317: "Rhode Island was not a Baptist College; it was a public college under Baptist patronage. Ezra Stiles, pastor of the Congregational Church at Newport and later president of Yale, wrote the college charter..." But this is manifestly inaccurate in light of the debate over the charter and the negative reaction to the draft charter that Stiles prepared for his Baptist friends in Newport. The charter process and documentation are traced in Walter C. Bronson, *The History of Brown University 1764–1914* (Providence: Brown University, 1914) 13–33.

liberal arts institution, it carried the aspirations of the denominational community and particularly of those involved in Christian ministry. Manning gave the institution his theological imprint and vision for theological education and, by extension, similarly influenced most American Baptists in the Revolutionary era.

Manning received his preparatory education at Hopewell Academy under Isaac Eaton (1724–1772), who was fond of Latin instruction. The young ministerial aspirant was also much influenced by Isaac Stelle, a Baptist minister at Piscataway, New Jersey. Among his academy mates was Oliver Hart, who would become a celebrated pastor in Charleston, South Carolina. In 1758, following the short administration of Jonathan Edwards, Manning matriculated in the College of New Jersey (later Princeton). There he learned ministry skills from observing the Reverend Samuel Davies and the Reverend Doctor Samuel Finley, successive presidents who also instructed him in Latin, Greek, and Hebrew. Finley was an evangelical Calvinist, much influenced by George Whitefield and Gilbert Tennent. The remaining faculty at the fledgling Presbyterian college were eminent Presbyterian clergymen from the Middle Colonies. Manning graduated in 1762, ranked second in a class of twenty-one.

Manning published nothing of note, but left extensive correspondence that profiles his religious values. The records of his service as pastor of the churches at Warren and later Providence reveal much. He was trinitarian, a Five Principle Calvinistic Baptist, and a close communionist who did not favor the "sixth principle"[8] as essential to communion. His piety included prayer, study of Scripture, a living faith in Christ, and fellowship with all those "walking orderly in the church of Christ."[9] As to instruction in the College, Manning prohibited any form of infidelity or the denial of the authenticity of the Scriptures.[10] Indicative of his stance, he responded negatively and directly to European authors such as Thomas Paine and Voltaire who had written that no book in the Bible was composed before the Exile. Theologically, President Manning met

---

[8] This is a reference to the Six Principle movement among General Baptists in England and the colonies. They held to a literal understanding of Hebrews 6:1–2, where among six obligatory practices, the laying on of hands at the time of baptism was the sixth principle. This position enjoyed wide acceptance in Rhode Island and for a time caused much division among colonial Baptists.

[9] "Warren Church Covenant," quoted in Guild, *Brown University,* 49.

[10] "Laws and Customs of Rhode Island College, 1774," quoted in ibid., 271–72.

the expectations for orthodoxy of a growing Baptist constituency. He quickly became a leading Baptist in New England and counted among his close associates men like Samuel Stillman, Isaac Backus, Hezekiah Smith, and Gardner Thurston—all regular Baptists.

Manning was an ardent promoter of revivals. He heard a number of the itinerant preachers as he traveled through the colonies in the 1770s to promote the college. His own preaching was consequently transformed and during 1775–76 a widespread "work of grace" broke out in Providence. Large crowds began to gather at public meetings in Providence's First Baptist Church. One hundred persons were baptized in about six months, including his wife. Perhaps most startling was the revival's impact upon the college. Manning reported that students gathered before class for prayer, and that instead of his planned lectures on logic and philosophy, he spoke to them about "matters of the Kingdom of God." He expressed great exultation to his English Baptist correspondent and friend, Benjamin Wallin.[11]

Manning was critical of what he considered aberrations of orthodox teachings. He preached against universal salvation, circulated a critique of Jemima Wilkinson as a pernicious teacher of error, and was openly critical of Elhanan Winchester's Unitarian/Universalist proclamations. By the conclusion of his career, Manning had established an appreciation for classical learning among Baptists and this would attract able students to formal education over the next century. His consistent Edwardsean Calvinism and warm evangelical pastoral heart were antidotes to those Baptists who held that education was superfluous or even harmful. Brown University, as Manning had laid the foundation, would have the potential to become a theological and educational standard for mainstream Baptists in the United States.

Jonathan Maxcy and Asa Messer followed Manning as presidents at Brown. Maxcy (1768–1820) was a brilliant alumnus of the college who became a tutor at nineteen, pastor of the Providence church in 1791, and Manning's successor at Brown in 1792. Maxcy had a penchant for theological openness, which became a matter of serious concern in the Baptist community. His public pronouncements, including his funeral eulogy for Manning, often took unexpected turns. For instance, in attempting to interpret death, he denied that spiritual death was implied

---

[11] Letter of James Manning to Benjamin Wallin, 12 November 1776, quoted in ibid., 296–97.

biblically in the punishment upon Adam and his posterity. He argued with perfect logic that if spiritual death was involved in God's curse upon Adam, then by virtue of the resurrection of Christ all would be raised to life—a kind of universal restoration. His view of sin was that it is voluntary, not inherited, and he made a distinction between sin and errors of judgment.[12] He opined, "I cannot induce myself to repose so small a share of confidence in the mercy of God, as to imagine, he will not pardon all the sincere errors of his creatures." In his view, a proven virtuous life counted for much.[13] Maxcy's flirtation with new ideas ultimately led him to reject the traditional views of the atonement for a governmental theory that was more in keeping with a new scientific consciousness and universal reason.[14] Fellow Baptist Isaac Backus thought Maxcy's positions were sometimes scandalous, and he was especially critical of Maxcy's historical elevation of Joseph Priestly over Jonathan Edwards. Fearing for the loss of support for the College, Maxcy moderated his public pronouncements and sought theological rapprochement with his longtime Baptist friends.[15]

Maxcy thought the sole basis of Christian unity was "love" and he recoiled at censuring persons of differing theological opinions. He believed diversity of religious opinion was to be expected. Tolerance was to be shown toward persons whose doctrines of the Bible differed from his own, and that included even known liberal thinkers such as Elhanan Winchester. "Perfect union in opinion and belief will not take place, till all men possess, not only the same kind of temper, but the same degree of capacity. Candor and forbearance ought always to mark the character of Christians. Nothing derogates more from their true dignity than to

---

[12] "A Funeral Sermon Occasioned by the Death of the Reverend James Manning, D.D., President of Rhode Island College. Delivered in the Baptist Meetinghouse in Providence, July 31, 1791," in Romeo Elton, *The Literary Remains of the Reverend Jonathan Maxcy, D.D., with a Memoir of His Life* (New York: A.V. Blake, 1844) 162–64. Maxcy acknowledged the work of a Congregationalist pastor in Stockbridge, Stephen West, titled *Scriptural Doctrine of the Atonement.*

[13] "A Funeral Sermon," preface, ibid., 151.

[14] E. Brooks Holifield, *The Gentlemen Theologians: American Theology in Southern Culture 1795–1860* (Durham: Duke University Press, 1978) 194, discusses the influence of Maxcy in his later career as president of South Carolina College.

[15] William G. McLoughlin, *Isaac Backus and the American Pietistic Tradition* (Boston: Little, Brown, 1967) 219.

censure or neglect others for difference of sentiment."[16] Maxcy first planted the seed of non-confessional, liberal Baptist thought at Brown, though it would take several generations to mature. Maxcy left Brown in 1802 to become president of Union College and later South Carolina College.

Asa Messer (1769–1836), who followed Maxcy as president between 1802–1826, was an able administrator and institutional leader. Like his predecessor, however, he became embroiled in doctrinal heterodoxy in the 1820s and it cost him his presidency. The son of a farmer, he prepared for college under Hezekiah Smith of Haverhill, Massachusetts, and graduated from Rhode Island College. First Baptist Church in Providence ordained him to the Baptist ministry and immediately thereafter he became a tutor in mathematics, philosophy, and languages at the college.

Like his two predecessors, Messer was an advocate of religious liberty and for many years his own theological perspective seems to have gone unchallenged. In 1818 his close friend, Samuel Eddy, secretary of the college corporation and a member of First Baptist, Providence, authored a pamphlet on the deity of Christ that many deemed heretical. He was "allowed to withdraw" from First Baptist and went over to the Unitarians. Messer often joined his friend for prayer at First Congregational Church, recently turned Unitarian, and this brought suspicion on the president of the college. In what may have been a test of orthodoxy applied especially against Messer, First Baptist Church declared it was disavowing fellowship with any who denied the deity of Jesus Christ. Responding, Messer wrote that Jesus possessed divinity as he proceeded from God as the pre-eminent Son of God. "He then is a Son and, as God has given him, so I would give him a name which is above every name." Much like contemporary Unitarian leaders, Messer could not equate Jesus with "the great Father of all, the self-existent, almighty, independent, underived, most holy, only wise God."[17] Given the transatlantic surge of popularity that the Unitarians enjoyed in those years and the strong antipathy against their teachings among the Baptists in England and America, a battle raged over theological confessionalism and trinitarianism that Messer was destined to lose. Citing John Gill, Jesus, and the apostles in his defense, and holding to other cardinal

---

[16] Ibid., 152.

[17] The documentation is cited in Bronson, *History of Brown University*, 186–89.

Baptist beliefs like profession of faith before baptism and immersion, the president publicly held his ground that "Jesus is the Christ, the Son of the living God."[18] Along the way, Messer managed to receive a Doctor of Sacred Theology degree from Harvard that enhanced his reputation among Unitarians.

Criticism of Messer's doctrinal position was joined with charges of poor administration of the curriculum, unmanaged student unrest, and a slander campaign in the Providence newspapers in 1826 that alleged that in the college "the head is sick and the whole heart fainteth." Messer objected vigorously when one of the trustees alleged "proof" against the president. Finally, worn down by controversy, he resigned. After thirty-nine years of service to the college, President Messer desired to live where he might "serve the living and true God without molestation," and he prayed somewhat cynically that the God of Abraham and Jesus would have "the seat of literature and all its patrons in his holy keeping."[19] Messer credited his undoing to the proponents of New England Baptist orthodoxy.

In many ways, his youth upon becoming president, his lack of pastoral experience, and his willingness to go beyond Calvinistic Baptist boundaries all contributed to the lack of support he gleaned from fellow Baptist clergy. Despite the level of suspicion that existed in the Baptist community regarding the college, Messer's legacy included three leading students who themselves would greatly influence the course of New England theology: Barnas Sears and Adoniram Judson among the Baptists, and Edwards A. Park among the Congregationalists. Alexis Caswell and Rufus Babcock, both future presidents of Baptist colleges, were also students during Messer's tenure.

Brown's reputation for educational leadership and theological orthodoxy in the Baptist community was salvaged by the university's fourth president, Francis Wayland (1796–1865). The new president was a towering figure among Baptists in the United States during the middle of the nineteenth century. Educated at Union College in New York—including in the field of medicine—Wayland had been recognized as a youth for his scholarly abilities and leadership. He was elected president of Brown University in 1827. During his four-decade career he led in the expansion of Brown, taught courses in religion and

---

[18] Ibid., 188.

[19] Messer's letter of resignation, quoted in ibid., 192.

ethics, and was a major figure in the evolution of the Baptist denomination. During the 1840s his position on slavery, an outgrowth of his ethical system, placed him at the forefront of northern antislavery advocates.

The early years of Wayland's life are instructive in understanding his theological perspective. His parents had been members of the Eagle Street Baptist Church in London before their immigration to New England. They joined the Fayette Street Baptist Church (afterwards the Madison Avenue Church) in New York, and eventually his father was called to the ministry. Wayland recalled that even as a child he had enjoyed regular exposure to classic Baptist and nonconformist writers such as Andrew Fuller, John Gill, Abraham Booth, John Newton, and Augustus Toplady. His father treasured a worn copy of John Cann's Bible.[20]

Wayland's initial studies were in language and general subjects that allowed him to qualify for admission to Union College. Once there, he embraced Republicanism and followed Episcopalian and Dutch Reformed religious influences. Upon his graduation in 1813 he took up medicine under two leading physicians in Troy, New York. A chance encounter with Luther Rice, who made an impassioned case for missions and conversion of the heathen, led to Wayland's conversion and changed his vocational direction toward the ministry. He discovered that formal Baptist educational opportunities were scant in Philadelphia and Massachusetts. Not satisfied with the typical methodology of learning one's ministry skills while "on the job" under the supervision of prominent pastors—such as William Staughton in Philadelphia and Jeremiah Chaplin in Danvers, Massachusetts—Wayland chose instead to attend the Congregationalist seminary at Andover. He was convinced his Baptist convictions would not be seriously challenged.

Wayland only spent a year at Andover, but it was an especially formative period. Among those with him in the incoming class of 1816 was another later-prominent Baptist, Irah Chase. The faculty consisted of Ebenezer Porter in Rhetoric, Leonard Woods in Theology, and Moses Stuart in Sacred Literature. Wayland naturally gravitated toward Scripture studies and found in Stuart a mentor and friend. Stuart had a

---

[20] Francis Wayland and H. L. Wayland, *A Memoir of the Life and Labors of Francis Wayland, D.D., L.L.D., Late President of Brown University* (New York: Sheldon and Co., 1867) 13.

mind for detail and demanded that his students dig deeply into the study of the Scriptures. Although a Congregationalist, a colleague recalled that, "in his creed the Bible was first, midst, last, highest, deepest, broadest. He spoke sometimes in terms too disparaging of theological systems...He read scholastic divines, but he studied the prophets and apostles."[21] Wayland also recalled that Stuart affirmed a modest regenerate believer position on baptism, that he concurred with the evangelicalism of Andrew Fuller, and provided a catholic learning atmosphere for his students.

Wayland left Andover after just one year of theological education, convinced that "the special peculiarity of the Baptist belief is, that the church of Christ is really composed of none but regenerate persons...and that pedobaptism, in all its forms, tends to obliterate this grand truth."[22] While much that was positive had been gained in his theological development during that brief tenure, he also developed some prejudices against education in seminaries. Over time, many of his role models would be characterized by their own development through the mentoring tradition of urban churches.

Following his brief season as a seminary student, Wayland took up the pastorate of First Baptist Church in Boston. Here he was exposed to several new theological influences. Initially he lived with Thomas Baldwin, and the two collaborated as editors of *American Baptist Magazine*. Baldwin esteemed the young Wayland as one with great potential for ministry. Baldwin was the pastor at Second Baptist and Daniel Sharp at Charles Street. With Wayland at First Baptist, the three formed a preaching trio that lifted an evangelical Christian voice to counter the widespread Unitarianism of Boston. After five years in pastoral work, however, Wayland returned to higher education. As president of Brown College, his administrative abilities were quickly noted as he pursued his objectives at the school with singular purpose: "I am built railroad fashion...I can go forward if necessary, and if necessary I can take the back track, but I cannot go sideways."[23]

---

[21] Ibid., 81.

[22] Ibid., 84.

[23] Quoted in "Stumbling Into Disorder," in Winthrop S. Hudson, *Baptists in Transition: Individualism and Christian Responsibility* (Valley Forge: Judson Press, 1979) 93.

Wayland dedicated the remainder of his life to collegiate higher education in the Baptist tradition. Early in his seminary studies, he wrote to his mother that he most desired a tutorship in some college.[24] He recognized the educational attainments of Congregationalists, Episcopalians, and Presbyterians over against the largely self-taught Baptists. He noted with chagrin the antagonism to education among many Baptists who largely preferred experience and piety as one's basic qualification for ministry. At the beginning of his career he commented on the number of second-career Baptist preachers who spoke extemporaneously and without care for language. This caused him to champion a classical collegiate education for those in the larger urban congregations of the denomination. He also promoted a higher standard of education for those who assumed lay leadership in the churches. He took it upon himself to teach moral science and Baptist practices in a rigorously organized way, the essence of his "systematic theology." Others who sat under him or who recognized value in the approach at Brown—notably A. C. Kendrick, E. A. Crawley, James P. Boyce, Henry G. Weston, and E.G. Robinson—emulated his approach elsewhere.

Francis Wayland's theological position is difficult to categorize. Some see in it the evolution of a great thinker, while others see a frustrating eclecticism. Norman Maring, in an incisive essay, held that although Wayland spent a year at Andover, he had little knowledge of theology and deemed it unimportant.[25] Certainly one can identify elements of an Anglo-American Baptist evangelical Calvinism in his writings. His strongest traits were a high view of the priority of Scripture and an unfailing personal piety. His use of Scripture and the imprint of exegete Moses Stuart on his religious consciousness, led Wayland to arrive at a naïve biblical theology that derived doctrine directly from the words of the text. When confronted with consistent Calvinism, Wayland stated he was a thoroughgoing "Edwardsian, after the first president Edwards and writers of that class."[26] But, when pressed to be specific, Wayland confessed he was actually a "moderate Calvinist," by which he meant he held in "divine contradiction" the sovereignty of God and the

---

[24] Ibid., 77.

[25] Norman H. Maring, "The Individualism of Francis Wayland," in *Baptist Concepts of the Church*, ed. Winthrop S. Hudson (Philadelphia: Judson Press, 1959) 138.

[26] Francis Wayland, *Notes on the Principles and Practices of the Baptist Churches* (Boston: Gould and Lincoln, 1858) 21.

freedom of man. "The sharp angles of Calvinism," he wrote, "which needed to be filed and hammered out in order to make a system, I desire to hold no opinion about."[27] It seemed to Wayland that the major flaw of all theological systems was that their "logical sequences" were inevitably imperfect interpretations drawn from revealed truth.

Francis Wayland's doctrinal expressions were an example of the effects of Baptist biblicism that subdued the emergence of a more elaborate, systematic theological system in one of the denomination's most influential thinkers. This point is of more than passing import due to Wayland's influence both upon individual Baptist thinkers and theological education. Much of his effort as president at Brown was spent in redirecting the piety and discipline of the student body. He did this by supporting revival services, meeting with individual students for prayer, and by teaching a regular Bible class in chapel. One student recalled what this meant for those preparing for ministry at Brown:

> The Bible class in his hands became a power, and gained a reputation extending far beyond the walls of the college. It even excited, it was rumoured, the jealousy of a theological institution then struggling for a place in the affections of the churches. It was hinted that the student preparing for the ministry at Brown, after attending the instructions given in that class for four years, did not feel that he greatly needed a course of lectures from a professor in didactic theology. It was hinted, indeed, that those who pursued their theological studies in a seminary, sometimes annoyed their instructors by too frequent allusions to the views and opinions which had been advanced in the chapel of their alma mater.[28]

Individualism in Christian experience was interlaced throughout Wayland's thought. In his moral system he understood each human being to be, by constitution, a separate and complete system. He wrote, "every human being is a distinct and independent individual...and every individual is free to resist or conform to the tendencies by which he is

---

[27] Wayland, *Memoir*, 125.
[28] Ibid., 290.

surrounded."[29] His doctrine of sin was consequently individualized. Perhaps even more indicative of an individualized religious perspective was his teleology: "May we not hope, then, that with the improvement of our race in piety, God will invigorate our powers of discovery...and we shall enter upon that career of improvement for which we were originally designed by our Creator."[30] Moreover, piety was linked with individualism in a revivalistic motif. This stemmed from young Wayland's own spiritual testimony and illustrated his bias against systematic theology:

> I do not remember any sermon that did me any good. The preaching, then as now, seemed to me to be too theological, devoted to explaining some doctrine of the gospel according to a particular system, with but little of that warm interest in man's salvation that appears suitable in the herald of a free and finished redemption. Occasionally I heard a plain man who poured out his soul in earnest for the salvation of men, and who affected me deeply; but in general the preaching left me as it found me.[31]

Wayland was instrumental in promoting several campus-wide revivals. One of his early students recalled the president's state of mind in 1834 as "truly heavenly...his conversations, his exhortations, his sermons, his prayers, seemed to me to be more eloquent and melting than anything I had ever heard from mortal lips."[32] Here was a direct carryover from his own morphology of conversion to his ministry in college teaching.

Wayland's first outstanding literary achievement was *Elements of Moral Science*, published in 1835. For several years he had lectured on moral philosophy using William Paley's *The Principles of Moral and Political Philosophy* (1785), which Wayland found increasingly problematic. In the making of his own work, he frankly admitted little dependence upon others, "to avoid the impression of using the labors of

---

[29] Francis Wayland, *Elements of Moral Science* (Boston: Gould and Lincoln, 1837) 202; Francis Wayland, *Salvation by Christ* (Boston: n.p., 1859) 91, as quoted in Maring, "The Individualism of Francis Wayland," 148.

[30] Francis Wayland, *Occasional Discourses*, 343.

[31] Wayland, *Memoir*, 50–51.

[32] Ibid., 291.

others without acknowledgement." Rather, pietistically, he prayed for the direction of God's Spirit to "enlighten, guide, and teach" him to write something that was true, and that would show "the necessity and excellency of the plan of salvation."[33] He did acknowledge his general indebtedness to Joseph Butler, and to J. J. Gurney for his work on the Sabbath. Wayland, though perhaps not recognizing the case, was also indebted in his intellectual framework to John Locke and Thomas Jefferson. Wayland's best-selling textbook was a conversation with the Enlightenment and American social and political ideals, couched in references to the Bible. His far-ranging topics included civic duties, personal morality, individual rights, Sabbath-keeping, veracity, oaths, family relations, benevolence, social structures, prayer, and property rights. Whole bits of contract theory of society, plus Lockean terminology about voluntary associations and individual rights and participation, were integrated with material derived directly from the Declaration of Independence of the United States of America. "Every man," he wrote, "is under moral obligation to pursue his own happiness in such a manner only as will leave his neighbor undisturbed." Ultimately, Wayland believed that "the more perfectly our wills are subjected to the will of God...the more ardent will be our devotion and the more filial the temper from which our actions proceed."[34] Here was an evangelical Baptist set of religious values fused with a conservative Republican social and political outlook.

Wayland addressed the thorny issues of personal responsibility and benevolence in *Limitations of Human Responsibility* (1838). Following Bishop Joseph Butler's notion (put forward in *Analogy of Religion* [1736]) that the relation of God to humanity is like that of a governor over servants, Wayland strongly asserted the divine imperative: "We are obliged to do whatever he [God] commands." Accordingly, Wayland argued that the first level of moral action was to respond directly to the specific commands of Scripture. Further actions in Wayland's system, however, were limited by one's circumstances: "We see that while our responsibility for the temper of the mind is unlimited and universal, our responsibility for the outward act is limited and special."[35] Wayland

[33] Ibid., 382, 380.
[34] Francis Wayland, *Moral Science*, 168, 193, 205.
[35] Francis Wayland, *The Limitations of Human Responsibility* (Boston: Gould, Kendall, and Lincoln, 1838) 16, 19.

thought that the circumstances under which one acts, coupled with other obligations by which one is bound, were ordained as well by God and posed the limits of one's actions. What he consequently created was a theory of limited benevolence that was circumstantially defined. This perspective was in sharp contrast to the perfectionism of evangelical ultraist and social reformers such as Charles G. Finney, and the Victorian voluntarist mindset that argued that individuals had an inherent responsibility to change their society by acts of unlimited benevolence. In the United States, Wayland drew fire from ardent evangelicals. In Britain, he was likewise subjected to heavy criticism. When he visited Bradford Academy in the north of England, the principal of the school informed him he could not open his pulpit to President Wayland on account of "some doctrines in your treatise on *The Limitations of Human Responsibility* have rendered you unpopular in England, and were I to do it, I should incur reprehension."[36]

It was in the field of ecclesiology that Wayland's theological thinking had its most enduring impact. Here his individualistic piety passed to the church. "I am a Baptist and an Independent," he wrote, "holding that believers alone are entitled to church membership and that each church…is competent in itself to all the purposes of government and discipline."[37] Seldom referring to the universal church, Wayland defined the church as "a class of persons possessing a particular moral character." Further, "a church of Christ is manifestly a voluntary association."[38] The object of the church is the conversion of souls; the confession of faith of a church was the New Testament. In his book, *Principles and Practices of Baptist Churches* (1856), Wayland postulated the complete independence of local congregations as the foundation of the doctrine of the church. "Each several church is a

---

[36] Wayland, *Memoir*, 13. This could also refer to a visit Wayland made to Stepney, where he met W. Harris Murch, the principal, and other British Baptist ministers, including John Dyer, Francis Cox, Joseph Angus, Charles Stovel, Edward Steane, and S. W. Greene. Wayland reported they conversed about slavery, the Bible issue, dissenters, and congregational polity. One of them present, who was reputed to be antagonistic to Wayland's theology, actually befriended him. See page 29.

[37] Wayland, *Human Responsibility*, 120.

[38] In another description, he put it this way, "every individual church is a voluntary association, subject to the laws which Christ hath enacted, empowered by him to execute those laws…and to leave to the conscience of every member precisely what Christ has left to his conscience." See ibid., 132.

Christian society on which is conferred by Christ the entire power of self-government."[39] There is no authority over the congregation, creed, confession, or church body that creates unity. Although early in his career he supported the establishment of Baptist denominationalism, he later reverted to local church protectionism. He came to feel that "moral questions cannot be decided by majorities nor can the law of God be ascertained by the vote of conventions." As soon as conventions and other extra-congregational bodies "assume to themselves the power of legislating over churches, and controlling the opinions and consciences of individuals…it will not be well…a church never invests its delegates to such assemblies with power to pledge it for anything."[40] In what one writer has called "the great reversal," Wayland single-handedly dismantled the Triennial Convention of 1826, and later even questioned the value of missionary organizations beyond the local church.[41] In doing so, he taught the freedom that each person has to read and interpret Scripture is the unifying element of the Christian household. Here Wayland relied upon the Enlightenment principle that "man is an intelligent and accountable being."[42]

As one might expect, Wayland carried a considerable brief for religious liberty. Again building upon John Locke's theories of the voluntary nature of religion, Wayland held that "the support of religion by law is at variance with the genius of the gospel." The gospel, he believed, supposed that all humans are voluntary in their service of God, mode of worship, and the selection and compensation of religious teachers. Ever the missionary, Wayland understood that the religion of Christ exerted its greatest power when it is left to have its effect upon the conversion of men.[43] This led him to conclude with early Baptists that

---

[39] Wayland, *Principles and Practices*, 14.

[40] Wayland, *Human Responsibility*, 137, 188.

[41] This in sharp contrast to his 1823 sermon, "The Moral Dignity of the Missionary Enterprise," delivered at First Baptist, Boston and widely circulated thereafter. See Wayland, *Memoir*, 164–67, and John A. Broadus, *Memoir of James Petigru Boyce, D.D., LL.D.* (New York: A. C. Armstrong, 1893) 34. Early in his career he supported the organization of Baptists into state conventions that might also support a national body. By 1855 "he rejoiced that the whole plan failed through sturdy common sense." Wayland, *Memoir*, 159.

[42] Ibid., 15.

[43] Wayland, *Moral Science*, 227.

"all application of force is gratuitous mischief,"[44] and he strongly held slavery in the United States to be a violation of personal liberty. Here he directly engaged the great issue of his day. First in *Limitations of Human Responsibility (1838)*, and later in a series of published debates with Richard Fuller of South Carolina, Wayland struck out at what he felt was a great moral deficiency of his day. But, the consistency of his limited benevolence placed boundaries on his position. "We are bound most scrupulously to avoid all measures... to infringe the rights of the South...we have no right to take any means...to excite the slaves to insubordination or civil war." Rather, Wayland believed, "we have a right to change the purpose of the master by argument." Here he clearly differed from many in the abolitionist movement. He did not believe activism in the matter issued from God's authority. Wayland was prepared to leave the resolution of the matter to God, "who is perfectly capable of vindicating his own laws and executing justice among the children of men."[45]

In a curious set of circumstances Wayland may well have transformed Brown College's institutional impact upon Baptist thought, broadened it from a primary focus on the ministry to include other professions. Given his own biases against a theologically trained ministry, it is not surprising to find his special appreciation for those in training to be lawyers. Prominent justices and lawyers in New England indicated pride at the very large proportion of eminent lawyers who benefited from Wayland's teaching, "since the main thing for a lawyer is the power of making a clear and complete analysis of the case."[46] Wayland's preoccupation with morals fit neatly the scheme of legal foundations. With the widespread adoption of *Elements of Moral Science* as a textbook and subsequently, *Elements of Political Economy* (1837), Wayland began to move in ever-broadening academic, social, and cultural circles. His advice or participation was sought in the establishment of the Smithsonian Institution, various statewide organizations, on political questions, and in support of social and religious institutions. Wayland designed and executed a thorough reform of Brown's curriculum in the 1850s that departed from a traditional emphasis on the classics and instead

---

[44] Ibid., 204.

[45] Francis, Wayland, *The Limitations of Human Responsibility* (Boston; Gould, Kendall & Lincoln, 1838), 182-183.

[46] Broadus, *Memoir of Boyce*, 35.

emphasized liberal education in the arts and sciences. The school's graduates now embarked upon a wide variety of pursuits quite distinct from the Christian ministry. Those who followed Wayland to lead Brown College would find themselves at the helm of an institution whose characteristic diversity resulted in a struggle over the nature of its Baptist identity and educational mission in contrast to the growing numbers of Baptist post-graduate theological seminaries.

Illustrative of this new direction was Barnas Sears (1802–1880), whose theological contributions will be discussed primarily in conjunction with Newton Theological Institution. He served as president of Brown University from 1855 to 1867 and developed an antagonistic relationship with his predecessor. Many of Wayland's reforms were rescinded in Sears's presidency and Wayland withdrew from participation in the college. Sears's tenure was further hampered by the War Between the States, and he returned to private educational pursuits after leaving Brown. Sears did follow Wayland's teaching program and taught courses to undergraduates in philosophy, history of philosophy, and Christian Evidences. Henry S. Burrage, a well-known historian who was a student during this period, recalled Sears's use of Joseph Haven's *Mental Philosophy* (1858) and Albert Schwegler's *A History of Philosophy in Epitome* (1856), both of which reflected a European bent. Sears also relied on Wayland's *Elements of Moral Science*. From all accounts, Sears gave much of his effort to character-building rather than the pursuit of rigorous scholarship. He hoped to teach students to think for themselves rather than accepting his or anyone else's thinking without question.[47] On balance, his pedagogical contributions at Brown were muted in comparison to those he would make later at Newton or Colgate.

The nineteenth century closed out with three Baptist ministers at Brown's helm, each of whom facilitated the now-familiar pattern of New England Baptist higher education. These were Alexis Caswell, Ezekiel G. Robinson, and Elisha B. Andrews. Caswell (1799–1877) graduated from Brown in 1822 with highest honors and went to Columbian College in Washington, D.C. He studied theology with William Staughton and taught ancient languages until the school went into receivership. In 1827 he was in Halifax, Nova Scotia, where he helped constitute First Baptist

---

[47] Alvah Hovey, *Barnas Sears: A Christian Educator, His Making and Work* (New York: Silver Burdette, 1902) 100–109.

Church and was there ordained.[48] Upon his return to Providence, Caswell became professor of mathematics and natural philosophy at Brown. Over the years his identity as a scientist grew beyond his ministerial credentials. He was nationally known in the scientific community and active in the Smithsonian Institution. He became president of the College at an advanced age, bringing needed change and new funding 1868–1872. Caswell's biographer noted that Caswell was truly a man of the nineteenth century whose religious faith and scientific views were never at variance.[49] "The mechanics of the heavens," Caswell wrote, "point with unending certainty to the superintending agency of an intelligent and infinite creator."[50]

Following the brief tenure of Alexis Caswell, Ezekiel Robinson enjoyed a seventeen-year presidency at Brown during which he also served as a lecturer in philosophy and ethics. While Robinson's theological contributions to broader Baptist thought are discussed below in connection with Rochester Theological Seminary, his work at Brown is not to be dismissed. One historian recalled him as neither scholarly nor a man of affairs, and unaware of the subtleties of New England conservatism.[51] Some conclude he held to traditional nineteenth-century modes of thought rather than embracing the emerging twentieth-century context. It is evident from student comments, however, that Robinson nevertheless excelled in some academic areas although his work at Brown did not reach the standards of excellence that were characteristic of his work at Rochester. At Brown, he moved between theology and philosophy, stressing the rational basis of Christianity and the need for rigorous thinking. In an institution known for memorization and recitation, he encouraged freedom of thought and classroom discussion. He stressed the immutability of the moral law as grounded in the nature of God. In the area of metaphysics, he followed carefully the school of

---

[48] Caswell left an indelible stamp of classical New England Baptist thought in the Maritimes. See William H. Brackney, "The Planter Motif among Baptists from New England to Nova Scotia 1760–1850" in *Pilgrim Pathways: Essays in Baptist History in Honour of B .R White*, ed. William H. Brackney and Paul Fiddes (Macon GA: Mercer University Press, 1999) 298–99.

[49] William Gamwell, "Memoir of Alexius Caswell D.D., L.L.D.: Ex-President of Brown University" *New England Historical and Genealogical Register* (July 1877).

[50] Quoted in *Dictionary of American National Biography*, ed. John A Garraty and Mark C. Carnes (New York: Oxford University Press, 1999) 565.

[51] Bronson, *Brown University,* 387.

Scottish Realism. Robinson had a considerable ministry in pulpits about Providence that students recalled as strongly apologetic for the finality of the Christian faith.[52] In 1882 his work as a theologian and homiletician was recognized in an invitation to deliver the Beecher Lectures in Preaching at Yale. Among Robinson's administrative achievements was the establishment in 1887 of earned graduate degrees at Brown—the Master of Arts and Doctor of Philosophy—the first such credentials to be awarded by an American Baptist denominational institution.[53]

Elisha B. Andrews (1844–1917), who succeeded Robinson, was a Civil War veteran who later completed his education at Brown and Newton. He served in the Baptist pastorate for a time and became president at Denison University, where he also occupied the chair in moral philosophy. While at Denison, he recruited William R. Harper for the faculty, exhibiting his appreciation for biblical studies of a progressive nature. He later returned East to take the chair in pastoral theology and homiletics at Newton. In 1882 he went to Brown for a post in history, traveled to Europe to study at the universities of Berlin and Munich, and ultimately assumed the New England school's presidency. During his tenure as president, Andrews introduced an expanding graduate education program, as well as a women's division that evolved into Pembroke College. Theologically speaking, Andrews seemed to identify with mainstream Baptist thought, though he was no friend of emerging premillennialism.[54] In 1897 a severe disagreement erupted between the president and some members of the faculty, resulting in Andrews's resignation. Many faculty supported Andrews, as did eventually the trustees, and his resignation was withdrawn, but not before national attention was drawn to issues of academic freedom at the Baptist university.[55] This incident would lay the foundation for Brown's increasingly independent stance from its traditional Baptist relationships.

---

[52] Ibid., 424–25.

[53] One of the two first recipients of the doctorate was a Canadian Baptist, Austen K. DeBlois in 1889, who became president of Shurtleff College and later Eastern Baptist Theological Seminary.

[54] In 1890 at the annual meeting of the American Baptist Missionary Union, he publicly referred to the position of prominent Brown alumnus A. J. Gordon as the "premillennial craze." Quoted in Gibson, *A. J. Gordon*, 199.

[55] Andrews's mercurial career is the subject of "Gallant, Stalwart Bennie: Elisha Benjamin Andrews 1844–1917: An Educator's Odyssey" (Ph.D. diss., University of

In the last year of the nineteenth century, William Herbert Perry Faunce (1859–1930) was elected president of Brown University. He was to lead the school to the point where its formal theological contributions to the Baptist movement would cease. Faunce received his A.B. and A.M. degrees from Brown and was also a graduate of Newton Theological Institution. He became a pastor in Springfield, Massachusetts, and later at New York's prestigious Fifth Avenue Baptist Church where he was widely acclaimed as a pulpiteer. In the 1890s he held adjunct positions at the University of Chicago and Harvard. In 1895 he studied the University of Jena during a sabbatical leave provided by his church. He spent over three decades at Brown and was responsible for rescuing the college from bankruptcy.

As Faunce's biographers have pointed out, he was conservative and traditional in educational matters but liberal in religious views. He was said to be "optimistic, activist, and catholic" and, unlike some of his Baptist theological allies, he was certain that science could substantiate the claims of Christianity. He taught mathematics at Brown early in his career, searching during that time for a coherent, organized theological system in light of the discoveries of the sciences. As a pastor in one of the wealthiest congregations in Baptist life, New York City's Fifth Avenue Baptist Church, he developed a progressive view of humanity and education. As Brown's president, one biographer saw him as "the best of evangelical liberal Protestantism of the first quarter of the twentieth century."[56]

Faunce initially had a significant impact upon popular Baptist thinking about the Bible and religious authority. Along with Harry Emerson Fosdick (which see), Faunce made it clear that higher education and certain presuppositions went hand in hand. He identified four "special thought forms" that characterized the new Western world: the world is not a finished product, but an unfolding process; a universal and invariable law in nature; the universal application of the scientific

---

Denver, 1969), and Edward Lach, Jr, "Elisha Benjamin Andrews," *Dictionary of American National Biography*, ed. Garraty and Carnes, vol. 1, 494–96.

[56] J. Walter Sillen, "William H. P. Faunce: A Representative Religious Liberal," *Foundations* 2/3 (July 1959): 239.

method; and the importance of higher education.[57] What this meant for an appropriate doctrine of Scripture was that it no longer could be assumed to be something along the lines of British Prime Minister Gladstone's "impregnable Rock of Holy Scripture." A cogent doctrine of Scripture was instead the result of "growth" in the context of biblical scholarship. He advised that the Bible is "not intended as a scientific treatise...Its profound moral and religious truth must be translated into the thought-forms of our generation."[58] It was not a new message, but considering Faunce's position as president of the Baptists's oldest and most prestigious educational institution in North America, and his well-known reputation as a premier American educator, his influence was large.

Faunce was relentless in his pursuit of new views on religious authority. There was even a strain of the newer forms of relativity-thinking in his Christology: "when we say Christ is the Son of God, we simply mean in morals and religion he is now and forever our master. Until a purer comes, he shall rule us."[59] In the 1920s, under the provisions of Brown's original charter, he successfully resisted an investigation of Brown's faculty by Northern Baptist fundamentalists and began the slow process by which the university ceased to be church-related. Further, as an articulate former pastor, he viewed the problem within the churches as a theological generation gap. The minister was at his best as an educational mediator who could "turn the hearts of the fathers to the children," by which he meant causing the older generation to accept the new views of the Bible.[60] Faunce thought the Old Testament was particularly useful for an appreciation of order and beauty of nature, while the New Testament was clearly the exponent of religious individualism. The "moral initiative and energy of the modern world" have their roots in the New Testament,[61] he urged fellow educators. Here was an old Baptist axiom borne along in clothing that many laypersons and pastors little appreciated.

---

[57] William Herbert Perry Faunce, *The Educational Ideal In Ministry: The Lyman Beecher Lectures at Yale University in the Year 1908* (New York: The Macmillan Co., 1908) 55–65.

[58] Ibid., 63–64.

[59] W. H. P. Faunce, "The Appeal of Christ to Men," *Proceedings of the Baptist Congress, 1906*, 166.

[60] Ibid., 44.

[61] Ibid., 103.

For Faunce, the essence of Christianity was not ritual, not creedal, not historical development, nor a moral system. He gave his evangelical Baptist critics much exercise with comments like, "If Christianity were creed, then orthodoxy would mean Christ-likeness, and those men and women who are most sound in the faith would be most unselfish and generous in character. But," he wryly observed, "history shows no such constant relation of theology to life."[62] Instead, Christianity was "Purpose," that is, "the revelation of the unchanging purpose of God, and the developing of that same purpose in the lives and institutions of men." God is immanent, Faunce believed, "making humanity's cause his own...a living personal power."[63] His published statements revealed intellectual dependence upon Albert Ritschl, B. P. Bowne and the personalists, and those in the experiential school such as W. N. Clarke. In his Cole Lectures at Vanderbilt University in 1912, he urged "tenacious loyalty to the purpose of Christ...and constant readjustment to the needs of humanity—that is efficiency and service."[64] One could also anticipate the modernism of Shailer Mathews and the influence of Gerald Birney Smith, the latter a close friend of Faunce through the years of his battles with fundamentalists.

In looking at the overall history of Brown University and its contribution to a theological tradition, the record is one of disappointment. Although the college was founded with the training of ministers clearly in view, it actually had only a modest impact upon the education of Baptist clergy. Unlike the British college tradition, as seen in the schools at Bristol and Stepney, Brown ultimately became an elite liberal arts school. Brown could not meet the growing institutional church needs that accompanied the rapid increase of Baptists, particularly outside New England. Further, the idea of a classical school program for training Baptist ministers became and remained a minority objective for the school. Most Baptist ministers were unable to afford the requisite four years of study, had little preparation for serious study of classical languages, and generally were less interested in academic pursuits. Those who did graduate from Brown tended to move into teaching careers, and to a lesser extent, to select urban pastorates or other

---

[62] William Herbert Perry Faunce, *What Does Christianity Mean?* (New York: Fleming H. Revell Co., 1912) 29, 40.
[63] Ibid., 39-40.
[64] Ibid., 56, 91–92.

arenas of institutional administration. Finally, Brown never developed a post-graduate seminary program, and consequently never hit the target audience Baptist pastors who aspired to enrich their educational portfolios. Thus, Brown's impact on the actual theological education of clergy was limited.

As an institution, Brown also experienced difficulties in maintaining generally accepted standards of Baptist orthodoxy. Some of its early leadership traveled beyond the pale of the theologically conservative Baptist church community, notably presidents Maxcy and Messer. It could also be argued that in its haste to identify young, bright, aspiring leaders, Brown tapped prodigies too young. That these students were outstanding undergraduate academic performers does not appear to have been universally translated into the skills necessary for dealing with the church community or the subtleties of administration that only years of experience bring. An experienced and effective senior pastor, though not as well educated in the classics, might have saved Brown for greater leadership among the churches.

Where America's first Baptist college did have a concerted and lasting impact was in training academic teachers and theologians. From Colby and Colgate, to McMaster and Baylor, the institutions founded by Baptists were often led by Brown alumni. The publishing outreach of key Brown presidents was also significant, as is given evidence by the large audience of the writings of Manning, Wayland, Robinson, and Faunce. Brown's leadership also served to warn more orthodox Baptists, often prone to eschew formal education, that ongoing theological interpretation of the faith was necessary if the community was to maintain its relevance as a people who carried the Word of God into the contemporary world.

THE PHILADELPHIA/WASHINGTON SCHOOL

As Brown University struggled to meet the demands of New England Baptists for a learned ministry, a second scholastic tradition arose in Philadelphia that provided a link with British Baptist theological traditions. Here the central figure was William Staughton (1770–1829). He was born in Coventry, educated at Bristol Baptist College, and took up his career in the United States during a period of great expansion for the denomination.[65]

Staughton was not a creative theologian, but he was the inaugurating force behind institutional Baptist theological education in the United States. His English West Country evangelicalism and his voluntaristic spirit fit neatly with American missionary motifs and the frontier context. At Bristol he studied with a faculty of three: Caleb Evans (principal), James Newton in the classics, and Robert Hall, Jr. Evans was a warm-hearted evangelical Calvinist who defended the Trinity in a well-publicized debate with Unitarians. His works on the atonement went through nine editions. Robert Hall was educated at Bristol and earned a degree at Aberdeen in the classics. Hall moved beyond traditional Calvinism, which he thought a straitjacket; he professed openness to all sorts of Christian positions. In the later eighteenth century, Bristol developed a reputation for emphasis in preaching, church planting, and academic rigor. Few doubt that Staughton was present as an active contributor in 1792 when the first Baptist overseas missionary society was formed.

It was Staughton's reputation as a preacher and minister that made of him a role model for younger preachers. A biographer suggested "the great excellence of the doctor consists in the fertility of his imagination, the rich and splendid fullness of his periods, the classic purity of his language, a most harmonious voice, and the most impressive action."[66] Existing portraits of Staughton are action poses of a great revivalist/preacher. The church edifice he designed on Sansom Street in Philadelphia was built for the preacher/communicator and he attracted large crowds. Young, aspiring ministers wanted to study his style and achieve his prominence. These circumstances would become a model for Baptist ministerial training through a mentoring process and in the development of church-related theological schools.[67] Staughton convened the first American Baptist theological school in his home in

---

[65] For an overall appreciation of his work, see Walter O. Lewis, "William Staughton," *Baptist Quarterly* 11/3 (July 1942): 74–78, and Rogers, *Richard Furman: Life and Legacy*, 78-84.

[66] S. W. Lynd, *Memoir of the Reverend William Staughton, D.D.* (Boston: Lincoln and Edmands, 1834) 129.

[67] For instance, Spurgeon's College in England (C. H. Spurgeon), Temple University School of Theology in Philadelphia (Russell H. Conwell), and Gordon Divinity School (A. J. Gordon).

Philadelphia and lectured for 11 years. Among his students were Daniel Sharp, John Mason Peck, Isaac McCoy, James Welch, Alexis Caswell, William Bullein Johnson, and James D. Knowles. In 1820 Luther Rice and Richard Furman persuaded Staughton to move his theological program to Washington D.C., where it became part of Columbian College. Staughton remained with the school until it was closed in 1828. He then accepted the presidency of Georgetown College and died enroute to Kentucky to assume the position.

As a teacher of theology, Staughton was remembered as deeply Christological. "Christ was his theme, the burden of all his pulpit exhibitions," wrote former student Samuel Lynd[68]. His classical studies at Bristol gave him impetus to ground his students in Latin, Greek, Hebrew, and a broad exposure to English literature. As the solitary teacher in his school, Staughton taught Bible content, ethics, preaching, and pastoral duties. His theological lectures emphasized inspiration of Scripture, Christian evidences, prophecy, and eschatology. He drew upon a broad theological variety in constructing his lectures, including John Gill, Matthew Henry, Phillip Doddridge, William Burkitt, Matthew Poole, John Trappe, and Adam Clarke. His devotion to Gill was more than passing, as evinced in his editing an abridged edition of Gill's *Body of Divinity* for an American audience. He encouraged his students to "read much" and work with languages.[69] The obvious bridge between English Baptist theology and the American Baptist scene, Staughton brought the emphases of Robert Hall, Jr., John Rippon, John Ryland, and Andrew Fuller to a new audience.

With the merger of Staughton's school and the new Columbian College in 1821–1822, Staughton taught history, belles letters, and philosophy in the Classical Department and preaching and divinity to the theological students. In Washington, Staughton brought to his side two important colleagues, Irah Chase and Alvah Woods. Staughton continued to lecture in "divinity" and Woods covered ecclesiastical history. Chase was assigned languages and biblical literature, which he taught in both the collegiate and theological divisions. Presumably his effort was largely given to Greek and Latin, with some attention eventually given to

---

[68] Lynd, *Staughton*, 161.
[69] Lynd, *Staughton*, 166.

Hebrew. Chase, however, was not fulfilled in the short-lived assignment.[70]

The Philadelphia/Washington tradition had insufficient time to develop into a permanent theological institution.[71] In some ways it was assumed into that of Newton Theological Institution because of the transfer of faculty. In other ways it ceased to exist with the departure of William Staughton. The principal result of this limited movement was the placement of virtually all of its "graduates" in missionary or ministerial service. Few theological schools could claim such a record of success.

NEWTON THEOLOGICAL INSTITUTION

Newton Theological Institution, located outside Boston, is the oldest formal post-graduate theological school among Baptists in North America. Boston area Baptist pastors like Daniel Sharp, Lucius Bolles, and Thomas Baldwin planned the institution as a denominational version of Andover Theological Seminary where some prominent Baptists had already studied.[72] The primary influence of Andover upon Newton was in the person of Andover professor, Moses Stuart. He was a rigorous Bible scholar who read and appreciated German critics and drilled his students in progressive theology like that of Nathaniel W. Taylor. Stuart was continually under scrutiny for his views on inspiration of Scripture, biblical conflicts with science, the atonement, and his resistance to

---

[70] William Hague, *Christian Greatness in the Scholar: A Discourse on the Life and Character of Reverend Irah Chase, D.D.* (Boston: Gould and Lincoln, 1866) 21.

[71] Columbian College was under the auspices of the General Missionary Convention until 1826. Its supporters were unable to fund its financial needs, and the Convention withdrew its support in 1826. This led to near insolvency and complete reorganization of the College. The entire faculty resigned and no degree in theology was ever conferred. The story of Columbian is best told in Elmer Louis Kayser, *Bricks Without Straw: The Evolution of George Washington University* (New York: Appleton-Century-Crofts, 1970) 38–55.

[72] Andover was a confessional school built upon the Westminster Shorter Catechism and a creed written by Congregationalist pastors Leonard Woods and Samuel Spring. The Andover curriculum, which served as a model for that of Newton, required students to study Bible and theology before church history and there were continual investigations by trustees and "Visitors" to ensure orthodoxy. Revivalist theology and missions were important conversionist emphases at Andover. The first two generations of appointments to the American Board of Commissioners for Foreign Missions graduated from the school, and many faculty and students participated in revival waves in the Northeast.

catechetical requirements. Yet, on balance, Stuart remained "the father of biblical learning" in the United States and he held forth at Andover Seminary until 1852, a constant friend and advisor to the Baptists.[73]

Newton, then in Andover's shadow, became the seminary of choice for Baptists who aspired to teach in theological schools or hold administrative positions. Its early theology was consistently Calvinistic, traditional, rationalistic and church-oriented. Representing the mainstream of Baptists in the United States, Newton was for up to a century the most influential theological school in the denomination, preparing pastors, missionaries, and aspiring faculty members for itself and other Baptist institutions. A 1925 survey by Austen DeBlois found that Newton graduates had been in key roles at Baptist colleges and universities such as Colby, Bates, Vassar, Columbian, Denison, Kalamazoo, Franklin, Chicago, Des Moines, McMinnville, and Shurtleff. Northern seminaries where Newton's graduates served included Rochester and Crozer among the seminaries. In the South, Newton men were found at Furman, Georgetown, and Western Theological Institution and Southern Baptist Theological Seminary. Newton's alumni played important roles in Canada at Acadia and McMaster universities.[74] By the first quarter of the twentieth century, no other institution matched the theological shadow Newton cast across American Baptist life.

Newton was also in the vanguard of exposing Baptist ministers in the United States and Canada to European ideas. This happened through faculty sabbatical leave travel and translation of textbooks into English. With the failure of a merger between Andover and Harvard due to conflict with Andover's confessional history, Newton eventually grew ever closer to Andover. In the 1920s, the two schools merged as Andover moved to the Newton campus. "Andover Newton" consequently evolved as a common enterprise "in the Reformed tradition."

Irah Chase (1793–1864) was Newton's founder. He was educated at Middlebury College in Vermont and Andover Theological Seminary. At Andover he revered the venerable Moses Stuart, who instilled in Chase

---

[73] Daniel Day Williams, *The Andover Liberals*: *A Study in American Theology* (New York: Octagon Books, 1970) 16–19. Williams thinks that Stuart was the fountainhead of liberal thought at Andover.

[74] Austen K. DeBlois, "Newton Men in Education" *Historical Addresses Delivered at the Newton Centennial, June, 1925* (Newton Centre: The Institution Bulletin, 1925) 42–63.

the desire to engage serious biblical study using the best methods suggested by contemporary European scholars.[75] Chase's sole Baptist colleague at Andover was Francis Wayland, who recalled Stuart's place in forming theological students: "With all this love of inquiry, his discipline was strict and exacting. He expected every man to be like himself, *totus in illis*...his reverence for the word of God was deep and all-pervading."[76] Young Chase fondly remembered on both a theological and personal level, "his convictions as a Baptist were treated with respect."[77] This would forge a lifelong affection between Andover and the founder of Newton Theological Institution. Upon graduation from Andover, Chase was offered a teaching position in languages at Waterville College as well as a position in theology at Columbian College. Columbian's impressive Dr. William Staughton was persuasive, and Chase went first to Washington D.C.

A biblical scholar more than a systematic theologian, Chase did set the standard for the training of theological educators. Convinced that European thought was advancing rapidly, he attended lectures in 1823 at the universities of Halle, Leipzig, and Göttingen, where he encountered Johann Friederich Blumembach (natural science), Arnold H. L. Heeren (classics), and Friedrich Carl Eichhorn (history).[78] Encouraged by the New England Baptist community, he put together America's first distinguished Baptist theological faculty, identifying colleagues with a similar interest in European scholarship. Chase assumed the teaching duties in theology and church history, Barnas Sears in theology, George

---

[75] Stuart was venerated in New England and much of Europe, but villified in some quarters. The esteemed evangelical Scottish Baptist, Robert Haldane, held that Stuart's work on Romans "perplexed and misled readers and overthrew their faith." Stuart "totally subverted the doctrine of justification by faith," wrote Haldane. See his essay "Mr. Stuart," in Robert Haldane, *Exposition of the Epistle to the Romans, with Remarks on the Commentaries of Dr. MacKnight, Professor Moses Stuart, and Professor Tholuck* (New York: Robert Carter & Brothers, 1857) 735–37.

[76] Wayland, *Memoir*, 69.

[77] Hague, *Irah Chase,* 13.

[78] Like other American theologians, Chase validated his use and knowledge of German sources by translating German works into English. His scholarly contribution was *The Work Claiming to be The Constitutions and Canons of the Holy Apostles, including the Canons; Whiston's Version, revised from the Greek, Translated by Irah Chase.* (New York: D. Appleton & Co., 1848).

Ripley in rhetoric, and Horatio B. Hackett[79] in biblical studies. Chase remained at the seminary until 1845, after which he retired to Boston to write.

Chase drew up the foundational curriculum plan for Newton, which gave promise to an entirely new approach to systematic theology. Rather than using a master formulary of doctrines, such as that developed by John Calvin or Francis Turretin, whereby the purpose of Scripture was to "proof-text" the propositions and "anticipate" the Scriptures, Chase reversed the equation. He instead urged students to become thoroughly grounded in the Scriptures themselves, "becoming Mighty ...by a mastery of their meaning, their scope, and of their applications."[80] The undergirding theological principle was essentially Baptist: namely that the inspired Word contained the requisites of religious knowledge, "the essential ideas that pertain to any set of defined statements that can deserve to be called a system of Christian theology."[81] Chase was shaped in large part by professors Gottlob Christian Storr (1746–1805) and Karl Christian Flatt (1772–1843) at Tübingen, whom Samuel Schmucker, the Lutheran professor of theology at Gettysburg, had introduced to North America through their philological and exegetical works, These orthodox stalwarts had resisted Schleiermacher's liberalizing approaches in favor of biblically-based dogmatic theology. Chase used Schmucker's textbook in his theology classes for many years.

From the trustee-approved description of Chase's chair in Newton, one sees the beginnings of a Baptist approach to theological systems as "biblical theology." Chase himself defined it this way: "Students should be prepared by a study of the teachings of the Bible to construct a theological system for himself...suited to meet the needs of his own mind, to the demands of his own age."[82] Here was a theology that was biblically oriented, characterized by a free hermeneutic, and retained a cultural sensitivity. It was a model that influenced all of the other Baptist schools of the nineteenth century. It was, however, the freedom Chase

[79] Although he worked in biblical studies, Hackett was well regarded in the school, particularly by alumni. According to Everett Carlton Herrick, *Turns Home Again* (Boston: Pilgrim Press, 1949), 30, he was one of the most brilliant proteges of Moses Stuart at Andover.
[80] Hague, *Irah Chase,* 23. Here he followed Moses Stuart, but was freed from Andover's confessional requirements.
[81] Ibid.
[82] Ibid., 26–27.

granted students to build their own systems that drew criticism of Chase and the new seminary at Newton. While the approach was baptistic at heart in allowing freedom of interpretation, some Baptists thought it far too heterodox.[83]

In his own writing, Chase developed a reputation for baptismal theology. In response to the controversy in the 1850s over baptismal regeneration among the Church of England and the Campbellites in the United States, Chase defended the Baptist position. From biblical data, he affirmed baptism by immersion for believers. Through quotation of a variety of ancient creeds, he demonstrated the inconsistency of infant baptism in church history.[84] Following the publication of Horace Bushnell's volume, *Christian Nurture* (1861), the Baptist community rushed to respond from a believer's church perspective. Near seventy years old, Professor Chase published *Infant Baptism: an Invention of Men* (1863) that addressed some of the chief concerns. In typical Baptist polemic[85], he set about to demonstrate that Bushnell's view on infant baptism contradicted both Scripture and common sense. He concluded "that infant baptism was not divinely instituted and sanctioned and that it opened the way for an untimely and unsuitable membership in the church."[86] Most importantly for Chase, the matter had Christological implications: Christ taught and commanded a believer's baptism.

Barnas Sears (1802–1880) was Chase's successor in theology and enjoyed a wide reputation for excellence in several institutions and in public education. He was educated at Brown University during the presidency of Asa Messer, whom he esteemed, and at Newton under Irah Chase. Chase's emphasis upon the biblical languages and Henry J. Ripley's work in New Testament were formative influences upon the

---

[83] A. H. Strong, *Miscellanies* (Philadelphia: Griffith and Rowland Press, 1912) 2:59–60.

[84] Irah Chase, *The Design of Baptism, Viewed in its Relation to the Christian Life* (Boston: Gould and Lincoln: 1851) 1–64; 163–84.

[85] It may be observed here that among the many contemporary German, British, and American sources Chase noted, he never mentioned Thomas Baldwin or other writers in the Baptist community in the United States. This leads one to conclude that Baptist theology did not flow in a direct line from one thinker to another. Instead, there is an individualistic strain to Baptist thought.

[86] Irah Chase, *Infant Baptism: an Invention of Men, or Dr. Bushnell's Arguments Reviewed* (Philadelphia: American Baptist Publication Society, 1863) 185–87.

young Sears, especially the opportunities afforded for further, personal studies under those teachers.[87]

Sears's most productive years as a theologian were spent at Newton, 1835–1848. He went to Newton fresh from studies overseas and earned a reputation for his knowledge of languages and German theological literature. During 1833–1835, as earlier done by Irah Chase, he traveled among the universities at Halle, Leipzig, Berlin, and finally Paris. He confessed to being enraptured with literature and languages, teaching himself in the classics and several modern languages. He developed a lifelong close friendship with F. A. G. Tholuck at Halle, being impressed with Tholuck's learned evangelicalism and concurrent pastoral ministry.[88] Of Tholuck, he wrote to his wife, "He attracts throngs of rationalists to hear his melting appeals in behalf of a religion pure and undefiled." He also wrote favorably of Georg Winer, Lebrecht F. Hermann, Joachim Neander, Ernst Hengstenberg, and Hermann Olshausen.[89] So overwhelmed was he with the German educational scene that one has the impression he would have stayed in Europe had the opportunity been presented.

Upon arriving at Newton, Sears took the title "professor of Christian Theology," succeeding Irah Chase who held the chair in "biblical theology." Sears wanted to blend the Baptist emphasis on Scripture with rational support of scholarship drawn from philosophy, psychology, history, and the natural sciences. According to a biographer, his motto was "religion is our atmosphere, knowledge should be our food, and discipline our exercise."[90] He also managed to lecture in church history and wrote extensively for scholarly journals. His main book length works were in German and included a biography of Luther. While selective in his choice of German theologians, Sears placed high value on German scholarship and wanted to see Americans work at the same scholarly levels.[91]

---

[87] Hovey, *Barnas Sears,* 18.

[88] On Tholuck's contribution, see Claude Welch, *Protestant Thought in the Nineteenth Century*, 2 vols. (New Haven: Yale University Press, 1972) 1:144.

[89] Ibid., 33–53, esp., 36.

[90] Alvah Hovey, *Barnas Sears, A Christian Educator: His Making and His Work* (New York: Silver, Bardette & Co., 1902) 56.

[91] Ibid., 58. It is a misreading of Sears to state that he wanted to "ward off a German menace," as Kenneth Short and Timothy George have written. Rather, he wanted to match the German scholarship with an American evangelical effort.

Methodologically, Sears was his own person. It is said he did not use a textbook in theology, nor did he develop one. He instead expounded upon events and people as he invited interaction among his students. His highest objective was to enable students to build the structure of their own belief systems. "I am simply anxious to teach you how to think," he told his students. "If you learn that, you may burn my lectures if you will."[92] He supplied a comprehensive bibliography for students to read, and he valued their becoming multi-lingual—a dubious skill for the pastoral ministry. Rejecting Friederich Schleiermacher and equally David Strauss, Sears tended toward a philosophical approach to education, using principles he derived from medieval writers. He acknowledged the emerging importance of science, remarking that "science cannot be overruled by theology." Moreover, "reason was a guide to matters presupposed by the Scriptures," and moral science and ethics were connected inextricably with Christian theology.[93] Sears's successor, Alvah Hovey, described his predecessor's theology as "biblical in its source and evangelical in tone." Others less enamored of the scholarly approach thought Sears taught little positive doctrine of any kind and that he led Newton away from an essentially conservative theological position.[94] Sears eventually left the school to become secretary of the Massachusetts Board of Education.

At the conclusion of the Sears era, Newton was at a crossroads. Many thought it should be combined with Brown College as a department of theology, lowering the cost of tuition and enhancing the literary atmosphere and prospects of enhanced academic repute for Brown.[95] Others felt that new, dynamic leadership was called for and that emerged in the person of Alvah Hovey (1820–1903). An upstate New Yorker by birth, Hovey was educated at Dartmouth College and Newton Theological Institution. A schoolteacher by profession, Hovey returned to the school in 1849 to teach church history and Hebrew. Upon the resignation of theology Professor Robert E. Pattison, Hovey assumed the chair in Christian Theology in 1855 and held that post until his death. In

---

[92] Hovey, *Barnas Sears,* 104.

[93] Ibid., 72–73.

[94] Strong, *Miscellanies,* 2:60.

[95] See the contemporary comments in Benedict, *Fifty Years Among the Baptists*, 220. Benedict assumed that most Newton students had done their undergraduate work at Brown.

1868 he became president at Newton, a post he retained for thirty years—a period in which his contemporaries included A. H. Strong at Rochester and Henry G. Weston at Crozer. He published his classroom lectures, titled *Manual of Theology and Ethics*, in 1877 through the American Baptist Publication Society. Compared with Ezekiel G. Robinson and A. H. Strong, Hovey was "critically orthodox" in his theological orientation and his leadership kept Newton within that orientation, throughout his long and illustrious career. To Hovey's credit, Newton became the most influential Baptist seminary of the mid-nineteenth century, counting four among five of the other Baptist seminary presidents as its alumni in 1868.

Hovey's work was widely accepted due to his reputation as a scholar, his inherent conservatism, and his position at the oldest Baptist seminary in America. His systematic work was skillfully reduced to seven categories, two on God and the remainder on man, the Bible, salvation, the church, and last things. In the second chapter of his *Manual of Systematic Theology*, Hovey struggled with the doctrine of Scripture. Much surrounded by the New Theology at Andover and Harvard, Hovey tried to accommodate science by arguing for a "religious dynamical theory of inspiration."[96] He moved away from claiming too much for Scripture, instead positing infallibility for Jesus and inspiration (which he defined along the lines of illumination) for the teachings of the apostles and their associates. "The New Testament Scriptures are worthy of full confidence as historical records," he wrote, affirming their general correctness, "but not the absence of minor inaccuracies."[97] Against the radical biblical criticism of F. C. Bauer and D. F. Strauss, Hovey appealed to the likes of Joachim Neander, Karl Ullman, Frederic Godet, and C. E. Luthardt. Not insensitive to the claims of the critical community, he acknowledged that the Bible possessed "varieties of style and verbal discrepancies, as well as essential harmony" in building his case for a doctrine of infallibility that was less than bibliolatry.[98] When confronted with the stark adverse effects of biblical criticism, he urged that the investigation of Scripture continue along modest, reverent,

---

[96] Alvah Hovey, *Manual of Systematic Theology and Christian Ethics* (Philadelphia: American Baptist Publication Society, 1880) 85.

[97] Ibid., 45.

[98] Ibid., 83. He described his view of inspiration as "dynamical."

patient, and cautious lines.[99] Hovey's position on biblical authority was shared by his protégés George D. B. Pepper and Henry G. Weston at Crozer, while others in the pastoral ministry "thought no other Baptist ever spoke with more *ex cathedra* influence than he."[100]

Hovey exhibited an essentially Calvinistic perspective in his understanding of original sin and its imputation to the human race. While mildly critical of other related views, he affirmed the federal theory that Adam and Christ are representatives of imputed sin and righteousness, respectively, thus offering a slight note of acknowledgement to the Westminster and Philadelphia (Baptist) confessions of faith. In his treatment of election, Hovey stood with St. Augustine, complete with Latin quotations, and affirmed God's unquestioned moral right to elect some and not others. Further, those so elected can rely on the sure perseverance of their state of grace.[101]

In much of Hovey's doctrinal discussions, he erred on the side of constructing an apparatus that was far too complex in scholarly obfuscation. In discussion of the church and ordinances, however, he stood firmly and clearly in his self-understanding as a Baptist. He equated the church with baptized believers and argued that, as such, the church retained the full right to accept only baptized believers into its fellowship. In the discussion current among Baptists about the universal nature of the church, Hovey took the position that the terminology of the New Testament clearly emphasized the church as essentially a local congregation. He stood against any form of hierarchy in leadership within the congregation, and like Francis Wayland before him and E. Y. Mullins after him, Hovey was wary of assigning responsibilities to extra-parish bodies. Winthrop Hudson saw this tendency in Alvah Hovey as a form of "permissiveness," whereby he stood with local church protectionists rather than helping to build an adequate doctrine of the church that responded to the needs of a new era.[102]

In his treatment of the ordinances, Hovey followed the well-worn Baptist pathways of the previous two centuries. He argued persuasively

---

[99] *Proceedings of the Baptist Congress*, 1883, 5.

[100] W. H. Allison, "Alvah Hovey," *Dictionary of American Biography*, ed. Dumas Malone 9:270.

[101] Hovey, *Systematic Theology*, 260.

[102] Winthrop S. Hudson, ed., "Shifting Patterns of Church Order," in *Baptist Concepts of the Church* (Philadelphia: The Judson Press, 1959) 215.

from older Baptist sources, notably Alexander Carson, Anders Wiberg, and Thomas J. Conant, for the appropriate meaning of the Greek word *baptizo* as immersion.[103] With respect to the Lord's Supper, after a nod to John Bunyan and Robert Hall as advocates of open communion, Hovey resided clearly in the closed communion camp, siding with R. B. C. Howell, and George D. B. Pepper, as demonstrated by his own widely circulated tract on "Close Communion" (1862).[104] In his attempt to be a consistent interpreter of Scripture with respect to matters of polity, Hovey disagreed with the inventiveness of recent "teetotalers" in calling for a "two wine theory" of the content of the cup in the Lord's Supper. Fully informed of all the scientific issues, Hovey maintained that the cup contained "proper wine, the fermented juice of grapes."[105] Like close communion, this was consistent with the understanding of the primitive churches, regardless of the emerging arguments for use of unfermented grape juice.

Hovey's doctrinal exposition concluded with Last Things. Here, at the beginnings of the influence of premillennial interpretation from groups like the Plymouth Brethren, he acknowledged "Many of the ablest German and English expositors believe in the premillennial return of Christ...not very distant from the present time." Against the rapture theories of Joseph Siess and C. A. Auberlen, he concluded that a careful Bible student finds the Scriptures inconclusive on the matter.[106] Hovey instead took the prevailing Baptist position and stressed the resurrection of the dead and the final judgment, ultimately citing a passage from Dante's *Paradiso*.

In general, Alvah Hovey lived in the theological consciousness of the nineteenth century, even more than his contemporary, Augustus Strong. Newton's theological position remained conservative in tone, even considering the work of Ezra P. Gould and Ernest Dewitt Burton. Gould, holder of the New Testament chair, provided Hovey and the Institution with a genuine challenge to its orthodoxy. As a young member of an

---

[103] Ibid., 316.

[104] Ibid., 337.

[105] Alvah Hovey, "What was the Fruit of the Vine Which Jesus Gave His Disciples at the Institution of the Supper?" *Baptist Quarterly Review* 9 (1887): 302–303, quoted in William H. Brackney, *Baptist Life and Thought, 1600–1980* (Valley Forge: Judson Press, 1983) 278–79.

[106] Ibid., 349.

aging faculty in the 1870s and 1880s, Gould made commentary in his classroom on matters pertinent to theology. As Hovey held tenaciously to an evangelical Calvinistic position that stressed the sovereignty of God and the justice of God in the atonement of Christ, Gould introduced ideas current with the New Theology. He held that Christ should be the center of theological understanding and discourse, and that the regnant characteristic of both God's and man's moral nature was love.[107] Hovey brought the situation to a head in 1882 with an investigation that produced the dismissal of Gould, insuring Newton's continued theological conservatism.[108] Ernest Burton, Gould's successor, taught New Testament at the school from 1883 to 1892, after which he joined William Rainey Harper at the University of Chicago. His work at Newton was praised for its textual thoroughness, but his career blossomed theologically when at Chicago he could articulate more contemporary theological findings that resulted from the application of his methods. The seeds of theological modernization were thus sewn during Hovey's distinguished career, but kept from full blossom until a later generation.

Nathan E. Wood (1849–1937) followed the venerable Hovey at Newton. Wood was educated at the University of Chicago and the Baptist Union Theological Seminary. Moving through the pastoral ministry to become pastor of First Baptist Boston, he became professor of Christian Theology and president following the long tenure of Alvah Hovey. He was author of *The Person and Work of Jesus Christ* (1909) and *Man and Sin* (1921). He served as professor of theology and president from 1899 until 1908.

Wood continued in the orthodox manner of Hovey, while acknowledging the emerging trends in theology. He considered himself a moderate Calvinist, holding a position that God's election of certain human beings is inscrutable, but at the point of man's "get-at-ableness,"

---

[107] Ezra P. Gould, "Is God Love?" *National Baptist* (12 October 1882): 641; and, "A Christocentric Theology," in ibid., 644.

[108] "The Removal of Prof. Gould," *National Baptist* (19 October 1882): 661. See Alvah Hovey, "Newton from 1875 to 1900," *Newtonian* 1/2 (June, 1903): 47 for Hovey's version of the Gould affair. He recalled that Gould "sometimes found it difficult to keep within the limits of his own department, preferring to discuss questions of theology on which his views were increasingly different from those of the officer in that chair [Hovey]....Everyone rejoiced when he found congenial work in another denomination and school."

he allowed it was somewhat "scrutable."[109] In this regard Wood appears to have been much influenced by George W. Northrup, Leonard Woods, and D. C. Davies. Likewise, in theorizing about the doctrine of the atonement, he posited that Christ's atonement was general and adequate. Rejecting atonement theories such as moral example, moral influence, governmental, and the Anselmic, Wood articulated what he called an "ethical/vicarious" theory, whereby both God's and man's ethical demands and needs are fulfilled in love and justice. This vicarious atonement thus produces "a new, obedient, and holy race."[110] In arriving at that position Wood exhibited influence from over fifty European and American theologians, ranging from orthodox to "New" theologians. Perhaps most startling to observers of Newton was Wood's insistence that it was not inspiration that validated revelation, but a Christian consciousness "that stubbornly asserts that God has made a revelation."[111]

Professor Wood appealed to historic Baptist positions in the majority of his thought. He expounded the scriptural basis of baptism in 1894, edited a commentary series on Pauline letters in 1896, wrote the history of First Baptist Church, Boston, and even managed to lecture on theology and missons at Gordon College. Like Hovey, Wood moved away from an affirmation of verbal inspiration—referring to that position as "the ten words of the law written by the finger of Jehovah...the very words of God"—to a "God realized in experience" test for anything that purported to be divine revelation. He believed Christian consciousness was a better arbiter of eternal fitness because it allowed for inquiry into the grounds of authority. Significantly, in his last published work (1925) he affirmed the divine inspiration of Scripture, doubtless in response to fundamentalism's attacks.[112]

Perhaps Wood's most revealing theological contribution to Baptist life was his essay, "Movements of Baptist Theological Thought During the Nineteenth Century" in A. H. Newman's *A Century of Baptist*

[109] Nathan E. Wood, *Lectures in Systematic Theology, As Given to the Classes in The Newton Theological Institution*, pamphlet (Newton MA: Newton Theological Institution, n.d.).
[110] "Atonement or Reconciliation,"in ibid., 46, 60.
[111] Quoted in Maring, "Baptists and Changing Views of the Bible." (Part 2),41.
[112] Nathan E. Wood, "Movements of Baptist Theological Thought" in A. H. Newman, *A Century of Baptist Achievement* (Philadelphia: American Baptist Publication Society, 1901) 430–31.

Achievement. In that much-circulated piece, Wood drew attention to changing patterns of Baptist thought about Scripture, the atonement, and the impact of the theory of evolution upon Baptist thought. From his standpoint, Baptists had not been led very far afield by "humanitarian views of Christ" and this was positive. He thought new studies of individual human freedom and responsibility were required because of the evolutionary hypothesis, yet he was wary of universal salvation, a trend he saw emerging among a small group of Baptists.[113] Wood was prepared to re-examine the nature of the atonement (only if this led to a conclusion that it originated in God). He was troubled by the implications of new evolutionary thinking on the doctrine of original sin, as well as with the ethical monism of A. H. Strong. His point was that after theorizing amongst theologians, Baptists (including himself!) should not obscure the cross of Christ as the "supreme manifestation of God in the salvation of men."[114] He was most heartened by the changes in world-view and ecclesiology in the denomination: "Baptists have grown out of the narrow ideas of a sect and into the world-view of a universal brotherhood in Christ and a universal church."[115] His general conclusion was that a theological "missionary spirit" drove Baptists. "If we shall ever be willing to become simply analytical, critical, self-content, and self-conceited," he mused, "God will bring us low and our crown of glory will be given to another."[116]

It is doubtful that Nathan Wood reflected many of the new emphases of his alma mater at Chicago. His education predated most of the more radical thinkers. Further, he was obviously tempered by interaction among the Baptist community in New England where Gordon College was making a conservative evangelical impression. In many ways Wood continued to use the theological rhetoric of the previous century, while appearing to be open to new discoveries and streams like monism, personalism, and the ethical nature of Christianity. It would be left to the

---

[113] Ibid., 434. This was either a veiled reference to A. H. Strong's position or the Chicago School.

[114] Ibid., 434. Actually, by 1901 he retreated to a more classic position of "two great and eternally separated classes" which seemed to recover the traditional Calvinistic particularism.

[115] Ibid., 436.

[116] Ibid., 437.

faculty he appointed, particularly his successor in theology, to move openly into the future of the New Theology.

Nathan Wood's successor in the chair of Christian theology at Newton was George Cross (1862–1929). Cross was educated at the University of Toronto, McMaster University, and the University of Chicago Divinity School. In 1900 at Chicago he earned a doctor of philosophy, completing a dissertation under George B. Foster on "The Theology of Frederich Schleiermacher." Cross became a leading American exponent of Schleiermacher's writings, publishing *The Theology of Schleiermacher, Creative Christianity,* and *What Is Christianity?* Prior to his appointment in theology at Newton he taught history at McMaster University.

At Newton, Cross taught the classic doctrine course to the main body of students in the bachelor of divinity program. It was in the graduate master of theology offerings that he pursued new trends. He taught courses in Ritschl, Schleiermacher, and one in comparative religions. In 1910 he introduced "evangelicalism" to comparative studies and guided theses on "The Bearing of Evolutionism on the Idea of Atonement" and "The Christian Idea of Immortality." The following year, Cross offered elective courses on the "Idea of Atonement" and "The Hope of Immortality." At the graduate level he examined the personal and social conceptions of salvation and the "Influence of Psychology on the Idea of a Future Life." The following year he moved to Rochester Theological Seminary to succeed the venerable A. H. Strong. He had opened Newton to the social gospel and a new form of comparative theology already evident at Colgate and Chicago.

Richard Miner Vaughan (1870–1954) followed Cross into Newton's transitional years. He was trained at Brown University and the University of Chicago Divinity School. Previously, he was dean and taught at Berkeley Baptist Divinity School (1908–1909) and the Pacific School of Religion (1910–1912). He occupied the chair in Christian Theology from 1912 to 1940. Vaughan was effusive about the influence of E. Benjamin Andrews upon his religious thinking as a student at Brown, but he had little to say about his theological training at Chicago.[117]

Vaughan provided a mediating influence during his long tenure in theology. He offered required "constructive" courses in theology, plus

---

[117] Richard M. Vaughan, "Turns in the Road," *Andover Newton Theological School Bulletin,* 1940, 9.

electives in modern thinkers (German theologians and New Theology advocates), comparative religions, and the theology of the poets, no doubt influenced by A. H. Strong at Rochester. He much accepted the Chicago principle that Christianity is an historical religion, but did not hold it accountable to meticulous historicism. Vaughan readily accepted the theory of evolution, yet held onto a soteriological understanding of revelation as the divine initiative in salvation. "God," he taught, "is not the everlasting silence, but the eternal Word forever self-expressive."[118] In the wake of the remarkable downfall of liberalism after World War I, Vaughn came to appreciate Karl Barth's idea of sin, a new emphasis upon the transcendence of God, the indisputable historicity of Jesus of Nazareth, and the evolution of a Christian culture that emphasized prayer, devotion and worship. Vaughan's doctrine of the church was held in creative tension on the one hand by the principle of voluntary association, and on the other by the ecumenical terminology of the Kingdom of God. Aware of the impact of fundamentalism, he believed that conservatives and liberals were meeting on what Hillyer Straton called the "common ground of essentialism."[119] Other than the occasional Sunday School lesson and infrequent lectures and journal articles, Vaughan was not a widely published theologian.

After Vaughan's retirement the predominating influence in theology at Andover Newton shifted from the Baptists to the Congregationalists. Nels F. S. Ferre, a Swedish graduate of Lund and Uppsala universities, and afterwards Harvard, brought international attention to Andover Newton for *The Christian Faith* (1942) and *Return to Christianity* (1943). Roger Hazelton, another Congregationalist appointed in philosophy of religion, followed Ferre in 1951 to what came to be known as the "Abbott Chair in Theology." Ferre returned to Andover Newton in 1957. A recovery of baptistic emphases was noticed in the short presidency (1947–51) of Harold Tribble, a Southern Baptist who had succeeded E. Y. Mullins at Southern Seminary. Tribble taught some theology courses with Ferre, but was quickly induced to become the president of Wake Forest College in North Carolina. Thereafter, prominent Baptist professors served in church history, missions, and

---

[118] Richard M. Vaughan, "The Meaning of History," *Andover Newton Theological School Bulletin* 1940, 15; Richard M. Vaughan, "Changes I Have Seen in Theological Thought," ibid., 11.
[119] Ibid., 14.

sociology. The school became renowned for its emphasis upon clinical education for ministry and historical/critical biblical scholarship through teachers like Norman K. Gottwald, Walter Harrelson, and Paul Minear. It also opened admissions to all, regardless of race or background.[120] With the upgrading of its programs in the 1960s, Gordon Divinity School began to assume an increasing share of pastoral training among Baptist students in New England, the heartland of Newton Theological Institution. While Andover Newton continued as a school related to the American Baptist Churches, its distinctive Baptist theological tradition may be said to have concluded as Newton affiliated with Andover in 1931.

THE COLGATE TRADITION

Colgate Seminary's roots are to be found in the development of theological education on the frontier of upstate New York. A missionary school, its first leaders were products of the Second Great Awakening. It continued to offer both liberal arts and theological programs throughout the nineteenth century as part of the literary and theological school (L&T) model of Baptist higher education.[121] Colgate was known in its earlier period for training pastors and missionaries. Over time it developed a reputation as a center for the emerging New Theology under the long-term influence of William Newton Clarke. Still later, the Colgate School became synonymous with the liberal tradition in American theology. In its long and distinguished history the school trained over two thousand students during the period of its peak Baptist influence, sent scores of persons to overseas missionary work on every continent, and was the educational center for the most active Baptist state convention of the first half of the nineteenth century in the United States. Considering such prominent religious educators as Barnas Sears, Miles

---

[120] A significant change occurred in the election of E. C. Herrick as president in 1925. Herrick abandoned his racial discrimination against Negroes, providing opportunities that Howard Thurman, Mordecai Johnson, and Benjamin Mays had been denied. See Richard I. McKinney, *Mordecai, The Man and His Message: The Story of Mordecai Wyatt Johnson* (Washington DC: Howard University Press, 1997) 149n.

[121] On the "L&T model," see William H. Brackney, "Nurseries of Piety or The School of Christ? Means and Models of Baptist Ministerial Education in Early America," in *Faith, Life and Witness: The Papers of the Study and Research Division of the Baptist World Alliance 1986–1990*, ed. William H. Brackney with Ruby J. Burke (Birmingham: Samford University Press, 1990) 120–23.

Bronson, Eugenio Kincaid, William Dean, and Jonathan Goble, Madison/Colgate's theological heritage genetically influenced the pioneer stages of Baptist thought in Europe, India, Burma, Africa, China, and Japan.

Colgate's first teacher of theology was Nathaniel Kendrick (1777–1848). Raised in the Upper Connecticut Valley, Nathaniel was a product of the first waves of a local revival that swept the region about 1797. What would become a "Second Great Awakening" occurred as scores of young people experienced conversion and many joined themselves to small Baptist congregations. Sensing a call to ministry, Kendrick took up studies with a series of pastor-mentors. The first was a Rev. Burroughs, a Congregational pastor in Hanover, New Hampshire. Burroughs gave young Nathaniel a four-month introduction to classical literature. From there Nathaniel moved on to develop a greater theological focus and worked with Asa Burton of Thetford, Vermont. Burton, a Congregationalist New Light pastor, was valued in the Valley for his "extensive prevalence of sound religion"[122]. Kendrick spent six months with Burton. Their method of study was a rigorous examination of texts, after which Kendrick wrote either sermons or essays which his teacher would critique. He kept many of these early written assignments for later reference, a remarkable record both of his mentoring and of the theological bibliography to which he was exposed.

Kendrick next took a position in Franklin, Massachusetts, under the esteemed pastor and teacher, Dr. Nathaniel Emmons, one of the more sought-after divines of western New England. Emmons led Kendrick through a series of exercises that focused upon a systematic treatment of Christian doctrine from an Edwardsean Calvinist perspective. Together they studied the atonement, God's decrees, grace, conversion, election, baptism, the Logos, and moral agency through writers as diverse as Whitby, Smalley, Edwards, and Dickinson. At the conclusion of these studies, Emmons issued Kendrick a certificate that read in part: "His mind is strong, inquisitive and penetrating. He is capable of conversing and writing upon theological subjects with ingenuity and accuracy...."[123] Kendrick's theological education continued through 1803 as he spent a profitable year under the tutelage of Thomas Baldwin, the distinguished

---

[122] S.W. Adams, *Memoirs of Rev. Nathaniel Kendrick, D.D. and Silas N. Kendrick* (Philadelphia: American Baptist Publication Society, 1860), 26.

[123] Ibid., 34-35. The Certificate is quoted herein

pastor of Second Baptist Church in Boston. There Baldwin and the eminent Samuel Stillman, the pastor at the city's First Baptist Church, critiqued his sermons. Kendrick also spent the year observing Baptist polity at work and the dynamics of the larger religious scene in Boston.

From 1803 to 1817 Kendrick served several congregations on the Vermont and New York frontiers. While part of the Shaftsbury Baptist Association he had occasion to visit western New York and Upper Canada on missionary forays, and he developed a burden for the frontier setting. In 1817 he moved to Eaton, New York, where he became part of a community of Baptist ministers and laymen interested in higher education. In 1818 the group, including notable pastors Daniel Hascall and Elisha Payne, formed the Baptist Education Society of the State of New York. The following year they obtained a charter to open the Hamilton Literary and Theological Institution, whose purpose was "to educate pious young men to the gospel ministry." Thus began an institutional heritage with a profound impact upon Baptists nationally and throughout the world: Madison University (1836), Colgate University (1888), the Theological Seminary (1853), and Colgate Rochester Divinity School (1928).

There were three primary theological influences upon the emerging tradition. The first was that the enterprise was Baptist. In contrast with Union College in Schenectady, the school in Hamilton was exclusively Baptist—trustees, faculty, and local church association. So deeply ingrained was its denominational ethos that a prominent Presbyterian thought it needed to be "unsectarianized." If the Baptists thought to move their school to Rochester during the "Removalist Controversy" to teach immersion, one writer opined others would have nothing to do with it.[124] The Hamilton Literary and Theological Institution, housed around and sponsored by the village's sole Baptist church, remained for generations a regional enclave of Baptist identity.

Second, the institution developed a missionary impulse in its nascent stages. "The fundamental idea," Hezekiah Harvey wrote, "was the training of men for work among the destitute; a God-called ministry, like the Apostles, who should preach Christ where he was not already

---

[124] *The First Half-Century of Madison University (1819–1860) or the Jubilee Volume Containing Sketches of Eleven Hundred Living and Deceased Alumni; with Fifteen Portraits of Founders, Presidents, and Patrons* (New York: Sheldon & Co., 1872) 71.

known."[125] Kendrick embodied this in his own experience. New York State was New England's mission field. Before the school opened, evangelists and church planters combed the forests of western New York to plant congregations in the region's various villages. Religious education tended to be given to the practical needs of these budding congregations and to continued missionary endeavor. Illustrative of these priorities was the formal title of the state's Baptist organization: The Baptist Missionary Convention of the State of New York. The domestic missionary ethos likewise contributed to a developing interest in the foreign missions field. This may be attributed to the visits of Luther Rice and the travels of leading Baptists such as Barnas Sears. Remarkably, the first graduating classes produced overseas missionaries of the highest calibre: Jonathan Wade, Eugenio Kincaid, Jonathan Goble, and William Dean, to mention a few.[126] In the 1830s Adoniram Judson was in close correspondence with the Hamiltonians about the nature of missionary training. He spent his only sabbatical at the school and his third spouse, Emily Chubbock, came from the campus community.

A third theological influence turned out to be of uneven value to the institution. Kendrick and others were friendly to the New Light movement of the early 1800s and promoted an evangelical, revivalistic theology and experience. The story was told that Kendrick had challenged the class of 1830 to be thorough in their assessment of doctrines and the majority of the students arrived at a troubling result. The startling announcement was made that they concluded that Jesus Christ was less than God, but more than human. Kendrick and his colleagues responded through protracted lectures and prayer sessions with the students. At length revival broke out, the recent heretical impulses vanished, and church attendance and baptisms increased. Kendrick reflected on what had happened, how the employment of "anxious benches" had led to some excitement, but that in the end "it was not the seats nor the saints important to salvation… but the life-giving energies of the Holy Spirit."[127] At length, this experience became the basis for a growing disaffection in the Hamilton faculty toward the New

---

[125] Harvey, "Foreign Mission Work of Madison University," in ibid., 139.

[126] A complete list of over 63 graduates to enter Baptist missions is found in Harvey, ibid., 139–57.

[127] *Memoirs of Reverend Nathaniel Kendrick D.D. and Silas N. Kendrick* (Philadelphia: American Baptist Publication Society, 1860), 102.

Light movement as graduates Jacob Knapp and Jabez Swan energized the community with new measures and represented the Removalist forces. When the distemper of that controversy died out, rather than becoming a rural school, the newly chartered and re-organized Madison University moved to adopt European scholarly interests and methods. To Kendrick's chagrin, the arts curriculum became dominant over the theological program.

Kendrick was named Professor of Christian Theology at Hamilton Literary and Theological Institution in 1820 and set the tone for the new school for a quarter century. He reflected the transition from Old School Calvinism to moderate or evangelical Calvinism. Timothy Dwight at Yale led in the restatement of evangelical doctrines, the divinity of Christ, and the sufficiency of divine grace in salvation, original sin, and the sovereignty of God. Some Congregationalists moved away from the traditional understanding of original sin as inherited from Adam, to a definition of human depravity as the voluntary sinfulness of each human being. Kendrick had met this position in his mentor Emmons, and rejected it for the more conservative view. In Augustinian terms, he held that "a full expression of God's essential glory is the ultimate end of all his operations."[128] One of his specialties was the doctrine of the atonement which, after Andrew Symington, a prominent Presbyterian theologian, Kendrick taught demonstrated and satisfied God's justice; it was substitutionary in that it superseded the punishment of sins for those who are regenerated. He taught strict predestination, holding salvation was sufficiently extensive for all mankind but effective for a definite number previously known and determined. As for the non-elect, it was the same as "rich entertainment" for spectators. Sometimes judged harshly, Kendrick's response was to repair to the question of whether one's contrary position could be found in Scripture.

Joining Kendrick in theological instruction was Daniel Hascall (1782–1852), the single most important founder of the Institution. Hascall was educated at Middlebury College and studied theology privately in Pittsfield, Massachusetts. Having served as a missionary pastor in upstate New York, he was elected principal and professor of rhetoric in Hamilton in 1820. He claimed that the concept for the Institution arose in his mind while reading a circular letter that Jeremiah

---

[128] Ibid., 197.

Chaplin had written in support of a similar Baptist literary and theological institution in Maine.[129] He taught in various fields as needed until his resignation in 1835. The institutional history indicates that Hascall's theology was markedly different from that of Kendrick. Hascall was an advocate of the general atonement theory, while Kendrick was of a "particular" persuasion. Hascall was said to be energetic in his positions, though the two seemed not to have differed personally. Hascall devoted his largest efforts to building the institution and left behind no significant theological writings.[130] His role at Hamilton Literary and Theological Institution reflected an important foundation of theological diversity that would be incorporated in the evolution of the institution as it later became Madison/Colgate University.

Barnas Sears, mentioned earlier in connection with Newton and Brown, can be considered to have been second-in-command at Hamilton, especially when Kendrick was traveling on behalf of the institution. Sears went to Hamilton to teach languages, and his position evolved into a new chair in biblical theology. One of his tasks was to design a curriculum that was rigorous and imitative of the other leading theological programs in the Northeast. The required textbooks from the first decade indicate his theological direction, especially the use of Moses Stuart's translation of Johann A. Ernesti, who introduced the "grammatical-historical" method of biblical interpretation.[131] Sears taught for three years (1829–1833), but was frustrated by the lack of students in the program and his own inadequacy to teach theology. A contemporary recalled his short tenure as "the pride and glory of the institution in its intellectual and literary character."[132] Sears determined to study in Europe and departed Hamilton in 1833, to return in 1836 for less than a year. He ruefully concluded the "school was young, more distinguished for its religious character and evangelical theology than for

---

[129] Ibid., 37. This detail forever connects the idea of the school in New York to its predecessor in Maine. Chaplin's son-in-law was Thomas Jefferson Conant, noted mid-nineteenth-century biblical critic at Madison University.

[130] Ibid., 86–87; 188.

[131] John H. Sailhammer, "Johann August Ernesti: The Role of History in Biblical Interpretation," *Journal of the Evangelical Theological Society* 44/2 (June 2001): 194–95.

[132] Hovey, *Barnas Sears,* 23; George W. Eaton, "Historical Discourse Delivered at the Semi-Centenary of Madison University" in *Madison University*, 46 refers to Sears as *venerabile nomen.*

a high standard of literary attainment."[133] Sears soon departed upstate New York to assume the chair in theology at his alma mater, Newton Theological Institution.

Sears's successor was John Sharp Maginnis (1805–1852).[134] Maginnis did not enjoy a widely-known reputation, but he did possess noteworthy credentials. He was educated at Waterville College, Brown University, and Newton Theological Institution. Appointed to the chair in biblical theology, he moved from the strict Calvinism proffered under Kendrick to a more pastorally-sensitive theology. He had a reputation for "feeding his pupils on the strong meat of the Word."[135] After 1840 Maginnis assumed most of Kendrick's classroom duties, in view of latter's advancing age. Maginnis was especially remembered for use of the Socratic method in teaching and for lucid lectures in theology.[136] Apparently, he was the first Madison/Colgate theologian to tackle the problem of epistemology from an experiential perspective. He wrote in his "Lectures on Systematic Theology: "The great business of man in the present life is to practice virtue, and search for truth." Further, "the first source of truth is experience." The second source was testimony, "the alleged experience of another." He then went on to use the works of Chalmers, Wayland, and Paine to build his system of theology and ethics in marked contrast with that of Nathaniel Kendrick.[137] In the 1840s Maginnis was intensely opposed to the presence of increasingly popular revivalism, and he became part of the forces supportive of removal to Rochester. Attempts were made to terminate his services twice, but these met with community and faculty opposition. Finally, when plans for the schools in Rochester seemed definite, Maginnis resigned in 1850 to accept the chair in theology at Rochester Theological Seminary. Maginnis's major contribution at Hamilton seems to have been to build a

---

[133] Ibid.

[134] Following Sears's departure, his chair was offered to William Williams of New York who refused to leave his pastorate, to Edmund Crawley at Acadia College who was prevailed upon to remain in Nova Scotia, and to Horatio B. Hackett, who remained at Brown University.

[135] DeBlois, "Newton Men in Education," 50.

[136] Williams, *History of Colgate University*, 59–60.

[137] "Notebook of George Washington Eaton." The second portion of this manuscript contains the "Lectures on Systematic Theology" written by John Sharp Maginnis. See pp. 1–6.

bridge to the future, opening new relationships and softening the older traditions.

When Professor Maginnis resigned to go to Rochester, the mantle of theologian at Madison University fell upon George W. Eaton (1804–1872), a graduate of Union College. Eaton was profoundly influenced by a brief stay at Princeton where he attended lectures in theology by Archibald Alexander. Eaton taught languages at Georgetown College before accepting the first chair in church history at Madison in 1837 as that theological program expanded to follow the New England model. Eaton moved to systematic theology in 1850 and became president of the university in 1856, limiting his work in theology. His own theological views included typical Calvinistic formulae of the era: the full deity and humanity of Christ, a vicarious atonement generally applied to all, and regeneration as a work of the Holy Spirit.[138] From 1859 to 1871 he taught doctrinal theology, practical theology, and the history of Christian doctrine. While Eaton was not generally distinguished as a scholar, he nevertheless fulfilled the need for a focus upon theology and was a popular classroom teacher who reinforced thinking, reflecting, and acting for oneself. His pedagogical efforts laid a foundation for a new kind of theological tradition at Madison University.[139]

Ebenezer Dodge (1819–1890) first came to Hamilton to teach biblical studies and joined Professor Eaton in theological instruction in 1861. Educated at Brown University and Newton Theological Institution, Dodge was for 36 years a faculty member, and president for 22 years at Madison University. Following a brief stint at Western Baptist Theological Institution where he taught with E. G. Robinson, and pastorates in rural New Hampshire, Dodge committed his loyalties to one institution, despite being offered chairs at Rochester and Newton. Not only did he have deep respect for his college teacher, Francis Wayland, but he was also converted during a revival meeting that Wayland had

---

[138] George W. Lasher, *George W. Eaton, D.D., L.L.D.: A Memorial* (Hamilton: Colgate University, 1913) 70–71. There is a copy of Eaton's Lectures on Systematic Theology that has gone missing from the Samuel Colgate Baptist Historical Collection in Rochester.

[139] George W. Eaton, *The Duty and Rewards of Original Thinking* (Hamilton: S. C. Griggs, 1847) 9.

planned. In seminary, Dodge referred to Barnas Sears as "the elemental man in New England theological life."[140]

Unlike other scholarly traditions where a genetic heritage might have been happenstance, Dodge was consciously building toward the future when he chose to remain at Madison. President Wayland advised him to stay in Hamilton and build up "an intellectual and spiritual temple,"[141] which he did through recruiting to the school such teachers as William Newton Clarke and others. Dodge's task was made all the more difficult because of the rift caused by the Removal Controversy and Hamilton's remote location. His own reputation as a teacher, plus the school's early record of training pastors and missionaries, was a prime factor in Madison's institutional recovery. To no one's surprise Dodge was selected president in 1868. During that time, he led the theological program from departmental status to that of a seminary on the New England model, he built a handsome edifice (Eaton Hall) to house both the theological faculty and its library, and he attracted the Colgate family fortune to establish a permanent endowment for the school. Under his presidency, Madison University became Colgate, and the school's status among Baptists was surpassed only by Brown University.

Dodge's theological identity matured with time. Students remembered him as "liberal, progressive, and yet conservative." At the beginning of his teaching career, he was clearly in line with classical New England Calvinist tradition. After only a short time in the classroom as professor of biblical criticism and interpretation, and doubtless under the influence of Barnas Sears, Dodge traveled to Europe where he studied at the University of Berlin under August Tholuck and Isaac Dorner.[142] Among the Germans he came to adopt a more critical methodology combined with a characteristic evangelical piety. He reacted coolly to Frederich Schleiermacher's work, and wrote "Religion is not mere feeling, but the union of thought, sensitivity and the will."[143] Dodge did follow carefully the experiential school, at one point claiming that he coined the terminology "Christian consciousness" as applied to New Testament hermeneutics, well before the Andover School did. He

---

[140] Charles H. Dodd, "Ebenezer Dodge: Pioneer in Experiential Theology," *Crozer Quarterly* 2 (1925) 285.

[141] Ibid., 285.

[142] On Dorner's contribution, see Welch, *Protestant Thought*, 1:274–82.

[143] Dodd, "Ebenezer Dodge," 287.

associated creation with redemption—"creative love became redeeming love"[144]—and moved in a new direction in his understanding of the atonement. "What was important about the incarnation," he wrote, " was Christ becoming human in order to have a justifying relationship with God the Father."[145] Here was a significant modification to the traditional substitutionary view of the atonement. Moreover, he argued for a general atonement but a particular redemption. Dodge was often critical of those in more orthodox circles he had moved beyond. For example, he characterized Charles Hodge's work as "medievalist."[146] At the conclusion of his career, he sounded like a devotee of the New Theology: "Revelation is a matter of experience in the Old and New Testaments. Everything is a matter of experience."[147] He spent a second study leave in Europe in 1858–59, again pursuing German theological trends.

Dodge managed to remain in the good graces of the Baptist community despite his embracing new directions. Close friend and benefactor, James B. Colgate, who had a "simple and childlike" conservative Baptist perspective on education and religion, granted part of his liberty. Colgate trusted Dodge explicitly. As a teacher of Christian Evidences to undergraduate students and a professor of theology to ministerial students, Dodge encouraged students to examine all kinds of ideas without restraint. One of his protégés, Nathaniel Schmidt, who was to push the boundaries of Madison's inquiring spirit, attributed his progressive religious views to Dr. Dodge's liberal attitudes.[148] Likewise, Dodge encouraged William Newton Clarke, "to take his own way."[149] Dodge was best known to scores of theological students through his 800-page *Lectures in Christian Theology* (1874–75), printed for students only. Impressive in its treatment of historical theology, it also covered comparative religions. He had previously published a more lay-oriented work on the matter, *Christian Evidences* (1869), for the broader denominational constituency. His theological and administrative

---

[144] Ibid, 298.

[145] Ibid, 299.

[146] Ibid, 293; E. Dodge, *Lectures on Christian Theology* (Hamilton: Colgate University, 1883), 399.

[147] Ibid., 299.

[148] Williams, *Colgate University,* 194, 195.

[149] William Newton Clarke, *Sixty Years with the Bible* (New York: Charles Scribner's, 1917) 88.

leadership was recognized across his career, being offered chairs in church history at Rochester and Christian theology at Newton.

During the Dodge era an important theological voice in the Madison University faculty was Hezekiah Harvey (1821–1893). Born in England, Harvey eventually immigrated to the United States. He was converted under the evangelistic ministry of Jacob Knapp and consequently took up studies at Madison University. Completing the undergraduate and theological courses, he entered pastoral ministry in upstate New York. In 1858 Harvey began a quarter-century career as professor of church history and pastoral theology at Madison, where he essentially defined Baptist ecclesiology at mid-century. "Not what one would term a brilliant scholar, but...thoroughly inclined to conservative views,"[150] he served as dean of the faculty of theology in the 1890s. His student and future colleague, William Newton Clarke, recalled Harvey as the one who had inspired him to the most fruitful studies of his life. Harvey's books, *The Church: Its Polity and Ordinances* (1879) and *The Pastor* (1879), were much quoted throughout the denomination and may well account for why theologians like Clarke did not include ecclesiology in their systematic theologies.

Doctrinally consistent with Baptist views on the authority of Scripture, Harvey began with the premise, "It is plain that Christ himself instituted the church and the ordinances and gave them a definite form."[151] Further, he held that the apostles were expressly inspired for the full establishment of Christian institutions. In searching the New Testament he found everywhere a uniformity of spiritual character and duties. Harvey went on to equate the Kingdom of God, prophesied in the Old Testament, to be fulfilled in Christ, "whose kingdom is not of this world and who was head over all things to the church."[152] Thus, his view of the church was entrenched in Christology. Harvey made his case for a believer's church that was both a local visible congregation as well as the invisible body of the elect. Importantly, he also argued against applying

---

[150] William Mangam Lawrence, "Historical Address-Colgate University—October 10, 1919," *Colgate University Centennial Celebration 1819–1919* (Hamilton: Colgate University, 1920) 69.

[151] Hezekiah Harvey, *The Church: Its Polity and Ordinances* (Philadelphia: American Baptist Publication Society, 1879) 17.

[152] Ibid, 23.

the term *ecclesia* to a universal visible church or to a national or denominational church.[153]

Harvey viewed the two recognized Baptist ordinances—baptism and the Lord's Supper—as entirely symbolic. He held each represented the vital truths of the gospel and wrote that only regenerate persons who profess a personal faith in Christ are proper subjects for baptism. Harvey also held that the appropriate mode of baptism was by immersion. As to the Supper, he taught that it is the church's responsibility to determine admission to the Supper and maintained that a restricted or closed communion was the position of nearly all Christians, Baptists included. He taught that union among denominations had no real advantages and might even lead to the destruction of church authority and discipline. He did disdain the contemporary language of evangelicalism, reasoning that "if the invitation is restricted to members of evangelical churches, then who shall determine what is an evangelical church?"[154]

Norman Maring's hunch is accurate that an important change occurred among Baptist academic theologians about 1870.[155] Most theological teachers had a firm conviction about the infallibility of Scripture, but a few were beginning to ask questions. While Ezekiel Robinson at Rochester had opened new vistas in the 1850s, he remained cautious and his successors even more so. The Theological Seminary at Madison University, however, appears to be the locus of the most searching new directions. President Ebenezer Dodge's mantle fell squarely upon William Newton Clarke (1841–1911) who ushered in a new era both at the school and in his denomination. Clarke was educated at Madison University for both his undergraduate and theological degrees. Of primary import to his thinking in college were Hezekiah Harvey, a traditional Baptist pastor/theologian, and Ebenezer Dodge. Most writers think that Clarke's tenure as pastor at Newton Centre, Massachusetts, was critical to his development because there he encountered Ezra P. Gould, the professor in New Testament who had been terminated at Newton Theological Institution for liberal thinking. While a pastor, Clark also became acquainted with Alvah Hovey, president at Newton, who was a moderate evangelical. Both probably

---

[153] Ibid., 28–29.

[154] Ibid., 238.

[155] Maring, "Baptists and Changing Views" (Part 1), 60–61; "Baptists and Changing Views of the Bible, 1865–1918" (Part 2), 1/4 *Foundations* (October 1958): 45.

influenced Clarke to think beyond his previously held, well-defined theological convictions that were rooted in traditional Baptist perspectives. His exegetical studies during that period led him to conclude, "Exegesis is revolutionary, too, and quite incompatible with permanent confidence in verbal inspiration."[156]

After pastoral ministry in Massachusetts and Quebec, he began his teaching career at Toronto Baptist College, later McMaster University (his Canadian contributions will be discussed below). Unwilling to fit into a tightening confessionalism, and due to poor health, he returned to upstate New York as pastor of the First Baptist Church in Hamilton, just off the campus of his alma mater. Upon the death of Ebenezer Dodge, whom he esteemed as a father, Clarke stepped in to take his unfinished classes and eventually was appointed the J. J. Joslin Professor of Theology, a post he retained for three decades. Highly influential, it is interesting that Clarke was described as "an unspectacular, slightly crippled, quietly impressive academic."[157]

Clarke was a pivotal figure not only in the Colgate tradition, but also among American theologians in general. Attempts to demonstrate his being influenced by Europeans aside, he was original in his thinking.[158] The first true "liberal" among Baptist theologians, he was comparable to Wilhelm Herrmann and Albert Ritschl in Germany. It is certain that he was aware of the work of Horace Bushnell, Borden Bowne, A. H. Strong, and D.C. MacIntosh.[159] But, Clarke was a deeply reflective person and immersed in the language of personal religious experience. He characterized his life as "Sixty Years with the Bible," by which he traced his views of Scripture from a view of the text as inerrant and factually historical, and his hermeneutical method as proof-texting, to a more "modern" use of Scripture. After 1880 he concluded, "The

---

[156] Clarke, *Sixty Years*, 47.

[157] William F. Hutchison, *The Modernist Impulse in American Protestantism* (Durham: Duke University Press, 1992), 117.

[158] His wife, Emily, observed that "the profound changes in his thought were his own, and purely the product of his own experience, study, and reflection ...an open-minded man who read somewhat widely." See Emily A. Clarke, ed., *William Newton Clarke, A Biography, with Additional Sketches by His Friends and Colleagues* (New York: Charles Scribner's Sons, 1916) 42.

[159] See his *Christian Doctrine of God*, 81; *Outline*, 89; D. C. MacIntosh, "Professor Clarke at Yale," in ibid., 258; and, Claude Howe, "The Theology of William Newton Clarke" (Th.D. diss., New Orleans Baptist Theological Seminary, 1959) 27.

Scriptures do not yield a single clear theology to which divine authority attaches."[160] Here was a clear departure from traditional Baptist dogma. Instead, he wrote, "The authority of the Scriptures is the authority of the truth they convey." He came to believe that it was moral and religious value that made the Bible a treasure that "satisfies one's reason and binds the conscience."[161] In his personal pilgrimage to the "New Theology," he held tenaciously to his personal piety.[162]

Two issues caused Clarke to begin revising his understanding of the Bible. First, was the introduction of the theory of evolution. Here he found the old religious explanations wanting and productive of a defensive kind of thinking. Before the Chicago School advanced the notion of the evolution of Christian doctrine and that doctrine must change in every age, Clarke applied the major scientific premise of his age to Christian experience and theology. In his major theological work he asserted, "The theology of any age is largely an expression of the Christian experience of that age."[163] Here he anticipated quite directly the work of Shirley Jackson Case and Shailer Mathews. Second, his church at Keene, New Hampshire, was deeply divided over the Millerite controversy, which taught him about some of the difficulties of understanding the Bible's chronology too literally. Clarke wrote in his systematic theology, "The more accurate the prediction, the surer thus far has been the disappointment...the Bible does not contain the material for successful prediction of coming events upon the earth. The entire labor of forecasting is misplaced."[164] Empowered by college teachers and congregations (especially First Baptist, Newton Centre, Massachusetts, and Olivet, Montreal) that gave him time for study and much liberty of thought, Clarke moved well ahead of conservative Baptists in accepting women in leadership, engaged in ecumenical cooperation, and questioned traditional hermeneutical approaches to the study of the New Testament.[165]

---

[160] William Newton Clarke, *The Use of the Scriptures in Theology* (New York: Charles Scribner's Sons, 1906) 42.

[161] Clarke, *Outline*, 42, 45.

[162] For an assessment of Clarke that places him in the context of W. A. Brown and H. C. King, see Welch, *Protestant Thought*, 2:232.

[163] Ibid., 19.

[164] Clarke, *Outline*, 433.

[165] William H. Brackney, "William Newton Clarke: A Canadian American Cross-Cultural Experience," *McMaster Journal of Theology* 3/2 (Spring, 1993): 62–81.

In addition to his changed attitude about the nature of the Bible, his interpretive hermeneutic changed as well. As he recalled it, the change began when he was minister at Newton Centre and he read Horace Bushnell's book, *The Vicarious Sacrifice Grounded in Principles of Universal Obligation* (1866). Although Newton President Alvah Hovey criticized Bushnell's approach, it transformed Clarke. He concluded that God acted consistently with his own character and that the guide to understanding God was revealed in Christ. From that point on, he interpreted Scripture in light of Christ and emphasized the ethical principles of Christianity. In an oft-quoted phrase, Clarke stylized his theological transition: "We are sure that the stars were there, though astronomies change; that the flowers are real, though botany alters its explanations."[166]

Clarke has often been called an "evangelical liberal." He was "evangelical" in that he continued to use the terminology of the Old School, but he often meant something entirely different. For example, presaging many in an anthropological approach, he separated "religion" from theology by defining the former as "the life of man in his superhuman relations...a function of the heart, the affectional nature." Theology came to be merely the unfolding and exposition of the conceptions that enter into religion. As a "liberal" thinker, he thought religion was universal to mankind and all the great religions contain some truth concerning religion. Christianity "claimed" to be the true religion, but it should not be contemptuous toward other religions. Clarke's positions sounded very much like European writers like August Sabatier, Wilhelm Herrmann, and Adolf Harnack and reflected the approach of Americans H. C. King and William Adams Brown. Attempts to demonstate that Clarke was significantly influenced by or dependent upon these other theologians have not proved productive. He was an original liberal thinker.

Having redefined his doctrine of biblical authority within the Christian religious tradition, Clarke's epistemology was fused with Christian experience. Building upon the thinking of his mentor, President Dodge, he further refined the idea of experience: "Power comes with feeling. Truth becomes effective by being felt to be truth...Not until someone feels that something is true does that something go out with

---

[166] Quoted in Robert Moats Miller, *Harry Emerson Fosdick: Preacher, Pastor, Prophet* (New York: Oxford University Press, 1985) 41.

effective power into the world. Unfelt knowledge is scarcely more fruitful than ignorance. Unfelt truth lies unused."[167] What validated the truth of Christianity for Clarke was that it was "experienceable and experienced." The Bible was a record of past experience. But, beyond Scripture, Clarke believed that Christian experience continues to be a "channel" through which Christian revelation enters to theology. His desire to apply evolutionary theory to theology led him to further conclusions; understandings of God, man, and salvation are shaped by the experience of a given age. Interpretation of Scripture and trends in religious thought are similarly shaped by their contexts. "If the theology of a time is various and changing, it is because the life of the time is various, growing, transitional."[168] A key to Clarke's understanding of experience was Christology. Jesus' supreme importance lay in his life among humans and his personally imparting spiritual truth to his followers. Clarke went further to argue that the Bible did not prescribe one form of Christian experience that was normative for all time, but a pattern that had to be experienced in subsequent historical differentiation. His evangelical nature shone through in his conviction that the Christian experience was missionary and could best be illustrated in the transformation of human hearts.

Clarke's courageous new directions came in the context of reports from Britain of the heresy trial of W. Robertson Smith and C. H. Spurgeon's attacks upon the work of Franz Delitsch. Closer to home, a heresy investigation at Andover Theological Seminary took place over the application of biblical criticism. As well, Clarke's pursuit of the "New Theology" cost him dearly among traditional Baptists who charged him with relativity and subjectivity.[169] Other important conservative evangelicals like Benjamin B. Warfield at Princeton charged him with "mere drifting" to an insecure final position.[170] To

---

[167] William Newton Clarke, *What Shall We Think of Christianity?* (Edinburgh: T & T Clark, 1899) 138.

[168] Clarke, *Outline*, 19.

[169] Ibid., 20.

[170] Warfield went so far as to say that "The new Bible Clarke has constructed for himself gives him a new Jesus, and his whole system of truth, brought into harmony with what he considers the new spirit of Jesus, is eccentric to the system of truth which is taught us by the real Bible which is placed in our hands by the real Jesus." Benjamin B. Warfield, "William Newton Clarke 1910," quoted in *Princeton Theology 1812–1921:*

those who were suspicious of Christian experience as too subjective, Clarke replied, "Welcome or unwelcome, experience enters and helps to form theology. To theologize outside the Christian consciousness of one's age is as impossible as to live outside the atmosphere... Experience cannot be set aside as mediator between theology and its chief source, the Christian revelation."[171] Adamant as he was, many of Clarke's Baptist theologian colleagues looked beyond his piety and unimpeachable Christian character and found his impact to be negative: "He has had a mighty influence in encouraging young men to seek to realize in themselves a like gracious combination of sanctified sweetness and light with liberal sentiments."[172] Clarke himself became increasingly wary of his theological adversaries in the Baptist community who from time to time rose up against his holding the chair in theology. He once confided to a student, "They will get me yet."[173] He was somewhat encouraged in 1901 when the University of Chicago awarded him the honorary doctorate and considered him for a position in theology. This was tempered, however, by opposition from George Burman Foster who thought Clarke too mystical and attached to the previous century.[174]

While at Colgate, Clarke came to understand Scripture in its historical context. He moved from teaching New Testament to theology. He

---

Scripture, Science, and Theological Method from Archibald Alexander to Benjamin Warfield, ed. Mark Noll (Grand Rapids: Baker Books, 1983) 308–310.

[171] Clarke, *Outline*, 20. To charges of his bowing to mere "feeling," he wrote: "Feeling, it may be objected, is no test of truth. We may feel, most intensely, something unreal; wherefore the sense of reality in the Christian testimony must not be taken as valid proof of that testimony. To this I should say that certainly feeling often takes hold on error, and becomes the stimulant of folly. Feeling is no proof of truth. But I would add that neither is feeling any proof that truth is absent...Is not feeling the normal accompaniment of truth? Reality and the sense of reality are inseparable companions." See *What Shall We Think*, 144–45.

[172] Newman, "Changes in Baptist Theology," 600. Newman had worked closely with Clarke at McMaster and knew of his personal charisma. This comment was doubtless a response to Clarke's concluding remarks to his systematic theology, reminiscing of his years at Colgate, "with our windows open to the morning light, teacher and pupils all students together, we talk without reserve of all things in earth and heaven that bear upon our high theme." (Clarke, *Outline*, 481.)

[173] Harry Emerson Fosdick, *The Living of These Days: An Autobiography* (New York: Harper & Brothers, 1956) 65.

[174] Edgar A. Towne, *Foundations* "A Single-Minded Theologian: George Burman Foster at Chicago, Part I" 20/1 (January 1977): 37.

enthusiastically embraced historical criticism.[175] He was more fond, however, of his own hermeneutical principle, namely that one seeks to identify what is the "Christian" element in the Bible, or "that which is in accord with what Christ revealed."[176] He concluded that doctrine, by its nature, evolves and new questions must be continually asked of it. The guiding principle of his new approach was, "a system of Christian theology with God at its centre, the spirit of Jesus as its organizing principle, and congenial truth from within the Bible and without for its material."[177] He and William Adams Brown, a Presbyterian at Union Theological Seminary in New York, became the great systematizers of the New Theology, for they found no adequate textbooks to use with their students.[178]

Consistent with other Baptist systematicians back to John Gill, Clarke held that the church belonged mostly to practical rather than systematic theology.[179] In one context, he seemed to reflect the emerging Chicago School in speaking of the church as a "help to his personal life" and the "social organ of Christianity." In his systematic version, the church was attached to his understanding of the Spirit. The Spirit performs his work in the church, thus it is a spiritual community. It is in this area of doctrine that Clarke was unquestionably baptistic. He opposed any organizational or sacramental view of the church, but held that any group of Christians gathered in Christ's name has the promise of Christ's presence. The Church was the sum of all actual organizations, but as an organization, had no promise of perpetuity. Rather, he thought a primary purpose of the church was to fulfill Christ's promise as the community among whom the Spirit will specially teach and impress truth because Christ's friends are prepared for such but the world was not. In the church, Christian people are guided into truth, men testify to Christ, and piety in fellowship with God is quickened. The Holy Spirit in the past "did not render Councils infallible, nor does he free individuals or churches from

---

[175] Ironically, as Claude Howe pointed out, Clarke, considered either an historian or Greek scholar, did not keep abreast of the results of biblical criticism: "The Theology of William Newton Clarke," 30–31.

[176] Clarke, *Use of the Scriptures*, 50, 56.

[177] Clarke, *Sixty Years*, 210.

[178] Browne believed Clarke was the true pioneer, but had not treated church and ministry and was lacking in historical data for the former's purposes. See Hutchison, *Modernist Impulse*, 121.

[179] Clarke, *The Circle of Theology*, 57; *Outline*, 381 ff.

all error now," language that was reminiscent of the Second London Confession.[180] Lastly, Clarke was of the opinion that the universal church was a comprehensive name for Christian people "in whom the spiritual work of Christ is going forward." While appreciative of his own denomination, and others like Luther and Wesley, Clarke also allowed "that Christianity may yet express itself in new forms, if the old prove insufficient or unadapted to growing needs."[181]

Clarke's eschatological treatments provide insight regarding a topic of high interest among Baptists of his era. One leader contemporary with Clarke pronounced Baptists, more than any of the reformed sects, identified with doctrines of premillennial interpretation.[182] However, instead of discussing doctrines of the end times under a heading such as "Last Things" or "Eschatology" that would have satisfied the contemporary public appetite, Clarke, a preeminent Baptist theologian, creatively used the terminology "Things to Come." By this he meant to focus less upon details of the parousia or the millennial kingdom, and more upon themes of immortality, judgment, and resurrection, questions that were patently more pertinent to people in day-to-day living. Specifically he rejected the Synoptic Gospels' view of Jesus' Second Coming in favor of the perspective found in the Fourth Gospel. "No visible return of Christ to the earth is to be expected," he concluded, "but rather the long and steady advance of his spiritual kingdom."[183] He turned aside discussion of the millennium, asserting "that there is no ground for a question of premillennial or postmillennial advent. The whole question has proceeded upon grounds that have no proper existence."[184] His perspective on the general resurrection followed closely his interpretation of the Second Coming of Christ. Clarke held that resurrection will not be simultaneous for all, but continuous or successive for each believer immediately upon death. Similarly, he believed that judgment was to occur for everyone individually at death rather than at some great gathering of the human race, basing his position

---

[180] See chapter 36, sec. 2 and 3, in William Lumpkin, *Baptist Confessions of Faith* 285–86.

[181] Clarke, *Systematic Theology*, 381–85.

[182] Ernest B. Gordon, *Adoniram Judson Gordon: A Biography* (New York: Fleming H. Revell Co., 1896) 357. See the discussion of Gordon below.

[183] Clarke, *Outline*, 444.

[184] Ibid., 434.

on his interpretation of Hebrews 9:27. Reminiscent of classic orthodoxy, Clarke did teach that as a result of judgment—which by its nature separates—there would be a blessed state beyond life advancing toward perfection. He believed as well that an evil state would be manifest, amounting to moral separation from God; an active life of progressive sin with no end in sight.[185] Needless to say, Clarke's eschatology possessed characteristics worthy of identification with the evangelical tradition, but also was characterized by enough creativity to mark him as a participant in the New Theology.

With Clarke's passing and his enormous immediate influence waning, Baptist thought in the United States was set upon entirely new footings. His initial successor in theology at Colgate was an understudy, Frank Aubrey Starratt (1865–1943). An instructor in theology toward the end of Clarke's career, Starratt eventually was appointed to the J. J. Joslin Chair in 1910 as the former reduced his teaching load and turned to ethics and apologetics. Starratt, a Canadian, was educated at Acadia University and Newton Theological Institution and studied theology for a time at the University of Chicago. He served churches in North Dakota and Texas, finally moving to Stoneham, Massachusetts. A distinguished pastor, he taught at Colgate until 1919. Virtually no written records remain to define him theologically.

John F. Vichert (1874–1948) followed Starratt. Vichert, also a Canadian, was educated at McMaster University. His McMaster divinity thesis was supervised by George Cross, later a colleague at Rochester Seminary. [186]He held the J. J. Joslin Chair in Theology from 1919 until 1923. In anticipation of a merger with Rochester Theological Seminary, Vichert transferred to Rochester in 1923 where he taught practical theology until 1940. Not widely published, Vichert nevertheless managed to engage the issues raised by fundamentalism. In 1922, while acting as dean of Colgate Theological Seminary, Vichert announced to the readers of a national Baptist newspaper, "I am a fundamentalist." Later the same year, he wrote, "We may fairly expect of our seminaries that they will lead their students into an intelligent apprehension of the fundamentals of our Christian faith," by which he meant "the faith once

---

[185] Ibid., 473.

[186] See "A Colleague's Tribute to Professor Vichert" in *Colgate Rochester Divinity School Bulletin* 20/4 (May 1948): 175–77.

delivered to the saints."[187] By such bold assertions he disclaimed any interest in the interdenominational World's Christian Fundamentals Movement, but enthusiastically endorsed the moderate Confession of Faith put forth at the Des Moines Convention of 1922. Vichert specifically affirmed the doctrine of the second advent, but rejected "lurid description of catastrophic events soon to occur." Following A. H. Strong, he revered the Scriptures but protected the careful, critical study of the Bible. In the field of education, he stood for progress in knowledge and thought, allowing religion not to interfere with science. While stressing evangelism, Vichert supported the social service implications of the gospel, not wanting in any manner to divide his denominational family. Above all else, he championed liberty of conscience under Christ as a mark of the spiritual heritage of Baptists. In positioning himself with the moderate fundamentalists, Vichert wanted to hold together the essentials of evangelical religion and Baptist principles.[188]

While Vichert tried to move Colgate toward a centrist theological position, many of William Newton Clarke's emphases were embraced by one of the school's more illustrious students, Harry Emerson Fosdick.[189] Completing an undergraduate degree at Colgate, Fosdick later returned for theological studies at Clarke's invitation. Fosdick admired Clarke's perspectives as "defying the obscurantism of old opinions and daring to phrase the Christian faith in the categories of modern thinking."[190] Clarke helped the young Fosdick rid himself of old trinitarian concepts and of other views the elder theologian considered inadequate expressions of the divinity of Christ. Fosdick was also drawn to Clarke's attack upon what was termed unbiblical Christian dogma and the priority of religious experience. He was also attracted to the writings of G. F. Hegel, Hermann Lotze, and F. D. E. Schleiermacher. Eventually, Fosdick was to embrace Borden Bowne's personalism as a mediating Christological

---

[187] John F. Vichert, "What Have We a Right to Expect from Our Theological Seminaries?" *Watchman Examiner* 10/46 (16 November 1922): 1475.

[188] John F. Vichert, "Fears and Hopes of a Fundamentalist" in *Watchman Examiner* 10/9 (2 March 1922): 266–67. In the same issue, moderate Baptist fundamentalists Curtis Lee Laws ("Just What Is Fundamentalism": 261) and Frank M. Goodchild ("The Spirit and Purpose of the Fundamentalists": 267) responded favorably to Vichert's concerns.

[189] See the discussion of Fosdick below. Fosdick credited Clarke as his mentor and had the great pipe organ in the sanctuary at Riverside Church in New York memorialized to Clarke.

[190] Fosdick, *Living of These Days*, 55.

position between literal biblicism and "metaphysical speculation." He paraphrased his mentor's famous words, "We must distinguish between abiding experiences and changing categories."[191]After one year, however, Fosdick found Hamilton, New York, too limiting and he looked to Union Seminary in New York City to further his theological education. Clarke doubtless supported his protégé in studying with William Adams Browne, who both admired Clarke and developed his theological system to greater lengths. At Union, Fosdick met not only a distinguished faculty of theologians, but also the teeming life of urban New York. He experienced theology that seminaries do not teach: poverty, filthy living conditions, and on an internship, rural primitivism in the Adirondack Mountains, as well as the traditional ways of the Old World on a trip to England.

Following his happy experience at Union Seminary, Fosdick went on to become a pastor in Montclair, New Jersey, and eventually the founding pastor of Riverside Church in New York City, a cathedral of American liberal thought. His friendship with Clarke continued, with the elder preaching at Fosdick's ordination in 1903. Fosdick was a prolific pastoral writer and his devotional writings covered prayer, service, character building, and the life of Christ. His preaching ministry was extended beyond the gothic walls of Riverside to the nation at large on the National Vespers Hour. What is often overlooked, however, were his professorial labors at Union Seminary. At Union he occupied the Morris K. Jesup Chair in Practical Theology and taught preaching and exposition of English Scripture, exploring the differences between the world of the Bible and contemporary society. His insights were found in a best-selling volume, *The Modern Use of the Bible* (1924). An earlier scholarly work, *The Meaning of the Faith* (1917), flowed from his work in apologetics. Along with Reinhold Niebuhr and Paul Tillich, Fosdick became a defining factor in the liberal heritage of Union Theological Seminary.[192]

Fosdick's eventual understanding of theology was far from traditional. Robert M. Miller has analyzed his library and sermons and finds prominent references to W. N. Clarke, B. P. Bowne and W. Rauschenbusch, as well as John Baillie, G. K. Chesterton, Henry

---

[191] Quoted in Miller, *Harry Emerson Fosdick*, 41.
[192] For Fosdick's contribution see Robert T. Handy, *A History of Union Theological Seminary in New York* (New York: Columbia University Press, 1987) 133.

Drummond, and Emil Brunner. He seemed to be well grounded in the Church Fathers and the reformers, though he confessed that Calvin's God was not his. Philosophy was an interest, with much attention given to William James. Personality was the key to understanding God, and the world was one—there was to him no separation between the natural and the supernatural. Fosdick spoke of God as "ever at work," "the Eternal Toiler," "the Great Adventurer."[193] God is revealed in evolution and in saints and world religious leaders. He believed the Bible to reveal God, not to be a revelation from God. The Bible was a "priceless treasure of spiritual truth," Fosdick wrote, which sounded close to the wording of the New Hampshire Confession; but in his book, *A Guide to Understanding the Bible*, he referred to inerrancy as "sheer nonsense."[194] This caused his critics to defame his theology as "sub-Christian."

Similarly, Fosdick stressed Jesus' humanity. When he thought of God, he saw Christ. Fosdick preferred to speak of divinity as a quality rather than an attribute of Christ. He believed God wanted to place this quality in all men. It was a quality of divinity that God called forth from underneath the frozen ground in the winter of humanity's lost condition, much as a seed awaits the spring.[195] The importance of the atonement lay in the demonstration of the costly love God willingly exercised on humankind's behalf. With respect to the literal resurrection, Fosdick was adamant: it was to be persistence of personality, not a resurrection of the flesh. More to his understanding of classical atonement doctrine, he argued that all humans are caught up in God's saving grace, inside or outside the Christian Church. As to the future, Fosdick denied the reality of eternal punishment in any geographical location like Hell, and he fell short of understanding immortality as "going on forever." Rather, he stressed the present effects of holding a belief in eternal life and chose to return to his commitment to "personal permanence" that stemmed from understanding creation as "anything but irrational and senseless."[196]

---

[193] Miller, *Harry Emerson Fosdick*, 402.

[194] Ibid., 404.

[195] Ibid., 409.

[196] Ibid., 417. I am greatly indebted to Miller for his cogent analysis of Fosdick's thought, a wide-ranging corpus of material. For useful unpublished studies of Fosdick's theology among over 20 doctoral and master's studies, consult Katharine Bonney, "Harry Emerson Fosdick's Doctrine of Man" (Ph.D. diss., Boston University, 1958); Hardy Clemons, "The Key Theological Ideas of Harry Emerson Fosdick" (Ph. D. diss., Southwestern Baptist Theological Seminary, 1966); Douglas Lawson, "The Idea of

When the Riverside preacher applied his theological perspective to a contemporary issue such as war, it exhibited his broad definitions. "Religion is a force," he wrote. "When religious faith supports war, when there is one by one, the wholesale destruction of children, starving them by millions, impoverishing them, spoiling the chances of unborn generations…We can have this monstrous thing or we can have Christ, but we cannot have both."[197] Exhibiting a capability to apply his theological revisioning to contemporary issues, he took up the issue of euthanasia and declared "God alone is not determining how long men and women shall live. Man is determining that, with his scientific medicine prolonging the average span of life…Man must shoulder the responsibility thus thrust upon him and devise some way of mercifully liberating the hopelessly ill from needless agony." [198] This publicly held ethical stance took him well beyond Baptist orthodoxy.

Fosdick came to personify theological modernism among Baptists. In the 1920s, at the apex of the fundamentalist attempt to seize control of the Northern Baptist Convention, Fosdick (who was then serving a Presbyterian congregation) was targeted especially as being on record denying practically every fundamental doctrine of the New Testament and of evangelical Christianity.[199] Anyone in step with Fosdick was an opponent of traditional Baptist orthodoxy. When it was rumored that he would leave his post at the Presbyterian church to accept John D. Rockefeller's invitation to Park Avenue Baptist Church, Baptist fundamentalists rose in an opposing chorus. They pointed to what they considered doctrinal deviations in Fosdick's published books. They especially complained about his offensive sermon, "Shall the Fundamentalists Win?" that severely indicted many whom his opponents called "good men." Some referred to Fosdick as a "Baptist bootlegger," the "Jesse James of the theological world," "an indescribable thing-in-human-form." Fosdick's response as he returned to minister among Baptists was, "Well, I am a heretic if conventional orthodoxy is the

Progress in the Theology of Harry Emerson Fosdick (Ph.D. diss., Duke University, 1963); and, Samuel Weaver, "The Theology and Times of Harry Emerson Fosdick" (Ph.D. diss., Princeton Theological Seminary, 1961).

[197] "The Unknown Soldier," (Sermon Preached at Riverside Church, 12 November 1933), quoted in William H. Brackney, ed., *Baptist Life and Thought: A Sourcebook,* rev. ed. (Valley Forge: Judson Press, 1998) 376.

[198] Fosdick, *The Living of These Days,* 285.

[199] Ibid., "Resolutions of the Baptist Bible Union," 358.

standard. I should be ashamed to live in this generation and not be a heretic."[200] Once he settled into the inclusive atmosphere of Riverside Church after 1930, Fosdick became less a theological pariah and more of an American liberal icon.

In many ways, the critical, broadly based liberal tradition that grew up at Hamilton was ideally fused with the Rochester Tradition in the merger of the two schools in 1928. As Colgate University closed out its formal relationship with the Baptists in the 1940s, it continued to value its favorite son, Harry Emerson Fosdick, as the best exemplar of its recent theological tradition.[201]

ROCHESTER THEOLOGICAL SEMINARY

Rochester Theological Seminary was a product of the "Removal Controversy" at Madison (later Colgate) University. In the 1840s upstate New York Baptist interests sought to relocate the university from its isolated Finger Lakes village of Hamilton to Rochester, one of the fastest growing urban areas in the United States. In the background of the controversy was a deep theological division created by the Second Great Awakening. Following a bitter battle in the court and among the churches, the Hamilton interests prevailed as far as the university campus was concerned. Those favoring the urban location ultimately went their own way and obtained charters for the University of Rochester and Rochester Theological Seminary, both of which opened in 1850. From their origins, the Rochester schools were less sectarian than their parent institutions in Hamilton. Many felt there would have been no charter for the University of Rochester if it had been exclusively Baptist and when the school first opened, three of its faculty were pedobaptists. The University, and in time the theological seminary, enjoyed the presence and direction of representatives from other than the Baptist denomination on its teaching staff.[202] This was to have long-term effects upon the new school's religious perspective and teaching traditions.[203]

---

[200] Fosdick, *The Living of These Days,* 176.

[201] Fosdick served on several of its boards and was honored with an endowment and a statue at the Hamilton campus.

[202] See the discussion in *Madison University*, 71. As far as I can determine this was the first usage of the term "liberal" in respect to the Rochester tradition.

[203] Glenn T. Miller's contention that "the Hamilton-Rochester competition was one of the great follies in the history of theological education...because the two schools were identical theologically" can only be validated if read backwards from the 1928 merger of

A stalwart theological heritage grew up in Rochester, featuring the names of Ezekiel G. Robinson, Augustus Hopkins Strong, and Walter Rauschenbusch. The first two exemplified the "Critical Orthodox" tradition, and the third pioneered liberal theology. Rochester Seminary was reorganized in the 1920s and merged with Colgate's theological seminary to form the Colgate Rochester Divinity School (CRDS) in 1928. CRDS has been much influenced by the Chicago School, as well as developing its own peculiar ethos in the social gospel tradition. In the twentieth century, Colgate Rochester became synonymous with the continued liberal tradition, despite a strong infusion in its ranks of Neo-Orthodoxy and Neo-Evangelicalism.

It seemed Rochester Seminary was destined to break new ground in the American Baptist tradition. Shortly after the seminary's opening, the school's charter holder—the New York Baptist Union for Ministerial Education—invited a convocation of educators to attend the graduation ceremony in 1853. The keynoter was President Francis Wayland of Brown University and others on the program included Barnas Sears, Johann G. Oncken, and George N. Briggs. The occasion proved to be a venting of the two competing models of theological instruction, and covertly, understandings of the Baptist doctrines of the church and ministry. Wayland defended a simplistic egalitarian model he described as "apostolic." Sears asserted a specialized calling for ministry that would evangelize America and protect orthodox ideals of the Reformation. Sears also had a passion for a minister-as-scholar role that could handle the levels of scholarship he had witnessed in Germany. The exchange between Wayland and Sears exhibited personal rancor between the leading theological educators in the Baptist family in America, as well as the intense competition between the Baptist institutions for limited support funds. Even more, the event marked a division between theological training of ministers at the collegiate undergraduate and seminarian post-graduate levels.[204] The dawning of the golden age of

---

the two seminaries. At the time of the controversy, there were deep theological differences and different constituencies. See further, Miller, "Piety and Intellect," 328.

[204] See Kenneth R. M. Short, "Baptist Training for the Ministry: The Francis Wayland-Barnas Sears Debate of 1853," *Foundations* 11/3 (July-September 1968): 227–34; Glenn T. Miller, "Piety and Intellect," ibid., 327–30; and, Timothy George "Baptist Contributions" in *Theological Education in the Evangelical Tradition*, ed. D. G. Hart and R. Albert Mohler, Jr. (Grand Rapids: Baker Books, 1996), 33. Short and others who have cited his article, have called this event a "Moment of Truth" for Baptist

theological seminaries and professional Baptist theologians was at hand and Rochester Theological Seminary was a clear harbinger of the future.

The first theologian to teach at the new seminary was John Sharp Maginnis. In 1850 he moved from Madison University to teach biblical and pastoral theology and set the course for a working relationship with the University of Rochester, where he also taught intellectual and moral philosophy. After the untimely death of Maginnis in 1852, leaders of the New York Baptist Union for Ministerial Education successfully induced Ezekiel G. Robinson (1815–1894) of Kentucky to accept the seminary's presidency. Robinson had been educated at Brown University and Newton Theological Institution. At the beginnings of his career, he represented the classical approach to Baptist theology as expressed in the New England tradition. He taught at the Western Baptist Theological Institution in Covington, Kentucky, and served in some key pastoral positions before being elected professor of theology at Rochester Theological Seminary in 1853.

As a student at Brown, the venerable Francis Wayland was a significant influence on Robinson, who later reflected that his education at Brown had been sorely lacking in content save for Wayland. It was not Wayland's advanced moral theories or knowledge of ethics that impressed Robinson. Rather, it was the experience of listening to Wayland expound his own personal views on subjects such as the slavery question or the limitations of human responsibility. Robinson was to succeed his role model and mentor as both professor and college president at Brown.

Even more than Wayland, Robinson came to esteem Horatio B. Hackett at Brown, under whom he studied Latin. When Hackett moved to the seminary at Newton to take the chair in Biblical Literature, the young Robinson followed to pursue studies in Hebrew. The two were destined to be colleagues at Rochester in the 1850s. Robinson referred to Hackett as the outstanding biblical scholar of the era. Newton's Irah Chase, who often wandered into theologically unorthodox paths, also brought formative influence to bear on the young Robinson.[205]

---

theological education and speculated about nativism and other cultural motives at work. In fact, the article itself is highly speculative, contains errors of fact, and reflects more of a snapshot of an evolving process already in place for two decades in the Northeast.

[205] See A. H. Strong's comments on Robinson's experience at Newton in "Theology of Ezekiel Gilman Robinson," in *Miscellanies,* 2:59–60.

Robinson claimed a superficial indebtedness to well-traveled American Baptist educator, Barnas Sears. As noted, in 1833–34 Sears was in Europe where he encountered German theologians at several institutions. Sears was in fact the only classroom source of theological understanding Robinson could claim. Robinson gained from Sears an eclectic pedagogical methodology that amounted to a great many quotations from contemporary scholars, especially among the German schools of thought. Sears was anything but a conservative thinker and exposed students to the most contemporary bodies of theological literature. Robinson recalled taking little of a dogmatic nature from Sears, who preferred students to draw their own conclusions. Sears's spirit of inquiry aroused in Robinson an insatiable desire to do likewise.[206] Robinson vowed to offer students more of his own thinking to cover the deficit in his Newton training.

Robinson began his career at the end of an era of unprecedented harmony among Baptists in the United States. Ordained by Jeremiah Bell Jeter in Richmond, Virginia, he served as chaplain at the University of Virginia in the 1840s. He moved from a church in Norfolk to Massachusetts and then to accept a professorship at the Western Baptist Theological Institute in Covington, Kentucky. There he taught Hebrew and Church History in a school designed on the Newton plan. Among those who sat under his early tutelage were William Ashmore, the missionary to China, and John R. Downer, soon to be a professor at Denison University. Among those especially touched at Covington by Robinson was Rufus C. Burleson, later to become president of Baylor University in Waco, Texas. Burleson had Robinson as a teacher in several classes and he recalled with high esteem Robinson's exacting demands, his desire to demolish skepticism, and his desire to see young preachers grounded in the faith.[207] The school at Covington ultimately became a victim of the slavery debate in the United States and closed in 1848, leaving Robinson to become a pastor in nearby Cincinnati. After three years in pastoral ministry, he moved to Rochester, New York, where the distinguished president of a new Baptist university there,

---

[206] E. H. Johnson, ed., *Ezekiel Gilman Robinson: An Autobiography* (Boston: Silver Burdette, 1896) 22. Prof. Maring thinks that Robinson more closely imitated Sears than Hackett, but this is not the impression left in Robinson's autobiography. See Maring, "Baptists and Changing Views of the Bible" 58.

[207] Johnson, *Robinson*, 239–40.

Martin Brewer Anderson, invited him to a professorship in Rochester
Seminary. Robinson succeeded John Sharp Maginnis, who had recently
died.

Robinson's role as seminary president had a definite impact upon his
public theological persona. Because of the fallout from the "Removal
Controversy",[208] he was ever aware of the need not to give his
institution's critics any reason to attack Rochester Seminary. "Even a
suspicion of heterodoxy," he wrote, "would be fatal to the Rochester
interest." This caused him to nuance his theological terminology,
preferring, for example, the word "experimental" to "experiential."[209] In
the year-long required theology course he began with the "Evidences of
Christianity." He used a diversity of teaching sources, including the
works of Theodore Parker, August Tholuck on inspiration, and Samuel
T. Coleridge's "Confessions of an Inquiring Spirit." Later he admitted
that he was reading just ahead of his students, that he freely mixed
German, American, and English thinkers, and that his own views on
doctrine were uncertain.[210] As one reads Robinson's evolving theology,
there are pathways that lead away from nineteenth-century orthodoxy.
He thought the doctrine of reprobation to be unscriptural, and his view
on the trinity was more historical and economic, primarily tied as it was
in his thinking to redemption and Christian experience rather than to the
attributes of God. On the important doctrine of justification, he admitted
the slightest subjectivity, holding that it involves not only "God's act for
man, but also God's act in man."[211] His eminent student, Augustus
Strong, also to become his successor, recalled that Robinson had only a
fragmentary understanding of dogma,[212] and a yet-to-be-developed
theological system: "He was still hewing out his theological lines."[213]

---

[208] The bitter struggle left antagonistic parties on either side. The Rochester party was
characterized by revival forces led in part by the fiery New School Baptist evangelist,
Jacob Knapp.

[209] Johnson, *Robinson*, 49.

[210] Ibid., 51.

[211] Ezekiel, G.Robinson, *Christian Theology*, (Rochester: E.B. Andrews, 1894) 300;
Henry, *Strong's Theology,* 43.

[212] Strong thought Robinson was more like Brown and Newton than Hamilton in this
regard. This is not surprising, due to the reactionary stance of Rochester to its parent
institution and Robinson's own educational heritage in New England. See Henry,
Strong's Theology, 20n.

[213] Ibid., 223.

Over the next thirty years, Robinson earned a reputation among
American theologians comparable to those of Charles Hodge, Horace
Bushnell, and Edwards A. Park.[214]

As time went on, however, Robinson's theological system did take a
definite shape. He reflected on the same issues and questions addressed
by Martin Kahler in Germany and P.T. Forsyth in Britain. Robinson
valiantly sought a position between the freethinking of New England and
the old-fashioned theology. At some points he was decidedly "Old
School," as in his conception of sin; at other points he pioneered new
pathways, as in the case of his conviction that justification of sinners is
not one-sided, but must involve regeneration as a simultaneous moral
change.[215] He also exhibited an interest in Scottish Common Sense
philosophy.[216] He considered European approaches, notably those of
George Calixtus at Helmstadt, Coccejus at Leyden, and A. T. Leydecker
at Utrecht, but favored a more topical method that had a threefold
division: God, man, and salvation, to which later was added eschatology.
In his context, Robinson was trying to be thoroughly modern, in that he
accepted two important premises. First, that theology is a progressive
science. As he put it: "The theology of today is the growth of all the
centuries since the beginning of the Christian era."[217] Secondly, he used a
scholarly technique in teaching and writing that demonstrated his
awareness of a variety of authors and their theological positions.[218] While
in his final years at Rochester, Robinson enjoyed an extended European
trip, during which he indulged his appetite for German theology, visiting
the universities at Berlin, Halle, and Heidelberg. His memoirs indicate

---

[214] So stated Benjamin O. True, professor at Rochester and a student of Robinson,
who recalled his work in advanced theological courses. In his retirement, Robinson
taught graduate students at Crozer and Chicago. See "Dr. Robinson as a Leader in Post-
Graduate Study," in Johnson, *Robinson*, 253.

[215] Robinson, *Christian Theology*, 318.

[216] Care must be taken not to overemphasize this point, however, as Gregory
Thornbury does in his essay "Augustus Hopkins Strong," in *Theologians in the Baptist
Tradition*, ed. Timothy George and David S. Dockery (Nashville: Broadman Holman,
2001) 149 ff. Robinson expressed disappointment in the content of Wayland's thinking
and was much more complex in his own evolution.

[217] Robinson, *Christian Theology*, 50-58.

[218] Robinson, *Christian Theology*, 4, 50 ff.

his affection for Dorner and von Ranke in particular, and less so for Hengstenberg.[219]

In his approach to the doctrine of God, Immanuel Kant especially influenced Robinson. Ultimately, he found a compelling case for God as the ultimate moral force in the cosmos.[220] Against the free-thinking theologians of New England, Robinson held that holiness was the fount from which all moral attributes were derived. This stance caused him to reject existing ideas of the atonement–Anselmic, imputation, governmental, or Socinian. He also appears to be among the first American theologians to adopt a *kenosis* understanding of the incarnation, meaning the self-limitation of the Logos in becoming human.[221] Much influenced by Neander's work in history, Robinson concluded that the importance of the death of Christ was the new life he brought into the world and the opportunity for participation in that new life. Moral law, Robinson taught, became the immutable aspect of God's character that carried forth in Christ.[222]

Like many Baptists of the nineteenth century, Robinson was an evangelical theologian who emphasized experience. He rejected the determinism of the Princeton School that had characterized his predecessor at Rochester, John S. Maginnis. Equally, however, he set aside the New England stream of thinking that was evolving into the New Theology. Robinson thought that direction was too subjective. He had a high view of Scripture against which all theological claims must be tested, although accommodation had to be made for the differences in the "occidental mind" and "orientalisms in Genesis."[223] The problems many modern critics were identifying with reports of miracles in the Bible could be resolved, he thought, by asking what the purpose of the miracle was rather than which laws or forces had been modified.[224] Like William Newton Clarke, he moved away from proof-text theology and theories of

---

[219] Johnson, *Robinson*, 96–99. In Berlin, Robinson attended a theological discussion group that included Charles A. Briggs of New York's Union Seminary.

[220] A. H. Strong observed that he was one of the first in the United States to subject the common arguments for the existence of God to a Kantian critique. Strong, *Miscellanies in Two Volumes, Vol. II Chiefly Historical* (Philadelphia: Griffith and Rowland Press, 1912), 65.

[221] Ibid., 214. Strong thought this was among Robinson's most noble achievements.

[222] Ibid., 59–60.

[223] Robinson, *Christian Theology*, 44-45.

[224] Ibid., 45, 107.

inspiration to holding that the entire early church was inspired and that inspiration belongs to the Bible as a whole. He tried to harmonize Scripture and the claims of science because he believed that the claims of science suffered severe limitations. To the chagrin of many, Robinson did not embrace the prevalent Princetonian theology, categorizing it instead as a series of "legal fictions."[225]

More than any other themes in Robinson's theology, his most original contributions were his emphasis upon Christian experience and his priority on the holiness of God. Christian experience, as circumscribed by Scripture, was the ultimate criterion of theology for Robinson: the personality and unity of God, God's attributes, and human redemption. In this regard he introduced to Rochester the same emphases that Ebenezer Dodge and William Newton Clarke were teaching at Madison (later Colgate) during the same period. Likewise, Christ's redemptive act—co-equal with creation—was voluntary and the direct implication of Christ's having assumed human nature. We learn this from the testimony of Scripture and applying it to one's own experience. In his inaugural address to Rochester Seminary Robinson declared: "A man's creed will always be just what he has experienced and no more. The formula of his faith will be just what his intellect has gathered from his heart... [Yet] experience has no authority at all, except what it borrows from the Bible."[226]

Regarding the holiness of God, Robinson taught that the regulative principle in all thinking about God is the idea of perfection. Speaking of the moral attributes of God, he held that love is an outgrowth of God's perfection and that God's love is manifested in the eternal and unchangeable law. For Robinson the law was not an artificial, external creation, but an illustration of the very nature of God; in other words, God's holiness. He held that both the Bible and human conscience teach this truth. This was the sure antidote to the virtually utilitarian systems of ethics and theology suggested in the New Theology. Doubtless in response to the holiness movement that made serious inroads in Western New York during Robinson's time at Rochester Seminary, he held sanctification to be a nurturing process that was part of justification and regeneration. He denied that perfection, or absolute holiness was

---

[225] Ibid., 61.
[226] Robinson, "Experimental Theology," in *Christian Theology*, 358, 360.

attainable in the present life.[227] Robinson thus stands where one might expect a progressively minded Baptist of his era to be, namely as a bridge between an orthodoxy of the evangelical nineteenth century and the emerging university scholarship anticipated in the New Theology of Yale, Union, and Chicago.

As a Baptist theologian, Robinson understood the church to be a religious and spiritual community, with no moral or social coercive power. Typically evangelical, he thought the church's purpose was to claim converts for Christ by proclaiming the gospel. Baptism was an entire surrender to the authority of the triune God. As to the ever present communion question, he held to closed communion, because no church had the right to celebrate the Lord's Supper with unbaptized persons. He inveighed heavily against "churchism," which he defined as extreme sectarianism.[228] Like other Baptist theologians of the period, he excluded ecclesiology from his systematic discussion while teaching church polity and pastoral theology as discrete fields in another class.[229]

Not unlike his fellow mid-century Baptist theologians with respect to eschatology, Robinson stayed close to the themes of divine consummation, eternal life of the soul, the resurrection of the dead by supernatural intervention, and the culmination of divine judgment in a single event. According to his most prominent student, A.H. Strong, Robinson rejected premillennialism and its associated sense of urgency because he believed that too much attention to the second advent of Christ "diminished or discredited the dispensation of the Holy Spirit which Christ himself declared to be better for the Church than his own presence."[230] In so doing, he distanced himself from contemporary Plymouth Brethren teaching and much of popular evangelicalism.[231]

---

[227] Ibid., 175; Carl F. H. Henry, *Personal Idealism and Strong's Theology* (Wheaton: Van Kampen Press, 1951) 26, 45.

[228] Augustus Hopkins Strong, "Ezekiel Gilman Robinson as a Theologian" in *Miscellanies*, 2:102.

[229] Something of his understanding of the church may be derived from Robinson's lecture, "The Relation of the Bible to the Church" in *Madison Avenue Lectures*, 387–419.

[230] Quoted in Henry, *Personal Idealism and Strong's Theology*, 46, n.243.

[231] Here Robinson was more classically Baptist and belonged in the nineteenth century rather than with the more modern thinkers. Even Henry Weston at Crozer, a distant contemporary of Robinson, engaged the popular side of evangelical thought positively and became a confidante of Dwight L. Moody.

A. H. Strong observed that there were a number of giants at the school during Robinson's tenure, but that the institution owed more of its character to him than any other person.[232] What Robinson created at Rochester was a style of theological inquiry that stressed breadth of exposure rather than strict systematic orthodoxy. He also blended into his own teaching emphases a combination of theory and praxis, teaching both theology and homiletics. His successors would build upon that foundation. Robinson also cast a large shadow over the Baptist ministry in the United States and training hundreds at three schools. Among his most devoted disciples and colleagues were George W. Northrup at Chicago, Ebenezer Dodge at Hamilton, Elias H. Johnson at Crozer, A. H. Strong in Rochester, and E. B. Andrews at Brown—a considerable apostolate.

Augustus H. Strong (1836–1921) was one of the most illustrious and heavily quoted Baptist theologians of his era. His wide scope of influence was due in part to the premier place in which he labored. Rochester Theological Seminary led student enrollment among the North American Baptist seminaries and boasted what was arguably the leading Baptist faculty at the end of the nineteenth century. Students arrived at Rochester from all corners of the United States and the British provinces to study theology, mostly with Strong. The other element in Strong's profile was his interest in maintaining dialogue with science and contemporary thought. While his writings may seem esoteric and scholarly to the point of pedantic to later generations, in Robinson's day they were considered sharply developed and conversant with the major philosophical issues of the day. By most assessments, he was a "critically orthodox" thinker who placed doctrine in its historical context and who attempted to show by means of logic, history, and experience that Christianity is valid.[233]

The Strong family name was virtually synonymous with Rochester, New York, and its religious heritage. Augustus's father, Alvah Strong, was the editor of Rochester's most prominent newspaper and a respected member of the community. He was active in bringing Baptists together in support of the University of Rochester and Rochester Theological Seminary. He had been converted in 1830 during the first crusade

---

[232] Ibid., 62. Among the emerging theologians with Robinson was George W. Northrup, who taught church history at Rochester from 1857 to 1867.

[233] Welch, *Protestant Thought*, 238n.

conducted in that city by Charles G. Finney. Augustus was himself brought to faith in Christ under Finney's influence in 1856[234]. Henry Strong, brother of Augustus, became a prominent physician and founder of the medical school of the University of Rochester.

A. H. Strong graduated from Yale with a bachelor of arts degree. There he found little beyond a strict recitation method, except in his interaction with Noah Porter who was president and professor of intellectual and moral philosophy. Porter introduced Strong to a new idea of conscience, namely that conscience is not separate from intellect and sensibility but a mode in which man is aware of moral relations and the feelings gathered in view of those relations. Porter's teachings, and his book titled *The Human Intellect*, were significant in the development of Strong's own theological repertoire.[235]

Following his years at Yale, the first important influence upon Strong was Ezekiel G. Robinson, the president and principal theologian of Rochester Seminary. Strong recalled being in awe of Robinson and barely spoke in Robinson's classes. In both positive and negative ways, Strong owed much to his teacher. Strong's only formal preparation to teach theology was the coursework he took with Robinson as a ministerial student. Robinson's greatest legacy was his constant asking of critical questions, which gave Strong a methodology, and Robinson's wide reading. Strong, for instance, credited Robinson with introducing him to the writings of Sir William Hamilton (1788–1856) of Edinburgh University, a devotee of Scottish Common Sense philosophy.[236] Later, however, Strong became quite critical of his teacher.[237]

A second influence on Strong is more difficult to trace. He confessed to being impressed with several German theologians, but when he began to encounter them is unclear. In 1872 Strong made his first trip to Europe, and since he visited German and Swiss cities, it is hard to believe he did not engage in dialogue about German theological studies. Also, some members of his traveling company were thoughtful pastors

---

[234] Strong's conversion is retold in "Theology and Experience" in A.H. Strong, *One Hundred Chapel Talks*, 12-14.

[235] Crerar Douglas, ed., *Autobiography of Augustus Hopkins Strong* (Valley Forge: Judson Press, 1981) 66.

[236] Ibid., 102. Hamilton was well read in German philosophy and critical of Hegel and John Stuart Mill.

[237] "Ezekiel G. Robinson as a Theologian" in *Miscellanies,* 2:63, 65, 108.

who knew he was soon to become a seminary professor. In 1884 and 1887 he made similar trips to Britain and Europe. Then there were Strong's associations with faculty colleagues in the German Department of Rochester Seminary, Albert Ramaker and August Rauschenbusch, who may have stimulated some of his thinking. Whatever his initial exposure, Strong came to appreciate several German writers, notably Isaac A. Dorner of Berlin, Gottfried Thomasius, Hermann Lotze, and Fredrich A. Philippi. Dorner was the mediating theologian who "most effectively held the citadel of Christian faith against the skepticism that had long infected European thought."[238] These writers whom Strong read with "avidity," took him well beyond his mentor. What he most appreciated about German theologians was their realism and dynamic nature.[239] They were open to revision and he would be as well after 1876.

In several editions of *Systematic Theology*, first issued in 1886[240] as published classroom notes, he appeared in print as a conservative, evangelical, and orthodox Baptist theologian. He spoke of Aristotle's influence in making theology a science, of Bishop Butler's writings on the moral constitution of human beings, and Jonathan Edwards's emphasis upon love in the creation story. To these he added premises from Scottish Common Sense thought wherein religion, as a science, rested upon philosophic foundations.[241] His first edition affirmed the sovereignty of God, the complete trustworthiness of Scripture, universal and original sin, an ethical theory of the atonement (which holds that the necessity of the atonement is grounded in God's holiness), traditional Calvinistic doctrines of election, perseverance, and an understanding of

---

[238] Hutchison, *Modernist Impulse*, 84.

[239] Douglas, *Strong*, 220.

[240] Augustus H. Strong, *Systematic Theology* (New York: A. C. Armstrong, 1886). The book first appeared as a compendium, *Lectures on Theology, Printed for the Use of Students in the Rochester Theological Seminary* (Rochester: E. R. Andrews, 1876). In the following decade, Strong added notes and illustrations based on his extemporaneous lectures, and the result was *Systematic Theology* (1886). The work went through 5 editions and produced 5,000 copies by 1915. He later again revised the work and produced a substantially different piece. Judson Press later reprinted the edition and it remains available.

[241] See the discussions in Henry, *Personal Idealism*, 55 and Thornbury, "Augustus Hopkins Strong," 151. The Thornbury essay must be used with care: specifics on the publication of Strong's writings and his influence upon other named theologians are inaccurate. Compare p. 140 with Henry's Appendix on details.

repentance that involved intellectual, emotional, and volitional elements. With respect to the church he was a classic Baptist, affirming a universal church, but carefully focused upon the local congregation as the concrete church. He held to closed communion and denied the sacramental character of the ordinances. His eschatology was traditional, holding to a literal Second Coming of Christ, according to a post-millennial scheme, followed by a final judgment as an event to vindicate God's righteousness.

Carl F. H. Henry has shown that as Strong's career unfolded his theology evolved dramatically. He traveled widely, offering lectures across the United States, engaged the intellectual elite in Rochester, and drank deeply from the work of German thinkers.[242] From the progress of theological discussion in the previous three decades, he valued views of heightened divine immanence, an understanding of evolutionary development as God's method, and higher criticism of the Bible.[243] He came to believe that his task was "to rescue theology from the realm of mere abstractions and to show its connections with literature and life."[244] In the 1880s Strong began to move in surprisingly new theological directions. Emphasizing that theology should be treated as a science, he accepted fully the results of higher criticism,[245] engaged the theory of evolution, more fully developed his idea of the ethical theory of the atonement, and became critical of Jonathan Edwards's theories of nature and substance. Strong's accommodation of contemporary scientific explanations for biblical phenomena was far-reaching and must have perplexed his traditional readers:

> I welcome every honest effort to reconcile science and scripture. God can use natural means for the accomplishment of his purposes, and when the natural will suffice, it is not necessary to postulate a supernatural working. Many so-called miracles may have their natural explanation, as an intensification

---

[242] Henry's published doctoral dissertation at Boston University, *Personal Idealism and Strong's Theology* (cited above), exhaustively categorizes Strong's theology. He was a member of the University of Rochester's elite Pundit Club, where papers on experimental topics were regularly presented.

[243] See A. H. Strong, "Fifty Years of Theology" and Henry's summary in his *Fifty Years of Protestant Theology* (Boston: W. A. Wilde, 1950) 23.

[244] Douglas, *Strong*, 220.

[245] Maring, "Baptists and Changing Views of the Bible" (Part 2), 46.

of natural processes. The parting of the Red Sea may have been caused by a blowing of the east wind, and the passage of the Jordan may have been made possible by a landslide that choked the river's course and temporarily dried up its bed. The angel of the Lord, who smote the host of Sennacharib, may have had at his command a simoom of the desert with which to overwhelm the Assyrians. The destruction of Sodom and Gomorrah may have been due to volcanic eruption, the effects of which are still seen in the asphalt of that region And so with regard to many other startling events of the Scripture record. If we knew all the latent powers of nature, we might be able to explain many narratives that now seem wholly supernatural.[246]

In a series of essays he explored modern idealism, various theories of monism, new approaches to the atonement question, and began to acknowledge a previously unrecognized dependence upon his former teacher, E. G. Robinson. He concluded eventually that Christ is the principle of evolution, that God's existence was best seen in the orderly system of nature, and—following the thinking of Lotze and numerous American university philosophers—he posited that Christ had become one with all mankind in creation. His earlier positions on Scripture now denied historical and scientific inerrancy, but spoke of infallibility. In place of traditional mechanical interpretations of nature, such as those found in German theologians like Ritschl, he saw Christ as the essence of the immanence of God, revealing the very nature of God in the world. Strong's 1907 *Theology*, containing about four times more material than his first edition, had myriad references to German theologians, and more references to Borden P. Bowne than to St. Augustine or John Calvin.[247]

Strong's most revealing and pioneering work was *Christ and Creation in Ethical Monism* (1899). The material first appeared in 1892 in a Rochester annual lecture series. Here was a fresh look at Christology, somewhat of a response to the new currents of theology

---

[246] Strong, *One Hundred Chapel Talks,* 192.

[247] Ibid., 145. Strong mused to his Rochester community that "the conservatives at Waco and Princeton think me too radical, and the radicals of Union and Chicago think me too conservative." For a survey of reactions to his work, see Grant Wacker, *Augustus Hopkins Strong and the Dilemma of Historical Consciousness* (Macon GA: Mercer University Press, 1985) 87–107, esp., 97.

prompted by German theologians. It was also a fulfillment of Strong's search from the 1870s for an adequate doctrine of creation in view of the theories proposed by Charles Darwin, Herbert Spencer, and others.[248] Strong earnestly desired to hold onto traditional formulations about Christ, which had endeared him to the Princeton School and other orthodox thinkers. But he also wanted to engage the philosophical ideas in theism and personalism.[249] A recent biographer has cast Strong's position in this regard as: "The fundamental import of ethical monism was, then, that Christ, the Logos, is the spark of human consciousness."[250] Consciousness developing across time becomes historical process. This line of thinking had widespread impact upon his articulation of other Christian doctrines. For instance, the imputation of human sinfulness became a major question for the Rochester theologian. In a series of intellectual steps across a decade, Strong thought it was one of his main theological contributions to assert that while Christ did not inherit original sin, he did carry its guilt. Therefore, in taking on human nature, Christ in reality was bound to die because God's holiness had been violated and Jesus carried the guilt. While Christians have depravity but not original sin guilt, so it was reversed with Christ who carried the guilt but not the depravity associated with humankind.

Strong pushed his developing Christological principle further by arguing that Christ had created humanity and thus was its life. Here was God's plan for the human race revealed before creation: that voluntarily, "Christ as life" would suffer for the guilt of humanity's sins and then rise to provide eternal life for the race. Ultimately, following the lead of Borden Bowne and Hermann Lotze, he determined that Christ was the life of the entire universe: "He is the revelation of God, the principle of physical and mental interaction, as well of evolution and moral unity."[251]

---

[248] See his lecture at Colby College in 1878, "The Philosophy of Evolution," in which he accepted Herbert Spencer's understanding of the mechanics of evolution.

[249] It is unclear how Strong encountered personalism. He reveals no personal acquaintance with either Lotze or Bowne, the latter having derived his ideas directly from Lotze. So, one is left to surmise that Strong read both theologians and sifted them through W. G. T. Shedd at Union Seminary and George Ladd at Yale. See Henry, *Strong's Theology*, 100n.

[250] Wacker, *Strong*, 66.

[251] Strong thought monism was the ruling idea of the times, and he wanted to give to it a Christian interpretation. He carefully distinguished his terminology from the personal idealism of Bowne and Lotze. See Ibid., 62, 107.

Strong referred to Christ's identification with humanity as ethical monism and thought he had discovered a new bridge between the emerging monism among scientists and philosophers at the turn of the century and theological discourse. With respect to the doctrine of creation, the new position allowed him to accept all of the values of evolution, thus affirming scientific modernity, and hold onto a strong form of Christology that he thought uncompromisingly evangelical. God worked by means, he reasoned, and laws of variation and selection were likely the methods in his design. Moreover, he declared, "Christ is the principle of evolution,"[252]

Although Strong argued strenuously that his new understanding in ethical monism was nothing more than the Apostle Paul claimed in asserting that all things consist in Christ, Strong's adversaries were numerous and harshly critical, labeling him a pantheist and a Buddhist. The eminent Charles Hodge at Princeton Theological Seminary thought Strong leaned toward a problematic *kenosis* idea of the incarnation that reduced the importance of Christ's humanity. Strong's longtime friend at Newton Theological Institution, Alvah Hovey, asserted, "This may be the coming philosophy, but we submit that it does not exalt or clarify one's conception of God."[253] On the liberal side, William Adams Brown at Union Theological Seminary was disappointed that Strong still held onto a traditional view of the inspiration of Scripture rather than turning to religious experience as most in the New Theology were doing. As it turned out, Strong's position won few actual devotees in the theologically liberal community and he had no adherents among the rising generation of conservatives and fundamentalists.

In the latter years of his teaching career, the much venerated seminary professor[254] had time to reflect and revise his system. He became increasingly concerned about the effects of higher criticism upon an individual's faith and the vitality of Christian witness. Holding Immanuel Kant and Albert Ritschl responsible for influencing a new generation of skeptics among American Christians, Strong believed the antidote was a reaffirmation of the authority of Christ and the Scriptures. Indeed, not unlike John Vichert at Colgate Seminary, Strong came to identify

---

[252] Strong, *Christ in Creation*, 11.

[253] Quoted in Henry, *Strong's Theology*, 218.

[254] His statue in Rochester Seminary illustrates him in an imperial draping robe. The main hall is named in his honor.

himself with moderate fundamentalists who understood the value of confessing a "faith once delivered to the saints."[255] In his *Autobiography,* A. H. Strong took the longer view and listed four guiding principles across the years of his work. First was his hospitality to new ideas. He came to agree with Augustine that all truth derived from God and that it was his duty to bring forth new ideas in tandem with older conceptions. Second, he understood truth to be derived also from sources many among the Baptist and evangelical orthodox would have held to be anathema, notably Baruch Spinoza and Aldous Huxley. Third, new ideas must be consistent with older truths if they are to be valid. Truth, despite its age or familiarity does not wear out and die, Strong thought. Finally, he saw himself as Bunyan's "Valiant for the Truth," even though others had not yet arrived at his positions.[256] Time, he thought, surely would vindicate him.[257]

Walter Rauschenbusch (1861–1918) was the second most influential *theological* theologian at Rochester Theological Seminary at the turn of the twentieth century. His father, August Rauschenbusch, representing a comfortable blend of German Pietism and American Evagelicalism, was a well-known German Baptist theologian and professor at the Seminary. August had been a student of Joachim Neander, whose principal legacy was his preoccupation with the Kingdom of God, about which August had much to comment as his son grew to maturity. Walter first attended Evangelisch Gymnasium zu Guetersloh, where he received a typical rigorous German post-secondary education and was accorded the distinction of *primus omnium.* Upon returning to the United States, he completed an undergraduate degree at the University of Rochester and enrolled in Rochester Theological Seminary, expecting to follow his father's path into the German Baptist ministry. As a promising theologian, he brought to Baptist life in America and Rochester Seminary in particular, a zeal for social critique similar to that of J. H.

---

[255] See his last published essay "Confessions of Our Faith" in *Watchman Examiner,* 7 July 1921, quoted in Thornbury, "Augustus Hopkins Strong," 146.

[256] Douglas, *Strong,* 256.

[257] Strong's legacy continues to be somewhat schizophrenic. Conservative evangelicals are drawn to his early work and reprint his early edition of *Systematic Theology,* hardly the fate presumed by Grant Wacker: "an immensely irrelevant dinosaur" (*Augustus Hopkins Strong,* xiii). Contemporary evangelicals see him as "left" (Erickson) or "inclusivistic" (Pinnock). More modernistic theologians and the Neo-orthodox think his ideas were interesting in context, but untenable in the long run.

Wichern, Adolf Harnack and Wilhelm Herrmann in Germany, and F. D.
Maurice and R. J. Campbell in Britain.

Walter's studies at Rochester Seminary proved directive throughout
his life. He worked with Howard Osgood, a conservative Old Testament
professor, and with William Arnold Stevens, a liberal New Testament
teacher. Others who influenced him positively were Benjamin O. True in
church history and T. Harwood Pattison in pastoral theology. True was
devoted to Neander's methods and Pattison was a product of Regent's
Park College in England. Perhaps the foremost influence on Walter was
Augustus H. Strong, president and the seminary's leading theologian.
Strong was in the conservative period of his development and carefully
guided Rauschenbusch through a project on the thought of Sabellius and
Horace Bushnell's theory of the atonement. Although Strong disliked
Bushnell's idea that Jesus voluntarily gave himself to show God's love
for mankind, Walter was drawn to it and to other leading thinkers in the
New Theology. He developed affinity for a wide variety of thinkers,
including Frederick Robinson, Frederick Tholuck, Samuel T. Coleridge,
and Frederick D. Maurice. His understanding of the Bible was unsettling
to the orthodox: "My inherited ideas about the inerrancy of the Bible
became untenable. I determined to follow the facts as divine, and let my
man-made theories go if they conflicted."[258] Rauschenbusch and Strong
became close personal friends and regular correspondents.[259]

Walter Rauschenbusch's contribution to Baptist life as a theologian
began in earnest with his pastorate in New York City.[260] Called in 1886
to serve the Second German Baptist Church in Hell's Kitchen, he learned
firsthand of the plight of tenement dwellers, exploited workers, and
broken families. He supported the evangelism of D. L. Moody, but also
resonated with urban economist/reformers like Richard Ely and Henry
George. Soon he formed a close fellowship with fellow Baptist pastors
Leighton Williams at Amity Baptist and Nathaniel Schmidt at First
Swedish Baptist, both of whom would join Walter in the work of the

---

[258] Quoted in Paul M. Minus, *Walter Rauschenbusch*: *American Reformer* (New York
: Macmillan, 1988) 40.

[259] Rauschenbusch thought his appointment to the Rochester faculty reflected a
liberalizing tendency in President Strong's thinking.

[260] A balanced assessment is found in Robert T. Handy, "Walter Rauschenbusch in
Historical Perspective," *Baptist Quarterly* 20/7 (1964): 313–21. Handy argued Walter's
liberalism was evangelical, not humanistic.

Baptist Congress and the Brotherhood of the Kingdom. As early as 1888 Rauschenbusch made his first literary foray into social Christianity to a pastor's gathering much enamored of others like Washington Gladden and Josiah Strong among the Congregationalists. In 1893 the three Baptist pastors and Samuel Zane Batten, William Newton Clarke, George Dana Boardman, and Mornay Williams formed officially the Brotherhood of the Kingdom, a "think tank" dedicated to social Christianity and reform.[261]

The new emphasis upon "kingdom theology" had deep ramifications. In an era of renewed interest among Baptists upon individualism, evangelism, and personal salvation, the Brotherhood pursued the "evangelization of the world." They believed in a kingdom of God on earth that could be realized in the political, industrial, scientific, and artistic life of humanity rather than an eschatological entity. The purpose of Rauschenbusch and his colleagues was to emphasize preaching and inspire hymns on the kingdom, as well as advocating public policy and influencing centers of power to emulate the ethical and social norms found reflected in the kingdom of God teachings. For them, "the kingdom embraced all pure aspirations God-ward, and all true hopes for the perfection of life…a perfect humanity on earth, living according to the will of God."[262]

In 1896 Strong invited Rauschenbusch to return to his beloved Rochester as a lecturer in the German Department of the Seminary. There he taught general arts courses and, in the theological areas, New Testament books and the life of Christ. This only served to deepen his Christological perspective. In 1901 he was appointed to the school's academic chair in church history and remained there until his death. In his role as church historian, Rauschenbusch produced various influential interpretive schemes such as the cyclical understanding of "adulteration-purification," and he came to test every institution, personality, or movement by the "spirit of Jesus." As a Baptist historian, Rauschenbusch believed the principal mark of that faith tradition was its advocacy of the original religion of Jesus.

---

[261] Minus links the Brotherhood to the gathering of Anglican theologians in 1889 that led to the publication of *Lex Mundi*. See Ibid., 86.

[262]Walter Rauschenbusch, "The Kingdom of God" **B***rotherhood Leaflet #4* (New York: Brotherhood of the Kingdom, 1894).

As time passed many of the turn-of-the-century the school's faculty came to retirement, including President Strong. Rauschenbusch had risen in prominence to become the outstanding theologian/teacher at Rochester, now the leading Baptist theological school in the world. More students were enrolled in the New York seminary than anywhere else and endowments were greater than $2 million, thanks to businessmen such as John D. Rockefeller. Although Strong felt the school slipping toward a more patent higher critical bent, the trustees wanted his successor to be in touch with emerging theological trends. Rauschenbusch was pleased with the choice of C. A. Barbour as president and he encouraged George Cross, a Canadian graduate of the University of Chicago, to become Strong's successor in theology on the promise of complete academic non-interference in his work. Rauschenbusch thought his own student, Justin Wroe Nixon, an ideal candidate for a teaching position in biblical studies.

In 1907 Rauschenbusch authored *Christianity and the Social Crisis*, an immediate bestseller and American social classic.[263] The book paid a personal tribute to the working people of his former parish in New York City. He called for its readers to undertake the task of creating a new social order. His theology emerged from his observation of human need: "There is certainly a great and increasing body of chronic wretchedness in our wonderful country. It is greatest where our industrial system has worked out its conclusions most completely."[264] Unlike many socialists of his era, Rauschenbusch was not critical of the accumulation of wealth in a capitalist system, but only of competitive commerce and its systemic abuse of the poor and underprivileged. He observed that it is the function of religion to teach the individual to value his soul more than the body, and moral integrity more than income. The church, he believed, had a great stake in the present (and any) social crisis: "It must either condemn the world and seek to change it, or tolerate the world and conform to it."[265]

---

[263] On the development of the social gospel, see Charles H. Hopkins, *The Rise of the Social Gospel in American Protestantism 1865–1915* (New Haven: Yale University Press, 1940) and Welch, *Protestant Thought*, 255–65.

[264] Walter Rauschenbusch, *Christianity and the Social Crisis* (New York: Macmillan, 1907) 246.

[265] Ibid., 341–42, 372.

In two important sequels to his first book, Rauschenbusch extended his case further under the rubric of kingdom theology. In *Christianizing the Social Order* (1912), he asserted that Jesus embodied the fullest revelation of God's purposes and that his disciples must likewise seek the Lord's ends and value what he did. All people were linked in a web of humanity, Rauschenbusch believed. People must join together in a Christian social order such that even "bad people would do good things."[266]

Quite contrary to the historic Baptist understanding of the separation of church and state, Rauschenbusch believed Christians should cooperate with the state and work through it to ensure the public good. He even encouraged an alliance between Christians and socialists to realize the aims of Christ through social reform. The 1917 Taylor Lectures at Yale University became the occasion for his *Theology for the Social Gospel* (1917). Although shy of the full-blown systematic theology of the social gospel, it was Rauschenbusch's best and most mature thinking. He warned that until Christians realized the nature of God's kingdom, they could not fully appreciate God's purposes in redemption. Those who thwarted the kingdom's progress, constituted a "kingdom of evil." In this masterpiece, he asserted the principle of social sin and reminded Christians that the Christ was crucified by an evil system and that social sin continues where the same forces were at work: oligarchy, corruption, bigotry, and militarism. Claude Welch wrote that this idea of "superpersonal sin" and righteousness was Rauschenbusch's greatest theological contribution.[267]

This perspective struck at the heart of Baptist individualism, rampant among most churches and thinkers of the era. It also challenged the common understanding of the sacraments/ordinances, suggesting that those who interpret God's kingdom as entirely a future event miss the ongoing growth toward the present realization of that divine realm. When one is baptized, Rauschenbusch believed, one renounces the kingdom of evil for the kingdom of God. The Lord's Supper symbolized the new community or "communion of the saints." Here was a novel interpretation of the sacraments/ordinances that was closer to a Catholic understanding than that of a radical Protestant.[268]

---

[266] Minus, *Walter Rauschenbusch*, 170.
[267] Welch, *Protestant Thought*, 2:265.
[268] Ibid., 189.

No less than the venerable Rochester historian, Winthrop S. Hudson, observed that the presidency of A. H. Strong was the end of an era. A transition to newer methods for a new age quickly took place at Rochester Theological Seminary. The appointment of George Cross (1912-1929) in systematic theology moved treatment of the field from a systematic to an historical basis.[269] Here liberal thought built upon the foundation that Rauschenbusch had laid. Cross's new faculty colleague in religious education, Henry Robbins, approached religion from the point of view of psychology, and Ernest Parsons was a pioneer in Form Criticism of the New Testament. Cross, Robbins, and Parsons reflected the new perspectives of university-trained theologians,[270]Cross being the senior and most creative theologian of the three.

By the time of his arrival in Rochester, Cross had attained a national reputation. He succeeded A. H. Strong as Robert K. Davies Professor of Systematic Theology and held that chair through 1929. In 1922 he delivered the prestigious Nathaniel W. Taylor Lectures at Yale Divinity School. His lectures, published as *Creative Christianity,* revealed his approach to theology. Essentially an historical theologian, Cross followed his Chicago mentors in positing that Christianity is an historical faith that has persisted through successive periods of time. It has been reshaped and institutionalized in its development. Accepting all of the premises of the New Theology, he wrote, "There can be no genuine knowledge of the universe in which we must live our life, except on the presupposition of the immanency, permanency, and integrated unity of the forces and laws of the universe."[271] Further, he operated on the assumption that modern critical interpretation of Scripture was the sole door of understanding the text of the Bible and the meaning of Jesus in particular. Retired president Strong characterized Cross's appointment as "the greatest calamity that has come to the seminary since its

---

[269] Justin W. Nixon and Winthrop S. Hudson, eds., *Christian Leadership in a World Society: Essays in Honor of Conrad Henry Moehlman* (Rochester: Colgate Rochester Divinity School, 1945) 6. Actually, Henry C. Mabie held the Davies Chair in Systematic Theology 1908–09, presumably in anticipation of a longer appointment for Cross.

[270] See Shailer Mathews's tribute to Robins, "Professor Robbins as a Thinker," and Shirley Jackson Case's "Professor Parsons as a Graduate Student," *Colgate Rochester Divinity School Bulletin* 13/4 (May, 1941): 116–20; 137–40.

[271] George Cross, *Creative Christianity: A Study of the Genius of the Christian Faith* (New York: Macm
    illan Co., 1922) 24.

foundation."[272] Cross's arrival in Rochester, he thought, signaled the intrusion of a series of agnostic, skeptical, and anti-Christan elements into the curriculum, personified in men like Robbins, Parsons, Nixon, and Conrad H. Moehlman—all who were sympathetic to Cross's views. A quintessential product of the Chicago School, Cross summarized his understanding of Christianity: "The Christian faith is identical with the spirit of loyalty to a historic figure of the past who is at the same time the ideal figure of the future."[273] He devoted himself to ultimate questions, like "What is the genius of Christianity?" His answer was that it lay in the perfect personality of Jesus and his transforming effect upon the making of a better world. Jesus' endurance of death, the grandeur of his self-affirmation in its presence, his power over men's hearts afterwards generations later, constitute the heart of the Christian faith. He questioned whether one could bear the guilt of another and believed that the atonement was neither priestly nor governmental, but a self-realization that Christ's death on the cross produces in humans the law of vicarious labor and suffering to bring good out of evil. The atonement thus happens across time and is perpetuated forever in the life of everyone who believes in Christ.[274] Cross believed that Christ transcended the boundaries of confessionalism, and he rejected such Calvinist ideas as election, because a communion of inner life "as wide as the race" can never be perfect except through individual personality.

Following the lead of Rauschenbusch in particular, Cross attached the vision of the Perfect personality to the theology of the Kingdom of God. He envisioned a lessening of emphasis upon the afterlife and a greater attention to a world in which all inhabitants possess the image of the Perfect Man.[275] Ultimately, the cosmic meaning of Christianity is expressed in platonic terms: "In the cosmos there is that which impresses itself upon us, awakens in us powers that we should otherwise never know to be ours and enacts its achievements anew in our souls... Jesus the Crucified through his vicariousness enables us to discover perfection in personality."[276] Unabashedly universalist in his own matured

---

[272] Douglas, *Strong*, 357.

[273] George Cross, *Christian Salvation: A Modern Interpretation* (Chicago: University of Chicago Press, 1925), 221.

[274] Ibid., 204, 206.

[275] Cross, *Creative Christianity,* 94.

[276] Ibid., 161-162.

'systematic theology,' *Christian Salvation* (1925), Cross wrote, "the Christian faith tends to raise up the whole community life of men never-ceasingly from baseness and weakness to refinement and strength." The future was certain, he believed, "because the eternity of existence is the necessary predicate of our sense of personal worth." [277]

Theology as a classic discipline at Colgate Rochester Divinity School fared unevenly in the era of the 1930s and 1940s. New emphases were placed upon Sociology of Religion, rural church work, public speaking, and Applied Christianity. The theological faculty included John Benjamin Anderson who was installed in a new position in 1929-1936 as the two seminaries consummated their merger: the William Newton Clarke Chair in Christian Theology and Ethics. He was a natural for the Clarke chair, having worked with Clarke at Colgate and following him in the Joslin Chair. Anderson was a graduate of Colgate University and its theological seminary. Born in England, he studied at the Universities of Berlin and Goettingen and taught first at Colgate 1906 to 1919 in Ecclesiology and English Bible, then he assumed the Joslin Chair in Christian Theology 1923-1928. Similar chairs were named in honor of James B. Colgate (History of Christianity), Augustus Hopkins Strong (History and Philosophy of Religion), Cornelius Woelfkin (Preaching), each of which made a mark for a rising liberal Baptist Christianity.

In 1936 Justin Wroe Nixon (1886-1958) was named to the W. N. Clarke Chair, and he held that position through 1952 when he moved to teach preaching in order to make a vacancy for William Hamilton. Nixon began his career in theological education in 1916 at Rochester Seminary in Old Testament studies, after which he held the chair in English Bible and Sociology. From 1924 to 1937 he was pastor of Rochester's Brick Presbyterian Church. Deeply Christological, he was a protégé of Walter Rauschenbusch and much enamored of the Presbyterian missionary, Robert E. Speer. Nixon commented that two movements, foreign missions and the social gospel had influenced him. He wrote, "Nothing seemed to us clearer than that economic, racial, and international relations …were largely in contradiction to the mind of Christ."[278]

In 1953 William Hamilton, a young upstate New Yorker, became the W. N. Clarke Professor at Colgate Rochester and the discipline regained

---

[277] Cross, *Christian Salvation*, 234, 241.
[278] Justin Wroe Nixon, "My Forty Five-Years in the Ministry" *Colgate Rochester Divinity School Bulletin* 26:2 (May, 1954): 14-15.

some of its lost prominence. Hamilton (1924-) came from Hamilton
College, had been educated at Oberlin College, Union Theological
Seminary in New York, and the University of St. Andrews in Scotland.
His St. Andrews Ph.D. dissertation was entitled "The Christian Doctrine
of the Body in Twentieth Century British Theology" and completed
under D. M. Baillie.[279] Paul Tillich and Dietrich Bonhoeffer also heavily
influenced him. In his fourteen years at the Divinity School, Hamilton
took theological definition to new boundaries of creativity and eventually
radical expression.

In the mid-1950s Hamilton evolved theologically from a liberal to a
radical position. In an article for a denominational journal he advocated
dialogue with fundamentalists and a much clearer statement of the
historic liberal position. He was fully committed to learning from
ecumenical discussions with other Protestants and Roman Catholics,
particularly on the spiritual life, the sacraments, and the role of laity.[280]
His patience with the failure of the liberal tradition, however, finally
seemed to run out. In a 1956 publication directed at the laity (actually an
outgrowth of his doctoral dissertation), *The Christian Man,* Hamilton
signaled some of his new directions. In exploring the demand of Christ
upon one's life and the real meaning of forgiveness, he asserted that only
through the act of sexuality do people see themselves in a deeper
Christian sense. Sexual intimacy was the ultimate expression of humility,
when one loses all pride and becomes truly humble, replicating humility
before the will of God. His idea of true Christianity was to embrace fully
the lordship of Jesus over the world and the challenges of imitating
Christ in one's life. Marriage held special significance for Hamilton for it
introduced the "feminine, the receiving, accepting, suffering side of
existence."[281]

Hamilton announced in *The New Essence of Christianity* (1966) that
theology must be done afresh in every generation. He found fault with a
"biblical-Augustinian-Reformed" way of speaking about God. Over
several years the traditional sovereign and omnipotent God became for

---

[279] Baillie was heavily influenced by Emil Brunner and sought to correct
Christological inadequacies in Barth. See Moody, *Word of Truth,* 29.

[280] William H. Hamilton, "The Ecumenical Responsibility of the Baptists,"
Foundations 1/2 (April 1958): 75–77.

[281] William Hamilton, *The Christian Man* (Philadelphia: Westminster Press, 1956)
74–78; *The New Essence of Christianity* (New York: Association Press, 1966) 156–59.

many a difficult God to perceive or meet. Drawing upon Freud and
Nietzsche, Hamilton exclaimed that God had withdrawn, that he was
absent, even that he was somehow dead. In so doing, he joined Gabriel
Vahanian at Syracuse University, Thomas Altizer at Emory University,
and Paul Van Buren at Temple University in the "Death of God"
movement. Suffering from a religious depression wherein general
religion had ceased to be a lively factor in human life, these "radical"
theologians concluded that "the world is not God, and it does not point to
God."[282] Hamilton ultimately rejected liberal Christianity's desire to
imitate Christ and he called for a lifestyle that was "reserved, tolerant,
and characterized by moral goodness."[283] His writings were replete with
references to Albert Camus, Charles Dickens, George Orwell, and Erick
Erickson, co-mingling theology, the social sciences, and literature.

Gradually Hamilton's reputation drew negative attention to Colgate
Rochester. While holding a faculty position in a school that prided itself
in preparing persons for pastoral ministry, Hamilton wrote, "The death of
God must be affirmed; the confidence with which we thought we could
speak of God is gone, and our faith, belief, experience of him are very
poor things indeed." A theologian in a Baptist seminary sadly concluded,
"Radical theology had not the desire nor the ability to serve the
Protestant Church in most of its present institutional forms."[284] The
reception of Hamilton's work among colleagues on the faculty was cool.
President Gene Bartlett observed that nineteen of the faculty were united
in opposition to the "Death of God" perspective. Only Hamilton
himself—the twentieth member of the twenty-person faculty—affirmed
that position. While Hamilton had been "scrupulous" to represent the
classical liberal orthodoxies in teaching the basic course in theology,
"students had found it difficult to keep him in perspective."[285] Hamilton
was asked to teach other courses, including Barth, Bonhoeffer, and
Modern Poetry. The negative pressure upon Professor Hamilton mounted
and in June 1967 he resigned the Clarke chair and joined the faculty of

---

[282] Hamilton, *New Essence of Christianity*, 58.

[283] Ibid., 58.

[284] Thomas J. J. Altizer and William Hamilton, *Radical Theology and the Death of God* (New York: Bobbs-Merrill, 1966) 7.

[285] Desmond Stone, "Save Face or Save Faith: The Big Debate 'Up on The Hill',"
reprinted article in the *Colgate Rochester Divinity School Bulletin* 38/2 (December,
1965): 1–2; "William Hamilton Resigns Post at Colgate Rochester," *Colgate Rochester Divinity School Bulletin* 39/4 (June, 1967): 1.

New College in Sarasota, Florida. While Hamilton assured Colgate Rochester that he was not leaving under protest, President Bartlett responded, "We're a particular kind of theological school, although we were founded by Baptists, we are today and have been for a long time, interdenominational...our traditions are liberal. We cast our lot with creative ministry."[286] To cover the theology course, John Macquarrie, an Anglican from Union Theological Seminary, commuted for a year to Rochester.

Mention should also be made of the contribution that Winthrop S. Hudson (1911–2001) made at Colgate Rochester during the years between 1950 and 1979. Hudson was essentially a church historian, trained at Kalamazoo College, Colgate Rochester Divinity School, and the University of Chicago. He studied with Sidney Mead and worked in the shadow of William Warren Sweet before returning to Rochester as the James B. Colgate Professor of the History of Christianity. He consequently held that post his entire career, except for a short period in the 1940s when he taught at Chicago University. Hudson carried the weight of Baptist identity for the school; he was active in the denomination, the American Baptist Historical Society, and ecumenical organizations. His primary theological interest was in the Baptist doctrine of the church, where he made longstanding contributions. Beginning in 1953, when he penned an article "Baptists Were Not Anabaptists," he defended the Puritan Separatist origins of the Baptists over against the Anabaptist kinship tradition.[287] This became a rallying point for American Baptists in contrast to the dominant Southern Baptist historical tradition. For many it was an affirmation of American Baptist ecumenical theology.[288] Further, Hudson's 1958 article, "The Associational Principle Among Baptists," confirming the longstanding idea of interdependence of churches dating from the eighteenth century, continued to build a case for a doctrine of the universal church.[289] Finally in 1963, Hudson and Norman H. Maring jointly published *A Baptist*

---

[286] Stone, "Save Face," 1.

[287] Winthrop S. Hudson, "Baptists Were Not Anabaptists," *Chronicle* 16/4 (December 1953): 171–79.

[288] See the comment in William R. Estep, *The Anabaptist Story* (Nashville: Broadman Press, 1963) 200–201.

[289] These and other classic essays by Hudson were reprinted in *Baptists in Transition*, and the earlier *Baptist Concepts*.

Manual of Polity and Practice, reflecting the congruency of Rochester's liberal theology with Eastern's "conservative, but progressive" stance in the American Baptist tradition. In that manual, which has become the training guide for new ministers over several generations, Hudson argued that Baptists had too long maintained an inadequate ecclesiology. He responded by raising the standard for a higher doctrine of the church. Influenced by British Baptist statements, Hudson taught the church constitutes the people of God, a servant people, a witnessing community, as well as a ministering and teaching community. He ended up agreeing with the British Baptist statement of 1926, "We believe in the Catholic Church, as the holy society of believers in our Lord Jesus Christ...Every local community thus constituted is regarded by us as both enabled and responsible for self-government...[leading] these communities to associate freely in wider organizations for fellowship and the propagation of the gospel."[290]

William Hamilton's career at Colgate Rochester had done deep damage even to the school's traditionally tolerant community of liberal Baptist support. Through a series of seemingly unrelated events in the next two decades, the Divinity School moved to the periphery of Baptist theological education in the American Baptist tradition.[291] Just when the liberal Baptist community most needed an outstanding center for developing leadership, Colgate Rochester essentially divested itself of its Baptist particularity.

THE CHICAGO SCHOOL

Perhaps the most illustrious and influential academic school of Baptist thought in America developed at the University of Chicago during the first decades of the twentieth century. Called the "Chicago School," its proponents advocated the application of the social sciences to the study

---

[290] Quoted in Norman H. Maring and Winthrop S. Hudson, *A Baptist Manual of Polity and Practice* (Valley Forge: Judson Press, 1963) 42. Hudson was not inclined toward E. Y. Mullins's ideas of soul competency and autonomy of the local church, which he felt spoke of too much individualism.
[291] These events included the "Black Students' Lockout," the conclusion of the turbulent administration of President Gene E. Bartlett, and the creation of the multi-denominational Rochester Center for Theological Studies. The William Newton Clarke Chair in theology was vacated permanently.

of religion.[292] In particular, they stressed contextualization of theological ideas and applied the evolutionary hypothesis to the development of ideas and institutions over the course of time. In theological terms, Chicago was the second institution after Colgate to adopt an unabashed acceptance of higher critical views of Scripture.[293] The development of a distinctive theological tradition paralleled similar progressive thought at the University in education, sociology, and psychology. The transition from one epoch to another allowed some to identify a "genetic" approach to theology. Because Chicago had a full-fledged graduate program of studies, many Baptist theologians were trained in the Divinity School or taught by its graduates. Still other Baptists chose to make Chicago the scapegoat of liberal, modernist Baptist thought. Several accounts have been written of the Chicago School, none of which focuses particularly upon its development within, and impact upon, the Baptist community. From its origin in the work of William Rainey Harper, to the 1940s when the university severed its ties with the Northern Baptist denomination, the Chicago School was a factor with which to be reckoned in the worlds of American evangelical and Baptist church-related higher education.[294]

A key pivotal figure in the Chicago story was George Washington Northrup (1825–1900). Northrup was the original theologian of the first theological school at Chicago. He received degrees from Williams College and Rochester Theological Seminary. He began his teaching career at Rochester Seminary and was known for his free-flowing discussion method rather than lectures and recitation. Northrup was heavily indebted to E. G. Robinson and remembered his teacher as "the greatest teacher of his generation." He admired Robinson's intellect, his free-flowing thought, and his openness to progress and triumph. It was Robinson who showed Northrup the way from an older substitutionary

---

[292] For a very useful bibliography, see "Bibliographic Guide to the Chicago School of Theology," in Charles Harvey Arnold, *Near the Edge of Battle: A Short History of the Divinity School and the "Chicago School of Theology" 1866–1966* (Chicago: Divinity School Association, 1966) 119–31.

[293] See Maring's analysis: "Baptists and Changing Views of the Bible" (Part 2), 45–46.

[294] There is a difference of opinion about exactly when the Chicago School emerged. Some argue that it was with the publication of G. B. Foster's *Finality of the Christian Religion* in 1906, while others posit the beginnings in Harper. See Arnold, *Edge of Battle*, and Bernard Meland, ed., *Theology as an Empirical Science* (Chicago: University of Chicago Press, 1969) 14.

theory of the atonement to one of moral influence. Likewise, Northhrup jettisoned his views of total depravity and reprobation under Robinson's influence.[295] As Robinson's faculty colleague at Rochester for a decade, Northrup affirmed without reservation Robinson's search for new patterns of truth.[296] A. H. Strong, who studied church history at Rochester with Northrup, praised him for his clarity of ideas, but noted, "there was something uncanny and abnormal about him that prevented either his piety or his thinking from getting the firmest hold upon students."[297]

As he left Rochester to preside over a new school in the West, Northrup adopted theology rather than church history as his primary discipline. He continued, however, to employ radical historical criticism in his theological understanding. "Theological theories are being discarded more and more," he mused, "ultra-Biblical speculations—fictions logical, metaphysical, and ethical—which have burdened Christianity for centuries, to its infinite injury, are rapidly giving way."[298] In 1867, Northrup became the first president and professor of systematic theology at the Baptist Union Theological Seminary in Chicago. During the ensuing two decades he gathered about him a collection of young luminaries for the faculty of what came to be known as the Morgan Park Theological Seminary, including Nathaniel Colver, J. C. C. Clark, Albert Arnold, William Hague, R. E. Pattison, and G. W. Warren.[299] In 1878 he brought a young William R. Harper to the vacancy in Hebrew. Northrup himself was probably the harbinger of much of what the Chicago School later would entail.

Northrup's theological system was typically "Reformed," and informed by American and European authors. His categories included a science-like division of primary theological themes, the doctrines of God, and most substantially, the inspiration and authority of Scripture. Teaching in the 1880s at Chicago, Northrup insisted on the supernatural origin of Scripture. He wrote extensively about Christian experience and

---

[295] George W. Northrup, "Ezekiel Gilman Robinson as a Seer," in Johnson, *Robinson*, 212–16.

[296] Many years later, Northrup was influential in bringing his elderly beloved teacher to the University of Chicago to continue to "illuminate and liberate religious thought."

[297] Douglas, *Strong*, 122.

[298] Northrup, "Robinson as a Seer," 216.

[299] On the original school, see Perry J. Stackhouse, *Chicago and the Baptists: A Century of Progress* (Chicago: University of Chicago Press, 1933) 81–82.

the limitations of science. His sources included Charles Hodge, W. G. T. Shedd, Theodore Parker, and from the German schools, Tholuck, Hagenbach, Francke, Bauer, and Turretin. Of the sciences he could still innocently write that they had not had a decided influence upon theological opinions, though he believed that they would become the source of error in the future.[300] A precursor to the importance it would take on among the next generation of the Chicago School adherents, Northrup believed that experience is infinitely progressive in strength. "It is possible for the believer," he wrote, "to have such experiences that he can no more doubt the truth of Christianity than he can doubt his own personal existence."[301] In response to the current interest in eschatology, Northrup asserted that it must involve "knowledge of the future beyond the reach of human sagacity."[302] In fact, he ridiculed premillennialists like A. J. Gordon with such pointed observations as that the advancement of heathenism in the nineteenth century had prolonged the millennium for a million years![303] When the university's first theological program was reorganized, Northrup was one of a small number of the faculty to be retained on the new staff.

Perhaps more than anyone of his era, Northrup was transformed from old orthodoxy to the New Theology. While he wrote and published comparatively little, his extant writings do exhibit the transformation in his thinking. A published essay from 1897 in particular set forth what would be the heart of a theological system that required development.[304] He began by reducing the relevance of historic dogmas such as the regal sovereignty of God, election, infant damnation, and reprobation. Those he termed errors of Catholicism that were only partially corrected in the Reformation. Once a rather stern Calvinist close to the Princeton Theology, Northrup turned on both strict and modified Calvinists, as well as on complex creeds that made the way to salvation ponderous. "Only an unreasonable and arbitrary despot would require assent to the

---

[300] G. W. Northrup, *Lectures on Systematic Theology*, vol. 1 (MS copied by A. H. Carman, 1880–1881) 23.

[301] Ibid., 110.

[302] Ibid., 140.

[303] "Report of the Seventy-Sixth Anniversary of the American Baptist Missionary Union," *Baptist Missionary Magazine* 70/7 (July 1890): 176.

[304] George W. Northrup, "The Fatherhood of God," *American Journal of Theology* 5/3 (July 1901): 473–95.

conditions upon salvation in the Athanasian Creed," he wrote.[305] Such "creed-scription" was unacceptable to a Baptist or an historian. He also set aside time-honored "Reformed" theologians including Augustine, Calvin, Spurgeon, Shedd, and Hodge.

In place of his earlier affirmations, Northrup exalted the Fatherhood of God. Here was the determinative idea of a contemporary Christian theology. He interwove four points in this primary theme: God the Father in creation, moral government, redemption, and retribution.[306] Drawing from his teacher, E.G. Robinson, Northrup concluded the fundamental idea about God was ethical perfection. Through God's fatherhood humankind was made kin to God, bore God's image, and enjoyed a "brotherhood of man." He thus avoided the oft-maligned position of the liberal theologians that through Christ humankind enjoyed the fatherhood of God and through Adam the brotherhood of man. Northrup's theological change brought delight to his colleagues in the new divinity school faculty, for it meant the total acceptance of the historical/critical method in Chicago.[307]

If Northrup was the original parent of Chicago, the foster parent of the "new" Chicago School was William Rainey Harper (1856–1906). He was educated at Muskingham College, the old Baptist Union Theological Seminary, and Yale University where he completed a doctor of philosophy at nineteen years of age under William Whitney, a Sanskrit philologist, and George E. Day, a Hebrew language and history scholar. Harper's dissertation was titled "A Comparative Study of the Preposition in Latin, Greek, Sanskrit, and Gothic." He began teaching at Denison University and then went to the Baptist Union Theological Seminary in Morgan Park where he both taught and earned his bachelor of divinity degree. In 1886 Harper went to Yale where he taught Hebrew and biblical subjects—he was so popular it was said his mail exceeded the amount received by the rest of the entire university! During the summer he devoted full energies to the Chautauqua Institute in Western New

---

[305] Ibid., 494.

[306] He could not escape the problem of one whom God fails to persuade, thus God by virtue of human choice shuts such persons away from the "realm of light."

[307] The essay was published posthumously by the AJT editors at the University of Chicago, who sought to demonstrate in a headnote the evolution in Northrup's views. See Ibid., 473.

York, spearheading popular lectures on Hebrew and religious topics.[308] In 1891 John D. Rockefeller and Thomas W. Goodspeed invited the "young man in a hurry" to become president of a new University of Chicago. Harper promptly accepted, designing and launching a graduate research university related to the Baptist denomination. His contributions as a Baptist included creation of a university-related theological school, superintendency of the Hyde Park Baptist Sunday School, and numerous assignments for Northern Baptist organizations. Harper was easily his generation's premier Baptist educator in the United States.

Baptist historian A. H. Newman observed of W. R. Harper that he influenced Baptist life and thought to an incalculable extent: "We have in his person an elemental force of the first magnitude for the liberalizing of the Baptist denomination."[309] The new president had deep convictions, derived from his scholarly pursuits, about personal and religious freedom. At one point he wrote, "Neither an individual, nor the state, nor the church has the right to interfere with the search for truth or with its promulgation when found."[310] Harper's full-scale commitment to scholarship, personified in his own Hebrew work, was held in a balance with his desire to democratize knowledge, forming what one recent historian has called a dialectic that characterized the formation of the University of Chicago.[311] The philosophical/theological legacy that Harper bequeathed to the university could best be described as critical and scientific, tending toward the historical and linguistic, humanist in its context. The application of these emphases to the teaching and articulation of theological subjects became the foundation of the divinity school. Harper was convinced that laypersons could not handle scientific theology, thus an institutional specialization was needed to advance theology as a science. The basis of this approach in the earliest years was

---

[308] Harper's importance in the study and promotion of the Hebrew language is detailed in Francis Brown's "Introduction," in Robert F. Harper, Francis Brown, and George F. Moore, eds., *Old Testament and Semitic Studies in Memory of William Rainey Harper* (Chicago: University of Chicago Press, 1908) xv.

[309] Newman, "Changes in Baptist Theology," 601.

[310] "William Rainey Harper," *American Biography*, 20:291.

[311] William J. Hynes, *Shirley Jackson Case and the Chicago School: The Socio-Historical Method* (Chicago: Scholars Press, 1981) 1–4.

philological; later it would become historical.[312] At the time of President Harper's death in 1906, what would soon be recognized as "the Chicago School" was well on its way to full emergence.

Harper recruited an exceptional team to build the first graduate school in the Baptist family. From the former university there were Galusha Anderson, Eri Hulburt, and George W. Northrup. Harper recruited from other schools Ernest Dewitt Burton (whom he had known since Denison days), Shailer Mathews, George Burman Foster, John Dewey, Albion Small, and Ezekiel G. Robinson.[313] These men faced squarely the overall problem of epistemology, or "how does one derive an adequate knowledge of truth from the sources available of religious knowledge?"[314]This, then, became the first task of the first generation of the Chicago School.

From its inception under president Harper, Chicago was iconoclastic not only among Baptist institutions, but among all Protestant schools in the United States. A new completely critical approach was brought forth at Chicago. Gone were the Calvinistic traditions identified with Princeton; gone also was any sense of a necessary commitment to evangelical orthodoxy, such as exhibited at Rochester, Newton, Crozer, and Southern seminaries. Theological scholarship at Chicago came to be synonymous with uninhibited academic searching for truth, no matter the outcome.

By 1894 Chicago was teeming with vigorous, creative, and energetic young scholars, all under forty years of age, such as Albion Small, Ernest Dewitt Burton, James Rowland Angell, and Harper.[315] A second wave of recruits brought Shailer Mathews (1863–1941) to the school. Mathews became for many the embodiment of the ideals held by the Chicago School. A native New Englander, he was educated at Colby College and Newton Theological Institution. At Newton, Mathews wrote a thesis under Ernest D. Burton that considered the influence of Paul's rabbinical

---

[312] His own philological skills were best demonstrated in his "Commentary on Amos and Hosea," *International Critical Commentary* (1905), his *Elements of Hebrew* (1881), and three other Hebrew language tools.

[313] Harper brought Robinson out of retirement as a nationally recognized Baptist educator. Robinson taught Christian Evidences and Christian Ethics in the Deptartment of Philosophy 1892–1894. See Johnson, *Robinson*, 135–36; 321.

[314] Arnold, *Edge of Battle*, 27.

[315] Miles H. Krumbine, ed., *The Process of Religion*: *Essays in Honor of Dean Shailer Mathews* (New York: Macmillan, 1933) 8.

career on his later teachings. This was to be the beginnings of his interest in an historical approach to Christian doctrine. In lieu of a graduate degree, Mathews spent two years at the University of Berlin working with Hans Delbruck, Ignaz Jastrow, Paul Scheffer-Boychost, Max Sering, and the economist, Adolf Wagner. During the academic year 1888–89, Burton became ill and Mathews took his place teaching New Testament at Newton. In 1894 Mathews moved to Chicago where he taught New Testament history, and later was appointed chairman of the Department of Christian Theology and Ethics, where he was also the first professor of historical theology. In 1908 Mathews succeeded Eri Hulburt as dean of the Divinity School of the University of Chicago, and arguably became its defining presence. Typologically, Mathews was a moderate in the Chicago School, a "modernistic liberal" who gradually became more radical as his career progressed.[316] Widely published, his best-circulated work was *The Faith of Modernism* (1924) and his best scholarship was *Experience with the Supernatural in Early Christian Times* (1929).[317]

Mathews was to American theology, and to the Chicago School in particular, what Ernst Troeltsch was to German theology. In fact, Mathews brought many of Troeltsch's approaches to America.[318] One writer has helpfully suggested that Mathews's thought stands on three legs.[319] First was his thoroughgoing commitment to the socio-historical method. Each religious tradition must be assessed in its historical context. Christianity, therefore, is a continuous movement of people committed to Jesus. Modernism, as defined by Mathews, was "the use of the methods of modern science to find, state, and use the permanent and central values of inherited orthodoxy in meeting the needs of a modern world." The second leg, comprised of two foci, were values and

---

[316] Cauthen, *Impact of American Religious Liberalism*, 148.

[317] For an assessment of Mathews's work and the application of his methods among his students, see John Thomas McNeill, Mathew Spinka, and Harold R. Willoughby, eds., *Environmental Factors in Christian History* (Chicago: University of Chicago Press, 1939); Kenneth L. Smith and Leonard Sweet, "Shailer Mathews: A Chapter in the Social Gospel Movement," *Foundations* 18/3, 4 (July and September 1975): 219–37; 296–320; and, 19/1, 2 (January, April 1976): 53–68; 152–69.

[318] On Troeltsch's contribution see Welch, *Protestant Thought*, 2:286–311.

[319] See the useful discussion in Leslie A. Murray, "Shailer Mathews: Introduction," in Creighton Peden and Jerome Stone, eds., *The Chicago School of Theology—Pioneers in Religious Inquiry*, vol. 1 (Lewiston: Edward Mellen Press, 1996) 119–23.

contemporary needs. Third, Mathews, like Samuel Zane Batten and Walter Rauschenbusch, was an advocate of social change through Christian values. Mathews was a curious kind of "evangelical egalitarian." As William Hutchison underscores, he often went to great lengths to show that modernists were evangelical Christians who were every bit as loyal to Jesus Christ as any fundamentalist.[320] Additionally, Mathews saw salvation from a social perspective that inferred the further maturation and development of the human personality. He particularly welcomed the "democratization of privilege," which he saw happening in the Progressive Era and the New Deal. Like Harper, Mathews thought one of his principal tasks was to articulate the faith of modernism to the masses, to real men and women in the midst of life's struggles. Consequently he spoke at camp meetings, denominational organizations, and ecumenical bodies, often writing specifically with the non-academic laity in mind.

For Mathews, the organizing principle of theology was historical in character. Theology was a set of presuppositions born of a community's social experiences. The standards of values and the essence of theology were to be found in specific communities, like the community in which Jesus was nurtured. In 1923 Mathews outlined the natural history of any given doctrine, noting that these begin with loyalties and hope, followed by the development of a vocabulary wherein words become symbols of a group's attitudes. At this stage, groups make certain words tests of membership and the group's beliefs come to be standardized. Eventually, Mathews found that subversive groups emerge within the community offering rival interpretations to previously unchallenged standards. Out of that struggle come agreements concerning given formulai to be accepted as legitimate symbols of a given group's majority attitudes. Finally, Mathews observed, strong emotional associations within groups are formed.[321]

What was most troubling about Mathews to many Baptists was his complete redefinition of theology. From his study of history, wherein he identified "social minds" that shaped the vocabularies of their respective communities, he thought theological doctrine to be essentially analogical.

---

[320] Hutchison, *Modernist Impulse*, 278–82 presents a personal side of Mathews not seen in his writings or administrative work.

[321] See Edwin Aubrey's discussion in "Theology and the Social Process," in Krumbine, *The Process of Religion*, 35.

Rather than being informed by a biblical tradition, Mathews wrote of a "cosmic interplay" which one may perceive but never fully comprehend. Christians use metaphorical language to express relative and redemptive realties to meet their felt needs. He had little time for philosophical inquiry, instead preferring to focus his attention on actual Christian communities. Vitally concerned churchmen and practicing congregations produced theology. In this way, Mathews defined empirical theology as "church-centered."[322] His language was baptistic, but his meaning moved well beyond their long-held orthodox traditions.

Next to Harper and Mathews in prominence was Shirley Jackson Case (1872–1947). He was reared a Canadian Free Baptist, with revival tradition and freedom of expression as strong values. This Freewill background gave Case a lifelong aversion to predestination, and a positively Arminian orientation to human freedom and responsibility.[323] He graduated from Acadia University with an undergraduate degree, followed by an M.A. in mathematics under Daniel F. Higgins. Later, he completed bachelor of divinity and doctor of philosophy degrees at Yale University under Benjamin W. Bacon and F. C. Porter. Bacon was a devotee of Julius Wellhausen and Adolf Juelicher, who introduced the theory of multiple authorship of the Pentateuch. Bacon's own work on Exodus radically altered biblical scholarship in the United States.[324] Case's New Testament dissertation was entitled "Sources of Information for a Study of Pre-Pauline Christology." Primarily a social historian, Case laid the groundwork for understanding the historical context of theology. As he put it, "History may be said to make religion." In his long career as professor of New Testament, early church history, and dean of the Divinity School at the University of Chicago, Case wrote sixteen books and over ninety articles. Significantly, he led in the American Society of Church History, the Association of Theological Schools, and the Northern Baptist Board of Education and the Federal

---

[322] Meland, *Empirical Tradition*, 20–21.

[323] There are two helpful biographies of Case: Louis B. Jennings, *The Bibliography and Biography of Shirley Jackson Case* (Chicago: University of Chicago Press, 1949), and the more recent insightful William J. Hynes, *Shirley Jackson Case*, 15–34.

[324] "Benjamin Wisner Bacon" in Vergilius Ferm, ed., *Contemporary American Theology: Theological Autobiographies* , 2 Vols. (New York Roundtable Press, 1932), II: 25–26. Bacon was a liberal Congregationalist.

Council of Churches. His distinguished students included Ernest Parsons, Ernest C. Colwell, John T. McNeill, and William Warren Sweet.[325]

Historical methodology, as Case used it, took novel and radical departures in New Testament studies and church history. In the New Testament context, Case assumed that there are primal units of tradition that construct a picture of Jesus at home in his Palestinian environment. These could be distinguished from traditions of a later origin; these spoke to a social situation quite different in the early church. What was sacrificed from a Baptist perspective was the uniqueness of Christ and the doctrine that follows suit. More important to Case was the Christ of History, which he could separate from the Jesus of history.[326] Moving to church history proper, Case rejected Christian or providential views of history as applied to what he called "human history." He meant instead to isolate and analyze the human causes and influences behind historic events. Case believed that history evolves and that observation demonstrates evidence of progress in material well-being, intellectual knowledge, and more slowly, society and spiritual life. The study of history must unquestionably include religion, and this must be done scientifically with a method of procedure that is strictly inductive of experimentally verifiable data. This approach allowed him to value constantly renewed activism: "Religion needs today, not less divine guidance, but more human virility."[327] Here was the germ of the Baptist understanding of the social gospel that connected him with other Chicago activists like Shailer Mathews and, of course, Walter Rauschenbusch at Rochester.

Case's understanding of Scripture turned his denomination's accepted doctrine upside down. In 1910 he spent a sabbatical year at the universities of Marburg and Berlin, acquainting himself with scholars such as Adolph Juelicher, Wilhelm Heitmuller, and Walter Bauer in New Testament, as well as Wilhelm Hermann and Martin Rude in theology.

---

[325] There are two excellent studies of Case's scholarship: Louis B. Jennings, "Shirley Jackson Case: A Study in Methodology" (Ph.D. diss., University of Chicago, 1964) and Claude Martin Shuler, "An Interpretation and Evaluation of the Work of Shirley Jackson Case as a Historian of Early Christianity" (Th.D. diss., Iliff School of Theology, 1964).

[326] Shirley Jackson Case, *The Historicity of Jesus: A Criticism of the Contention That Jesus Never Lived, a Statement of the Evidence for His Existence, an Estimate of His Relation to Christianity* (Chicago: University of Chicago Press, 1912) 309.

[327] Shirley Jackson Case, *The Christian Philosophy of History* (Chicago: University of Chicago Press, 1943) 56–67, 187.

He would write: "The historian knows that the Bible is an incidental outgrowth of the Hebrew and Christian religions over a thousand year period...It did not generate them, they generated it...To treat the Bible as though it were the one authentic deposit of religion in its final form—a body of revelation once for all delivered to the saints—is to substitute a part for the whole."[328] Case acknowledged limits to the scientific methodology of approaching historical (and so, theological) studies: "The scientific study of history proposes to determine only what has been in the past; it claims no authority to issue decrees upon what ought to be in the present and future."[329]

The problem of what had become of theology under the scrutiny of historical criticism was left for resolution to Case's colleagues George Burman Foster and Gerald Birney Smith. Foster (1858–1918) was a Lincolnesque figure from West Virginia who was educated at West Virginia University and Rochester Theological Seminary.[330] In seminary and long after, he always considered himself one of President Strong's "boys." A prodigy, he served a congregation at Saratoga Springs, New York, after which he turned to teaching theology at McMaster University in Toronto. To further his awareness of contemporary trends in theology, Foster studied in Germany under Julius Kaftan, Adolf von Harnack, Wilhelm Hermann, and Albert Ritschl. He soon caught Harper's attention, who considered the young teacher one of "the greatest thinkers in his line." Harper relentlessly pursued Foster over a four-year period, 1891–95, to come to Chicago to "improve the efficiency of the theological department" and strengthen the graduate doctoral program. Eventually, Foster succeeded George Northrup in the theology chair at Chicago.

Foster became part of the "Ritschlian School" that virtually replaced philosophical theology with moral life as illustrated in the biography of Jesus. Following Immanuel Kant, he arrived at virtually the same place Shirley Jackson Case had in de-emphasizing confidence in Scripture and traditional doctrine in favor of "faith." Labeled a "naturalistic theist" or even a pure humanist, Foster wrote of the "finality of the Christian

---

[328] Ibid., 169.

[329] Shirley Jackson Case, "The Religious Meaning of the Past," *Journal of Religion* 4 (1924): 576–91.

[330] For a fine biography and theological analysis, see Hjalmar W. Johnson, "The Religious Thought of George B. Foster" (Ph. D. diss., Yale University, 1931).

religion." By this he meant that, in Jesus, God was given realized personality and his humanness in turn gave successive generations the divine gifts of authentic freedom and moral consciousness. For Foster, historical and literary criticism had eliminated the "Christ of faith" in favor of the "Jesus of history," who became a supreme example of "dying to live."[331] In his major work, *The Finality of the Christian Religion* (1906), he argued that the certitude of the Christian faith was established within the consciousness of an individual and this produced an ultimate and perfect truth, despite change and development in life. He utterly rejected "authority religion," by which he meant traditional scholarship, the Bible, the church, and theologians. "The religion of Jesus," he believed, "is personality religion...religion is too simple for the theologians. They cannot teach religion any more than they can teach grass to grow, birds to sing, or lovers to love."[332]

Foster did not become a widely read theologian. Many thought his writings incomprehensible. One observer quipped, "The difficulty of his prose protected him. Had he been as clear as, say, H. L. Mencken, ...Foster would have been a more vilified figure in our intellectual history."[333] His reception in the university and among local Baptist churches, however, soon became contentious. He clashed with university officials in 1901 over the possible appointment of William Newton Clarke to the school, and in 1904 he was moved to the Philosophy of Religion Department when Shailer Mathews took up the chair in theology. The publication of Foster's book declaring the finality of the Christian religion deeply divided Baptists in Chicago and in Illinois generally. While he survived an assault on his teaching position and ministerial credentials in 1906, the ax fell in 1909. Opposition to the book spread quickly in the ministerial community, which in turn produced a resolution from the Baptist Ministers Meeting that "the views set forth in this book are contrary to the Scriptures and that its teachings and tendency are subversive of the vital and essential truths of the Christian faith."[334] Foster was expelled from the Ministers Meeting (which amounted to a regional clergy trial) and the ministers asked his church, Hyde Park Baptist, to drop him from its membership upon pain

---

[331] Maring, "Baptists and Changing Views of the Bible" (Part 2), 44.

[332] George B. Foster, *The Finality of the Christian Religion* (1906) 6–7.

[333] Hutchison, *Modernist Impulse*, 215.

[334] The resolution is quoted in Stackhouse, *Chicago and the Baptists*, 169–70.

of the congregation being disfellowshipped from the Association.[335] Even the ever-tolerant Harper wavered in his support: "He keeps putting his foot into trouble as rapidly as any man I have ever known. We have stood by him bravely, but he seems to have no thought that people must be educated before they can enjoy…or even approve of his position."[336]

Harper's successor, Harry Pratt Judson (also president of the Northern Baptist Convention), was not as supportive and quickly sought to reduce the impact of Foster's work on the university. Foster's impact on the school's Baptist constituency went from bad to worse. He became the unwitting catalyst that spawned the financial support of Los Angeles millionaire Lyman Stewart for the preparation of the *Fundamentals* (1910–1915),[337] as well as the establishment of the Northern Baptist Theological Seminary in 1913. In the midst of the turmoil, Foster responded with characteristic sarcasm: "I don't know whether they want me to get out of the conference, or get out of the church, or get off the earth." He nevertheless affirmed his historic faith: "Never in my life have I denied the divineness of Jesus Christ…Jesus is the best we know, human or divine…the problem is not whether Jesus is as good as God, but whether God is as good as Jesus is."[338]

Foster is said to have raised the difficult questions confronting modern man. Tortured by Nietsche's writings, Foster moved haltingly from Ritschlianism to pragmatism, and finally to his own form of humanism. Having rejected biblical religion, he pursued a contemporary, contextual faith. As he moved to discredit "authority religion," he abandoned traditional language about God that used terms such as "theism" and "transcendence." Not surprisingly, some have identified

---

[335] The maker of the original resolution and a staunch opponent of Foster was Austen Kennedy DeBlois, Canadian-born pastor at First Baptist, Chicago, and later president of Shurtleff College. DeBlois was the second president of Eastern Baptist Theological Seminary, a conservative evangelical Northern Baptist school in Philadelphia. For a sample of his thought, see *Evangelism in the New Age* (Philadelphia: Judson Press, 1933).

[336] Creighton Peden, *The Chicago School: Voices in Liberal Religious Thought* (Bristol IN: Wyndham Hall Press, 1987) 26–27.

[337] Edgar A Towne, "George Burman Foster: Introduction," in *The Chicago School of Theology–Pioneers in Religious Inquiry*, vol. 1, ed. W. Creighton Peden and Jerome A. Stone (Lewiston NY: Edward Mellen Press, 1996) 2.

[338] Quoted in Edgar A. Towne, "A Single-minded Theologian: George Burman Foster at Chicago" (Part 1), *Foundations* 20/1 (January 1977): 168–70.

Foster as the first "death of God" theologian in America.[339] His concept of "radical immanentism" invested God with all of the ethical and rational values, physical energies, and ontological attributes of the older conception of God, but none of the authoritarian deity of an ancient faith. In his second major work, *The Function of Religion in Man's Struggle for Existence* (1909), Foster wrote that religion had arisen in part as the creation of human beings in response to their own needs. "Man made the gods do for him what he could not do for himself,"[340] he asserted. As Foster vacillated between despair and creativity, he concluded that it was unacceptable to endeavor "to give up a real God, a real man, and a real world."[341] Constantly under fire, he retreated to his self-understanding as "a typical, loyal, old-fashioned Baptist, believing and trusting in the grace of God." Lamentably, Foster died before he was able to resolve the conflicts in which he found himself and had also involved the Chicago School.[342] His most outstanding protégés were Eustace Haydon and Douglas C. MacIntosh.

Similar to Foster, but much less radical, was Gerald Birney Smith (1868–1929).[343] Smith was educated at Brown University, Union Theological Seminary and Columbia University. At Union he studied theology with William Adams Brown, who provided an overseas study opportunity for Smith. Under Brown's tutelage, he was especially drawn toward Ritschlianism In Europe, Smith spent a year with Wilhelm Hermann at Marburg, and shorter periods with Adolf von Harnack in Berlin and Auguste Sabatier in Paris. Sabatier's dialectical method of separating relative and transient doctrines from that which endures and must be re-contextualized was attractive and useful to Smith.[344] In 1900

---

[339] Peden, *Chicago School*, 133.

[340] George B. Foster, *The Function of Religion in Man's Struggle for Existence* (Chicago: University of Chicago Press, 1909), 49.

[341] Quoted in Hutchinson, *Modernist Impulse,* 218–19.

[342] Foster continues to be a negative benchmark for conservative Baptists. In a recent essay, Timothy George treats him as a "high caliber" heretic: "The Baptist Tradition," in Hart and Mohler, *Theological Education*, 44.

[343] For a useful analysis of Smith, see Larry L. Greenfield, "The Theology of Gerald Birney Smith" (Ph.D. diss., University of Chicago, 1978).

[344] Auguste Sabatier (1839–1901) taught theology at the University of Strasbourg, and later at the University of Paris where he was dean of the Protestant Theological Faculty. His method is well presented in *The Religions of Authority and the Religion of*

he was appointed an instructor in theology in the University of Chicago Divinity School and over the next thirteen years rose to full professor of theology. He was an administrative understudy of Shirley Jackson Case and exerted a wide influence in the academy, editing the *Journal of Religion* and helping to found the American Theological Society. Less well known than his colleagues, he remained involved in the Chicago School a generation beyond Foster and was articulate and effective in his relations with the churches. Smith is considered a bridge between naturalism and empiricism, a moderate among the modernists. His most important work was *Social Idealism and the Changing Theology* (1913).[345] Later in his career, however, Smith was less interested in the complexities of theology in dialogue with science and turned to the symbols and structures of the arts to inform theological ideas.[346]

Smith was influenced in many ways by his colleagues among the Chicago faculty. He looked to their experience to develop ways in which he might apply critical methodology to systematic theology. He accepted the socio-historical method and used it to construct a new theological understanding, outlining a fourfold task for theology: establishing historical understanding, analysis of contemporary needs, interpretation of those needs in a practical way, and creating an apologetic defense of the convictions one reached. Taking a clue from but soon moving beyond William Newton Clarke at Colgate, who thought theology derived its material from virtually "anywhere," Smith turned toward a more scientifically disciplined approach in his pursuit of a contemporary and relevant critical theological apparatus.[347]

During the earlier years of his career, Smith concentrated on applying recently considered connections between democracy and science to the discipline of theological inquiry. From John Dewey in Chicago's Department of Philosophy, he took the dynamic of evolutionary change, proposing that theology evolves and adjusts to its environment and must meet contemporary needs in order to maintain relevant vitality. As time went on, Smith showed evidence of influences from William James,

---

the Spirit, originally published in 1897. Sabatier was a key component in the transition from a theology of authority to emphasizing religious experience.

[345] See the introductory essay by Larry L. Greenfield, "Gerald Birney Smith," in Peden and Stone, *Chicago School of Theology,* 1:187192.

[346] Meland, *Empirical Theology,* 26.

[347] Ibid., 217; Clarke, *Outline,* 10.

Henri Bergson, and other philosophic evolutionists. For much of his career, Smith was greatly enamored of science and sought to make theological discourse accountable to it. Instead of doctrine standing apart in supernatural revelation, Smith held that "it must be susceptible of verification by repeated experiments; it must be seen to fit in with the conclusions of other sciences."[348] A theologian, he held, must be an investigator rather than an advocate. Investigation will show that "so sacredly guarded a doctrine as the Trinity has a history which includes an interesting variety of interpretations." For him, "the key to a proper understanding of doctrine is to be found in correct apprehension of the problems which demanded solution."[349] Smith set out four tasks that enable contemporary formulation of religious beliefs: historical understanding of one's social inheritance; analysis of present religious beliefs; interpretation of religious belief that demonstrates practical efficiency and is rationally defensible; an apologetic defense of those religious convictions reached. Here he connected closely with the theological and religious modernism advocated by Shailer Mathews.

An additional word needs to be said about Smith's position on democracy and theology. He saw higher criticism as a modern response to authoritarianism. Criticism was therefore a liberating, democratic force: "Now criticism in the realm of biblical study means that the utterances of Scripture are subjected to the judgments of men, exactly as democracy in government means the deeds of the ruler are to be judged by the citizens of the country." Smith was an incurable optimist and believed that democracy was the vehicle to carry Christianity into the future. "Democracy," he wrote, "by its very nature, is a gigantic experiment…freedom to experiment carries with it freedom to make mistakes…to insist prematurely on dogmatic finalities would be to defeat the best outcome of human progress."[350] Democracy—still a novel experiment in modern Western history—and science went hand in glove, for experimentation produces glimpses of truth. Only an attitude of democracy produces a "forward-looking faith." Here Smith exhibited an appreciation for the democratic idealism of American president, Woodrow Wilson. Inevitably, Smith knew, "democracy is more

---

[348] Gerald B. Smith, "Task and Method of Systematic Theology," *American Journal of Theology 14/2 (April 1910)* 232–33.

[349] Ibid., 222.

[350] Ibid., 347.

interested in the possibilities of the future than the sanctities of the past."[351] Democratic idealism was the means by which he made contemporary what was previously historic Christianity. But Smith's contributions to American Baptist life through the study of democracy and theology had profound negative implications for his Baptist constituency. As he advocated that an intelligent citizenship is preferred over the "inculcation of dogmatic propaganda," he called upon clergy to "stop preaching about a supernatural, autocratic God and minister to contemporary needs."[352] In so doing, Smith dismissed the average Baptist minister who continued to believe in and teach about God's kingdom in terms of a supernatural world.

Gerald Birney Smith also had an important impact on formal Baptist theological education. This was reflected in his classic essay titled "The Indispensable Minimum of the Theological Curriculum" (1918), into which he incorporated the teaching principles and theological emphases of the Chicago School. Smith contrasted the older tradition of Baptist theological education and its preoccupation with the Bible to contemporary religious ideals as expressed by modernism. Instead of enthroning "divine rights," he argued for popular or democratic rights. Religious and social conformity needed to be replaced with open-ended inquiry. With classical studies and theology giving way to vocational and technical studies, it was the Chicago School that first applied the terminology "professional education" to the seminary curriculum. Smith held that the provincialism of the past was giving way to a "world conscience." He argued that the nature of Baptist theological instruction had to change, and he quoted his friend E. Y. Mullins of Southern Baptist Seminary in that vein: "The most important thing for a minister is that he shall live as a citizen in the world in which he has got to live."[353]

In connection with the Chicago School, mention must also be made of Douglas Clyde MacIntosh (1877–1948).Having completed his bachelor's degree at McMaster University, MacIntosh subsequently earned graduate degrees from the University of Chicago. While he was not on the

---

[351] Gerald Birney Smith, "Christianity and the Spirit of Democracy," *American Journal of Theology* 21/3 (July 1917): 350.

[352] Quoted in Peden, *Chicago School*, 47.

[353] Gerald Birney Smith, "The Indispensable Minimum of Theological Curriculum." Paper Delivered at the Conference of Baptist Theological Seminaries (Massachusetts, 1918) quoted in Brackney, *Baptist Life and Thought*, 320–23.

Chicago faculty, he was exemplary of the first generation of the Chicago School, and he remained close to its faculty throughout his career. He taught briefly at Brandon College, a Baptist university in western Canada, before going to Yale University for over three decades as professor of theology and philosophy of religion. Most historical theologians classify him as an empirical theologian in the Modernist tradition.[354] He liked to characterize himself as "untraditionally orthodox."[355]

MacIntosh refused throughout his career to be separated from his evangelical roots. His mother implanted a firm faith in him that was later confirmed in a revivalistic setting. He wrote in 1932, "I have not been able to shake off the conviction that to retain its vitality Christianity must find a way to continue to be evangelistic. The outer forms of evangelism may need to be changed from time to time, but when the evangelistic spirit is dead the end is not far off."[356] His educational pilgrimage, however, pushed him in new, radical directions. James TenBroeke at McMaster and Frederick Tracy at the University of Toronto introduced him to William James, Immanuel Kant, John Stuart Mill, and Rudolph H. Lotze. TenBroeke in particular emphasized the prejudicial aspects of both rationalism and evangelicalism.[357] McIntosh credited George Cross in the History Department with introducing him to German theologians. The Yale influence was strong in his undergraduate years and he left McMaster with rebellious spirit, given to questioning all that was traditional in the Baptist expression of religious faith.

MacIntosh's work at the University of Chicago produced in him just the opposite effect. There the liberal teaching of the Chicago School caused him to be constructive and want to conserve the essentials of the Christian faith. Although he planned to study at Chicago and then move on to Yale, he found fulfillment at Chicago. He was drawn to George Burman Foster, who introduced him to Ritstchlianism. His doctoral dissertation, "The Reaction Against Metaphysics in Theology," was done under Foster and Gerald B. Smith. Like his teachers and friends of the

---

[354] Cauthen, *American Religious Liberalism*, 171–73; Hutchison, *Modernist Impulse*, 213–15.

[355] "Douglas Clyde MacIntosh," in *Contemporary American Theology*, 1:318.

[356] Ibid., 289.

[357] James TenBroeke, "Biblical Criticism in Some of Its Theological and Philosophical Relations," *Biblical World* 2/6 (December 1893): 444–51.

Chicago School, Macintosh rejected dogmatic theology as well as the Christocentric emphases of the evangelical liberals. Instead, he argued for a religious faith that is squarely rooted in reason and religious experience. He devoted much of his life's effort to devising a workable methodology for theology as an empirical science. In this regard, he was materially different from his friends at Chicago. What MacIntosh meant by empirical theology was not grounded in social process, but the religious experience of ordinary people. He held that methodology, intuition, observation, and reflection were of equal importance in theological reflection.[358]

MacIntosh began with trying to establish a body of experimentally tested religious knowledge, to which could be added other postulates. He was concerned with empirical religious data, provided by social science methods, theological laws derived from these data, and theoretically valid propositions about God that bore the probability of truth. For his sources of religious data, he was willing to admit material from any world religion. His "laws" were predicated on the logical notion that God acts consistently with respect to human needs and requests and that this action may be observed across time. Further, theological postulates arise from the concerns of religious thought, such as the moral nature of God, the relation of God to history, and the future of all things. An example of MacIntosh's thinking is his assertion that "there ought to be a God, i.e., it would be well for humans if there were a God." Further, in his view, it was theoretically possible there is a God; prominent philosophers and scientists pointed to the necessary being or real possibility of the divine. MacIntosh followed the pattern of the Chicago School in his Christology, finding in Jesus a moral example and a symbol of God's redeeming power while rejecting the relevance of the classical theory of atonement. For MacIntosh the importance of Jesus lay in his life, teachings, in leading people to an experience of God.

There is insight into MacIntosh's doctrine of the church late in his career in the foreword that he wrote for W. R. McNutt's *Polity and Practice of Baptist Churches* (1935). MacIntosh understood the church to be a "God-ruled" body of believers, a realm where God's will is voluntarily done. He believed the sovereignty of God and the freewill of man were reconciled in the local church. Once regenerated, believers

---

[358] See the helpful essay by Bernard Meland, "Introduction: The Empirical Tradition in Theology at Chicago," in *Empirical Theology*, 11.

could act competently under God, to capture E. Y. Mullins's contemporary terminology. MacIntosh also spoke of the church as a fellowship of the religiously competent. It was to be independent of ecclesiastical and political authority to follow the will of God as the only absolute and all-sufficient law. In this regard, he was especially protective against governmental laws and regulations over the church, so evident from his own life experience in being denied U.S. citizenship. Further, like other Baptist theologians, he linked his understanding of the Baptist ordinances to ecclesiology. Baptism and the Lord's Supper are "dramatic professions of faith," but nevertheless more a matter of pledges than performances of grace. He considered them indispensable to the psychology of healthy religious experience, but never indispensable for fellowship in the church.[359]

Through his teaching at Yale and mentoring scores of graduate students, MacIntosh left a deep imprint on the process of academic theological inquiry for many Baptists. While he took a radical position methodologically, he did not lose his basic understanding of theistic Christianity. While most think his attempt to establish theology as an empirical science failed,[360] he was utterly devoted to restoring theology as a serious academic endeavor.

Another Chicago School product whose genetic influence in Baptist life should not be overlooked was Edwin Ewart Aubrey (1896–1956). Born in Scotland and educated at Bucknell University and the University of Chicago, Aubrey received his doctorate in Christian theology under Shailer Mathews and Shirley Jackson Case.[361] After teaching at Carleton College, Miami University, and Vassar College, Aubrey returned to Chicago in 1929 to teach Christian theology, where he eventually became the department chairman. In *Man's Search for Himself* (1940),

---

[359] Douglas C. MacIntosh, foreword in W. R. McNutt, *Polity and Practices of Baptist Churches* (Philadelphia: Judson Press, 1935) i-iv.

[360] Claude Welch described MacIntosh's formulas as "either sterile or comical, not doing justice to the Baptist piety out which they sprang." He also points out that none of MacIntosh's students took up his project in a continuing pursuit. Welch, *Protestant Thought*, 2:228.

[361] According to Mathews's son, Aubrey was the choice of Dean Mathews to assess his theology. See Robert Eldon Mathews, "Shailer Mathews: A Biographical Note," and Aubrey's own contribution, "Theology and the Social Process," in Miles H. Krumbine, ed., *The Process of Religion: Essays in Honor of Dean Shailer Mathews* (New York: Macmillan, 1933).

Aubrey drew new lines for a doctrine of mankind. Following the lead of his Chicago mentors, he found that sociology and psychology enable human beings to understand themselves in light of their participation in social fellowship. Further, the authentic—spiritual, social, moral, and ethical—transformation of persons, destined to set them free, is a work of divine enablement through the activity of the Holy Spirit in and through community. "Consequently," he argued, "the whole range of social life comes under the scrutiny of the church."[362] From biblical sources he affirmed that "Men ought to love each other" and that "no better embodiment of love in a dynamic world is to be found than Jesus Christ."[363] Like many Protestant theologians between the world wars of the twentieth century, Aubrey found himself needing either to justify existing theology or develop a new system. It seemed to him that theology had become too much an individualistic matter, plagued by conflicts with science and an economy of abundance.[364]Here he was referring to the "privatization" of religious faith at the individual level. Calling for a radical examination of faith, Aubrey argued for a creative theology that longed for peace, contended against secularism, resolved the tension between individualism and collectivism, and could effectively be applied to actual circumstances. His view was that "theology originates in social communication of Christian experience, and its pertinence is in the social experience of Christian people."[365]

Baptist antagonism toward the Chicago School during the 1920s reached a fevered pitch. Local ministers had long denounced Professor Foster for his attacks upon "scriptural Christianity," and Shirley Jackson Case won no friends in the midst of World War I for his denunciation of premillennialism as "a wild and relatively harmless fancy."[366] As Fundamentalist factions among the Northern Baptists coalesced to form the Baptist Bible Union in 1922, efforts were made to investigate and halt the perceived modernism and apostasy in Baptist schools, notably at Chicago and Crozer Theological Seminary. When a Committee of Nine

---

[362] Edwin E. Aubrey, *Man's Search for Himself* (Nashville: Cokesbury, 1940) 198.

[363] Ibid., 214–15.

[364] Edwin E. Aubrey, *Present Theological Tendencies* (New York: Harper Brothers, 1936) 211–26.

[365] Edwin E. Aubrey, *Living the Christian Faith* (New York: The Macmillan Co., 1939) 117

[366] Shirley Jackson Case, "The Premillennial Menace," *Biblical World* 52 (1918): 17.

was appointed to gather evidence of teachings inconsistent with Baptist principles, the University of Chicago did not respond to the questionnaires. Leaders among the fundamentalists like Jasper C. Massee then openly accused Dean Shailer Mathews of heresy. The resultant rift between the Chicago School and the denomination of its religious heritage proved irreparable.[367]

Baptist relationships with the Chicago School continued to deteriorate dramatically after the 1940s. More and more faculty were recruited for the Divinity School who were not Baptist. New names like Wilhelm Pauck (United Church of Christ), E. S. Ames (Disciples of Christ), Albert Eustace Haydon (Baptist turned universalist), and Henry Nelson Wieman (Presbyterian) dominated Morgan Park. In 1944 the Northern Baptist Convention approved major changes in the school's charter, lessening Baptist influence on the institution's board of trustees and removing the requirement that the school's president be a Baptist. Beginning in the late 1940s Baptist faculty prospects bypassed Chicago in significant numbers for positions at nonsectarian universities and theological school doctoral programs not besieged by institutional strife.[368] Some hold that the Chicago School, insofar as it is identified with the socio-historical method of interpretation, ended in the late 1940s as the personnel recruited by Shirley Jackson Case retired or left the Divinity School.[369]

How could a leading voice for the historical-critical approach to Christianity develop in a denominational tradition that historically valued the authority of Scripture, the piety of Christian experience, and was characterized by a deep embrace of the supernatural nature of the faith? One answer lies in the organizing principle of Baptist life, namely the local congregation. By the late nineteenth century, most Baptists in the Northern states concluded that there was no earthly authority greater than

---

[367] See the discussion in Hynes, *Case and the Chicago School,* 6–8.

[368] Among those institutions I have identified as providing graduate degrees for aspiring Baptist faculty were Boston University, Princeton Theological Seminary, Temple University, University of Pennsylvania, Yale University, Columbia University/Union Theological Seminary, Duke University, McMaster University, Vanderbilt University, Southern Baptist Theological Seminary, Northern Baptist Theological Seminary, New Orleans Baptist Seminary, Southwestern Baptist Seminary, Dallas Theological Seminary, and the combination of the University of California at Berkeley/Graduate Theological Union.

[369] Hynes, *Case and the Chicago School*, 31.

the local church despite the wide differentiation among churches and associations. Where modernist thinkers clustered for education, they were nurtured by strong local congregations such as Hyde Park Baptist in Chicago, the leading Baptist churches of Rochester (New York), Newton Centre (Massachusetts), Granville (Ohio), Philadelphia (Pennsylvania), as well as many of the older urban congregations across the denomination. For the most part, the wealthy, socially conscious churches welcomed the new ideas and approaches that graduates of Chicago, Rochester, Newton, and Crozer brought to them.

A second explanatory factor lies in the deep desire of many congregations and leaders to have a truly learned progressive ministry that participated shoulder to shoulder with other Protestants. A rising tide of ecumenical opportunities in the period 1880 to 1920 called upon Baptists as the leading evangelical thinkers of mainline Protestantism. In accepting that role, Baptist leaders did not account for the discontinuity between their identity up through the mid-nineteenth century and what they were becoming under the later influences of New Theology and higher education.

COBB DIVINITY SCHOOL AND THE FREEWILL BAPTISTS

The impact of professional academic theology may even be traced in the smaller Baptist bodies, notably the Freewill Baptists. The sect was founded by Benjamin Randal and a small coterie of rural New England itinerants. As time went on a strong interest in education developed among the Freewill Baptists, resulting in the founding of schools in New York, New England, and the Midwest. One of the most prominent was Bates College in Lewiston, Maine. From its inception the school had a Bible department. That department eventually evolved into a theological program known as Cobb Divinity School. Small but influential in both New England and the Maritime Provinces, Cobb's reputation was attributed early to the labors of John J. Butler.

Educated in the academies of New England, then at Bowdoin College and Andover Theological Seminary, John J. Butler (1814–1891) rose to lead the institutional development of the Freewill Baptists. In 1854 he became the principal lecturer at New Hampton Institute and was the premier theologian at Cobb for nineteen years, after which he taught briefly at Hillsdale College in Michigan. From his Andover days, Butler was well-versed in Reformation thought and the classical English and

American theologians. His reading included Luther, Calvin, Edwards, Gill, Wesley, and Hopkins, plus the more contemporary Timothy Dwight, Nathaniel W. Taylor, and Charles G. Finney. He had a deep appreciation for Johann G. Knapp, the noted German theologian who stressed evangelical emphases. Butler represented a significant intellectual link between the Baptist Academy and the holiness movement, maintaining a deep appreciation for the writings of the antislavery Wesleyan Methodist, Luther Lee.

Butler broke with the traditional Baptist theological systems, however, on some key points. He held intellectual culture to be insufficient, because "abstract study and scientific exercises will lessen the spirit of devotion."[370] The starting point of Christian theology for Butler was the nature of ministry. The ministry is essentially supernatural and the purpose of theology is to elucidate "Gospel Redemption." The study of any system of theology was for that reason most suited to its practical applications in the life of the church. He consequently included a substantial section in his systematic theology on "The Church and Its Institutions."

The predictable Freewill or Arminian Baptist positions were well articulated in Butler's volume. He held that limited atonement was "wholly foreign from the scriptural representation of the subject."[371] He listed nine propositions in support of general atonement, including the benevolence of God that was open to all persons, that Christ died for all persons, Scripture's record of indiscriminately offered gospel invitations, and that all persons are required to exercise faith in Christ. Following Thomas W. Jenkyn on the matter, Butler asserted "The gospel is an authoritative warrant to induce every sinner to believe that his salvation is a possible case."[372]

Perhaps the best-rationalized statements of the freedom of human will from a Baptist perspective is found in Butler's work. Treating the "will" under the general heading of moral agency, Butler argued that for an act to be moral it must be free—that is one must have the power of contrary choice respecting it. The government of God extends over all moral beings; and all are under an unchangeable obligation to do right. All in

---

[370] John J. Butler, *Natural and Revealed Theology: A System of Lectures* (Dover, NH: Freewill Baptist Printing Establishment, 1861), 27.
[371] Ibid., 227-228.
[372] Ibid..

this world, or in any other, have the ability to do their duty. This is a moral axiom. There is no reason to doubt but even the lost are ever sinning as well as ever suffering. Much more, therefore, must it be allowed, that all in a state of probation, are free to obey and live, or to sin and perish in their sins.[373]

CROZER THEOLOGICAL SEMINARY

Founded in 1867 in Chester, Pennsylvania, an industrial city to the south of Philadelphia, Crozer's theological tradition is one of the more fascinating among the American Baptist institutions. The school began as a post-Civil War family enterprise of the descendants of John Price Crozer (1793–1866), a textile manufacturer. His son, Samuel P. Crozer, gave generously to found the institution and acted directly in the recruitment of its inaugurating faculty. Chosen as the school's first president was an orthodox pastor from Peoria, Illinois, Henry Griggs Weston (1820–1909). A man possessed at the core with a pastoral temperament, Weston was well-versed in the English New Testament. His labors placed a four-decade stamp of pastoral and evangelical Baptist identity on the school. Writing at the turn of the nineteenth century, a conservative Baptist historian found that Crozer under Weston was "safely among the positive forces for the conservation of Baptist orthodoxy."[374]

Weston was chosen president of the seminary and first faculty appointment because of his outstanding reputation as a leading orthodox Baptist pastor. Throughout his years at Crozer, his mission was to ensure Crozer's orthodoxy in the midst of the Philadelphia Baptist Association, home to numerous prestigious pulpits of the denomination. Norman Maring characterized Weston's view of Scripture as "a dogged belief in inspiration, without being able to define it."[375] Yet, Weston successfully kept the New Theology out of Crozer for two generations, as he himself participated in many events and projects of the revivalistic and dispensationalist schools. He was a contributing editor of the *Scofield Reference Bible* (1909) and a eulogist at Dwight L. Moody's funeral.

Following President Weston was Milton C. Evans (1909-1934), who led in the modernization movement that resulted in Crozer's becoming

---

[373] Ibid., 168.

[374] Newman, "Changes in Baptist Theology," 606.

[375] Maring, "Baptists and Changing Views of the Bible" (Part 1), 58.

one of the storm centers of theological liberalism. Crozer had an interest
in the Southern Baptist community of the upper South (Kentucky, West
Virginia, Virginia and North Carolina) and attracted numerous students
who found their own denominational family too confining. Later in the
century, Crozer generated a social activism that overwhelmed its identity
as a training ground for religious ministry and ultimately led to its
demise as a freestanding institution. It relocated in 1969–70 to Rochester,
New York, in federation with Colgate Rochester Divinity School, Bexley
Hall, an Episcopal School, and St. Bernard's Seminary, a Roman
Catholic diocesan school. Martin Luther King, Jr., a graduate of Crozer,
has become synonymous with its later development.

Crozer's first systematic theologian was George Dana Boardman
Pepper (1833–1913). Pepper was trained at Amherst College and Newton
Theological Institution. At Newton he so imbibed Alvah Hovey's
thought that he wrote, "My theology is largely his."[376] In his first years
out of seminary, Pepper became a leading pastor serving the First Baptist
Church of Waterville, Maine, (1860–1865) the campus church of
Waterville College. Newton called upon Pepper to teach ecclesiastical
history which he did for two years. His greatest passion was theology
and he responded with enthusiasm when invited by Weston to become
the first professor of systematic theology at Crozer Theological Seminary
in 1868. Weston doubtless chose Pepper for his first appointment in the
discipline because of their common trust in Hovey and the younger
man's own conservative approach.

Pepper set Crozer upon an orthodox course for fourteen years
(1868–1882). His published lectures, *Outlines in Systematic Theology*
(1882) reveal his high doctrine of Scripture and his classic orientation in
theology. [377] Following his years of teaching at Crozer, Pepper returned
to Maine to become president at Colby College. After experiencing
health problems, he concluded his career in religious education by
teaching biblical literature at Colby from 1892 until 1900.[378]

President Weston chose Elias Henry Johnson (1841–1906) to succeed
Pepper. Johnson taught theology at Crozer from 1882 to 1906. A major
contributor to the theological tone of Crozer's early years, Johnson

---

[376] G. R. Hovey, *Alvah Hovey*, 192.

[377] George D. B. Pepper, *Outlines in Systematic Theology*

[378] On Pepper's later career, see Ernest Cummings Marriner, *The History of Colby
College* (Waterville: Colby College Press, 1962) 219–32.

completed his bachelor's degree at the University of Rochester and later earned a graduate degree from Brown University. In Rochester, Johnson was much influenced by E. G. Robinson. Johnson's theological perspective is found in his *An Outline of Systematic Theology* (1891, 1895), compiled in conjunction with a section by Henry Weston on ecclesiology. Among the contemporary Baptist attempts at a systematic work during that period, Johnson's was written in the most "student-friendly" style: it is clear, concise, and carries references at the end of each section. His sources are readily apparent. The book represents his classroom lectures in theology to the middler and senior students at Crozer. He recognized that theology had taken on scientific aspects and that theology itself had been subcategorized into natural, biblical, historical, and dogmatic aspects.[379]

Like many of his American contemporaries in theology, Johnson attempted to bridge the widening gap between traditional orthodoxy and the newer sciences. In this regard, he was rightly at home with the "critically orthodox." He was aware of the distinction between the New Theology where Christian experience was the vehicle for interpreting the Bible, and conservative orthodoxy that considered such emphasis of experience an inevitable invitation to the subversion of Scriptures. Johnson endeavored to mediate between the two extremes, offering moral conviction as the criterion to which all religious doctrines are subjected. He nevertheless concluded, "the Bible remains the only trustworthy rule of faith and practice."[380] He went on to discuss the effects of the Darwinian theory of evolution and natural selection, accepting a theistic evolution hypothesis himself. Johnson was skeptical of monistic theories arguing they were unbiblical and pantheistic. In discussing various theories of the Second Coming of Christ, he concluded the premillennial position embraced by the Plymouth Brethren lacked persuasive argument. His own position was that of a suspended verdict.

Henry Weston added a section on the New Testament church to the second edition of Johnson's textbook (1895). Weston used a strictly biblical approach to ecclesiology, defining the church as " a body of professed believers in Christ, baptized on a credible confession of faith in

---

[379] E. H. Johnson, *An Outline of Systematic Theology* (Philadelphia: American Baptist Publication Society, 1895) 1.

[380] Johnson, *SystematicTheology,* 13.

him, associated for worship, work, and discipline."[381] In response to the
Landmarkist Movement, Weston declared that baptism was a church-
wide ordinance, not an individual or ministerial act, and that churches
should adhere to a discipline of restricted or closed communion. Weston
and Johnson agreed that open communionists had no tenable ground to
substantiate their position. Here the Crozer luminaries' consistency with
historic American Calvinistic Baptist practices was apparent.

Significant changes transpired at Crozer following Weston's death in
1909. Milton G. Evans (1862–1939) became the school's new president
and pointed Crozer in a fundamentally different theological and
educational direction.[382] Following trends at Colgate, Rochester, Newton,
and particularly imitating the Chicago School, Evans sought faculty with
critical scholarly training and he built one of the strongest theological
libraries in the United States. Edward B. Pollard, a doctoral graduate
from Yale, joined the faculty in 1906. In 1908 Frank Grant Lewis
became the first doctoral graduate from Chicago to teach at Crozer.

In 1905 Evans reached an agreement with the University of
Pennsylvania whereby the two schools would allow degree candidates
from either institution ready access and mutual accreditation for course
work taken. This greatly enhanced the seminary's reputation among
other Baptist institutions. Evans reorganized the theology program in
1909 to include "Comparative Theology" and "Practical Theology." The
former included coursework in other world religions, tribal and native
religions, as well as an examination of the claims attributed in Scripture
to Jesus Christ. Christian theology was formulated in response to the
academic findings of the History of Religions. Anthropology was for
Evans an important emerging field. To announce Crozer's arrival in
theological scholarship, he began publication of *The Crozer Seminary
Bulletin* in 1909 and *The Crozer Quarterly* in 1924, both of which
showcased faculty work. A contemporary observer noted with
admiration, "It was Dr. Evans who was most influential in bringing the

---

[381] Weston, as quoted in ibid., 324.
[382] The last vestiges of conservative Baptist thought were gone from Crozer by 1918
with the retirement of Barnard C. Taylor. Norman Maring, who was born on the Crozer
campus while his father was a student there, traced the bibliographic evolution in ibid.,
2:47, 61n.171.

school to a full realization of the importance of the principle of academic freedom."[383]

At the turn of the twentieth century, Crozer had become well established in its conviction that without freedom, true Christianity would become anemic. "To be bound by ignorance, superstition, ecclesiasticism, or domination by the state," wrote Rittenhouse Neisser, "would rob Christianity of its high calling."[384] Among those who worked closely in the "new" Crozer was Henry Clay Vedder (1853–1935). Vedder came to the seminary as editor of *The Examiner* and *The Baptist Quarterly Review*. He soon picked up responsibilities for teaching church history and managing the denominational archives. Vedder himself went through the modernization process at Crozer. At length he became a lightning rod among the anti-fundamentalists. He absorbed many of the editorial assaults of the conservatives. According to his biographer, Vedder achieved a positive view of socialism between 1908 and 1911 and applied his evolving perspective to the teaching of church history. The result was a theological shift from evangelicalism to evangelical liberalism and a completely reconstructed theological framework.[385]

When in 1920 Vedder began to receive severe criticism for his publicly stated views on the Bible (he was referred to as a "Bapto-Unitarian"), he responded first in the words of his Rochester seminary teacher, A. H. Strong, that the Bible was the record of a progressive divine revelation. He later exhibited his new-found modernism, as he underscored the historical development of Scripture and the occurrence of imperfections in the text due to the human element in revelation and inspiration. At another point, he rejected substitutionary and expiative views of the atonement in favor of what he called a "partnership, ... social sin-bearing" view of the death of Christ.[386] On the matter of teaching the theory of evolution, he thought it confirmed by fact and reason. He ridiculed those who held on to the old theological traditions with comments such as: "Theology might be defined as that science

---

[383] Rittenhouse Neisser, "Crozer At the Dawn of the Century," *Chronicle* 7:3 (July 1944): 121.

[384] Ibid., 124.

[385] Robert B. Hanley, "Henry Clay Vedder: Conservative Evangelical to Evangelical Liberal," *Foundations* 5/2 (April 1962): 135–57.

[386] Henry C. Vedder, "My Teaching on the Atonement," *Baptist* (20 November 1920): 1471.

which has for its end the finding of bad reasons for our good beliefs."[387]
He held that the theory of evolution had given humankind a new world, a
real God, a new religion stressing the teachings of Jesus, a new hope
through which people could possibly be organized into ideal social
relations and a resultant perfecting of individuals. He wrote: "Evolution
and the gospel complement each other; together they are invincible."[388]
Vedder challenged his critics to demonstrate where he had deviated from
the essence of Baptist orthodoxy and the freedom to interpret the Bible
for oneself.[389] While he did not teach theology *per se*, he was widely read
and quoted. More combative than shy, Vedder as much as any faculty
member at Crozer helped to cast the stamp of scholarly modernism on
the school.

There were those during Crozer's first years who had a quiet
influence upon the school's early conservative theology. The pastor of
nearby Upland Baptist Church, where many of the faculty worshiped was
one such person. James M. Pendleton (1811–1891) had a long pastoral
and educational career across the nineteenth century, mostly in the South.
In the early 1850s he met James R. Graves and began to write for
Graves's paper, *The Tennessee Baptist*. Pendleton produced two classics
for the Landmarkist movement, *Three Reasons Why I Am a Baptist*
(1856) and *An Old Landmark Reset* (1854). In 1865 he became pastor at
Upland and produced a *Church Manual* (1867) and *Christian Doctrines*
(1878). His influence strengthened the traditional Baptist identity of the
seminary community.

Spencer B. Meeser (1859–1939) was also a long-term contributor to
Crozer's theological tone. Meeser graduated from Bucknell University
and Crozer. He taught systematic theology from 1909 to 1930. His
assignment was to maintain courses in traditional systematic theology
while Evans blazed new paths in comparative theology. Though lacking
a graduate degree, Meeser was well acquainted with contemporary
theologians, ranging from William Newton Clarke at Colgate, William
Adams Brown at Union, and O. A. Curtis of Drew Theological School,

---

[387] Henry C. Vedder, "Evolution and Its Contribution to Religious Thinking-The
Matriculation Address for 1923," *Bulletin of Crozer Theological Seminary* 15/4 (October
1923): 128.

[388] Ibid., 126–35.

[389] Henry C. Vedder, "What I Teach about the Bible," *Baptist* (30 October
1920):1357-1358.

to Isaac Dorner, James Orr, Abraham Kuyper and Charles Hodge. In his 1909 inaugural address at Crozer, Meeser rejected the notion that theology was no longer to be seriously considered an academic discipline, or that in its place students should study the social sciences. His approach was broadly characterized by empiricism, "to state the facts of our knowledge of God in orderly manner, to relate them, give clear, balanced expression to them, reveal their meaning and give spiritual and moral force to them for our life."[390] He did introduce at least one significant challenge to the typical nineteenth-century Baptist understanding that theology was appropriately limited to the examination and doctrinal interpretation of faith as restricted by biblical texts. "If it be urged that we have in the Bible a sufficient body of doctrines and that we may do with them as they are," he wrote, "the appropriate reply is that Christian doctrines, as a miscellany of uncorrelated statements, do not constitute a theology."[391] Systematic theology, he was certain, had to be more than a collection of Bible teachings.

Meeser was not a well-published scholar, but some glimpses of his methodology are available. For instance, the content of his systematic theology course for the second-year students indicates a focus on the doctrine of God. He demonstrated an awareness of personalism as well as the unity of God, displaying some dependence upon Strong. "Only in a revelation of God through personality may we come to a complete knowledge of God We assume that He is personal...The ultimate ground of religious life and morality is in personality; is in a personal God."[392] Meeser's Christology, however, was not so modern. Against the Chicago School and historical criticism, he warned against engaging the attempt to separate apostolic interpretations of Jesus from Jesus' own religion. Following the Spirit, the Apostles were "close upon the heels and teachings of Jesus." They were, he held, not a diversion nor subversion but a normal expression of Jesus' teaching. Reflecting contemporaries such as E. Y. Mullins, Meeser found ultimate certainty of religious knowledge in Christian experience. "All certainty," he thought, "is by way of faith in whatever is accredited to the soul in experience in that realm of life where the subject of the faith lies; whether it be scientific,

---

[390] Spencer B. Meeser, "Systematic Theology: A Rationale," *Bulletin of the Crozer Theological Seminary* 2/1 (October 1909): 4–5.

[391] Ibid., 4.

[392] Ibid., 10.

philosophic, aesthetic, or religious certainty."[393] With respect to the doctrine of the atonement, Meeser evinced a modern view of God's justice. It was a "longing will to recover man," rather than a strict payment or penalty.[394] In the same connection, he discussed the principles of prayer and the credibility of miracles.[395] Lacking the opportunity to present a full-orbed systematic theology, much of Meeser's written effort was sent to denominational periodicals.

Among Evans's appointments that had most far-reaching impact theologically upon the life of the school were Isaac G. Mathews (1871–1959) and Morton Scott Enslin (1897–1980). In 1921 Matthews was brought from McMaster University via New Haven, Connecticut, where he had run afoul of fundamentalists for his teaching. He succeeded the conservative Barnard C. Taylor, one of Weston's appointments.[396] Enslin was the youngest appointment to the rank of full professor in any U. S. institution when he arrived at Crozer in 1924. He was a graduate of Newton and received his doctorate from Harvard. Enslin certainly strengthened the seminary's connection with the academic world, but he also managed to inflame the Baptist community with his hypercritical scholarship and iconoclastic public remarks.[397]

Under the leadership of President James H. Franklin (1934–1944), Crozer faced a severe crisis in the years of the Great Depression. The point is illustrated by the evolution of its curriculum. Classical liberals like Mathews and Enslin, who favored a traditional program of studies based in the languages and traditional theological disciplines dominated the faculty. In 1928 Evans had appointed William Roy McNutt, a prominent New England pastor, to develop a progressive practical theology chair. McNutt was trained at Colby College, Ottawa University

---

[393] Ibid., 14–15.

[394] Spencer B. Meeser, "Systematic Theology," (pamphlet in the American Baptist Historical Society files: n.p.; n.d.) 24.

[395] Ibid..

[396] Matthews published *Old Testament Life and Literature* (1923) and *The Religious Pilgrimage of Israel* (1947). Professor Taylor became so distressed about the course of theology at Crozer that he came out of retirement in 1925 to be a founding professor at Crozer's rival, the Eastern Baptist Theological Seminary. Prof. Enslin, who lived near the Eastern campus, recalled no further contact between Taylor and his Crozer colleagues.

[397] His works included *Christian Beginnings* (1938) and *From Jesus to Christianity* (1964). He is said to have quipped that "he would have been a Christian if Jesus had never been born."

(Bachelor of Arts), Crozer (Bachelor of Divinity), and the University of Pennsylvania (Master of Arts). He attempted to usher in a program that emphasized internship in ministry and more attention to Crozer's church constituency. He soon crossed swords with Franklin who made it difficult, if not impossible, for McNutt to accomplish his goals. Franklin opposed the prominent place given the social sciences and forced retrenchment by keeping a significantly restrictive budget. McNutt retired in 1944, protesting that he had been circumscribed, hedged in, and humiliated.[398]

Despite the difficulties surrounding his career at Crozer, McNutt did effect some long-term impact on Baptist thought. His chief work titled *Polity and Practice in Baptist Churches* (1935), published by Judson Press, filled a need for such a piece in the middle of the twentieth century. With a preface by D. C. MacIntosh, a friend who was in accord with McNutt's perspectives, the book articulated a progressive understanding of ecclesiology. Referring directly to E. Y. Mullins's work, McNutt affirmed soul competency and soul freedom. These affirmations in turn mandated that "all conduct within the realm of religion must bear the stamp of voluntariness, else it is a bastard and not a son."[399] Competency involved resistance to legalism, creedalism, and every form of coercion. The church was to be an organized group of baptized disciples, independent and democratic by nature. Answering the Landmarkists in the South, McNutt argued that the church and the kingdom are not synonymous, as the church is an agent of the kingdom. In the theocratic tradition of New England, what bound the church together for McNutt was a voluntary covenant.[400] The covenant, though a voluntary commitment, had the potential to limit absolute and unrestrained freedom. As a Baptist rooted firmly in the associational principle, McNutt also affirmed the need for churches to cooperate voluntarily in associations, conventions, missionary societies, and on philanthropic boards. His work translated Mullins's individualistic perspectives into the Northern Baptist community as its regional and state organizations reached their zenith of institutionalization.

---

[398] "The Story of Practical Theology at Crozer, 1924–1947," *The Voice: Crozer Centennial Issue 3* 60/3 (July 1968): 5.

[399] McNutt, *Polity and Practice*, 23, 104.

[400] Ibid., 26–31.

A second area to which McNutt contributed was an expansion of Baptist understandings of the authority of Scripture. Quoting the time-honored phraseology of the Confession of 1677—"the Bible is a sufficient authority and guide in matters of faith and practice"—he argued that its guidance was, by its very nature, neither foolproof nor absolute. Rather, there is wide liberty for a teacher. The teacher, he thought was Christ first of all, but Christ gives only "sufficient" guidance. It is left to the exercise of every human's competency to make many contemporary moral decisions. God himself is the ultimate Teacher and provides competent teachers of the gospel, rather than authoritarian enforcement of doctrine, through the church.[401] Here McNutt was doubtless responding to the fundamentalist position that elevated Scriptures to supreme authority.

Angus Stewart Woodburne (1881–1938) represented a transitional theological appointment toward the end of the Evans era. Woodburne was a Canadian, educated at McMaster University where he completed bachelor degrees in the arts and divinity. He served from 1906 to 1914 as a missionary in India under appointment of the Canadian Baptist Foreign Mission Society. Returning to the United States between 1914–1917, he earned master's and doctoral degrees at the University of Chicago. His dissertation was entitled, "The Relation between Religion and Science: A Biological Approach." In the 1920s he was professor of philosophy at Madras Christian College in India, from which in 1930 Crozer called him to its chair in theology. Evans had hoped to bring to the school both another Chicago School doctorate and a scholar familiar with world religions, in the person of Woodburne. Unfortunately, the missionary and professor died unexpectedly while overseas in 1938.

The coming of Edwin E. Aubrey in 1944 to Crozer as president signaled that institution's full acceptance of the Chicago School, at least among the faculty and trustees. Aubrey (1896–1956) arrived at Crozer with the accolades of a well-read American theologian and religious educator. At Chicago he had written a master's thesis titled "A Sketch of the Divine Attributes of God in Pre-Exilic Prophets," and a bachelor of divinity thesis titled "Introduction to the Student Religious Problem." His doctoral dissertation was titled "An Experiment in College Religious Education." After only five years at Crozer, however, he moved to the

---

[401] Ibid., 109–111.

University of Pennsylvania to teach in the field of religious philosophy and thought. Something of his new secular approach was revealed in the 1952 Ayer Lectures he gave at Colgate Rochester Divinity School. Aubrey took exception to the Christian case against secularism, in part because secular forces had repeatedly influenced Christianity. He went so far as to argue that there are spiritual values in secular movements that Christianity could not claim. He urged a theology that was "at once humbler, and bolder, less plaintive and more responsible."[402] Still clinging to the visible church, Aubrey redefined it as "a fellowship gathered around the Christ, ...the seedbed of attitudes which refine and ennoble life day by day."[403] Aubrey was convinced the church had no monopoly on spiritual gifts or assets: it needed to avail itself of the cooperation of secular groups and individuals.

George Washington Davis (1902–1960) followed Aubrey as a professor of theology at Crozer. Davis was a graduate of the University of Pittsburgh, Colgate Rochester Divinity School, and Yale University, where his doctoral thesis was titled "Conversion in Hindu India." A James H. Franklin appointee, he remained at Crozer from 1939 to 1961. Among his more famous students was Martin Luther King, Jr. Davis became a defining spokesperson for the liberal tradition within the Baptist family. Upon observing the various factions at the 1948 Northern Baptist Convention meeting, he wrote that liberalism's perspective of truth was an attitude: "Truth is an ever-unrolling phenomenon that humans are under an obligation to be open to its perennial wonder and enlargement.... For the liberal only some of the facts are in and the end of truth is open."[404] He published *Existentialism and Theology: An Investigation of the Contribution of Rudolf Bultmann to Theological Thought* (1957) in which he accepted Bultmann's demythologization of the life of Christ to recover the personality of Jesus. Like liberal theologians before him, Davis valued religious experience. Following Hegel and Schleiermacher, he wrote, "God is a being of rational order

---

[402] Edwin E. Aubrey, *Secularism a Myth: An Examination of the Current Attack on Secularism* (New York: Harper Brothers, 1953) 12–13.
[403] Ibid., 178–79.
[404] George W. Davis, "In Praise of Liberalism," *Theology Today* 4/4 (January, 1948): 487, 491.

whether his activity is discerned in nature or religious experience."[405] He believed strongly in the power of pronouncements of prophets and institutions, as well as appeals to history.

Following the difficult years of World War II, Davis held that liberal thought had been supplanted by Neo-Orthodoxy. Crozer was consequently in search of a renewed theological vision. One of the more articulate liberal theologians of his era, he critiqued his tradition for being superficial and not understanding the Bible as a whole. He called for a "theology of depth," wherein would be described a new moral foundation of reality, the necessity of God's spiritual control would be realized, and Jesus would be seen as the "personal and loving will of God." He came to believe that excessive individualism had caused a loss of moral and spiritual moorings, and that Protestantism had succumbed to a "crude supernaturalism that feeds on unexpected miraculous thrusts from heaven."[406] Davis succinctly stated the core of his own theological stance in 1951: "Christians know God. They may approach him through Christ. Most of them do. But they finally know God as an essentially personal Being, with will and purposes of his own, controlling the world, and reaching his children in the deepest places of their being. Such religious experience is determinative."[407]

W. Kenneth Cauthen (b. 1920) was the last of the Crozer theologians. He was educated at Mercer University, Yale Divinity School, Emory University, and Vanderbilt University. His Vanderbilt dissertation, "Types of American Liberalism 1900–1935," under the guidance of Langdon Gilkey and Roger Shinn, was published as *The Impact of American Religious Liberalism* (1962) and was for many years a standard reference on the topic. Raised in a Southern Baptist family, he reflected Crozer's interest in conveying the liberal tradition to Southern Baptists. He taught theology and related subjects at Crozer Theological Seminary from 1961 until 1970, when Crozer moved to Rochester. Cauthen concluded his academic career in Rochester, continuing to advocate the ethos of Crozer and to embody the founding spirit behind the John P. Crozer Griffith Professorship in Theology.

---

[405] George W. Davis, "Liberalism and a Theology of Depth" *Crozer Quarterly* 28/3 (July 1951) 211.

[406] Ibid., 206–211.

[407] Ibid., 210.

Later in his career, Cauthen compiled a textbook titled *Systematic Theology: A Modern Protestant Approach* (1986). Published by a small press, the work did not gain the notoriety it might otherwise have enjoyed, but it did circulate as an example of theology in the liberal Baptist tradition. In the preface, Cauthen indicated his plan to present an orientation from "the non-conservative academic tradition in modern American Protestant theology."[408] Cauthen euphemistically equated this with the "Yalenunion" approach, meaning that perspective taught at Yale Divinity School and Union Theological Seminary in New York, the closest institutional allies of Colgate Rochester and Crozer. Akin to Robinson and the Rochester tradition, Cauthen presents various positions on doctrinal particularities from a variety of writers, Neo-orthodox, Process, Black, Liberationist, Feminist, Traditional Liberal, and Evangelical/Fundamentalist. He tried to keep his own opinions out of the discussion, in order to give the range of options and issues in the past and present. Cauthen's work is a collection of scholarly commentary on theological categories rather than dogmatic or confessional dictum.

As to his baptistic identity, Cauthen reveals much in his discussion of the church and the sacraments. Following the lead of the World Council of Churches, he sees the church as a community of the Holy Spirit. Specifically, the church is the "community of the Endtime called into being by the redemptive work of Christ. It is the congregation of those who have been introduced into the new age and who await the final consummation of the purpose of God."[409] Unwilling to mandate what he calls a "subjective pole, individual principle" (baptistic) idea of the church, he wants to accommodate fully the ecumenical vision. A process theologian himself, Cauthen has been more interested in what the church will become than he is in finding an identifiable pattern in its historical record.

Unlike most Baptists in North America, but very much in the Liturgical Renewal and the Anglo-Protestant traditions, Cauthen uses the term "sacrament" to orient his readers to his discussions of baptism and the Lord's Supper. He takes the position that baptism is essentially a rite of initiation, as though one were joining a family. This is in contrast to the believers' churches for which baptism is considered akin to a

---

[408] W. Kenneth Cauthen, *Systematic Theology: A Modern Protestant Approach* (Lewiston NY: Edward Mellen Press, 1986) viii.
[409] Ibid., 230.

marriage involving covenant and personal commitment. Interestingly, his references to baptismal thought in the Baptist tradition hearken to the early twentieth century British scene, including the writings of H. Wheeler Robinson at Regent's Park College, Oxford, and A. C. Underwood at Rawdon College. Given more significance is Karl Barth's affirmation of believer's baptism.[410] One finds in Cauthen's theology the use of familiar terms with entirely new meanings, a rhetorical strategem typical of the Liberal and Post-Modern schools. With the conclusion of Cauthen's writing and teaching career, the Crozer tradition may be said to have come to an end.[411]

SUMMARY

The development of schools of thought associated with theological institutions and colleges provided a source of professional theologians for the budding American Baptist community. As candidates for ministry entered colleges or seminaries, the mentor system of training ministers ceased to exist on a broad scale. Each of the schools produced signal theologians, upon whose theological reputations the schools flourished or waned. It was customary that the institutions took care to appoint theologians who would seamlessly tie together study programs of biblical languages, church history, theology, and the practice of ministry. Emerging schools of thought, associated with the various institutions, began to produce systematic theologies that were published first for student use and then distributed more broadly among pastors and other interested readers. The emergence of professional theologians from Baptist ranks was a hallmark of the mid-nineteenth century religious experience in America. The genetic theological influences set in place by these first professionals are most obviously traced among those who attended the various schools, colleges, universities, and seminaries in which these pioneering professors taught.

---

[410] Ibid., 326.

[411] One might be tempted to include Kenneth L. Smith (1925–1992) in the Crozer Tradition because Smith made claims about his influence in social ethics upon people like Martin Luther King, Jr., and others. In reality, Smith's work was largely historical and written at a popular level, advocacy in nature. He produced no major theological treatises. See for instance, Kenneth L. Smith and Ira Zepp, *Search for the Beloved Community*, and with Thomas McKibbens, *The Life and Works of Morgan Edwards*.

The most marked degree of change in Baptist thought occurred first within the institutional settings of their academies. From there, those changes slowly filtered out into the local churches and the broader Baptist community. The trend in theological ideology evolved from a Calvinistic orthodoxy to a "critically orthodox" position, and finally to a bifurcation between conservatives and liberals. First and foremost, theology began to be spoken of as a science rather than treated as dealing exclusively with a body of revealed doctrinal truths. Published systematic theologies began by acknowledging this shift in perspective, though among Baptists it was popular to remind readers that theological understanding was still essentially a matter of faith and piety. The launching of a graduate school in theology at the University of Chicago became the high water mark of scientific theology among Baptists.

The evolution of full-time teachers of theology in Baptist circles was also important to the genetic influences brought to bear upon the tradition. Some were pastors, but increasingly people prepared for this vocation by securing advanced academic degrees and significant collegiate-level teaching experience. Their accountability came to be to the academy, specifically their institutions, and not necessarily to the local churches. This provided a freedom to experiment, while also producing some alienation from the church community. Such was especially true when theologians transgressed cherished doctrinal boundaries, such as challenging common affirmations of the nature of Scripture's authority. Experimentation led to the development of entirely new genetic pathways, most obviously the social gospel movement.

The exposure of Baptists in America to European theologians had a profound impact upon Baptist schoolmen. It was not only fashionable to study in Germany, Switzerland, or France, but became necessary to complete one's academic credentials. It is noteworthy that by and large Baptists from the North American academy were not attracted to Europe's conservative confessionalists in those critical decades of change, but to progressive and liberal theologians.[412] No other factor is as important in the process of pushing Baptist thought to acknowledge historical and contextual factors, the social needs of the church, the role of religious experience, and the empirical nature of the sciences as

---

[412] For a careful study of the transatlantic conservative tradition, see Walter H. Conser, Jr., *Church and Confession: Conservative Theologians in Germany, England and America 1815–1866* (Macon GA: Mercer University Press, 1984) esp., 13–95.

applied to theological issues. The primary personalities identified as catalysts toward modernization were Barnas Sears at Brown University, who had the same impact on Colgate Seminary; at Colgate, William Newton Clarke; at Rochester, A. H. Strong and Walter Rauschenbusch; at Crozer, Milton G. Evans and Henry C. Vedder; and at the University of Chicago, it was Shailer Mathews and Gerald Birney Smith.

One must not overestimate the impact practically or genetically upon the larger American Baptist community of the schoolmen. First, a large number of those ordained to the Baptist ministry until 1920 did not pursue college or seminary degrees. Second, as the modernization process continued within the schools, reactions set in where it became a badge of honor among many churches to have a minister not trained or dependent upon the new ideas. This erupted most forcefully in the fundamentalist movement of the period 1915 to 1945. Gradually the liberalizing theologies of the schoolmen had to compete for the hearts of Baptists with new evangelical thought emerging from communities like the Evangelical Alliance, or from fundamentalist or evangelical Baptists who considered themselves "in diaspora."

CHAPTER 7

SOUTHERN BAPTISTS AND THEIR SCHOOLS

Keep the Seminary lashed to the cross. If heresy ever comes in the teaching, take it to the faculty. If they will not hear you, and take prompt action, take it to the trustees of the Seminary. If they will not hear you, take it to the convention that appoints the Board of Trustees, and if they will not hear you, take it to the great common people of our churches. You will not fail to get a hearing there.

B. H. Carroll, 1914

Because of their proliferation and unique qualities, we turn to a separate treatment of Baptists in the American South. From the planting of the first Baptist congregations in the Southern colonies, two factors were fairly obvious. First, Baptists would thrive in the South in an unusual way. Second, the nature of Baptist identity in the South would emphasize particular cultural qualities. By the eighteenth century, a distinct theological tradition began to emerge in the Baptist South. The differentiating factors were regional, experiential, and theological. Southern regions of the late colonial and early national period developed differently than the communities of the Middle States and New England. Where variegated immigration and urbanization occurred on a wide scale in Pennsylvania, New Jersey, and New York, pluralistic theologies came forth and a sense of "denominationalism" emerged. Elsewhere, closely-knit towns dotted the New England landscape from coastal Maine to Connecticut and their Christian theological expressions tended to emphasize covenantal themes. Baptists in that region had much in common with Congregationalists.

The South, by contrast, was characterized by the development of isolated rural communities and relatively few urban areas. Individualism was fostered in the isolated settings and interaction with larger cultural trends limited. In religious terms, narrative experience[1] was more highly valued than liturgy, confessionalism, or a learned ministry. Educational opportunities were limited and aspiring leaders often had to leave the South to pursue formal education. An in-bred, unique religious character evolved in the South that was reinforced across the region well into the nineteenth century.[2] This was strengthened by a culture of revivalism and constant attention to reinforcing existing ideals. Baptist congregations were typically isolated, developing strong parochial perspectives and antipathy toward other Christian groups. Religion in the South provided a self-oriented "legitimating impetus" for the entire region.[3]

Southern Baptist historians have long debated the primary characteristics of Southern Baptist theological culture. Walter Shurden argued persuasively for four foci: Charleston, Sandy Creek, Georgia, and Tennessee (or Landmark) traditions.[4] Of the four, H. Leon McBeth wrote that Landmarkism was the defining element in Southern Baptist understanding of the church. "Perhaps no other movement," McBeth observed, "has done more to shape the self-identity and intense

---

[1] By "narrative experience," I mean one's "personal testimony." This remains the validating factor in much of popular Southern Baptist spirituality.

[2] As Ellen Rosenberg has shown, Texas, more than anywhere else in the South, is the heartland of Baptist life, "where Southern Baptists have literally inherited the earth." See her *Southern Baptists: A Subculture in Transition* (Knoxville: University of Tennessee Press, 1989) 15.

[3] John Lee Eighmy, *Churches in Cultural Captivity: A History of the Social Attitudes of Southern Baptists* , rev., with an introduction, conclusion, and bibliography by Samuel S. Hill (1972; Knoxville: University of Tennessee Press, 1987) 202.

[4] Walter Shurden, "Carver-Barnes Lectures," *Outlook* 30 (March–April 1981) 5–10, and "The Southern Baptist Synthesis: Is It Cracking?"*Baptist History and Heritage* 16/2 (April 1981): 2–12. The Charleston tradition is a version of the Philadelphia tradition, and the Sandy Creek tradition reflects the revivalistic Separate ethos. The Georgia tradition was especially influential at the founding of the Southern Baptist Convention in 1845, as illustrated in the first presidential address of the Southern Convention written by William Bullein Johnson, in which Johnson played down any doctrinal differences of Baptists north and south: "The Southern Baptist Convention, To the Brethren in the United States; to the congregations connected with the respective churches; and to all candid men," *Proceedings of the First Triennial Meeting of the Southern Baptist Convention Held in Richmond, Virginia 1846* (Richmond: H. K. Ellyson, 1846) 17. See also the discussion of a "voluntarist/evangelical" typology and an accompanying critique in James Leo Garrett, Jr., E. Glenn Hinson, James E. Tull, eds., *Are Southern Baptists Evangelicals?* (Macon GA: Mercer University Press, 1983) 148–64, 199.

denominational loyalty of Southern Baptists."[5] This nineteenth-century theological tradition laid stress upon the exclusivity of Baptist churches, a direct line of apostolic succession from the New Testament, and that the true church is manifest in local congregations. Landmarkism gave churches and Baptist thought a quality that matched the unique character of historic Southern and Southwestern cultures. It continues to be notably present in the theological genes of many contemporary Southern Baptists.

Historian John B. Boles has traced another important genetic characteristic related to Southern Baptist life, revivalism, to the Great Revival at the turn of the century in Kentucky. He found that the fruits of the revivals at Cane Ridge, Kentucky, were diverse: ministerial activism, evangelization, a new hymnology, extemporaneous preaching, millennial optimism, and for many Baptists, eventually an aversion to religious extremes. What these constituted as a whole was a Southern evangelical cast of mind whose leading characteristic was a theology of individualism.[6] Individual sinners were the targets of revival preachers, and autonomous local congregations were the institutional result of the revivals. British social philosopher John Locke's definitions of churches as voluntary societies were quoted among leading Baptists like Richard Furman as each denomination was forced to make its case to individuals. An individual sanctification experience followed individual conversion, providing a continuation of the revival motif. Across the South as a "spiritual region," widely scattered settlements, a heritage of dissent, revivalistic preaching, and a stress on an inward piety created a Southern Protestant ethos across a variety of denominations.[7] Baptists carved out their niche in this individualistic economy by adhering to Andrew Fuller's evangelical Calvinism and it served them well.

By the later nineteenth century, the distinctiveness of Southern religious ideals had become a definable tradition that within itself exhibited diversity. Its character traits included a religious experience expressed in pietistic terms for some, while for others security was found

---

[5] H. Leon McBeth, *The Baptist Heritage: Four Centuries of Baptist Witness* (Nashville: Broadman Press, 1987) 446.

[6] John B. Boles, *The Great Revival, 1787–1805: Origins of the Southern Evangelical Mind* (Lexington: University Press of Kentucky, 1972) 110, 125–27.

[7] Ibid., 129.

in a confessional tradition.[8] Local congregational independence, individualistic spirituality, theological otherworldliness, and a preoccupation (some would call it an obsession) with the Bible as the primary revelation of divine truth permeated both strands of the tradition. Where the Bible was concerned, most Southerners affirmed a literalistic interpretation that matched their strict constructionist legal and social perspectives.[9] One trait, however, had come to overshadow all the others, as John Lee Eighmy and Samuel S. Hill have argued: "Whether the issue is social responsibility, the nature of the church, basic theology, or the meaning of salvation, Southern Protestants think dominantly in individual terms. Images of theology and mission are thus not social in character."[10]

As in the Northern states, evidence of the nature of Southern Baptist thought is initially found in the records of pastoral ministries. Walter Shurden has argued correctly that a primary vehicle for theologizing among Baptists in the South was the sermon. Because it was primarily an oral phenomenon, a sermon's effects were often difficult to assess. Sermons helped shape people's theology, as did hymns often written by pastors. W. W. Sweet and E. Brooks Holifield suggest that Southern Baptist preachers were typically "farmer/preachers" or "gentlemen preachers." Farmer/preachers such as Daniel Marshall and John Taylor embodied the religious sentiments of the common people in simplest

---

[8] An interesting synthesis that combines these two strands is that of W. Wiley Richards who argues for three stages of evangelicalism in understanding Southern Baptist theology: Calvinistic evangelicalism, ecclesiological evangelicalism, and evangelistic evangelicalism. See his *Winds of Doctrines*: *The Origin and Development of Southern Baptist Theology* (Lanham MD: University Press of America, 1991) xi.

[9] In support of this contention, see Rosenberg, *Southern Baptists*, 12.

[10] Ibid., 201. Some analysts object to this thesis as it appears to deny Southern Baptists of social perspectives on major issues and crises of the antebellum era. For this debate, compare Rufus B. Spain, *At Ease in Zion: A Social History of Southern Baptists* (1967, 2003) with Wayne Flynt, *Alabama Baptists: Southern Baptists in the Heart of Dixie* (Tuscaloosa: University of Alabama Press, 1998) 266-298, social perspectives on major issues and crises of the antebellum era. While Baptist associations and the Convention itself certainly took positions on cultural issues like the Civil War, the thesis of W. W. Barnes that the Southern Baptist Convention in the nineteenth century was essentially a decentralized ecclesiology weighs in heavily in support of individualism and local church protectionism. See William Wright Barnes, *The Southern Baptist Convention: A Study in The Development of Ecclesiology* (Fort Worth: Self-published, 1934) 1, 51, 78–79.

terms. The more urbane, rationalistic, and well-informed gentlemen preachers such as Basil Manly, Sr., Jeremiah B. Jeter, and Jesse Mercer strove for assurance, acceptability, and gentility in village and city churches. The farmer preachers more often carried the genes of the Separate Baptist anti-confessionalism that stressed religious experience and the Bible. On the other hand, the gentlemen preachers exhibited the "Charleston Association" traits of appreciation for confessions of faith and a well-ordered ecclesiology. Many of them possessed collegiate educations, and as time went on, seminary educations as well. They were predominantly Calvinistic, which manifested itself in an Edwardsian or later Fullerite Calvinism that was rational and easily suggested systematic articulation.[11] Southern Baptist "modified-Calvinists" found equal disaffection with Northern Calvinists who had moved toward Nathaniel W. Taylor and the New Divinity that produced various forms of ultraism, including antislavery, and Arminians who were better known as Methodists.[12]

Gradually institutions such as seminaries, colleges, and the Sunday School Board emerged to incarnate this "Southern Baptist" educational tradition and train its leaders. But formal education accounted for only a minority of Baptist preachers and pastors in the South well into the twentieth century. Theological identity was more often an inherited and self-informed tradition, reinforced by tried and true literature. Whenever influences from outside the region were introduced, such as biblical criticism, the evolutionary hypothesis, or the social gospel, they were met with reaction that ranged from suspicion to severe opposition. The Southern region became one of quintessential religious conservatism, as other regions moved with contemporary trends and various forms of modernization. Arguably, Southern Baptist theological sources reflect these regional genes more faithfully and consistently than other denominations of the South. It became perhaps, to embellish a phrase already coined, a tradition in "cultural and theological captivity."

---

[11] E. Brooks Holifield, *The Gentlemen Theologians: American Theology in Southern Culture 1795–1860* (Durham: Duke University Press, 1978) 251n33.

[12] On the types, see ibid., 25–49, and Sweet, *Religion on the American Frontier: The Baptists*, (New York: Henry Holfis, 1931), 22–23. Walter Shurden helpfully pulls together the importance of Southern Baptist pastor-theologians in "The Pastor as Denominational Theologian in Southern Baptist History," *Baptist History and Heritage* 15/3 (July 1980: 15–22.

The oldest of the scholarly traditions among Southern Baptists is associated with Mercer University in Macon, Georgia. By the later nineteenth century, Southern Baptist Theological Seminary in Greenville, South Carolina, and later Louisville, Kentucky, overshadowed Mercer's role. Southern Baptist Seminary is considered the "mother" of all theological schools in the Southern Baptist family; its history parallels that of institutions in the Northern states such as Newton, Colgate, and Rochester. Later, Southwestern Baptist Theological Seminary in Fort Worth, Texas, developed advanced degree programs and a unique Texas-style evangelistic theology. New Orleans Baptist Theological Seminary (formerly the Baptist Bible Institute), the only other Southern Baptist institution with an academic doctorate in theology, was much influenced by faculty from Southern Seminary, though it has had a decidedly conservative flavor about it since the 1960s.

MERCER UNIVERSITY

Largely self-taught and pastorally oriented in his early career, John Leadley Dagg (1794–1884) was the pre-eminent theologian of the early years of Southern Baptist life, reinforcing a "Georgia Tradition" set forth by William B. Johnson and Isaac T. Tichenor.[13] Dagg's systematic theology was intended for Baptist ministers in the South and was in fact the first book imprinted by the Southern Baptist Publication Society. As a young person, Dagg's intensive study of languages and Scripture ruined his eyesight, a circumstance that little hampered his effectiveness as a pastor, administrator, writer, and teacher. He began his educational career in 1834 as president and professor of theology at Haddington Institute, an early effort of the Philadelphia Baptist Association. In 1844 he became president and professor of theology at Mercer University, where he made his mark as "the representative religious thinker among

---

[13] Johnson was trained at William Staughton's theological school in Philadelphia and leaned toward a consensus of Baptist theology that included Baptists north and south. Tichenor (1825–1902) had only a secondary education under the tutelege of graduates of Waterville College at Taylorsville Academy in Kentucky, but was a champion of the establishment of a southwide seminary in Greenville, South Carolina, in 1859. He was also the longtime secretary of the Home Mission Board in Atlanta, Georgia, from which he made numerous advances for Southern Baptist work.

Baptists in the antebellum South."[14] His work was simple, direct, and free of controversy. Experiential and pietistic, Dagg wrote for informed pastors on themes consistent with evangelical Calvinism. "The study of religious truth ought to be undertaken and prosecuted from a sense of duty," he wrote. Further to study theology, "for the purpose of gratifying curiousity, or preparing for a profession, is an abuse and profanation of what ought to be regarded as most holy."[15]

Dagg began his monumental work by affirming the Bible as the principal source of religious knowledge. In three short pages he detailed what he thought relevant about natural theology, which was inferior to the Scriptures. His assertions about the inspiration of the Bible, plus an appendix on the subject, laid a sure foundation for future Southern Baptist preoccupation with the Bible. Other than his own organization of the Bible's internal claims for its authority, Dagg revealed only a slight dependence upon Andrew Fuller's works.[16]

In a forthright presentation, Dagg's *Manual* discussed the doctrines of God, God's decrees, Man (humankind), Christ, Holy Spirit, Grace, and Last Things. Using the language of prevailing Calvinism, Dagg spoke of covenantal obligations and depravity. Following the Reformed tradition, he employed the word "covenant" to denote the revelation of God's will to Adam. But, "all men are by nature, totally depraved," he wrote. Further, "a thorough conviction of our total depravity is necessary to humble us before God." This in turn calls upon "the everlasting covenant in Jesus Christ, the blessing of which is salvation." The covenant of grace involves the perseverance of the saints, the sovereignty of God's grace, the election of God's people, particular redemption, and the reprobation of the unsaved. In response to those who question reprobation, Dagg displayed his modified Calvinism by asserting that "according to God's method of grace, the salvation of men is made dependent on their belief of the gospel." His eschatology consisted of separate treatments of

---

[14] Robert G. Gardner, "John Leadley Dagg: Pioneer American Baptist Theologian" (Ph.D. diss., Duke University, 1957) 14. In fact, Dagg wrote most of his theological treatises after he left Mercer, but he clearly established a tradition there.

[15] John L. Dagg, *Manual of Theology in Two Parts.* (Charleston: Southern Baptist Publication Society, 1858) 13. For an assessment of Dagg's theology in the evolving Southern Baptist tradition, consult Mark E. Dever, "Representative Aspects of the Theologies of John L. Dagg and James P. Boyce: Reformed Theology and Southern Baptists" (Th.M. thesis, Southern Baptist Theological Seminary, 1987).

[16] Ibid., 31.

immortality, resurrection, judgment, heaven, and a lengthy exposition on hell.[17]

Dagg's position on the doctrine of the church and the ordinances, constituting the second part of his system,[18] became standard fare for non-Landmarkists across the Southern Baptist family. According to his major scholarly biographer, his positions were similar to those of Thomas Baldwin, William T. Brantly, and Andrew Broaddus. Among British Baptists, Dagg was close to Andrew Fuller, Abraham Booth, and John Gill. Like Alexander Carson and John Ryland before him, Dagg held tenaciously to a universal church and regarded believer's baptism as "a Christian ordinance of perpetual obligation"[19]

Dagg's historical scholarship is perhaps nowhere more evident than in his discussion of baptism. Like earlier British writers, he carefully surveyed the meanings of the Greek terms for "baptize" and met objections to Baptist exegesis. He boldly asserted the "believership" required for baptism. Especially following Alexander Carson, Dagg insisted the design of baptism was primarily for the profession of one's faith and constituted the essential rite of the Christian tradition,[20]

It is in discussing the doctrine of the church that Dagg created the ground where mainstream Southern Baptists would stand. He believed the primary application of the term *ecclesia* was to local congregations. He unleashed a mighty apologetic against John Dick, a contemporary Presbyterian on this point. Dagg was comfortable with the nineteenth-century terminology of "independence" as applied to congregations: "each church as a distinct organization, was independent of every other church."[21] Following Johann K. L. Gieseler's *Compendium of Ecclesiastical History* (1840), he agreed that the history of the church demonstrated its gradual infringement upon original church order. What most differentiated Dagg's idea of the church from others was his treatment of the "church universal." In particular, contesting contemporary works like *Theodosia Ernest* (1856–57), Dagg insisted that there was a generic usage of "church" in Scripture. It was the general body of

---

[17] Ibid., 144, 157, 258, 341–78.
[18] He called it "A Treatise on Church Order."
[19] J.L. Dagg, *A Treatise on Church Order* (Charleston: Southern Baptist Publication Society, 1858), 13.
[20] Ibid., 70.
[21] Ibid., 83.

believers in Christ, he taught. He conceded that sometimes because of deceit, the church universal might not be coincident with a local church. This was not to deny that the church universal was not an organization but to affirm it as a spiritual reality in all ages. Unlike Landmarkists, Dagg believed that baptism was not the door to a local church or the church universal because regeneration must occur prior to baptism and some regenerate persons may remain unconnected to any local church.[22] For the sake of maintaining fellowship, Dagg thought local churches should exercise toleration toward each other in matters of specific discipline.

In his discussion of the Lord's Supper, Dagg gave evidence of understanding the differences between the terminology of "ordinance" and "sacrament." He recognized the use of terms like "eucharist" and "Communion," and leaned toward a Calvinistic usage "that we receive him as our spiritual nourishment, but by faith." Following the theology of "memorialism," he simply stated, "the rite is commemorative."[23] Dagg spent a good deal of discussion on the arguments, Baptist and non-Baptist, for open or mixed communion. He concluded that arguments in support of open communion were invalid and that a congregation has a responsibility to practice sound discipline: "To admit unbaptized persons to membership is to subvert a known law of Christ". Conversely, in response to Robert Hall or "mixed communionists," to practice strict communion is "to do the Lord's will."[24] To those Baptists who had turned the washing of feet into an ordinance, Dagg held that Christ did not institute a new rite but enforced a class of moral duties.

William Williams (1821–1877) succeeded Dagg in the "Georgia Tradition" when the latter took up duties as president of Mercer. Williams was educated at the University of Georgia, graduating first in his class. He later finished the course at Harvard Law School and became a leading young attorney in Montgomery, Alabama. Sensing a call to ministry, he was ordained and became pastor of the Baptist congregation at Auburn, Alabama. After five years, he took up responsibilities at Mercer as professor of systematic theology. Williams joined Henry Tucker (homiletics) in a faculty of theology intended to be three in number. Williams lectured in both theology and ecclesiastical history. In

---

[22] Ibid., 135.
[23] Ibid., 209.
[24] Dagg. *Treatise on Church Order*, 224.

theology he used John Dick's *Lectures on Theology* (1834), Joseph Butler's *Analogy,* Thomas Chalmers' *Institutes of Theology* (1849), and the text of Scripture. The theological course lasted two years. In the historical area, he used Johann Gieseler and Johann L. Mosheim, both standard texts for the early nineteenth century. Students also took Greek, Hebrew, and courses in pastoral duties. Williams likely helped as well with these courses.

As a scholar, Williams was well informed. Sensing the impending error of Baptist successionism, Williams vitiated the case for such a selective interpretation of Scripture and called for the recognition that religious authority lay wholly in the Word of God.[25] He was equally vocal about proper Trinitarian doctrine against hints of modalism or Sabellianism among Georgia congregations.[26]

FURMAN UNIVERSITY

As plans were laid for the establishment of a theological seminary at Furman, William Williams became the clear choice as that seminary's first leader in 1859. He had a wide reputation as an orator, his broad and orthodox work at Mercer had laid an educational foundation trusted among Baptists, and his pastoral collegiality had endeared him to many. In addition, he brought rare educational credentials to the new enterprise.

The initial attempt to create an institutional theological tradition at Furman University began in the 1850s. The school's first professor of theology was James S. Mims (1817–1855). Mims was educated at the University of North Carolina and Furman. He completed the theological course at Newton Theological Institution. Like his colleague of many years at Furman, Peter C. Edwards, he imbibed the newer approaches at Newton, especially with respect to Calvinist doctrines like "imputation." In 1848 Mims was the subject of a somewhat bitter controversy and appeared before the Furman trustees on the matter of his orthodoxy.[27] His sole published work was *The Gospel, the Instrument of Human*

---

[25] William Williams, "Cramp's Baptist History," *Christian Index* 48/6 (1 July 1869).

[26] William Williams, "The Sin Against the Holy Spirit," *Christian Index and Baptist* (21 January 1875); "More Gratified than Aggrieved," *Christian Index and Baptist* (18 March 1875).

[27] Mims's position is found in his published defense, *Orthodoxy: An Address Delivered Before the Board of Trustees of the Furman Theological Institution, on the day of the Annual Commencement, June 19, 1848.* (Columbia SC: I. C. Morgan, 1848).

Salvation (1851). His untimely death allowed for a youthful James P. Boyce to begin his teaching career at Furman in 1855.[28]

THE SOUTHERN BAPTIST THEOLOGICAL SEMINARY

The Southern Baptist Theological Seminary has long been esteemed as the flagship post-undergraduate theological school of Southern Baptists. It was founded before the Civil War and recognized as a nationally prominent seminary, in league with Newton, Colgate, Rochester, and Western. Its significant growth in the twentieth century was a mark of its worldwide acceptability. Southern conferred the first theological doctorates among the Baptist family in 1894 and organized a separate School of Theology in 1953.

While most accounts of the establishment of Southern Baptist Theological Seminary credit James P. Boyce as "founder," arguably Basil Manly, Jr. (1825–1892) was the theological parent of the institution. Manly was the son of a prominent Alabama Baptist minister and educator, Basil Manly, Sr. A child prodigy, the son graduated from the University of Alabama at eighteen. He next entered Newton Theological Institution, then in its prime. He was much taken by Horatio Hackett in Hebrew, but the course of national political events changed Manly's course. After a year at Newton, the Southern state Baptist organizations withdrew from the American Baptist societies over the issue of slavery, and Southern students no longer felt comfortable in New England.[29] Manly happily transferred to Princeton Theological Seminary, where he wrote fondly of professors Archibald Alexander, Samuel Miller, and Charles Hodge. Following seminary, he served churches, notably the prestigious First Baptist, Richmond, Virginia, and he gained a favorable reputation equal to any in the South for establishing the Richmond Female Institute.[30]

---

[28] John A. Broadus, *Memoir of James Petigru Boyce, D.D., LL.D.* (New York: A. C. Armstrong, 1893) 101. Boyce's biographer believed Boyce was well aware of the theological controversy at Furman. In his capacity as editor of the *Southern Baptist* newspaper, Boyce published papers on the two sides of the controversy.

[29] In particular, Manly had attempted a relationship with Francis Wayland at Brown, but found Wayland arrogant and dismissive of his youth. See Mueller, *History of Southern Baptist Seminary*, 88, where a letter about Wayland is quoted.

[30] For scholarly assessments of Manly, see James M. Manley, "The Southern Baptist Mind in Transition: A Life of Basil Manly, Jr., 1825–1892" (Ph.D. diss., University of

It was to Manly that Boyce turned in 1859 to articulate the doctrinal basis of the new seminary. The school's guiding Abstract of Principles was a collection of twenty articles summarizing succinctly the Christian faith in Reformed theological terms. Beginning with an article on the authority of Scripture, other articles were devoted to the Trinity, election, Christ, sanctification, the perseverance of the saints, the church, the ordinances, last things, and liberty of conscience. The article on sanctification spoke of a progressive work, the church was composed of all true disciples identified in local churches or societies, and final judgement was meted out both to the righteous and the damned. The article on liberty of conscience was clearly derived from early English Baptist phraseology, if not from Thomas Helwys himself: "God alone is Lord of the conscience."

In the crucial early years of Southern Seminary, Manly proved his worth to the school. As the second professor appointed to teaching duties at the seminary, he was responsible for courses in biblical introduction and the Old Testament. One has to understand the high priority that Boyce, Williams, and Manly placed upon Scripture (and the Southern Baptist tradition thereafter) to grasp the importance of Manly's role. He taught virtually every introductory course where the issue of biblical authority might have come up and, with Boyce, shaped the additional curriculum on the Bible. In 1879, as he returned to the seminary to fill the vacancy created by Crawford H. Toy, he wrote, "The main objective of a theological education was a practical knowledge of the Scriptures." Further, he believed that "every school and department of the Seminary is mainly valuable as it promotes the elevation of the Word of God and the practical application of its teachings."[31]

Manly's understanding of the doctrine of Scripture proved to be definitive for many Southern Baptists for many generations. He wrote extensively of his position following the departure of Crawford Toy from Southern in 1879 due to doctrinal and methodological controversies surrounding the teaching of the Old Testament. He styled himself a "plenary theorist," by which he meant "the Bible as a whole is the Word of God, so that every part of Scripture there is both infallible truth and

---

Florida, 1999), and the earlier work of Joseph P. Cox, "A Study of the Life and Work of Basil Manly, Jr. (Ph.D diss., Southern Baptist Theological Seminary, 1954).

[31] Quoted in Mueller, *History*, 97.

divine authority."[32] Following the venerable J. L. Dagg in the Southern tradition, Manly rejected the widely accepted dictation theory, holding instead to a two-fold authorship position regarding the Scriptures: "The whole Bible is truly God's Word written by men."[33] He had little interest in how the Bible was inspired, because he believed its self-declaration and thought the process beyond revelation. His notes reveal that he was well read among nineteenth-century evangelicals on the subject, liberally quoting James Bannerman, George T. Ladd, Alexander Carson, B.F. Westcott, and L. Gaussen.

James P. Boyce (1827–1888) was the preeminent personality in founding Southern Baptist Theological Seminary. Raised in a distinguished Baptist family, and a son of historic First Baptist Church of Charleston, Boyce had unusual opportunities for a Southern lad. His father desired him to attend Brown University and to continue a post-graduate education in any of the outstanding schools of the Baptists in the United States, regardless of geographical location. As an undergraduate, Boyce was deeply impressed by the president of his college, Francis Wayland. He was awed by Wayland's stature as a published scholar, even by his ability to debate the sensitive issue of slavery. He emulated Wayland's speech, his demeanor, and leadership skills. But, most of all, Boyce was a product of Wayland's evangelistic efforts. In the spring of 1846 Wayland preached to impenitent undergraduates and caused Boyce to reflect on his spiritual condition. Weeks later in South Carolina during protracted meetings held by Richard Fuller, Boyce made a decision to accept Christ and was baptized. Years later a biographer credited Wayland with the beginnings of that process.[34] Boyce must also have imbibed Wayland's preoccupation with what came to be known as "biblical theology." One biographer reported: "Mr. Boyce adopted, when he became a teacher of theology, President Wayland's method of analytical recitations, without questioning."[35]

Wayland's influence upon young Boyce was soon supplemented by his experience in seminary at Princeton. He intentionally chose Princeton

---

[32] Basil Manly, Jr., *The Bible Doctrine of Inspiration, Explained and Vindicated* (New York: A. C. Armstrong, 1888) 59, 62.

[33] Ibid., 62.

[34] Broadus, *Memoir of Boyce*, 43–45.

[35] Ibid., 35.

over Newton, doubtless because of Newton's reputation to be
unorthodox and because it was farther north in the colder climate of
Boston. In the stronghold of Presbyterian orthodoxy, theology reigned
supreme among the faculty and the dominant figure was Charles Hodge,
the great systematician. Though in poor health, Hodge was informing
and inspiring; Boyce was more influenced by Hodge than anyone else,
save Francis Wayland.[36] Hodge convinced his students that Calvinism
was really Pauline truth and that their theology should be well organized.
At Princeton Boyce also pursued homiletics and frequently filled local
pulpits. He did not finish the course, considered several options,
including study in Europe, but finally went into the pastoral ministry.

In 1855 Boyce began a teaching career in theology at Furman
University. He succeeded Professor J. S. Mims in systematic theology
and remained at Furman for two years. Instructing in the biblical
languages, church history, and theology, Boyce was strongest in
theology. Like most in the orthodox, Reformed tradition, he used John
Dick's textbook on theology. Later he would turn to Johannes J. Van
Oosterzee's *Practical Theology: A Manual for Theological Students*
(1878), Alvah Hovey's *Manual of Theology* (1877), that he valued for its
"clear, sound, and vigorous approach," and finally A. A. Hodge's
Outlines of Theology (1860; 1878) that he deemed an excellent volume.
None, however, completely suited Boyce's pedagogy and so over the
course of his years in the classroom he developed his own textbook. The
Baptist key to his theological method was the authority of Scripture. "We
are led to value each of the doctrines of the Word of God," he wrote.
"Each is true. Each has been revealed that it might be believed."[37]

At length Boyce became a prime mover in the creation of a
theological institution distinctly for Southern Baptists.[38] Boyce articu-

---

[36] On the Princeton influence, see W. Wiley Richards, "A Study of the Influence of
Princeton Theology upon the Theology of James Petigru Boyce and His Followers with
Special Reference to the Works of Charles Hodge" (Th.D. diss., New Orleans Baptist
Theological Seminary, 1964).

[37] James P. Boyce, *Abstract of Systematic Theology* (Philadelphia: American Baptist
Publication Society, 1887) 7.

[38] Southern Baptist historians attribute the theological character of Southern
Seminary to Boyce, Basil Manly, Jr., and John A. Broadus. Of the three, Broadus is
celebrated as the preeminent *professor* because of his huge contribution in preaching, his
reputation beyond the South, especially as the Beecher Lecturer at Yale. He was the only
person for whom the Convention had a memorial service. In this context, of specifying

lated his understanding of theology in a classic definition of a unique model of theological education. First, he had an egalitarian theology of ministry, holding value not just for an elite trained in the best of undergraduate schools, but also those who gave evidence of gifts and a call to ministry without formal education. His mentor, Francis Wayland, had advocated this approach three years before in a Rochester, New York, address titled "The Apostolic Ministry." Boyce's role models in this regard also included John Bunyan, Robert Semple, Andrew Broaddus, Jesse Mercer, and John Gano, mostly early Southern pastors. Second, he wanted to develop advanced curricula for teaching and scholarship so that Baptists would be less dependent upon European (or for that matter Northern American) institutions. Here was the formal genesis of a Southern education for Baptists, as well as one of the seeds of bias against Continental and Northern Baptist theological scholarship among many Baptists in the South. Finally, Boyce argued persuasively for a doctrinal statement that would serve as a guide for instructors at the seminary. He took a different tack than either Newton's interest in open, critical scholarship, or Princeton's Calvinistic orthodoxy. Rather, for Baptists and other "Bible Christians," the test of theological doctrine was "the principles and practices sanctioned by the authority of Scripture and by the usage of our people."[39] The first curriculum of the new seminary placed biblical studies at the head of both the curriculum and the departmental organization.[40] In Boyce's mind, a Bible culture already existed among his Southern Baptist constituency, and sound theological education must reflect that cultural reality.

Boyce's published theology, first issued in 1882 for his students, was for several generations the leading textbook on theology among Southern Baptists. In his preface, he acknowledged the perspective of the 1880s that treated theology as a science in the way it can be organized and considered. Boyce cautioned, however, that it could never be an exact science. In his organizing plan he was careful to arrange the material in one hundred recitations, which meant that he had to exclude some

---

theological instruction and curricular development, plus his overall influence upon the consistent Princetonian Calvinism of the Seminary during his years of service, persuade this writer to affirm Boyce as the theological pacesetter at Southern. On Broaddus's own "reasoned" Calvinistic perspective, see *Memoir of Boyce*, 310.

[39] Quoted in Broadus, *Memoir of Boyce*, 140.

[40] Ibid., 156.

material, notably the doctrine of the church. This was covered in a separate course that he called "Church Government." He also taught a Latin Theology course from time to time, reading sources from classic Christian writers like Thomas Aquinas and Francis Turrettin. Throughout his treatment of doctrines that followed fairly closely Charles Hodge's plan, he articulated an evangelical Calvinist theology. The overarching theme was the doctrine of God, and "much that some theologians would treat exclusively under the doctrine of Man...was presented in the doctrine of the divine nature, attributes and purposes."[41] Boyce further modified this by what he called "biblical dogmatics," in which theological study followed less a single, pre-arranged system, and more the patterns of Scripture that he understood to be revealed truth.

Of particular interest because it reflects Boyce's consistency with predecessor Calvinists, were his chapters on the atonement and sanctification. Having surveyed several theories of the atonement, including that propounded by Andrew Fuller (whom Boyce found inadequate in this regard), he underscored his support for the "limited purpose" theory. Boyce quoted extensively from Archibald Alexander Hodge, who following the Westminster Confession, asserted: "After the manner of the Augustinian schoolmen, Calvin, on 1 John 2:2, says, 'Christ died sufficiently for all, efficiently only for the elect.'"[42] In the geographic and historic midst of a revival of holiness thought, Boyce set forth a progressive understanding of sanctification that stood against perfectionism. Paraphrasing John Wesley's words, and concurring with Manly in the Abstract of Principles, Boyce wrote: "It is not, like justification, a single act, but is a continuous process. The work goes on through the lifetime of the believer, nor is it completed before death."[43]

Boyce was definitive for seminary life in other ways and means. As a teacher of theology, he required candidates for a degree to undergo a course in classical Latin writers that clearly gave a larger historical context to Baptist thought. Evidence of his Princeton upbringing was here clearly present as he guided students through study of the works of Turrettin, Augustine, Anselm, and Aquinas. Methodologically, Boyce conducted his classes according to a rigorous drill routine that required

---

[41] Ibid., 308.
[42] Boyce, *Abstract*, 339.
[43] Ibid., 413.

great amounts of memorization and recitation.[44] For him, theology was fixed and controlled one's approach to all other disciplines, including the study of Scripture.[45] *A priori* systematics left little patience for philological nuances, and Boyce bantered with his Old and New Testament colleagues about their disinclination toward his proof-texts. Boyce's method undergirded a third characteristic of Southern Baptist theological discourse, namely its Calvinistic flavor. "Although the young men were generally rank Arminians when they came to the Seminary," a biographer wrote, "few went through this course under him without being converted to his strong Calvinistic views."[46] Apparently, this was an antidote for students who went to churches in the Upper South where they encountered the New Theology, various forms of liberalism and "advanced thought."[47] Finally, Boyce filled in the gaps in Baptist polity and practice, doubtless on the foundation laid by Francis Wayland. He lectured on church government, parliamentary practice, and pastoral duties, and was praised for the impact he had on the larger church polity of the Southern Baptist family.

At a time when Baptist theologians in the older American seminaries were making accommodations to the "New Theology," and significant changes were occurring in the British Baptist community, James P. Boyce remained steadfast in his commitment to the more traditional

---

[44] Boyce's methods, exacerbated by inadequate pre-seminary preparation of many Southern students, resulted in standards below those of other Baptist theological schools. Walter Rauschenbusch visited the seminary in 1884 and observed that the graduating orations at Rochester were superior to those at Southern, where they resembled those of a secondary school. See "Walter Rauschenbusch to Munson Ford, June 14, 1884," quoted in Winthrop S. Hudson, ed., W*alter Rauschenbusch: Selected Writings* (New York: Paulist Press, 1984), 51.

[45] This in part explained the division that erupted at Southern seminary in the late 1870s over the work of C. H. Toy, who was ultimately dismissed for his evolutionary linguistic approaches to the study of the Old Testament. See Broadus, *Memoir of Boyce*, 260–64; Pope A. Duncan, "Crawford Howell Toy: Heresy at Louisville," in George R. Schriver, ed., *American Religious Heretics: Formal and Informal Trials In American Protestantism* (Nashville: Abingdon Press, 1966) 65–69. For an assessment of Toy's impact, Crawford H. Toy, *The Claims of Biblical Interpretation on Baptists* (New York: Lang and Hillman, 1869), and Billy G. Hurt, "Crawford H. Toy as Interpreter of the Old Testament" (Ph.D. diss., Southern Baptist Theological Seminary, 1965).

[46] Broadus, *Memoir of Boyce*, 265.

[47] Ibid., 266.

theological perspectives.[48] As one reviewer in 1888 put it while assessing Boyce's systematic theology, "Dr. Boyce is not afraid to be found 'in the old paths.'"[49] Another assessment found he was "conservative and eminently Scriptural...after the model of 'the old divines.'"[50] As some sought to shed the religion of authority and confessionalism, Boyce renewed Calvinism through a baptistic lens and left an indelible imprint on Southern Baptist thought.[51]

Joining Boyce and Manly, William Williams was a transitional figure between Mercer and the first manifestation of Southern Baptist Theological Seminary. Following his short stay at Mercer, he was one of the original Southern faculty, hired in 1859 to teach ecclesiastical history and church government, as well as ministry topics. He is mentioned here because in the continuous absence of James Boyce for fundraising purposes, in 1872 Williams assumed the chair of Systematic Theology. Quiet and unassuming, he related effectively to the churches and attempted to do several different assignments at the seminary. He was a genuine intellectual and used a traditional lecture method in teaching theology. Williams's lectures apparently were terse and well organized. But, his frail health failed and his scholarly effort was limited.[52] His few publications include *Apostolical Church Polity*.

At the conclusion of a long and influential era in the development of a theological tradition at Southern Seminary, Dr. Boyce handpicked Professor Franklin Howard Kerfoot as his theological successor. Kerfoot (1847–1901) graduated from Columbian College (Washington, D.C.), having completed a master of science and the L.L.B. degrees. He served

---

[48] Boyce was equally leery of Dispensationalism and Restorationism. His treatment of eschatological matters focused upon immortality, resurrection, the second coming, and judgment, following upon his discussion of the perseverance of the saints. He supposed the thousand years of Rev 20:1–6 to be an indefinite period and rejected flatly any notion of restoration of the damned. See Boyce, *Abstract*, 435–92.

[49] Boyce was so successful in this regard that James R. Graves, leader of the Landmarkist movement, declared that Boyce was a "Landmark" Baptist. Graves deduced this from statements Boyce reputedly made in 1876 about alien immersions and non-Baptist pulpit affiliations in a convention meeting in Mississippi. See James R. Graves, *Old Landmarkism: What Is It?* (Memphis: Baptist Book House, 1880), 120.

[50] Editorial from *The Standard*, quoted in Broadus, *Memoir of Boyce*, 308–309.

[51] On the Princeton School, see Claude Welch, *Protestant Thought in the Nineteenth Century*, 2 vols. (New Haven: Yale University Press, 1972) 1:200–207.

[52] Broadus, *Memoir of Boyce*, 169, 247–48.

in the Confederate Army during the War Between the States. Led to prepare for ministry, he started studies at Southern Baptist Theological Seminary, but finished the course at Crozer in 1871. He studied in the Holy Land and Egypt, finally attending the University of Leipzig for a year. Partially disabled by a fall, he was anxious to leave pastoral ministry to return to the seminary. He was hired in 1886 at Southern Seminary as a co-professor of systematic theology with James Boyce and three years later took full responsibilities in theology for the next ten years.[53] Indications are that Kerfoot followed Boyce's recitation method and used his *Abstract of Theology*. He also continued the basically Calvinist bent of the Seminary established under Boyce, affirming as late as 1905 "that nearly all Baptists believe what is usually termed the doctrines of grace." [54] Kerfoot's chief published work was a revised edition of Boyce's *Abstract*, issued in 1899.

Upon the departure of Southern Seminary's president W. H. Whitsitt, Kerfoot advanced his case for the post but failed to persuade those who would select the next incumbent. Kerfoot eventually took a position with the Southern Baptist Home Mission Board, and his career as a teaching theologian was concluded. Beyond contributions in theology, Kerfoot reflected a new trend toward a European theological orientation at Southern Seminary in the late nineteenth century.[55]

Students of Southern Baptist theological development see a marked transition at this point from the old orthodox Calvinism of the seminary founders to a "de-Calvinized" theological perspective. James Leo Garrett, following others, thought Baptists in the South never fully embraced what he called "Bezan Calvinism," (which few would have understood!), and that neither the doctrine of limited atonement nor harsh statements of human depravity were prevalent among Baptists in the

---

[53] See the material on Kerfoot in ibid., 317, 336, 340.

[54] Kerfoot's administrative aspirations to become Broadus's successor no doubt hindered any scholarly intentions. In 1899 he became corresponding secretary of the Southern Baptist Home Mission Board. The quotation is from Tom Nettles, *By His Grace and for His Glory: A Historical, Theological, and Practical Study of the Doctrines of Grace in Baptist Life* (Grand Rapids: Baker Books, 1986) 50, but lacks citation of the original source. Some care must be taken with the meaning of "doctrines of grace" which has taken on more heavily Calvinistic tones since the 1980s.

[55] There is some indication that Boyce changed his attitude toward continental theologians. In the 1870s he began to study German in order to read current theological works.

South. "The clearest surviving aspect...was the doctrine of the perseverance of the saints."[56] According to this line of thinking, the general twentieth-century Southern Baptist view was that they stood historically in the heritage of St. Paul, Augustine, Martin Luther, John Calvin, and Andrew Fuller. To wit, "God's sovereignty is always coupled with and qualified by God's gracious purpose to save."[57] Later theologians, especially at Southern Seminary, would change that course considerably. In this respect, Southern Seminary mirrored the transition of other nineteenth century Baptists in North America and Britain in the gradual lessening of old orthodox formulations and openness to new theological trends. Among Southern Baptists it was later and much less obvious than elsewhere.

Edgar Young Mullins (1860–1928) represents a giant stride into the next major era of theological tradition associated with the Southern Baptists's flagship school, and as such within the Southern Baptist family as well. Mullins was educated at the Texas State Agricultural and Mechanical College (later Texas A&M University), and Southern Baptist Theological Seminary. During his Baltimore pastorate he took courses in logic and speech at Johns Hopkins University. Among those whom he found influential at the beginning of his ministry was John A. Broadus at Southern Seminary, Edward Judson (whose lectures on missions he enjoyed), William R. Harper (whose admonitions to serious Bible study he heeded), and A. J. Rowland (whose preaching he esteemed).[58] While a pastor in Newton Centre, Massachusetts, Mullins became a close friend of Alvah Hovey at Newton Theological Institution and he had a tangential encounter with William Newton Clarke, former pastor of the

---

[56] While this may be reflected in the theological teachers of Southern Seminary, it is seriously open to challenge when applied to "Baptists in the South." I do not equate "Southern Baptists" and "Baptists in the South." Excluded from this majoritarian view are those in the self-taught traditions, the Old School Baptists of varying kinds and those who, like revivalistic types, continued to identify traditional Calvinistic doctrines (such as reprobation) in various forms among their doctrinal tenets.

[57] James Leo Garrett, "Are Southern Baptist Evangelicals?" in *Are Southern Baptists Evangelicals?* 89–90, and Robert T. Kendall, "The Rise and Demise of Calvinism in the Southern Baptist Convention" (M.A. thesis, University of Louisville, 1973).

[58] Isla May Mullins, *Edgar Young Mullins: An Intimate Biography* (Nashville: The Sunday School Board, 1929) 55, 66.

Newton Centre Church.[59] In his long educational ministry, he corresponded with virtually everyone of note on the Baptist scene, including
Dean Shailer Mathews at the University of Chicago, who he felt had
given up his evangelicalism for scientific modernism.[60] If Mullins's
contemporaries A. H. Strong and Alvah Hovey can be described as
"critically orthodox," Mullins was "cautiously critically orthodox."

During his long career, E. Y. Mullins became a leading figure among
Baptist statesmen, clearly the prominent Southern Baptist of his era and
arguably ever. With the reorganization of Southern Baptist Theological
Seminary in the 1990s under president Albert Mohler and the return to
giving emphasis to historic Calvinism, Mullins has again become a
benchmark theologian. Some frame him as an agent of theological
mediation that led to compromises far removed from the Calvinist roots
of founder James P. Boyce and unclear stances on all the important
issues of his day.[61] Others, however, still see him as a careful guide
between extreme positions with a knack of weighing all ideas in light of
the Bible, retaining what was useful, and discarding the rest. It is not
overstating the case to see Mullins hailed as an heroic figure to
theological moderates in the Southern Baptist family, while for others he
has become a significant villain.[62] As a recent biographer has argued,

---

[59] Ibid., 96, 114. Hovey much appreciated his Southern pastor and Mullins highly
esteemed Hovey's scholarship. Isla May Mullins was actually a direct connection with
Clarke, who encouraged E. Y. Mullins through her to take the presidency of Southern
Baptist Theological Seminary.

[60] Correspondence quoted in William E. Ellis, *A Man of Books and a Man of the
People: E. Y. Mullins and the Crisis of Moderate Southern Baptist Leadership* (Macon
GA: Mercer University Press, 1985) 171.

[61] In a new edition of Mullins's works, Albert Mohler details eight areas of concern
about Mullins: contacts with liberals in the North; a reliance upon religious experience as
a source of knowledge; a division between religious and scientific knowledge; a refusal
to declare himself on the evolution issue; a refusal to identify the Bible as revelation; a
moderation of traditional Calvinistic doctrines; an emphasis upon autonomous
individualism; soul competency. See E. Y. Mullins, *Axioms of Religion*, comp. R. Albert
Mohler (Nashville: Broadman Press, 1997) 7–20.

[62] A moderate interpretation is in Russell Dilday, "Mullins the Theologian: Between
the Extremes," *Review and Expositor* 96/1 (1999): 75– 86, which lifts up Mullins as a
"denominational cosmopolite, a functional practitioner, an innovative theologian, and a
redeemer of non-evangelical ideas." Contrast this with a more fundamentalist view in R.
Albert Mohler, Jr., "Baptist Theology at the Crossroads: The Legacy of E. Y. Mullins,"
Southern Baptist Journal of Theology 3/4 (Winter 1999).

Mullins lived in a border state region and he was a consummate conciliator, attempting an evangelical system that was open to newer trends of thought.[63]

No matter what view one has of the "enduring Mullins," he was responsible for defining new emphases in Southern Baptist thought, as well as introducing a new vocabulary in popular Baptist usage. Given his opportunities as president of the Southern Baptist Convention, president of the Baptist World Alliance, and a well-traveled seminary president, coupled with the propagation of his books through the mission boards and the Sunday School Board, it is not surprising he was so influential. Three terms more or less coined or emphasized by E. Y. Mullins, elucidate his contribution: soul competency, autonomy of the local church, and the priority of Christian experience.

To understand the theological system of E. Y. Mullins, one needs first to define his understanding of the authority of the Bible, a common point of departure for Southern Baptist thinkers. Mullins held that the post-Reformation concepts of scriptural authority in the various schools of criticism produced only intellectual assent. Rather, he argued, the Bible should produce a demonstration of the Spirit and of power.[64] "The Bible is not an authority on all subjects," he wrote, acknowledging the struggles of Baptist colleagues in the last century, " but in religion it is final and authoritative." Similar to contemporaries in the Chicago School, Mullins agreed that "authority" religion, whether vested in pope, church, or Bible, was not acceptable.[65] Instead, he posited a combination of the "objective" and "subjective" that certainty of truth could be found. In Christ is to be found the supreme revelation of God's grace. The Scriptures are the authoritative source of the knowledge of that revelation. Finally, "in his own soul, the Christian finds a working of God's grace that enables him to know Christ and understand Scripture."[66] In very similar language three decades before, W. N. Clarke had stated that "a person's theology...should be inspired in him through the Bible by the Holy Spirit...the authority of the Scriptures is the authority of the truth that they convey." Like Clarke, Mullins believed that Christian

---

[63] Ellis, *A Man of Books*, 220.
[64] Mullins, *Axioms,* 10.
[65] Ibid., 10–11.
[66] Ibid., 11.

experience became the empowering agency for a spiritual understanding of Scripture.[67]

Without doubt, Christian experience became a dominant motif in Mullins's theology.[68] In his magnum opus, *The Christian Religion in Its Doctrinal Expression* (1917), it occupied pride of place in the first four chapters, before Christ, the Holy Spirit, God, the works of God, the Christian life, and last things. In the context of Frederich Schleiermacher, Albert Ritschl, Theodore Munger, William Adams Browne, and Baptists like W. N. Clarke, D. C. MacIntosh, and the Chicago School, Mullins made his foray into defining experience. In his words:

> We can understand the nature of Christian experience only as we keep in mind the fact that it is a transaction between the divine and human. The key to correct understanding of the matter is the idea of personality. It has to do with man, not as intellect, or feeling, or will, or conscience simply, but with man in the totality of his spiritual nature. The Christian experience thus completes the ideal of religion, since it is not only man submitting himself to God, but also God communicating himself to man.[69]

Importantly, Mullins held that Christ was the source of Christian experience, and the greatest testimony to the deity of Christ was the moral transformation within man. Echoing the disturbing question raised by George B. Foster about the "finality of the Christian religion," Mullins answered resoundingly that "Christ becomes final for man, final for his reason, final for his conscience, final for his will, final for his intellect and most of all, final for his faith, his hope, his love, his aspiration. Nothing higher can be conceived."[70] Mullins demonstrated his engagement with contemporary writers on the subject of religious experience further in an article published in the inaugural issue of

---

[67] Clarke, *Sixty Years*, 200–203; *Outline*, 42; Hutchison, *Modernist Impulse*, 120.

[68] Wiley Richards observes that experience permeated everything Mullins wrote, and that Mullins often used the terminology "human experience" interchangeably with "Christian experience." See *Winds of Doctrines,* 154.

[69] Edgar Y. Mullins, *The Christian Religion in Its Doctrinal Expression* (Philadelphia: Judson Press, 1917) 50.

[70] Edgar Y. Mullins, "The Testimony of Christian Experience," repr., *Southern Baptist Journal of Theology* 3/4 (Winter 1999): 84.

Southern Seminary's first faculty journal. He much affirmed the "Christ-exalting" positions of Frank Hugh Foster, professor of theology at Hartford Seminary and L. F. Stearns at Bangor Theological Seminary, who pointed to Christ as the source of Christian experience.[71] He was disturbed by William James's otherwise helpful analysis of religious experience that corresponded with an objective reality that James "stubbornly" refused to identify uniquely as Christ.[72] Mullins was convinced that the Christian norm of religious experience could be intellectually vindicated to a candid inquirer, because as a theory, it accounted for all the facts. When it became a personal experience, and men felt its power, the certainty for Mullins became absolute.[73]

In so defining Christian experience in 1917, Mullins demonstrated his dependence upon Borden P. Bowne and William N. Clarke in particular. Bowne was influential in underscoring personality through his "personalist" approach, while Clarke underscored the nature of Christian theology as essentially experiential. Religious experience was an individual matter for Mullins. His "religious axiom" asserted the principle of individualism, by which he defined the divine/human relationship as one between individuals. "As Christ is the mediator between God and man, man's religious life is established and maintained through Christ," he wrote.[74] Religious duty and access are first and foremost individual matters, and Mullins thought this seemed abundantly clear from Scripture. Nothing, the church, liturgy, the sacraments—certainly not creeds—could come between God and humanity. Should this occur, spiritual tyranny would result. For the believer, a major responsibility was to interpret Scripture for oneself, in order to discover God's revelation and answer directly to God for faith and conduct. This was the essence of Christian experience for Mullins.

---

[71] L. F. Stearns, *The Evidence of Christian Experience: Being the Ely Lectures for 1890* (New York: Charles Scribners Sons, 1890); F. H. Foster, *Christian Life and Theology; or The Contribution of Christian Experience to the System of Evangelical Doctrine* (New York: Fleming H. Revell, 1900).

[72] William James, *The Varieties of Religious Experience: A Study in Human Nature, Being the Gifford Lectures in Natural Religion, delivered at Edinburgh 1901–02* (London: Longmans, Green, & Co., 1902) 508.

[73] E. Y. Mullins, "Is Jesus Christ the Author of Religious Experience?" *Baptist Review and Expositor* 1/1 (1904): 69.

[74] Mullins, *Axioms*, 94–95.

The outstanding definition of soul competency came in Mullins's book, *The Axioms of Religion*. Recovering the ever-popular Landmarkist terminology of "axioms," Mullins sought to reduce Baptist principles to popular phraseology.[75] Years later, Mullins recounted how his "axioms" came to be: "They just this moment came to me—like a flash—the whole thing!"[76] Simply put, soul competency, which became the lynchpin of his dogmatic structure, is "a competency under God, not a competency in the sense of human self-sufficiency...it is both exclusive and inclusive."[77] Underlying Mullins's concept was the Renaissance intellectual principle of "man's capacity and right in the exercise of freedom" and what he called the "Anglo-Saxon principle of individualism."[78]

Theologically, he built his case upon medieval thought, assuming that man is made in God's image and that God is a personality able to be revealed to man. He wrote, "Man has capacity for God, and God can communicate with man."[79] Mullins further asserted that "it excludes at once all human interference, such as episcopacy and infant baptism, and every form of religion by proxy...Religion is a personal matter between the soul and God."[80] Soul competency was new terminology to many Baptists and some objected. In the Northern Baptist community questions were raised about its consistency with more time-honored terms like "soul liberty," "soul freedom," "freedom of conscience," or "freedom of the will."[81]

Some British Baptists, like H. Wheeler Robinson, liked the concept, but somewhat derisively characterized Mullins's angle of approach as "naturally American."[82] Mullins found in soul competency human capacity to receive revelation, a capacity for moral progress, personal responsibility, individual moral freedom, and a personal relationship with

---

[75] See Graves, *Old Landmarkism*, 21 ff.

[76] Mullins, *Christian Religion*, 139.

[77] Apparently, Mullins was unaware of John Howard Hinton's use and definition of the term: *The Theological Works of The Rev. John Harvard Hinton, M.A. Vol. I – Systematic Divinity* (London: Houlston & Wright, 1864), I: 455-459.

[78] Mullins, *Axioms*, 67.

[79] Ibid., 68.

[80] Ibid., 54.

[81] Cited in E. Glenn Hinson, "E. Y. Mullins as Interpreter of the Baptist Tradition," *Review and Expositor* 96/1 (1999): 117.

[82] H. Wheeler Robinson, *The Life and Faith of the Baptists* (London: Methuen, 1927) 18.

God. For Southern Baptists, this became the very essence of Baptist identity, a much-celebrated dogma.[83]

Mullins introduced the terminology "autonomy of the local church" to the American public in 1898. Obviously influenced within his geographic region by the Landmarkist movement, autonomy of a local congregation became a collective theological corollary to soul competence. This latter term means the self-governance of a local church without interference from external authorities, such as a convention, council, bishop, or assembly. Extreme forces within the Southern Convention, notably the Gospel Mission Movement and the Haydenite Controversy[84] in Texas, not to mention the presence of those like J. Frank Norris, caused Mullins and others to engage in local church protectionism. In contrast, at precisely the same period in denominational history, British Baptists were celebrating the church as a voluntary association that linked with others of like faith and order, and Northern Baptists were engaging in collective social action and participating in the ecumenical movement.

As Mullins used it, the term "autonomy of the local church" was rooted in the Baptists' seventeenth-century London Confession that affirmed each congregation was a "compact and knit citie in itself."[85] In so doing, he affirmed ancient English and American Baptist genetic ecclesiological principles. Further, it could be traced to the reality of isolated congregations on the moving American frontier. There was little available to scores of congregations beyond their own human and material resources and the term "autonomous" legitimately described their survival. The writers of the "Baptist Faith and Message" of 1925

---

[83] The celebrations of Mullins on this account are legion. See for instance, James Dunn, "Church, State, and Soul Competency," *Review and Expositor* 96/1 (1999): 61–71. Dunn notes that Karl Barth credited Mullins with the invention of the phrase, "competency of the soul."

[84] On the Gospel Mission Movement, see T. P. Crawford, *Evolution in My Mission Views* (Fulton, KY: J. A. Scarboro, 1903) and Adrian Lamkin, "The Gospel Mission Movement" (Ph.D. diss., Southern Baptist Theological Seminary 1980). Likewise on the Haydenite consult Joe Early, Jr., "The Haydenite Controversy: A Detailed Examination of the First Major Altercation of the Baptist General Convention of Texas" (Ph.D. diss., Southwestern Baptist Theological Seminary, 2002).

[85] "The London Confession, 1644, Art. XLVII" in Lumpkin, *Baptist Confessions of Faith*, 169.

were obviously also indebted to the New Hampshire Confession of Faith, the classic statement of local church theology.

There is another dimension to the use of the term autonomy that may be an additional clue to understanding Mullins in his appropriate context. Theologian Kenneth Cauthen has used the word to denote an emphasis on human reason and experience over against the orthodox stress upon authoritative revelation of God contained in biblical propositions. This was especially evident in the New Theology of the late nineteenth century that eventually may be identified as the liberal tradition. Cauthen noted that it was seen in degrees as most theologians generally tried to include both reason and revelation, but inevitably tilted one way or the other.[86] Nothing could more aptly describe Mullins; it is ironic that he used terms like "soul competence" and "autonomy" to anchor his theological axioms. Mullins frequently discussed his positions in what appears to be unclear phraseology, either because he was not sure himself or he was providing necessary camouflage for new ideas among his conservative constituency. His remarks before the 1904 Baptist Congress meeting illustrate this tendency:

> Experience is the starting point in constructing theology. Experience is not the sole principle in constructing theology. The other principle is revelation. Revelation as a principle involves experience but may be more than experience. ...I say experience should be the progressive apprehension of the transcendent God and the transcendent Christ, and the revelation through Christ is the method by which the transcendent God is reaching down to the place where we can reach up and grasp him.[87]

Mullins's preoccupation with Christian experience reveals a related context within his theology that often has been overlooked. While some contemporary writers have tried to trace Mullins's understanding to a "Whirlpool of Experience" and noted affinities with Frederich

---

[86] Cauthen, *Impact of American Religious Liberalism*, 12–13.

[87] E. Y. Mullins, "On Religious Experience" *Annual Session of the Baptist Congress for the Discussion of Current Questions, Held in Broadway Baptist Church, Louisville, Kentucky November 8, 9, 10, 1904* (New York: Baptist Congress Publishing Co., 1905) 93, 95.

Schleiermacher, William Newton Clarke, and Shailer Mathews,[88] Mullins was in fact caught up in the leading theological debates of the late nineteenth century. As William Hutchison has shown, the later nineteenth century gave rise to trends in theology in American denominations that caused Baptist writers to lay aside old concepts of religious authority, the predominance of the Bible as a source for Christian theology, heavy emphases on sacramentalism, for scientific methods of biblical criticism, an appreciation of the social and communal dimensions of Christianity, the notion of human progress in civilization and moral order, and the importance of religious experience. American theologians on leave in Europe discovered these ideas in the work of men like Dorner, Ritschl, Strauss, Tholuck, and, of course, Schleiermacher. Many among the Baptist schools in the Northeast, notably Ebenezer Dodge, Barnas Sears, Ezekiel Robinson, A. H. Strong, and W. N. Clarke developed these emphases in their classrooms and systematic theologies.

Mullins brought at least some of the trappings of the New Theology to his Louisville presidency in 1899. He had enjoyed recent intimate contact with Alvah Hovey and the Newton community, had read the papers of the Baptist Congress, and was encouraged by a distant friendship with William Newton Clarke at Colgate. He considered A. H. Strong at Rochester as having made "an able and suggestive contribution" to theology and sent a protégé to study there.[89] Beyond the Baptist community, Mullins gave clear evidence of interaction with Horace Bushnell, Richard Ely, Aldous Huxley, F. D. Maurice, and Robert Browning in England. He was clearly beyond the orthodoxy of the Princeton School that held Charles Hodge captive to an inconsistent sacramentalism.[90] He had a deep but not uncritical appreciation for Schleiermacher and Ritschl.[91] But, there were limits to the reception of the new theological currents in the Southern family. While he read the

---

[88] Curtis W. Freeman, "E. Y. Mullins and the Siren Songs of Modernity," *Review and Expositor* 96/1 (1999): 26–28.

[89] E. Y. Mullins, "The Theological Trend," in *Proceedings of the Baptist World Congress* 1905, (London: Baptist Union Publication Dept., 1905), 145-153. The protégé was W. T. Conner, later to serve at Southwestern Baptist Seminary in Texas.

[90] Mullins, *Axioms*, 108–111.

[91] Mullins thought Schleiermacher was lacking in comprehension of "facts" or evidence, and Ritschl, though having saved many from unbelief, propounded a system every bit as demanding as the most thorough Calvinism, that everyone, including Mullins was attempting to improve upon. See "Theological Trend," 257.

writings of fellow Baptist Walter Rauschenbusch, he shied away from terms like "social gospel," preferring instead the more awkward theoretical terms, "sociological gospel" or "social theology." He acknowledged the abuses of child labor, rampant materialism, and the corruption of family life, but refused to relinquish "regenerated individualism." Contrary to social Christianity, Mullins wrote: "It is by means of regenerated individuals associated together as churches that Christianity becomes a leaven to transform the social order...This is primary and fundamental."[92]

In response to the liberal trend among theologians such as Charles M. Sheldon or Washington Gladden who cast and limited Jesus to the role of a great teacher or moral example, Mullins drew a distinction between "copying" and "imitating" Christ. Again, his words: "To copy Christ is to attempt to feed the hungry thousands by a miraculous multiplication of loaves and fishes. To imitate Christ is to labor for equitable social conditions, just laws, and equal privileges for men that they may earn their own bread."[93] In contrast to most major mainline denominational leadership, Mullins studiously avoided identification with political parties or labor reform movements. He held that the theological identity of Southern Baptist Seminary and its denomination had been wrought on the anvil of the Bible and biblical theology, the directions he pursued. As William Ellis concluded, "Mullins's role as a theologian suffered because his evangelical predilections and the Southern Baptist atmosphere precluded any real theological innovation." Russell Dilday is nevertheless correct in observing that Mullins "obviously was a major influence on theology in the twentieth century" and that he continues to be a guide for much Southern Baptist theology in the twenty-first century.[94]

E. Y. Mullins found that the terminology he had chosen did not always equate with earlier Baptist usage and the New Testament connection was often tenuous. Baptist theologians in the Northern states and in Britain hailed the efforts, but quibbled over his terminology. Mullins persevered in his intellectual development and in the end aided in at least the temporary modernization of his denominational family. He

---

[92] Mullins, *Axioms,* 169–70.

[93] Mullins, *Axioms*, 172.

[94] Ellis, *Man of the Books*, 221; Russell Dilday, "Mullins the Theologian: Between the Extremes," *Review and Expositor* 96/1(1999): 75.

was a complex figure who continues to spark debate among biographers and theologians. His chief theological contributions included the simplification of Baptist theology and the internationalization of his part of the tradition. His axioms of religion became a kind of shorthand for Baptist distinctives. This was perhaps the first of countless attempts, particularly among Southern Baptists, to codify Baptist characteristics in convenient lists of five, six, or seven traits. Mullins also carried well beyond the traditional boundaries of the American South a definition of being Baptist that read very much "Southern Baptist." Not only did the publishing arms of the Sunday School Board and mission presses propagate seemingly to every corner of the earth a Southern Baptist perspective, Southern Baptists in the meantime became the generic standard by which all Baptists were defined. In much of the most widely circulated literature about Baptists, the religious ideals of the American South shine through without much reference to, or even awareness of, other Baptist kinds or perspectives. These include individualism, autonomy, religious experience, and biblicism. Herein lies the enduring genetic contribution of E. Y. Mullins to Baptist thought.

Southern Seminary theologian Harold W. Tribble (1899–1986) continued many of Mullins's emphases, but with less of a national or international forum. He completed his graduate education at Southern Seminary and was clearly a product of the Mullins/Robertson tradition. His 1925 New Testament doctor of theology dissertation was titled, "*Hagios* and *Hagiadzo* in the Johannine Literature." Tribble left Southern in 1947 to become president of Andover Newton Theological School. He would later be appointed president of Wake Forest University. Tribble's theological publications included a simplified version of the republished *Axioms of Religion* (1935). He called Mullins "the greatest thinker Southern Baptists produced up to this time."[95] Tribble added a discussion of the Kingdom of God to preface *Axioms* and concluded the revision with a "spiritual" interpretation of Christianity in the context of realized efforts toward church union among several denominations. He also deleted some of the detailed scholarship of the original axioms (notes from church history and Reformation theologians)

---

[95] Harold W. Tribble, "Edgar Young Mullins," *Review and Expositor* 49/2 (1952): 125. The new edition was a handbook sized item, carrying both Mullins's and Tribble's names. A subtitle explained that the original work had been rewritten and adapted by H. W. Tribble.

and omitted the nuances of the 1920s that Mullins had used to contemporize the first discussion, particularly with respect to Baptist denominational identity. Most helpful to a new, lay-characterized audience, Tribble added a set of study questions at the conclusion of each chapter.

Texas-born and theologically bred in the revivalist tradition, Dale Moody (1915–1992) has been called "the most significant Southern Baptist theologian of the latter half of the twentieth century."[96] He was educated at Baylor University, Dallas Theological Seminary, Southern Baptist Theological Seminary, and Oxford University. He wrote two doctoral dissertations: "The Problem of Revelation and Reason in the Writings of Emil Brunner" for the doctor of theology degree at Southern under the direction of W. O. Carver; and for the doctor of philosophy credential from Oxford he wrote "Discipline and Instruction: A Critical Study of the Theology of Infant Baptism with Special Reference to Recent Thought (1937–1964)" under the supervision of S. L. Greenslade, Regius Professor of Ecclesiastical History in Christ Church, and G. Henton Davies at Regent's Park College. His Oxford work was published as *Baptism: Foundation for Christian Unity* (1967).

During his long teaching career at Southern Seminary as the Joseph Emerson Brown Professor of Theology, Dale Moody took additional study at Union Theological Seminary in New York under Paul Tillich, as well as Karl Barth, Oscar Cullmann, and Walter Eichrodt at Basel, and at Zurich under Emil Brunner. At Union he read rationalistic theologians and assisted Henry P. Van Dusen at Columbia in teaching the history of Western thought. While at Oxford he also interacted with and had deep appreciation for Joachim Jeremias of Goettingen University, who served to reinforce Moody's proclivities for biblical studies. At the conclusion of his long career, Dale Moody confessed to being "nearer to Pannenberg and Moltmann than to any other German theologians."[97] He authored seven theological works and influenced hundreds of students at Southern

---

[96] Dwight Moody, as quoted in Timothy George, "Systematic Theology at Southern Seminary," *Review and Expositor* 82/1 (1985): 40.

[97] Dale Moody, "Perspectives on Scripture and Tradition: A Response by Dale Moody," *Perspectives in Religious Studies* 15/1 (1988): 14.

Seminary.[98] It is not overstating the case to say that Dale Moody was the theological determinant of the seminary while he taught there.

Moody's major theological work, *The Word of Truth* (1981), was a folksy summary of over four decades of his classroom lectures in systematic theology. Its subtitle, "A Summary of Christian Doctrine Based on Biblical Revelation," revealed Moody's approach was that of a biblical theologian. Because he perceived that theology in the United States had been dominated by systems other than biblical materials, he proposed that the structure of sound theology rests upon the solid foundation of historical revelation.[99] His categories followed a classic formulation beginning with God, God's works, sin, salvation, Christ, the Church, and Last Things. With a base clearly in his own generation of negative reaction to American fundamentalism and European Neo-Orthodoxy, he was in dialogue with biblical criticism, theology of worship, and ecumenical thought, particularly Roman Catholicism. He thought the light of God's revelation extended far through the various traditions of the church. Indeed, his view of Scripture was more open than most Southern Baptists: "Scripture is supreme and developing apostolic tradition is secondary," he wrote, "but it is surely right to give attention to experience and revelation, culture and reason also."[100] As a result, the book is riddled with citations from a wide variety of contemporary theologians, including Jürgen Moltmann, Ninian Smart, Hans Küng, Helmut Thielicke, and John Cobb.

What distinguished Moody's work from others are his views on apostasy, eschatology, and the universal church. Two were combative responses to fundamentalist theology of his era, the other a response to Landmarkism. On the matter of apostasy, Moody sought to correct the prevailing Calvinist dogmatic system of "perseverance of the saints". From clear and neglected biblical data, Moody demonstrated the presence of apostate believers in the early church and throughout the history of the church. He laid blame for perversion of biblical teaching on a line of thinkers from Augustine to Calvin, John Owen, the

---

[98] The best biographical account of Moody's life is E. Glenn Hinson, "Dale Moody: Bible Teacher Extraordinaire," *Perspectives in Religious Studies* 14/4 (1987): esp., 12.

[99] Dale Moody, "The Crux of Christian Theology," *Review and Expositor* 46/2 (1949): 167.

[100] Dale Moody, *The Word of Truth*: *A Summary of Christian Doctrine Based on Biblical Revelation* (Grand Rapids: Eerdmans, 1981) 40.

Landmarkists, L. S. Chafer of Dallas Seminary, and in his own era, R. T. Kendall of Westminster Chapel in London.[101] In 1941 Moody credited A. T. Robertson for "helping him out of eternal security," and he devoted a good deal of his pulpit effort from that time forward to refuting the error.[102] Labelling John Owen's work an ordeal of verbosity, he mused, "A reading of the old Augustine and the old Calvin raises the question whether old men should discuss predestination, perseverance and apostasy at all!"[103]

Likewise, Moody was scathing in his rebuke of fundamentalist eschatology. He rejected the dispensationalist preoccupation with the restoration of Israel in favor of a kingdom of God motif. In the coming kingdom, Moody theorized, the Jews and the Gentiles will constitute a *pleroma*, the fullness of the Body of Christ, the Church. In dealing with literalistic pretribulationism, he asserted the "language of Zion, the concrete symbolism that speaks to those saturated with the words of Holy Scripture."[104] All of biblical revelation points to the future when God as Creator and Sustainer will redeem fallen creation. The *pleroma* will be realized at the *parousia* (the appearing of Christ in the last times). More than the fulfillment of millennial kingdom details, Moody longed for both cosmic and personal redemption.[105] In his textbook on eschatology, *The Hope of Glory* (1964), he plumbed the depths of both biblical data and modern scholarship only to conclude that God is the ultimate personal reality and "man's relationship with God is eternal, either without or within the Holy City."[106] He freely and humbly admitted that behind all the biblical images and symbols, and behind the seeming exactitudes of theological systems, there remained much uncertainty about details of the "last things."

---

[101] Ibid., 362. Moody noted that R. T. Kendall's M.A. thesis, "The Rise and Demise of Calvinism in the Southern Baptist Convention" (Southern Baptist Theological Seminary, 1973) was an attempt to refute Moody's position with respect to his rejection of Calvinism. Kendall later moved to accept some of Moody's views.

[102] Moody was especially fond of I. Howard Marshall's doctoral thesis at the University of Aberdeen in 1963, because Marshall's exegetical findings supported Moody's theology. Ibid., 353.

[103] Ibid., 359, 361.

[104] Ibid., 591.

[105] Ibid., 566–75.

[106] Dale Moody, *The Hope of Glory* (Grand Rapids: Eerdmans, 1964) 170, 278–80.

Moody strongly rejected the Landmarkist tendency in Southern Baptist life. His theology of the church extended from plain teaching of Scripture and could be summarized as witness, service, and fellowship. Moody's contemporary Wayne E. Ward, who followed him at Southern Seminary as Joseph Emerson Brown Professor of Theology, astutely showed how his predecessor's concept of the Church was trinitarian, using biblical metaphors as "people of God," "bride of Christ," and "fellowship of the Spirit."[107] Moody further emphasized the multiplicity of patterns in the New Testament community, and across the span of church history, four stages of church structure that parallel the work of Catholic theologian, Hans Küng. Moody found in his own experience the drawing of God's Spirit toward greater unity in the one Lord of the Church.[108] In retrospect, it was Moody's doctoral work on baptism at Oxford that truly transformed his idea of the church universal. He later recalled the early sixties as "exciting days of Pope John XXIII" when theological dialogue was ongoing throughout the Christian world. He tackled the well-worn track of baptismal theology, owing a great debt to Anglican tradition. At one level Moody believed the Reformation was incomplete without baptismal reform. Practically speaking, however, he realized that pedobaptists would not likely accept a "believer's baptism" position and vice versa. Through an Anglican formation, he came to recognize the two forms of baptism for different purposes in the "wholeness" of the Body of Christ.[109] This led him to appreciate large sections of the visible church outside usual Baptist circles, as well as increased recognition of his own work in the ecumenical scene.

Not only did his scholarship reflect his larger ecclesiology, but Moody's associations did so as well. He was a member of the Faith and Order Commission of the World Council of Churches at a time when Baptists were uncertain about the ecumenical movement. He openly conversed with Roman Catholic theologians and prelates. Moody lectured at the Gregorian University in Rome, the first Baptist to do so. Twice he participated in The Tantur Ecumenical Institute for Advanced

---

[107] Wayne Ward, "Dale Moody's Ecclesiology," *Perspectives in Religious Studies* 14/4 (1987) 86–87.

[108] A keen insight into Moody's eccelesiology is found in Duke K. McCall, *What Is the Church?* (Nashville: Broadman Press, 1958), that Moody helped to compile.

[109] Dale Moody, *Baptism: Foundation for Christian Unity* (Grand Rapids: Eerdmans, 1967) 304.

Theological Research in Jerusalem. Beeson Divinity School theologian Timothy George has noted Moody's influence in the 1963 *Baptist Faith and Message* article on the Church: "the Body of Christ which includes all of the redeemed of all the ages."[110]

Related to the Moody era at Southern Baptist Seminary were William Mueller, Wayne E. Ward, Eric Rust, and James Leo Garrett. As Moody defined theological studies, specialization and segmentation in the theological curriculum at Southern ensued. Mueller (1902–2001) gravitated to historical theology and particularly the Reformers and devotional classics. Mueller not only wrote the centennial history of the seminary, but also *Church and State in Luther and Calvin* (1954). Ward (b. 1921), whose doctoral work at Southern Seminary was supervised by Mueller and William Davis, wrote his dissertation on "The Concept of Holy Scripture in Biblical Literature." Ward also studied at the University of Basel with Karl Barth. As a professor at Southern, he initially took the New Testament as his area of theology, complementing Eric Rust in Old Testament. Ward also taught systematic, contemporary, and Baptist theology across his career, and assumed the Brown chair in theology when Dale Moody stepped down. His major books included *The Drama of Redemption* (1966) and *The Word Comes Alive* (1969).

Eric Rust (1910–1991), who came to Louisville from Rawdon College in Britain as Professor of Apologetics, emphasized pastoral theology, Christian philosophy, and science and religion. Much influenced by Neo-Orthodox thinkers Barth, Brunner, and Niebuhr, his first important work was *The Christian Understanding of History* (1947), that remained a classic for many years in Christian historiography. Later he wrote *Science and Faith: Towards a Theological Understanding of Nature* (1967). In contrast to Rust was W. T. Conner's Texan protégé, James Leo Garrett. He spent almost two decades in Louisville emphasizing historical theology and managing to further his studies at Harvard. In the post-World War II era, Southern Seminary developed unparalleled leadership in the breadth of theological studies offered in its department. No other theological institution had the faculty resources, the student support, or the research agenda in its graduate programs as did the Baptist seminary. Its graduates ranged broadly around the Baptist world across the next five decades until reorganization in the 1990s. The

---

[110] Timothy George, "Systematic Theology at Southern Seminary," *Review and Expositor* 82/1 (1985): 41.

members of "Moody's team" were responsive to the broader theological currents of the era and decidedly Neo-orthodox, personalist, and historical in approach.[111] Here they reflected more gradually the patterns already in place in British Baptist and Northern/American Baptist theological schools. They also portended a growing disaffection with academic theologians in Southern Baptist Convention schools at the grass-roots level of the denomination.

The theological tradition at Southern Baptist Seminary has been characterized over time by its preoccupation with biblical tradition, an openness to general theological trends in the United States and Europe, and a self-image of being a theological "pace-setter" in the denominational family.

SOUTHWESTERN BAPTIST THEOLOGICAL SEMINARY

Next in order of prominence among Southern Baptist schools is Southwestern Baptist Theological Seminary in Fort Worth, Texas. An outgrowth of the Bible Department of Baylor University, Southwestern had auspicious beginnings. Probably the most conservative of all the North American Baptist seminaries in 1910, it was a bulwark of Baptist distinctives. Its early faculty included Albert H. Newman and Calvin Goodspeed (of Canadian notoriety) behind the resourceful leadership of Texan B. H. Carroll. The seminary grew rapidly under its Texas presidents, stressing pastoral ministry and evangelism. In 1905–06 the school offered its first doctoral program and became a competitor of Southern Seminary. The growth of the school in Fort Worth warranted a separately organized School of Theology in 1923 that anticipated other programs for women, music, and religious education. Yet, the perception of Southwestern's academic standing among Southern Baptists has always been overshadowed by Louisville, and its theological tradition has been marked by Texas cultural individualism and popular piety. In many ways, its strength has been greater in the area of church history than in theology. Southwestern Seminary has been the institutional home to noted historians such as A. H. Newman, William W. Barnes, Robert A. Baker, William Estep, and H. Leon McBeth.

---

[111] In assessing the period, Rust emphasized the personal character of God as a primary motif among the faculty in theology. See Eric C. Rust, "Theological Emphases of the Past Three Decades," *Review and Expositor* 78/12. (1981): 260–61.

In its earliest development, Benajah Harvey Carroll (1843–1914) was the shaper of Southwestern's theological position. He graduated from Baylor University and became one of its most loyal sons. L. R. Scarborough, Carroll's successor as president, credited Carroll's defense of New Testament life and theology as pastor of First Baptist, Waco, and as a prime organizer of the Bible program at Baylor in the 1880s. He was a widely regarded preacher and revivalist who published a number of tracts and a multi-volume Bible commentary that reflected traditional Calvinistic interpretations of key passages.

Carroll first made certain that the new school was under tight control of the Baptist General Convention of Texas. He suggested a process that would become a theological guarantor in generations ahead, namely that orthodoxy was to be assured first by the faculty, then the trustees, if necessary the Convention, and ultimately the supportive churches. Next, he proposed the New Hampshire Confession of Faith as the doctrinal basis. The only modification he suggested was the removal of the term "visible" [with respect to the church], and the addition of the term "particular." L. R. Scarborough, who taught evangelism at the seminary for several decades, wrote: "If the heart of an institution burns hot with the fires of soul-winning, it is not likely to drift in its theology from the fundamentals of its New Testament faith."[112] Here he carried forth the simple, direct Bible apologetic set in place by Carroll.

Robert Baker's recent version of the seminary history indicates that Carroll was greatly enamored of C. H. Spurgeon's stand against theological liberalism in the Baptist Union of Great Britain and how he directed the college that took his name to avoid such unsavory tendencies.[113] This helps to explain Carroll's continuous references to liberal, modernist tendencies against which the new school would stand unashamed. In this regard, Carroll's tendency toward Landmarkism must be noted. As one writer has pointed out, "he magnified the authority of the local church" in a 1903 published lecture, and with respect to the controversy raised at Southern Baptist seminary in Louisville over President Whitsitt's interpretation of Baptist history, Carroll supported a Landmarker position. It is likely that he had maintained a friendship with

---

[112] Lee R. Scarborough, *A Modern School of the Prophets: A History of the Southwestern Baptist Theological Seminary* (Nashville: Broadman Press, 1939) 153–62.

[113] Robert A. Baker, *Tell the Generations Following: A History of Southwestern Baptist Theological Seminary 1908–1983* (Nashville: Broadman Press, 1983) 96–97.

the venerable James R. Graves, whose following in Texas was enormous.[114] Certainly Carroll's theological position would have been broader without the dominance of Landmarkist thought in Texas.

Calvin Goodspeed joined the faculty at Baylor University, later Southwestern, in 1905. Lured to Texas by his former McMaster University colleague, A. H. Newman, the latter described him as "teaching a thoroughly orthodox theology, repelling what he conceives to be erroneous innovations."[115] While teaching in Texas, Goodspeed completed work on the "Genesis" volume in the American Commentary that Daniel Weldon had started prior to his death. Goodspeed gave first-rate evidence of his own abilities in biblical exegesis and of familiarity with a wide range of scholarship. Apparently, under Alvah Hovey's editorial guidance and his own fidelity to Weldon's work, Goodspeed was compelled to answer the Old Testament radical critics. A self-described "conservative," he took lengthy exception to the Graf-Wellhausen Hypothesis of post-Mosaic authorship and the evolutionary school of thinking. Goodspeed believed that the logical tendency of radical scholarship was toward anti-supernaturalism. That, in turn, led to denial of the incarnation of the Son of God, as well as his resurrection and vicarious work. Goodspeed held that the new theories resulted in reducing Christianity to an ethical code and to the same class as other religions. Those great doctrines "held by the most royal men of all the Christian centuries" were to be preserved tenaciously. Goodspeed feared that holding too critical a view of Scripture would lead to unitarianism characteristic of fellow Baptists Nathaniel Schmidt, H. P. Smith, and Julius Kaftan of Berlin.[116]

Along with Southwestern's esteemed founder, B. H. Carroll, Goodspeed became an early theological apologist for the Texas seminary. In a series of essays on selected articles of faith, Goodspeed defined Southwestern's position on some key doctrines. On "Sanctification" he spoke of a believer becoming more like God himself.

---

[114] Ibid., On the other side, Baker also suggests that Carroll was an opponent of the Gospel Mission movement and that he was in fact the target of the verbal abuse of S. A. Hayden's anti-conventionism, both of which were Texas-nurtured manifestations of Landmarkism. On the Haydenite Controversy see Early, "The Haydenite Controversy".

[115] Newman, "Recent Changes in The Theology of Baptists," *American Journal of Theology* 10/4 (October 1906): 606.

[116] Calvin Goodspeed, "Introduction," *An American Commentary on the Old Testament* (Philadelphia: American Baptist Publication Society, 1909) xxxvi.

He rejected instantaneous and entire sanctification (a popular Wesleyan position) in favor of a progressive work that he called "biblical", because "no class can claim to be a sanctified aristocracy."[117] In a second essay on the "Perseverance of the Saints", he took a position congruent with the New Hampshire Confession of Faith, essentially proof-texting the divine foundation of perseverance.[118] The last piece that he wrote focused on the relationship of the Law to the Gospel. Here he became pastoral and quoted a number of texts from the Apostle Paul to demonstrate that the Gospel did what the Law could not accomplish. "Preaching", he said, "must have the tough fiber of righteousness as well as the tenderness of love."[119] It is more than likely that Goodspeed assisted Carroll in the writing of the seminary's original Articles and was thus in an excellent position to interpret them. He was clearly a "tower of strength" for accepted Baptist doctrine and practice: conservative, biblical, and moderately Calvinistic.

Walter Thomas Conner (1877–1952) followed Goodspeed. Conner, a longstanding theologian at Southwestern from a Southern revivalistic background, was educated at Simmons College and Baylor University, followed by theological studies at Rochester Theological Seminary. His doctoral work, completed at Southern Baptist Theological Seminary, focused upon pragmatism and theology at the University of Chicago. Conner was the principal writing theologian at Southwestern Baptist Theological Seminary from1910 until 1949.

Among several influences on the young Conner were John S. Tanner, B. H. Carroll, A. H. Strong, the Chicago School, and E. Y. Mullins, all Baptist stalwarts of the first years of the twentieth century. While a student at Baylor University, Tanner gave Conner a deep sense of mission-mindedness that caused him to ask the practical questions of all theological reflection. B. H. Carroll's influence was less positive: Conner declined to follow Carroll's eschatological system and thought Carroll was too rigid in his orthodoxy. He referred to Carroll's thought as "a combination of strange elements...an inflexible system of theology

---

[117] Calvin Goodspeed, "Our Articles of Faith: Sanctification," *Southwestern Journal of Theology* 7/3 (1923): 55–63.

[118] Calvin Goodspeed, "Our Articles of Faith: The Perseverance of the Saints," *Southwestern Journal of Theology* 7/4 (1923): 28–36.

[119] Calvin Goodspeed, "Our Articles of Faith: Harmony of the Law and the Gospel," *Southwestern Journal of Theology* 8/1 (1924): 29.

which had much of the character of medieval scholasticism elements."[120] At Southwestern Baptist Seminary, Conner was much influenced by Calvin Goodspeed who had arrived from Canada just after A. H. Newman. It was Goodspeed's advice that led to Conner's study at Rochester Seminary. In the Rochester environment 1909–10, Conner was favorably impressed with Strong, then Rauschenbusch, and finally with H. C. Mabie. He later pursued one year of theological studies at the Divinity School of the University of Chicago, an experience he found unsettling. Conner thought Shailer Mathews was shallow in his assessment of doctrine, that Foster was helpful philosophically, and that Gerald Birney Smith was radically eclectic and critical. Conner wrote of his experience at Chicago: "They teach a number of things which they call theology, but it is bad philosophy with a false brand."[121]

At Southern Baptist Theological Seminary, Conner was most impressed with E. Y. Mullins. Beginning with Mullins's preoccupation with "soul competence," Conner learned to distinguish between experiential religion and theological propositions. His theological system came to be characterized by Christian experience. Mullins helped him appreciate the work of Borden P. Bowne at Boston University in the "personalist school," though Conner himself did not fully embrace the approach. Much concerned for the "practicalness" of theology, Conner completed a Th.D. dissertation at Southern Seminary in 1916 titled "Pragmatism and Theology." He later submitted a second dissertation at Southern in 1931, "The Idea of the Incarnation in the Gospel of John" for the Ph.D.[122]

An assessment of Conner's thought and writing indicates that he was widely read and relied upon over fifty major theologians and philosophers in his formal work. [123]Later influences included P. T. Forsyth, E. J. Goodspeed, and James Denny. He read Karl Barth, A. H. Newman, and H. E. Dana with appreciation. A study of various theologians in Conner's works reveals more references to Mullins,

---

[120]Ibid., 91..

[121] James Leo Garrett, Jr. 'The Theology of Walter Thomas Conner (Th. D. dissertation, Southern Baptist Theological Seminary, 1954), 98-131.

[122] Quoted in Stewart A. Newman, *W.T. Conner: Theologian of the Southwest* (Nashville: Broadman Press, 1964), 89-90.

[123] James Leo Garrett, Jr. "Walter Thomas Conner" *Theologians of the Baptist Tradition*, 206.

Strong, Denny, and Barth than others. Conner published fifteen books from 1924 to 1954, ranging from his systematic theology to popular works on Bible doctrines and the Christian life. His position at Southwestern placed him among the most widely read theologians among Southern Baptists of the twentieth century.

From an institutional perspective, James Leo Garrett (b.1925) was W. T. Connor's successor at Southwestern and belongs in his predecessor's tradition. He was educated at Baylor University, Southwestern Baptist Theological Seminary, and Harvard University. Although Garrett taught at Southern Baptist Theological Seminary and later directed Baylor University's J. M. Dawson Institute for Church-State Studies for eight years, he is primarily known as a Southwestern Seminary theologian. Garrett has edited several important works, including *Baptist Relations with Other Christians* and *Calvin and the Reformed Tradition* (1980). His most important authored work was *Systematic Theology: Biblical, Historical, and Evangelical* (2 volumes, 1995).

Leo Garrett has been an important theologian on the Baptist scene for several decades. His appreciation for the larger world in which Baptists live is particularly notable. In 1965 he wrote a helpful introduction to Baptist understanding of Vatican II, *Baptists and Roman Catholicism,* in which he surveyed and classified two centuries of Baptist writings about the papal system and Catholic doctrine. He pointed out the dilemma facing the Baptist community: either respond to an invitation to engage in inter-religious dialogue or continue to consider Catholics as subjects for evangelization. He was pro-dialogue in order to clarify common ground against non-Christians, to encourage use of new study materials produced by Catholics and Protestants, and to extirpate the pagan influences from international Catholicism. Garrett also strongly believed in the "purifying judgment of God" over all "ecclesiastical structures."[124] His later book, *Baptist Relations with Other Christians* (1974), was a collection of essays detailing international Baptist relations with other Christian bodies and councils. Garrett himself encouraged looking at the Baptist position between "churches" and "sects" and called upon Baptists to consider more carefully the contemporary needs of Christian cooperation in areas like evangelism, missions, education, and

---

[124] James Leo Garrett, Jr., *Baptists and Roman Catholicism: A Survey of Baptist Writings about the Roman Catholic Church, with an Interpretation of Recent Developments* (Nashville: Broadman Press, 1965) 45.

publication. He advised reference to "Concepts of Unity and Models of Union Consultation" sponsored by the World Council of Churches. To his denomination's credit, Professor Garrett represented Baptists in varying contexts for bilateral conversations, notably with Roman Catholics in the 1980s and briefly the Orthodox Churches in the 1990s. At a time when a nearly xenophobic fundamentalist resurgence has dominated his own Baptist family, Leo Garrett has been a courageous witness for ecumenism.

As one thumbs through the fourteen-hundred pages of Garrett's *magnum opus* dealing with systematic theology, it is evident that he is rightly considered A. H. Strong's successor in the second half of the twentieth century. Like Strong, Garrett exhaustively surveys each topic, supplying an impressive array of references to predominantly contemporary literature. His own unique contributions include defining theology as a practical or ministry-oriented discipline whose aspects include those that are fixed and those that reflect change.[125] A committed systematician, Garrett tenaciously holds on to the utility of systematic theology in the face of numerous Baptist and evangelical theologians who question the very concept. Garrett claims that his own formulation of doctrine follows locating and correlating Old and New Testament texts and the more significant statements from the patristic period to the modern age.[126] In defense of his understanding of theology as "evangelical," Garrett asserts that the tasks of theology are polemical, apologetic, ethical, and missionary.

With respect to the authority of Scripture, Garrett equates the terms dependability, trustworthiness, infallibility, and inerrancy. He further announces that no essential Christian doctrine is in jeopardy from any perceived discrepancies in the Bible, unless it is inerrancy. For him the authority of the Bible—indeed for all of Christianity—rests squarely upon the authority of a sovereign God. God's authority commands and persuades, but does not coerce.[127] On the doctrine of Christ, Garrett likewise affirms historic orthodoxy in a contemporary phrase, "Christians should reverently acknowledge the unfathomable, non-analogical mystery of his person." Garrett appears to find, even if

---

[125] James Leo Garrett, Jr., *Systematic Theology: Biblical, Historical, and Evangelical,* 2 vols. (Grand Rapids: Eerdmans, 1990; 1995), 1:10.
[126] Ibid., ix.
[127] Ibid., 167, 182.

somewhat haltingly, that Millard Erickson is persuasive regarding the preponderance of the biblical witness in favor of a universal atonement. His position on the theories of atonement is a combination of triumph, satisfaction, and regeneration, following P. T. Forsyth and John Stott.[128]

One of Garrett's particular strengths is his work on the doctrine of the church. A theologian much involved in ecumenical dialogues, he maintains a cooperative and engaging ecclesiology. For example, when comparing Jesuit scholar Avery Dulles and Southern Baptist Harold Songer, Garrett finds the church to be a combination of four models: redeemed community, gospel herald, suffering servant, and institution. Not surprisingly, he connects his discussion of the mission and ministry of the church with the ordinances, membership and polity of the churches, while modestly dismissing Landmarkism.[129]

Baptists in North America have been much occupied in the twentieth century with eschatological issues. Garrett devoted a major section of his systematic to that topic; including almost two hundred pages dealing with judgment, heaven, and hell. Following a survey and critique of positions regarding the millennium, Garrett concludes the key to unlock the meaning of Revelation 20:1–6 has yet to be found. For those who have argued for a position other than eternal punishment, he warns that the weight of tradition is strongly in favor of the doctrine. His treatment, and indeed his systematic theology, happily concludes with heaven defined as "the complete manifestation of God's glory."[130]

James Leo Garrett's systematic theology is more and less than it appears. As a type of theological literature that hearkens back to the nineteenth century—even to John Gill in its comprehensiveness—it is a feast for the Baptist student in a theological school. Garrett gives his writing a collegial tone and renders the systematic theology in parallel with a typical seminary curriculum. There is some disappointment in the new directions Garrett offers. More often than not, after surveying the extant literature on a particular issue, he accepts a predictable position or combines the best of several existing writers.

---

[128] Ibid., 2:54, 65.
[129] Ibid., 480; 531–32; 741–42.
[130] Ibid., 2:768, 807, 821.

SUMMARY

Southern Baptists occupy an important place and role in the development
of overall Baptist thought. Over the course of their development, they
exhibited first a dependence upon Baptist mentors and schools in the
North as well as the Presbyterian Princeton Theological Seminary. In
fact, the Princeton influence held sway for decades through the end of
the nineteenth century. Later, the school of thought associated with
Southern Baptist Theological Seminary moved cautiously along the
continuum of modernization behind E. Y. Mullins and Dale Moody,
before being reorganized by resurgent fundamentalist and Calvinistic
movements in the 1990s. That resurgence at the institutional levels of
the denomination led to a dispersion of Southern Seminary's traditionally
moderate theological representatives. Southwestern Baptist Theological
Seminary remained closer to its revivalistic heritage and influenced
thousands of pastors throughout the Convention family. Between 1994
and 2003, however, it too was re-organized along fundamentalist lines
and its formerly influential faculty and theological rubric dispersed.

As we have surveyed the theological development of Southern
Baptists, three features may be particularly noted. First is the overall
Reformed orientation of the Convention and its schools. This can hardly
be denied in the training of early faculty and curricula of Southern
Seminary. Second, James Thompson has observed that whether
fundamentalist or not, all Southern Baptists approach Scripture as God's
Word "constantly aware of the difference between it and the inspired
works of men."[131] This means that while other major components of the
Baptist family have embraced biblical criticism to one degree or another,
such an approach to the Bible's texts and their interpretation presented a
serious problem for Southern Baptists. Third is the pervasive influence of
Landmarkism or local church protectionism. This nineteenth century
phenomenon has strengthened expressions of the doctrine of the church,
while limiting theological conversation outside the Southern Baptist
tradition. Finally, it must be noted that with the exception of E. Y.
Mullins, Dale Moody, and James L. Garrett, few Southern Baptist
theologians have transcended their own denominational family and few

---

[131] James J. Thompson, Jr., *Tried As By Fire: Southern Baptists and the Religious
Controversies of the 1920s* (Macon GA: Mercer University Press, 1982) 85.

are recognized as players in the worldwide Baptist family, not to speak of evangelical or liberal Protestantism.

CHAPTER 8

AFRICAN AMERICAN
BAPTIST TRADITIONS

> Our theology is not, as has been suggested, a poor imitation
> of the white man's religion.[1]
>
> Joseph H. Jackson

The African American Baptist experience is a category to itself, while also displaying genetic traits relating to the entirety of the Baptist tradition. African American Baptists span a history for a period from at least the mid-eighteenth century to the present. Significantly, Baptists constitute the largest single category of Christians among African Americans. The priority of identifiably Baptist themes and emphases among other African American Christians is unmistakable both because of the chronological contribution of Baptists in establishing churches and institutions, and the prominence of Black Baptist leaders in the evolution of black theology.[2] It is a theological tradition that encompasses the slave and free churches, as well as mainstream, evangelical, and liberation theologies. Along with evangelical Calvinism, religious liberty, and the social gospel, African American Baptist thought made primary and uniquely Baptist contributions to Christian theology.

Black Baptist theology is a category of African American thought and follows several oft-repeated themes. A "compensatory" pattern developed whereby in spirituals and recorded prayers it is said that God is on the side of the African Americans, knows their plight, and will

---

[1] J.H. Jackson, *A Story of Christian Activism: The History of the National Baptist Convention USA, Inc.* (Nashville: Townshend Press, 1980), 590.

[2] See for instance, Milton C. Sernett, ed., *Afro-American Religious History: A Documentary Witness* (Durham NC: Duke University Press, 1985) 43–50; 337–48;423–64; and Gayraud S. Wilmore, *Black Religion and Black Radicalism: An Interpretation of the Religious History of Afro-American People* (Maryknoll: Orbis Books, 1983) 5, 128.

reward them in this life or the next. Heaven became a place where the servant will be free of trials and tribulations. Powerful metaphors stirred the people under great duress: "God fights battles;" "God is a rock in a weary land;" "God is shelter in a mighty storm."[3] There was also another set of themes that may be categorized as uplifting to the African American: "God is against slavery;" "God created all races;" "the Negro is not an inferior person;" and "God will bring slaveholders to their just rewards."[4]

Benjamin Mays found that after 1914 African American imagery of God took another direction. Following World War I, social changes were needed. This-worldly themes replaced the earlier other-worldly themes in vocabulary of Black religious language. Life was recognized as a hazardous undertaking, and therefore protection from danger, disease, death, hell, and enemies in this world was necessary. Yet a third set of themes stressed that the African American was God's perfect handiwork, that the entire human family is united in God, and that the Black person was on a special errand for God in this difficult period. A note of hope was captured in the sentiment that peace and goodwill finally would come when the races recognized their unity in God.[5] Part of the result of the American social reality for the Black community in the 1920s and 1930s was disillusionment, worsening segregation, doubt, and cynicism. Persons entrenched in what was referred to as the old Negro church stressed more than ever that their cause was just and that God was going to see them through the times of continuing injustice. Booker T. Washington, for example, elucidated the tradition that is firm in faith in God, while W. E. B. DuBois was clear about God, but unsure that God was of any help in the struggle for social parity following the emancipation of the enslaved African Americans.[6] The character of the African American social experience and how it was interpreted within that community gave shape to the unique contributions of Black Baptist theological expression.

Historically, African American Baptist thought has been dominated by personalities who served as pastors within their communities. Miles

---

[3] Benjamin E. Mays, *The Negro's God as Reflected in His Literature* (Boston: Chapman & Grimes, 1938) 79–82, 116–18.

[4] Ibid., 247.

[5] Ibid., 249–50.

[6] Ibid., 139, 249–54.

Fisher, W. E. B. DuBois, and later historians have pointed out the connections between slave preachers and African priests. Whether slave exhorters or recognized clergy, the preacher/pastors were the theologians of the black communities.[7] John Jasper (1812–1901) was an important early leader in the development of African American Baptist genetic heritage. A former slave, Jasper was regionally known as a great orator who exploited the metaphors of Scripture by the employment of a "black vernacular," sometimes with outlandish results.[8] He served as pastor of Sixth Mount Zion Baptist Church in Richmond, Virginia, for over three decades. His sermon "De Sun Do Move" was a remarkable piece of slave idiom. Jasper demonstrated that Black Baptist thinking was richly experiential and he helped establish a foundation for a stream of theology that would rise from the biblical narratives.[9] Andrew Bryan in Georgia, Lott Carey in Virginia, and Thomas Paul in New England and later New York, also exemplified this pastoral and theological role.

A new breed of Black leaders emerged under the nurture of the American Baptist Home Mission Society following the War Between the States. Chief among these was William James Simmons (1849–1890). Educated at Madison University, the University of Rochester, and Howard University, Simmons took up a career in school teaching, worked as a dental apprentice, and also served in the Civil War. Simmons's motto was "God, my race, and denomination." As Black Baptist life took shape following the Civil War, his education and pastoral skill drew him by increasing measure to significant leadership roles. In 1880 he became president of the Normal and Theological Institute of Louisville, Kentucky, where "he awarded numerous Doctor of Divinity degrees, ministered to a local church, trained leading clergy, organized political events, edited a newspaper and presided over a

---

[7] Milton C. Sernett, *Black Religion and American Evangelicalism: White Protestants, Plantation Missions, and the Flowering of Negro Christianity, 1787–1865* (Metuchen: Scarecrow Press, 1975) 94–101.

[8] Walter F. Pitts, *Old Ship of Zion: The Afro-Baptist Ritual in the African Diaspora* (New York: Oxford University Press, 1993) 67.

[9] On Jasper, see William E. Hatcher, *John Jasper: The Unmatched Negro Philosopher and Preacher* (New York: Fleming H. Revell, 1908); and Richard Ellsworth Day, *Rhapsody in Black: The Life Story of John Jasper* (Philadelphia: Judson Press, 1953) esp., 95–111.

denomination....In short Simmons was an ecclesiastical politician with a powerful patronage system."[10]

In 1886 Simmons began to build support for his dream of a united Black Baptist organization. In an open letter to churches, Simmons characterized the Black church as a place to promote piety, sociability, and a better knowledge of each other. Further, he believed the church could encourage literary gifts and discuss the important questions of the day. Behind a simple ecclesiology was a conviction of the church as an agent of much-needed social transformation.[11] As an agent of morality, the theological underpinning of the church would reach into every area of life. His dream was realized in short order. Simmons became president of the American National Baptist Convention 1886–1890 and left an indelible legacy of Christian ministry and hope to this body. While other Black organizations focused upon redeeming the African homeland, Simmons focused entirely upon the circumstances of the American Black.

Theologically and programmatically, Simmons was concerned with the problems that Black Baptists faced. The Convention embarked upon a course that stressed "self-elevation" of Blacks through social and educational renovation. For him, "the Baptist host is like a cube; throw them aside and they always land on an equal side, and you need never despair when in your trials and doubts in your several churches; remember the God of battles is on your side and that the ages have only increased his glory."[12] Further, he recognized early that within the African American experience there was an inherently unique quality. "The spirituality of this race was not diminished in slavery."[13] Although they copied much from their masters, Simmons observed that in African Americans there was "a vigorous, vital, God-like spirituality" that needed nourishment. His desire was therefore "to exalt his people, snatch their lives from obscurity to become household matter for conversation."[14] A prolific author, he wrote countless essays on Baptist

---

[10] James Melvin Washington, *Frustrated Fellowship*: *The Black Baptist Quest for Social Power* (Macon GA: Mercer University Press, 1986) 159–60.

[11] See Owen Pelt and Ralph Smith, *The Story of the National Baptists* (New York: Vantage Press, 1960) 88–91.

[12] William J. Simmons, *Men of Mark*: *Eminent, Progressive, and Rising* (Nashville: Rowell Co., 1887) 16.

[13] Ibid., 2.

[14] Ibid., 2–3.

polity and thought, as well as compiling a hagiographic dictionary for "Men of Mark."

Other Black leaders in the Progressive Era were Elias Camp Morris (1855–1922) and Lewis G. Jordan (c. 1860–1940). Morris was born into slavery, apprenticed as a shoemaker, self-educated, and ultimately attended Roger Williams University in Nashville. The Alabama State Normal Institute awarded him a doctor of philosophy degree, and in his later years the State University in Kentucky conferred an honorary doctoral degree upon him. Morris built educational institutions to improve the future of Black Baptists and joined the chorus in favor of a Black Baptist ecclesiology. Likewise, Jordan was reared in slavery and used the narratives of his experience to create an appreciation of the African American's pilgrimage and unique spirituality. He was educated at Roger Williams University and served congregations in San Antonio and Waco, Texas, and Philadelphia, Pennsylvania. Jordan was convinced that the future of Black Baptists required that they develop their own identity and community resources. Against conservatives who favored a slower course in recognizing the gains of religious freedom, he moved boldly along the same lines as Simmons. Inevitably, this led to schism in the formation of the Lott Carey Foreign Mission Convention. Among others who favored a separation from white structures, and eventually white thought, were Walter H. Brooks of Washington, D.C., and Richard H. Boyd of Texas. These men would sew the seeds of a movement that sought to establish a distinctive Black consciousness.[15] Historian James Washington has noted the contribution of Black women in the making of the African American Baptist experience of the later nineteenth century.[16]

Miles Mark Fisher (1899–1970) was one of the first nationally recognized African American Baptist scholars. He was educated at Morehouse College, later receiving his seminary degree from Northern Baptist Theological Seminary. At the University of Chicago he wrote a

---

[15] See James D. Tyms, *The Rise of Religious Education Among Negro Baptists: A Historical Case Study* (New York: Exposition Press, 1965) 150–51.

[16] Washington, *Frustrated Fellowship*, 139n. See also Evelyn Brooks, "The Feminist Theology of the Black Baptist Church, 1880–1900" in *Class Race, and Sex: The Dynamics of Control*, ed. Amy Swerdlow and Hanna Lessinger (Boston: G. K. Hall, 1983) 31–59; and her other article, "Nannie Helen Burroughs and the Education of Black Women" in *The Afro-American Woman: Struggles and Images*, ed. Sharon Harley and Rosalyn Terborg-Penn (Port Washington NY: Kennikat Press, 1978) 97–108.

doctoral dissertation titled "Negro Slave Songs in the United States" under the supervision of William Warren Sweet, Sidney Mead, Amos Wilder, and Joachim Wach. He served at Richmond Theological Seminary as Hoyt Professor of Church History and later at Shaw University Divinity School in Raleigh, North Carolina. For many years he was pastor of White Rock Baptist Church in Durham, North Carolina.

Fisher followed in the footsteps of his distinguished father, Elijah John Fisher (1858–1915) who was the pastor of Olivet Baptist Church in Chicago for eight years. The elder Fisher was born and raised in slavery in LaGrange, Georgia. He became a "floor preacher" and taught himself rudimentary theology from reading Boyd's *Eclectic Moral Philosophy*, Adam Clarke's *Commentaries*, and the *Works of Josephus*. Later he studied at Atlanta Baptist Seminary (Morehouse College) and the University of Chicago. At an early stage in ministry, the senior Fisher published essays on "The Influence of Baptist Principles on Other Denominations" and "A Regenerated Church Membership and Why."[17] He was well known for his love of Scripture, writing, "The fundamental principle is our belief in the supreme authority and absolute sufficiency of the Word of God. Relying on God's Word, we believe in a scriptural church, hence a regenerated membership.... and we believe that our religion should be spiritual, direct, and practical, instead of formal, meditative and creedal."[18]

In his years of service to the denomination, Elijah Fisher became a leader in the National Baptist Convention movement, asserting that it was time for American Blacks to place their support in institutions that they could own and control. He was positively influenced by the work and thought of Booker T. Washington, who from time to time encouraged Fisher.[19] In Chicago he heralded a new era of "Negro theological education"[20] and stressed action through the church and denominational structures, virtually introducing organized effort to the African American community. Olivet Baptist Church, said to be the largest Protestant congregation in the world at his retirement, became a

---

[17] Miles Mark Fisher, *The Master's Slave*: *Elijah John Fisher* (Philadelphia: Judson Press, 1922) 43.

[18] Ibid., 91.

[19] Ibid., 83; 103–105.

[20] The school was called the Chicago Religious Training Seminary, and Fisher taught various subjects, including theology.

focal point for the development of an African American Baptist theological tradition. To the point of his importance in developing Black Baptist thought, Elijah Fisher was a "race man," that is, he supported issues that would improve the lot of his people. He created at Olivet a model of help for the needy, training for youth, and various enterprises to assist Black families and industry.

In education and influence, Elijah Fisher's son, Miles, carried the influence of his father's work significantly forward. His work on slave songs brought prominence to the genre as well as meaning to the peculiar themes of his own denomination. As a child, he recalled the pride of his father in recounting stories about Africa. Following upon the earlier work of William Francis Allen, Charles Richard Ware, and Lucy McKim, Fisher pointed out that the spirituals reflected the harsh social conditions under which the enslaved Blacks were forced to live. "Negroes evidently had something that offset the wretched and unmoral pictures that were usually drawn of their total situations," he wrote, "something that gave them the strength to survive overwhelming hardships."[21] He demonstrated that the slave song was a master index to the mind of the slave. Fisher determined that the doctrinal content of slave songs was only superficially Christian, because they were the extensions of the traditional African beliefs expressed in secret meetings. Music from percussion instruments, repetition of simple phrases, and a limited vocabulary, all contributed to the limits of an indigenous developing African American Baptist theology. The source of Baptist thought among the slaves was more likely the teaching of the missionaries from white publications, Fisher thought. This explains the dependence upon white, especially American Baptist, theology and polity evident in the early Black Baptist movement. Behind the missionary context, however, lay a solid foundation in African expression. In identifying this character, Fisher would bring to Black Theology a pursuit of its legitimately African heritage, and this would find expression in Black liturgical motifs and hermeneutics.[22]

---

[21] Miles Mark Fisher, *Negro Slave Songs in the United States* (New York: Russell and Russell, 1953) 190.

[22] J. Deotis Roberts, "Thurman's Contributions to Black Religious Thought" in *God and Human Freedom: A Festschrift in Honor of Howard Thurman*, ed. Henry James Young (Richmond IN: Friends United Press, 1983) 145.

Fisher's second great achievement in helping to create a Black Baptist identity was to write the first history of Black Baptists. Published by the National Baptist Sunday School Board in Nashville, Fisher's *A Short History of the Baptist Denomination* (1933) was designed to demonstrate that his people—early-on referred to as Negro Baptists—were part of the larger Baptist family, yet unique in their heritage and emphases. In the preface he reminded his readers that in the United States, the Black Baptist population was twice that of Northern Baptists and equal in number to the membership of the Southern Baptists. His historical mentors were Carter G. Woodson, Lewis G. Jordan, Norman Cox (Southern Baptist), William Warren Sweet, and Garnett Ryland (Virginia Baptist), a varied and distinguished coterie. Deferring to the more contemporary findings regarding the origins of the Baptist tradition, Fisher acknowledged the Anabaptist possibilities but summarily rejected any successionist theory.[23] As his story of Baptists in England and America unfolded, he carefully wove in the account of the Negro Baptist saga—in both white churches and in their own congregations. He included major sections on the slavery controversy and the incongruity of slavery with Baptist emphases on freedom.[24]

Fisher believed Black churches that remained branches of white organizations thwarted and obscured the religious history of the African American Baptists. In tracing the development of the older Negro organizations, he created the foundations of race consciousness. He commented on the frequent lack of cooperation between Black Baptists and Northern Baptists: "For them to cooperate meant subordination. They were unconsciously expressing the opinions of any submerged group that appropriates the culture and ideals of the dominant race or nationality and at the same time reinterprets them in terms of aspirations of their own. It is important to understand this racial consciousness to account for the progress of Negro Baptists."[25] Fisher did go on to show appreciation for the social gospel, the lyrics and tunes of evangelical Protestantism, and the theological approach of the Northern Baptist

---

[23] Miles Mark Fisher, *A Short History of the Baptist Denomination* (Nashville: Sunday School Publishing Board, 1933) 1–2. The book unfortunately suffers from some egregious editing errors in fact and details. For instance, John Gill is cited as John Dill.

[24] At one point, p. 57, he cites evidence that even Negro leaders Andrew Bryan and John Berry Meachum kept slaves. Ibid., 93.

[25] Ibid., 111.

family in helping to define the Black Baptist identity. Of particular note
was the publication of *The Freedman's Book of Christian Doctrine*
(1865) by the American Baptist Publication Society, the first book of its
kind. Fisher was especially appreciative of Colgate, Rochester, and the
University of Chicago divinity schools, while also stressing the
importance of Black schools operated by Black leaders.

Theologically speaking, Fisher wanted his students to locate Black
Baptists among the mainstream Calvinistic Baptists of England and the
United States. He gave credit as being formative of Baptist theological
opinion to Roger Williams (an architect of religious liberty), the Second
London Confession of Faith, the New Hampshire Confession of Faith,
and the writings of E. Y. Mullins.[26]

The circumstances of the African American community in the United
States following World War I produced new streams of theology, some
of which were discontinuous with earlier Black Baptist thought.
Important influences could be traced to social thought in the liberal
Baptist community of the Northeast. For example, Howard Thurman
(1899–1981) had a major impact upon African American and Baptist
thought. Thurman was educated at Morehouse College, Columbia
University, and Rochester Theological Seminary. In his autobiography
he told the story of his being denied admission to Newton Theological
Institution on the grounds of race. Like Mordecai Johnson and Benjamin
Mays, Thurman sought theological studies elsewhere, finally being
cordially received at Rochester.[27] There he encountered the social gospel,
liberal theology, and the comparative approach to the study of religion.
Rather than pursue a graduate degree as his friends urged, he entered the
pastoral ministry in Oberlin, Ohio. He taught at Morehouse and Spelman
Colleges and became dean of the chapel at Howard University in
Washington, D.C. Later he held a similar chaplaincy at Boston
University. In 1943 he founded the Church for the Fellowship of All
Peoples in San Francisco, the first multi-racial, intercultural congregation
in the United States. During his early career he cultivated the friendship
of leading African Americans, including Mary McLeod Bethune, Nannie

---

[26] Ibid., 174–75.

[27] Howard Thurman, *With Head and Heart: The Autobiography of Howard Thurman*
(New York: Harcourt, Brace Jovanovich, 1979) 45; Richard I. McKinney, *Mordecai, The
Man and His Message: The Story of Mordecai Wyatt Johnson* (Washington DC: Howard
University Press, 1997) 30–31.

Helen Burroughs, and A. Philip Randolph. His Howard University elite circle of intellectuals included Mordecai Johnson, E. Franklin Frazier, and Alain Locke, and in Atlanta, W. E. B. Dubois. Thurman was for several decades an important mentor in the development of Black Baptist and African American leadership.

There were three important sources to the thought of Howard Thurman. The first was his seminary experience at Rochester Theological Seminary, primarily guided by George Cross, and to a lesser degree by Henry Burke Robbins and Conrad H. Moehlman. Cross, characterized as an "evangelical liberal," sought to establish the "essence" of Christianity apart from the entire overlay of history and evolving cultures. He taught Thurman to look for a quality of spiritual life, as evidenced in Jesus Christ. It was an applied form of religion, realized in human fellowship that has a power for social redemption. Christian salvation, Thurman learned, is to be found in a "perfect community." Thurman was also taught to recognize that the creative essence of Christianity is never complete, being future-oriented and ultimately involving personality. True to his Chicago School training, Cross emphasized the evolutionary character of Christianity. Cross served as a mentor for Thurman, urging him "as a sensitive Negro," to turn away from social questions to "the timeless issues of the human spirit." He recalled fondly of his teacher, "He had a greater influence on my mind than any other person who ever lived."[28]

Two other faculty members at Rochester also influenced Thurman. Henry Robbins taught religious education and missions at the seminary, as well as philosophy of religion. Following the theme that Cross had introduced, Robbins showed Thurman that there was a single spiritual essence underlying all world religions. Understanding this religious essence enabled him to appreciate other religious traditions. Robbins also utilized Rauschenbusch's terminology of the kingdom of God to characterize the perfect community. For Robbins also, personality kept religion vital in an otherwise evolutionary process. Doubtless, Thurman was also impressed with Robbins's chapel ministries and would draw upon those recollections as he pursued his own course at Howard and

---

[28] Luther E. Smith, Jr., *Howard Thurman: The Mystic as Prophet* (Lanham MD: University Press of America, 1981) 19–23; Thurman, *With Head and Heart*, 55, 60–61. Cross, a white man, attempted to empathize with Thurman as a Negro and planned a mentorship for his protégé that never happened because of Cross's untimely death.

Boston Universities. Moelhman was a towering scholar who introduced Thurman to an historical understanding of theology, noting particularly the creedal battles that had been waged within the church over the course of its existence.[29]

A second formative influence upon the young Thurman was the mystic Quaker, Rufus Jones (1863–1948). Thurman encountered Jones while attending Haverford College in 1929 as a special student. Jones helped Thurman redefine his Rochester ideas about religious essence in terms of mysticism. Mysticism became for Thurman an avenue to address contemporary contextual problems such as oppression. Building upon Cross's foundations, Jones helped Thurman understand the race question as essentially a religious issue. Jones doubtlessly helped direct Thurman to broader vistas of Christian fellowship.

The third major influence upon Thurman and his developing theology was Nancy Ambrose, Thurman's grandmother. Her contribution was to suggest that spirituality sustains one in the midst of trying circumstances. Like her slave ancestors, she looked to her inner-self to cope with the matter of survival and the issue of identity. She discouraged her grandson from reading the letters of St. Paul because they spoke of relations between masters and slaves.[30] Thurman's book, *Jesus and the Disinherited* (1949), was attributable to Nancy Ambrose's Christological perspectives.

Like many twentieth-century African American thinkers, Thurman preferred to work in ethics rather than theology *per se*. He was fond of Walter Rauschenbusch's dictum that it is safer to be eloquent about the immortality of the soul than to address the ethical demand the soul makes for a living wage. For him the task of the Black minister was "to interpret life in terms of a creative expansive idealism…He must be aware of the findings in all of human knowledge and interpret their meaning in terms of the Kingdom of God."[31] His own interpretation was greatly enhanced in 1935–36 when he made a trip to India where he saw firsthand how poorly Christianity related to other world religions. During that trip he was especially attracted to Bhakti mysticism. He met Gandhi personally

[29] Thurman, *With Head and Heart*, 54.
[30] Ibid., 32–33.
[31] Walter Earl Fluker and Catherine Tumber, eds., *A Strange Freedom: The Best of Howard Thurman on Religious Experience and Public Life* (Boston: Beacon Press, 1998) 199.

and introduced the saga of the American Negro to the Indian philosopher. Thurman was profoundly impressed with the interchange.[32] Subsequently, he made another trip to India to develop avenues that would encourage dialogue and reconciliation between the races in America. The report of his experiences concluded that Indians and Black Americans were victims of color prejudice at the hands of white conquerors. Thurman observed that since the American Black and White populations were committed to the same Christian ideal of brotherliness, then "unbrotherliness" was to be classified as sinful and unchristian. Much of his life's energy was thus given to the goals of dialogue and reconciliation between the races.

What constituted a doctrine of God for Howard Thurman was mediated through his heritage, with the background of slavery pressing very near his generation. His immediate ancestors once had no identity and with emancipation achieved their first sense of self. Thurman would write: " To be known, to be called by one's name, to find one's place and hold it against all the hordes of hell....it is to honor an act as one's very own, it is to live a life that is one's very own, it is to bow before an altar that is one's very own, it is to worship a God who is one's very own."[33] Some writers think that Thurman was especially influenced in this direction by William Ashby's 1915 book, *Redder Blood*, wherein the author argued that God gives to each person a selfhood into which even God cannot enter uninvited.[34]

Thurman's Christology was unique and influential. In his search for a proper interpretation of Jesus, he found traditional theologians defining Jesus as an object of worship and devotion. Thurman saw Jesus as a religious subject in quest of moral community and spiritual dignity. Jesus' solution for the evils of his world was to work for the redemption of all the cast-down people in every generation. "Living in a climate of deep insecurity," Thurman wrote, "Jesus was faced with so narrow a margin of civil guarantees, that he had to find some other basis upon which to establish a sense of well-being.... Deep from within that order he projected a dream, the logic of which would give to all the needful security." There would be room for all, and no one person would be a

---

[32] Thurman, *With Head and Heart*, 131–33.

[33] Howard Thurman, *The Inward Journey* (New York: Harper & Row, 1961), 37.

[34] Mays, *Negro's God*, 253. Mays thought his close friend Thurman was an exception to the radicals that did not slip into atheism.

threat to another.[35] The similarity of the social position of Jesus in his context to that of the African American could not be missed.

Reconciliation became for Howard Thurman a major doctrine. He defined it as the simple human desire to understand others and to be understood by others. "Every man," he wrote, "wants to be cared for and... this is essential to the furtherance and maintenance of life in health."[36] Of primary importance to Thurman's idea of reconciliation was the applied concept of nonviolence. Here he was indebted to Mahatma Gandhi as much as to the teachings of Jesus. Nonviolence for him created an attitude that inspired wholeness and integration.[37] In classic Christian theological terms, the parable of the prodigal son taught that the way between God and humankind must be kept open so that humanity and God the Father may have free access to one another.[38] Thurman was convinced that the primary obstacles to reconciliation were the existence of "tight circles of security," such as those found in the proscriptions that accompany institutionalized religious faith and political ideology, or are reflected in the quest for some particular definition of social purity.

Ecclesiologically, Howard Thurman behaved like a Baptist. His ministry was directed through the local church that he envisioned as a genuine experiment in Christian community. In his youth he had been exposed to rigorous Baptist discipline where doctrinal matters were highly specified and church process was of the essence. He reacted negatively to both.[39] In his congregation membership was typically open to any who shared the commitments and responsibilities that defined the Christian faith. He wanted to work within the framework of historical Protestantism, though without reference to a particular denomination. Thurman's overarching objective was to create a fellowship without a dominant group. He had little interest in the associational principle behind the ecclesiastical affairs of Baptist churches insisting instead, "We must put a vast faith in the contagion in the Spirit of Jesus rather

---

[35] Fluker and Tumber, *Strange Freedom*, 147.

[36] Ibid, 164-164.

[37] Ibid., 172.

[38] Ibid., 179.

[39] As a student at Rochester Seminary, Thurman worked at First Baptist Church of Roanoke, Virginia, where at the time of his ordination he answered questions about the Trinity unsatisfactorily and he objected to the laying on of hands until he rationalized the act in his own mystical thinking. See *With Head and Heart*, 55–58.

than in the building of organizations to perpetuate his Spirit." [40] Within a congregation itself there were sufficient integrative activities and programs to emulate what Edward Judson referred to as an "institutional church." Thurman held a profound conviction that meaningful experiences between peoples were more compelling than ideologies and prejudices that may divide them. The variety of programs was exceeded only by the variety of racial/ethnic groups involved—some six altogether.[41]

What distressed many black Baptist leaders about Thurman over the years was his tendency toward universalism. His stance in support of reconciliation and dialogue led him to say that he was not interested in converting people of another faith to Christianity. Rather, he encouraged all to discover their own heritage and "affirm its revelation of the divine." Here he followed Paul Tillich and others in theorizing that to be the ultimate answer, "Christianity had to break through its own particularity."[42] This of course caused many Black Baptists to distance themselves ecclesiastically from Thurman, while at the same time drinking deeply from the deep well of his thought.

Howard Thurman was baptistic and yet more. His theological perspective reached back into the African American slave experience and identity of his grandparents. His influence on the American religious scene in the twentieth century was felt in two primary ways. First, while he did not trumpet their relationship, he had a profound impact upon Martin Luther King, Jr. Thurman and Martin Luther King, Sr., had been fellow students at Morehouse. Thurman respected young Martin's courage and supported him personally. According to Lerone Bennett, King read and re-read Thurman's widely published book, *Jesus and the Disinherited*, during the 1956 boycott.[43] It is very tempting to posit a significant genetic dependency here, though Thurman retreated from such a claim.[44] It is, however, unmistakable that Thurman certainly

---

[40] Fluker and Tumer, *Strange Freedom*, 195.

[41] There is a complete description by Thurman of the church in ibid., 220–24, and *With Head and Heart*, 148–54.

[42] Smith, *Howard Thurman*, 76–77.

[43] Lerone Bennett, Jr., *What Manner of Man: A Biography of Martin Luther King, Jr.* (Chicago: Johnson Publishing Co., 1964) 74–75.

[44] Referring to the Civil Rights Crusade, Thurman stated, "We did not ever discuss in depth the progress, success, or failure of the movement itself." In *With Head and Heart*, 255.

reinforced Gandhi's thought in King's mind, which King later cited as a major transforming influence. Second, through his writings and his legacy at Rochester Seminary, Thurman continued to be a figure of theological and ethical direction for young Black leaders.

Similar in influence among Black Baptist religious educators in the same generation with Howard Thurman was Mordecai Wyatt Johnson (1890–1976). Johnson rose from poor circumstances in Tennessee to attend Roger Williams University, Howe Institute, and Morehouse College. For a time he taught English and economics at Morehouse, while in the summers earning a second bachelor's degree in social sciences at the University of Chicago. Johnson served in the pastoral ministry in Ohio and at First Baptist Charleston, West Virginia (an African American congregation), where he championed the labor rights of coal miners and helped to organize the NAACP and several community cooperatives. His dream to enter theological studies at Newton Theological Institution was denied because of his race. A biographer notes the importance of this in terms of his future discontent with denominations and his commitment to the social tenets of the gospel.[45] Newton's loss became Rochester's gain. Johnson earned two theological degrees, one from Rochester Theological Seminary (bachelor of divinity), the other from Harvard University (master of sacred theology). At Rochester, where he graduated at the head of his class, Johnson developed an affection for Walter Rauschenbusch's work on the social gospel. Rochester also provided the nearby opportunity to hone his pastoral skills at Second Baptist, Mumford, New York. He was ordained there with seminary president Clarence Barbour participating in the service. Johnson, at 37 years of age, was called to the presidency of Howard University in Washington, D.C. and became America's youngest Black college president.

In his youth, Johnson signaled new directions by which to understand the church and the possibilities of a Black theology. In his Harvard University commencement address of 1922, he declared a growing differentiation between "white man's religion and white man's understanding of democracy." He saw segregation as a national, not just a Southern problem and called for laying the foundations of "a Black

---

[45] McKinney, *Mordecai*, 30–31.

empire, a Black religion, and a Black culture."[46] He seemed convinced that the American Black could not expect to acquire economic, political, and spiritual liberty in the United States. He believed the Blacks' religion must deal with that reality. His address went on to discuss radical Negro organizations:

> They are home-grown fruits...their power lies in the appeal that they make to the Negro to find a way out of his trouble by new and self-reliant paths. The larger masses of the colored people do not belong to these more radical movements. They retain their belief in the Christian God, they love their country, and they hope to work out their salvation within its bounds. But they are completely disillusioned ... Now they have come to the place where their faith can no longer feed on the bread of repression and violence. They ask for the bread of liberty, of public equality, and of public responsibility. It must not be denied them.[47]

He concluded by asking whether the Christian religion could bind together a multicolored world in brotherhood. Surely this was one of the epicenters from which the Black Theology movement would emerge in later years.

To the surprise of personal benefactors and leaders at Howard University, Johnson turned aside an early offer to assume a Baptist professorship and work with Baptist students at Howard. His vision was to be nonsectarian. A few years later in his inaugural address as president of Howard, he revealed his vision for a school of religion that would enable the entire Black Church: "The simple, unsophisticated, mystical religion of the Negro cannot continue to endure unless it is reinterpreted over and over to him by men who have a fundamental and far-reaching understanding of the significance of religion in its relation to the complexities of modern civilzed life."[48] He proposed a nonsectarian graduate school of religion delivering people from superstition and

---

[46] Carter G. Woodson, *Negro Orators and Their Orations* (Washington DC: Associated Publishers, 1925) 146–48.

[47] Ibid.

[48] Quoted in McKinney, *Mordecai*, 257–58.

uncharitable sectarianism, one that bound them in cooperation. His models were Harvard and the University of Chicago.

Johnson's influence was in the areas of Black education and the encouragement of scholarship. As president of Howard University, he developed a stellar faculty and encouraged several young scholars in their career development, notably J. Deotis Roberts, Howard Thurman, and Richard McKinney. Under his leadership, Howard University Divinity School and Department of Religion became accredited centers of theological training for Black Baptist ministers. The congregations in the Middle Atlantic States in particular benefited from Howard's programs, and Benjamin Mays sent many prized Morehouse graduates to Howard for theological studies. In 1978 Colgate Rochester Divinity School recognized the important contribution of Johnson by establishing the Mordecai Wyatt Johnson Institute of Religion.

J. Deotis Roberts was an exception to Benjamin Mays's generalization that African Americans in that period were producing few theologians because Black thinkers were not much interested in fine theological or philosophical discussions about God.[49] Roberts was influenced by both Miles Mark Fisher and Mordecai Johnson. He became a leading philosophical theologian, forging a bridge of dialogue between Black Theology and other major categories of Christian theological discourse.

Roberts (b. 1927) was educated at Johnson C. Smith College (B.A.), Shaw University Divinity School (B.D.) where he was a student of Miles Fisher, and Hartford Seminary Foundation (B.D., Th.M.). He completed a doctoral work at the University of Edinburgh in philosophical theology. His dissertation, "The Rational Theology of Benjamin Whichcote: Father of the Cambridge Platonists," was written under the direction of John Baillie and Charles Duthie.[50] Roberts taught at Georgia Baptist College and Shaw University before accepting an invitation from Mordecai Johnson at Howard University to be a professor of religion at the school in the nation's capital. He later served on the faculties of Virginia Union School of Theology, Interdenominational Theological Center, George Mason University, and Eastern Baptist Theological Seminary.

---

[49] Mays, *Negro's God*, 255.

[50] Duthie awakened in Roberts an interest in Blaise Pascal, about whom Roberts had written at Hartford Theological Seminary.

Somewhat out of step with his own contemporaries in Black Theology, Roberts has long emphasized the importance of philosophical theology and the need for Christians to encounter other religions and cultures. For him it is a matter of "faith seeking understanding," and an outgrowth of his graduate research. Coming as it did during the outburst of radical Black theologians, Roberts's book titled *From Puritanism to Platonism in the Seventeenth Century England* (1968) signaled that Black theologians were connected to the great intellectual traditions of Western culture. In 1964 an extensive journey through India and Asia profoundly influenced his theology. Similarly, in 1971 Roberts traveled to the heart of Africa and observed the foundations of African American thought.

Roberts has embodied an important statement about Black thinkers and Black themes in his own scholarly and ecclesial development. He sought the best education he could attain, and his work among classical theologians has been hailed by American and continental theologians as a genuine contribution. He has sought to demonstrate that Black thinkers can make contributions at the most advanced academic levels, while at the same time carrying a burden for a theology of an oppressed people. His contribution to Black Theology has been to describe and contextualize. He is less interested in Black power and Black Theology as an assertion of Black racism over against white racism, than Black Theology as an intellectual and spiritual endeavor that will open dialogue with other theological traditions. It is vitally important to Roberts that Black theology be understood in light of the Black experience. To that end, Roberts has been active in various parts of the Black Baptist denominational traditions and with local churches. He has contributed energetically to interpreting the life and work of Martin Luther King, Jr., in various church programs. This has created a context for his overarching question, "What does it mean to be Black and Christian in the United States?"

In 1974 Roberts published *A Black Political Theology* in which he made an ethical case for liberation as a goal. In 1980 *Roots of a Black Future* appeared, focusing upon the Black church and family from African roots to the New World. Next came *Black Theology Today* in 1983, wherein Roberts critically evaluated the work of prominent Black theologians. In 1987 *Black Theology in Dialogue* brought a global awareness of a maturing Black Theology. In 1994 he brought out a second edition of *Liberation and Reconciliation* in which again he called upon Black churches to discover the healing nature of the gospel. Roberts made the case again for a "holistic" foundation of the gospel. Themes like the beauty and dignity of all human beings, particularly Blacks, the equality of Blacks and Whites, and the relevance of seeing the Messiah from a Black perspective, all appear regularly in Roberts's thinking.

Of paramount import to Roberts is the concept of reconciliation. He cast himself as an ameliorating force: "I will not go into a tirade," he wrote, "regarding the confusion and omission of White scholars. I am pro-Black and not merely anti-White."[51] He believed that James Cone had done the work of demolition and that as a consequence someone had to embrace the task of reconstruction. Because he believed Black theologians needed to address a wider community than other Blacks, he wrote, "Reconciliation is the more excellent way. Christ the Liberator is likewise Christ the Reconciler… We are called forth as agents of reconciliation. Reconciliation has to do with overcoming estrangement, mending fences, breaking down walls of separation between men."[52]

For Roberts theology is both a confessional and an activist enterprise. In *Christian Beliefs* (1980) he defined the basic doctrines of Christianity. The next year he wrote a commentary on the Sullivan Principles, an anti-Apartheid statement on financial investments. He entered yet another phase of his scholarship in the 1990s, bridging the thought of Martin Luther King, Jr. and Howard Thurman, again to provide a dialogue between disparate theologies. Roberts also crossed important boundaries in his teaching career, moving from predominantly African American institutions like Howard University, Interdenominational Theological Center, and Shaw University, to hold distinguished chairs or visiting professorship roles at Eastern Baptist Theological Seminary, Duke University Divinity School, Baylor University, and Southern Baptist Theological Seminary.[53]

---

[51]Ibid, 327.

[52] J. Deotis Roberts, "Black Theology in the Making," *Review and Expositor* 70/3 (1973): 324.

[53] There is a useful biographical sketch on Roberts, limited to pre-1990 in Gerald Thomas, "James Deotis Roberts," *Baptist Theologians*, 627–39. Roberts considered David Emmanuel Goatley a pastor-theologian in the National Baptist Convention of America as his protégé. Goatley is an offspring of W. J. Simmons of Louisville, Kentucky.

Unlike Howard Thurman and Mordecai Johnson who moved afield of traditional African American Baptist thought, Joseph H. Jackson (1900–1991) was devoted to the denominational vision of E. C. Morris and was himself another of the outstanding Black Baptist leaders of the later twentieth century. While others moved outside the bounds of denominationalism, Jackson worked from within the National Baptist Convention, USA Inc, the second largest family of Baptists in the world. He was part of the heritage of the Olivet Baptist Church in Chicago, a heritage first set in place by Elijah Fisher. Jackson was educated at Jackson College, Colgate Rochester Divinity School, and did further study at Creighton University, the University of Pennsylvania, and the University of Chicago. He served pastorates in Omaha, Philadelphia, and Chicago, where his congregation, Olivet, became a leading Black church in the denomination and the United States.

Jackson's theological stance was summarized later in life by a chapter in his history, "Toward a National Baptist Theology." In keeping with his forbears and despite recognizing that "many National Baptist preachers do not know the deep theological terms and have not mastered the science of theology in the academic sense of the word," Jackson did believe Black Baptists made a unique contribution. For him they were evangelical, meaning there can be no great preaching without faith in God. "If theology can successfully be reduced to merely 'God-Talk,' it will have no substance or reality." What all National Baptists had in common, he believed, was "an idea of God that they inherited from Jesus Christ."[54] This Christological approach led Jackson to argue that God is essentially "spirit." As spirit, "God is an invisible principle, a living force or being, a personality or an entity that is not limited to time and space. Therefore Black Baptists make no attempt to bring God down to something of earth…We are unprofitable creatures in our quest of Him. One of the implications of this theology is that worship can never be by pigmentation, but by principles of adoration, appreciation, and praise."[55] His adoption of the social gospel, or more properly Rauschenbusch's doctrine of the kingdom shows clearly: "The National Baptist Convention USA, Incorporated, is an example of what can happen when an organization will be both active for the growth of itself and for its

---

[54] J. H. Jackson, *A Story of Christian Activism: The National Baptist Convention, USA, Incorporated* (Nashville: Townsend Press, 1980) 582–83.
[55] Ibid., 588–89.

fellowmen in obedience to God our maker and to our Lord, Jesus Christ."[56] The contributions to the cause of the relief of the poor and the oppressed, and the progressive influence of the lovers of the nation (that is American Patriots) "of the nation" may need more explanation, were manifestations of the kingdom. Jackson was energetic in pursuit of engagement in the Baptist World Alliance as the largest expression of his ecclesiological ideals and he often brought the emphases of National Baptists to Alliance sessions.

Concurrent with the later years of Jackson's ministry was the Black Power movement, also manifested in Black Theology. "In the materialistic conception of life, some want to reduce all theology to a matter of color. They may bring some "beautiful theories and philosophies" that may encourage sincere minds devoted to civil rights and to the struggle of the race, but Jackson held firmly, "This has nothing to do with the theological notion of God as spirit."[57] His Christological sensibilities were on occasion offended by Black Theology because it caused serious theologians to think that the views of African Americans are some kind of "half-baked response to the outgrown and feeble drifting of the white race." Rather, Jackson insisted, "The theology of the participating members of the National Baptist Convention comes from the lips of the Man of Galilee."[58] The biblical foundations for this insistence were reflected in John 4:24 and 2 Corinthians 3:17. He sincerely believed that the message of Black leaders must not be restricted only to the African American community.

Christology was a major emphasis in Jackson's thought. He maintained a firm and evangelical view of Jesus Christ as Savior and Lord. In the Sermon on the Mount, Jesus' key ideas were articulated. In the cross is seen the Lord's ultimate revelation of truth. Jackson wrote, "We are drawn to Him by His divine character and by His redemptive love and mercy...and by His sacrificial life, death, and resurrection, all sinners are invited and made welcome into His eternal kingdom."[59] Jesus became the ultimate example of how life was to be lived. He led no

---

[56] Ibid., 591.

[57] Ibid., 586.

[58] Ibid.

[59] Quoted from the 1971 Annual Meeting of the National Baptist Convention USA in Peter Paris, *Black Religious Leaders: Conflict in Unity* (Louisville: Westminster/John Knox Press, 1991) 68.

boycotts, picket lines, or mass demonstrations. His suffering and death were the norms of humanity's sufferings. Consequently, Jackson saw sins of bitterness, racism, revenge, and war as violations of the teachings and life of Christ. Mercy, forgiveness, and justice should replace evil. Jackson understood evil in the same terms as Reinhold Niebuhr; it is essentially rooted in the emotions, which are a part of the whole person. Only God in Christ could overcome evil.

Theologically, Jackson held fast to the doctrine of freedom. "Freedom is the right of all human beings and should be granted to all God's people. All human beings who have tasted bondage and have known the bitter experience of servitude, must hate the chains that bind their bodies."[60] The Christian church cannot ever become less than a fellowship of believers dedicated to the ideals and principles of Jesus Christ. The church cannot be divorced from the need to eliminate human affliction and suffering. The Baptist leader, Jackson taught, must be interested in civil rights and cooperate with legitimate organizations through finances, words of encouragement, and fellowship.[61] Jackson thought protest was dangerous if out of control and that Blacks should appeal to their strengths which is under the directives of the U.S. Constitution. Failing such an appeal, Blacks risk loss of self-respect, personality, and spirit as well as being taken over by enemies of a democratic society. This meant that "official" mainstream organizations like NAACP and the Southern Christian Leadership Conference (organized by the NBC-USA) were to be the vehicles by which social ills were best addressed. Having organized the Convention for all sorts of social and political engagement, Jackson believed that the time would come when "out of our own genius and experience we may help to supply the psychology for the disconsolate, and the creative philosophy for the oppressed and teach men in all walks of life the correct use of all available resources in the spirit of love without being poisoned by the incubus of hate."[62]

Joseph Jackson's "theology" in the larger sense of the word was revealed in a kind of credo issued in 1959. The "Re-Affirmation of Our Faith in the Nation" is at once a statement of theology and ethics in a nationalistic crucible. After initially affirming the ideals of democracy

---

[60] Jackson, *Story of Christian Activism.,* 235.
[61] Ibid., 237.
[62] Ibid., 366.

inherent in the United States constitution, it proceeded to build a case for minority improvement and the neglect of minorities as a sin. The statement affirmed racial coalitions and cooperation between races as people of good will work for complete democracy. The "battle for freedom" is God's just cause because God made out of one blood all races to dwell in peace. The doctrine of the church became in the statement a "community of believers held together by a common loyalty to Jesus Christ" and " a redemptive influence and a vital part of the soul of the nation."[63] Finally, the leadership of the Convention proclaimed, "We believe in God, the Creator of heaven and earth; we believe in the dignity of man, in the triumph of justice, and in the victory of the truth."[64]

But, Jackson's theology was far from static, as might be implied in the "Re-Affirmation." He was an active ecumenist and recognized the limitations of some long accepted precepts. "A theological concept that is outmoded," he reflected in the 1960s, "by the facts of science or the findings of philosophy or the testimony of advancing life cannot be employed in the service of moral and spiritual truths." He saw this reality in the ecumenical movement of Vatican II, where he served as an observer to the official proceedings and heralded its changes.[65] Here Jackson's panoramic understanding of the church was manifest. Rather than tearing down the organized church, Jackson believed the church should embody unity. This unity should also be evident in denominational plurality. The task of the church in any age is to make its society the beloved community of God.

The beginnings of a new direction in Jackson's thinking occurred at Philadelphia in 1960. Prior to the annual meeting of the National Baptist Convention, USA, over which Jackson had presided fourteen years, there was an organized attempt to unseat him in favor of Gardner C. Taylor. A "Baptist sit-in" was organized that held up Convention business in order to get the number of votes necessary to elect Taylor. Those organizing the opposition to Jackson, besides Taylor, included Martin Luther King, Jr., and Marshall Shepard. The Taylorites lost and Jackson remained the

---

[63] Ibid.

[64] Rev. Owen D. Pelt and Ralph Lee Smith, *The Story of The National Baptists* (New York: Vantage Press, 1960) 182.

[65] See Joseph Jackson, *Many But One: The Ecumenics of Charity* (New York: Sheed and Ward, 1964) 40. Pope John XXIII personally invited Jackson to attend.

Convention's president. Taylor eventually left the National Baptists to form the Progressive National Baptist Convention.[66] What truly motivated the controversy was an understanding of Christian activism that differed markedly between Jackson's supporters and the King/Taylor advocates. When Jackson initially pressed for the assurance of African American civil rights in 1956, he was in the vanguard of the nascent movement. Gradually, however, King built a competing base of Black support in the Deep South. Jackson was identified with a more cautious approach to civil rights activism than that associated with the NAACP. King wanted to pursue activist strategies that would garner more immediate results. Repeatedly, Jackson moved the Convention away from the independent civil rights crusade. Jackson noted in his published version of the matter: "The National Baptist Convention rejected both the philosophy and the methodology of the leaders of these two negative protest movements as sound principles for racial improvement and as sound principles in a democratic government. The convention also rejected the so-called civil disobedience movement that the White Citizen's Council group of Mississippi tried to bring against the Supreme Court decision of 1954."[67] Jackson believed this meant a rejection of a theology of a class society. He considered his resistance a positive refusal to condone a perspective of a God of discrimination and a creed of racism. "The Convention," he wrote, "has not reduced its worship to a cult of race, or nationality, and has not put the gospel of color above the Christ of God."[68] To Jackson, particularities of race, nationality, or rank were unacceptable that demanded inappropriate theological compromise by negating the universality of the love of God.

Jackson eschewed what he called negative tools of social transformation. Paramount among these was non-violent civil disobedience. Such public behavior, he thought, can be a ready-made weapon for weakening or sabotaging any ordered society. Jackson instead sought to "work with all Americans and all other citizens

---

[66] See the fullest account in Albert A. Avant, Jr., *The Social Teachings of the Progressive National Baptist Convention, Inc. Since 1961: A Critical Analysis of the Least, the Lost, and the Left-Out* (New York: Routledge, 2004) 21-26; there is a brief historical sketch in Clarence Taylor, *The Black Churches of Brooklyn* (New York: Columbia University Press, 1994) 147–49.

[67] Jackson, *Story of Christian Activism*, 493.

[68] Ibid., 491.

dedicated to the growth of a democratic republic." Some referred to the
Taylor movement as "Progressives," a differentiation to which Jackson
reacted negatively and strongly. He rejected the idea of exempting
African Americans from critical evaluation and assignment of partial
responsibility with respect to the circumstances of the social order of the
day. Such exemption and privilege was, in essence, the position taken by
the Black Power movement when it came to public dialogue about the
day's social ills with respect to race relations. "We are entitled to know
the truth, to be told the truth, and to be held to the consequences
whenever the true principles of life are ignored or sinned against. This
does not mean that we absolve America for what she has not done."[69]

The conflict between the Jackson conservatives and the Taylor/King
activists was personalized in many ways. Jackson, who had worked hard
over decades to be a spokesman among the powerful of Chicago and
nationally for Blacks, resented King's rapid and heroic advance. With
King directly in focus, Jackson rebuked the entire activist movement for
civil rights: "This is no time for the making of false heroes or pseudo-
leaders for the Negro race. We must reject those members of our race
who appear as saints among white observers and then expect to be our
spokesmen and who try to set the standard by which all of us are
judged."[70] Their own people because of the love and respect the leaders
have won, Jackson taught, select the true leaders of the Negro
community. Unlike King who saw social prophets as those who confront
systemic injustice and wrong-doing, Jackson thought a prophet was "a
religious seer whose personality demonstrates a higher order to which
society should be conformed."[71] In some of his strongest language on the
matter, Jackson wrote, "Negroes will not—and cannot—be blessed by
those eloquent speakers who counsel their Negro brothers to curse white
people on whom such hypocrites secretly rely for finance, aid, and
support."[72] At the ecclesial level, Jackson opposed dual alignment with
predominantly white conventions of Baptists, because they are not
permitted to exercise the freedoms that were taken for granted in the
Negro conventions. "Many of us have made supreme sacrifices to make
our own churches and conventions as great and meaningful as

---

[69] Ibid., 493.
[70] Ibid.
[71] Paris, *Black Religious Leaders*, 72.
[72] Jackson, *Many But One,* 493.

possible."[73] Here was a sense of Black identity that William J. Simmons or Elias Camp Morris might have articulated a century earlier.

Another Black Baptist leader in the tradition of Mordecai Johnson was Benjamin E. Mays (1894–1984). Mays held degrees from South Carolina State College, Bates College, and the University of Chicago where he earned a doctoral degree. His original plans to enter Newton Theological Institution were frustrated because of racial discrimination. While a student at Bates, a Newton recruiter told Mays to apply to Virginia Union School of Theology because of his race. The result was that he permanently set aside aspirations for seminary studies.[74] He went on to teach mathematics at Morehouse College, while also serving a local Baptist church and completing graduate school. He worked for the Urban League and conducted sociological research for the Institute of Social and Religious Research. His Chicago dissertation was titled "The Development of the Idea of God in Contemporary Negro Literature." In 1934 Mays was named dean of The School of Religion at Howard University and president of Morehouse College in 1940. While at Morehouse he encouraged countless young Black men through his chapel talks, inspiring a quest for excellence in many future leaders such as Martin Luther King, Jr.. An ecumenist among Black Baptists, Mays was a major speaker at the Evanston (Illinois) Assembly of the World Council of Churches in 1954.

An important facet of Mays's theological outlook was his own realism about social change and theology in general. Mays believed that the African American idea of God grew out of the community's social situation, particularly developed during points of social crisis. "His ideas of God," Mays wrote of a typical Black person, "are chiseled out of the very fabric of the social struggle."[75] He also observed that Blacks' lives have been too unstable and precarious, too uncertain for them to become sufficiently objective to gain competence in theologizing or philosophizing about God. He urged would-be Black theologians to consider schools such as the University of Chicago, whose application of the social sciences to religious disciplines could help African American degree candidates transcend the classical scholarship of the mainstream

---

[73] Ibid., 494.

[74] The incident is described in Benjamin E. Mays, *Born to Rebel* (New York: Charles Scribner's Sons, 1971) 61.

[75] Mays, *The Negro's God*, 255.

Baptist community. But Mays also recounted in his autobiography that he experienced more discrimination in Chicago—both in that community and in the school itself—than at any other previous time. That experience helped to shape his theological outlook.[76]

Mays pointed out in his groundbreaking study on the Black church, that African Americans first achieved freedom in the Christian churches. The first entirely Black church was Baptist. He further pointed out that a segregated church was a boon to his people's development and identity as it fostered self-expression and leadership. Black churches and pastors thus enjoyed "unrestrained freedom" in Baptist churches where, "four laymen and three ordained ministers [might] start a Baptist church." Mays found that the minister is God's ambassador on earth, and that the minister and the church are to be held sacred. This elevated status was not necessarily impeached if the minister's conduct fell short of expectations. The idea that the church is God's house and the minister is God's prophet, were leading expectations of the early "Negro churches."[77] As Mays's thinking about the church matured, he embraced a greater cooperative attitude toward working with other Baptists and Christians of all ilks. He served faithfully as a delegate to the World Council of Churches and in other national denominational responsibilities. An influential force behind enabling a theological school for Blacks to survive, Mays fostered a plan to unite Gammon and Turner Theological Seminaries with the Morehouse School of Religion, thus establishing Atlanta's Interdenominational Theological Center. With this development Black Baptists gained a fully accredited, ecumenical institution on par with other ecumenical centers in California, Chicago, Rochester, and Boston.[78]

Mays's most outstanding protégé was Martin Luther King, Jr. (1929–1968), a Baptist minister and one of the most influential American Christian leaders of the twentieth century. While studies abound of his religious upbringing and political agenda,[79] King's influence upon

---

[76] Mays, *Born to Rebel*, 65.

[77] Benjamin Elijah Mays and Joseph William Nicholson, *The Negro's Church* (New York: Negro Universities Press, 1933) 10–11.

[78] Mays, *Born to Rebel*, 234 ff.

[79] Steven Oates, *Let The Trumpet Sound: The Life of Martin Luther King, Jr.* (New York: Harper and Row, 1982) makes an attempt to address King's religious orientation, but erroneously reports (see pp. 24 and 35) that Crozer Seminary was non-denominational and that King graduated with a B.A. in divinity.

Baptist life and thought has yet to be fully assessed. The essentials of his background include that he was the son of a prominent Black Baptist pastor in Georgia, Martin Luther King, Sr.; his Baptist education at Morehouse College and Crozer Theological Seminary; and his assumption of pastoral ministries at Dexter Avenue Baptist Church in Montgomery, Alabama, from 1954 until 1958. To these basics can be added the influence of J. Pius Barber (1894–1974), the long-term pastor at Calvary Baptist Church in Chester, Pennsylvania, under whose watchful eye young Martin interned during his seminary years. Barbour was the first Black graduate of Crozer who completed a master's degree at the University of Pennsylvania, specializing in studies on theories of religious knowledge. He was convinced that socialism was a means of reversing White economic exploitation, and his pulpit often resounded with this type of pro-African American social theory.[80]

"Daddy King," as the elder Martin was known, was a formidable influence on his son. Fundamentalistic in doctrinal understanding and baptistic to the core of his ecclesiology, Martin Sr. was the foundational theological influence on young Martin's life. Daddy King was reared in a poor family and struggled to obtain a college degree from Morehouse College. Upon his graduation, he assumed the pastorate of Ebenezer Baptist Church in Atlanta, Georgia, where he remained until his death. He inherited the pastoral role from his father-in-law, A. D. Williams, the long time minister at Ebenezer. The elder King was typical of Black preachers whose lives were circumscribed by their congregations, affirmed the authority of Scripture, vividly related Scripture to life's circumstances, and was active in the community. His advocacy of equal rights and human dignity was the bedrock of his son's burgeoning sense of social concern. He also bequeathed to Martin Jr. a penchant for excellence in education.[81]

Next in line influencing the development of the younger King were Morehouse College mentors George D. Kelsey and Benjamin E. Mays. Kelsey, the head of the Department of Religion, was King's favorite teacher. He led Martin out of a confining literalism to a critical

---

[80] The most detail yet found on Pius Barbour is in Richard Lischer, *The Preacher King: Martin Luther King, Jr., and the Word that Moved* (New York: Oxford University Press, 1995) 67–70.

[81] For a warm-spirited insight into the elder King, see Martin L. King, Sr., *Daddy King: An Autobiography* (New York: William Morrow, 1980) esp., 80–102.

understanding of the Bible. King later wrote that, thanks to Kelsey, "The shackles of fundamentalism were removed from my body."[82] Martin revered President Mays as a towering Black thinker who dismissed "Black accommodationism" in favor of an educational philosophy of "liberation through knowledge." His chapel talks were filled with encouragement to engage social realities rather than find "socially irrelevant patterns of escape."[83] Mays had confirmed through research that emotionalism in religious expression was on the wane. He found evidence among minorities that commitment to other-worldly religion was giving way to an embrace of activism aimed at challenging socio-economic structures primarily dedicated to satisfying the predilections of ruling majorities.[84] As an undergraduate, King often lingered after chapel or class lectures to debate or discuss Mays's topics and a lifelong friendship between the two men developed. After King completed his doctoral work at Boston University, Mays offered him a teaching position at Morehouse. King declined the offer to become pastor at Dexter Avenue Baptist Church.[85]

In seminary, two Crozer professors were especially important in King's development: George Washington Davis and Kenneth L. Smith. In Davis's theology courses, King drank in neo-orthodoxy, especially that of Reinhold Niebuhr, he was put off by Friedrich Nietzsche, and came to criticize both Karl Marx and capitalism.[86] Davis also had an intense interest in Mahatma Gandhi and his concept of *satyagraha*.[87] In Smith's ethics class, King re-encountered Walter Rauschenbusch, Paul Tillich, and the Social Gospel. But, he was troubled by Rauschenbusch's optimism and equally so by Niebuhr's doctrine of human evil and his desire to identify with oppressed peoples and to confront evil with the power of love. He stood between powerful explications of the Kingdom

---

[82] Quoted in ibid., 19.

[83] Ibid.

[84] Mays and Nicholson, *The Negro Church*, 92–93.

[85] Mays, *Born to Rebel*, 266.

[86] The best discussion of King's seminary struggles is David L. Lewis, *King: A Critical Biography* (New York: Praeger Publishers, 1970) 27-34.

[87] *Satyagraha (satya*=truth and *love*; *graha*=force) was a program of nonviolent activism espoused by Gandhi. It involved agitation, boycotting, non-cooperation, civil disobedience, and usurpation of government functions. See King, Jr.'s explanation in his *Strength to Love* (Philadelphia: Fortress Press, 1981), 151. Davis had devoted his Ph.D. dissertation to Indian spirituality. See above, pp. 379–80.

of God and its purpose. King also maintained continuous conversation with Crozer president Sankey Lee Blanton. Also important were lectures on campus by visiting personalities or that King attended at other institutions in the Philadelphia area. He remembered, for example, a guest lecture by A. J. Muste, Executive Secretary of the Fellowship of Reconciliation and founder of the Congress of Racial Equality, who offered an impassioned and well-reasoned endorsement of nonviolent organization in the pursuit of social justice. At the University of Pennsylvania, he heard Mordecai Johnson of Howard University lecture on Gandhi's spiritual leadership and its results in India. As King left Crozer, a prize-winning student at the head of his class, he was sensitive to racial discrimination, sympathetic to oppressed people, and intent on demonstrating his passion for social justice.

Boston University was the final venue for King's formal intellectual formation. He registered in the Faculty of Philosophy to work with Edgar S. Brightman and to work closely with members of the School of Theology. He took courses at Harvard in the area of existentialism and corresponded with Reinhold Niebuhr at Union and Paul Tillich in Germany. On Boston's campus, the esteemed preacher, Howard Thurman was dean of chapel and shared one year in Boston with King. Martin initially thought to work with Edgar S. Brightman, but Brightman died after King's first year. After plunging into the thought of Personalism, and working through the classic writings of Borden Bowne and Hermann Lotze under the direction of L. Harold DeWolf and A. C. Knudson,[88] King submitted a dissertation titled, "A Comparison of the Conceptions of God in the Thinking of Paul Tillich and Henry Nelson Wieman." Rejecting what he thought to be the impersonal God of Tillich and Wieman, King found in Personalism two conclusions: first, that God's nature is personal and, second, that God's personality is the basis for the dignity and worth of all personality.[89] Further, God's will is that all humanity should acknowledge God's parenthood and resultant kinship. This, coupled with his growing appreciation for Gandhi, would be the basis of King's theology for the years of engagement ahead. As he

---

[88] This combination of Boston University mentors at roughly the same time gave shape to Carl F. H. Henry.

[89] Paris, *Black Religious Leaders*, 106, is convinced that King was an original thinker more than becoming a disciple of anyone. His use of the dialectical method was critical to appreciating truths from a variety of thinkers.

would later write, "In the truest sense of the word, God is a living God. In him there is feeling and will, responsive to the deepest yearnings of the human heart: *this* God both evokes and answers prayer."[90]

Reflecting on his relatively short career in 1963, King declared that while in seminary he became a devoted theological liberal. Nothing in the biblicism of fundamentalism seemed to him to be effective. "I became so enamored of the insights of liberalism," he wrote, "that I almost fell into the trap of accepting uncritically everything it encompassed. I was absolutely convinced of the natural goodness of man and the power of human reason."[91] When he encountered Neo-orthodoxy, however, he concluded that liberalism had been too sentimental toward human nature. His continuing task was to synthesize liberal and neo-orthodox thought. King endeavored to do that through existentialist critique, particularly that perspective's concept of humankind's finite freedom. King connected that freedom with the social activism of Rauschenbusch and Gandhi. His preaching, as Coretta Scott King recalls, was a transformation of biblical narrative to contemporary circumstances. He moved far from the strict historical literalism of White hermeneutics to a far more figurative approach.

During the Montgomery bus boycott in 1955, Martin reminded his followers "the basic conflict is not really over the busses. Yet we believe if the method we use in dealing with equality on the busses can eliminate injustice within ourselves, we shall at the same time be attacking the basis of injustice—man's hostility to man."[92] King often took familiar Scripture passages and rewrote them in current idiom with a moral apologetic, as in his famous sermons, "A Tough Mind and a Tender Heart" and "Paul's Letter to American Christians." King was often impatient with the biblically prominent love ethic. Rather than hoping and waiting for love to rule the day, people needed to make forthright—even difficult—commitments to God and to each other to instill a legitimate sense and experience of community between the races. Humanity, he believed, must cooperate actively with God to eradicate evil. This is where his ecclesiology came to bear, namely that the church is the conscience of society. It must guide and critique the state and join the struggle for racial justice. "If the church," he wrote, "will free itself

---

[90] King, Jr., *Strength to Love*, 155.
[91] Ibid., 147.
[92] Ibid., 5.

from the shackles of a deadening status quo, …and will speak fearlessly and insistently in terms of justice and peace, it will rekindle the imagination of mankind and fire the souls of men."[93]

King's full impact upon Baptist thought, prominently manifested through his work with the Southern Christian Leadership Conference (SCLC) and the Atlanta Improvement Association, was neither limited to these nor ended with his assassination. He considered himself to be, at the core, a minister of the gospel and a representative of a valuable religious tradition: "In the quiet recesses of my heart, I am fundamentally a clergyman, a Baptist preacher."[94] In 1961, in a bold move, he, Gardner Taylor, and other prominent civil rights-oriented ministers bolted from the National Baptist Convention and formed the Progressive National Baptist Convention. Its eccelesiology, a clue to that of King, was ecumenical, interracial, and activistic. Perhaps his final theological and institutional legacy was in mentoring a coterie of Black Baptist ministers in the SCLC, including Ralph Abernathy, Wyatt T. Walker, Jesse Jackson, and Andrew Young.

One of the more radical Black Baptists in the twentieth century was Adam Clayton Powell, Jr., scion of a unique Black Baptist tradition. Powell (1909–1972) represented congregational leadership applied to political agendas and he managed to open the way for others to follow in his political opportunities, if not his theological understanding. Powell was born into a prominent Baptist minister's family and received an excellent education. He graduated from Colgate University and did further study at Union Theological Seminary in New York.

Adam Clayton Powell, Jr., was destined to follow the pathway laid by his father, Adam Clayton Powell, Sr. A light-skinned Black raised in poverty-stricken West Virginia, he was educated at Howard University and Wayland Seminary (later Virginia Union University School of Theology). Powell Sr. also spent a year of study at Yale University. He served several churches, in Minnesota, Philadelphia, and New Haven, before accepting the challenge of pastoral ministry at New York's Abyssinian Baptist Church in 1908. A widely recognized lecturer on topics like "The Stumbling Blocks of the Race," he considered himself of like-mind with the self-help conservative tradition of Booker T.

---

[93] King, Jr., *Strength to Love*, 47.
[94] Quoted in Lischer, *Preacher King*, 5.

Washington.[95] Fundraising and preaching were the particular gifts Powell took to Abyssinian, a congregation long known for its dictatorial, erratic, and mercurial pastors. As Peter Paris has pointed out, the elder Powell earnestly believed that God designed racial harmony as the noblest end of a democratic state. Many were drawn to this vision, including Dietrich Bonhoeffer, who taught Sunday School at Abyssinian and preached there on Sunday evenings. A young Leon Sullivan came from West Virginia to be mentored by Powell and served as youth minister at the church. For many observers, Abyssinian Baptist Church became an example of the appearance of racial harmony.[96] At the time of his retirement in 1937, Pastor Powell urged his son to "preach with all the power of your soul, body, and mind the old time simple Gospel, because it is a fountain for the unclean, food for the hungry, drink for the thirsty, clothing for the naked, a solace for the sorrowing, medicine for the sick, and eternal life for the dying."[97] One of the starkest differences between the elder and the younger Powell was that the former understood the words metaphorically and the latter as a literal agenda for action.

Upon Powell Jr.'s graduation from Colgate, it was apparent that the elder Powell desired his son to be his successor. As one church member at Abyssinian quipped, " His father called him to preach—not the Lord."[98] The younger Powell's pilgrimage would little resemble that of his illustrious father. Instead, he would preach racial and economic justice and the massive congregation he inherited was to be his political headquarters for four decades. In the immediate Harlem community were the young leaders of a new Black activism: W. E. B. Dubois, A. Philip Randolph, Roy Wilkins, and Ben Davis. These were the shapers of Powell Jr.'s thinking as he delivered spellbinding rhetoric from the pulpit of America's most distinguished Black Church.

Powell hated the realities of racial discrimination in America. He had experienced the color barrier himself, and linked the abject poverty of his community with racial prejudice. His viewed the church as a gathering of significant power, prestige, and money with which Blacks could make a

---

[95] On Adam Clayton Powell, Sr., see his *Against the Tide: An Autobiography* (New York: Richard R. Smith, 1938).

[96] Paris, *Black Religious Leaders*, 154.

[97] Wil Haygood, *King of the Cats: The Life and Times of Adam Clayton Powell, Jr.* (New York: Houghton Mifflin, 1993) 73.

[98] Ibid., 73.

difference in ameliorating economic injustices. Unlike his father, he had little interest in and did not pursue membership in the larger Black Baptist organizations. Gradually, as Powell looked to his own enlarging political future, he began to dismiss many of the Black civil rights leaders. In the early days of Martin Luther King's rise to prominence, Powell considered the young minister an upstart and was not supportive of efforts in the South to confront and eradicate racial discrimination. Powell had trouble identifying with "Black" leaders because he was lighter-skinned than most.[99] and he frowned on many members of his own racial community. In the words of his most recent biographer, Powell was a loner.

Powell's sermons and two autobiographical books are the only real gauge of his theology. Each was a statement of activism. He considered himself a mystic, which one writer describes as the powerful influence between the spirit of humanity and the absolute Spirit that rules the universe.[100] God was ultimate truth and knowable through ideals of truth, beauty, and love. Powell moved far beyond the bounds of orthodoxy, however, rejecting specific teachings about the afterlife and even biblical authority. He essentially adopted a contemporary Marcionite and politically sculpted canon: "We do not believe in the Bible as the word of God. It is too filled with contradictions. We believe in the Thomas Jefferson Bible. Carefully that brilliant Founding Father cut from the New Testament only those words that Jesus spoke. Then in logical order he put them together until he had created a new Bible, a new Bible of old words."[101]

Powell's doctrine of Christ was well developed if not generally orthodox. Noting that Jesus was the bearer of God's absolute truth, Powell saw in the words of Jesus the mandate of Scripture. Rejecting notions of human depravity, Powell described sin as self-evident wrong that is perceived by human conscience. When under the pangs of a stirred conscience, a person responds to God's salvation. By this process, a person is set free and cleansed of hatred toward one's neighbors. White

---

[99] Haygood, *King of the Cats: the Life and Times of Adam Clayton Powell, Jr..*, 10-11, 52 argues that Powell often passed himself off as a white man, sometimes causing scandal.

[100] Paris, *Black Religious Leaders*, 145.

[101] Adam Clayton Powell, Jr., *Adam by Adam: The Autobiography of Adam Clayton Powell, Jr.* (New York: Dial Press, 1971) 43.

man's religion failed, Powell believed, in its inability to stir love for one's neighbor. "America is not a Christian country," he wrote. "It is a country of pretensions, of 'churchianity' where the institution of Christianity has been perverted into an instrument to perpetuate, if not to propagate...anti-Christian doctrines of segregation and discrimination."[102] He developed a theory of two kingdoms in conflict; one the kingdom of God, the other a kingdom of humanity. Not unlike Walter Rauschenbusch, Powell held that the kingdom of God was not future but realized in history as human beings work to achieve fully God's will. His ecclesiology included the metaphor that the church is a family, and also a transforming agent to usher in the kingdom of God with healing and reconciliation.

Powell's genetic influence can be seen traced in two types of followings he developed. First were those who served with him at Abyssinian. Notable among these were David Licorish, a fiery West Indian, and Wyatt Walker, a more conservatively-minded man who disapproved of Powell's increasingly lavish lifestyle. Second, there was the group of Baptist ministers who admired his application of ethics to politics. These included Jesse Jackson from Chicago and William Epps, a student activist who had attended Andover Newton Theological School. Gardner Taylor considered Powell a friend, and Samuel D. Proctor, a nationally recognized educator, actually succeeded him as senior minister at Abyssinian.

One of the most beloved African American Baptist personalities of the later twentieth century has been Gardner C. Taylor (b. 1918). Taylor was educated at Leland College, Southern University, and later Oberlin College School of Theology. He served smaller churches in Louisiana and Ohio, before accepting a call at 30 years of age in 1948 to Concord Baptist Church in Brooklyn, New York. He remained there for 42 years, growing that congregation to over 14,000 members. Taylor's great contribution to Black Baptist identity came through his pulpit ministry and his collegial advocacy for change in the national movements of Black Baptists. Known as the "poet laureate of American Protestantism," critics of all theological stripes regard him as one of the best pulpiteers of the American Christian historical experience. His fidelity to the pastoral ministry marked his agenda with a singleness of purpose that many of his

---

[102] Ibid.

more politically oriented contemporaries, with the exception of Joseph H. Jackson, lacked.

SUMMARY

The African American Baptist theological heritage is unique. As Harvey Cox has observed, "Black churches do not exist to provide a theological challenge to white churches, or to supply some kind of inspiration to white Christians. They exist to bring the hope of the gospel into lives of people whom history...has tried to rob of hope."[103] It displays definite genetic traces culled from mainstream Baptist ideas, while moving through its own context to produce perhaps the purest form of contextualization seen to-date in Baptist thought. One can identify within this Baptist stream a preoccupation with Scripture, a strong Christology, the power of religious experience, the dignity and worth of all persons before God, and an assertive understanding of the kingdom of God. Of all the influences that help shape the African American Baptist tradition, it was primarily the slave experience and liberal Baptist thought between 1890 and 1930 that were most determinative in that community. Rochester Theological Seminary was foremost in fostering and encouraging a core group of Black Baptist thinkers and ministers.

A significant challenge for any analysis of Black Baptist theological development in America and the Western hemisphere, is its close connection with political activism. A significant number of Black theologians, as well as their church-based counterparts in the Christian ministry, have gained widespread public recognition in the political or educational spheres. Their political writings often carry a veneer of theological ideas and use religious rhetoric, but move well beyond the realm of the religious into social and political ideologies. In many ways, Black theology and Black social thought in America and the West are inseparable.

One must take care not to over-emphasize the Baptist component in Black Baptist thought. Generally speaking, African American theology is African, American, and multi-confessional more than it is tied to historic Baptist emphases. No better illustration of this reality can be found than in the writings and ministry of Howard Thurman. A final observation about Black Baptist theology is that it seems to have reached a creative

---

[103] Harvey Cox, *Just As I Am*, 56.

peak in America and the West during the years between 1950 and 1980, thus far in its development.

CHAPTER 9

CANADIAN BAPTIST
THEOLOGICAL TRADITIONS

> The peculiar affliction of the Baptists in Canada has been foreign interference and influence—at one end, too English—at the other, too American. Society in Canada is neither like that of England, nor that of America; and it is as absurd to insist upon conforming it in every respect to either, as it would be, upon making Corinthian metal, pure silver or pure brass.[1]
>
> Robert A. Fyfe, 1851

Not to be overlooked in the saga of Baptist thought in North America were the Baptist theologians and institutions of Canada. Baptist life in British North America (after 1867 to be called Canada) was sufficiently developed to produce its own unique theological mosaic. The resulting Canadian Baptist character is eclectic, revealing both British and American Baptist genes. Canadian Baptist theological identity has been shaped by four historic factors: the Maritime revivalistic experience, British Baptist classical theology, American Baptist schools, and a unique form of Canadian Prairie fundamentalism.

MONTREAL AND MCMASTER

If Canadian Baptists have a unique theological tradition, it may be seen in the development of the schools in the McMaster University heritage. The roots of this tradition were British and missionary. As English missionaries planted the first churches in Montreal, and later along the Lake Ontario shoreline, the need for theological instruction began to be recognized. The primary models available were Bristol Baptist College,

---

[1] J. E. Wells, *Life and Labors of Robert Alex Fyfe, D.D.* (Toronto: W. J. Gage Co., 1868) 226.

the Haldane Seminary,[2] and the Academical Institution at Stepney. The latter school became the dominant model in the early Canadian Baptist story. The first British Baptist missionaries in Canada, John Gilmour and John Edwards, were anxious to ensure that the first steps toward founding such a school be sure. They invited Benjamin Davies (1814–1876), an erudite young theologian, to begin the work of establishing a college to serve the Canadian provinces in 1838. Davies brought a doctoral degree in languages from Leipzig to the Canada Baptist College of Montreal and built the first outstanding theological library in that province. Frustrating his efforts to recruit students to the school was that its program of studies was better suited to the British educational system and he was constantly grappling with inadequate funding. This first Canadian Baptist institution closed in 1849, but not without having accomplished some important gains for regional theological study at a university level with attendant expectations for significant curricular content and the pursuit of academic excellence.

A second stage of institutional growth ensued with the re-establishment of theological education through the Canadian Literary Institute at Woodstock, Ontario, in central Canada. Robert A. Fyfe (1816–1878), a young pastor and instructor at Montreal, improved on the earlier enterprise by dropping the heavy language requirements and stressing pastoral skills. Fyfe was trained at Madison University for one year and later at the Newton Theological Institution. In his years at the Canadian Literary Institute, he taught nearly every course in the curriculum and attracted a wide array of colleagues. While relatively small in size, the Institute brought together the best of both the American and British Baptist streams. With funding provided by the generosity of William McMaster, a member of the Senate of Canada, the enterprise moved to Toronto in 1881. As Toronto Baptist College, it drew to itself a coterie of bright young theologians, including Albert H. Newman of Mercer University and Rochester Seminary, Calvin Goodspeed of New Brunswick, William Newton Clarke of Colgate, Theodore H. Rand of Acadia University, and O. C. S. Wallace of Acadia University and Newton Theological Institution. By the 1890s the college was constituted as McMaster University, affiliated with the University of Toronto, and enjoyed a growing student body as well as placement in an axis of

---

[2] The primary influence of the Haldane Movement and its seminary was evangelical zeal. As an institution, it did not long survive, but its ideals remained for generations.

relationships with the best Baptist institutions of North America: University of Chicago, Colgate University, Bucknell University, Rochester Theological Seminary, and Newton Theological Institution. Its early graduates included Thomas Trotter, George Cross, and D. C. MacIntosh.

Of the several professors of theology who taught and wrote at McMaster or its predecessors, Calvin Goodspeed (1842–1912) was foremost. Goodspeed was a New Brunswicker with broadly expanded horizons. He was educated at the University of New Brunswick and eventually graduated from Newton Theological Institution. Between degrees he studied at Spurgeon's Pastor's College and Regent's Park College in London. Shortly after he was appointed professor of systematic theology at Canadian Literary Institute in Woodstock, he again returned overseas to study at the University of Leipzig. Following pastoral and editorial years in the Maritimes, he returned to central Canada where he was taught systematic theology and apologetics at McMaster University. There he gained a formidable reputation as a leading Baptist theologian. Jones H. Farmer, dean at McMaster, recalled Goodspeed as "one whose scholarship was accurate and who possessed a keen, analytic mind, his reasoning was surefooted and his thinking constructed."[3]

Goodspeed's earlier writings reveal the typical Free Church perspective of the late Victorian era. In his book, *The Peculiar Principles of the Baptists* (1878), he extolled the virtues of congregational governance, the separation of church and state, and affirmed the general doctrinal stance of the New Hampshire Confession of Faith. In building a case for believer's baptism, he wrote *Baptism: An Argument and Reply* (1882), in which he criticized John Calvin for not being consistent with Scripture. In 1900 Goodspeed published a study of eschatology, *Messiah's Second Advent*, in which he took a postmillennial stance to expound key biblical passages related to the Second Advent. He declined emerging dispensationalism, and preferred to stress the relational aspects of the kingdom of God, referring to theories of a separate "rapture" as a "figment of the imagination." In a minor work, *The Christian Sabbath* (1895), he moved against sabbatarians by arguing that the first day of the

---

[3]Allison A. Trites, "A Forgotten Scholar: Professor Calvin Goodspeed" *An Abiding Conviction: Maritime Baptists and Their World,* ed. Robert S. Wilson (Hantsport: Lancelot Press, 1988), 202.

week was divinely instituted as the Lord's Day. As McMaster's leading theologian in its first generation, Goodspeed was a significant theological voice among Canadian Baptists.[4] His variant positions on certain themes positioned his theological perspectives as important alternatives to many of those of the commonly popular American evangelicals.

As a theological tradition, McMaster had a wide influence among Canadian Baptists. Several of its graduates or faculty later taught at Acadia University. McMaster graduates were found in most of the burgeoning urban and village churches of Ontario. In the West, it was McMaster graduates who helped plant congregations in the Prairie Provinces and start a Baptist college at Brandon, Manitoba. Overseas, McMaster graduates pioneered schools in India and Bolivia that aspired to the stature of McMaster. In its early years, under men like Rand and Wallace, McMaster was the exemplar of Baptist orthodoxy. Several distinguished theologians taught early in their careers at McMaster and then went on to schools like the University of Chicago and Yale University where a more open attitude toward academic inquiry existed. Notable among these were George Burman Foster and Douglas Clyde MacIntosh.

In its continual pilgrimage to keep pace with first-rank American schools and the British Baptist traditions, McMaster overreached itself theologically. When the second generation of educators retired between 1915 and 1925, additions were recruited for academic reputations rather than from among students who were most interested in continuing within the doctrinal life of the Canadian churches. The institution's independence and its status as university produced several rifts with local churches over faculty appointments. After 1925 a line of liberal arts educators, sometimes possessing the barest of church credentials, re-shaped the university in an open and progressive fashion. These included Theodore Harding Rand, Thomas Trotter, A. C. McCrimmon, H. P. Whidden, and Jones Hughes Farmer.[5] Their academic models were the

---

[4] Allison A. Trites, "Calvin Goodspeed: An Assessment of His Theological Contribution," in Jarold K. Zeman, ed., *Costly Vision: The Baptist Pilgrimage in Canada* (Wolfville; Acadia Divinity College, 1988) 23–43.

[5] George Rawlyk credited Whidden and his successors with "pushing McMaster into a liberal and secular position." See his *Is Jesus Your Personal Saviour? In Search of Canadian Evangelicalism in the 1990s* (Montreal: McGill Queens University Press, 1996) 45.

University of Chicago, Brown University, and Rochester Theological Seminary. McMaster easily became prey to theologically conservative critics, with the result being the loss of Baptist support and the diminution of theological studies within the university.

One Baptist minister in particular helped to sharpen McMaster's theological identity. Thomas Todhunter Shields (1873–1955), pastor of Jarvis Street Baptist Church in Toronto for most of his career, used McMaster as a whipping post for his fundamentalistic diatribes. Shields was British-born, self-taught, and a gifted orator. Due to his position as pastor of the late Senator William McMaster's congregation and the church-home of many university faculty, Shields expected to enjoy a premier role, if not a faculty position, in the school. Disappointed with the school's inattention to his hopes, he became an antagonist who challenged many of McMaster's faculty appointments, beginning in 1915 with that of Isaac Matthews.

Shields organized his supportive followers to oppose granting an honorary degree to American Baptist liberal and Brown University president, William H. P. Faunce, at the meeting of the Canadian Baptist Convention in the early 1920s. He next turned against L. H. Marshall's appointment to teach theology at the school in 1925. Marshall was an advocate of the historical critical method and the pastor of an "open membership"[6] church in Liverpool, England, before his appointment. In editorials, from his pulpit, and across the country, Shields attacked Marshall and the university, accusing the man and the institution of failure to uphold the full authority of the Bible and for accepting less than classic Baptist standards of doctrinal discipline. These attacks forced Jones H. Farmer, dean of theology at McMaster, to respond in support of Marshall and openly support a more progressive stance toward theology. Farmer absorbed the attacks of the fundamentalists for three decades and produced at McMaster a Canadian version of the University of Chicago. The Baptist community in Ontario split, McMaster holding tenuously onto the regular convention churches.

The decades of the 1940s through the 1970s were theologically uneventful for McMaster. Robert James McCracken (1904–1973) taught theology at the school until he left to accept the pastorate of Riverside

---

[6] Open membership in this context identifies the practice of accepting members from other than Baptist backgrounds who may not have been baptized as believers or by immersion. In this era it signalled an ecumenically – oriented stance.

Church in New York, the successor to Harry Emerson Fosdick.[7] McCracken had two degrees from University of Glasgow and had served various congregations in Scotland. Prior to accepting an appointment to McMaster, he taught systematic theology at the Scottish Baptist College in Glasgow. In Canada he became professor of Christian Theology and Philosophy of Religion, later serving as head of the department at McMaster. While not a writing scholar, McCracken produced *Putting Faith to Work* (1960) and *What Is Sin? What is Virtue?* (1966). After McCracken, followed Russell F. Aldwinckle (1911–1992) who oversaw the transition of the school's department of theology to a professional divinity college in which advanced theological courses were discontinued. Aldwinckle, a protégé of H. Wheeler Robinson and Ernest Payne, was educated at Oxford University (theology), and subsequently at the University of London (medieval history). Later at the University of Strasbourg under a Baptist Union scholarship to study abroad, he pursued a doctoral degree in the philosophy of religion under Victor Monod. The title of his dissertation was "The Object of Christian Worship: A Study of the Notion of Objectivity in Relation to Religious Experience," which he actually completed under Charles Hauter because Monod died. For over thirty years Aldwinckle valiantly maintained at McMaster a dialogue on substantive theological issues, producing a number of writings on Christ and baptism. He endeavored to offer an orthodox response to the ever more popular process theologians, while also offering a contemporary understanding of baptism in ecumenical context. His last work titled *The Logic of the Believing Mind* (1995), published posthumously, was an attempt to bridge perceived gaps between theology and the philosophy of religion by arguing that the incarnation of Christ was the foundation for the logic of a believing mind.

Eventually, with declining membership among the churches of the Baptist Convention of Ontario and Quebec, fewer students enrolled in the theological school and constituent pressure from organized evangelicals led McMaster to be more accommodating to the evangelical tradition, albeit with a relatively open, scholarly, and ecumenical spirit.[8]

---

[7] While at Riverside Church, McCracken also served as adjunct professor of practical theology at Union Theological Seminary.

[8] In addition to Pinnock's appointment, evidences of this shift are seen in the reorganization of the Divinity College under Canadian book-publisher John W. Irwin,

When Aldwinckle retired in 1977, the trustees made a token evangelical appointment in Clark H. Pinnock of Regent College. In recent decades, theologically speaking, McMaster has had less of an influence upon its Baptist constituency than that exercised by the Evangelical Fellowship of Canada, various parachurch organizations, and evangelical voices from the United States.

ALLINE AND ACADIA

A somewhat unique regional theological tradition developed in the Canadian East. In its formative stages, this tradition was unique to the Maritimes region, but imitative of the Great Awakening in New England. Among the Maritime Baptists a tension has existed for over two centuries between revivalistic, experiential theology common in the churches and a desire among leading pastors for a more staid, educated ministry. The Maritime revivalistic experience is the direct result of the itinerant preaching of Henry Alline (1748–1784). In a second stream of tradition, Acadia University is the result of the desire for an educated ministry among Baptists. The two emphases interacted creatively and for the most part positively.

Baptist historiography has with certainty established the importance of the Allinite tradition in the making of Canadian Baptist life and thought. Converted in 1775, Henry Alline was called to preach and was the fountainhead of a major revival in Nova Scotia in 1776. He became an itinerant preacher in Nova Scotia and New England, a chief advocate of New Light theology. He was a mystic, full of enthusiasm for the experienced gospel. A self-taught Arminian theologically, Alline held Calvinism to be blasphemous and contrary to Scripture. Instead, he drew upon a variety of writers, including John Fletcher, Edward Young, John Milton, and William Law. While he was recognized by Baptists and certainly influenced their development, he remained above denominational distinctions. For Alline, while baptism was voluntary, the experience of the new birth in Christ was a necessity.[9] In his legacy were the hymns he wrote, those persons directly converted under his

---

and the principalship of William H. Brackney, 1989–2000. See Rawlyk, *Is Jesus Your Personal Saviour*, 46.

[9] James A. Beverly and Barry Moody, editors, *The Life and Journal of the Reverend Mr. Henry Alline* (Hantsport: Lancelot Press, 1982) 14–20.

ministry, his much-reprinted tract, *Two Mites*, strong lay participation in churches, and radical enthusiasm in public religious gatherings.

The Allinite tradition was carried on in the nineteenth century by disciples of Alline and revivalistic pastors. Known among Canadian Baptists as the "Maritime Fathers," these include Edward Manning (1766–1851), Theodore S. Harding (1773–1855), James Manning (1763–1818), Thomas H. Chipman (1756–1830), Joseph Dimmock (1768–1846), Harris Harding (1761–1854), and Joseph Crandall (1775–1858). These men were pastors of prominent churches in the Annapolis Valley or New Brunswick. They held regional revivals, organized the associational structures, standardized theological understandings, and wrote the history of Baptist life in the Maritimes. The "Fathers" form a constant point of reference for understanding Maritime Baptist identity.[10]

The institutional side of the Maritimes story reflects energy and diversity. Acadia University's faculty in theology exhibited anything but a policy of exclusivism. Graduates of Acadia and others with American, European, and Canadian backgrounds were sought to fill the faculty ranks. One historian has observed, "Acadia's comparatively liberal hiring practices brought to the campus men of diverse backgrounds, training and ideas, certainly adding to the complexity and strength of the institution."[11] British Baptist classical influences entered the Canadian streams via John Mockett Cramp (1796–1881) and much later through a cluster of immigrants associated with McMaster University from the 1920s through the 1980s. Cramp was an educational missionary of the Canada Baptist Missionary Society in 1844. By all accounts, his work in Montreal was both rewarding and frustrating. He built a significant theological library at Canada Baptist College and raised funds important to its sustenance. He edited newspapers in Montreal and promoted Madame Feller's evangelical mission to the French. But the college's curriculum was esoteric and too academic for a frontier of planting

---

[10] See for instance, I. E. Bill, *Fifty Years with the Baptist Ministers and Churches of the Maritime Provinces of Canada* (Saint John: Barnes and Co., 1880); Edward M. Saunders, *History of the Baptists of the Maritime Provinces* (Halifax: John Burgoyne, 1902); and more recently, George Rawlyk, *Ravished By the Spirit* (Kingston, Ontario: McGill Queens University Press, 1984).

[11] Barry Moody, "Acadia College: Breadth of Vision, Breadth of Mind, the Baptists and Acadia College," in George Rawlyk, *Canadian Baptists and Christian Higher Education* (Kingston Ontario: McGill Queens University Press, 1988) 18.

churches. It closed after only eleven years of life. In 1850 Cramp was invited to another young institution that was struggling for its place on the Canadian landscape. At what evolved as Acadia College in Nova Scotia, Cramp remained for two decades and was at the forefront of the developing Maritime Baptist theological heritage. He taught theology at Acadia from 1854 until his death in 1881.[12]

Cramp's theological perspective was shaped at Stepney under William Newman. He was widely read and wrote with authority on subjects as diverse as baptism, the life of Christ, the Lord's Supper, Baptist church polity and practice, and Reformation themes. His *Textbook of Popery, Comprising a Brief History of the Council of Trent and a Complete View of Roman Catholic Theology* (1831) is an exhaustive compilation of research not only on Roman Catholic dogma, but also on various Protestant responses. In the spirit of the anti-Catholic surge of the mid-century, Cramp's strong denunciation of the non-Christian aspects of Catholicism doubtless fueled much resentment towards Rome. He held extremely high academic expectations for the Baptist ministry and this surely played a role in the modest numbers of Maritime ministerial candidates that attended the school during his tenure. Cramp's ecclesiology was perilously close to Landmarkism. "No society," he wrote, "founded on principles opposed to those of Christ is worthy to be called a Christian church. If it consists of an indiscriminate population, obtaining membership by birth...if it is governed by royal edicts or acts of parliament—it may be a human institution, a worldly corporation, but it is not a Christian Church."[13]

Cramp was no religious obscurantist. At his induction as president of Acadia, he boldly asserted his optimism about freedom of inquiry. "Is this an age of freedom and light? Christianity is the religion of freedom and light. Is it the age of science? Christianity harmonizes with science. Is it an age of bold inquiry? Christianity invites and will repay such inquiry."[14] In his interpretation of the Second Coming of Christ, he

---

[12] For a useful overview of the structural, institutional evolution of theology at Acadia, consult Owen Darrel Cochran, "The Development of Theological Education at Acadia University" (B.D. thesis, Acadia University, 1954).

[13] John M. Cramp. "The Kingdom of Christ" in *Lectures for These Times* (London: Houlston and Stoneman, 1844) 66.

[14] John M. Cramp, *The Inaugural Address Delivered by the President June 20, 1851.* (Halifax: James Bowes, 1851) 18–20.

exhibited dispensational language within an amillennial framework, typical of most Baptist interpretations at mid-century that treated the text of the Bible as a source of specific historically and chronologically locatable details.[15] Punctuating much of what Cramp wrote was a continuous Protestant anti-Roman ethos that favored biblical authority over any form of historic church council and papal legislation.

Closely associated with Cramp was Edmund Albern Crawley (1799–1888), Acadia's first professor of theology. Crawley was a Baptist convert from Anglican roots. He had practiced law and was well-grounded in academic studies at the University of Kings College, Canada's oldest Anglican school, in Windsor, Nova Scotia. He entered Baptist ranks under the pastorate of Alexis Caswell at Granville Street Baptist Church in Halifax. Originally he had hoped for a Baptist faculty position at Dalhousie University, but was denied the position. Following Caswell to the United States, Crawley took the theology course at Newton Theological Institution and later spent a year of advanced work at Brown University. Crawley's indebtedness to Newton was unmistakable and would be reflected in several generations of Maritimes schoolmen trained at Acadia University. His career at Acadia was largely given to teaching theology and biblical languages.

In 1881 when Crawley retired, Daniel Morse Weldon (1831–1904) was appointed the next teacher of theology and biblical languages at Acadia. Having received a bachelor's and master's degrees at Acadia, he earned a doctoral degree at Leipzig, becoming Acadia's first theologian to hold that credential. After only a brief time on the faculty, he went to Toronto Baptist College (later McMaster University) to continue his career. The president of Acadia, Artemas Wyman Sawyer (1827–1907), consequently offered the lectures in theology and philosophy, which he called "moral science," likely in emulation of Francis Wayland's approach at Brown University. Sawyer was trained at New London Academy, Dartmouth College, and Newton Theological Institution. His great influence in the classroom was largely felt among undergraduates who recalled his revivalistic piety and devotional life.[16]

---

[15] J. M. Cramp, D.D., *The Second Coming of Our Lord: An Essay* (Halifax: Messenger Printing Office, 1879) 16–17.

[16] On Sawyer, see A. C. Chute, *The Religious Life of Acadia* (Wolfville, Acadia University, 1933) 82–88.

Theological instruction slipped into the background at Acadia during the 1880s and in fact was transferred for a time to Toronto Baptist College in Upper Canada. This plan to consolidate Baptist theological education in Toronto failed because a national program did not materialize soon enough, the Maritimes students did not see their regional emphases being given sufficient priority, and most of all, the seminary of choice continued to be Newton.[17] In 1896 when theological instruction at Acadia again resumed, Thomas Trotter (1853–1918) was appointed to the newly established Pazant Chair in theology. Trotter had studied theology at Toronto Baptist College and the University of Toronto, and helped to establish what historians call the "new Acadia." He came to the Maritimes as a pastor and followed Sawyer as college president. Trotter's teaching fields were Apologetics and Pastoral Theology. He left the presidency of the school in 1906 to engage pastoral ministries.

In some important respects, Acadia's theological contribution came of age in the twentieth century. The prestige of the school's department of theology was enhanced with the appointment of Arthur Crawley Chute (1853–1936) as dean in 1901. Chute, the son of a Baptist minister and a graduate of Acadia, moved far beyond the traditions of the Baptist Maritimes in his own theological pilgrimage. As an undergraduate, he knew Crawley and Cramp, thus connecting him to Acadia's origins. He held both President Sawyer and Professor Trotter in high regard. Chute nevertheless chose to attend the Baptist Theological Seminary at Morgan Park in Chicago for his degree in divinity, taking one year at Newton. He was squarely among the progressive wing of Northern U.S. Baptists and brought a new broader scientific perspective to theology at Acadia. He was dean of the theological department from 1901 to 1922, and it was during his tenure that theological courses came to be classified as "professional studies," following the new terminology of the University of Chicago.

Essentially a generalist and biblical specialist himself, Dean Chute appointed a 1897 graduate of Acadia, Simeon Spidle (1867–1954), to a professorship in church history and theology. This appointment was a

---

[17] For a detailed discussion of this project, see the pamphlet titled "Correspondence between a Committee of the Maritme Baptist Convention and the Authorities of Toronto Baptist College," published by the Maritime Convention, Wolfville NS, 1886 (Acadia University Archives).

bellwether for the critical period of the 1920s. In addition to his Acadia credentials,[18] Spidle had pursued studies at Newton Theological Institution and Clark University, obtaining a doctorate from the latter school. He taught systematic theology and church history at Acadia from 1911 until 1936 and served as the dean of theology between 1922 and 1936.

Spidle developed thoroughly modern views of the academic topics he addressed, while still retaining terminology that sounded traditional. Methodologically, he opened new vistas by moving beyond mere textual analysis to the application of social science techniques to biblical hermeneutics. His doctoral dissertation under G. Stanley Hall at Clark University was titled "The Belief in Immortality" and was defended before the faculty of that university's department of psychology. At that time in the United States, Hall was a leading pioneer in the field of examining the psychological bases of religious behavior. Having surveyed various philosophical and religious approaches to the subject of immortality, Spidle conducted an opinion survey of thirty subjective questions among a population of his acquaintances—Americans and Canadians. He concluded that the vast majority of people clung to a belief in personal immortality, but were uncertain of the details regarding that realm or plain of existence. Spidle reasoned that the benefits of a belief in immortality include its humanizing effects and its moral aspects. "Immortality enriches one's life," he wrote, "and induces a man to do good."[19]

As a teacher of logic, metaphysics, theology, and ethics, Spidle drew upon a wide variety of mainly contemporary authors. He used the work of Northwestern University professor Edmund Soper in comparative religions, A. E. Taylor of St. Andrews University in philosophy and psychology, and Columbia University philosopher W. P. Montague for epistemology. A syllabus from one of Chute's theology courses indicates high appreciation for Adolf von Harnack, Frank Hugh Foster, and James Orr, as well as Baptists William Newton Clarke, E. Y. Mullins, W. T. Conner, and A. H. Strong. Rejecting a dictation theory of the Bible's inspiration, he fully embraced an historical theory of progressive revelation. In an era filled with references to literal interpretations of

---

[18] Spidle and Acadia president, George B. Cutten, were undergraduate classmates.

[19] Simeon Spidle, "The Belief in Immortality," repr., *Journal of Religious Psychology*, 5/1 (1912): 44–48.

scientific details in the Scriptures, Spidle concluded, "the Bible is not a textbook on the subject of science." [20] Following Hezekiah Harvey, E. C. Dargan, and Edward Hiscox, Spidle held typically Baptist views of the church as a democratic fellowship, the practice of baptism for adults only, and a Zwinglian/Anabaptist view of the Lord's Supper.[21] Predictably, he turned the contemporary issue of eschatology toward his own area of expertise on immortality. His students remembered him as "crystal clear, honest, and well-informed."[22]

Spidle received heightened public attention during a celebrated trial in 1935 known as the "Kingston Parsonage Case". The issue of the ownership of the Baptist parsonage at Kingston, Nova Scotia, was secondary. The real battle was waged between fundamentalists who claimed the Baptist Convention was modernist, and those who supported the Convention and particularly Acadia University. As dean of theology, Spidle defended "historic Baptist principles." Labeled by fundamentalists an elitist who was essentially a "liberal evangelical," Spidle did not answer questions under interrogation directly, seeming evasive to some and certainly a modernist to most. He refused to define terms, to categorize specific positions, or even to comment upon clear eschatological questions. From that time on, both Acadia and its dean were suspect among the more conservative and the fundamentalist evangelicals.[23]

At the end of his career, Spidle produced two manuscripts for use as textbooks. Neither was published, but each reveals his theological positions. His textbook on ethics was written in response to the aftermath of two world wars and his perception of widespread moral laxity. Rather than engaging in a biblical commentary on the topic, he discussed current moral issues in light of classic positions. Likewise, his "Outline of Theology" was intended to be a helpful survey for a beginning student in Christian theology. Without citing sources or indicating general references, Chute adopted more popular Baptist positions on open

---

[20] Simeon Spidle, "Syllabus of Systematic Theology," 18. (Baptist Archives, Acadia University, Wolfville, N.S.)

[21] Ibid., 56.

[22] "In Memoriam" *Acadia Bulletin*, 40/6 (1954): 3.

[23] See George Rawlyk, "Fundamentalism, Modernism, and the Maritime Baptists in the 1920s and 1930s" *Acadiensis, 17/1* (Autumn 1987): 24–27, and "Kingston Baptist Parsonage Case" (May 1935), record of the *Kingston Nova Scotia Court*, proceedings file no. 5259.

communion, believer's baptism, and a limited view of the universal
church. The final section of the outline was given to the topic of
immortality rather than eschatology.[24]

Acadia's theological direction was next set by Robert MacGregor
Fraser (1890–1967), who joined the theology faculty of four in 1938 that
included three Yale University graduates. Fraser completed
undergraduate and theology degrees at McMaster. He studied Gaelic
literature and theology at New College, Edinburgh, and theology at Basel
and Marburg, all the while serving in various locations as a pastor. Later,
at Yale University, he completed master's and doctoral degrees, while
serving as pastor of a German-speaking congregation. His Yale
dissertation was titled "A Study of the Philosophy of Wilhelm Dilthey,"
and was written under the direction of H. Richard Niebuhr, professor of
Christian ethics. Dilthey was a well-known German philosopher at Basel
and later Berlin, who attempted to create a methodology for the
humanities that was free of the natural sciences. Both Niebuhr and Fraser
thought Dilthey might be applicable to the theological disciplines.
Perhaps the most broadly oriented theologian ever to teach at Acadia,
Fraser was much enamored of Friederich Schleiermacher and delivered a
"mild variety of classical liberalism."[25]

Professor Fraser was devoted to the Socratic method of teaching. He
presented multiple views and opinions,[26] often not revealing his own in
order to challenge students to pursue truth wherever it might lead them.
In at least one case this was to give Fraser a heightened public image that
turned negative. In 1947, Earle K. Hawksworth of Wolfville, Nova
Scotia, prepared a thesis under Fraser's direction for his bachelor of
divinity degree at Acadia. Hawksworth's thesis essentially denied the
necessity of belief in the virgin birth of Jesus Christ as a prerequisite to
the Christian experience. The faculty accepted his thesis and
Hawksworth graduated. At the 1947 session of the Maritime Examining
Council for Ordination, however, Hawksworth encountered serious

---

[24] Chute's "Outline of Theology" appears to have been a private retirement project
for friends and former students. Copies are located in the Acadia University archives.

[25] So recalled his successor, M. R. Cherry, in an interview by author, Wolfville, Nova
Scotia, 30 July 2001.

[26] The fallout from this circumstance prompted Dean of Theology, Evan Whidden, to
make a speech at the Convention in support of continued funding for the school, and the
Committee on Ministerial Standing admonished the faculty to take care to insure the
orthodoxy of future candidates for the ministry.

difficulties and was approved only after a lengthy debate in which Fraser defended his student's right to take the controversial position. As a result, Fraser and Acadia University lost further credibility among many conservative and evangelical Canadian Baptists. Those who favored the establishment of a Bible institute as a response to Acadia's perceived liberalism experienced renewed hope for their project.[27] Professor Fraser completed his distinguished career at Acadia teaching philosophy and translating German and Gaelic literature.

When Fraser retired in 1957, the search led to Southern Baptist Theological Seminary in Louisville, Kentucky. Acadia president Watson Kirkonnell persuaded a young doctoral graduate, Millard R. Cherry (b. 1922), to teach theology at the Canadian university for at least a two-year period. Southern Seminary was at that time enjoying its most progressive era, with Dale Moody, a prominent Neo-orthodox devotee, occupying the Joseph Emerson Brown Chair in theology. Cherry, whose stated career objective was to be a "well-trained country preacher," completed a dissertation in biblical theology titled "The Christology of Philippians 2:5–11" under the supervision of Moody, Olin Binkley, and Eric Rust. The apparent strategy at Acadia in calling Cherry was to move away from the candidates proposed by warring camps within Maritime Baptist life to a Southern Baptist appointee trained in biblical theology who appeared to be orthodox and evangelical. Cherry's two-year appointment evolved into a teaching and administrative career that spanned four decades and produced for the school a *de facto* de-emphasis of classic systematic theology. Cherry taught theology full-time but published little and was best remembered for his devotion to the students. He used the works of E. Y. Mullins, Emil Brunner, and Dale Moody as class textbooks.[28]

---

[27] On this event, see "Report of the Examining Council for Ordination," *Yearbook of the United Baptist Convention of the Maritime Provinces of Canada* (1947): 192. See also Earle K. Hawksworth, "The Incarnation" (B.D. thesis, Acadia University, 1947) 42; and his "Confusion Amid the Elect (1947)," in *The Years of the Locusts* (privately published personal memoir, 1986) 63–64. The matter was rejoined in a special session of the Convention of the Maritime Provinces of Canada in 1950. See *Yearbook of the United Baptist Convention of the Maritime Provinces of Canada* (1950): 24–25.

[28] Acadia president, Watson Kirkonnell, contacted Duke K. McCall, president at Southern Seminary. McCall and Sydnor Stealey, dean of the seminary's School of Theology, recommended M. R. Cherry, a recent graduate in theology (Th.D.) serving in a rural parish at Little Mount, Kentucky.

With the Cherry appointment and subsequent personnel shifts, emphasis at Acadia was placed upon practical theology and evangelism. Given the vocally competing camps within the Maritime Baptist Convention organized by modernists and conservatives, this was a key strategic move on the part of the school's administration. They were committed to positioning the seminary as broadly "evangelical" and "trustworthy." More important to Acadia's future were: the reality that an increasing number of students were being trained at Gordon College and Divinity School (later Gordon Conwell) in the United States; a surge of Southern Baptist interest in the Maritimes as a mission field; and, the potential loss of constituency to the New Brunswick Bible Institute at Woodstock and the fledgling United Baptist Bible Training School in Moncton.[29]

The theological tradition that grew up at Acadia was a derived tradition within the New England orbit of Newton. Newton became the primary seminary of choice for those who aspired to significant pastorates or teaching posts in the Maritimes. Moreover, New England Baptists wanted to preserve Acadia as a feeder institution to Newton. Over several generations, Acadia faculty additions were drawn from Newton, who themselves influenced others to attend there. Responsible for the initial Acadia–Newton connection was Alexis Caswell, who had first induced Edmund Crawley to further his studies at Newton. One searches in vain to find any critical assessment of Newton's theology among Acadia theologians.

The second primary influence on Acadia was McMaster University. McMaster was perceived as the senior Baptist center of theological training and scholarship in Canada and several of its graduates taught at Acadia. As one historian put it, Acadia was a virtual replica of McMaster.[30] To the detriment of Acadia, several promising faculty members transferred to McMaster to pursue careers in a more urbane setting. As Newton and McMaster waxed more theologically liberal over

---

[29] To counter this trend, two pastors became successively principals of the college, Abner Langley and Harold Mitton. Andrew D. MacRae, general secretary of the Baptist Union of Scotland, was appointed in 1983 to a chair in evangelism. Later, as principal, he appointed Roy Williams, a non-Canadian Trinity Evangelical Divinity School graduate specializing in Puritan theology, to the historic role in Theology. MacRae expected Acadia would take its place among leading North American evangelical schools.

[30] George Rawlyk, *Canadian Baptists*, ix.

the course of the twentieth century, the Maritime community became less enamored of their approaches and or welcoming of their graduates. Acadia eventually was controlled by the more conservative and fundamentalist factions of Canadian Baptist life, producing a long-term cleavage between the two Baptist universities. Acadia's leaders still attempted to bring progressive theologians to campus for the sake of the university's overall reputation, but the more traditional revivalistic ethos of the churches won out. Eventually, it would be the conservative evangelical streams in the United States, plus the fundamentalism inherent in the region itself, that would shape Acadia's theology.[31]

ABERHART AND THE PRAIRIES

The Canadian Prairies were a formidable challenge to the institutional development of Baptist schools in the later-nineteenth and early-twentieth centuries. Vast stretches of territory were sparsely settled, mostly by a wide variety of immigrant groups from Europe and Asia. Baptists, like Methodists and Presbyterians, struggled to provide a witness and plant churches among the villages and poor farms. Beginning in the 1880s, student summer evangelists and pastors from McMaster University, and later Brandon College, began to work in isolated locations and the rudiments of Baptist union of churches was begun. These beginnings proved inadequate, in part because access to institutionally directed leadership training were inaccessible and the majority of regional pastoral leaders were consequently self-taught. Between 1910 and 1940 Bible colleges sprang up in Manitoba, Saskatchewan, and Alberta to meet the need. These schools focused upon lay training and were much influenced by American and British evangelicals. While the central Canadian penchant for theology was expressed in the university context, and the Maritime Provinces were characterized by a tradition of revivalist theology, the Prairie phenomenon developed its own unique theological identity.

William Aberhart (1878-1943) was raised in Ontario and completed a bachelor's degree through correspondence from Queens University. A

---

[31] The leaders of the school widely advertised it as an evangelical institution and recruited faculty on that basis. Symbolically, relationships were built with Canadian and American evangelical organizations such as the Evangelical Fellowship of Canada, the Fellowship of Evangelical Seminary Presidents, and SCUPE (Seminaries Committed to Urban Professional Education.)

Presbyterian by upbringing, he had planned to prepare for ministerial studies at Knox College, but took a school teaching position in Calgary, Alberta. In addition to teaching and work in school administration, he taught Bible classes at the Presbyterian and Methodist churches in his neighborhood. When a preaching opportunity arose at Westbourne Baptist Church, a mission of First Baptist Church of Calgary, Aberhart responded and there developed a reputation as a Bible-teaching pastor. His Bible class grew in such popularity that he moved it to the Calgary Public Library and renamed it the Calgary Prophetic Bible Conference. His popularity as a lay minister became a concern to the Baptist Home Mission Society and they tried to remove Aberhart from his pastoral role in the church.[32] Aberhart eventually was recognized as a lay minister by Baptist clergy leadership and he sought believer's baptism as part of a "Jesus Only" tradition then moving about the West among Pentecostal groups. Aberhart's ministry was peripheral to mainstream Baptist ecclesiocracy, but well ensconced among the people.

Aberhart was a thoroughgoing dispensationalist. He admired religious personalities such as Arno C. Gabelein and Dwight L. Moody, as well as many writers and teachers among the Plymouth Brethren. Beginning with a doctrine embracing an infallible, inerrant Bible, his rallying cry was, "The Bible, the whole Bible, and nothing but the Bible."[33] His specific teachings included a rapture of Christians before the tribulation, the emergence of an Antichrist superhuman being, a Yellow Race War, a Russian resurgence, a Battle of Armageddon, and a literal reign of Christ for 1,000 years. He appealed to people to gain new insight from their newspapers by studying "Bible prophecy." He invited hearers to become Christians to avoid the tribulation. This type of popular Bible teaching and its related forms of evangelism became standard fare for a monthly newspaper titled *The Prophetic Voice* (1924–1942), lectures at the Palace Theater in Calgary, and in 1927 it comprised the core curriculum at the Calgary Prophetic Bible Institute. In 1925 Aberhart's lectures were broadcast for the first time in radio history as "Back to the Bible" on CFCN to homes across Alberta and the Canadian Prairie Provinces. Aberhart's connection with other Baptist dispensationalists was evident.

---

[32]Minutes of the Westbourne Baptist Church, 16 January 1918 p.132, cited in David R. Elliott & Iris Miller, *Bible Bill: A Biography of William Aberhart* (Edmonton, AB: Reidmore Books, 1987), 30, 52n.
[33] Elliott and Miller, *Bible Bill*, 36.

He invited the Toronto fundamentalist pastor at Jarvis Street Baptist Church, T. T. Shields, to hold meetings in Calgary, and William Bell Riley of Minneapolis to dedicate officially the Institute's new building in 1927. Aberhart's educational plan was imitated among the Pentecostals, Nazarenes, Mennonites, and Independents at schools across western Canada, including the Prairie Bible Institute and Briercrest Bible College.

Beyond his dispensational theology and unusual Baptist persuasion, Aberhart became a devotee of the "Douglas System of Economics" in 1933 and created a new political movement that swept across the dire economic circumstances of the Great Depression. The Social Credit movement focused on social justice. "Every citizen should be able to secure food, clothing and shelter from the country he lives in," he wrote.[34] Specifically, this meant that every citizen would recive $25.00 per month credit from government credit houses. On a ticket known as the "Co-operative Commonwealth Federation," Aberhart was mandated into power in 1935 as premier of the Province of Alberta. He retired in 1943 in ill health, having successfully fused dispensational theology with social welfare politics. "It should be clear to every student of the Bible," he wrote, "that the British Commonwealth, the United States, and their allies are truly God's battle axe at this time."[35]

From 1945 until the 1970s Baptists in the Canadian West depended upon a ministry locally trained at various Bible colleges in the Prairie Provinces and a steady stream of McMaster graduates to serve the larger urban churches. As McMaster moved toward a kinship with the United Church style of theological education, Western Baptists planned to develop their own theological program. Unable to mount a freestanding seminary, the Baptist Union looked at possible cooperation with North American Baptist College and Seminary in Edmonton and a new Brethren school in Vancouver. The result was the establishment of Carey Hall, a Baptist foundation that maintained a permanent relationship with Regent College, an independent lay training program. In the 1990s, Carey Hall evolved into Carey Theological College while still in connection with Regent. Baptist theologians associated with the enterprise included Clark Pinnock, Samuel Mikolaski, Roy Bell, and Stanley Grenz. Pinnock's contribution will be fully treated below.

[34] Quoted in ibid., 120.
[35] Quoted in ibid., 306.

Mikolaski held a doctoral degree from Oxford in philosophical theology and taught at New Orleans Baptist Seminary and other schools in Canada and the U.S. Roy Bell concentrated on ethics and Grenz, who came from North American Baptist Seminary in Sioux Falls, South Dakota, was trained at Conservative Baptist Seminary in Denver and in Germany under Wolfhart Pannenburg.[36] Regent has provided a conservative evangelical stamp on the character of the Baptist community in the Canadian West, with a decided tilt toward British evangelicals of a Calvinistic orientation.

SUMMARY

Three theological traditions mark the development of Baptist communities in Canada. A British tradition grew up from Montreal to Toronto that was fostered in what became McMaster University. Close ties were eventually forged among McMaster, Rochester Theological Seminary, and the University of Chicago. The tradition's theological character was mildly liberal, not being as critical in methodology nor as oriented to social activism as were its American institutional counterparts.

In the Maritime Provinces, eighteenth-century revivalism continued to define the majority of the Baptist churches and Acadia University long after the tradition's "founding fathers" were deceased. Acadia was tied closely to New England Baptist thought, particularly Newton Theological Institution and, to a lesser extent, Brown and Colgate Universities. As conservatism reacted against these institutions in the 1920s, another Baptist school in New England, Gordon College, grew in prominence.

Finally, beyond the reach of university schoolmen-theologians, the dispensational theology of William Aberhart and a Bible college-level of training characterized Baptist life on the Canadian Prairies well into the twentieth century. In the 1960s as Baptist institutional life in the West matured, there was continuing aversion to university-style theology. The Baptist Union of Western Canada pursued its own course of evangelical

---

[36] Grenz has written extensively in the areas of ethics and theological topics. Among his theological works are *Theology for the Community of God* (1994), *Beyond Foundationalism: Shaping Theology in a Postmodern Context* (2001), and *The Social God and the Relational Self: A Trinitarian Theology of the Imago Dei* (2001).

ecumenism in creating a partnership with Brethren and Anglicans in Carey Theological College.

CHAPTER 10

BAPTIST THEOLOGIANS IN DIASPORA

> I saw in rapid succession on the parade ground in my mind the futility and intellectual bankruptcy of my former strategy and the wonderful freeing strategy of Barth's theological method. I could be just as free a person in theology as I could be if I were an experimental scientist. With the full permission of the truth of God in Holy Scripture, I could fearlessly read, study, and listen to all options and opinions in theology.[1]—Bernard Ramm, 1957

ACADEMICIANS AND PASTOR-THEOLOGIANS

Following World War II, three significant changes occurred among Baptist theologians. First, less systematic theology was undertaken and academic theologians contented themselves with writing on topics relating to current ecumenical or evangelical issues. Illustrative of the point, only a dozen systematic theologies were produced in part or in whole by Baptists between 1950–1999.[2] Second, a large amount of formal theology being done by Baptists was outside of Baptist institutions. For many of these theologians, "being Baptist" was less important than other identifying religious characteristics. Third, a significant amount of the Baptist theology produced in this period was a product of iconoclastic, pastoral leadership throughout the denomination. These "disasporic" pastor-theologians produced a wider range of theologically oriented literature than in any other comparable period among Baptists of all stripes.

---

[1] Bernard Ramm, "Helps From Karl Barth" *How Karl Barth Changed My Mind*, ed. Donald McKim (Grand Rapids: Eerdmans, 1986), 121.

[2] These include Carl F. H. Henry, Edward Carnell, Millard Erickson, Stanley Grenz, Kenneth Cauthen, James Leo Garrett, Dale Moody, David Smith, James W. McClendon, J. Deotis Roberts, Bernard Ramm, and Robert P. Lightner.

The theological enterprise of Carl F. H. Henry (1913–2003) was a harbinger of things to come among Baptists. Raised in the German American immigrant tradition, he possessed three degrees from Wheaton College, a ministerial degree and a theological doctorate from Northern Baptist Theological Seminary, and a second doctorate from Boston University. Henry taught at Northern Baptist and Fuller Theological Seminaries, and later on a concurrent basis at Eastern Baptist Theological Seminary and Trinity Evangelical Divinity School. He earned an international reputation as editor of *Christianity Today* (1956–67). His work became the point of departure for the "neo-evangelical movement" in American theology. This group of thinkers held on to orthodox doctrine while also engaging in dialogue with the liberal and ecumenical traditions. Henry's cohorts included Bernard Ramm, Clark Pinnock, Gordon Fee, Donald Bloesch, Harold Lindsell, and Kenneth Kantzer.[3] One biographer has asserted, "Carl Henry has helped evangelicalism emerge from the exile of the 1930s, regain a sure theological footing, and overcome the shocks of the harsh fundamentalist-liberal religious war…his influence in theology…is unparalleled among evangelicals."[4]

Later in life, Carl Henry identified numerous influences on his thought and religious pilgrimage.[5] At Wheaton College, he appreciated President J. O. Buswell, Henry C. Thiessen, a Dallas Seminary-trained theologian, Gordon H. Clark, a consistent Calvinist in philosophy, and Herbert Moule in history. These teachers helped Henry to inculcate Wheaton's "Christian world-view." Particularly important was Clark, who taught him medieval and modern philosophy, and whom Henry considered without peer among evangelical philosophers. After

---

[3] Henry was often critical of these very people. For instance, of Clark Pinnock, he thought him more eager to attempt to adduce empirical evidence from the cosmos and history than to accept the inspired teaching of the Bible. Similarly, he thought Bernard Ramm wrongheaded about propositional revelation and the nature of the language of myth. Of his longtime editorial colleague, Harold Lindsell, he perceived unhelpful pragmatic tendencies that attempted to prove Scripture in experience. See Carl F. H. Henry, *God, Revelation, and Authority: The God Who Speaks and Shows*: Vol. I *Preliminary Considerations* (Waco: Word Books, 1976) 1:67, 230; 4:163.

[4] Bob E. Patterson, *Makers of the Modern Theological Mind: Carl F. H. Henry* (Waco: Word Books, 1983) 56, 169.

[5] Carl F.H. Henry, *Confessions of Theologian: An Autobiography* (Waco: Word Books, 1986).

undergraduate studies, he enrolled in the John Dickey Memorial
Theological Seminary Course at Wheaton and concurrently at Northern
Baptist Theological Seminary. At Northern he recalled with appreciation
Peder Stianson in church history, Julius Mantey in New Testament, and
William E. Powers in philosophy of religion. It was Powers, an ardent
evangelical, who introduced Henry to shapers of the twentieth-century
mind, including William James, John Dewey, Henry N. Wieman, Karl
Barth, and Emil Brunner. Upon completing his doctorate at Northern
Baptist, he became professor of systematic theology and philosophy at
the seminary, 1942–1947. His Northern Baptist doctoral dissertation was
subsequently published under the title, *Successful Church Publicity: A
Guidebook for Christian Publicists*.

Henry continued his educational quest to broaden his evangelical
credentials. He took graduate courses at Indiana University under
philosophers W. Harry Jellema, a staunch Calvinist, and Henry Veitch, a
Thomist. At Loyola University, he delved into Duns Scotus and Thomas
Aquinas. Initially he had planned to study at the University of Chicago,
but Henry N. Wieman's doctrinaire commitment to the scientific method
redirected him to Boston University. The program at Boston University
signaled the kind of theologian he aspired to be. Working in the
Department of Philosophy under Edward Brightman, Albert C. Knudson,
and L. Harold DeWolf, a distinguished group of Methodist liberal
thinkers, Henry considerably broadened his theological awareness. From
Knudson, he learned the metaphysical significance of personality, how
religious belief is voluntaristic, and that God is essentially immanent.[6]
Under Brightman he heard that religious experience is invaluable for data
on religious truth, which is essentially metaphysical, and that "all
experience is the experience of persons."[7] DeWolf gave him an
appreciation for a classic liberal Protestant theological perspective.
Henry's own academic research work at Boston was titled "The
Influence of Personalistic Idealism on the Theology of A. H. Strong." He
thoroughly examined the influences upon young Strong, and the changes
that occurred in Strong's career-long search for a credible orthodox
theological position. He concluded that a comparison of Strong's

---

[6] A. C. Knudson, "A Personalist Approach to Theology," in Vergilius Ferm, ed.,
Contemporary American Theology: Theological Autobiographies , Vol. I(New York
Roundtable Press, 1932) 234–38.

[7] Edgar S. Brightman, "Religion as Truth," in ibid., 58, 73 ff.

Lectures on Theology (1876) with his revised *Systematic Theology* (1886–1907) demonstrated substantial shifts away from orthodoxy and toward a compromising personalist philosophical position, not unlike that of his contemporary Borden P. Bowne at Boston University. Strong, for Henry, had replaced biblical authority in theology with a new source of religious knowledge. Henry's study thus demonstrated what several Baptists had suspected about these turn-of-the century theologians: there had been a shift to acceptance of some, if not many, liberal tenets among the academic theologians, and thus subtly into the wider denomination. It became Henry's self-described task to restore biblical authority to the Baptist community and to Protestant theology in general. The young theologian was prepared to remain in mainstream Baptist life as long as the Northern Baptist Convention retained its fidelity to the New Hampshire Confession of Faith.[8]

In 1947 Carl Henry began an eight-year teaching career in theology at the new Fuller Theological Seminary in California. He joined Wilbur Smith and Everett Harrison as the original faculty of the first evangelical seminary on the West Coast of the United States. As he began his tenure at Fuller, Henry authored *The Uneasy Conscience of Modern Fundamentalism* (1947), one of two works that would define his career. In *Uneasy Conscience* he criticized fundamentalism for its withdrawal from society, its pessimism about evangelism, and its despairing view of world history. Rather than resisting the character of early twentieth-century liberalism's "kingdom-now mood," Henry challenged evangelicals to reapply the redemptive message of the gospel to the global predicament, to stress "great evangelical agreements in a common world front," and to revisit eschatology in a way that would not "unnecessarily dissipate evangelical strength in controversy over secondary positions."[9] With subtlety, the book began using the term "fundamentalist" to describe those adhering to biblical Christianity. It transformed that nomenclature to "evangelical," by which Henry meant those espousing a "supernaturalistic world and life view." Instead of a revolt against fundamentalism, he called for an application of the

---

[8] Earlier in his career, he and Leonard Lewis planned a thorough revision of Strong's theology with more evangelical emphases. See Carl F. H. Henry, *Confessions of a Theologian: An Autobiography* (Waco: Word Books, 1983) 106.

[9] Carl F. H. Henry, *The Uneasy Conscience of Modern Fundamentalism* (Grand Rapids: Eerdmans, 1947) 50, 57.

fundamentals of the faith.[10] The book was very well received among moderate evangelicals and fundamentalists in transition to more open theological positions. While at Fuller, Henry's influence among evangelicals grew exponentially and he traveled widely across America and in Europe. In 1955 Billy Graham offered him the opportunity to become the founding editor of *Christianity Today*, an evangelical magazine to be published fortnightly. In that role Henry progressively came to be an influential voice among American religious conservatives.

Henry published a second defining work in 1950 that established him as one among the most prominent twentieth-century theological and philosophical thinkers. *Fifty Years of Protestant Theology*[11] grew out of his courses in seminary. On the one hand, it was a jargonistic, stilted discussion of the course between liberal theology and neo-supernaturalistic theism (he termed it "idealistic immanentism").[12] On the other hand, it was also a call for serious theologians to re-engage biblical theology. A student of the leading German theologians, he had personal encounters with some of the mid-twentieth-century's most respected scholars, including Karl Barth, Emil Brunner, Rudolf Bultmann, Paul Tillich, Helmut Thielicke, and Gustaf Aulen.

Henry not only read contemporary theologians voraciously, he was himself a bridge between evangelicals and the theological left.[13] He was deeply critical of Barthianism because it had resulted in a lessened sense of biblical authority and theological confusion among evangelicals at mid-century. The promise of an American evangelicalism that would correct the errors of British and continental ways, however, was for Henry a bright prospect. He wrote: "Let us see to it that the United States shall retain its strategic importance for missions and evangelism...Let us

---

[10] Ibid., preface.

[11] The title echoed A. H. Strong's book by the same title of 1899, for which Henry had great esteem. Strong had extolled the rediscovery of the immanent God, while Henry pressed for a transcendent God. Carl F. H. Henry, *Fifty Years of Protestant Theology* (Boston: W. A. Wilde, 1950) 23.

[12] Influenced by his Boston University teacher, A. C. Knudson, Henry did not like the term "neo-orthodoxy" because it placed a positive interpretation on what he thought was a defective pattern of thought. He defined "neo-supernaturalism" as "a catchall for upward-moving liberals, discontented evangelicals, and relativists who watch the tides of thought." Ibid., 60, 78.

[13] See *Uneasy Conscience*, 74, where he affirmed the value of "an efficient united nations organization" as a post-war political model for dialogue.

help to make the next half century in America at least, great years of theological thought, and not fifty years in which, in the name of enlightened scholarship and Christian insight, Biblical revelation is again dissolved into secular philosophies of religion."[14] A protracted period of missed theological opportunities to clarify important evangelical doctrines, Henry believed, would reduce evangelicalism to the status of a cult.

Eventually Carl Henry's openness with the theological center cost him credibility with the backers of *Christianity Today*. He stepped down as editor in 1968 and from a continuing "at large" role in 1971.[15] Henry returned to the academy to give theological education another try.[16] In 1969 J. Lester Harnish, the new conservative evangelical president of Eastern Baptist Theological Seminary in Philadelphia invited Carl Henry to be a signal of thorough reform at the seminary and within the American Baptist denomination. Henry accepted the assignment, but only halfway, as he continued to be a visiting distinguished professor at Trinity Evangelical Divinity School in Illinois. His self-imposed limited role hurt his leadership chances at Eastern—he was on campus only the first term each year and virtually invisible to students and faculty colleagues. He taught senior theology and had a reputation for harsh grading practices. His brother-in-law, Thorwald Bender, also taught theology at the seminary and was openly opposed to Henry's presence on the faculty. After only three years, Henry "retired" from both seminary teaching and American Baptist life. While he was at Eastern/Trinity, he produced a dictionary of Christian ethics and spearheaded Key '73, a pan-evangelical evangelistic effort that launched American evangelicals into a more cooperative phase.

Following his departure from theological education, Carl Henry spent five years as a lecturer for World Vision and he traveled widely as a distinguished evangelical spokesman. During this time he issued the six-volume *God, Revelation, and Authority* (1976–1983). Henry's noted friend, Bernard Ramm, called the work, "the broadest, the most learned, the most incisive comprehensive work on revelation in our current

---

[14] Henry, *Fifty Years*, 92.

[15] Henry had a longstanding disagreement with magazine board members, Presbyterian millionaire J. Howard Pew and Harold Lindsell. See ibid., 279–87.

[16] For an assessment of Henry's breach with evangelicals, see Larry Dean Sharp, "Carl Henry: Neo-Evangelical Theologian" (Ph.D. diss., Vanderbilt University, 1972).

evangelical tradition," while a prominent newspaper editor hailed it as "the most definitive work on biblical theology in this century." University of Chicago historian Martin Marty thought it set the future course for evangelical theology.[17]

As a theologian, Carl Henry was part journalist and part critic. His writing style in later works was lucid and he included commentary on matters not generally associated with academic theological treatises, including the impact of the mass media and an assessment of the Jesus People movement. He continued to take pleasure in dialogue with a variety of prominent religious writers: Karl Barth, Emil Brunner, Rudolf Bultmann, Gordon Clark, Leon Morris, Charles F. D. Moule, and Cornelius Van Til. In his magnum opus, *God, Revelation and Authority*, Henry held that the task of theology is "to exposit and elucidate the content of Scripture in an orderly way."[18] Here he was in keeping with generations of Baptist forbears. He built his entire system on the nature of the revealed Word: "Divine revelation is the source of all truth, reason is the instrument for recognizing it; Scripture is its verifying principle."[19] In the same vein, Henry has been an ardent defender of propositional revelation: "God in his special revelation has spoken in sentences, that is propositionally" and the prophets and apostles to whom special revelation came attest this.[20] As far as his estimation of biblical inerrancy is concerned, Henry opines: "The generation that possessed the apostolic autographs viewed them as the veritable Word of God. The fact of inerrant autographs is both theoretically and practically important. If the originals were errant, then textual criticism would expect to give us not more truthful readings but only more ancient ones."[21]

Henry's identity as a Baptist theologian is worth discussion. As biographers have pointed out, he was a Baptist by choice, mostly in the Northern/American Baptist tradition. He was licensed to the ministry in a Northern Baptist congregation and ordained in a German Conference Baptist Church.[22] Henry himself wrote appreciatively of Baptist

---

[17] Ibid., 366.

[18] Henry, *God, Revelation, and Authority*, 1:238.

[19] Ibid., 215.

[20] *God, Revelation and Authority*, 3:481.

[21] Ibid., 4:209.

[22] Henry, *Confessions*, 84, 95, 104, and Carl F. H. Henry, "Twenty Years a Baptist," *Foundations* 1/1 (1958): 47. He was baptized in 1937 at Babylon Baptist Church, Long Island, New York. Two years later he was licensed to preach there. In 1941 the Humboldt

distinctives: the final authority of Scripture above all creeds and speculation, the priesthood of all believers, believer's baptism by immersion, the autonomy of the local church, and the separation of church and state.[23] He taught at two Northern/American Baptist theological schools. His scholarship was set in the context of Baptist theological teachers, though that became significantly broader as time went on. Henry valued American Baptist assessments of his work and seemed sincerely to desire relating to them. On the negative side of the ledger, he was pained at being dropped from the denominational pension fund when he went to Fuller and always seemed to feel that he worked at the margins as a confessing evangelical.[24] He also became critical of what he called Baptist "distractions," by which he meant a retreat from the primary authority of Scripture, a perceived sympathy for ecumenical theology, and "the disheartening spectacle of political maneuvering" that was indicative of the deep divisions within denominational life. He confessed to being deeply concerned about "theological amnesia" among fellow Baptists.[25]

Not surprisingly, Carl Henry has enjoyed acclaim amongst Baptists, particularly Southern and other conservative Baptists who declare a high view of Scripture. Ironically, Henry has enjoyed an uneven relationship with Southern Baptists.[26] Over the years, he seemed to shy away from what he perceived to be the disjunction in Southern Baptist thinkers between evangelism and biblical authority. He also decried the lack of ecumenical interest in the South and his perception that "Southern Baptists often close their theological history with E. Y. Mullins or W.T.

Park Baptist Church in Chicago ordained him to become its pastor. During a major part of his career his membership was at Capitol Hill Metropolitan Baptist Church in Washington D.C., and later at Cherrydale Baptist Church in Arlington, Virginia. Cherrydale was an independent congregation led by Alton Jackson. Jackson was aligned with dispensational-fundamentalists at Capital Bible Seminary.

[23] Henry, "Twenty Years a Baptist," 47.

[24] Henry, *Confessions*, 118, 174, 219. He complained that while a University of Chicago professor, Henry Wieman, was retained by the pension board, Henry was dropped. Years later, Henry was much gratified when Robert Handy, the American Baptist church historian at Union Seminary in New York, recognized the impact of Henry's 1957 editorial, "Dare We Revive the Modernist-Fundamentalist Conflict?" by including it in his co-edited 1963 two-volume sourcebook, *American Christianity*.

[25] Henry, "Twenty Years a Baptist," 49–51.

[26] In the late 1940s he decried the duplicitous position of Southern Baptists on tobacco-smoking and mixed public bathing: See *Uneasy Conscience*, 21.

Conner."[27] In his 1949 institutional survey of the effects of Barthianism among American seminaries, Henry found a "vigorous point of contact" for Barth at Southern Baptist Seminary. In 1958 he marveled at the energetic organizational life of Southern Baptists, but was unable "to reconcile their strong claims to biblical fidelity with allowing biblical criticism to infiltrate biblical theology."[28] In the 1970s he mingled with those at Southwestern and Southern Seminaries who wanted to reestablish an inerancy-based perspective on biblical authority within the institutions and throughout the Southern Baptist community. In recent years, he has been well received by some resurgent fundamentalists in the Southern and Independent Baptist communities, but never fully drawn into the circle of new theological leadership in the Southern Baptist Convention.[29]

Similar to the work of Carl Henry was that of Edward J. Carnell (1919–1967). Carnell earned divinity and master's degrees from Wheaton College and Westminster Theological Seminary, before finishing doctoral degrees at Harvard ("The Concept of Dialectic in the Theology of Reinhold Niebuhr") under Johannes A. C. F. Auer and Nels F. S. Ferre[30], and at Boston University ("The Problem of Verification in Soren Kierkegaard")[31] under E. S. Brightman. At Wheaton, Gordon H. Clark was his mentor, while at Westminster he was greatly taken by Cornelius Van Til. Carnell taught theology at Gordon College and at Fuller Theological Seminary, serving as its first resident president from 1948 through 1954. He returned to the classroom in 1955 as a teaching

---

[27] Henry, "Twenty Years a Baptist," 53.

[28] Henry, *Fifty Years*, 75; Henry, "Twenty Years a Baptist," 49, 53. These may well have been asides directed at Southern Seminary's Dale Moody, a devoted anti-fundamentalist who used the values of biblical criticism in creating his "biblical theology." Henry was also aware of the theological trends at the newly formed Southeastern Baptist Seminary in Wake Forest, North Carolina.

[29] Perhaps the most devoted follower of Carl F. H. Henry among Southern Baptists is Albert Mohler, currently president of Southern Baptist Theological Seminary, who cast Henry as "the premier theological representative of the evangelical movement of the last half of the twentieth century." Mohler's dissertation, "Evangelical Theology and Karl Barth: Representative Models of Response" (Ph.D. diss., Southern Baptist Theological Seminary, 1989) deals with Henry, as does Mohler's biographical sketch of Henry in *Theologians in the Baptist Tradition*, ed. Timothy George and David S. Dockery (Nashville: Broadman Holman, 2001) 518–33.

[30] He also studied with Elton Trueblood and A. J. Nock.

[31] Published as *The Burden of Søren Kierkegaard* (Grand Rapids: Eerdmans, 1965).

scholar. Carnell's life ended tragically with an overdose of sleeping pills, after a long struggle with suicidal depression.[32]

Like Henry, Carnell was a presuppositional theologian. The predominant perspective in his published works was his Westminster Seminary orthodoxy. He was concerned with abusive fundamentalism, which he characterized as "orthodoxy gone cultic." He would have met this type of Christianity in his youth as he witnessed the battles among Northern Baptist fundamentalists, then as a student at Wheaton College, and again at Westminster Seminary where J. Gresham Machen was overpowering in recent memory and lived on in the teaching of Oswald T. Allis, E. J. Young, and Van Til.[33] Carnell considered the fundamentalist akin to a knight-errant, going forth with the illusion that holding the correct doctrine concerning the Word of God is synonymous with the possession of virtue. No one can understand fundamentalism, Carnell wrote, "until he understood the degree to which he himself is tinctured by the attitudes of fundamentalism."[34] Fundamentalists were ideologues, dominated by rigid principles, self-exempted from an awareness of the effects of original sin.[35] In his own approach he tried to find a middle way between extreme fundamentalism and the weakness of denominational Christianity that he labeled "orthodoxy." His two most outstanding works were *An Introduction to Christian Apologetics* (1948) and *The Case for Orthodox Theology* (1959).

Carnell's theological identity was further shaped by his association with the Neo-evangelical movement and Fuller Theological Seminary. Carl F. H. Henry, Harold J. Ockenga, Harold Lindsell, and Wilbur Smith were close associates. An inerrantist, he was much intrigued with the relationship between gospel and culture. Carnell's apologetic was in many ways a reflection of his own spiritual struggle. In his award-winning *Introduction to Christian Apologetics* (1948) he asserted, "The Christian religion is indeed based upon the act of faith, but faith that is

---

[32] The saga is recounted in Rudolph Nelson, *The Making and Unmaking of an Evangelical Mind: The Case of Edward Carnell* (Cambridge: Cambridge University Press, 1987) 209–231.

[33] Carnell admired Van Til as a student, but afterwards seriously disagreed with him methodologically. Ibid., 44–45.

[34] Carnell, *Case for Orthodoxy*, 125.

[35] Ibid., 114.

not grounded in knowledge is but respectable superstition."[36] After working his way through the maze of typical challenges to rational Christianity, such as biblical criticism, evil, miracles, and science versus Scripture, Carnell concluded, "Truth is propositional correspondence to God's mind and the test for truth is systematic consistency." Ultimately, he held, the Christian turns to the Bible for the blessings and privileges of special revelation. Carnell was genuinely convinced that the Christian had as much right to advance the hypothesis of the Bible's inerrancy as the scientist had when he appealed to the law of gravity, for he believed each was an inference based upon the observation of specific facts.[37]

Carnell's doctrine of the church revealed his discomfort with his Baptist past. In fact, it is fair to say that Carnell's identity as a Baptist was dubious. Preoccupied by the sense of original sin and its effects upon both the individual and corporate Christianity, he wrote, "Denominational distinctives are an index to our blindness." His father had been a victim of disrupted pastoral ministry in a denominational family at war with itself. Although ordained and nurtured in the Baptist community, his educational pilgrimage had been pursued in other venues.[38] He came to conclude that ordination had little to do with Christian ministry and was essentially an initiation into a cult. He was little interested in local church ecclesiology, and affirmed instead a classical view of the church whose ideals were witnessed by Christ and the apostles, not by separatists. His references to church polity included Charles Hodge, James Hastings, and W. H. Griffith Thomas, a collection of Presbyterian and Anglican writers from the previous century. He equated the Baptist view of immersion with the Episcopal view of succession, the Lutheran view of the real presence, the Methodist view of holiness, and the Pentecostal view of speaking in tongues. Quoting Herman Melville, he held that "Presbyterians and Pagans alike are all dreadfully cracked about the head and sadly need mending."[39] Some of his evolved ecclesiology doubtless stemmed from the frustration that

---

[36] Edward J. Carnell, *An Introduction to Christian Apologetics* (Grand Rapids: Eerdmans, 1948) 65.

[37] Ibid., 354. Further, "Upon every important theoretic problem of life, the Bible has reliable, logical judgement to offer...yielding a system of thought which is horizontally self-consistent and which vertically fits the facts of life" (ibid., 356).

[38] On details of his father's ministry and Carnell's struggles in this regard, see Nelson, *Making and Unmaking*, 16–27.

[39] Carnell, *Case for Orthodoxy*, 131.

Fuller Seminary experienced in its early days over rejection of its program and graduates from mainline denominational ministries.

While he was raised in the Baptist tradition, Carnell moved to the Congregational Church in California. He did not identify his denominational orientation and he was particularly distressed by fundamentalist "cultic mentality." As he pointed out in his essay defending orthodoxy, "the Reformed faith, despite its shortcomings, is the most consistent expression of orthodoxy." It is not surprising, then, that the only Baptist theologian Carnell gave credit to, was John Gill, and that only as he begged forgiveness in Gill's words for any shortcomings.[40]

Bernard Ramm (1916–1992), with Carl Henry, was one of the most outstanding Baptist thinkers of his era. Ramm first pursued a career in science and engineering, receiving his undergraduate degree at the University of Washington. Pursuing an interest in theology, he graduated from Eastern Baptist Theological Seminary and went on to complete a master's and doctoral degrees in the history of philosophy at the University of Southern California. His master's thesis was titled "The Idealism of Jeans and Eddington in Modern Physical Theory." His doctoral dissertation was titled "An Investigation of Some Recent Efforts to Justify Metaphysical Statements from Science with Special Reference to Physics." Across his half-century teaching career, his academic assignments reflected his evolving theology: Biola College, Baylor University, Los Angeles Baptist Seminary, Bethel Theological Seminary, Eastern Baptist Seminary, and finally as Pearl Rawlings Hamilton Professor of Christian Theology at the American Baptist Seminary of the West. He authored 27 books and scores of articles.

Ramm was a bridge-builder between advocates of disparate religious perspectives throughout his career. He worked to bring intellectual respectability to conservative evangelical scholarship. For example, he made several attempts to establish contemporary dialogue with issues in science. In 1955 he published *A Christian View of Science and Scripture* in which he argued that the battle to keep the Bible as a respectable book among learned scholars was fought and lost in the nineteenth century. Ramm thought that a combination of narrow biblicism and the legacy of Plymouth Brethren thought had buried the noble tradition of biblical

---

[40] Ibid., 13, 14. L. Joseph Rosas III, "Edward John Carnell," in *Baptist Theologians*, 616, missed the Gill reference.

authority whose origins were in the Middle Ages. He hoped to reverse the unwholesome attitude toward science among fundamentalists as well as to recognize the contribution of committed Christians to science. Because Ramm thought evolution could be harmonized with Scripture, the book caused quite a stir on both sides, the fundamentalists thinking he had conceded too much to evolutionists and scientists critiquing that his understanding of science was inadequate. In his conclusion, he wrote, "it is impossible to separate Christianity from history and Nature....Christianity is a religion, not a science."[41]

Ramm continued to work at his themes, writing in 1957, "It is impossible for an evangelical who truly understands his position to be an obscurantist."[42] His reputation soared after the publication of *Protestant Biblical Interpretation* in 1956. Ramm successfully convinced numerous evangelicals to accept his understanding of biblical hermeneutics as a science in which a competent interpreter must also believe in divine inspiration. He inveighed against erratic hermeneutics that made of the Bible a state of confusion, rather than a source of light. Ramm proposed ten hermeneutical principles that included the unity of the Bible, the priority of the original languages, and progressive revelation. These became standard fare across the Baptist family, including the very conservative traditions.[43] For him, a renewed understanding of the term "evangelical" included fundamentalist readers as well as Lutherans and those in the Reformed tradition; he also was among the first to begin to include Pentecostals in the mix. By the mid-1950s, Ramm had become a leading, if not the premier voice among Neo-evangelicals.[44]

Ramm studied at the University of Basel, Switzerland with Karl Barth during the 1957–1958 academic year. His interactions with Barth in the English seminars and careful reading of Barth's *Dogmatik*, gave Ramm a

---

[41] Bernard Ramm, *The Christian View of Science and Scripture* (Grand Rapids: Eerdmans, 1955) 17, 348.

[42] *Christianity Today,* Vol I, No. 10, p. 14. 18 February 1957.

[43] Bernard Ramm, *Protestant Biblical Interpretation: A Textbook of Hermeneutics for Conservative Protestants* (Boston: W. A. Wilde, 1956) 3. Note the book is dedicated to the dean of the Conservative Baptist Seminary in Denver, Colorado.

[44] For an overall assessment of Ramm's theology, see David W. Miller, "The Theological System of Bernard L. Ramm" (Ph.D. diss., Southwestern Baptist Theological Seminary, 1982). A helpful listing of his lifetime work is Murdina MacDonald, "A Bibliography of the Works of Bernard L. Ramm," *Perspectives in Religious Studies* 17/4 (Winter 1990): 87–101.

reputation as a leading Barthian scholar. For him, Barth had restored the lost luster of theology. Marcus Barth, for instance, observed that Ramm was one of two outstanding English-speaking interpreters of his father's work. Profoundly influenced by Barth's spiritual and scholarly freedom, Ramm appreciated his mentor's grasp of historical theology and Barth's perspective that theology done for the church must be more than merely an academic religious or philosophical endeavor. He also favored Barth's ability to link historical criticism with a solid understanding of the inspiration of Scripture.[45] Ramm again built bridges in attempting to demonstrate how Barth could inform evangelical theology; this was the thrust of his 1983 book, *After Fundamentalism*. He believed evangelicals had not yet decided how to blend theological thinking with modern knowledge and that a new paradigm was needed to offer such a methodology. For Ramm, Barthian thought was the best paradigm upon which to build and he spoke to such themes as the Scripture, freedom, man, the existence of God, universalism, and eschatology in a Christological motif. Especially having fundamentalists in mind, Ramm challenged theologians to cultivate a greater sense of humor and a lesser sense of self-importance, much as had Barth.[46]

Ramm remained aloof of the then current "battle for the Bible" of the 1970s and 1980s. He was a nuanced inerrantist, one who sought to emphasize the ministry of the Holy Spirit in revelation. He explored this theme in *The Witness of the Spirit* (1959) and concurred with Calvin and others in the Reformed Tradition that Scripture is primary, but must involve a *testimonium* that conveys the understanding of the Holy Spirit. Without the witness of the Spirit, Ramm contended, the Bible is a paper book and lacks the vitality of the Word of God. Moreover, it is to be understood Christologically and interpreted as both a divine and a human book. Again he nuanced his position by declaring that liberalism had no *testimonium* and fundamentalism had given Scripture a counterfeit life of its own. It has been observed that Ramm moved gradually in the 1960s from an "evidentialist" approach to that of an apologist, illustrated in his 1972 work titled *The God Who Makes a Difference: A Christian Appeal to Reason.*

---

[45] Bernard Ramm, "Helps from Karl Barth" 121, 123.

[46] Bernard Ramm, *After Fundamentalism: The Future of Evangelical Theology* (San Francisco: Harper & Row, 1983) v.

Many consider Ramm's finest work his two 1985 books, *An Evangelical Christology* and *Offense to Reason: The Theology of Sin*. Both were answers to Carl Henry's assessment of *After Fundamentalism* that challenged Ramm to create a neo-evangelical theology in light of the Barthian corpus.[47] Ramm's Christological study is a grand apologetic for the understanding of the person of Jesus Christ as the bedrock of historic Christianity. Ramm took on the radical critics of New Testament studies, especially Rudolf Bultmann, and found them able to produce "only a technical, piecemeal, analytical, and dissective result."[48] Ramm was especially critical of Frederich Schleiermacher, who he thought led the attack upon historic Christology. He held that twentieth-century Christology was "reprocessed Schleiermacher."[49] In contrast, Ramm argued that the theologian must affirm the clear teaching of Scripture and the historic creeds that Jesus Christ is a savior who can really save.

Especially important to Ramm's Christology is *Christus Praesens*, the presence of Christ with individual believers and in the Church. In studying sin, Ramm restated Blaise Pascal's famous comment, "The doctrine of original sin is beyond our ability to explain it, but without it we can explain nothing."[50] His own hamartiology doctrine of sin was amazingly Calvinistic and evangelical: a human fall, apostasy from God, the broad effects of sin, the displeasure of God, and the only hope of redemption lying in the reconciling work of Jesus Christ. Ramm broadly surveyed the effects and images of sin from pollution of the planet's air and abuse of other natural resources, to corruption in religious organizations. He concluded that a (doctrine of sin) clarifies personal existence, social relations, and the course of history, rendering a sense of clarity about the whole of life as no other single religious construct is able to provide. Ramm did not consider the idea of sin uniquely Christian, for it belongs to all religious groups that endeavor to explain commonly recognized misfortunes witnessed in life.

As the multi-faceted character of his career suggests, Ramm was in many ways larger than any single denominational tradition. A lifelong

---

[47] Ibid., 121.

[48] Bernard Ramm, *An Evangelical Christology: Ecumenic and Historic* (Nashville: Thomas Nelson Publishers, 1985) 27.

[49] Ibid., 100.

[50] Bernard Ramm, *Offense to Reason: A Theology of Sin* (New York: Harper and Row, 1985) 1.

Baptist in the American, Swedish, and Southern Baptist traditions, his basic Baptist tenet was that the church should build its own theology as well as draw its ethics from the New Testament. As a Baptist and a leading voice within the New Evangelical movement, in 1979–1980 Ramm became an unwitting major player in a debate among Southern Baptists about their identity as evangelicals. On one side of the fracas was James Leo Garrett of Southwestern Baptist Seminary, who clearly identified Southern Baptists as "denominational evangelicals" and Bernard Ramm as a leading and important Baptist voice among the New Evangelicals. On the other side was E. Glenn Hinson of Southern Baptist Seminary, who argued that Baptists are distinct from evangelicals in that they place a priority of a voluntary faith response over any "objective" Word of God. He saw Ramm as a respected theologian who "preferred to think of himself as an Evangelical rather than a Baptist."[51] Throughout the papers presented in the debate, Ramm's definition of an evangelical as "one who places the priority of the Word and Act of God over faith responses of men" was used constantly as a point of departure.[52] Throughout his career, Ramm was considered by some a fountainhead for the enrichment of evangelical theology at the international level. Others considered his methodology a threat to traditional evangelical perspectives. All camps will likely agree that Ramm was singularly responsible for initiating and sustaining dialogue—whether factious or not—among academy, theology, science, and religious traditionalists.

Canadian-born, well traveled, and without a formal theological education, Clark Pinnock (b. 1937) is truly the "pilgrim theologian" of latter-day Baptists. He earned two degrees, a bachelor of arts from the University of Toronto in Near Eastern Studies and a doctor of philosophy from the University of Manchester. His doctoral dissertation was titled "The Pauline Concept of the Holy Spirit" and written under the supervision of Frederick Fyvie Bruce. Pinnock was mentored as a young person by Orthodox Presbyterian Francis Schaeffer at L'Abri, a religious community in Switzerland. Returning to the United States following his studies at Manchester, Pinnock secured a position a New Orleans Baptist Theological Seminary (1965–1968), one of the more theologically conservative schools within the Southern Baptist Convention. While at

---

[51] James Leo Garrett, Jr., E. Glenn Hinson, James E. Tull, eds., *Are Southern Baptists Evangelicals?* (Macon GA: Mercer University Press, 1983) 213.
[52] Ibid., 169.

New Orleans, Pinnock rubbed shoulders with all sectors of Southern Baptist life and was persuaded to identify with an emerging fundamentalist coterie headed by Judge Paul Pressler of Houston, Texas. Many consider the meeting Pinnock had with Pressler at Antoine's Restaurant in New Orleans to be the beginnings of the fundamentalist domination of the Southern Baptist Convention.[53] In 1969 Pinnock moved to Trinity Evangelical Divinity School where he spent a tumultuous five years. Thereafter, he returned to Canada to teach at Regent College, a new lay-oriented school in Vancouver, British Columbia. In 1978 Pinnock accepted a teaching post at McMaster Divinity College in Hamilton, Ontario.

During the first period of Pinnock's theological development he stressed his affinity for a high view of biblical authority and his preference for a self-confident and well-delineated Christian apologetic. As a young person he was much taken with popular evangelical writers like J. I. Packer, Martyn Lloyd-Jones, Carl F. H. Henry, and Cornelius Van Til. Pinnock was confident these theologians offered an antidote to "liberal" churches, such as the one in Toronto in which he was raised.[54] He was critical of his Baptist experience in noting "a twenty minute sermon with three illustrations and a tearful invitation is simply insufficient grounds for requesting an intelligent decision for Christ." His first book, *Set Forth Your Case* (1967), was a clear statement of apologetic, underscoring the infallibility of Scripture. "We need a group of well-trained scholars capable of following the myths of our day to their source and exposing them there," he wrote.[55] In 1967 he also authored *In Defense of Biblical Infalliblity*, staking out territory that drew fundamentalists and evangelicals alike to his constituency. The following year at a meeting of Southern Baptist conservatives, he challenged them to maintain their belief in the evangelical truths of an

---

[53] Judge Paul Pressler, *A Hill on which To Die: One Southern Baptist's Journey* (Nashville: Broadman and Holman, 1999) 58–59. This meeting has also been located at the Café DuMonde in New Orleans.

[54] While Pinnock refers to this congregation as part of his "pilgrimage," it is debatable whether it could truly be labeled "liberal." The congregation was more likely mainstream in its relation to the Baptist Convention of Ontario and Quebec, and was situated theologically within the McMaster tradition.

[55] Clark H. Pinnock, *Set Forth Your Case: Studies in Christian Apologetics* (Nutley NJ: The Craig Press, 1968) 8, 88.

inerrant Bible. His apologetic was squarely rooted in the declaration of a specific message.[56]

During the eight years he spent at conservative evangelical schools, he began to show variation from typical evangelical lines. Ray Roennfeldt finds evidence of a major shift in Pinnock's overall theology during this period.[57] Pinnock confessed to I. Howard Marshall at Aberdeen in 1975 that the latter's book, *Kept by the Power of God* (1969), had exercised a decisive influence on his thinking about perseverance and apostasy. Pinnock subsequently recommended its republication among North American evangelicals.[58] When he accepted a position at McMaster Divinity College in systematic theology, he hoped to bring that historic institution back to its evangelical moorings. McMaster had been in decline and the subject of a major campaign among Canadian Baptist evangelicals either to reform the school according to their likes or to have it closed. Pinnock's appointment to the chair long held by Russell Aldwinckle was an experiment among a faculty that was not sympathetic to his appointment.

Pinnock was largely ostracized within the institution and he took advantage of the isolation at McMaster to shift his thinking in radically new directions. First, he became interested in renewal theology. "I am not writing theoretically or abstractly," he wrote. "As a theologian, I work where the battle for gospel truth rages fiercely; as a church member and deacon, I long for the church to come alive under God. As a Canadian citizen, I grieve over the decline of North America into the secular abyss."[59] In *The Scripture Principle* he began to soften his inerrancy position and soon was reconsidering his stances on freedom of the will and the gifts of the Spirit. "The reason I believed in inerrancy," he wrote, "is that I desperately wanted it to be true."[60] As he considered

---

[56] Clark Pinnock, *Evangelism and Truth* (Tigersville: Jewel, 1969) 18–19; "Parameters of Biblical Inerrancy," in *Proceedings of the Conference on Biblical Inerrancy 1987* (Nashville: Broadman Press, 1987) 96.

[57] Ray C. W. Roennfeldt, "Clark H. Pinnock's Shift in His Doctrine of Biblical Authority and Reliability: An Analysis and Critique" (Ph.D. diss., St. Andrews University, 1990).

[58] I Howard Marshall, "The Problem of Apostasy in the New Testament," *Perspective in Religious Studies* 14/4 (Winter, 1987) 66.

[59] Clark H. Pinnock, *Three Keys to Spiritual Renewal* (Minneapolis: Bethany, 1985).

[60] Clark H. Pinnock, gen. ed., *The Grace of God, the Will of Man: A Case for Arminianism* (Grand Rapids: Academie Books, 1989) 26–27.

the work of other Baptists such as Millard Erickson and James McClendon, who dealt with issues of culture and modernity, Pinnock became unsatisfied with "timeless propositions" or "contextual relativity." He defined what he thought was a unique place he called "Christian narrative," whereby he sought in a new approach to Scripture the story of God's interaction in history for human salvation. The result was *Tracking the Maze* (1990).

Another change of direction in Pinnock's doctrinal perspective was his move away from Calvinism to Arminian thought. In succession he began to rethink the decrees of God, divine election, predestination, human depravity, the atoning work of Christ, divine immutability and omniscience. This resulted in *Grace Unlimited* (1975) and *The Grace of God and The Will of Man* (1989), and a new theological position Pinnock referred to as "Free-will Theism." This doctrinal journeying was emblematic of Pinnock's continuing struggle with the Calvinist hegemony in evangelicalism, who he believed were the ones who controlled schools, publishing, and managed the inerrancy movement. "I wanted to do something, however modest," he declared, "to give a louder voice to the silent majority of Arminian evangelicals."[61] He coined the term, "Calvinian," to describe the dominating evangelical theology and identified the late Gordon Clark of Wheaton College and John Gerstner of Trinity Evangelical Divinity School as its major defenders.[62] Needless to say, Pinnock's older Calvinistic Baptist following eroded significantly, particularly among Southern Baptists.

During his McMaster years, Pinnock had the freedom to pursue new frontiers and directions relating to the doctrine of the Holy Spirit. This characterized his third period of theological productivity. He engaged in debates with Delbert Brown and process theologians like Kenneth Cauthen and John Cobb. He wrote on diverse topics like *The Openness of God, A Wideness in God's Mercy*, and *Flame of Love*. Losing much of his earlier uncompromising fundamentalist attitude, Pinnock embraced Pentecostalism and the Toronto Blessing in the 1990s, further leading to modifications in his ideas of church renewal. Though he was part of a renewal movement at Baptist-related McMaster, he frequently told his students he did not write from an intentionally baptistic perspective and openly encouraged charismatic worship and healing services.

---

[61] Ibid., 27.
[62] Ibid.

One of the most startling changes in Pinnock's thought occurred with respect to his idea of the Holy Spirit. Speaking of his faculty role in a small university divinity school and as a member of a small suburban Baptist congregation, he wrote of the 1980s and 1990s: "The spiritual vitality so evident in Scripture is rare and thin in the religious circles I inhabit. The atmosphere is restrained and the style highly cognitive…I am tired of spiritless Christianity with only rumors and occasional glimpses of wonder and signs."[63] In *Flame of Love* (1996), Pinnock's personal story defined his newly embraced charismatic theological outlook. "I have long been sure that God is pouring out the Spirit in Pentecostalism…cessationist attitudes still impede reform, but they are in retreat."[64] Reaching out to Catholic Christians, he also generously quoted Pope John Paul II and documents from Vatican II in calling for a "new Pentecost." Along the way, he wanted to de-emphasize the theology of substitutionary atonement in favor of a participatory theology of the atonement. He proposed that infant baptism, followed by real confirmation, provided the same ordinal power as did the baptismal practices of Baptists.[65] His theology of the Holy Spirit even extended to other religions, because "it would be strange if the Spirit excused himself from the very arena where people search for meaning." Pinnock discovered a new freedom in the Spirit and summarized its impact upon his theological task: "There are gifts of God scattered over a wide variety of places in the church. They need to be gathered together."[66]

Clark Pinnock is chiefly known for his interaction with other theologians from a basically evangelical stance. He writes as a reluctant Baptist, as do many other "Baptist/Evangelicals." Pinnock has produced provocative reflections of his "pilgrim career" through liberalism, fundamentalism, Calvinism, post-modernity, and overly formalized styles of Christianity, but no major integrative treatise. Pinnock has seemed Quixotic to some. In the late 1990's he joined the "open theism" movement that argues that God limited his own capabilities in dealing

---

[63] Clark H. Pinnock, *Flame of Love*: *A Theology of the Holy Spirit* (Downers Grove: Intervarsity Press, 1996) 247.

[64] Ibid., 240. His encouragement of tongues-speaking often focused on academic people "who are trained to guard their speech, so as not to blurt out something they are not sure they want to say. It can be hard for them to yield to tongues." See ibid., 173.

[65] Ibid., 9, 126, 227.

[66] Ibid., 203, 238.

with humans in order to guarantee the free response of humans. This
stance was taken to be anathema by traditional evangelicals, who nearly
voted eapuleim from the Evangelical Theological Society for pinnacle.[67]
One of his critics has written, "In arguing passionately against the
establishment, Pinnock occasionally is unconvincing, if not mistaken."[68]
One cannot deny, however, that Clark Pinnock's theology is derived
from deeply meaningful personal experience.

One of the most widely used systematic theologies among Baptists in
the past two decades is that of Millard J. Erickson (b. 1932), a graduate
of the University of Minnesota, Northern Baptist Theological Seminary,
University of Chicago, and Northwestern University.[69] The title of his
doctoral dissertation at Northwestern was "The Apologetical Theology of
the New Evangelicalism," later published as *The New Evangelical
Theology* (1968). Erickson taught first at Wheaton College in Bible and
philosophy. For most of his subsequent career at Bethel Theological
Seminary, a school in the Swedish Baptist tradition where Erickson was
also dean, he continued to teach in those disciplines. In recent years he
has been a distinguished visiting professor at George W. Truett
Theological Seminary of Baylor University. Erickson met Bernard
Ramm at Bethel College and acknowledged the latter as his first
theology teacher. He was particularly influenced by E. J. Carnell and in
graduate school by his mentor, William Hordern, a Lutheran specialist
interested in Barth and Luther. From Wolfhart Pannenburg, Erickson
affirmed the value of recognizing and dealing fairly with differing
theological positions.[70]

Millard Erickson has published twenty-two books and numerous
articles across three decades. One of his first books, *Relativism in*

---

[67] See Doug Koop, "Closing the Door on Open Theists" *Christianity Today* 47/1,
9January 2003): 24-25.
[68] Robert K. Johnston, "Clark Pinnock" in Walter Elwell, ed., *Handbook of
Evangelical Theologians* (Grand Rapids: Baker Books, 1993) 443.
[69] Like other neo-evangelical Baptists, Erickson first wanted to study at the
University of Chicago, but preferred to major in theology rather than philosophy, so he
went to a Methodist institution that was theologically inclusive of several positions. Carl
F. H. Henry did likewise at Boston University.
[70] For biographical details and implications of Erickson's thought, see David S.
Dockery, ed., *New Dimensions in Evangelical Thought: Essays in Honor of Millard J.
Erickson* (Downers Grove: Intervarsity Press, 1998), and Bradley G. Green "Millard J.
Erickson" *Theologians of the Baptist Tradition*, 317-337.

Contemporary Christian Ethics (1974) was a critique of Joseph Fletcher's *Situation Ethics*. He took up the doctrine of the Trinity with *God in Three Persons: A Contemporary Understanding of the Trinity* (1995), and dealt with the thorny question of the unsaved in *How Shall They Be Saved? The Destiny of Those Who Do Not Know of Jesus* (1996). In this last title he upheld the appropriateness of God's justice in condemning the unsaved as "all have known God, if not effectually, because they suppressed the truth."

As he formulated his systematic theology, Erickson was advised by Clark Pinnock to make it sing like a hymn rather than read like a telephone book. Erickson was conscious of the exhaustive treatments that characterized the golden age of Strong and others. His three-volumes (later published as one thick book) concentrated on clear presentation and firm conviction. Dedicating his magnum opus to his three teachers, Ramm, Hordern, and Pannenburg, he used a nine-step method to address theological topics, involving assembling biblical data and finding a central interpretive motif, seeking illumination from sources other than the Bible, and maintaining a positive attitude toward culture. His overarching theme is the magnificence of God. His doctrine of Scripture, predictably, unashamedly upholds inerrancy… "whatever statements the Bible affirms are fully truthful when they are correctly interpreted in terms of their cultural setting and the purpose for which they were written."[71] In declaring himself an inerrantist, Erickson, however, cautions that "there will never be complete confirmation of all the propositions in the Bible," nor does the doctrine instruct Christians on how to interpret scripture.[72]

Erickson's theology presents a "moderately Calvinistic" approach, such as in holding that God works congruously with the will of the individual. Likewise on the doctrine of atonement, Erickson posits a penal substitution theory as the best understanding of an essentially substitutionary view that fully accounts for the total depravity of all humans. He further finds that advocating a limited atonement is not very persuasive. Instead he holds that God provided full salvation for all and then elected some to receive it, involving a subjective element of their acceptance. Erickson is careful to place himself near the sublapsarian

---

[71] Millard J. Erickson, *Christian Theology* (Grand Rapids: Baker Book House, 1983–1985) 238.

[72] Ibid.

position of A. H. Strong, and under the B. B.Warfield label "congruism," but far from Arminianism.[73] In matters of eschatology, he divides his treatment evenly, discussing individual destiny, the Second Coming of Christ, millennial and tribulational views, and final states. He prefers historic premillennialism, and thinks the post-tribulational position is more probable. On the issue of what older theologians referred to as "reprobation," Erickson argues for eternal punishment by degrees, making the nature of future states far more intense than anything known in this life.[74] As his critics and students have observed, Millard Erickson's theology is less intimidating than that of Carl F. H. Henry, far more reasonable than that of A. H. Strong, and more creative and less comprehensive than that of James Leo Garrett. He is seen as a definite advance beyond Walter Conner, E. Y. Mullins, and Dale Moody.[75] Given the translation of his work into languages other than English, he has cast a long shadow in and beyond the English-speaking Baptist community.

James William McClendon (1924–2001) is a diasporic Baptist theologian whose work reflected his vocational and professional pilgrimage. He received an undergraduate degrees from the University of Texas, a divinity degree and a theological doctorate from Southwestern Baptist Theological Seminary, and a master's degree in theology from Princeton Theological Seminary. At Southwestern his doctoral dissertation was "The Doctrine of Sin in the First Epistle of John: A Comparison of Calvinistic, Wesleyan, and Biblical Thought" written under the supervision of John Newport and James Leo Garrett. McClendon taught at Golden Gate Baptist Theological Seminary, Temple University, Pacific School of Religion, the University of San Francisco, and finally Fuller Theological Seminary where he was Distinguished Scholar in Residence at the time of his death. He characterized himself as "a Baptist scholar teaching in an ecumenical setting." Over the course of his career, McClendon taught philosophy of religion, theological ethics, doctrinal and narrative theology.

Early in his career, McClendon began to press beyond traditional systematic theology. In a slightly noticed work co-authored with James Smith, *Understanding Religious Convictions* (1975), he analyzed religious language and religious convictions, concluding that there is no

---

[73] Ibid., 359, 835.
[74] Ibid., 1241.
[75] Dockery, *New Dimensions*, 31.

conviction-free place from which to understand religious discourse objectively. The objective study of religion is a fiction, they wrote. Similarly in *Biography as Theology* (1974), McClendon argued that professions of faith are related to life contexts and doctrinal statements fail the test if they cannot be lived out. In a work co-authored with Axel Steuer, *Is God GOD* (1981), they suggested that within community one's concept of God was of primary importance, even more so than arguments for the existence of God. One knows God, they concluded, in trust, worship, and obedience. Ever so gradually, McClendon initiated a course that would identify an important new direction in theological method, now referred to as "non-foundationalist." McClendon and others came to conclude that the future of theology did not lay with a regressive set of foundational principles that are non-negotiable, but in the way in which a community understands and practices theology. For McClendon, foundational theology had its origins certainly in Descartes, if not Plato, but through the Enlightenment it had achieved a failed methodology. Illustrative of the point, he found the writings of classic Baptist theologians such as E. Y. Mullins (*Axioms of Religion*) ultimately untenable. With theologians such as Ronald Thiemann and George Lindbeck, McClendon found theology to be a "second order discourse" describing and sometimes reforming the primary language of religion, that is prayer, preaching, and confessing. As one of his devoted protégés put it, "It was Baptist McClendon, stripped of Constantinian pretensions, but clothed with courage and the wisdom of the Gospel, who has led us into this wonderful new land of theology without foundations."[76]

His magnum opus, over two decades in preparation, reflected his attempt to recover a "Baptist vision." Much influenced by Radical Reformation thought, McClendon took the mantles of John Howard Yoder and Harold Bender to create a generic form of the "baptist vision," symbolized in the miniscule form of the word "baptist." He wanted to include such heirs of the Radical Reformation as the Christian Church (Disciples of Christ), Mennonites, Plymouth Brethren, Adventists, Quakers, Church of God, Church of the Brethren, some Methodists, Assemblies of God, and Southern, British, European, and American

---

[76] Stanley Hauerwas, Nancey Murphy McClendon, and Mark Nation, *Theology Without Foundations: Religious Practice and the Future of Theological Truth* (Nashville: Abingdon Press, 1994) 31. The comment belongs to Nancey Murphy McClendon and the book was a festschrift in honor of McClendon.

Baptists. Here he followed the historical path of Glenn Stassen and others who found undeniable links between Anabaptists and Baptists of the seventeenth century.[77] In the tradition of H. S. Bender, each community shares the "vision": ownership of the biblical narrative, witness of liberty, discipleship, and community. "By such a vision," he wrote, "I do not mean some end result of theoretical reflection, remote from the daily life of a rather plain people...I mean the guiding stimulus by which a people shape their life and thought as that people or combination."[78]

In his three-volume theological treatise (1986–2001), McClendon mused that Baptists have produced little theology in comparison with Lutherans and Methodists, and considered John Gill, John Dagg, A. H. Strong, W. N. Clarke, Walter Rauschenbusch, E. Y. Mullins, D. C. MacIntosh, W. T. Conner, Dale Moody, Carl F. H. Henry, and Gordon Kaufman as systematicians worthy of special honor.[79] McClendon began his theological discourse at a different non-foundationalist starting point than previous similar Baptist enterprises. Rather than beginning with doctrine, McClendon's system began with ethical considerations.[80] In his second volume, he rearranged traditional ideas of doctrinal theology under three headings: the Rule of God, the Identity of Christ, and the Fellowship of the Spirit. For the theologian, doctrine is what the church—as a community of participants—must teach to the church. In areas specific to the Baptist theological enterprise, McClendon found value in all three approaches to understanding the atonement of Christ, but concluded that the most relevant of the midrashic metaphors is probably the theme of sacrifice in the sense that Horace Bushnell used the term.[81]

---

[77] McClendon took a direct translation of the German "Taufer" and posited that they were not unified by description, but by fidelity to Scripture and response to human life.

[78] James W. McClendon, Jr., *Systematic Theology: Ethics* (Nashville: Abingdon Press, 1986) I: 27.

[79] Ibid., 1:37. Wenger and Kaufman were Mennonites.

[80] For useful reviews of McClendon's first volume and basic approach, see : a Mennonite point of view, Dale Brown's review in *Brethren Life and Thought* 33/3 (Summer 1988): 250–52; and the debate over narrative ethics in Max Stackhouse's critique in *Journal of the American Academy of Religion* 55/3 (Fall 1987): 615–17 and Richard J. Mouw's "Ethics and Story: A Review Article" in *Reformed Journal* 37/7 (July 1987): 22–27.

[81] McClendon, 2:232.

The heart of his third volume deals with a "baptist" understanding of the church cast in an ecumenical age, reflecting a quest for community that places stress upon being Spirit-filled and mission-oriented, with a discipleship always shaped by a practice of discernment. While Baptist churches are to emulate the primitive church as closely as possible, there is not yet a complete community, for "Christian ecclesiology is provisional ecclesiology; it looks toward a fulfillment not yet achieved."[82] Again and again he warned that Baptists must not be mere primitivists, but they must act in their own context with their own identification with Jesus' first disciples.[83] In an *excursis* on authority, McClendon argued, with Roger Williams, that authority amounts to "the love of God enjoyed, the grace of Christ written, the fellowship of the Spirit gathered." In other words, the matter of authority was forever settled in Jesus Christ.[84]

McClendon's was a bold attempt to launch "baptist" thought out into a new cosmos: cultural, post-modern, and interactive with other disciplines. With his wife, Nancey Murphy as co-author, he titled the work "Witness" (in contrast with "Ethics" and "Doctrine") and ventured into a "theology of culture." The foundation was laid in the thought of Peter Berger, Robert Bellah, and Paul Tillich. The work of Julian N. Hartt, and John Howard Yoder marked McClendon's theological trajectory. On his theological horizon were science, native spirituality, and art and literature. For him, witness was a series of stories, sometimes conflicting narratives, that have their conclusion in glorification and the encounter with the Coming One. Along the way, McClendon offered a critique of "baptists" for having no first rank university and he challenged the "real" university to reinvigorate theology in its curriculum even against the stalwart claims of secularism. Here he consciously followed Edwin E. Aubrey, formerly of Crozer Theological Seminary, who rejected the scorn of culture in Neo–Orthodoxy and called for Christianity to engage culture fully.[85]

None of the groups listed among McClendon's "baptists" has yet acknowledged his role as their defining theological spokesman. Some moderate Southern Baptists, notably at Baylor University, acknowledge

---

[82] Ibid., 344.
[83] Ibid., 395.
[84] Ibid., 484–87.
[85] McClendon, *Witness*, 3:419.

personal indebtedness, while others ponder his "cultural approach." Part
of McClendon's challenge was his use of terms in nuanced ways, his
references to non-traditional theological resources, and his penchant to
launch out in creative new directions. He upended "doctrine" in favor of
"ethics" and turned the distinctive traditional identity of the Baptist
community into a generic "baptist" communion. For biblicists and
literalists, he made too much of metaphor in volume two. In the third
volume, he cited sociologists and Flannery O'Connor, dedicating two
chapters on Ludwig J. J. Wittgenstein (1889–1951) with little substantive
result. Unlike many of his contemporaries, in search of A. H. Strong's
mantle, McClendon moved on in fresh directions. In this regard his genes
lie close to Baptist theologians like Thomas Grantham, Robert Hall,
Andrew Fuller, H. Wheeler Robinson, Walter Rauschenbusch, and W. N.
Clarke.

Another theologian who well represents the diasporic nature of
Baptist theologians in the second half of the twentieth century is Harvey
Cox. Harvey Cox (b. 1929) is a theologian at the liberal end of the
Baptist tradition, whose work was seminal among Baptists and far
beyond. Nurtured in a community of Pennsylvania Baptist piety, he
received his undergraduate degree at the University of Pennsylvania
where he was much influenced by E. E. Aubrey, a religious naturalist
who had once taught at the University of Chicago and more recently had
been president at Crozer Seminary.[86] Cox chose Yale Divinity School for
his theological degree where he was much enamored of H. Richard
Niebuhr. He was ordained an American Baptist minister, and entered
university chaplaincy at Temple University and later Oberlin College.
Doctoral studies at Harvard exposed him to Paul Tillich, Gabriel Marcel,
Robert Bellah, and Wilfred Cantwell Smith. He chose for his mentor,
James Luther Adams, a Baptist turned Unitarian. Framed in the history
and philosophy of religion, Cox's dissertation was titled "Religion and
Technology from the Renaissance to the Present."[87]

Harvey Cox's teaching career commenced at Andover Newton
Theological School in 1962; he was absent from his installation to the
chair in theology and culture due to being imprisoned in North Carolina

---

[86] Cox, *Just As I Am,* 52; 146-147.

[87] Harvey Cox, "Afterward and Forward" in *Religion in a Secular City: Essays in
Honor of Harvey Cox*, ed. Arvind Sharma (Harrisburg, PA: Trinity Press International,
2001), xv-xvi. This volume includes a comprehensive bibliography of Cox's works.

as part of a Southern Christian Leadership Conference civil rights demonstration. In 1965 he joined the faculty of Harvard Divinity School as associate professor of church and society and in 1970 became the Victor Thomas Professor of Divinity. During his storied pilgrimage, Cox has lectured in Mexico and Latin America, much involved in Liberation Theology and written or edited fourteen books. His influence upon the American Baptist Convention in the 1960s was large, as a program associate mentoring several leaders and closely monitoring the social conscience of the American Baptist Home Mission Society and the Ministers and Missionaries Benefit Board, pressing both to support the civil rights agenda of Martin Luther King, Jr.

The first stage of Cox's written theological contribution came as an outgrowth of his mission experience in urban areas in the U.S. and in East Berlin with the Gossner Mission. *The Secular City* (1965), his first book, was also an outgrowth of his doctoral work on urbanization. He argued that western civilization, in which Christianity figured prominently, moved through socio-economic stages to the urban organization that is characterized by diversity, disintegration of tradition, and impersonality.[88] Religion no longer holds an integrating place and the language of God is outmoded, relating to bygone eras of development. Cox sympathized with the radical death of God theologians and critiqued them, but had more hope about a God who is hidden and yet transcendent and who moves through secularity to achieve his purposes. Though Cox thought there should be a moratorium on talking about God, he foresees a prophetic role for the church as God's "avant-garde."[89] Appreciative of biblical truth, he saw several transitional periods in the history of Israel where the people of God had to reformulate their understanding and language about God. The book went through several editions, sparked a vigorous debate among Christian theologians, and spoke to new groups of persons not necessarily a part of the Christian community. In 1999 the Protestant Theological Faculty of the University of Marburg chose *Secular City* as one of the two most decisive books of the twentieth century, along with Karl Barth's *Epistle to the Romans*.

---

[88] Harvey Cox, *The Secular City: Secularization and Urbanization in Theological Perspective* (New York: Macmillan, 1965), 4.

[89] Ibid, 103-129.

Also a part of Cox's first stage thinking was his ministry among American Baptists and others. His book, *God's Revolution and Man's Responsibility* (1965), published by the denominational press, was a call to a church in apathy to place less emphasis upon church renewal and get about the renewal of the world. Speaking to a national Baptist student conference at Green Lake, Wisconsin, in 1963, Cox warned that the church needed to focus upon reconciliation, the shalom of God. Rejecting traditional ideas of sacrament and priestly hierarchies, Cox instead called for ministry in places of crises like the cold war or racial discrimination. In a bold stroke, he informed his Baptist friends "the most helpful image of the ministry today is *not* the priesthood of all believers. He reminds us that the term never appears in the New Testament. Rather, a far more frequent figure for describing the ministry of the church is that of the athlete, the soldier, the farmer, and even the servant.[90] Rounding out Cox's initial work were two popular books, *The Feast of Fools: A Theological Essay on Festivity and Fantasy* (1969) and *The Seduction of the Spirit: The Use and Misuse of People's Religion* (1973). In the former he reminded his following that Christianity was not all social change, but also celebration, and in the latter he engaged in personal narrative to build a case for theology as "a satirizing activity that debunks destructive myths."[91]

A second stage of Cox's thought emerged as religion made an unexpected comeback to Cox's secular city. Brought about by a militant fundamentalism that Cox saw embodied in the Rev. Jerry Falwell of Lynchburg, Virginia, and the election of Pope John Paul II, Cox actually heralded the fundamentalist critique of liberal theology, but denied that fundamentalism had the answers. Rather, he wrote in 1984 that postmodern theology would come from the bottom and the edge. He saw a new reformation, sparked by a powerfully biblical idea, the resurrection: "God alive in the world, life defeating death."[92] In 1985 when the Brazilian Franciscan theologian Leonardo Boff was formally silenced by the Vatican for his criticism of church hierarchy and

---

[90] Harvey Cox, *God's Revolution and Man's Responsibility* (Valley Forge: Judson Press, 1965), 114.

[91] Harvey Cox, *The Seduction of the Spirit: The Use and Misuse of People's Religion* (New York: Simon and Schuster, 1973), 319.

[92] Harvey Cox, *Religion in the Secular City: Toward a Postmodern Theology* (New York: Simon and Schuster, 1984), 263.

articulation of Liberation Theology, Cox joined the cause as an advocate. For Cox, who had become a devotee of Liberation Theology himself, the Boff silencing became for him a test of whether the Church could become "the people," and "whether Christianity, for so many centuries a largely western and "northern" faith, and live in and speak to the tribes and nations of the whole world."[93] His book, *The Silencing of Leonardo Boff: The Vatican and the Future of World Christianity* (1988) became a report on the historic incident and a call for open theological debate and a new sense of unity among Christians. One of the most vivid aspects of this phase of Harvey Cox's shift was his reclamation of his Baptist identity: "In the two decades since *The Secular City* was published I have gained the reputation of being a 'liberal' theologian, I have never been satisfied with the label. Born and raised in a conservative Baptist milieu, I have never really abandoned that tradition. ...These two disparate streams of Christian faith do not seem contradictory to me ... I can feel at home in both."[94]

In the third stage of his career, Cox became much enamored of Pentecostalism. As a child he had visited a local Pentecostal church and marveled at its spirituality. A keen observer of American religious trends, he recognized that the Pentecostals had resisted the religious decline of the sixties and had in fact become a major world Christian phenomenon. Moreover, in Pentecostalism he found many elements he had affirmed in the black religious experience. Following a world tour and scores of encounters and interviews, Cox ascertained that Pentecostals were in fact deeply divided between fundamentalists and experientialists, with a small group of emerging Latin American Pentecostal liberationists, to which he was especially drawn. Cox believes that ultimately Pentecostals will emerge "on the side of the angels," because Pentecostal spirituality is "emotional, communal, narrational, hopeful, and radically embodied." Its strength lies in its radical "outposts of the kingdom," by which Cox, a Baptist theologian, made reference to the local church.[95]

---

[93] Harvey Cox, *The Silencing of Leonardo Boff: The Vatican and the Future of World Christianity* (Oak Park, IL: Meyer Stone Books, 1988), 185.

[94] *Religion in the Secular City,* 267.

[95] Harvey Cox, *Fire From Heaven: The Rise of Pentecostal Spirituality and the Reshaping of Religion in the Twenty-First Century* (Reading, MA: Addison Wesley Publishing Co., 1995), 319-320.

In recent years and still on faculty at Harvard Divinity School, the "theologian of secularization" continues to reach out to new avenues of religious interest, affirming much of his life-long Baptist identity. He is well known to a growing number of Baptist students in the Divinity School, speaks broadly among Baptists, and occasionally provides hospitality for Baptists on the campus of Harvard University.[96]

PASTORS AND EVANGELISTS

Baptist pastors and evangelists have made large contributions in the past half century to theological discussion, noticeably on the conservative and/or fundamentalist side. Their impact goes beyond the denomination and thus offends the religious world at large, particularly North America.They include W. Amos Criswell, Billy Graham, and Jerry Falwell. Each represents a discrete position among Baptists "in diaspora."

W. Amos Criswell (1909–2002), the long-time former pastor of First Baptist Church in Dallas, Texas, had a major impact upon the course of fundamentalistic theology in the Southern Baptist tradition. First Baptist Church had long been a flagship congregation of the denomination. Under Criswell's leadership it became a congregation of importance on the national and international religious scenes. Criswell, a graduate of Baylor University and Southern Baptist Theological Seminary, became critical of both schools in the 1960s. He saw in them sources introducing troubling liberal theology into the denomination. Criswell led a crusade against Baylor's Department of Religion and Dale Moody's theological directions at Southern Baptist Seminary. Beyond this, he publicly chastised the leadership of the Baptist General Convention of Texas and the Southern Baptist Convention for similarly perceived shortcomings.

Criswell's book, *Why I Preach the Bible Is Literally True* (1969), was a major catalyst in the beginnings of the inerrancy movement among Southern Baptists. Pinning his argument on his understanding of the Bible as " the literal, inspired, God-breathed truth of heaven," he drew upon the earlier biblicism of L. Gaussen, Arthur W. Pink, Benjamin B. Warfield, and John Urquhart. Criswell painted a picture of an apostate ministry where "there are ministers and professors of divinity without

---

[96] In March 2001, for instance, Cox hosted a delegation from Baylor University, including this writer, that sought to open dialogue between America's oldest theological faculty and confessing evangelicals.

number who undermine the written word and deny the incarnate Word."[97] He assailed liberal and Neo-Orthodox theologians whose higher critical methods had wrought nothing but confusion. Ironically, he used Henry Vedder as a source of Baptist solidarity with his position on Scripture, the same Henry Vedder who led the Modernist position at Crozer Seminary in the 1920s. Instead of falling into "a fool's paradise of rationalism," Criswell challenged his Southern Baptist colleagues in evangelism, the pastorate, education, and missions to "stand by the Book, preach its treasures, love its words, serve its Saviour, and humbly seek to obey its mandates."[98]

At the heart of Criswell's theological understanding were the tenets of a bygone fundamentalism. In sermonic form, he dealt with the literalness of the Genesis creation stories, the "bestial" theory of evolution, and a literal return of Jesus Christ. He also took passing swipes at Plato, Aristotle, and Sigmund Freud, who were unequal to the power of Scripture in meeting and ministering to human need. For Criswell, the value of the Bible lay in its fulfilled prophecies, the testimony of archaeology, and its truthfulness about the moral blemishes of most of its characters. He ultimately took the position of verbal plenary inspiration and warned preachers in particular not to yield from that stance.

Because W. A. Criswell had a pulpit ministry to thousands, and a regionally televised ministry, his initial influence was greatest in the Southwest. His book on inerrancy sold well outside of Texas, however, and he was subsequently elected president of the Southern Baptist Convention in 1969. Criswell's preaching circuit had become national in scope. Never satisfied to join the existing fundamentalists in his vicinity, he opened the Criswell Bible Institute in 1970, which soon became Criswell College. The purpose and curriculum at the College is defined by the defense of the doctrine of Scripture's inerrancy. At length many of Criswell's protégés at First Baptist and graduates of the college went on to lead the political takeover of the Southern Baptist Convention in the 1980s. W. A. Criswell had been a defining element in continuing Southern Baptist thought and negatively in the establishment of offshoot Southern Baptist coalitions like the Alliance of Baptists and the Cooperative Baptist Fellowship.

---

[97] W. A. Criswell, *Why I Preach the Bible Is Literally True* (Nashville: Broadman Press, 1969), 7.
[98] Ibid., 154, 160.

One of the most influential theological voices among Baptists from the 1950s through the 1990s was William F. "Billy" Graham (b. 1918). Graham has not overly emphasized his being Baptist and many of his biographers are silent on his denominational affiliation.[99] His relationship to the Baptists began while he was a student at Florida Bible Institute, where in 1938 he held his first revival at East Palatka Baptist Church. Shortly thereafter he was baptized by immersion at nearby Peniel Baptist Church and the majority of his support came from local Florida Southern Baptists. He was ordained an evangelist in a congregation of St. John's Baptist Association of Northern Florida. Graham's first full-time ministry further connected him to Baptists. William Bell Riley, a noted Baptist fundamentalist pastor and educator, made Graham his successor in 1947 as president of the Northwestern Schools in Minneapolis, Minnesota.[100]

In 1953, after being well-established as a national evangelical voice, Graham held a four-week crusade in Dallas, Texas, during which he joined that city's First Baptist Church. The pastor of the church was W. Amos Criswell, the bombastic Southern Baptist discussed previously. Graham quipped that if he had joined a church near where he lived, they would have asked him to be active in church affairs. While at home in North Carolina, he attended his wife's Presbyterian church. Internationally, Graham identified with Baptists, as was especially the case in Poland, Hungary, and the Soviet Union. In these places he was sometimes able to negotiate with repressive governments on behalf of evangelical Christians and secure gains with respect to religious liberty, a cherished Baptist ideal. Beginning in 1972, Billy became a regularly invited speaker at the Southern Baptist Convention annual meetings and at notable meetings of the Baptist World Alliance.[101] An important personal connection in later years has been the family relationship between his daughter, Anne, who married Dan Lotz the brother of

---

[99] There are several useful biographies of Graham, including his autobiography, *Just As I Am: The Autobiography of Billy Graham* (San Francisco: HarperCollins/Zondervan, 1997). The most detailed account that follows his baptistic leanings is William Martin, *A Prophet with Honor: The Billy Graham Story* (New York: William Morrow, 1991) esp., 76, 152.

[100] On Riley, see C. Allyn Russell, *Voices of American Fundamentalism,* 79-106.

[101] For a critical view of Graham's Southern Baptist relationship, particularly of his membership at First Baptist, Dallas, see Joe E. Barnhart, *The Billy Graham Religion* (Philadelphia: Pilgrim Press, 1972) 219–26.

Denton Lotz, General Secretary of the Baptist World Alliance since 1990.

As an evangelist, Billy Graham made no pretense to being a professional theologian. The widespread popularity of his thinking, however, merits some analysis. His 1953 book, *Peace with God*, has served for many as a kind of systematic statement of the evangelist's theology. He builds his perspective upon a high view of Scripture: "The Bible qualifies as the only book in which God's revelation is contained." Speaking of its inspired qualities, he sees thirty authors who acted as scribes for God. "They acted as channels for God's dictation; they wrote as He directed them; and under His inspiration they were able to see the great and enduring truths."[102] After discussing Scripture and God, Graham next writes about sin, the devil and the afterlife. Within his discussion of sin, he argues for a person's free will to choose and reveals a modest dispensationalist direction in speaking of a "period of Grace" to benefit man's acceptance of God's plan. Soteriologically, the book reflects a substitutionary view of the atonement that extended to all peoples of all generations. With respect to the doctrine of the church, he teaches the unity of one universal church, and acknowledges the denominational reality of many local churches with differing customs, emphases, and structures. The great outreach of the church should include both evangelistic and humanitarian concerns. Somewhat surprising to some, Graham included a chapter on social obligations of Christians that include good citizenship, charitable giving, positive labor-management relations, a wholesome view of sexuality, racial harmony and justice, and commentary on the plight of suffering humanity. In that early book, Graham quoted Wilbur Smith and H. C. Thiessen, known conservatives, and the work of the World Council of Churches whose 1954 theme was "Christ, the hope of the world."[103] In published works written over a three-decade ministry, Billy Graham also embraced premillennial thought, religious liberty, family issues, and an active Christian response to cultural issues.

Graham's theological influence has been a defining standard for Baptist evangelism. A chair in evangelism was created at Southern Baptist Theological Seminary in Graham's honor in 1965. He has sponsored pastor's conferences, held schools of evangelism, and written

---

[102] Billy Graham, *Peace with God* (New York: Doubleday, 1953) 24.
[103] Ibid., 204.

eighteen books on popular themes such as the authority of the Bible, conversion, the Second Coming, discipleship, and moral values. By the 1990s Graham had become something of a patron saint to many Baptists, and virtually an American icon of sound religious enterprise. His theological perspective has doubtless influenced millions of followers in the United States and around the world.

As Billy Graham's stellar international career as an evangelist and popular theologian slowed, that of Jerry Falwell (b.1933) seemed to gain sudden momentum. Falwell, not a trained theologian, has become another major influence upon Baptist thought in the United States. He attended Lynchburg College for two years and then graduated from Baptist Bible College in Springfield, Missouri. With no seminary training he entered the ministry and started a congregation in Lynchburg, Virginia, the Thomas Road Baptist Church. Falwell was much influenced by a coterie of "come-outer" Southern—mostly Baptist—evangelist preachers such as G. Beauchamp Vick, B. R. Lakin, John Rawlings, Noel Smith, John R. Rice, and to a lesser degree, Bob Jones, Sr. In his autobiography, Falwell identified the importance to his conversion of listening to Charles Fuller's Old Fashioned Revival Hour on the radio. Eventually, Falwell's own radio and telecast ministry would be called the "Old Time Gospel Hour."

The growth of Falwell's congregation to over ten-thousand in Sunday School by 1968 afforded him prominence in Virginia. He embarked upon educational ministries that eventually included an institution extending collegiate and graduate degrees. First in 1971 came Lynchburg Baptist College (later renamed Liberty University). Falwell had asked Dallas Theological Seminary graduate and religious educator, Elmer Towns, to be at the forefront in the effort to establish the new school. Next, Falwell and Harold Wilmington founded Thomas Road Bible Institute (1972), followed by Lynchburg Baptist Theological Seminary (1973) that Robert Hughes helped to shape. Falwell was named chancellor of the institutions and was the controlling presence in all of the ventures, while continuing to serve the church as pastor. Falwell has used the institutions and the church to define what he calls the Moral Majority, a coalition of like-minded people whose money and ideology embrace perspectives such as anti-abortion, male headship in the family, anti-gay rights, pro-school prayer, a strong national defense, anti-drug liberalization, free enterprise, and pro-Israeli ethics. He identified with Republican Party political interests in the 1970s, supporting Richard Nixon, George Bush, Ronald Reagan (his favorite president), Gerald Ford, and George W. Bush. His television broadcasts, that focus upon the sermons *in situ* at Thomas Road Baptist Church and fundraising appeals, have created a powerful vehicle of social influence for Falwell and his socio-religious agenda. He is a frequent representative of evangelical, fundamentalist, and Baptist identity in the media. In the late 1990s Falwell, an Independent Baptist, began a slow, quiet pilgrimage into the heart of Southern Baptist life, first as the media's idea of the most important person among Southern Baptists, then as a frequent speaker at schools like Southeastern Baptist Theological Seminary, and finally as the chosen speaker at the national pastor's conference immediately preceding the 2002 annual meeting of the Southern Baptist Convention. Through a newly organized Southern Baptist body in Virginia, Falwell and his church have become cooperating members of the Southern Baptist Convention.

Falwell's doctrinal view can be best described as "fundamentalist Baptist." In keeping with the World Baptist Fellowship, Baptist Bible Fellowship, and Southwide Baptist Fellowship, this type of fundamentalism is driven by aggressive evangelism and open criticism of mainstream denominations, including Baptists of moderate stripe. Early in the evolution of Thomas Road Baptist Church, Falwell described his doctrinal position: "We believe in Christian witness. Getting people saved is everything. And we believe that salvation is forever. Once it's done, it is done! Once you've accepted Christ as Lord and Savior, you are in."[104] He affirmed the inspiration and infallibility of Scripture, the deity of Christ, substitutionary atonement, the literal resurrection, and the literal Second Coming of Christ. He and co-authors Ed Hindson and Ed Dobson marked their congruency with the *Fundamentals* pamphlets of the early twentieth century and particularly identified with the Hal Lindsey/John Walvoord forms of dispensationalism.[105] They go on to discuss a set of ethical standards, including ecclesiastical separation and an aversion to ecumenical evangelism. The "stronger" a group, the more definitive its prohibitions are, they believe. Falwell described his understanding in a folksy but telling manner: "Our Baptist code is

---

[104] Falwell, *Strength for the Journey*, 221.
[105] Jerry Falwell, ed., *The Fundamentalist Phenomenon: The Resurgence of Conservative Christianity*, with Ed Dobson and Ed Hindson (Garden City: Doubleday-Galilee Original, 1981) 6–12, 228n.

simple, sometimes way too simple. We don't drink. We don't smoke. We don't believe in immorality whatever form it takes. We have our dress codes and a few other 'spiritual trademarks'."[106] The fundamentalist ethic was neatly fused with patriotism and this became the clarion call of Falwell's 1980 book, *Listen, America!* In that book, he charged the Moral Majority with carrying the Christian standard to the nation: "Right living must be reestablished as an American way of life. We as American citizens must recommit ourselves to the faith of our fathers and to the premises and moral foundations upon which this country was established. Now is the time to begin calling America back to God, back to the Bible, back to morality."[107]

With respect to Baptist doctrines and identity, Falwell has asserted a fusion of Successionist and Anabaptist Kinship theories, not unlike those in the South and southwestern Southern Baptist family: "The Church has reference to a distinct group within history who through the medium of preaching has accepted the gospel of Jesus Christ by faith and has separated itself unto righteousness."[108] In keeping with a "Free Church" typology suggested by Gunnar Westin, Falwell traced the trail of Baptist nonconformity from Montanists, Marcionites, Donatists, Novatians, Waldensians, Wycliffe and Savonarola. Of the Mennonites in particular, he wrote, "Their history became one of the most tragic chapters in all the pages of church history. Martyrs by the thousands gave their blood for their baptistic beliefs."[109] The local church being completely independent, to Falwell the symbolic nature of the ordinances are a contemporary sign of religious non-conformity with the establishment churches: "To us, taking the bread and wine (most of us use grape juice) is simply a memorial of Christ's death. He is not literally present in the elements. And eating and drinking the juice does not guarantee His grace in our lives."[110] In so doing, there is an identification with the historic believers' churches. While Falwell and his colleagues early argued for the principle of religious liberty, citing Church of the Brethren historian Donald Durnbaugh and as evidenced primarily in the corollary of

---

[106] Falwell, *Strength for the Journey*, 221.

[107] Jerry Falwell, *Listen, America!* (Garden City: Doubleday & Co., 1980) 265.

[108] *Fundamentalist Phenomenon*, 27.

[109] Ibid, 28–38; 40. The force of Falwell's position lies with those nonconformists who held in common opposition to mainline Christianity.

[110] Falwell, *Strength for the Journey*, 276.

separation of church and state, their position has evolved. More recently Falwell seems to have determined that religious liberty in and of itself is not a biblical precept.[111]

SUMMARY

Those Baptist theologians and pastors classified here as in *diaspora* are not so grouped because they fit into none of the other categories. I have placed them here because in their own contexts they have moved beyond the center of traditional Baptist schools, organizations or labels, while still practicing Baptist principles or remaining members of Baptist congregations. Each still manifests a baptistic perspective on matters of scripture, salvation, Christ, and the church. In the case of Carl Henry, Bernard Ramm, Clark Pinnock, and Millard Erickson, each worked energetically at developing and maintaining an evangelical theological identity. In contrast, McClendon walked away from Baptist particularism to a generically baptistic set of principles. From within a Baptist frame of reference questions of a particular type are predictable with respect to major, enduring Baptist tenets. These include pondering the nature of the church, the matter of the atonement of Christ, and the authority of Scripture. By contrast, topics such as the interplay of God's grace and human free will, the relationship of evangelism and social action, or the gifts of the Spirit often have been given higher priority by the theologians and pastors considered in diaspora.

In some cases the diasporic context has been destined by the theologian, in others theologians have intentionally broadened their reach. Some thinkers have felt too limited by their denominational family (Edward Carnell, Clark Pinnock), while others have been drawn into dialogue well beyond the scope of Baptist church life (James McClendon, Bernard Ramm). Ironically, for those who have worked hard at Baptist identity within Baptist institutions and organizations, the marginal personalities often characterize what being Baptist means. Fundamentalists have often been definitive in the popular religious press in this regard. While many of the characters in the diasporic category have moved away from insisting upon a clearly baptistic identity, some have reversed the trend. Billy Graham has continually affirmed his

---

[111] Falwell, *Fundamentalist Phenomenon*, 54–55.

Baptist ties to a local Baptist church and the B.W.A., and Jerry Falwell has moved closer to a mainstream regional convention Baptist identity.

CHAPTER 11

THEMES AND THEOLOGICAL GENES IN RETROSPECT

> I cannot guarantee that my ideas will measure up to the full Baptist stature. Indeed, the likelihood is all the other way. No one man is likely to see the whole, nor even to say the whole of what he sees. If I fall short, this is a free country, and anybody is at liberty to hoist the Baptist colors on a taller pole than mine.[1]
>
> Walter Rauschenbusch, 1905

The Baptist heritage in Britain and North America represents a major category of Free Church theological development. Baptist thought has developed over four centuries and has been shaped by a wide diversity of writers, thinkers, and practitioners, including pastors, lay spokesmen, professional theologians, and poets. Virtually every social class is represented in the development of Baptist theological thought. Few other Christian denominations can claim such diversity or inclusiveness over so long a period. Moreover, Baptists are found in every locale of Britain and North America, not to speak of their spread to the farthest corners of the globe.

At its heart, Baptist theology is an ongoing attempt to understand God and humanity in a theologically and historically orthodox framework, while recognizing the power of religious experience and swell of human circumstance. Baptist theology is not only about the classic doctrines of God, Christ, humanity, and salvation, but also about the community of faith, the struggle of the people of God in life settings, and the ultimate meaning and direction of life itself. Therein lies a central difficulty. Orthodoxy, tightly defined, and religious experience that constantly changes, can be mutually exclusive forms of religious authority and

---

[1] Walter Rauschenbusch, *"Why I am Baptist* – Prelude" *Rochester Baptist Monthly* (November 1905): 3, 20/3

knowledge. As a whole, Baptists have tried to keep these two streams of epistemology in creative tension, though these have more often represented a traditional dividing line among differing types of Baptists. There are confessional Baptists and there are those who hold to the importance of religious experience in defining religious character; there is often too little friendly dialogue between the two.

At face value, Baptist thought may appear to be hopelessly atomized. For the historical theologian some stratagem or cohesive tissue is needed to provide a usable mosaic that tells the Baptist story. A "genetic approach" promises the potential of such a cohesive account. When one sees among Baptists the personal, educational and social interrelationships, as well as dependencies, reactions and scholarly citations, a larger tradition does indeed emerge from what to many seems merely a swirl of never-ending controversy. That larger tradition may be described as follows: Baptist theology is a biblically oriented, Christologically centered, evangelical Christian tradition that values religious experience, congregational identity, and freedom of conscience in a racially and ethnically diverse heritage. It took at least two centuries for this profile of the Baptist tradition to take definite shape and develop a body of literature to explain adequately and sustain the community. Essentially, though not exclusively, Baptist theological identity has been written in the English language and shaped in an Anglo-North American cultural context.[2]

Within the boundaries of that profile, from its earliest stages, genetic theological connections can be identified. Ideas pass from one pastor to another, or from a tract to a treatise. These enduring ideas are the "genes" of Baptist thought. First and foremost among the genetic traits for Baptists has been the authority of Christ, the Living Word. An inheritance from their Puritan forbears (and equally the Anabaptists), the doctrine of Christ overwhelms Baptist character. He is spoken of in the confessions as Savior, Redeemer, Lord, Messiah, Head of the Church, Lawgiver, and Logos. He is believed present in the Church, defining its members and relationships, receiving its worship, each congregation being "complete in Christ." Freedom in Christ was the impulse of Baptist teaching on religious liberty. The proper understanding of the atonement of Christ—its extent or application—was an important theological

---

[2] In a future volume, I hope to assess Baptist thought beyond Britain and North America.

question that Baptists wrestled with for over two centuries. As the evangelical tradition became preoccupied with the written texts of Scripture, most Baptists sought solace in the living Christ as head of the Church and the Lord of the "Great Commission" (see Matt. 28:18–20). The missionary advance of Baptists in church planting, education, translation efforts, and benevolent work was empowered by their embrace of Christ's commission to the disciples and the church.

On the definitively liberal side of the traditon, for many Baptists Christ in the New Theology became the Example, the Incarnation of God's fullness, the chief interpreter of Scripture and ethics. Those in the historicist traditions, like the Chicago School, emphasized Christ as an historical figure who shaped the core or *kerygma* of Christianity and whose teachings became the timeless authoritative parts of Scripture. All Baptists understand a personal experience with Christ as essential to a definition of true Christianity. Typically, Baptists understand eschatology as a historic reunion with Christ. The "Kingdom of Christ (or God)" is a familiar term in both Landmarkist and Social Gospel literature. Baptist artwork, not a prolific genre, more often than not depicts scenes from the life of Christ, notably his baptism and presiding role at the Last Supper.

The doctrine of Christ as a genetic mark for Baptists has produced some fascinating implications for Trinitarian dogma. The Fatherhood of God, for example, is not an area of Baptist teaching that is well articulated. The Fatherhood of God did receive great attention among non-trinitarian Baptist thinkers in the eighteenth and early nineteenth centuries, and later among more liberal theologians who explored immanence and/or process theologies. Similarly, Baptists seem not to have a clear perception of the Holy Spirit, pointing essentially to his role as teacher, guide to Christ, and source of gifts in the Church. The Holy Spirit's role in evangelism, sanctification, and empowerment of believers was developed by other evangelical groups and entered Baptist thought in a limited way through writers like A. J. Gordon and Clark Pinnock and schools of thought that resulted from such movements as the Keswick and Northfield meetings. To the present, mainstream Baptists retreat from Pentecostal or charismatic expressions of spirituality in favor of Christological affirmations. Among African American Baptists, however, there is frequent reference and response to the Spirit through active worship traditions.

The next most recognizable genetic trait among Baptists is undeniably the priority of Scripture. Among the earliest Baptist theologians, Scripture was the starting point for a new doctrine of the church. They found the charter and practices of a New Testament form of Christianity in the Bible free from the corruption of ecclesiastic machinery. Little wonder that their use of Scripture was according to a proof-text methodology. Likewise, their confessional statements lifted the phraseology of Scripture off the page and rearranged it into convenient catechetical form. An early era significantly influenced by Calvinism sought to defend itself against later systems by continual reference to Scripture. In the eighteenth century, advocates of various theological positions, from "freewillers" to Unitarian Baptists, tried to demonstrate that their understanding of the Bible was most in keeping with its literal meaning.

What many evangelical commentators miss in assessing the advent of liberal theology among Baptists is their preoccupation with Scripture. Virtually all of the biblical scholarship, as well as the systematic work done in the name of "New Theology" by Baptists, confessed a strong dependency upon Scripture. Baptist "heretics" like Nathaniel Schmidt and Crawford H. Toy in the 1880s and 1890s were trying to understand Scripture from a newly shaped interpretive perspective and were inextricably given to "biblical theology." As systematic theology waned altogether at the conclusion of the nineteenth century, thinkers like H. Wheeler Robinson and A. H. Strong still supported their approaches based on the authority of Scripture. Even the Chicago School was convinced that only a careful study of the context and evolution of Scripture would reveal its true meaning and possible implications for later generations of the church. Men like Shirley Jackson Case and Shailer Mathews may be found in support of this assertion. Finally, who would deny that both the Baptist fundamentalists of the 1920s and the Neo-evangelicals of the mid-twentieth century contended for a biblically based approach to theology? Baptists simply must align themselves theologically with Scripture in order to assert credibility for their doctrinal constructs.

A third "gene" among Baptist thinkers has involved religious, or more specifically, Christian experience. Early Baptists were driven by a pressing desire to move beyond liturgical confessionalism to a form of Christianity that was fully experiential. Perhaps owing to their working class identity, or their close proximity to other dissenters like Ranters, Seekers, Fifth Monarchists, and Quakers, Baptists wrote a good deal about experience. At one level, religious experience was at the heart of their understanding of the church. Candidates for church membership must "give evidence of their new life in Christ." Baptism became for Baptists not merely a symbol of spiritual truth, but a vivid corporate experience. Similarly, the Lord's Supper was a full re-enactment of the drama of the Passover Meal in which all true disciples are invited to participate. As time went on, Baptists recognized that interpretation of Scripture required the element of experience to be valid. It was not a matter of mere human experience, but how the activity of the Holy Spirit in the believer's life shed light on the eternal truth of the Scriptures. The advent of revivalism brought to the Baptist movement a new form of outward experience whereby people could give public witness of their response to an invitation to accept Christ or deepen a commitment to the faith. The recounting of one's experience, called a "personal testimony," has long been an integral part of Baptist life.

Baptist song-making is an example of a premier experiential component of Baptist thinking. Baptists delight to express themselves individually and collectively in songs of the faith. They remember these from generation to generation and teach the faith to their offspring through the songs they sing. Here more than many other places, Baptists have been ecumenically oriented, including songs of faith from many Christian faith traditions in our hymnals and songbooks. More often than not, it seems Baptists can sing a line of doctrine before easily recalling a passage of Scripture or a theological discourse regarding that tenet.

In this regard, we see the roots of the Black Baptist theological contribution as an outgrowth of the Baptist appreciation of religious experience. Interpreters of Black theology remind us continually of the importance of the slave experience in the early United States, as well as the continuing struggle of that community against racism and deprivation of social and economic opportunity. Deotis Roberts has recently written of the desire of African American thinkers to reflect theologically upon their African experience, again reinforcing the importance of religious experience in the theology of the Black community.

The fourth major genetic influence that has shaped Baptist thought is a modified Reformed theological tradition. It is clear that Baptists were a part of the second generation of Protestants, owing their religious character to earlier ideals like *sola scriptura, sola fidei,* the priesthood of all believers, and justification by faith, as well as a disestablishmentariansm that characterized the nature of the seventeenth century reformations. The first Baptists were mostly an evolved form of the Reformed family, with eclectic embellishments drawn from Anglican, Lutheran, and anabaptistic formulae. While no one can discount the connections of the first Baptist-like congregations with Puritan/Separatist forbears, Baptist theological identity did not appear in history as a solitary religious perspective, but developed from a modified variety of Reformed thought. The early confessions of faith evince an unmistakable Reformed tone in their expressions of the sovereignty and perfection of God, the sinfulness of humans, the atonement of Christ and grace of God, and some perception of the chosen nature of God's people. Even those Baptists of the "general atonement" tradition are in keeping with the majority of Reformed tenets.[3] Well into the nineteenth century most Baptists acknowledged their debt to the "doctrines of grace," while holding firmly to the free offer of salvation.

What modified the predominantly Calvinistic outlook of most Baptists in Britain and the United States was the influence of progressive thought on the old formulae. Frank Hugh Foster demonstrated the evolution of Calvinism from the Puritans and Jonathan Edwards to Edwards A. Park at Andover Theological Seminary. He noted the changes in emphasis and meaning of key doctrines such as the atonement of Christ, the decrees of God, sin, and future punishment in a shift from the "inability" of Calvinism to a theology where the love of God became the determinant principle.[4] With respect to parallel Baptist theological expressions, the theologies of John Clifford, H. Wheeler Robinson, and Ernest Payne in the British tradition, and A. H. Strong, W. N. Clarke, A. Hovey, E. Y. Mullins and Dale Moody in the United States, remind repeatedly of the desire to move away from rigid doctrines of determinism, human depravity, and soteriological elitism to a theology that is more open, accepting, diverse, enlightened, and egalitarian. James Leo Garrett has argued persuasively that even among Southern Baptists in the United States, where a latent Calvinism held on into the twentieth

---

[3] See Stephen Brachlow, "Puritan Theology and General Baptist Origins," *Baptist Quarterly* 31/4 (1985): 179–94.

[4] Frank Hugh Foster, *A Genetic History of the New England Theology* (Chicago: University of Chicago Press, 1907) 491.

century, the surviving aspect was perseverance of the saints, with far less emphasis upon doctrines of limited atonement, predestination, or the sovereignty of God.[5] For others, moving away from Calvinism—understood as the "old Orthodoxy"—was tantamount to affirming human autonomy and a progressive, historical understanding of Christianity. This was the contribution of the Chicago School.

Calvinistic emphases also produced a negative reaction among Baptists. The basically egalitarian mindset of Baptists, wrought by religious persecution from their earliest days, caused some to recoil against harsh predestinarianism and later against elite ideas of election. This led inevitably to an open-ended soteriology that pushed seventeenth-century General Baptists toward universalism and encouraged eighteenth-century Regular Baptists to back away from the doctrine of reprobation. Not all Baptists followed suit with liberal theologians among the Congregationalists in eschewing determinist thinking; some merely wandered there by reading the New Testament from a perspective of the unbounded love and mercy of God. Likewise, a literalistic reading of Scripture also caused important Baptist thinkers in the eighteenth century to question the biblical warrant for trinitarianism, as well as the divinity of Christ. There is a wide range of leading Baptist thinkers who found difficulties with the Calvinist system to one degree or another: Thomas Grantham, Andrew Fuller, Archibald McLean, Dan Taylor, Elias Smith, Benjamin Randal and Clark Pinnock, to name a few.

The Calvinist tradition has enjoyed several resurgences at key points in Baptist history. In the British family, as leaders of the General Baptists and Particular Baptists began to move closer to union between 1831 and 1892, many congregations that espoused a Calvinistic theology protested and reshaped themselves around definitive Calvinistic emphases.[6] A similar reaction occurred among Baptists in America where the influence of Freewill Baptists and the missionary movement in the mainstream Baptist family led hundreds of congregations in the Northeast to become part of the anti-missionary, hardshell, or Primitive Baptist movement. C. H. Spurgeon's interest in resurrecting the Puritan classics was an important catalyst in a transatlantic revival of Calvinist theology among

---

[5] James Leo Garrett, Jr., E. Glenn Hinson, James E. Tull, eds., *Are Southern Baptists Evangelicals?* (Macon GA: Mercer University Press, 1983) 89–90.

[6] For the subtle nuances, see Kenneth Dix, "Varieties of High Calvinism among Nineteenth-Century Particular Baptists," *Baptist Quarterly* 38/2 (1999): 56–69.

many Baptists between 1880 and the 1920s. Finally, in the past twenty years of Southern Baptist history in the United States, there has been a reawakening of old Calvinism at Southern Baptist Theological Seminary, Samford University, and to a lesser degree at Southwestern Baptist Seminary.[7] What is evident in each of these examples is that many Baptists hold that Baptist thought is rooted in a modified Reformed confessionalism, and when theology has strayed too far from its confessional roots for the comfort of conservatives, it is correctable by reference in particular to the Calvinistic tradition, historically interpreted in the Princeton School of the nineteenth century. The roots of much of American conservative evangelicalism, fostered by publications such as *Christianity Today* and in doctrinal characteristics of schools like Wheaton College, lie in a particular view of the Reformed tradition. Both have their devotees among the Baptist community.[8]

It is evident from any reading of Baptist literature that much of the energy of Baptist theology has been applied to polity and order. Among many confessional traditions other than Baptist, these matters are not included in classical theological discourse because they are considered matters of praxis. When Baptists reflect on issues like baptism and the Lord's Supper, evangelism, the nature of church membership, the visibility of the church as a congregation, and democratic decision-making, they are exploring an extended doctrine of the church, a fifth gene.

The constituency of the *ecclesia*, or the church's membership, is for Baptists a theological issue. Membership involves an understanding of humanity that is voluntary in spirit and communal in nature. One joins the people of God on God's invitation through personal response. Every member is equal in standing, though different in gifts, with other members before God. Here an egalitarian doctrine of the atonement is at work as well as a practical manifestation of the *Imago Dei*. Baptists understand the church as a congregation or visible manifestation of the grace of God that makes their ecclesiology empirical. Matters of

---

[7] Garrett edited a sourcebook of Calvinistic material for a special series Broadman published. For his assessment of Calvinism, see *Calvin and the Reformed Tradition* (Nashville: Broadman, 1980) 23–39.

[8] From time to time Baptists have served as contributing editors of *Christianity Today* and several schools recruit faculty candidates from among the Christian College movement.

discipline, order, structure, and relationships have theological implications rather than mere organizational meaning.[9] Landmarkists may be faulted for their overly-exclusivist understanding of the church, but it is the mark of an ancient Baptist gene to identify local congregations empirically as the people of God.

For Baptists, the ordinal elements of water, wine, and bread are purely symbolic because they act as metaphors to remind Christians that the nature of the church is essentially spiritual. Consequently, Baptists have agreed with Reformation writers who understand from the Scriptures that the sacraments/ordinances are essentially memorials or reminders of spiritual realities. Likewise, Baptists for the most part have set aside the debates of the sixteenth century over the "visible" versus the "invisible" church, preferring to focus upon the visible church. Here matters of personal decision, faithfulness, and Christian ethics become the essence of the people of God, not a sacramental or forensic understanding. As such, one can see the ideological continuity of such matters between John Smyth's *Differences in the Churches of the Seperation*, Andrew Fuller's *Gospel Worthy of All Acceptation*, James R. Graves's *Old Landmarkism*, W. T. Conner's *Christian Doctrines,* and Millard Erickson's *Christian Theology.*

A sixth genetic trait of Baptists is their evangelical nature. Here the term is used most carefully to avoid the misunderstandings of the past one and one-half centuries. From their earliest gatherings, Baptists have sensed urgency about their role as God's people and their obligations under the gospel. For some it has been expressed in the "Great Commission," for others in their witness as the people of God in worship and service. For yet others, the urgency has been translated into social activism or ecumenical relationships. Baptists have not been a quiet people about their positions on sharing the love of God in Christ, justice, mercy, and human rights. In this regard, they have been for the most part an outwardly directed people rather than introspective or communitarian. Baptists were not Seekers or Quakers in the seventeenth century; they were not Mennonites or Hutterian Brethren in later development. They were among the first advocates of general atonement and open communion in the seventeenth and eighteenth centuries respectively. Theologians

---

[9] See, for instance, B. R. White, "Open and Closed Membership Among English and Welsh Baptists," *Baptist Quarterly* 24/4 (1972): 330–34, where the author demonstrates the theological connections with traditional Calvinistic and Arminian schools.

like E. Y. Mullins openly embraced ideas such as autonomy and competency as axiomatic principles of faith. For some, this tendency has led to the edges of orthodoxy and beyond, as we have witnessed the possibility of universalism among Baptists. The term "evangelical," used here as an adjective ("gospel-oriented") describes an inherent gene in Baptist life.

The final shared genetic trace among Baptists to note is that of freedom or liberty. Closely tied to both Christology and anthropology, Baptists have developed and promoted a clear understanding of religious liberty. Early Baptists like Thomas Helwys and John Murton laid the foundations for the expression of religious liberty within an ordered society. Later, Baptist pastors and lay leaders experienced violations of religious freedom and wrote of their experiences as an apologetic for liberty. Among these were Roger Williams, John Clarke, Isaac Backus, John Leland, William Carey, John Clifford, James Rushbrooke, Adoniram Judson, E. Y. Mullins, and Martin Luther King, Jr. But the principle of religious liberty is also seen in the yearning of Baptist pastors and biblical scholars to interpret Scripture unencumbered, as reflected in the stories of Robert Robinson, Elhanan Winchester, Nathaniel Schmidt, C. H. Toy, and W. R. Harper, and Ralph Elliott. Methodologically, professional Baptist theologians like D. C. MacIntosh, W. S. Hudson, W. R. McNutt, and Walter Rauschenbusch likewise display the trait. One might even argue that the stridency and tenacity of fundamentalist Baptists like William Bell Riley, J. Frank Norris, T. T. Shields, or the contemporary ranks of resurgent fundamentalists, reflect a freedom of expression and license not common to other hierarchical or presbyterial polities. It is said that the hallmark of the international representation of many Baptists, the Baptist World Alliance, is religious liberty.

In any genetic map, there is always evidence of offshoots that become important branches or expressions of the basic character of the source organism. The most creative manifestations of the Baptist character do not fall neatly into predictable evolutions, but can be understood from a perspective of contextual growth. These include: the development of a missionary theology, the rise of social gospel, and evolution of Black Theology. Evangelical Calvinism, as Andrew Fuller expressed it, closely akin to Dan Taylor's and Benjamin Randal's Arminian positions, evolved seamlessly into theologies of mission. Baptists translated the need to receive Christ as personal Lord and Savior into an obligation to preach the gospel to the nations. Their penchant for organization followed closely upon their theology, and the notable achievement of their missionary efforts was the result. Later in the nineteenth century, in large part due to Walter Rauschenbusch's experience as a pastor in Hell's Kitchen, and that of his brother-in-law, John E. Clough, in poverty-stricken India, Baptists responded to the gospel call with heightened appreciations for social concern. That response had transformational effects on many Baptists' theology of the Kingdom of God, as well as on their doctrines of Christ and salvation. Finally, directly related to Rauschenbusch's theology of the social gospel, African American Baptists changed their theological direction away from accommodation to unjust social structures, instead affirming the dignity of all persons and establishing a theological foundation for social change activism. These three genetic outgrowths are not marginal, but essential components of Baptist identity.

Having summarized the character of the Baptist theological heritage, there is a final sobering note about the forums in which Baptist theological ideas have been debated and carried forth. After an initial period of self-definition in which there was a good deal of interaction with Puritans, other Nonconformists, and Anglicans, Baptists from England to the United States largely talked to each other. Their issues were in many instances lost on mainstream Protestant theologians and when opportunities came to interact with Congregationalists, Unitarians, Methodists, and Presbyterians, Lutherans, or Catholics, Baptist writers were more often acrimonious than irenic. Very conservative positions on the authority of Scripture, the nature of a true church, and the exclusiveness of their understanding of evangelistic witness assured Baptists of an undisturbed (and perhaps uninteresting!) theological position. One searches long in the eighteenth and nineteenth centuries for Baptist thinkers who are quoted with appreciation outside the denominational presses. The list is short: John Gill, C. H. Spurgeon, Francis Wayland, and William Newton Clarke. In the next century, the list is even shorter: Walter Rauschenbusch, A. H. Strong, H. Wheeler Robinson, and Martin Luther King, Jr. Much more awareness of Baptist theologians occurs with the entry of post-World War II thinkers who reached into the broader evangelical and liberal spheres, leaving behind their denominational orientations. It is, therefore, difficult to chart how other Christian communities assess Baptist theological discourse. Some hint comes in Daniel Day Williams's characterization in 1958: "Here is a form of the Christian community which rests upon an experience of the Gospel which is personal, easily intelligible, vividly symbolized, calling for personal dedication, and open to the promptings of the Spirit."[10] The theological dialogues of the Baptist World Alliance with various world Christian communions also provide dialogical texts. Here again, Baptists have been more than extremely cautious, their leading theologians often not at the tables of conversation.[11]

Baptist thought has brought forth a vast array of theological opinion, often the cause of bitter conflict. As part of the Free Church stream of Christian spirituality that stresses the individual, Baptists have had to struggle to secure synthesis—they lack the all-important cohering function brought about by human administrative authority, such as might be rendered by organizationally empowered elders, bishops, or inter-church councils. Progress in theological understanding has come only with painful, intense debate, often characterized by dislocation and breaking of fellowship between persons who claim to follow the same Lord revealed in Scripture. As progress toward more openness of ideas occurs, among Baptists there has always been a conserving tendency. More likely than not, this persistent attitude is attributable to the core Baptist genetic trait, a concern for the authority of Scripture. It is only as thinkers and ideas are seen to conform with the Word of God that acceptability among Baptists is achieved.

---

[10] Daniel Day Williams, "The Mystery of the Baptists," *Foundations* 1/1 (1958): 9.

[11] The Baptist World Alliance (BWA) has engaged in conversations with Roman Catholics, Lutherans, Reformed Churches, Mennonites, Eastern Orthodox, and Anglicans. One searches in vain to find the input of Carl F. Henry, Bernard Ramm, Harvey Cox, Clark Pinnock, or Millard Erickson in similar discussions. Two Southern Baptist theologians, Dale Moody and James Leo Garrett, have made substantial contributions to ecumenical dialogue, but their own part of the denomination has retreated from such efforts.

BIBLIOGRAPHY

BAPTIST THEOLOGY — GENERAL, BACKGROUNDS

Baird, Robert. *Religion in America, or An Account of the Origin, Relation to the State, and Present Condition of the Evangelical Churches in the United States*. New York: Harper and Brothers, 1856.

Brackney, William H. *Baptist Life and Thought, 1600–1980*. Valley Forge PA: Judson Press, 1983.

Brackney, William Henry. *The Baptists*. New York: Greenwood Press 1988.

Campbell, Douglas. *The Puritan in Holland, England, and America*. 2 volumes. New York: Harper and Brothers, 1892.

Conser, Walter H., Jr., *Church and Confession: Conservative Theologians in Germany, England and America 1815–1866*. Macon GA: Mercer University Press, 1984.

Davies, Horton. *Worship and Theology in England*. 5 volumes. Princeton: Princeton University Press, 1961–1970.

Estep, William R. *The Anabaptist Story*. Nashville: Broadman Press, 1963.

Ferm, Vergilius, editor. *Contemporary American Theology: Theological Autobiographies*. 2 volumes. New York: Round Table Press, 1932.

Foster, Frank H. *Christian Life and Theology; or The Contribution of Christian Experience to the System of Evangelical Doctrine*. New York: Fleming H. Revell, 1900.

Foster, Frank Hugh. *A Genetic History of the New England Theology*. Chicago: University of Chicago Press, 1907.

Garrett, James Leo, Jr., *Baptists and Roman Catholicism: A Survey of Baptist Writings about the Roman Catholic Church, with an Interpretation of Recent Developments*. Nashville: Broadman Press, 1965.

Garrett, James Leo, Jr., editor. *Calvin and the Reformed Tradition*. Nashville: Broadman Press, 1980.

George, Timothy. "Dogma Beyond Anathema: Historical Theology in the Service of the Church." *Review and Expositor* 84 (Fall 1987): 691–713.

Glover, Willis B. *Evangelical Nonconformists and Higher Criticism in the Nineteenth Century*. London: Independent Press, 1954.

Goen, C. C. *Revivalism and Separatism in New England 1740–1800*. New Haven: Yale University Press, 1962.

Halevy, Elie. *England in 1815*. Translated by E.I. Watkins and D. A. Barker. New York: Peter Smith, 1949.

Hauerwas, Stanley, Nancey Murphy, and Mark Nation. *Theology Without Foundations: Religious Practice and the Future of Theological Truth*. Nashville: Abingdon Press, 1994.

Henry, Carl F. H. *Fifty Years of Protestant Theology*. Boston: W. A. Wilde, 1950.

Hodgson, Peter C. and Robert H. King, editors. *Christian Theology: An Introduction to Its Traditions and Tasks*. Philadelphia: Fortress Press, 1982.

Hostetler, John A. *Hutterite Society*. Baltimore: Johns Hopkins University Press, 1974.

Hubmaier, Balthasar. *Balthasar Hubmaier: Theologian of Anabaptism*. Volume 5 of *Classics of the Reformation*. Translated and edited by H. Wayne Pipkin and John H. Yoder. Scottdale PA: Herald Press, 1989.

Hudson, Winthrop S. *Baptist Concepts of the Church: A Survey of the Historical and Theological Issues Which Have Produced Changes in Church Order*. Valley Forge: Judson Press, 1959.

———. *Baptists in Transition: Individualism and Christian Responsibility*. Valley Forge: Judson Press, 1979.

———. "Baptists Were Not Anabaptists." *The Chronicle* 16/4 (December 1953): 171–79.

———. "Shifting Patterns of Church Order." In *Baptist Concepts of the Church*. Edited by Winthrop S. Hudson. Philadelphia: Judson Press, 1959.

Hutchison, William F. *The Modernist Impulse in American Protestantism*. Durham: Duke University Press, 1992.

James, William. *The Varieties of Religious Experience: A Study in Human Nature, Being the Gifford Lectures in Natural Religion, Delivered at Edinburgh 1901–1902*. London: Longmans, Green, & Co., 1902.

Keeble, N. H. *The Literary Culture of Nonconformity in Later Seventeenth Century England*. Leicester: Leicester University Press, 1987.

Kendall, R. T. "The Nature of Saving Faith from William Perkins to the Westminster Assembly." D.Phil. dissertation, Oxford University, 1976.

Lovegrove, Deryck. *Established Church, Sectarian People: Itinerancy and the Transformation of English Dissent 1780–1830*. Cambridge: Cambridge University Press, 1988.

Maring Norman H. and Winthrop S, Hudson. *A Baptist Manual of Polity and Practice*. Valley Forge: Judson Press, 1963.

McBeth, H. Leon. *The Baptist Heritage: Four Centuries of Baptist Witness*. Nashville: Broadman Press, 1987.

McGregor, J. F. "The Baptists: Fount of all Heresy." In *Radical Religion in the English Reformation*. Edited by J.F. McGregor and B. Reay. Oxford: Oxford University Press, 1984.

Newman, Albert H. *History of the Baptist Churches in the United States*. Philadelphia: American Baptist Publication Society, 1898.

Noll, Mark A. *American Evangelical Christianity: An Introduction*. Oxford: Blackwell Publishers, 2001.

———., editor. *The Princeton Theology 1812–1921: Scripture, Science, and Theological Method from Archibald Alexander to Benjamin Warfield*. Grand Rapids: Baker Books, 1983.

Nuttall, Geoffrey. *Visible Saints: The Congregational Way, 1640–1660*. Oxford: Basil Blackwell, 1957.

Patterson, W. Morgan. *Baptist Successionism: A Critical View*. Valley Forge: Judson Press, 1969.

Robert, Dana L. "The Crisis of Missions: Premillennial Missions Theory and the Origins of Independent Evangelical Missions." In *Earthen Vessels: American Evangelicals and Foreign Missions 1880–1980*. Edited by Joel A. Carpenter and Wilbert R. Shenk. Grand Rapids: Eerdmans, 1990.

Sabatier, Auguste and Louise Seymour Houghton. *Religions of Authority and the Religion of the Spirit*. New York: McClure, Phillips & Co., 1904.

Sailhammer, John H. "Johann August Ernesti: The Role of History in Biblical Interpretation." *Journal of the Evangelical Theological Society* 44 (June 2001): 193–206.

Smith, H. Shelton, Robert Handy, and Lefferts A. Loetscher. *American Christianity: An Historical Interpretation with Representative Documents*. 2 volumes. New York: Charles Scribner's Sons, 1960–1963.

Snyder, Arnold. "Beyond Polygenesis: Recovering the Unity and Diversity of Anabaptist Theology." In *Essays in Anabaptist Theology*. Edited by H. Wayne Pipkin. Elkhart: Institute of Mennonite Studies, 1994.

Stearns, L. F. *The Evidence of Christian Experience: Being the Ely Lectures for 1890*. New York: Charles Scribner's Sons, 1890.

Torbet, Robert G. *History of the Baptists*. Valley Forge: Judson Press, 1963.

Trinterud, Leon J. "The Origins of Puritanism." *Church History* 20 (March 1951): 54.

Underwood, A. C. *History of the English Baptists*. London: Carey Kingsgate Press, 1947.

Underwood, William. *The General Baptist Denomination, Its Past History, Distinctive Peculiarities, and Present Position*. London: Henry James Tresidder, 1864.

Vedder, Henry C. *Balthasar Hubmaier, The Leader of the Anabaptists*. New York: G. C. Putnam's, 1905.

———. *A History of Baptists in the Middle States*. Philadelphia: American Baptist Publication Society, 1898.

Walker, Williston. *The Creeds and Platforms of Congregationalism*. New York: Charles Scribner's Sons, 1893.

Webster, John. "Confession and Confessions." In *Nicene Christianity: The Future for a New Ecumenism*. Edited by Christopher Seitz. Grand Rapids: Brazos Press, 2002.

Welch, Claude. *Protestant Thought in the Nineteenth Century*. 2 volumes. New Haven: Yale University Press, 1972.

Wenger, John C. "The Schleitheim Confession of Faith." *Mennonite Quarterly Review* 19/3 (October 1945): 244–53.

White, B. R. *The English Baptists of the Seventeenth Century*. Didcot: Baptist Historical Society, 1996.

Whitley, William T. *History of the British Baptists*. London: Carey Kingsgate Press, 1923.

Williams, Daniel Day. "The Mystery of the Baptists." *Foundations* 1/1 (January 1958): 7–9.

Wood, Nathan E. "Movements of Baptist Theological Thought." In *A Century of Baptist Achievement*. Edited by A. H. Newman. Philadelphia: American Baptist Publication Society, 1901.

Yuille, George, editor. *History of the Baptists in Scotland*. Glasgow: Baptist Union Publication Committee, 1926.

THE CONFESSIONAL TRADITION

Baines, Arnold H. J. "Signatories to the Orthodox Confession, 1679" *Baptist Quarterly* 17 (April 1957): 74–86.

———. "Signatories to the Orthodox Confession, 1679" *Baptist Quarterly* 17 (July 1957): 122–28.

The Baptist Catechism, Or a Brief Instruction in the Principles of the Christian Religion, Agreeably to the Confession of Faith. Boston: Manning and Loring, 1795.

"Baptist Faith and Message." *Southern Baptist Annual, 1925,* Nashville: Marshall & Bruce, 1925: 72–73.

Barnes, William Wright. "The New Hampshire Confession of Faith, Its Origins, and Use." *Review and Expositor* 39/1 (January 1942): 3–8.

Broadway, Michael, James W. McClendon, Curtis Freeman, Elizabeth Newman, Barry Harvey, and Phillip Thompson. "Re-Envisioning Baptist Identity: A Manifesto for Baptist Communities in America." *Baptists Today,* June 26, 1997, 8–10.

A Confession of Faith of Several Churches of Christ in the County of Somerset and of some Churches in the Counties neer adjacent. London: Henry Hills, 1656.

Carter, James E. "American Baptist Confessions of Faith: A Review of Confessions of Faith Adopted by Major Bodies in the United States." In *The Lord's Free People in a Free Land: Essays in Baptist History in Honor of Robert A. Baker.* Fort Worth: Southwestern Baptist Theological Seminary, 1976.

Collier, Jay Travis. "The Sources Behind the First London Confession." *American Baptist Quarterly* 21 (June 2002): 197–214.

Englerth, Gilbert R. "American Baptists: A Confessional People?" *Foundations* 4 (June 1985): 131–45.

Estep, W. R. "Baptists and Authority: The Bible, Confessions, and Conscience in the Development of Baptist Identity." *Review and Expositor* 84 (Fall 1987): 599–615.

The Feast of Fat Things. Middletown NY: G. Beebe's Sons, 1832.

Gillette, Abram D., editor. *Minutes of the Philadelphia Baptist Association 1707–1807.* Philadelphia: American Baptist Publication Society, 1851.

"Goodchild Confession at Fundamentals Conference at Des Moines." *The Baptist* (Chicago) July 2, 1921:684m 701.

Goodchild, Frank. "Fundamentals Conference, Des Moines, Iowa." *The Chronicle* (1943): 57–58.

Hayden, Roger. "The Particular Baptist Confession of 1689 and Baptists Today." *Baptist Quarterly* 32 (October 1988): 403–417.

Heimann, Franz. "The Hutterite Doctrine of the Church and Common Life: A Study of Riedemann's Confession of Faith." *Mennonite Quarterly Review* 26 (January 1962): 142–60.

Lumpkin, William L. *Baptist Confessions of Faith.* Chicago: Judson Press, 1959.

McClendon, James W., Jr. "The Voluntary Church in the Twentieth Century." In *The Believer's Church: A Voluntary Church.* Edited by William H. Brackney. Waterloo ONT: Pandora Press, 1998.

McGlothlin, W. J. *Baptist Confessions of Faith.* Philadelphia: American Baptist Publication Society, 1911.

Powell, Vavasour. *A Confession of Faith, drawn Up by Mr. Vavasour Powell, Concerning the Holy Scriptures.* n.p., 1660?.

Routley, Erik. *Creeds and Confessions: From the Reformation to the Modern Church.* Philadelphia: Westminster Press, 1962.

Riedemann, Peter. *Account of Our Religion, Doctrine and Faith, Given by Peter Riedemann of the Brothers Whom Men Call Hutterians.* Rifton NY: Plough Publishing House, 1970.

Renihan, James M. "An Examination of the Possible Influence of Menno Simons' Foundation Book upon the Particular Baptist Confession of 1644." *American Baptist Quarterly* 15/3 (September 1996): 190–207.

Report of The Committee on Baptist Faith and Message," *Southern Baptist Annual,* 1925, Nashville, 71.

Schaff, Philip. *Bibliotheca Symbolica Ecclesiae Universalis: The Creeds of Christendom, with a History and Critical Notes.* Volume 3. New York: Harper and Brothers, 1877.

Shurden, Walter B. "Southern Baptist Responses to Their Confessional Statements." *Review and Expositor* 76 (Winter 1979): 69–84.

Stassen, Glen Harold. "Opening Menno Simons's *Foundation-Book* and Finding the Father of Baptist Origins Alongside the Mother—Calvinist Congregationalism." *Baptist History and Heritage* 33 (Spring 1998): 34–44.

Underhill, Edward Bean. *Confessions of Faith and Other Public Documents Illustrative of the History of the Baptist Churches of England in the 17th Century.* London: Haddon Brothers, 1854.

Wood, Nathan E. *The History of the First Baptist Church of Boston (1665–1899).* Philadelphia: American Baptist Publication Society, 1899.

HYMNS, MUSIC, AND BAPTIST THEOLOGY

Adey, Lionel. *Class and Idol in the English Hymn.* Vancouver BC: University of British Columbia Press, 1988.

Arnold, Richard, editor. *English Hymns of the Eighteenth Century: An Anthology.* New York: Peter Lang, 1991.

Broaddus, Andrew. *The Virginia Selection of Psalms, Hymns and Spiritual Songs.* Richmond VA: R. I. Smith, 1835.

Burrage, Henry S. *Baptist Hymn Writers and Their Hymns.* Portland ME: Brown, Thurston & Co., 1888.

Collis, Michael J. "The Lord's Supper in British Baptist Hymnody in the Twentieth Century." *Baptist Quarterly* 38 (April 2000): 290–305.

Duffield, Samuel Willoughby. *English Hymns: Their Authors and History.* New York: Funk & Wagnalls, 1886.

Garside, Charles. "The Origins of Calvin's Theology of Music, 1536–543." *Transactions of the American Philosophical Society* 69 (1979): 5-33.

———. *Zwingli and the Arts.* New Haven: Yale University Press, 1966.

Gibson, J. Daniel. "A Homiletical Hermeneutic for the Re-Writing of Hymn Texts." M.Th. thesis, Waterloo Lutheran Seminary, 2000.

Haeussler, Armin. *The Story of Our Hymns.* St. Louis: Eden Publishing Co., 1952.

Hein, David. "S. F. Smith and 'America.'" *Baptist Quarterly* 32 (July 1987): 134–40.

Hustad, Donald P. *Jubilate II: Church Music in the Evangelical Tradition*. Carol Stream IL: Hope Publishing Co., 1981.

Johnson, James Weldon. *The Book of American Negro Spirituals*. Binghamton NY: The Vail-Bollan Press, 1925.

Manly, Basil and Basil Manly, Jr., "Before the Pool A Sufferer Lay." In *The Baptist Psalmody: A Selection of Hymns for the Worship of God*. Charleston SC: Southern Baptist Publication Society, 1850.

McElrath, Hugh T. "The Hymnbook as a Compendium of Theology." *Review and Expositor* 87 (Winter 1990): 11–31.

Music, David W. "Music in the First Baptist Church of Boston, Massachusetts, 1665–1820." In *Singing Baptists: Studies in Baptist Hymnody in America*. Edited by Harry Eskew, David W. Music, and Paul A. Richardson. Nashville: Church Street Press, 1994.

Nettl, Paul. *Luther and Music*. Translated by Frieda Best and Ralph Wood. Philadelphia: Fortress Press, 1948.

Price, Milburn. "What Every Pastor Should Know About the Hymnal: The Hymnal as a Worship Sourcebook." *Review and Expositor* 87 (Winter 1990): 33–41.

Reynolds, William J. "Baptist Hymnody in America." In *Handbook to the Baptist Hymnal*. Nashville: Convention Press, 1992.

Richardson, Paul A. "Baptist Contributions to Hymnody and Hymnology." *Review and Expositor* 87 (Winter 1990): 59–74.

Routley, Erik. *Hymns Today and Tomorrow*. Nashville: Abingdon Press, 1964.

Schilling, S. Paul. *The Faith We Sing*. Philadelphia: Westminster Press, 1983.

Sharpe, Eric. "Bristol Baptist College and the Church's Hymnody." *Baptist Quarterly* 38 (January 1979): 7–16.

Singer, David. "God and Man in Baptist Hymnals." *Midcontinent American Studies Journal* 9 (Fall 1968): 14.

Staehlin, Wilhelm. "The Church Hymn and Theology." In *Response*. St. Paul: Lutheran Society for Worship, Music, and the Arts, 1958.

Stansbury, George. "The Music of the Billy Graham Crusades 1947–1970." Ph.D. dissertation, Southern Baptist Theological Seminary, 1969.

Stennett, Joseph. *Hymns Compos'd for the Celebration of the Holy Ordinance of Baptism*. Edited by Don Sandford. Janesville: Seventh Day Baptist Historical Society, 2001.

Temperley, Nicholas. *The Music of the English Parish Church*. Cambridge: Cambridge University Press, 1971.

Thomson, Ronald W. "Anne Steele, 1716–1778." *Baptist Quarterly* 21 (October 1966): 369.

Baptist Hymnal. Nashville: Convention Press, 1991.

Hymnal of the Baptist Federation of Canada. Mississauga ONT: Baptist Federation Press, 1973.

Vincent, William. *Considerations on Parochial Music*. London: n.p., 1787.

Walker, Wyatt T. *Somebody's Calling My Name: Black Sacred Music and Social Change*. Valley Forge: Judson Press, 1979.

Whalum, Wendel Phillips. "Black Hymnody." *Review and Expositor* 70 (Summer 1973): 341–55.

Whitley, William T. "The First Hymnbook in Use." *Baptist Quarterly* 10 (July 1941): 374–75.

Worship and Service Hymnal for Church, School, and Home. Chicago: Hope Publishing, 1957.

Young, Robert H. "The History of Baptist Hymnody in England from 1612 to 1800." D.M.A. dissertation, University of Southern California, 1959.

BRITISH BAPTISTS — BIOGRAPHICAL AND HISTORICAL

Acworth, James. *A Discourse Occasioned by the Decease of the Rev. William Steadman, D.D.* London: Simpkin, Marshall & Co., 1837.

Archer, Robert. "Like Flowers in the Garden: John Bunyan and His Concept of the Church." *Baptist Quarterly* 36 (April 1996): 280–93.

Bacon, Ernest W. *Spurgeon: Heir of the Puritans.* London: George Allen and Unwin, 1967.

Baines, Arnold H. J. "Signatories to the Orthodox Confession, 1679." *Baptist Quarterly* 17 (January 1957): 35–42.

Ban, Joseph D. "Was John Bunyan a Baptist?: A Case Study in Historiography." *Baptist Quarterly* 30 (October 1984): 367–76.

Beasley-Murray, Paul. *Fearless for Truth: A Personal Portrait of the Life of George Beasley-Murray, 10 October 1916–23 February 2000.* Carlisle PA: Paternoster Press, 2002.

Bebbington, D. W., editor. *The Baptists in Scotland: A History.* Glasgow: Baptist Union of Scotland, 1988.

Bebbington, David. "Spurgeon and British Evangelical Theological Education." In *Theological Education in the Evangelical Tradition.* Edited by R. Albert Mohler, Jr. and D. G. Hart. Grand Rapids: Baker Books, 1996.

Brachlow, Stephen. "Puritan Theology and General Baptist Origins." *Baptist Quarterly* 31/4 (October 1985): 179–94.

Brown, Louise F. *The Political Activities of the Baptists and the Fifth Monarchy Men in England During the Interregnum.* Washington, DC: American Historical Association, 1912.

Butt-Thompson, F. W. "William Vidler." *Baptist Quarterly* 17 (January 1957): 3–10.

Byrt, G. W. *John Clifford: A Fighting Free Churchman.* London: The Kingsgate Press, 1947.

Calder, R. F. "Robert Haldane's Theological Seminary." *Transactions of the Congregational Historical Society* 13 (1937): 59-63.

Champion, Leonard G. "The Baptist Doctrine of the Church." *Foundations* 1 (January 1958): 27–39.

―――. "The Theology of John Ryland: Its Sources and Influences." *Baptist Quarterly* 38 (January 1979): 17–29.

Clipsham, E. F. "Andrew Fuller and Fullerism: A Study in Evangelical Calvinism." *Baptist Quarterly* 20 (April 1963): 268–76.

————. "Andrew Fuller and Fullerism: A Study in Evangelical Calvinism." *Baptist Quarterly* 20 (July 1963): 99–114.

————. "Andrew Fuller and Fullerism: A Study in Evangelical Calvinism." *Baptist Quarterly* 20 (October 1963): 146–54.

Coggins, James. *John Smyth's Congregation: English Separatism, Mennonite Influence and the Elect Nation.* Scottdale PA: Herald Press, 1991.

Crosby, Thomas. *The History of the English Baptists from the Reformation to the Beginning of the Reign of King George I.* 4 volumes. London: Crosby, 1738–740.

Culpeper, R. Alan. "George R. Beasley-Murray." In *Baptist Theologians.* Edited by Timothy George and David S. Dockery. Nashville: Broadman Press, 1990.

Daniel, Curt. "Hyper-Calvinism and John Gill." Ph.D. dissertation, University of Edinburgh, 1983.

Davies, Michael. *Graceful Reading: Theology and Narrative in the Works of John Bunyan.* Oxford: Oxford University Press, 2002.

Dix, Kenneth. "Varieties of High Calvinism Among Nineteenth Century Particular Baptists." *Baptist Quarterly* 38 (April 1999): 56–69.

Drummond, Lewis. "Charles Haddon Spurgeon." In *Theologians of the Baptist Tradition.* Edited by Timothy George and David S. Dockery. Nashville: Broadman & Holman, 2001.

Early, W. T. "The Doctrine of Revelation in the Theology of H. Wheeler Robinson." Th.D. dissertation, Union Theological Seminary, 1963.

Ella, George M. "John Gill and the Charge of Hyper-Calvinism." *Baptist Quarterly* 36 (October 1995): 160–77.

Fuller, Thomas Eakins. *A Memoir of the Life and Writings of Andrew Fuller.* London: J. Heaton, 1863.

Gloer, Hulitt, editor. *Eschatology and the New Testament: Essays in Honor of George Beasley-Murray.* Peabody: Hendrickson, 1988.

Garrett, Duane A. "H. Wheeler Robinson." In *Baptist Theologians.* Edited by Timothy George and David S. Dockery. Nashville: Broadman Press, 1990.

Gould, George. "The Origins of the Modern Baptist Denomination." In *Transactions of the Baptist Historical Society.* Volume 2 (1911): 193–212.

Greaves, Richard. *John Bunyan.* Abingdon: The Sutton Courtenay Press, 1969.

Haldane, Alexander. *The Lives of Robert Haldane of Airthrey and His Brother James Alexander Haldane.* London: Hamilton and Adams, 1853.

Handbook of the Baptist Union, 1899-.

Hayden, Roger. "Champion, Leonard George, 1907–1997." *Baptist Quarterly* 37 (January 1998): 211–12.

Haykin, Michael A. G. *Kiffin, Knollys, and Keach: Rediscovering Our English Baptist Heritage.* Leeds: Reformation Today Trust, 1996.

————. "Particular Redemption in the Writings of Andrew Fuller (1754–1815)." In *The Gospel in the World: International Baptist Studies.* Edited by David Bebbington. Carlisle, Cumbria: Paternoster Press, 2002.

————. *Recovering our English Baptist Heritage: Kiffin, Knollys, and Keach.* Leeds: Reformation Today Trust, 1996.

Haymes, Brian and Roger Hayden, editors. *Bible, History and Ministry*. Festschrift of Leonard Champion. Bristol: Bristol Baptist College, 1997.

Hopkins, Mark T. E. "The Downgrade Controversy: New Evidence [S. H. Booth Correspondence]." *Baptist Quarterly* 35 (1994): 262–78.

———. "Spurgeon's Opponents in the Downgrade Controversy." *Baptist Quarterly* 32 (1988): 274–94.

Hughes, Gordon W. "Robert Hall of Arnesby 1728–1791." *Baptist Quarterly* 10 (October 1941): 444–48.

Hughes, Graham W. *Robert Hall*. London: The Carey Press, 1943.

Ivimey, Joseph. *History of the English Baptists*. 4 volumes. London: Holdsworth, 1823.

James, Sharon. "Revival and Renewal in Baptist Life: The Contribution of William Steadman 1764–1837." *Baptist Quarterly* 37 (April 1998): 263–82.

Johnson, Dale A. *The Changing Shape of English Nonconformity, 1825–1925*. New York: Oxford University Press, 1999.

Kliever, Lonnie D. "General Baptist Origins: The Question of Anabaptist Influence." *Mennonite Quarterly Review* 36 (1962): 291–321.

Kirkby, Arthur H. "Andrew Fuller-Evangelical Calvinist." *Baptist Quarterly* 15/5 (January 1954): 195–202.

Land, Richard D. "Doctrinal Controversies of the English Particular Baptists 1644–1691, As Illustrated by the Career and Writings of Thomas Collier." D.Phil. dissertation, Oxford University, 1979.

Laws, Gilbert. "Andrew Fuller 1754–1815." *Baptist Quarterly* (1924–1925): 76–84.

Lawson, William W. "Robert and James Haldane." *Baptist Quarterly* 8 (1934–1935): 276–86.

Lord, F. Townley. "A Moderate Estimate of Calvinism." *Baptist Quarterly* (1928–1929): 82–89.

MacDonald, Murdina D. "London Calvinistic Baptists 1689–1727: Tensions Within a Dissenting Community Under Toleration." D. Phil. dissertation, Regent's Park College, Oxford University, 1982.

Manley, Ken R. "John Rippon D. D. (1751–1836) and the Particular Baptists." D.Phil. dissertation, Oxford University, 1967.

Marchant, James. *Dr. John Clifford, c.h.: Life, Letters, and Reminiscences*. London: Cassell and Co., 1924.

Maroney, Nina Reid. "Spurgeon and British Evangelical Theological Education." In *Theological Education in the Evangelical Tradition*. Edited by Albert Mohler. Grand Rapids: Baker Book House, 1996.

Mason, Rex. "H. Wheeler Robinson Revisited." *Baptist Quarterly* 37/5 (January 1998): 213–26.

Moon, Norman S. *Education for Ministry: Bristol Baptist College 1679–1979*. Bristol UK: Bristol Baptist College, 1979.

Murray, Derek. "The Scotch Baptist Tradition in Great Britain." *Baptist Quarterly* 33/4 (December 1987): 186–98.

Nichols, Michael. "The Downgrade Controversy: A Neglected Protagonist." *Baptist Quarterly* 32 (April 1988): 260–73.

Oliver, Robert W. "The Emergence of a Strict and Particular Baptist Community Among the English Calvinistic Baptists, 1770–1850." Ph.D. thesis, CNAA/London Bible College, 1986.

Payne, Ernest A. "Abraham Booth 1734–1806." *Baptist Quarterly* 26 (January 1975): 28–42.

———. *The Baptist Union: A Short History*. London: Carey Kingsgate, 1958.

———. "Dr. Dakin." *Baptist Quarterly* 23 (January 1970): 193–94.

———. *Free Churchmen, Unrepentant and Repentant, and Other Papers*. London: Carey Kingsgate Press, 1965.

———. *Henry Wheeler Robinson: Scholar, Teacher, Principal*. London: Nisbet, 1946.

———. "More About the Sabbatarian Baptists." *Baptist Quarterly* 14 (October 1951): 161–66.

Reid, Adam A. "Benjamin Keach, 1640." *Baptist Quarterly* 10 (April 1940): 77.

Rinaldi, F. W. "The Tribe of Dan: The New Connexion of General Baptists 1770–1891: A Study in the Transition from Revival Movement to Established Denomination." Ph.D. dissertation, University of Glasgow, 1996.

Robinson, O. C. "The Particular Baptists in England 1760–1820." D.Phil. dissertation, Oxford University, 1963.

Robinson, Theodore H. "Reminiscences of George Pearce Gould." *Baptist Quarterly* 9 (1938–1939): 311–13.

Robison, Olin C. "The Legacy of John Gill." *Baptist Quarterly* 24 (July 1971): 111–25.

Rushbrooke, J. H. "John Clifford: Pastor, Social Reformer, National Leader, First President, the Baptist World Alliance." *Baptist Quarterly* 11 (October 1944): 288–94.

Sadler, Lynn Veach. *John Bunyan*. Boston: Twayne Publishers, 1979.

Saito, Goki. "An Investigation into the Relationship between the Early English General Baptists and the Dutch Anabaptists." Th.D. dissertation, Southern Baptist Theological Seminary, 1974.

Sellers, Ian. "John Howard Hinton: Theologian." *Baptist Quarterly* 33 (July 1989): 123.

Seymour, R. E. "John Gill–Baptist Theologian." Ph.D. dissertation, University of Edinburgh, 1954.

Spears, W. E. "The Baptist Movement in England in the Late Seventeenth Century as Reflected in the Work and Thought of Benjamin Keach, 1640–1704." Ph.D. dissertation, University of Edinburgh, 1953.

Staughton, William. *Gill's Body of Practical and Doctrinal Divinity*. Philadelphia: n.p., 1810.

Steadman, Thomas. *Memoir of the Rev. William Steadman, D.D.* London: Thomas Ward and Co., 1838.

Sweatman, Kent E. "The Doctrines of Calvinism in the Preaching of Charles Haddon Spurgeon." Ph.D. dissertation, Southwestern Baptist Theological Seminary, 1998.

Vaughn, J. Barry. "Benjamin Keach." In *Baptist Theologians*. Edited by Timothy George and David S. Dockery. Nashville: Broadman Press, 1990

White, B. R. "John Pendarves, the Calvinistic Baptists, and the Fifth Monarchy." *Baptist Quarterly* 25 (April 1974): 251–72.

———. "Open and Closed Membership Among English and Welsh Baptists." *Baptist Quarterly* 24 (December 1972): 330–34.

————. "Samuel Eaton (d. 1639): Particular Baptist Pioneer." *Baptist Quarterly* 24 (January 1971): 10–21.

Waugh, Percival. "The New Dawn and the Rise of the Scotch Baptists." In *History of the Baptists in Scotland*. Edited by George Yuille. Glasgow: Baptist Union Publication Committee, 1926.

West, W. M. S. *To Be a Pilgrim: A Memoir of Ernest A Payne*. Guildford UK: Lutterworth, 1983.

BRITISH BAPTISTS — INSTITUTIONAL

Carter, A. C. *A Popular Sketch Historical and Biographical of the Midland Baptist College*. London: Kingsgate Press, 1925.

Green, Samuel. *Education for the Ministry, Being One of the Papers Read to the Baptist Union of England and Wales, At Its Annual Session in Northampton, September 1871*. London: Yates and Alexander, 1871.

————. *Inaugural Address of the President, the Rev. Samuel Green, B.A. September 1863*. London: J. Heaton & Son., 1863.

Greenhough, J. G. *Inaugural Address of Rev. J. G. Greenhough as Warden of Midland Baptist College 1892–1893*. Darby: Williams Printing, 1893.

Gummer, Selwyn. "Trosnant Academy." *Baptist Quarterly* 19 (1938–1939): 417–23.

Hayden, Roger. "Evangelical Calvinism among Eighteenth Century Baptists, with Particular Reference to Bernard Foskett, Hugh and Caleb Evans, and the Bristol Baptist Academy." Ph. D. dissertation, Keele University, 1991.

Johnson, E. H. *The Baptists of Wales and Ministerial Education: Also the Nonconformist Theological Colleges of Wales, etc*. London: Hughes and Son, 1902.

Kidd, Richard. "Northern Baptist College." *American Baptist Quarterly* 18 (June 1999): 94–105.

————., editor. *Something to Declare: A Study of the Declaration of Principle Jointly Written by the Principals of the Four English Colleges in Membership with the Baptist Union of Great Britain*. Oxford: Whitley Publications, 1996.

Payne, Ernest. "The Development of Nonconformist Theological Education in the Nineteenth Century, with Special Reference to Regent's Park College." In *Studies in History and Religion, Presented to Dr. H. Wheeler Robinson, M.A. on His Seventieth Birthday*. Edited by E. A. Payne. London: Lutterworth, 1942.

————. "Regent's Park College, Oxford: The First Half Century." *Baptist Quarterly* 27 (January 1978): 225–33.

Philpot, J. H. *The Seceders: The Story of a Spiritual Awakening as Told in the Letters of Joseph C. Philpot and William Tiptaft*. London: Farncombe, 1930.

Quicke, Michael J. and Ian M. Randall. "Spurgeon's College." *American Baptist Quarterly* 18 (June 1999): 118–31.

Rimmington, Gerald T. "L.H. Marshall's Ministry in Leicester 1930–1936." *Baptist Quarterly* 36 (October 1996): 404–412.

Roberts, R. Philip. "Andrew Fuller." In *Theologians of the Baptist Tradition*. Edited by Timothy George and David S. Dockery. Nashville: Broadman, Holman, 2001.

————. *Continuity and Change: London Particular Baptists and the Evangelical Revival 1760–1820*. Wheaton: Richard Owen Roberts, 1989.

Stroud, W. S. "John Clifford." *Baptist Quarterly* 6 (1932–1933): 304–311.

Thomas, J. Hobson. "Bunyan the Baptist." *Baptist Quarterly* 4 (1928): 97–103.

Thompson, David. "John Clifford's Social Gospel." *Baptist Quarterly* 31 (January 1986): 199–218.

Wilmott, A. E. *Greater Things: A Popular History of Spurgeon's College.* London: The College, n.d.

BRITISH BAPTISTS — THEOLOGICAL WORKS

Acworth, James. *The Scripture Doctrine of the Trinity, in A Circular Letter of the East and West Ridings of the Yorkshire Baptist Associations of Baptist Churches.* Bradford: Scarlett and Northgate, 1857.

Booth, Abraham. *An Apology for the Baptists.* London: E. and C. Dilly, 1778.

———. *The Reign of Grace, from Its Rise to Its Consummation.* Grand Rapids: Eerdmans, 1949.

———. *A Defense [sic] for the Baptists, Being A Declaration and a Vindication of Three Historically Distinctive Baptist Principles, Compiled & Set Forth in The Republishing of Three Books.* Paris AR: The Baptist Standard Bearer, 1985.

Bunyan, John. *The Works of John Bunyan with an Introduction to Each Treatise, Notes, and a Sketch of His Life, Times, and Contemporaries.* Edited by George Offor. 3 volumes. Edinburgh: Banner of Truth Trust, 1991.

———. *Differences in Judgment about Water-Baptism, No Bar to Communion.* London: John Wilkins, 1673.

———. *A Holy Life, The Beauty of Christianity or An Exhortation to Christians to be Holy.* London: Benjamin Alsop, 1684.

———. *Miscellaneous Works of John Bunyan.* Edited by Roger Sharrock. Volume 7. Oxford: Oxford University Press, 1989.

Campbell, John McLeod. *The Nature of the Atonement.* London: Macmillan 1869.

Carson, Alexander. "The Doctrine of the Atonement, set forth in an Address to the Public, on the Nature and Importance of the Gospel." In *The Works of the Rev. Alexander Carson, LL.D.* Volume 1. Dublin: William Carson, 1847.

———. *Baptism: Its Mode and Subjects Considered and a Reply to the Arguments of Mr. Ewing and Dr. Wardlaw Refuted.* Edinburgh: Waugh and Innes, 1831.

———. *The Works of the Rev. Alexander Carson, LL.D.* 5 volumes. Dublin: William Carson, 1852.

Clifford, John. *Battle of the Sacred Books.* London: E. Marlborough, 1888.

———. *The Inspiration and Authority of the Bible.* London: James Clarke, 1895.

———. *Is Life Worth Living: An Eightfold Answer.* London: E. Marlborough & Co., 1894.

Collier, Thomas. *Several Resolutions and Answers of Queries.* London, n.p., 1657.

Cramp, John M. "The Kingdom of Christ." In *Lectures for These Times.* London: Houlston and Stoneman, 1844.

Evans, Percy. *Infant Baptism Today.* London: Carey Kingsgate Press, 1948.

Fuller, Andrew. *The Complete Works of the Rev. Andrew Fuller: With a Memoir of His Life by Andrew Gunton Fuller.* 3 volumes. Revised, with additions by Joseph Belcher. Philadelphia: American Baptist Publication Society, 1845.

————. *Calvinistic and Socinian Systems Examined and Compared, as to Their Moral Tendency, in a Series of Letters, Addressed to the Friends of Vital and Practical Religion*. Boston: Lincoln & Edmunds, 1793.

————. *Strictures on Sandemanianism, in Twelve Letters to a Friend(!)*. Nottingham UK: C. Sutton, 1810.

Fuller, Andrew, and William Vidler. *Letters to Mr. Vidler on the Doctrine of Universal Salvation*. Boston: Manning & Loring, 1803.

Gotch, F. W. "The Inspiration of the Holy Scriptures." *A Discourse Delivered before the Bristol Association of Baptist Churches June 12, 1851*. London: Hamilton, Adams, 1851.

Gracey, David. *Precision in Doctrine: A Paper Read at the Baptist Union 1869*. London: n.p., 1869.

————. *Sin and the Unfolding of Salvation, Being the Three Years' Course of Theological Lectures Delivered at the Pastor's College, London*. London: Passmore and Alabaster, 1894.

Greenhough, J. G. *The Conduct of Public Worship*. London: Baptist Union, n.d.

Haldane, Robert. *Exposition of the Epistle to the Romans, with Remarks on the Commentaries of Dr. MacKnight, Professor Moses Stuart, and Professor Tholuck*. New York: Robert Carter & Brothers, 1857.

Hall, Robert. *Help to Zion's Travelers: Being an Attempt to Remove Various Stumbling-blocks Out of the Way Relating to Doctrinal, Experimental, and Practical Religion*. Boston: Lincoln and Edmands, 1824.

————. *Modern Infidelity, Considered with Respect to Its Influence on Society in a sermon preached at the Baptist Meeting in Cambridge*. Cambridge: privately published, 1799.

Helwys, Thomas. *A Short Declaration of the Mystery of Iniquity*. Edited by Richard Groves. Macon GA: Mercer University Press, 1998.

Hinton, John Howard. *The Test of Experience or The Voluntary Principle in the United States*. London: A. Cockshaw, 1851.

Keach, Benjamin. *Gospel Mysteries Unveiled*. London: n.p., 1701.

————. *A Medium Betwixt Two Extremes*. London: Andrew Bell, 1698.

McCaig, Archibald. *The Grand Old Book, Being Lectures on Inspiration and the Higher Criticism*. London: Russian Missionary Society, 1923.

————. *The Works of Mr. Archibald M'Lean, Late Pastor of the Baptist Church, Edinburgh, with a Memoir of His Life, Ministry, and Writings in Six Volumes*. Compiled by William Jones. London: William Jones, 1823.

Monck, Thomas. *A Cure for the Cankering Error of the New Eutychians Who (Concerning the Truth) Have Erred, Saying, That Our Blessed Mediator Did Not Take His Flesh of the Virgin Mary, Neither Was He Made of the Seed of David According to the Flesh, and thereby Have Overthrown the Faith of Some*. n.p., 1673.

Reynolds, H. R., editor. *Ecclesia: A Second Series of Essays on Theological and Ecclesiastical Questions*. London: Hodder and Stoughton, 1871.

Robinson, H. Wheeler. *The Life and Faith of the Baptists*. London: Methuen, 1927.

————. "The Principle of Authority in the Christian Religion." (Paper Read at Regent's Park College, 13th April 1942.) In Ernest A. Payne, *Henry Wheeler Robinson: Scholar, Teacher, Principal.* London: Nisbet, 1946.

Spurgeon, Charles H. *The Downgrade Controversy: Collected Materials Which Reveal the Viewpoint of the Late Charles Haddon Spurgeon.* Pasadena TX: Pilgrim Publications, n.d.

Taylor, Adam. *Memoirs of the Rev. Dan Taylor: Late Pastor of the General Baptist Church, Whitechapel, London, with Extracts from His Diary, Correspondence, and Unpublished Manuscripts.* London: Adam Taylor, 1820.

Taylor, Dan. *Universality of the Savior's Death: A Letter to the Churches.* London: n.p., 1796.

Tymms, T. Vincent. *The Christian Idea of Atonement.* London: Macmillan, 1904.

————. *First Principles of Christian: A Sermon Preached at the Downs Chapel, Clapton October 17, 1875.* London: Yates and Alexander, 1875.

————. *The Mystery of God: A Consideration of Some Intellectual Hindrances to Faith.* London: Elliot Stock, 1885.

AMERICAN BAPTISTS — BIOGRAPHICAL AND HISTORICAL

Barnhart, Joe E. *The Billy Graham Religion.* Philadelphia: Pilgrim Press, 1972.

Beebe, Gilbert. "Autobiography of Elder Gilbert Beebe." In *History of the Church of God, from the Creation to A.D. 1885; Including Especially the History of the Kehukee Primitive Baptist Association.* Edited by Cushing Biggs Hassell. Revised by Sylvester Hassell. Middletown: Gilbert Beebe's Sons, 1886.

Bicknell, Thomas W. "John Myles and Religious Toleration in Massachusetts." *Magazine of New England History* 2 (1892): 213–42.

Bonney, Katharine. "Harry Emerson Fosdick's Doctrine of Man." Ph.D. dissertation, Boston University, 1958.

Brackney, William H. "Nurseries of Piety or The School of Christ? Means and Models of Baptist Ministerial Education in Early America." In *Faith, Life and Witness: The Papers of the Study and Research Division of the Baptist World Alliance 1986–1990.* Edited by William H. Brackney, with Ruby J. Burke. Birmingham AL: Samford University Press, 1990.

————. "William Newton Clarke: A Canadian American Cross Cultural Experience." *McMaster Journal of Theology* 3 (Spring 1993): 62–81.

Bronson, Walter C. *The History of Brown University 1764–1914.* Providence RI: Brown University, 1914.

Burrage, Henry S. *History of the Baptists in Maine.* Portland ME: Marks Printing House, 1904.

Cauthen, Kenneth. *The Impact of American Religious Liberalism.* New York: Harper & Row, 1962.

Cherry, Conrad. *Hurrying Toward Zion: Universities, Divinity Schools, and American Protestantism.* Indianapolis: Indiana University Press, 1995.

Clarke, Emily A., editor. *William Newton Clarke, A Biography, with Additional Sketches by His Friends and Colleagues.* New York: Charles Scribner's Sons, 1916.

Clarke, William Newton. *Sixty Years with the Bible.* New York: Scribner's, 1909.

Clemons, Hardy. "The Key Theological Ideas of Harry Emerson Fosdick." Ph. D. dissertation, Southwestern Baptist Theological Seminary, 1966.

Coker, Joe L. "Sweet Harmony vs. Strict Separation: Recognizing the Distinctions between Isaac Backus and John Leland." *American Baptist Quarterly* 16 (September 1997): 241–49.

Davies, Hywel. *Transatlantic Brethren: Rev. Samuel Jones and His Friends: Baptists in Wales, Pennsylvania, and Beyond*. Bethlehem PA: Lehigh University Press, 1995.

Dockery, David S., editor. *New Dimensions in Evangelical Thought: Essays in Honor of Millard J. Erickson*. Downers Grove IL: Intervarsity Press, 1998.

Dodd, Charles H. "Ebenezer Dodge: Pioneer in Experiential Theology." *Crozer Quarterly* 2 (1925): 285.

Elton, Romeo. *The Literary Remains of the Rev. Jonathan Maxcy, D.D., with a Memoir of His Life*. New York: A. V. Blake, 1844.

Falwell, Jerry, editor, with Ed Dobson and Ed Hindson. *The Fundamentalist Phenomenon: The Resurgence of Conservative Christianity*. Garden City: Doubleday, 1981.

Gamwell, William. "Memoir of Alexus Caswell D.D., L.L.D.: Ex-President of Brown University." *New England Historical and Genealogical Register* (July 1877).

Gardner, Robert G. "John Leadley Dagg: Pioneer American Baptist Theologian." Ph.D. dissertation, Duke University, 1957.

Gaustad, Edwin S. *Baptist Piety: The Last Will and Testimony of Obadiah Holmes*. Grand Rapids: Eerdmans, 1978.

———. "The Backus Leland Tradition." *Foundations* 2 (April 1959): 131–52.

George, Timothy and David S. Dockery, editors. *Theologians of the Baptist Tradition*. Nashville: Broadman & Holman, 2001.

Gibson, Scott M. *A. J. Gordon: American Premillennialist*. Lanham MD: University Press of America. 2001.

Gordon, Ernest B. *Adoniram Judson Gordon: A Biography*. New York: Fleming H. Revell Co., 1896.

Hague, William. *Christian Greatness in the Scholar: A Discourse on the Life and Character of Rev. Irah Chase, D.D.* Boston: Gould and Lincoln, 1866.

Handy, Robert T. "Walter Rauschenbusch in Historical Perspective." *Baptist Quarterly* 20 (1964): 313–21.

Hanley, Robert B. "Henry Clay Vedder: Conservative Evangelical to Evangelical Liberal" *Foundations* 5 (April 1962): 135–57.

Hansen, James E. "Gallant, Stalwart Bennie: Elisha Benjamin Andrews 1844–1917: An Educator's Odyssey" Ph.D. dissertation, University of Denver, 1969.

Harper, Robert F., Francis Brown, and George F. Moore, editors. *Old Testament and Semitic Studies in Memory of William Rainey Harper*. Chicago: University of Chicago Press, 1908.

Henry, Carl F. H. *Personal Idealism and Strong's Theology*. Wheaton: Van Kampen Press, 1951.

———. "Twenty Years a Baptist." *Foundations* 1/1 (January 1958): 46–54.

Hopkins, Charles H. *The Rise of the Social Gospel in American Protestantism 1865–1915*. New Haven: Yale University Press, 1940.

Hovey, Alvah. *Barnas Sears: A Christian Educator, His Making and Work.* New York: Silver Burdette, 1902.

Hovey, G. R. *Alvah Hovey, His Life and Letters.* Philadelphia: Judson Press, 1928.

Howe, Claude. "The Theology of William Newton Clarke." Th.D. dissertation, New Orleans Baptist Theological Seminary, 1959.

James, Sydney V. *John Clarke and His Legacies: Religion and Law in Colonial Rhode Island 1638–1750.* University Park: Pennsylvania State University Press, 1998.

Johnson, E. H., editor. *Ezekiel Gilman Robinson: An Autobiography.* Boston: Silver Burdette, 1896.

Johnston, Robert K. "Clark Pinnock." In *Handbook of Evangelical Theologians.* Edited by Walter Elwell. Grand Rapids: Baker Books, 1993.

Kendrick, Nathaniel and Silas Kendrick. *Memoirs of Rev. Nathaniel Kendrick D.D. and Silas N. Kendrick.* Philadelphia: American Baptist Publication Society, 1860.

Lach, Edward, Jr. "Elisha Benjamin Andrews." In *Dictionary of American National Biography.* Volume 1. Edited by John A. Garraty and Mark C. Carnes. New York: Oxford University Press, 1999.

Lasher, George W. *George W. Eaton, D.D., L.L.D.: A Memorial.* Hamilton: Colgate University, 1913.

Lawson, Douglas. "The Idea of Progress in the Theology of Harry Emerson Fosdick." Ph.D. dissertation, Duke University, 1963.

Lewis, Walter O. "William Staughton." *Baptist Quarterly* 11 (July 1942): 74–78.

Lynd, S. W. *Memoir of the Rev. William Staughton D. D.* Boston: Lincoln and Edmunds, 1834.

MacIntosh, D. C. "Professor Clarke at Yale." In *William Newton Clarke, A Biography, with Additional Sketches by His Friends and Colleagues*, ed. Emily Clarke. New York: Charles Scribner's Sons, 1916.

Maring, Norman H. "Baptists and Changing Views of the Bible, 1865–1918, Part 1." *Foundations* 1 (July 1958): 52–75.

———. "Baptists and Changing Views of the Bible, Part 2." *Foundations* 1 (October 1958): 30–61.

———. "The Individualism of Francis Wayland." In *Baptist Concepts of the Church.* Edited by Winthrop S. Hudson. Philadelphia: The Judson Press, 1959.

Martin, William. *A Prophet with Honor: The Billy Graham Story.* New York: William Morrow, 1991.

MacDonald, Murdina. "A Bibliography of the Works of Bernard L. Ramm." *Perspectives in Religious Studies* 17 (Winter 1990): 87–101.

Marshall, I. Howard. "The Problem of Apostasy in the New Testament." *Perspectives in Religious Studies* 14 (Winter 1987): 65–80.

McKibbens, Thomas R. and Kenneth L. Smith. *The Life and Works of Morgan Edwards.* New York: Arno Press, 1980.

McLoughlin, William G. *Isaac Backus and the American Pietistic Tradition.* Boston: Little, Brown, 1967.

———. *New England Dissent 1600–1833: The Baptists and the Separation of Church and State.* 2 volumes. Cambridge: Harvard University Press, 1971.

Miller, David W. "The Theological System of Bernard L. Ramm." Ph.D. dissertation, Southwestern Baptist Theological Seminary, 1982.

Miller, Robert Moats. *Harry Emerson Fosdick: Preacher, Pastor, Prophet.* New York: Oxford University Press, 1985.

Minus, Paul M. *Walter Rauschenbusch: American Reformer.* New York : Macmillan, 1988.

Mohler, Albert. "Carl F. H. Henry." In *Baptist Theologians.* Edited by Timothy George and David S. Dockery. Nashville: Broadman Press, 1990.

Mouw, Richard J. "Ethics and Story: A Review Article." *The Reformed Journal* 37 (July 1987): 22–27.

Nelson, Rudolph. *The Making and Unmaking of an Evangelical Mind: The Case of Edward Carnell.* Cambridge: Cambridge University Press, 1987.

Newman, Albert H. "Recent Changes in the Theology of Baptists." *American Journal of Theology* VI:3 (October 1906): 587–609.

Nixon, Justin W. and Winthrop S. Hudson, editors. *Christian Leadership in a World Society: Essays in Honor of Conrad Henry Moehlman.* Rochester: Colgate Rochester Divinity School, 1945.

Patterson, Bob E. *Makers of the Modern Theological Mind: Carl F. H. Henry.* Waco: Word Books, 1983.

Proceedings of the Baptist Congress, 1881–1912. Various publishers.

Rosas, L. Joseph, III. "Edward John Carnell." In *Baptist Theologians.* Edited by Timothy George and David S. Dockery. Nashville: Broadman Press, 1990.

Roennfeldt, Ray C. W. "Clark H. Pinnock's Shift in His Doctrine of Biblical Authority and Reliability: An Analysis and Critique." Ph.D. dissertation, St. Andrews University, 1990.

Russell, C. Allyn. *Voices of American Fundamentalism: Seven Biographical Studies.* Philadelphia: Westminster Press, 1976.

Seventh Day Baptists in Europe and America: A Series of Historical Papers Written in Commemoration of the One Hundredth Anniversary of the Organization of the Seventh Day Baptist General Conference, Celebrated at Ashaway, Rhode Island, August 20–25, 1902. 3 volumes. Plainfield NJ: American Sabbath Tract Society, 1910.

Sharp, Larry Dean. "Carl Henry: Neo-Evangelical Theologian." Ph.D. dissertation, Vanderbilt University, 1972.

Sillen, J. Walter. "William H. P. Faunce: A Representative Religious Liberal." *Foundations* 2 (July 1959): 235–49.

Smith, Kenneth L. and Ira Zepp. *Search for the Beloved Community: The Thinking of Martin Luther King, Jr.* Valley Forge: Judson Press, 1974.

Smith, Kenneth L. and Leonard Sweet. "Shailer Mathews: A Chapter in the Social Gospel Movement: Part 1." *Foundations* 18 (July–August 1975): 219–37.

———. "Shailer Mathews: A Chapter in the Social Gospel Movement: Part 2." *Foundations* 18/4 (October–December 1975): 296–320.

———. "Shailer Mathews: A Chapter in the Social Gospel Movement: Part 3: Sin and Salvation" *Foundations* 19 (January–March 1976): 53–68.

————. "Shailer Mathews: A Chapter in the Social Gospel Movement: Part 4: The Kingdom and the Church." *Foundations* 19 (April–June 1976): 152–70.

Stone, Edwin Martin. *Biography of Rev. Elhanan Winchester*. Boston: H. B. Brewster, 1836.

Sweeny, Joseph R. "Elhanan Winchester and the Universal Baptists." Ph.D. dissertation, University of Pennsylvania, 1969.

Taylor, Jeff. "For Their Rock Is Not as Our Rock; Primitive Baptist Self-Definition During the Crucial Years of Movement Formation, 1832–1848." Ph.D. dissertation, Baylor University, 2000.

Thomas, Gerald. "James Deotis Roberts." In *Baptist Theologians*. Edited by Timothy George and David S. Dockery. Nashville: Broadman Press, 1990.

Thornbury, Gregory. "Augustus Hopkins Strong." In *Theologians of the Baptist Tradition*. Edited by Timothy George and David S. Dockery. Nashville: Broadman & Holman, 2001.

Tinder, Donald G. "Fundamentalist Baptists in the Northern and Western United States, 1920–1950." Ph.D. dissertation, Yale University, 1969.

Torbet, Robert G. "Baptist Thought About the Church." *Foundations* 1/2 (April 1958): 18–37.

————. *Venture of Faith" The Story of the American Baptist Foreign Mission Society and the Women's American Baptist Foreign Mission Society 1814–1955*. Philadelphia: Judson Press, 1955.

Wacker, Grant. *Augustus Hopkins Strong and the Dilemma of Historical Consciousness*. Macon GA: Mercer University Press, 1985.

Wayland, Francis and H. L. Wayland. *A Memoir of the Life and Labors of Francis Wayland, D.D., L.L.D., Late President of Brown University*. New York: Sheldon and Co., 1867.

Weaver, Samuel. "The Theology and Times of Harry Emerson Fosdick." Ph.D. dissertation, Princeton Theological Seminary, 1961.

Witte, John, Jr. "The Theology and Politics of The First Amendment Religion Clauses: A Bicentennial Essay." *Emory Law Journal* (1991): 490–507.

AMERICAN BAPTISTS — INSTITUTIONAL

DeBlois, Austen K. "Newton Men in Education." *Historical Addresses Delivered at the Newton Centennial, June, 1925*. Newton Centre: The Institution Bulletin, 1925. 42–63.

Guild, Reuben Aldridge. *Early History of Brown University, Including the Life, Times, and Correspondence of President Manning 1756–1791*. Providence RI: Snow and Farnham, 1896.

Handy, Robert T. *A History of Union Theological Seminary in New York*. New York: Columbia University Press, 1987.

Harvey, Hezekiah. "Foreign Mission Work of Madison University." In *The First Half Century of Madison University (1819–1860) or the Jubilee Volume Containing Sketches of Eleven Hundred Living and Deceased Alumni; with Fifteen Portraits of Founders, Presidents, and Patrons*. Edited by Benjamin F. Bronson and Jirah D. Cole. New York: Sheldon & Co., 1872.

Herrick, Everett Carlton. *Turns Home Again*. Boston: Pilgrim Press, 1949.

Hovey, Alvah. "Newton from 1875 to 1900." *The Newtonian* 1/2 (June 1903): 47.

Kayser, Elmer Louis. *Bricks Without Straw: The Evolution of George Washington University*. New York: Appleton-Century-Crofts, 1970.

Lawrence, William Mangam. "Historical Address-Colgate University—October 10, 1919." In *The Colgate University Centennial Celebration 1819–1919*. Hamilton: Colgate University, 1920.

Marriner, Ernest Cummings. *The History of Colby College*. Waterville ME: Colby College Press, 1962.

Miller, Glenn T. *Piety And Intellect: The Aims and Purposes of Ante-Bellum Theological Education*. Atlanta: Scholars Press, 1990.

Neisser, Rittenhouse. "Crozer At the Dawn of the Century." *The Chronicle* 7 (July 1944): 121.

"The Removal of Prof. Gould." (An editorial.) *The National Baptist* (October 19, 1882): 661.

"Report of the Seventy-Sixth Anniversary of the American Baptist Missionary Union." *Baptist Missionary Magazine* 70 (July 1890): 176.

Short, Kenneth R. M. "Baptist Training for the Ministry: The Francis Wayland-Barnas Sears Debate of 1853." *Foundations* 11 (July–Sept. 1968): 227–34.

Stone, Desmond. "Save Face or Save Faith: The Big Debate 'Up on The Hill.'" *The Colgate Rochester Divinity School Bulletin* 38 (December 1965): 1–2.

"The Story of Practical Theology at Crozer, 1924–1947." *The Voice: Crozer Centennial Issue III*. 60 (July 1968): 5.

Vichert, John F. "What Have We a Right to Expect from Our Theological Seminaries?" *Watchman Examiner* 10 (November 16, 1922): 1475.

Vaughan, Richard M. "Turns in the Road" *The Andover Newton Theological School Bulletin,* (1940): 9.

"William Hamilton Resigns Post at Colgate Rochester." *The Colgate Rochester Divinity School Bulletin* 39 (June 1967): 1.

Williams, Daniel Day. *The Andover Liberals: A Study in American Theology*. New York: Octagon Books, 1970.

Williams, Howard D. *A History of Colgate University*. New York: Van Nostrand Reinhold, 1969.

AMERICAN BAPTISTS—THEOLOGICAL WORKS

Aubrey, Edwin E. *Living the Christian Faith*. New York: Macmillan, 1939.

———. *Man's Search for Himself*. Nashville: Cokesbury, 1940.

———. *Present Theological Tendencies*. New York: Harper Brothers, 1936.

———. *Secularism a Myth: An Examination of the Current Attack on Secularism*. New York: Harper Brothers, 1953.

Altizer, Thomas J. J. and William Hamilton. *Radical Theology and the Death of God*. New York: Bobbs-Merrill, 1966.

Backus, Isaac. *Church History of New England*. Philadelphia: Baptist Tract Repository, 1839.

————. *A History of New England with Particular Reference to the Denomination of Christians Called Baptists*. 2nd edition. Edited with notes by David Weston. Newton MA: The Backus Historical Society, 1871.

————. *Isaac Backus on Church, State, and Calvinism: Pamphlets*. Edited by William G. McLoughlin. Cambridge: The Belknap Press, 1968.

Baldwin, Thomas. *The Baptism of Believers Only, and The Particular Communion of the Baptist Churches Explained and Vindicated in Three Parts*. Boston: Manning and Loring, 1791.

Benedict, David. *Fifty Years Among the Baptists*. New York: Sheldon, 1860.

Carnell, Edward J. *The Burden of Soren Kierkegaard*. Grand Rapids: Eerdmans, 1965.

————. *The Case for Orthodox Theology*. Philadelphia: Westminster, 1959.

Cathcart, William. *The Papal System*. Philadelphia: Griffith and Rowland Press, 1872.

Chase, Irah. *Infant Baptism: an Invention of Men, or Dr. Bushnell's Arguments Reviewed*. Philadelphia: American Baptist Publication Society, 1863.

————. *The Design of Baptism, Viewed in its Relation to the Christian Life*. Boston: Gould and Lincoln: 1851.

————. *The Work Claiming to be The Constitutions and Canons of the Holy Apostles, including the Canons; Whiston's Version, revised from the Greek Translated by Irah Chase*. New York: D. Appleton & Co., 1848.

Clarke, John. *Ill Newes from New-England, or, A Narative of New-Englands Persecution wherin Is Declared That While Old England Is Becoming New, New-England is Become Old*. London: Henry Hills, 1652.

Clarke, William Newton. *The Christian Doctrine of God*. New York: Charles Scribner's Sons, 1909.

————. *Sixty Years with the Bible*. New York: Charles Scribner's, 1917.

————. *The Use of the Scriptures in Theology*. New York: Charles Scribner's Sons, 1906.

————. *What Shall We Think of Christianity?* Edinburgh: T & T Clark, 1899.

Cross, George. *Christian Salvation: A Modern Interpretation*. Chicago: University of Chicago Press, 1925.

————. *Creative Christianity: A Study of the Genius of The Christian Faith*. New York: MacMillan Co., 1922.

Davis, George W. "In Praise of Liberalism." *Theology Today* 4 (January 1948): 487.

————. "Liberalism and a Theology of Depth" *Crozer Quarterly* 28 (July 1951): 193-211.

DeBlois, Austen Kennedy. *Evangelism in the New Age*. Philadelphia: Judson Press, 1933.

Eaton, George W. *The Duty and Rewards of Original Thinking*. Hamilton: S. C. Griggs, 1847.

Edwards, Morgan. *The Customs of the Primitive Churches, or a Set of Propositions Relative to the Name, Materials, Constitution of a Church*. Philadelphia: Andrew Stuart, 1768.

————. *Two Academical Exercises on Subjects Bearing the Following Titles: Prescience, God's Purpose. Predestination, Election, Reprobation, Regeneration, Conversion, Holy Lump, Delivered in 1742 and 1743*. Philadelphia: Dobson & Lang, 1788.

Enslin, Morton Scott. *Christian Beginnings*. New York: Harper and Brothers, 1938.

———. *From Jesus to Christianity*. Boston: Beacon Press, 1964.

Falwell, Jerry. *Listen, America!* Garden City: Doubleday & Co., 1980.

———. *Strength for the Journey: An Autobiography*. New York: Simon and Schuster, 1987.

Faunce, William Herbert Perry. "The Appeal of Christ to Men." *Proceedings of the Baptist Congress, 1906*, 166.

———. *The Educational Ideal In Ministry: The Lyman Beecher Lectures at Yale University in the Year 1908*. New York: The Macmillan Co., 1908.

———. *What Does Christianity Mean?* New York: Fleming H. Revell Co., 1912.

Fosdick, Harry Emerson. *The Living of These Days: An Autobiography*. New York: Harper & Brothers, 1956.

Furman, Richard. *America's Deliverance and Duty: A Sermon Preached at the First Baptist Church of Charleston, on the Fourth Day of July, 1802*. Charleston: privately printed. 1802.

Goodchild, Frank M. "The Spirit and Purpose of the Fundamentalists." *Watchman Examiner* 10/9 (March 2, 1922): 267.

Gordon, A. J. *The Holy Spirit in Missions*. New York: Fleming H. Revell, 1893.

———. *The Ministry of the Spirit*. Philadelphia: American Baptist Publication Society, 1894.

———. *The Twofold Life*. Boston: Howard Gannett, 1882.

———. "Modern Evangelism." In "Minutes and Proceedings of the First Annual Autumnal Conference Held at Brooklyn, New York, 1882." Typescript, American Baptist Historical Society.

Gould, Ezra P. "A Christocentric Theology." *The National Baptist* (October 12, 1882): 644.

———. "Is God Love?" *The National Baptist* (October 12, 1882): 641.

Graham, Billy. *Peace with God*. New York: Doubleday Publishers, 1953.

Grenz, Stanley. *Theology for the Community of God*. Nashville: Broadman & Holman, 1994.

Grenz, Stanley, and John R. Franke. *Beyond Foundationalism: Shaping Theology in a Post-Modern Context*. Louisville: John Knox Press, 2001.

Hamilton, William H. *The Christian Man*. Philadelphia: The Westminster Press, 1956.

———. "The Ecumenical Responsibility of the Baptists." *Foundations* 1 (April 1958): 75–77.

———. *The New Essence of Christianity*. New York: Association Press, 1966.

Harvey, Hezekiah. *The Church: Its Polity and Ordinances*. Philadelphia: American Baptist Publication Society, 1879.

Henry, Carl. F. H. *Confessions of a Theologian: An Autobiography*. Waco: Word Books, 1983.

———. *The Uneasy Conscience of Modern Fundamentalism*. Grand Rapids: Eerdmans, 1947.

Hovey, Alvah. "What Was the Fruit of the Vine Which Jesus Gave His Disciples at the Institution of the Supper?" *Baptist Quarterly Review* 9 (1887): 302–303.

Jones, Samuel. *The Doctrine of the Covenants. A Sermon Preached at Pennepack in Pennsylvania, September 14, 1781.* Philadelphia: F. Bailey, 1782.

Laws, Curtis Lee. "Just What Is Fundamentalism?" *Watchman Examiner* 10 (March 2, 1922): 261.

McNutt, William Roy. *Polity and Practice in Baptist Churches.* Philadelphia: Judson Press, 1933.

Nixon, Justin Wroe. "My Forty Five Years in the Ministry." *Colgate Rochester Divinity School Bulletin* 26 (May 1954): 14–15.

Northrup, George W. "The Fatherhood of God." *American Journal of Theology* 5 (July 1901): 473–95.

Parker, Daniel. *A Public Address to the Baptist Society and Friends of Religion in General, on the Principles and Practices of the Baptist Board of Foreign Missions.* Vincennes IN: Stout and Osborn, 1820.

————. *Views on the Two Seeds, Taken from Genesis 3d Chapter, and Part of the 15th Verse.* Vandalia IL: Robert Blackwell, 1826.

Pinnock, Clark. *Evangelism and Truth.* Tigerville SC: Jewel, 1969.

————. *Flame of Love: A Theology of the Holy Spirit.* Downers Grove IL: Intervarsity Press, 1996.

————. "Parameters of Biblical Inerrancy." In *Proceedings of the Conference on Biblical Inerrancy (1987: Ridgecrest, N. C.).* Nashville: Broadman Press, 1987.

————. *Set Forth Your Case: Studies in Christian Apologetics.* Nutley NJ: The Craig Press, 1968.

————. *Three Keys to Spiritual Renewal.* Minneapolis: Bethany Press, 1985.

Pressler, [Judge] Paul. *A Hill on Which To Die: One Southern Baptist's Journey.* Nashville: Broadman & Holman, 1999.

Ramm, Bernard. *The Christian View of Science and Scripture.* Grand Rapids: Eerdmans, 1955.

————. *An Evangelical Christology: Ecumenic and Historic.* Nashville: Thomas Nelson Publishers, 1985.

————. *After Fundamentalism: The Future of Evangelical Theology.* San Francisco: Harper & Row, 1983.

————. "Helps from Karl Barth." In *How Karl Barth Changed My Mind.* Edited by Donald McKim. Grand Rapids: Eerdmans, 1986.

————. *Offense to Reason: A Theology of Sin.* New York: Harper and Row, 1985.

————. *Protestant Biblical Interpretation: A Textbook of Hermeneutics for Conservative Protestants.* Boston: W. A. Wilde, 1956.

Rauschenbusch, Walter. *Christianity and the Social Crisis.* New York: Macmillan, 1907.

————. *A Theology for the Social Gospel.* New York: Macmillan, 1917.

————. *Walter Rauschenbusch: Selected Writings.* Edited by Winthrop S. Hudson. New York: Paulist Press, 1984.

Robinson, Ezekiel Gilman. "The Relation of the Bible to the Church." In *Madison Avenue Lectures,* 387–419. Philadelphia: American Baptist Publication Society, 1867.

Smith, Elias. *The Life, Conversion, Preaching, Travels, and Sufferings of Elias Smith.* Portsmouth: Beck and Foster, 1816.

Strong, Augustus H. *Autobiography of Augustus Hopkins Strong*. Edited by Crerar Douglas. Valley Forge: Judson Press, 1981.

————. *Christ in Creation and Ethical Monism*. Philadelphia: The Roger Williams Press, 1899.

————. *Miscellanies*. 2 volumes. Philadelphia: Griffith and Rowland Press, 1912.

————. *Philosophy and Religion*. New York: A. C. Armstrong, 1888.

————. *The Present Outlook in Theology*. Louisville: Southern Baptist Theological Seminary, 1909.

Strong, A. H. and Mullins, E. Y. *Forty Years of Progress in Theology: Upon the Retirement of President Augustus H. Strong*. Rochester: Rochester Theological Seminary, 1912.

Tillman, Thomas. *The Fourth Principle of Christian Religion, or, The Foundation Doctrine of Laying on of Hands Asserted and Vindicated by Way of Answer to Such Arguments as by Lieutenant Colonel Paul Hobson Have Been Presented against This Gospel Ordinance*. London: Printed by E.C. for Henry Eversden, and are to be sold by William Hucheson of Durham, 1655.

Vaughan, Richard M. "Changes I Have Seen in Theological Thought." *The Andover Newton Theological School Bulletin* (1940): 11.

————. "The Meaning of History." *The Andover Newton Theological School Bulletin* (1940): 15.

Vedder, Henry C. "Evolution and Its Contribution to Religious Thinking: The Matriculation Address for 1923." *Bulletin of Crozer Theological Seminary* 15 (October 1923): 128.

————. "My Teaching on the Atonement." *The Baptist* (November 20, 1920): 1471.

————. "What I Teach about the Bible." *The Baptist* (October 23, 1920): 1357-1358.

Vichert, John F. "Fears and Hopes of a Fundamentalist." *Watchman Examiner* 10 (March 2, 1922): 266–67.

Wayland, Francis. *Occasional Discourses, Including Several Never before Published*. Boston: James Loring, 1833.

————. *Salvation by Christ*. Boston: n.p., 1859.

————. *The Limitations of Human Responsibility*. Boston: Gould, Kendall, and Lincoln, 1838.

THE CHICAGO SCHOOL

Arnold, Charles Harvey. *Near the Edge of Battle: A Short History of the Divinity School and the "Chicago School of Theology" 1866–1966*. Chicago: Divinity School Association, 1966.

Berthold, Fred, and Bernard E. Meland, editors. *The Future of Empirical Theology*. Chicago: University of Chicago Press, 1969.

Case, Shirley Jackson. *The Christian Philosophy of History*. Chicago: University of Chicago Press, 1943.

————. *The Historicity of Jesus: A Criticism of the Contention That Jesus Never Lived, a Statement of the Evidence for His Existence, an Estimate of His Relation to Christianity*. Chicago: University of Chicago Press, 1912.

————. "Professor Parsons as a Graduate Student." *The Colgate Rochester Divinity School Bulletin* 13 (May 1941): 137–40.

————. "The Premillennial Menace." *Biblical World* 52 (1918): 17.

————. "The Religious Meaning of the Past." *Journal of Religion* 4 (1924): 576–91.

Foster, George B. *The Finality of the Christian Religion.* Chicago: University of Chicago Press, 1906.

Greenfield, Larry L. "Gerald Birney Smith." In *The Early Chicago School, 1906–1959: G. B. Foster, E. S. Ames, S. Mathews, G. B. Smith, S. J. Case.* Volume 1. Edited by Creighton Peden and Jerome Stone. The Chicago School of Theology—Pioneers in Religious Inquiry series. Lewiston: Edward Mellen Press, 1996.

————. "The Theology of Gerald Birney Smith." Ph.D. dissertation, University of Chicago, 1978.

Hynes, William J. *Shirley Jackson Case and the Chicago School: The Socio-Historical Method.* Chicago: Scholars Press, 1981.

Jennings, Louis B. *The Bibliography and Biography of Shirley Jackson Case.* Chicago: University of Chicago Press, 1949.

————. "Shirley Jackson Case: A Study in Methodology." Ph.D. dissertation, University of Chicago, 1944.

Johnson, Hjalmar W. "The Religious Thought of George B. Foster." Ph. D. dissertation, Yale University, 1931.

Krumbine, Miles H., editor. *The Process of Religion: Essays in Honor of Dean Shailer Mathews.*

Mathews, Shailer. "Professor Robbins as a Thinker." *The Colgate Rochester Divinity School Bulletin* 13 (May 1941): 116–20.

Meland, Bernard, editor. *The Future of Empirical Theology.* Chicago: University of Chicago Press, 1969.

————. "Introduction: The Empirical Tradition in Theology at Chicago." In *The Future of Empirical Theology.* Edited by Fred Berthold and Bernard E. Meland. Chicago: University of Chicago Press, 1969.

————, editor. *Theology as an Empirical Science.* Chicago: University of Chicago Press, 1969.

McNeill, John Thomas, Mathew Spinka, and Harold R. Willoughby, editors. *Environmental Factors in Christian History.* Chicago: University of Chicago Press, 1939.

Murray, Leslie A. "Shailer Mathews: Introduction." In *The Chicago School of Theology—Pioneers in Religious Inquiry.* Volume 1. Edited by Creighton Peden and Jerome Stone. The Chicago School of Theology—Pioneers in Religious Inquiry series. Lewiston: Edward Mellen Press, 1996.

Peden, Creighton. *The Chicago School: Voices in Liberal Religious Thought.* Bristol IN: Wyndham Hall Press, 1987.

Shuler, Claude Martin. "An Interpretation and Evaluation of the Work of Shirley Jackson Case as a Historian of Early Christianity." Th.D. dissertation, The Iliff School of Theology, 1964.

Smith, Gerald Birney. "The Task and Method of Systematic Theology." *American Journal of Theology* 14/2 (April 1910): 215–32.

————. "Christianity and the Spirit of Democracy." *The American Journal of Theology* 21/3 (July 1917): 347.

Stackhouse, Perry J. *Chicago and the Baptists: A Century of Progress.* Chicago: University of Chicago Press, 1933.

Towne, Edgar A. "George Burman Foster: Introduction." In *The Chicago School of Theology—Pioneers in Religious Inquiry.* Volume 1. Edited by Creighton Peden and Jerome Stone. The Chicago School of Theology—Pioneers in Religious Inquiry series. Lewiston: Edward Mellen Press, 1996.

————. "A Single-minded Theologian: George Burman Foster at Chicago, Part 1." *Foundations* 20/1 (January 1977): 163–80.

THE SOUTHERN BAPTIST THEOLOGICAL TRADITION

Baker, Robert P. *Tell the Generations Following: A History of Southwestern Baptist Theological Seminary 1908–1983.* Nashville: Broadman Press, 1983.

————. *Adventure in Faith: The First Three Hundred Years of First Baptist Church, Charleston, South Carolina.* Nashville: Broadman Press, 1982.

Barnes, William Wright. *The Southern Baptist Convention: A Study in the Development of Ecclesiology.* Seminary Hill: by the author, 1934.

Bogard, Ben M., editor. *The Baptist Way-Book: A Manual Designed for Use in Baptist Churches.* Texarkana: Baptist Sunday School Committee, 1946.

Boles, John B. *The Great Revival, 1787–1805: Origins of the Southern Evangelical Mind.* Lexington: University Press of Kentucky, 1972.

Broadus, John A. *Memoir of James Petigru Boyce, D.D., LL.D.* New York: A. C. Armstrong, 1893.

Bruce, Dickson. *And They All Sang Hallelujah: Plain-Folk Camp-Meeting Religion, 1800–1845.* Knoxville: University of Tennessee Press, 1974.

Burkitt, Lemuel and Jesse Read. *A Concise History of the Kehukee Baptist Association, from Its Original Rise Down to 1803.* Philadelphia: Lippincott, Grambo, and Co., 1850.

Carroll, J. M. *The Trail of Blood: Following the Christians Down Through the Centuries, or The History of Baptist Churches from the Time of Christ, Their Founder, to the Present Day.* Lexington KY: Ashland Avenue Baptist Church, 1931.

Cox, Joseph P. "A Study of the Life and Work of Basil Manly, Jr." Ph.D dissertation, Southern Baptist Theological Seminary, 1954.

Crawford, T. P. *Evolution in My Mission Views.* Fulton KY: J. A. Scarboro, 1903.

Criswell, W. A. *Why I Preach the Bible Is Literally True.* Nashville: Broadman Press, 1969.

Dever, Mark E. "Representative Aspects of the Theologies of John L. Dagg and James P. Boyce: Reformed Theology and Southern Baptists." Th.M. thesis, Southern Baptist Theological Seminary, 1987.

Dilday, Russell. "Mullins the Theologian: Between the Extremes." *Review and Expositor* 96 (1999): 75–86.

Duncan, Pope A. "Crawford Howell Toy: Heresy at Louisville." In *American Religious Heretics: Formal and Informal Trials In American Protestantism.* Edited by George R. Schriver. Nashville: Abingdon Press, 1966.

Dunn, James. "Church, State, and Soul Competency." *Review and Expositor* 96 (1999): 61–73.

Early, Joseph E., Jr. "The Haydenite Controversy: A Detailed Examination of the First Major Internal Altercation of the Baptist General Convention of Texas." Ph.D. dissertation, Southwestern Baptist Theological Seminary, 2002.

Eighmy, John Lee. *Churches in Cultural Captivity: A History of the Social Attitudes of Southern Baptists with an Introduction and Epilogue by Samuel S. Hill.* Knoxville: University of Tennessee Press, 1972.

Elliott, Ralph H. *The Genesis Controversy and Continuity in Southern Baptist Chaos: A Eulogy for a Great Tradition.* Macon GA: Mercer University Press, 1992.

Ellis, William E. *A Man of Books and a Man of the People: E. Y. Mullins and the Crisis of Moderate Southern Baptist Leadership.* Macon GA: Mercer University Press, 1985.

Freeman, Curtis W. "Can Baptist Theology Be Revisioned?" *Perspectives in Religious Studies* 24 (Fall 1997): 273–310.

Freeman, Curtis W. "E. Y. Mullins and the Siren Songs of Modernity" *Review and Expositor* 96 (Winter 1999): 23–42.

Garrett, James Leo, E. Glenn Hinson, and James E. Tull, editors. *Are Southern Baptists "Evangelicals"?* Macon GA: Mercer University Press, 1983.

George, Timothy. "Systematic Theology at Southern Seminary." *Review and Expositor* 82 (Winter 1985): 31–47.

Graves, James R. *Old Landmarkism: What Is It?* Memphis: Baptist Book House, 1880.

Hassell, Cushing Biggs, and Sylvester Hassell. *History of the Church of God, from the Creation to A.D. 1885; Including Especially The History of the Kehukee Primitive Baptist Association.* Middletown NY: Gilbert Beebe's Sons, 1886.

Hinson, E. Glenn. "Dale Moody: Bible Teacher Extraordinaire." *Perspectives in Religious Studies* 14 (Winter 1987): 3–17.

————. "E. Y. Mullins as Interpreter of the Baptist Tradition." *Review and Expositor* 96 (Winter 1999): 109–122.

Holifield, E. Brooks *The Gentlemen Theologians: American Theology in Southern Culture 1795–1860.* Durham: Duke University Press, 1978.

Hurt, Billy G. "Crawford H. Toy as Interpreter of the Old Testament." Ph.D. dissertation, Southern Baptist Theological Seminary, 1965.

Johnson, William Bullein. "The Southern Baptist Convention, To the Brethren in the United States; to the congregations connected with the respective churches; and to all candid men." In *Proceedings of the First Triennial Meeting of the Southern Baptist Convention Held in Richmond, Virginia 1846.*

Kendall, Robert T. "The Rise and Demise of Calvinism in the Southern Baptist Convention." M.A. thesis, University of Louisville, 1973.

Lampkin, Adrian. "The Gospel Mission Movement." Ph.D. dissertation, Southern Baptist Theological Seminary, 1980.

Manly, Basil, Jr. *The Bible Doctrine of Inspiration, Explained and Vindicated.* New York: A. C. Armstrong, 1888.

Manley, James M. "The Southern Baptist Mind in Transition: A Life of Basil Manly, Jr. 1825–1892." Ph.D. dissertation, University of Florida, 1999.

Martinez, Salvador T. "Southern Baptist Views of the Scriptures in Light of the Elliott Controversy." Th.M. thesis, Southern Baptist Theological Seminary, 1966.

McCall, Duke K. *What Is the Church?* Nashville: Broadman Press, 1958.

Mims, James S. *Orthodoxy: An Address Delivered Before the Board of Trustees of the Furman Theological Institution, on the day of the Annual Commencement, June 19, 1848.* Columbia SC: I. C. Morgan, 1848.

Mohler, R. Albert, Jr. "Baptist Theology at the Crossroads: The Legacy of E. Y. Mullins." *The Southern Baptist Journal of Theology* 3 (Winter 1999).

————. "Evangelical Theology and Karl Barth: Representative Models of Response." Ph.D. dissertation, Southern Baptist Theological Seminary, 1989.

Moody, Dale. *Baptism: Foundation for Christian Unity.* Grand Rapids: Eerdmans, 1967.

————. "The Crux of Christian Theology." *Review and Expositor* 46 (1949): 164–80.

————. *The Hope of Glory.* Grand Rapids: Eerdmans, 1964.

————. "Perspectives on Scripture and Tradition: A Response by Dale Moody." *Perspectives in Religious Studies* 15 (Spring 1988): 5–16.

Mueller, William A. *A History of Southern Baptist Theological Seminary.* Nashville: Broadman Press, 1959.

Mullins, E. Y. "Is Jesus Christ the Author of Religious Experience?" *The Baptist Review and Expositor* 1/1 (April 1904): 69.

————. "On Religious Experience." *Annual Session of the Baptist Congress for the Discussion of Current Questions, Held in Broadway Baptist Church, Louisville, Kentucky November 8, 9, 10, 1904.* New York: Baptist Congress Publishing Co., 1905.

————. "The Testimony of Christian Experience." *The Southern Baptist Journal of Theology* 3 (Winter 1999): 84.

————. "The Theological Trend." In *Proceedings of the Baptist World Congress* 1905. London: Baptist Union Publication Department, 1905), 145-153.

Mullins, Isla May. *Edgar Young Mullins: An Intimate Biography.* Nashville: Sunday School Board, 1929.

Nettles, Tom. *By His Grace and for His Glory: A Historical, Theological, and Practical Study of the Doctrines of Grace in Baptist Life.* Grand Rapids: Baker Books, 1986.

Norman, R. Stanton. *More Than Just a Name: Preserving Our Baptist Identity.* Nashville: Broadman & Holman, 2001.

Patterson, T. A. "The Theology of J. R. Graves and Its Influence on Southern Baptist Life." Th.D. dissertation, Southwestern Baptist Theological Seminary, 1944.

Richards, W. Wiley. *Winds of Doctrines: The Origin and Development of Southern Baptist Theology.* Lanham MD: University Press of America, 1991.

Richards, Walter W. "A Study of the Influence of Princeton Theology upon the Theology of James Petigru Boyce and His Followers with Special Reference to the Works of Charles Hodge." Th.d. dissertation, New Orleans Baptist Theological Seminary, 1964.

Rogers, James A. *Richard Furman: Life and Legacy.* Macon GA: Mercer University Press, 1985.

Rosenberg, Ellen. *The Southern Baptists: A Subculture in Transition.* Knoxville: University of Tennessee Press, 1989.

Rust, Eric C. "Theological Emphases of the Past Three Decades." *Review and Expositor* 78 (1981): 259–70.

Scarborough, Lee R. *A Modern School of the Prophets: A History of the Southwestern Baptist Theological Seminary*. Nashville: Broadman Press, 1939.

Shurden, Walter B. "The Baptist Identity and the 'Baptist Manifesto.'" *Perspectives in Religious Studies* 25 (Winter 1998) 321–40.

————. *The Baptist Identity: Four Fragile Freedoms*. Macon GA: Smyth and Helwys, 1993.

————. "Carver-Barnes Lectures." *Outlook* 30 (March–April 1981): 5–10.

————. *Not a Silent People: Controversies that Have Shaped Southern Baptists*, Nashville: Broadman Press, 1972.

————. "The Pastor as Denominational Theologian in Southern Baptist History." *Baptist History and Heritage* 15 (July 1980): 15–22.

————. "The Southern Baptist Synthesis: Is It Cracking?" *Baptist History and Heritage* 16 (April 1981): 2–11.

Smith, Harold S. "A Critical Analysis of the Theology of J. R. Graves." Ph.D. dissertation, Southern Baptist Theological Seminary, 1966.

Thompson, James J., Jr. *Tried As By Fire: Southern Baptists and the Religious Controversies of the 1920s*. Macon GA: Mercer University Press, 1982.

Toy, Crawford H. *The Claims of Biblical Interpretation on Baptists*. New York: Lang and Hillman, 1869.

Tribble, Harold W. "Edgar Young Mullins: Founder's Day Address." *Review and Expositor* 49 (April 1952): 125–38.

Tull, James. "An Open Question?" In *Are Southern Baptists Evangelicals?* Edited by James Leo Garrett, E. Glenn Hinson, and James Tull. Macon GA: Mercer University Press, 1983.

————. *High Church Baptists in the South: The Origin, Nature and Influence of Landmarkism*. Macon GA: Mercer University Press, 2000.

Ward, Wayne R. "The Baptists and the Transformation of the Church, 1780–1830." *Baptist Quarterly* 25 (October 1973): 167–84.

————. "Dale Moody's Ecclesiology." *Perspectives in Religious Studies* 14 (Winter 1987): 81–97.

Williams, William. "Cramp's Baptist History." *The Christian Index* 48/26 (July 1, 1869): 101.

————. "More Gratified than Aggrieved." *The Christian Index* 54/13 (March 18, 1875): 5.

————. "The Sin Against the Holy Spirit." *The Christian Index* 54/3 (January 21, 1875): 2.

AFRICAN AMERICAN BAPTIST THOUGHT

Bennett, Lerone, Jr. *What Manner of Man: A Biography of Martin Luther King, Jr.* Chicago: Johnson Publishing Co., 1964.

Brooks, Evelyn. "Nannie Helen Burroughs and the Education of Black Women." In *The Afro-American Woman: Struggles and Images*. Edited by Sharon Harley and Rosalyn Terborg-Penn, 97–108. Port Washington NY: Kennikat Press, 1978.

———. "The Feminist Theology of the Black Baptist Church, 1880–1900." In *Class Race, and Sex: The Dynamics of Control*. Edited by Amy Swerdlow and Hanna Lessinger, 31–59. Boston: G. K. Hall, 1983.

Day, Richard Ellsworth. *Rhapsody in Black: The Life Story of John Jasper*. Philadelphia: Judson Press, 1953.

Fisher, Miles Mark. *The Master's Slave: Elijah John Fisher*. Philadelphia: Judson Press, 1922.

———. *Negro Slave Songs In the United States*. New York: Russell and Russell, 1953.

———. *A Short History of the Baptist Denomination*. Nashville: Sunday School Publishing Board, 1933.

Fluker, Walter Earl and Catherine Tumber, editors. *A Strange Freedom: The Best of Howard Thurman on Religious Experience and Public Life*. Boston: Beacon Press, 1998.

Hatcher, William E. *John Jasper: The Unmatched Negro Philosopher and Preacher*. New York: Fleming H. Revell, 1908.

Haygood, Wil. *King of the Cats: The Life and Times of Adam, Clayton Powell, Jr.* New York: Houghton Mifflin, 1993.

Jackson, J. H. *Many But One: The Ecumenics of Charity*. New York: Sheed and Ward, 1964.

———. *A Story of Christian Activism: The National Baptist Convention, USA, Incorporated*. Nashville: Townsend Press, 1980.

King, Martin Luther. *Daddy King: An Autobiography*. New York: William Morrow, 1980.

King, Martin Luther, Jr. *Strength to Love*. New York: Harper and Row, 1963.

Lischer, Richard. *The Preacher King: Martin Luther King, Jr., and the Word that Moved*. New York: Oxford University Press, 1995.

Mays, Benjamin E. *Born to Rebel*. New York: Charles Scribner's Sons, 1971.

———. *The Negro's God as Reflected in His Literature*. Boston: Chapman & Grimes, 1938.

Mays, Benjamin Elijah and Joseph William Nicholson. *The Negro's Church*. New York: Negro Universities Press, 1933.

McKinney, Richard I. *Mordecai, The Man and His Message: The Story of Mordecai Wyatt Johnson*. Washington DC: Howard University Press, 1997.

Oates, Steven. *Let The Trumpet Sound: The Life of Martin Luther King, Jr.* New York: Harper and Row, 1982.

Paris, Peter. *Black Religious Leaders: Conflict in Unity*. Louisville: Westminster/John Knox Press, 1991.

Pitts, Walter F. *Old Ship of Zion: The Afro-Baptist Ritual in the African Diaspora*. New York: Oxford University Press, 1993.

Powell, Adam Clayton, Jr. *Adam by Adam: The Autobiography of Adam Clayton Powell, Jr.* New York: Dial Press, 1971.

Powell, Adam Clayton. *Against the Tide: An Autobiography*. New York: Richard R. Smith, 1938.

Pelt, Owen and Ralph Smith. *The Story of the National Baptists*. New York: Vantage Press, 1960.

Roberts, J. Deotis. "Black Theology in the Making." *Review and Expositor* 70 (Summer 1973): 321–30.

Roberts, J. Deotis. "Thurman's Contributions to Black Religious Thought." In *God and Human Freedom: A Festschrift in Honor of Howard Thurman*. Edited by Henry James Young. Richmond IN: Friends United Press, 1983.

Smith, Luther E., Jr. *Howard Thurman: The Mystic as Prophet*. Lanham MD: University Press of America, 1981.

Thurman, Howard. *The Inward Journey*. San Diego: Harcourt, Brace and Jovanovich, 1984.

———. *A Strange Freedom: The Best of Howard Thurman on Religious Experience and Public Life*. Edited by Walter Earl Fluker and Catherine Tumber. Boston: Beacon Press, 1998.

———. *With Head and Heart: The Autobiography of Howard Thurman*. New York: Harcourt, Brace and Jovanovich, 1979.

Sernett, Milton C., editor. *Afro-American Religious History: A Documentary Witness*. Durham: Duke University Press, 1985.

Sernett, Milton C. *Black Religion and American Evangelicalism: White Protestants, Plantation Missions, and the Flowering of Negro Christianity, 1787–1865*. Meteuchen MA: The Scarecrow Press, 1975.

Simmons, William J. *Men of Mark: Eminent, Progressive, and Rising*. Nashville: Rowell Co., 1887.

Taylor, Clarence. *The Black Churches of Brooklyn*. New York: Columbia University Press, 1994.

Tyms, James D. *The Rise of Religious Education Among Negro Baptists: A Historical Case Study*. New York: Exposition Press, 1965.

Washington, James Melvin. *Frustrated Fellowship: The Black Baptist Quest for Social Power*. With new forewords by Cornell West and Quinton Dixie. Macon GA: Mercer University Press, 2004; org. 1986.

Wilmore, Gayraud S. *Black Religion and Black Radicalism: An Interpretation of the Religious History of Afro-American People*. Maryknoll: Orbis Books, 1983.

Woodson, Carter G. *Negro Orators and Their Orations*. Washington DC: The Associated Publishers, 1925.

CANADIAN BAPTISTS — BIOGRAPHICAL AND HISTORICAL

Bill, I. E. *Fifty Years with the Baptist Ministers and Churches of the Maritime Provinces of Canada*. Saint John NS: Barnes and Co., 1880.

Brackney, William H. "The Planter Motif among Baptists from New England to Nova Scotia 1760–1850." In *Pilgrim Pathways: Essays in Baptist History in Honour of B .R White*. Edited by William H. Brackney and Paul Fiddes. Macon GA: Mercer University Press, 1999.

Chute, A. C. *The Religious Life of Acadia*. Wolfville NS: privately published, 1933.

Cochran, Owen Darrel. "The Development of Theological Education at Acadia University." B.D. thesis, Acadia University, 1954.

"Correspondence between A Committee of the Maritime Baptist Convention and the Authorities of Toronto Baptist College." Printed pamphlet (1886) by the Maritime Convention. Copy in Acadia University Archives, Wolfville NS.

Court Record, Supreme Court of Nova Scotia (justice Humphry Mellish, presiding) "Kingston Baptist Parsonage Case", May 1935, No. 5259.

Elliott, David and Iris Miller. *Bible Bill: A Biography of William Aberhart.* Edmonton AL: Reidmore Books, 1987.

"In Memoriam." Acadia Bulletin, 40 (November 1954): 3.

Moody, Barry. "Acadia College: Breadth of Vision, Breadth of Mind, The Baptists and Acadia College." In *Canadian Baptists and Christian Higher Education.* Edited by George Rawlyk. Kingston ONT: McGill Queens University Press, 1988.

Rawlyk, George, editor. *Canadian Baptists and Christian Higher Education.* Montreal: McGill-Queen's University Press, 1988.

———. "Fundamentalism, Modernism, and the Maritime Baptists in the 1920s and 1930s." *Acadiensis* (1987): 24–27.

———. *Is Jesus Your Personal Saviour? In Search of Canadian Evangelicalism in the 1990s.* Montreal: McGill Queens University Press, 1996.

———. *Ravished By the Spirit.* Kingston ONT: McGill Queens University Press, 1984.

"Report of the Examining Council for Ordination." *The Yearbook of the United Baptist Convention of the Maritime Provinces of Canada 1947.* St. John: United Baptist Convention, 1947: 192.

CANADIAN BAPTISTS — THEOLOGICAL WORKS

Beverly, James A. and Barry Moody, editors. *The Life and Journal of the Rev. Mr. Henry Alline.* Hantsport: Lancelot Press, 1982.

Cramp, John M. *The Inaugural Address Delivered by the President June 20, 1851.* Halifax: James Bowes, 1851.

———. *The Second Coming of Our Lord: An Essay.* Halifax: Messenger Printing Office, 1879.

Gibson, Theo T. *Robert A. Fyfe* Burlington ONT: Welch Publishing Co., 1988.

Goodspeed, Calvin. "Introduction." In *An American Commentary on the Old Testament.* Philadelphia: American Baptist Publication Society, 1909.

———. "Our Articles of Faith: Harmony of the Law and the Gospel." *Southwestern Journal of Theology* 8 (January 1924): 29.

———. "Our Articles of Faith: Sanctification." *Southwestern Journal of Theology* 7 (July 1923): 55–63.

———. "Our Articles of Faith: The Perseverance of the Saints." *Southwestern Journal of Theology* 7 (October 1923): 28–36.

Hawksworth, Earle K. "Confusion Amid the Elect (1947)." In *The Years of the Locusts.* privately published, 1986.

———. "The Incarnation." B.D. thesis, Acadia University, 1947.

Matthews, Isaac G. *Old Testament Life and Literature.* New York: MacMillan Co., 1923.

———. *The Religious Pilgrimage of Israel.* New York: Harper, 1947.

Saunders, Edward M. *History of the Baptists of the Maritime Provinces.* Halifax: John Burgoyne, 1902.

Spidle, Simeon. "The Belief in Immortality." Reprint from *Journal of Religious Psychology*, 5 (January 1912): 44–48.

————. "Outline of Theology." Notes in Acadia University Archives.

————. "Syllabus of Systematic Theology." Notes in Acadia University Archives.

Ten Broeke, James. "Biblical Criticism in Some of Its Theological and Philosophical Relations." *The Biblical World* 2 (December 1893): 444–51.

Trites, Allison A. "Calvin Goodspeed: An Assessment of His Theological Contribution." In *Costly Vision: The Baptist Pilgrimage in Canada.* Edited by Jarold K. Zeman. Wolfville NS: Acadia Divinity College, 1988.

Wells, J. E. *Life and Labors of Robert Alex Fyfe, D.D.* Toronto: W.J. Gage Co., 1868.

BAPTIST SYSTEMATIC THEOLOGIES

Boyce, James P. *Abstract of Systematic Theology*. Philadelphia: American Baptist Publication Society, 1887.

Brown, Dale. "Review of Systematic Theology: Ethics by McClendon, James Wm., Jr." *Brethren Life and Thought* 33 (Summer 1988): 250–52.

Butler, John J. *Natural and Revealed Theology*. Dover DE: Freewill Baptist Printing Establishment, 1861.

Dagg, John L. *Church Order: A Treatise*. Philadelphia: American Baptist Publication Society, 1871.

————. *Manual of Theology in Two Parts*. Charleston: Southern Baptist Publication Society, 1858.

"Notebook of George Washington Eaton." The second portion of this manuscript contains the "Lectures on Systematic Theology" written by John Sharp Maginnis. See pages 1–6. Unpublished msss., Colgate Archives.

Carnell, Edward J. *An Introduction to Christian Apologetics*. Grand Rapids: Eerdmans, 1948.

Cauthen, W. Kenneth. *Systematic Theology: A Modern Protestant Approach*. Lewiston NY: Edward Mellen Press, 1986.

Clarke, William Newton. *An Outline of Christian Theology*. New York: Charles Scribner's Sons, 1899.

Conner, W. T. *A System of Christian Doctrine*. Nashville: Sunday School Board, 1924.

Erickson, Millard J. *Christian Theology*. Grand Rapids: Baker Book House, 1983–1985.

Garrett, James Leo, Jr. *Systematic Theology: Biblical, Historical, and Evangelical*. 2 volumes. Grand Rapids: Eerdmans, 1990.

Gill, John. *A Complete Body of Doctrinal and Practical Divinity or A System of Evangelical Truths Deduced from the Sacred Scriptures*. London: John Gill, 1769.

Grantham, Thomas. *Christianismus Primitivus, or, The Ancient Christian Religion, in its Nature, Certainty, Excellency, and Beauty, (Internal and External) Particularly Considered, Asserted, and Vindicated from the Many Abuses which Have Invaded that Sacred Profession, by Humane Innovation, or Pretended Revelation*. London: Francis Smith, 1678.

Henry, Carl F. H. *God, Revelation, and Authority*. 6 volumes. Waco: Word Books, 1976—1983.

Hovey, Alvah. *Manual of Systematic Theology and Christian Ethics*. Philadelphia: American Baptist Publication Society, 1880.

Johnson, E. H. *An Outline of Systematic Theology*. Philadelphia: American Baptist Publication Society, 1895.

Lightner, Robert P. *Evangelical Theology: A Summary and Review*. Grand Rapids: Baker Books, 1986.

McClendon, James W., Jr. *Systematic Theology*. 3 volumes. Nashville: Abingdon Press, 1986–2001.

Meeser, Spencer B. "Systematic Theology." Pamphlet in American Baptist Historical Society files: (n.p.; n.d.): 24.

———. "Systematic Theology: A Rationale." *Bulletin of the Crozer Theological Seminary* 2 (October 1909): 4–5.

Moody, Dale. *The Word of Truth: A Summary of Christian Doctrine Based on Biblical Revelation*. Grand Rapids: Eerdmans, 1981.

Mullins, Edgar Young. *The Axioms of Religion*. Compiled by R. Albert Mohler. Nashville: Broadman Press, 1997.

———. *The Christian Religion in Its Doctrinal Expression*. Philadelphia: Judson Press, 1917.

Northrup, G. W. *Lectures on Systematic Theology* Volume 1. Mss. copied by A. H. Carman, 1880–1881. (John Hay Library, Brown University).

Pepper, George D. B. *Outlines in Systematic Theology: Printed Solely for Classes under the Author's Instruction*. Philadelphia: Jas. B. Rodgers, 1873.

Robinson, Ezekiel G. *Christian Theology*. Rochester: E. B. Andrews, 1894.

Strong, Augustus H. *Systematic Theology*. 1886. Second edition, New York: A. C. Armstrong, 1908.

Wayland, Francis. *Elements of Moral Science*. Boston: Gould and Lincoln, 1837.

———. *Notes on the Principles and Practices of the Baptist Churches*. Boston: Gould and Lincoln, 1858.

Wood, Nathan E. *Lectures in Systematic Theology, As Given to the Classes in The Newton Theological Institution*. Pamphlet published by the Institution, n.d.

INDEX

Southeastern Baptist Theological Seminary, 523
Southern Baptist Home Mission Board, 403
Southern Baptist Publication Society, 390
Southern Baptist Sunday School Board, 389, 414
Southern Baptists, 42, 47-61, 343, 380, 385-429, 496, 513, 519-520, 523, 524, 534; Bible Culture, 399; in Virginia, 523
Southern University, 464
Speer, Robert, 340
Southern Baptist Theological Seminary, 91, 184, 199, 252, 253, 395-402, 415, 428, 448, 481, 518, 519, 534; Abstract of Principles, 396, 400; Billy Graham Chair in Evangelism, 521-522; James Buchanan Harrison Chair, 199; Joseph Emerson Brown Chair, 415, 418, 481
Southern Christian Leadership Conference, 451, 461, 515
Southwestern Baptist Theological Seminary, 253, 350, 420-427, 423, 496, 503, 510, 534
Soviet Union, 520
Spencer, Herbert, 331
Spidle, Simeon, 477-478
Spilsbury, John, 26, 28, 105
Spinoza, Baruch, 333
Spurgeon, C.H., 33, 106, 150-156, 157, 161, 193-194, 195, 201, 247, 308, 348, 421, 533, 537; *Sword and Trowel*, 154-155; Age of Spurgeon, 163
Spurgeon's College, 175, 188, 195-200
St. Bernard's Seminary, 370
Staehlin, Wilhelm, 65
Stanley, Charles, 55
Starratt, Frank Aubrey, 312
Stassen, Glenn, 512
Staughton, William, 118, 234, 236, 260, 269, 275-277, 280
Steadman, William, 166, 169, 189-191
Stealey, C.P., 48
Steane, 170
Stearns, L.F., 408
Steele, Anne, 78-80
Stelle, Isaac, 255
Stennett, Joseph, 26, 68-70
Stephens College, 48
Steuer, Axel, 511
Stevens, William Arnold, 334

Stewart, Lyman, 357
Stianson, Peder, 490
Stillman, Samuel, 86, 203, 218, 225, 229, 234, 250, 256, 295
Stonehouse, George, 231
Storr, Gottlob Christian, 281
Stott, John, 427
Stovel, Charles, 34, 178
Stowe, Baron, 86, 203
Stowe, Phineas, 91
Straton, Hillyer, 292
Strauss, David, 284, 285, 412
Strict Baptists (UK), 42, 145, 146-147, 158
Strong, Augustus Hopkins, 285, 290, 291, 292, 305, 325, 326-334, 346, 373, 384, 405, 412, 423, 426, 478, 490, 509, 512, 514, 530, 532, 537
Strong, Josiah, 335
Stuart, Moses, 137, 260-261, 262, 278, 298
Student Christian Movement, 187
Sullivan, Leon, 462; Sullivan Principles, 448
Sully, James, 180
Sutcliff, John, 38, 124, 169
Sutton, Amos, 81-82
Swann, Frederick, 101
Sweet, William Warren, 343, 388, 435, 437
Symington, Andrew, 297
Syracuse University, 342

T. & T. Clark, Publishers, 160
Tantur Ecumenical Institute for Advanced Theological Research, 418-419
Tasker, R.V.G., 198
Tenner, John S., 423
Taylor, A.E., 478
Taylor, Barnard C., 376
Taylor, Dan, 105, 124, 147-149, 175, 233, 533, 536
Taylor, Gardner C., 452-453, 461, 464-465
Taylor, John, 388
Taylor, Michael, 194-195
Taylor, Nathaniel W., 38, 278, 368, 389
Temple University, 254, 342, 510, 514
Ten Broeke, James, 362
Tennent, Gilbert, 255
Terrill, Edward, 166
Texas A & M University, 404
Theology of individualism, 387
Thieliche, Helmut, 416, 492
Thiemann, Ronald, 511

University of Pennsylvania, 231, 254, 372, 377, 379, 449, 457, 514; See also College of Philadelphia
University of Pittsburgh, 379
University of Rochester, 317, 327, 334, 371
University of San Francisco, 510
University of Southern California, 499
University of St. Andrews, 172, 341, 478
University of Strassbourg, 181, 472
University of Toronto, 291, 362, 468, 477, 503
University of Utrecht, 322
University of Wales, 199
University of Washington, 499
University of Zurich, 174, 254, 415

Vahanian, Gabriel, 342
Van Buren, Paul, 342
Van Deusen, Henry P., 415
Van Horn, William, 231
Vanderbilt University, 254, 380; Cole Lectures, 274
Van Oosterzee, Johannes J., 398
VanTil, Cornelius, 494, 496, 497, 504
Vassar College 279, 364
Vaughn, Richard Miller, 291
Vedder, Henry Clay, 42, 373, 384, 519; referred to as a "Bapto-Unitarian", 373
Veitch, Henry, 490
Vichert, John F, 312, 333
Vick, G. Beauchamp, 522
Victoria University of Manchester, 193
Vidler, William, 127, 129-130
Vines, Jerry, 56
Virginia Union University, 446
Voltaire, 255
Voluntarism, 473, 503, 534
Voluntary Church, 217, 267, 276

Wach, Joachim, 435
Wade, Jonathan, 296
Wagner, Adolf, 351
Wake Forest University, 414
Waldensians, 524
Walker, Wyatt T., 98, 461, 464
Walker, Williston, 12
Walvoord, John, 523
Wall, William, 147, 227
Wallace, O.C.S., 468
Wallin, Benjamin, 73-74, 256

Wallis, Joseph, 176
Ward, W.R., 149
Ward, Wayne, E., 418, 419
Ware, Charles Richard, 436
Wardlaw, Ralph, 133
Warfield, Benjamin, 308, 510
Warren, G.W., 346
Warren Baptist Association, 36
Washington, Booker T., 431, 435, 461-462
Washington, James M., 434
Watry Tomb, 69
Watson, Thomas, 197
Watt, James, 133
Watts, Isaac, 70, 86, 94, 148; "Alas! And did my Savior bleed?" 70-71
Wayland, Francis, 129, 197, 259-266, 275, 280, 286, 299, 300, 301, 318, 397-398, 401, 476, 537
Wayland Seminary, 461; See also Virginia Union University
Webster, John, xi-xiii, 8n
Welch, Claude, 3, 337
Weldon, Daniel, 422, 476
Wellhausen, Julius, 353
Welsh Baptists, 30, 35, 76, 86, 102, 189, 207-208, 217, 219
Wesleyan Methodists, 368
Wesley, John, 24, 156
Wesley, John, 147, 169, 231, 233, 311, 368, 400, 510
West, W. Morris S., 174-175, 188, 201
West Country Evangelicalism, 85, 124, 168, 174, 222, 276
West Virginia University, 355
Westcott, B.F., 397
Western Baptist Theological Institute, 252, 279, 300, 319, 320

Western Congregational College, 173
Westin, Gunnar, 524
Westminster Theological Seminary, 496, 497
Weston, Henry G., 262, 285, 369-372
Whately, Richard, 178
Wheaton College, 489, 496, 508, 534; John Dickey Memorial Theological Seminary Course, 490
Whichcote, Benjamin, 446
Whidden, H.P., 470
White, Barrington R., 15, 188